CAMBRIDGE SURVEYS OF ECONOMIC LITERATURE

LABOR SUPPLY

CAMBRIDGE SURVEYS OF ECONOMIC LITERATURE

The literature of economics is expanding rapidly, and many subjects have changed out of recognition within the space of a few years. Perceiving the state of knowledge in fast-developing subjects is difficult for students and time consuming for professional economists. This series of books is intended to help with this problem. Each book will be quite brief, giving a clear structure to and balanced overview of the topic and written at a level intelligible to the senior undergraduate. They will therefore be useful for teaching, but will also provide a mature yet compact presentation of the subject for economists wishing to update their knowledge outside their own specialism.

Other books in the series
E. Roy Weintraub: Microfoundations: The compatibility of microeconomics and macroeconomics
Dennis C. Mueller: Public choice
Robert Clark and Joseph Spengler: The economics of individual and population aging
Edwin Burmeister: Capital theory and dynamics
Mark Blaug: The methodology of economics or how economists explain
Robert Ferber and Werner Z. Hirsch: Social experimentation and economic policy
Anthony C. Fisher: Resource and environmental economics
Morton I. Kamien and Nancy L. Schwartz: Market structure and innovation
Richard E. Caves: Multinational enterprise and economic analysis
Anne O. Krueger: Exchange-rate determination
Steven M. Sheffrin: Rational expectations

GP84 01321

Labor supply

MARK R. KILLINGSWORTH

Department of Economics
Rutgers – The State University

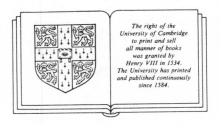

The right of the
University of Cambridge
to print and sell
all manner of books
was granted by
Henry VIII in 1534.
The University has printed
and published continuously
since 1584.

CAMBRIDGE UNIVERSITY PRESS

CAMBRIDGE

LONDON NEW YORK NEW ROCHELLE

MELBOURNE SYDNEY

Published by the Press Syndicate of the University of Cambridge
The Pitt Building, Trumpington Street, Cambridge CB2 1RP
32 East 57th Street, New York, NY 10022, USA
296 Beaconsfield Parade, Middle Park, Melbourne 3206, Australia

First published 1983
Reprinted 1985

Printed in the United States of America

Library of Congress Cataloging in Publication Data
Killingsworth, Mark R., 1946–
Labor supply.
(Cambridge surveys of economic literature)
Bibliography: p.
Includes index.
1. Labor supply.   I. Title.   II. Series.
HD5706.K57   1983   331.12   82–14598
ISBN 0 521 23326 7 hard covers
ISBN 0 521 29916 0 paperback

To Vivienne

CONTENTS

Contents ix

TABLES AND FIGURES

Tables

PREFACE

The analysis of labor supply has an important bearing on a wide variety of issues of economic and social policy. Debates about welfare payments, the Social Security system, and the income tax system inevitably involve questions about work incentives. Recent attempts to develop methods of economic growth accounting and indices of economic welfare bring up questions about the valuation of an important "good," leisure, that is not included in the national income and product accounts. Controversies about unemployment, wage rigidity, and other macroeconomic problems often raise questions about microeconomic choices between labor and leisure; discussion of male–female wage differentials and household behavior often focuses on male–female differences in labor–leisure choices.

Because of its intrinsic interest, because of its relevance to these and other issues, and – in no small way – because of healthy dollops of research funding, the study of labor supply in the past two decades has resulted in an enormous body of theoretical and empirical work. The purpose of this book is to summarize much of this work on labor supply, to give it some coherence and structure, to note unresolved problems, and to suggest a few directions for future research. My hope is that this survey will be useful, albeit in somewhat different ways, to several kinds of readers. First, specialists may find it helpful to have a summary and synthesis of many of the leading theoretical and empirical studies of static and dynamic labor supply models, together with commentary and discussion. Second, nonspecialists – economists working on subjects other than labor economics, persons in other disciplines – may find this survey both a useful overview of recent work on labor supply and a source of references and ideas for research involving questions about labor supply. Finally, I hope that students – advanced under-graduates and graduate students – will find this book useful in at least two respects: as a thorough introduction to and exposition of labor supply models, and as an illustration of some of the ways in which economists apply basic techniques of theoretical and empirical analysis.

In discussing theoretical models, I have tried to avoid mathematical detail; in discussing empirical work, I have generally eschewed econometric arcana. For the most part, readers familiar with the elements of a mathematics-for-economics course at the level of Chiang (1974) or Allen (1938) will not encounter much mathematics that is difficult or unfamiliar; readers familiar with the elements of statistics and econometrics at the level of Wonnacott and Wonnacott (1977) or Theil (1978) will be able to follow my discussions of empirical work. In some places – particularly Chapters 4 and 5 – I have felt it not only useful but essential to include relatively formal discussions that rely on mathematics or econometrics. Readers with little experience in using such tools may find these sections of the book heavy going at first. If you are in this category, *I urge you to persevere*. I have tried to put an informal intuitive discussion in front of each dose of more formal analysis, in the hope that it will provide a useful handhold (or resting place!). When the going gets rough, read the intuitive discussion carefully; read it again; then read *between* the lines of the following technical discussion – *without* worrying about each step in the argument – to see where it is going. After that, read the technical discussion again, this time more slowly, working out how each step follows from the previous one. Close attention to the heuristics that precede the more formal analyses, together with patient and repeated reading of the formal analyses themselves, will pay important dividends. It deepens understanding of the analyses that others have done; more important, it develops skills for use in original work.

A few guidelines on style may be worth mentioning for the reader. First, equations, tables, figures, and sections of chapters are always preceded by the number of the chapter in which they appear. Thus, for example, equation (6.3) refers to the third equation in Chapter 6,

Section 4.1 refers to the first section in Chapter 4, and so on. Second, in order to avoid awkward phrasing, I have used the masculine pronoun in the generic sense to mean "he or she" where appropriate.

This book began as a short manuscript that I wrote about ten years ago, largely in an attempt to force myself to think clearly about what, even at the time, was already a rather large body of literature. Whether the present work – by its much greater length or by what it reveals about my capacity for thought on the subject – shows that I should have stopped at that point I leave for the reader to decide. For better or for worse, however, I began to revise and expand the manuscript, and its rate of expansion began to increase appreciably thanks to an invitation from Orley Ashenfelter to spend a year at the Industrial Relations Section, Princeton University. He is not responsible for what I have written, but the fact that I have written it is, in an important sense, the result of his encouragement and assistance, for which I am profoundly grateful.

For a time, Ashenfelter and I expected that the Section would publish the survey as part of its monograph series, and Ellen Seiler began editing the manuscript, ultimately going through most of it. But, like Topsy, the projected monograph just grew. At about the time that it was becoming obvious that the survey was getting to be much longer than the usual Industrial Relations Section monograph, Colin Day of the Cambridge University Press began looking for a manuscript on labor supply and, in the course of his inquiries, called Ashenfelter. After an amicable transfer of responsibility, Day and Mark Perlman took over the task of nagging me to get the manuscript finished.

Many colleagues and friends commented on the manuscript in one or more of its numerous versions; while not responsible for the opinions expressed here, they have been of invaluable assistance. They include Michael Abbott, John M. Abowd, Orley Ashenfelter, Gary Becker, Alan Blinder, Farrell Bloch, Lee Edlefsen, Malcolm Fisher, Belton Fleisher, Wolfgang Franz, Herschel Grossman, Anne Hill, Deborah Milenkovitch, Jacob Mincer, Robert Moffitt, Derek Robinson, Michael Taussig, and Antoni Zabalza. I owe a special debt of gratitude to David Bloom, James J. Heckman, Thomas Kniesner, John Pencavel, and Cordelia W. Reimers, who read huge chunks of the penultimate draft of this book and provided extensive suggestions, criticisms, and encouragement. The figures in the text were drawn by staff of the Cambridge University Press, to whom I am most grateful. Susan Winick, who copyedited the text, was both professional and painstaking far beyond the call of duty.

M. R. K.

1

The simple static model of labor supply

"Economic agents may be taken to reach their decisions in the light of what they want and what they can get" (Arrow and Hahn, 1971, p. 22). Thus, in neoclassical models, labor supply decisions – like consumption decisions, and for that matter all other decisions – are the result of utility maximization ("what agents want") subject to constraints ("what they can get").[1]

In the simplest version of the static labor supply model, the individual's utility or well-being depends on his tastes and on the amount of market (i.e., consumer) goods C and hours of leisure time L that he consumes per period.[2] In maximizing utility, the

[1] As Abbott and Ashenfelter (1976) have stressed, it is natural to analyze labor supply decisions along with consumption decisions, treating leisure time (the complement of labor supply) as one among many consumer goods. For surveys of theoretical and empirical work on consumer behavior as such, see Barten (1977), Brown and Deaton (1972), Deaton and Muellbauer (1981), Goldberger (1967), H. A. J. Green (1971), Houthakker (1961), Katzner (1970), Phlips (1974), and Theil (1975, 1976). Several labor economics texts, such as Ehrenberg and Smith (1982) and Fleisher and Kniesner (1980), discuss the simple labor supply model at length; Abbott and Ashenfelter (1976) and Gilbert and Pfouts (1958) provide mathematical treatments that complement the intuitive account given here.

[2] A few definitional and measurement issues are worth mentioning here. First, "well-being" and "utility" are usually taken to be equivalent, even though, strictly speaking, utility and indifference curves are concerned with desires or preferences rather than with the actual satisfaction of desires. Second, the C of this model refers to consumption of the services of goods rather than to actual expenditures or outlays. Thus, for example, it refers to the stream of services that an individual derives per period from an auto (or other durable good) rather than to the money spent purchasing such

1

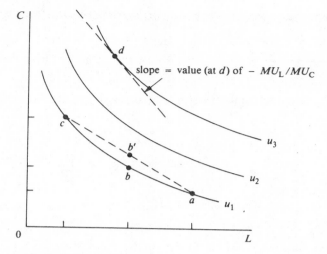

Figure 1.1.   Indifference curves

individual faces several constraints. First, the price of a unit of C is P, and the "price" of an hour of L is a fixed amount W, the wage per hour: That is, the individual must forgo or sacrifice W when he devotes an hour to leisure rather than to work. Second, the total amount of time available to the individual per period is fixed at T hours and may be allocated to work hours H and leisure hours L. Finally, in the absence of borrowing, saving, transfer payments to the individual, or tax payments by the individual, spending on market goods PC must equal total income from work WH and other income V derived from sources that are unrelated to work, such as property. In effect, then, the model assumes that the individual acts as if he had neither a past nor a future and were concerned only with the present.

a good. Moreover, an individual may do some consuming at or through the workplace (e.g., drinking "free" coffee, using company recreational facilities, and the like), without paying directly for such C. Thus, some of the C of the model may not appear in any conventional "budget" data for the individual. Third, the L of the model refers to time not spent actually working, and therefore, in principle, includes time spent *at* work that is not devoted *to* work (e.g., time spent on coffee breaks or making personal telephone calls). All this may pose problems for empirical studies, since the C to which the model refers is not necessarily measured by the individual's own outlays for consumption goods, and the L of the model is not necessarily measured by the time the individual spends away from work.

This process of maximization is shown graphically in Figures 1.1–1.3. The individual's tastes or preferences are represented by indifference curves, as depicted in Figure 1.1. Each of these shows different combinations of C and L that give the individual the same level of satisfaction or utility u, where u is given by a utility function $u = u(C, L)$. At any given point – that is, at any given (C, L) combination – the slope of an indifference curve is equal to $- MU_L/MU_C$, the negative of the ratio of the marginal utility of leisure to the marginal utility of consumer goods, at that point.[3] The ratio itself is called the *marginal rate of substitution of consumer goods for leisure*. The individual is assumed always to prefer "more" to "less," so indifference curves that lie farther from the origin entail more utility. Finally, indifference curves are assumed to be convex (that is, bowed away from the origin). This means that if the individual lost successive equal amounts of L (e.g., went from point a to point b and then from point b to point c), then he would require successively larger amounts of C in order to remain at the same level of utility. It also means that the individual prefers any *average* of a "desirable" and a "less desirable" combination of C and L to the "less desirable" combination itself.[4] (For more on

---

[3] That is, when C and L change by amounts dC and dL, respectively, then, since $u = u(C, L)$, the resulting change in utility, du, may be written as $du = (\partial u/\partial C)dC + (\partial u/\partial L)dL$, where $\partial u/\partial C$ is the rate of change of utility with respect to a change in C (the marginal utility of consumption) and $\partial u/\partial L$ is the rate of change of utility with respect to a change in L (the marginal utility of leisure). Along an indifference curve, utility is constant and so $du = (\partial u/\partial C)dC + (\partial u/\partial L)dL = 0$ as one moves along an indifference curve by changing C and L. Rearrange this expression to obtain the slope of the indifference curve, dC/dL, as $dC/dL = -(\partial u/\partial L)/(\partial u/\partial C) = - MU_L/MU_C$. See Dunn (1978, 1979), MacCrimmon and Toda (1969), Mosteller and Nogee (1951), Rousseas and Hart (1951), Thurstone (1931), and Wallis and Friedman (1942) for discussion of attempts to derive empirical indifference curves using experimental or interview data. It is interesting to note that laboratory experiments appear to suggest that even (?) nonhumans – rats, pigeons, and so forth – seem to have "indifference curves"; for one recent study, see Battalio, Green, and Kagel (1981).

[4] In terms of Figure 1.1, this means that points lying on the dashed line $ab'c$ in between points a and c on indifference curve u_1 are regarded as better than any of the points below them. Note that the points on this dashed line are averages of the (C, L) combinations at point a and at point c: The points on the dashed line that are closer to a have a greater proportion of the a-bundle of C and L, whereas points that are closer to c have a greater proportion of the c-bundle.

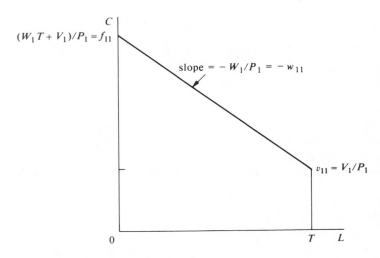

Figure 1.2. Budget line

indifference curves, see H. A. J. Green, 1971, or Henderson and Quandt, 1971.)

The constraints facing the individual are summarized by a budget line, as shown in Figure 1.2. For example, suppose that the individual receives property income of V_1, gets a wage of W_1 for each hour of work, and faces a price level of P_1. If he does not work at all and devotes all available time T to leisure, then he can consume $v_{11} = V_1/P_1$ in consumer goods. If he devotes all available time to work and takes no leisure, then he can earn $W_1 T$ by working and will enjoy a total income of $V_1 + W_1 T$ and hence consume $f_{11} = (V_1 + W_1 T)/P_1$ in consumer goods. Finally, the (C, L) combinations the individual can "purchase" if he divides his time between leisure and work are given by the straight line drawn between v_{11} and f_{11} in Figure 1.2, because in this simple analysis the wage is assumed to be independent of hours of work. (Thus, the slope of the line between v_{11} and f_{11}, equal to $-W_1/P_1 = w_{11}$, where w denotes the real wage, is constant.) In sum, the individual's budget line is $Tv_{11}f_{11}$. Points that lie beyond it are unattainable because – relative to his property income V and the price level P – the individual's wage is too low to permit him to purchase any (C, L) combination that lies beyond it. On the other hand, points lying between the origin and the budget line are all feasible: Given the values of V, P, and W facing him, the individual can purchase any such combination in that region.

In formal terms, the individual's problem is to maximize utility, which is a function of C and L, that is,

(1.1) $u = u(C, L)$

by choosing C and L values that give him the highest value of u that is consistent with the budget constraint

(1.2) $PC = WH + V$

where total available time per period, T, may be allocated between leisure and work, that is,

(1.3) $H + L = T$

Note that (1.2) may be rewritten as an equation for C, that is,

$$C = (W/P)H + (V/P)$$

which indicates that (i) the slope of the line $v_{11}f_{11}$ in Figure 1.2 is indeed W/P, the "real wage"; (ii) the amount of C the individual can enjoy when $H = 0$ is indeed $V/P = v_{11}$, "real property income"; and (iii) the amount of C the individual can enjoy when $H = T$ (so that all available time is devoted to work) is indeed $(W/P)T + (V/P) = f_{11}$. Now, f_{11} is sometimes called *full income* (Becker, 1965); it represents maximum attainable real income (since it is the greatest possible amount of the consumer good the individual can have). In particular, note that one can insert (1.3) into (1.2) and rearrange terms to obtain

$$WT + V = WL + PC$$

The left-hand side of this expression is "full income," expressed in nominal terms (e.g., dollars). The first term on the right-hand side is "expenditure" on leisure (valued at the wage rate, i.e., at the "cost" of leisure), whereas the second is expenditure on the consumer good. Following Becker (1965), one may therefore say that the individual "spends" his "full income" $V + WT$ – that is, the maximum income attainable when all time is devoted to work – on leisure and on consumer goods so as to maximize utility, where WL and PC represent his "expenditures" on leisure and consumer goods, respectively.

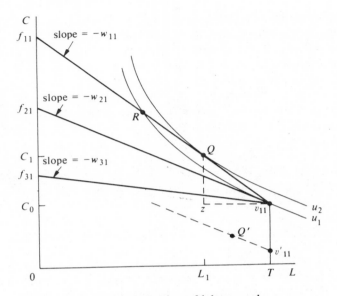

Figure 1.3.   Determination of labor supply

The *optimal* (C, L) combination is the one lying on the highest possible indifference curve that is consistent with the requirement that the individual remain on or below the budget line $Tv_{11}f_{11}$. In terms of Figure 1.3, when the wage is W_1, the price level is P_1, and property income is V_1, the optimal point is Q. At Q, the individual consumes $0C_1$ in consumer goods and $0L_1$ in leisure, works $0T -$ $0L_1 = L_1T = H_1$ hours, and reaches a level of satisfaction given by indifference curve u_2. At Q, the constraints are just satisfied, and the individual gets the greatest possible utility consistent with those constraints. Q just touches the budget line $Tv_{11}f_{11}$; points on any higher indifference curve lie entirely above the budget line (and so are not feasible); and whereas some points on lower indifference curves are feasible, they do not yield as much satisfaction as Q. All available time has been allocated between leisure and labor, so that $0T = 0L_1$ $+ L_1T$; total expenditure on consumption is exactly equal to total income from work and property, so that $0C_1 = w_{11}L_1T + Tv_{11}$.[5]

---

[5] Note from Figure 1.3 that w_{11} is the absolute value of the slope of the line from Q to v_{11}; $L_1T = zv_{11}$; and $Tv_{11} = 0C_0$. So consumption at Q, $0C_1 = 0C_0 + C_0C_1$, is in turn equal to $Tv_{11} + zQ = Tv_{11} + w_{11}zv_{11}$ = property income + labor income.

Now, at Q, the indifference curve is tangent to the budget line, so at this point the slopes of the budget line and the indifference curve u_2 are equal, that is, $MU_L/MU_C = W_1/P_1 = w_{11}$. In other words, at the optimum, $MU_L/W_1 = MU_C/P_1$. So at Q, the utility that would be gained (lost) from spending one more (less) dollar on C and one less (more) dollar on L would be just offset by the utility that would be lost (gained) by the reduction (increase) in L. Any further reallocation of time from leisure to work, or vice versa, would therefore be pointless. Moreover, if the individual were located at some other point on the budget line, such as R in Figure 1.3, then he would always desire to get back to Q. For example, at R, the individual would have utility of only u_1. Because the slope of the indifference curve u_1 at R is greater than the slope of the budget line $Tv_{11}f_{11}$ at R, the individual would have $MU_L/W_1 > MU_C/P_1$ there. Hence, he could raise his utility by taking a dollar away from consumption (that is, work less and therefore earn a dollar less) and devoting it instead to leisure: Moving from R to Q would be an improvement.

Now, the optimum at Q is called an *interior solution* – one in which C, L, and H are all positive. At lower values of W or higher values of V, a *corner solution*, with $H = 0$, may be optimal. For example, in terms of Figure 1.3, suppose that the wage falls to W_2 (that is, to $w_{21} = W_2/P_1$ in real terms). Then the budget line becomes $Tv_{11}f_{21}$ and the optimal solution is now the point v_{11}, with $MU_L/W_2 = MU_C/P_1$, $L = T$, and $H = 0$. If the wage fell still further – say, to W_3 (that is, to $w_{31} = W_3/P_1$ in real terms) – then the slope of the budget line would be less than the slope (at point v_{11}) of the indifference curve u_1. This is the highest possible curve consistent with the new budget constraint $Tv_{11}f_{31}$, in which the wage is W_3. At this wage, the optimal point is still v_{11} – but note that now $MU_L/W_3 > MU_C/P_1$ at the optimum.

This has a simple and natural economic interpretation: Leisure is so "cheap" (W is so low) relative to the price level P and the individual's property income V and the utility "lost" by transferring time from leisure to work (and hence into market goods C) is so large in relation to what would be gained from work (in the form of additional earnings and hence additional C) that the individual devotes all available time to leisure and none to work. Thus, in the simple model, the "value" of the time of people who do work is given, at the margin, by their wage rate W; but the marginal value of time to nonworkers exceeds the wage they could earn. Note also from Figure 1.3 that if the individual had v_{11} in property income and faced a real wage of w_{21}, then he would face a budget line of $Tv_{11}f_{21}$ and would be indifferent between working and not working. Hence, when his property income is $v_{11} = V_1/P_1$ in real terms, w_{21} is his "reservation wage" in real terms: In other words, w_{21} is the highest wage at which the individual will not work. Thus, when the wage is below the reservation level, *changes* in the wage will not change behavior. (For example, when the real wage changes from w_{31} to w_{21}, labor supply remains at zero.) Of course, if V changes, then the reservation wage will change. For example, other things being equal, people with less property income cannot "afford" to be choosy about working and will have to be prepared to work for a lower wage.[6]

Finally, note that the individual decides *simultaneously* not only how many hours to work but also whether to participate in the labor force. This is because, in the world of perfect certainty and perfect information portrayed by the simple model, the participation decision and the hours-of-work decision are really one and the same.[7]

[6] In other words, the reservation wage is the slope of the line that is tangent at point v_{11} to the indifference curve that just touches the top of the line Tv_{11}; and as v_{11} (= property income in real terms) falls, so does the reservation wage. To see this, assume that C and L are normal goods and that the individual currently faces budget line $Tv_{11}f_{21}$ (and, therefore, is indifferent between working and not working). Now decrease his property income from v_{11} to some lower level v'_{11}. This will shift his budget line to some lower level; a portion of this new budget line appears in Figure 1.3 as the dashed line drawn between v'_{11} and Q'. Because C and L are both normal goods, the individual will react to the drop in property income by consuming less of each and so will move from his old equilibrium at v_{11} to a new point such as Q' in Figure 1.3. At this new equilibrium, the relevant indifference curve will be tangent to the new budget line $Q'v'_{11}$, and the new budget line has the same slope as the old one. In other words, even though he was formerly indifferent about working at the wage w_{21}, he will now work at this wage because his property income has dropped – which means that his reservation wage must have gone down. Consequently, as property income rises or falls, so does the reservation wage, other things being equal.

[7] In a world of imperfect information and risk, however, the individual will first have to look for a job (find a wage offer) before he can decide how many hours to work. In this case, unless he is lucky enough to land an offer immediately, the decision to participate in the job market and the decision about hours of work are separate not only in logic but also in time. For more on such issues, see Burdett and Mortensen (1978), Lippman and McCall (1976a, b), and Pissarides (1976).

For example, if the real wage rose from w_{21} to w_{11}, then the individual would decide both to participate and to supply H_1 hours of work.

The effects of changes in variables such as W, V, or P on the variables L, H, and C are usually discussed in terms of income and substitution effects. First, consider the effect of a wage increase on L. A wage increase makes it possible to earn more income and get greater satisfaction or utility at any given relative price ratio $w = W/P$; it will therefore have an income effect on leisure. By definition, if leisure is a "normal" good, then the income effect of the wage increase will cause leisure time to rise (and labor supply to fall): The wage increase makes the individual better off, so he can "afford" to consume more leisure time. However, a wage increase also makes an hour of leisure more "expensive" – that is, makes an hour of work more remunerative – relative to market goods at any level of income or satisfaction. Thus, a wage increase will also have a negative substitution effect on the consumption of leisure time (and a positive substitution effect on labor supply): the wage increase makes work more attractive, so the individual consumes less leisure time and works longer, thus substituting consumption goods (purchased out of earnings) for leisure.

If leisure is a normal good, as seems likely, then the income and substitution effects on leisure time (and therefore on labor supply) pull the individual in opposite directions. The net effect of this tug-of-war will depend on whether the positive substitution effect on labor supply outweighs the negative income effect, or vice versa. This is shown in Figure 1.4, which shows two different individuals, A and B. These two individuals face the same budget line before the wage increase ($Tv_{11}f_{11}$) and after ($Tv_{11}f_{21}$) but have different tastes: A's indifference curves are u_{A1} and u_{A2} whereas B's are u_{B1} and u_{B2}. Before the wage increase, A and B are at points Q_{A1} and Q_{B1}, respectively; after the increase, they move to Q_{A2} and Q_{B2}, respectively. Hence the wage increase caused A to decrease his labor supply (from $L_{A1}T$ to $L_{A2}T$) but caused B to increase her labor supply (from $L_{B1}T$ to $L_{B2}T$). This is because A's income effect was larger than his substitution effect, whereas for B the reverse was true.

To measure A's income and substitution effects, draw a line AA' that is parallel to the original budget line ($v_{11}f_{11}$) and tangent to the indifference curve u_{A2} at which A reaches his new equilibrium. Let

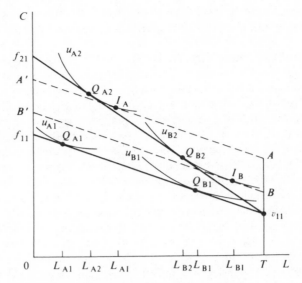

Figure 1.4. Income and substitution effects

the point at which AA' and u_{A2} are tangent be I_A. When the budget line shifts from $v_{11}f_{11}$ to AA', individual A's utility is increased by just as much as when the wage rose, but the relative price ratio $w = W/P$ stays at what it was before the wage increase. Hence, such a shift portrays the income effect (that is, the effect of increasing satisfaction by the amount attributable to the rise in the wage but with no change in relative prices w). Evidently, the income effect of the wage increase on A is the change from Q_{A1} to I_A and led to a rise in A's leisure time from L_{A1} to L_{AI} (see Figure 1.4).

The substitution effect of the wage increase on A may be portrayed as a shift in the budget line from AA' to $v_{11}f_{21}$: This shift keeps utility constant but changes relative prices from their old level (given by the slope of AA', equal to w_{11}) to their new level (given by the slope of $v_{11}f_{21}$, equal to w_{21}). Evidently, the substitution effect on A is the change from I_A to Q_{A2} and led to a reduction in A's leisure time from L_{AI} to L_{A2} (see Figure 1.4).

On balance, the negative substitution effect on A's leisure time (from L_{AI} to L_{A2}) was smaller than the positive income effect (from

L_{A1} to L_{AI}), so A's labor supply decreased and A's leisure time increased. Just the opposite happened to B, whose behavior in response to the wage increase can be analyzed in a similar manner using the "income-effect budget line" BB'.

At this point, the reader who is familiar with income and substitution effects in the context of conventional consumer demand theory but is unfamiliar with labor supply models may feel slightly puzzled. After all, conventional consumer demand theory says that if a good such as lettuce is a normal good, then *both* the income *and* the substitution effect of an increase in the price of lettuce will *decrease* its consumption – yet the labor supply model outlined above says that if the good known as leisure is a normal good, then the income and substitution effects of a rise in the price of leisure (that is, in the wage) will work in *opposite* directions, with the substitution effect reducing leisure consumption but with the income effect raising the demand for leisure time.

Has someone made a fundamental mistake? No, and it is worth noting why. Conventional consumer demand models are concerned with people who *consume* the goods to which such models refer but who do not *sell* those goods. In contrast, as previously implied, an individual not only consumes leisure but may also "sell" it to an employer (in which case it is, of course, called *work time*). To turn things around, then, consider a farmer who not only consumes but also grows and sells lettuce and ask how a rise in the price of lettuce will affect his consumption of lettuce. True, lettuce is now more expensive, so to some extent the farmer will substitute other goods in place of lettuce. However, the increase in the price of lettuce will also raise the farmer's real income (unless he eats more lettuce than he grows). Here, then, as in the case of someone who both consumes and sells leisure time, the income and substitution effects of a price change work in opposite directions when the good in question – be it leisure or lettuce – is a normal good.

Figure 1.4 has a variety of implications that will prove important later on, so it is worth pausing a moment at this point to discuss them. First, a technical observation: One may measure the substitution effect of a wage change by pivoting an income-effect budget line, such as AA', along the indifference curve that is attained after the wage change – in other words, by switching the slope of the budget line from the old relative price ratio w_{11} to the new one w_{21} while staying on the same "post-wage change" indifference curve (u_{A2} in A's case). However, this is the same as changing the relative price ratio from the level implied by the income-effect budget line AA' to the new level implied by the post-wage change budget line while simultaneously reducing property income (in A's case, from TA to Tv_{11}) so as to keep the individual at the same level of utility (in A's case, u_{A2}). Hence, the substitution effect of a wage change is sometimes called an *income-compensated* effect, that is, the effect of a change in the wage with property income altered so as to keep utility the same.

Second, Figure 1.4 implies that, at least in principle, a wide variety of empirical labor supply schedules is consistent with the simple static model of labor supply. For example, A supplies a relatively large amount of labor (and consumes a relatively small amount of leisure) but reduces his labor supply in response to a wage increase, whereas B supplies a relatively small amount of labor but increases her labor supply in response to a wage increase. So labor supply schedules may have positive or negative slopes, depending on whether the income effect of a wage increase on labor supply is smaller or larger than the substitution effect. For example, if the substitution effect dominates at low wage levels but is outweighed by the income effect at higher wage levels, then the labor supply schedule will bend backward, with first a positive and then a negative slope.[8]

---

[8] Analysis of the impact of wage changes in terms of income and substitution effects is now second nature to labor economists. However, until the 1930's economists did not always recognize that a wage change would have both kinds of effects. Some argued that an increase in the wage would necessarily reduce labor supply (they were of course thinking only of the income effect); others, that it must raise labor supply (they were of course thinking only of the substitution effect). For example, see Robbins (1930) and the references cited therein. The notion of income and substitution effects has its roots in Slutsky's (1915) seminal paper, but it was not applied to labor supply until Hicks (1932, 1946) and Robbins (1930). Buchanan (1971) argues that although the substitution effect of a wage increase on *leisure* is always negative, the substitution effect on *work hours* is always positive only if one is somewhat imprecise in defining "substitution effect." For discussions of "backward-bending" labor supply schedules, see Barzel and McDonald (1973), Buchanan (1971), Finegan (1962a), Hanoch (1965), Huang (1976), Jones and Barnes (1973), Krueger (1962), Leijonhufvud and Buchanan (1973), and Vatter (1961, 1962). Note that even if nearly all *individuals* have backward-bending labor supply schedules, the *aggregate* labor supply schedule will still slope upward if wage increases draw in enough new entrants

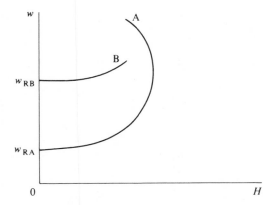

Figure 1.5. Labor supply schedules in simple model

Third, Figure 1.4 makes clear that differences in tastes – that is, in indifference curves – may play a powerful role in individual differences in labor supply: A and B face the same budget constraint but have quite different levels of labor supply at any given wage and respond quite differently to changes in wages. This is solely because they have different tastes (that is, because their indifference curves have different shapes).

Fourth, considered along with Figure 1.3, Figure 1.4 implies that the labor supply schedule (i) is zero at all wage levels at or below the reservation wage, w_R; (ii) runs into the vertical, or w, axis at w_R; and (iii) is continuous and implies positive labor supply at all wage levels in excess of the reservation level w_R. For example, as shown in Figure 1.5, the model implies that A begins to supply labor when the wage reaches his reservation level w_{RA} and continues to supply some labor at all wage levels in excess of w_{RA}. B has a higher reservation wage w_{RB}, but, again, for wages in excess of that level, she always supplies some labor.[9]

to offset reductions in supply from persons already working. See Wallace (1981) for discussion of some of the macroeconomic implications of a backward-bending labor supply schedule.

[9] Of course, Figures 1.4–1.5 are for illustration only. By suitably altering the shapes of the indifference curves of A and B, one could guarantee that A would supply more labor and raise labor supply in response to a wage increase, whereas B would supply less labor and reduce labor supply in response to a wage increase. Likewise, that the labor supply schedules of A and B do not cross in Figure 1.5 is purely arbitrary; in

Fifth, responses to changes in V or P can also be analyzed in terms of income and substitution effects. A change in consumer prices gives rise to both income and substitution effects (the former because a change in prices alters purchasing power and hence income in real terms; the latter because a change in prices alters the price of leisure relative to the price of consumption goods). A change in V, property income, affects income but not the relative price $w = W/P$ and so has a "pure" income effect only. The total effect of simultaneous changes in W, V, and P will obviously depend on the relative magnitudes of these changes; but an interesting implication of the model is that if W, P, and V all change by the same percentage, then leisure time (and labor supply) will not change at all. In mathematical terms, this means that the individual's demand for leisure (and likewise his demand for C) is homogeneous of degree zero in W, P, and V; in words, this means that labor supply is not subject to "money illusion" and that behavior is determined by *real* wages and *real* property income, $W/P = w$ and $V/P = v$, rather than the nominal variables W, V, and P. It is not hard to see why this is so: If W, P, and V all change by the same proportion (e.g., exactly 100 percent), then neither the slope, W/P, nor the vertical or horizontal intercepts of the individual's budget line – $(WT + V)/P$ and V/P, respectively – will change at all, so the budget line itself will stay unchanged.

Sixth, another technical matter: The labor supply function for a given individual may be written as $H = H(W, V, P)$ or, because of the absence of money illusion, more compactly as $H = H(W/P, V/P)$. This defines the *optimal* or *utility-maximizing* level of labor supply. By the same token, the optimal C for a given individual may be written as $C = C(W/P, V/P)$, since C is determined along with and as part of the same process that determines leisure and labor supply.[10] Moreover, utility is simply $u = u(C, L)$, or, because $H +$

principle, almost anything is possible, and what appears there is simply one possibility.

[10] Note that these functions refer to a *given* individual and that the *shapes* of these functions will differ from one individual to another because different individuals have different tastes. (Recall the discussion of Figures 1.4 and 1.5.) To make this explicit, one could write these functions as $H = H(W/P, V/P, e)$ and $C = C(W/P, V/P, e)$, where e is a measure of tastes. Thus, as implied by, for example, Figure 1.4, individuals who have the same W/P and V/P may nevertheless have quite different H and C due to differences in e – that is, in tastes.

$L = T$, $u = u(C, T - H)$. Substitute the C and H functions into this expression for utility to obtain

$$(1.4) \qquad u^* = u[C(W/P, V/P), T - H(W/P, V/P)]$$

This looks rather complicated, but its meaning is simple. Because the key economic variables W, V, and P determine the optimal levels of C and H (and therefore L) for a given individual with given tastes, they also determine the individual's maximum or maximized utility u^*. Indeed, the particular version of the utility function given by (1.4) is known as the *indirect or maximized utility function*: C and L directly determine the level of u, but W, V, and P directly determine the optimal C and L – so, indirectly, W, V, and P determine what maximized utility will be, just as (1.4) implies. Further, since the C and L functions are derived from a utility function, it follows that demand functions for C and L (or, equivalently, $H = T - L$) necessarily imply some kind of utility function, and vice versa. A result known as *Roy's Identity* (Roy, 1947) states some very specific conditions about the close relation between the demand functions for C and L and the indirect utility function, (1.4) (for a proof, see pp. 239–45):

$$(1.5) \qquad H = T - L = MU_W/MU_V$$
$$(1.6) \qquad C = -MU_P/MU_V$$

(1.5) says that, *at the optimum*, the amount of labor supplied is equal to the ratio of the marginal utility of a higher wage to the marginal utility of more property income, as derived from (1.4); (1.6) says that, *at the optimum*, the amount of the consumer good C demanded is equal to the ratio of the negative of the marginal utility of a higher price to the marginal utility of more property income, as derived from (1.4). This implies that "[g]iven [a] function of prices [, wages,] and income which is homogeneous of degree zero in all its arguments, demand functions, fully consistent with utility theory, may immediately be generated" from (1.4) by finding the marginal utilities (in mathematical terms, first-order partial derivatives) and using equations (1.5) and (1.6). (See Brown and Deaton, 1972, p. 1201.) This simplifies the process of generating appropriate demand functions for C and L (or, equivalently, a supply function for H), since it means that it is not necessary to start with a utility function as such: One can instead use equations (1.5) and (1.6) and a function that is homogeneous of degree zero in prices, wages, and property income.

Of course, in the real world, individuals consume a great variety of different consumer goods rather than a single commodity such as the C of Figures 1.1–1.4. However, Hicks (1946, pp. 312–13) has in effect shown that as regards labor supply analysis it makes no difference how many consumer goods there are, so long as the prices of these goods stay in the same relation to each other. This remarkable result is known as the *composite commodity theorem*. In somewhat more formal language, it says that if the prices of each of a group of goods remain in fixed proportions, then the group of goods may be treated as a single commodity – and all of the results previously discussed for the simple labor supply model with just one consumer good remain valid. There is one proviso: The composite good is a price-weighted sum of its individual components, so that it should be regarded as proportional to expenditure on the set of consumer goods comprised within it. Thus, if there are a total of n consumer goods, the ith such good being denoted by C_i and its price by P_i, then one may regard the C of Figures 1.1–1.4 as a relative-price-weighted sum of the individual C_i's – that is, as $\Sigma_i C_i(P_i/P_j)$, where the relative prices P_i/P_j are the weights and P_j is the price of any arbitrarily selected consumer good C_j. One may then proceed exactly as before, interpreting the slope of the budget line as W/P_j.

Although the simple model presented in Figures 1.1–1.4 is certainly simple, this discussion suggests that the model is nevertheless both flexible and powerful. (The theoretical notion of income and substitution effects has proven to be a particularly useful analytical construct.) Moreover, there is more in the simple model than meets the eye at first glance.

As one example, consider how the simple model may be used to understand two important "stylized facts" about labor supply behavior during the course of the business cycle. On the one hand, overall labor force participation (the proportion of the population that is working or seeking work) generally falls as the overall unemployment rate rises – a phenomenon that is called the *discouraged-worker effect*. On the other hand, labor force participation among married women whose husbands are unemployed is generally higher than it is among women whose husbands are employed – a phenomenon that is called the *added-worker effect*.

How may these two seemingly contradictory patterns be reconciled? As regards the discouraged-worker effect, note that a cyclical downturn generally reduces real wage rates – meaning that, other things being equal, some individuals who previously found that the real wage rate available to them exceeded their reservation wage (and who therefore were in the job market) will now find that the real wage rate is less than their reservation wage; they will no longer desire to work. However, "other things" are not equal for some workers, including, of course, persons whose spouses become unemployed during a cyclical downturn. As noted in Chapter 2, a decline in one's spouse's income may (under certain conditions) be treated as the equivalent of a reduction in property income, V; and (as explained in note 6) a reduction in V tends to reduce *reservation* wages. Provided the reduction in one's reservation wage (caused by the unemployment of one's spouse) exceeds the reduction in one's market wage (caused by changes in market conditions that accompany a general cyclical downturn), one will be more likely to seek work – hence, the added-worker effect among persons in households in which some members are (or have recently become) unemployed. (See Burdett and Mortensen, 1978; Finegan, 1981; Lundberg, 1981; and Mincer, 1966; for discussion of the added-worker and discouraged-worker effects.)

As a second example of the usefulness of the simple model, note that that model implies not only a labor supply function, for H, but also a consumption function, for C. Now, this consumption function says that consumption spending depends on real wage rates and property income (and, of course, tastes) – in contrast with simple so-called Keynesian models encountered in most introductory and intermediate macroeconomics textbooks in which consumption depends on "real income." Of course, *when labor supply is fixed*, "real income" and "the real wage rate and real property income" amount to the same thing, that is, real income $= (W/P)\overline{H} + (V/P)$, where $\overline{H}$ is a fixed level of labor supply. However, except when labor supply is fixed, the so-called Keynesian consumption function and the labor supply model consumption function are potentially quite different. (For more on this, see the discussion of models of labor supply "rationing" in Section 2.4.)

On the other hand, however, there is also less in the model than some of its critics (and some of its advocates) seem to realize. First, for example, the simple model is sometimes criticized on the grounds that it assumes something that is contrary to observed fact: that the length of the working day or week is completely flexible. However, this criticism is misdirected. The different hours-of-work possibilities implicit in budget lines, such as the one shown in Figure 1.2, do not necessarily refer to possibilities that are available with a given employer: Different points on (or segments of) the budget line could just as well refer to different employers, and individuals who change their hours of work (like individuals A and B in Figure 1.4) may do so – indeed, may *have* to do so – by changing employers. Moreover, the simple model assumes only that hours can be varied over *some* period of time (e.g., one year or five years); and the adjustment of hours need not be instantaneous (Larson, 1981). Thus, even if all employers have an 8-hour day or a 40-hour week, individuals may still be able to vary their hours of work per year through absence from work (absenteeism, vacations), overtime, moonlighting, and the like. Of course, the budget line may not be a straight line: Its slope may change (for example, the wage a moonlighter gets when he moonlights may differ from the wage he gets at his "first" job), and it may also have "holes" (for example, it may not be possible to work between zero and four hours per week). Although it is obviously convenient to assume that the budget line is a continuous straight line, this is hardly an essential feature of any labor supply model. (For more on "noncontinuous" budget lines, see Chapter 2.)

Second, the simple model focuses on labor supply as an aspect of individual choice. However, contrary to what various writers at either extreme of the political spectrum sometimes seem to infer, this has no ideological implications. In particular, the claim that "'individual choice' implies that individuals are responsible for their income positions; if they starve it is their choice, if they are rich it is their choice" (Berch, 1977, p. 97) is unfounded. For in the simple model (and, indeed, in most economic models) decisions are subject to *constraints* – notably, in the present case, the value of the wage and of property income. The fact that these constraints are "tight" or "loose" (e.g., that the wage is high or low) may also be a consequence of the individual's own choices (laziness, dropping out of school); but it may also be a result of actions by others (discrimination, an inferior school system). Changing the constraints will change labor supply. Thus, to say that the simple labor supply model implies that an individual's low earnings are simply "his choice" is either to ignore the role that constraints play in labor supply decisions or else to assume something that the simple model does not: that the constraints themselves are wholly "his choice" too. (See Ulph, 1978.)

Third, not surprisingly, the simple model focuses on the role of pecuniary variables – notably, the wage and property income – in labor supply decisions. However, this does not mean that the model implies that such factors "explain" (in any sense) "all" (measured in any manner) of an individual's labor supply or that individuals respond only to (changes in) pecuniary factors.[11] Indeed, small changes in the wage will not affect the labor supply of individuals when the wage is below the reservation level or when income and substitution effects exactly offset each other. Thus, the model does not even imply that changes in pecuniary factors will *always* change labor supply. Moreover, as previously noted, the simple model also implies that "tastes" – that is, preferences or, more technically,

---

[11] Thus, for example, Piore (1979, p. 53) writes: "Most economic theory is predicated on the notion that the production of income . . . is the *only* function of work, and that people will thus move around from one job to another in response to variations in economic rewards.

"But to the considerable extent that the job, and the work that it entails, serves itself to define our social and personal selves, there are decided limits upon what we feel willing and able to do simply to earn money . . . .

"The social role of the job itself limits considerably the degree to which people will respond to economic incentives." (Emphasis added.) The second clause of the first sentence just quoted is correct, particularly if one inserts the phrase, "other things being equal, some" before the word "people": There are indeed "decided limits upon what we feel willing and able to do simply to earn money" (which is another way of saying that different people have different, and occasionally quite high, reservation wages). This, however, hardly means that even the simplest labor supply model ignores limits on "the degree to which people will respond to economic incentives" or assumes that "the production of income . . . is the only function of work." For example, in Figure 1.3, an increase in the real wage from w_{31} to w_{21} will have absolutely no effect on the labor supply of an individual with indifference curve u_1. Likewise, as writers since Adam Smith (1776, esp. Book I, Chap. 10) have recognized, choices about work are based not only on pecuniary factors (wage rates and property income) but also on nonpecuniary factors, such as the pleasantness or unpleasantness of the work – which may be a function of individual tastes, the "social role" of the work, and so forth.

indifference curves – affect labor supply decisions. (See, in particular, Figure 1.4 and the previous discussion of individuals A and B.) In terms of econometrics, one can say that the simple model does assert that the relationships between labor supply and various variables measuring pecuniary factors (the wage rate, property income) will usually be "statistically significant" (subject to the exceptions just noted); but it does not assert that such pecuniary factors alone necessarily have a high "explanatory power" (in the sense of producing a high value of R^2).

In sum, the notion that the simple model treats suppliers of labor as persons who make decisions solely on the basis of pecuniary factors is a fundamental misconception. Indeed, although the simple model previously outlined assumes that time devoted to leisure has a direct effect on utility whereas time devoted to work does not, it is straightforward to modify that model to allow for the possibility that time devoted to work may contribute directly to utility.[12]

Similarly, it is a relatively simple matter to incorporate taxes and transfers into the model. If taxes and transfers do not affect the shape of indifference curves (see Chapter 6 for more on this question), then introduction of taxes or transfers merely alters the shape of the individual's budget line. Specifically, the post-tax (post-transfer) budget line lies below (above) the original budget line; the vertical distance between the two lines measures the amount of taxes paid (transfers received). At any level of work hours, the slope of the post-tax (post-transfer) line is flatter than the original budget line: The reason is that some of the wage gains from work are "taxed away" in the form of higher tax payments (lower transfer benefits).

---

[12] In other words, in the simple model, utility is given by the function $u = u(C, L)$; hours of work H are "purely instrumental" because they affect utility only "indirectly" (in the sense that an increase in H reduces L and, by increasing earnings, raises C). However, one can easily modify this utility function to make $u = u(C, L, H)$, so that H affects utility "directly" as well as "indirectly." See Hamermesh (1974) for details. In such a model, analytical conclusions (e.g., about the signs of income and substitution effects) differ little from those derived from the simple model. However, normative conclusions (e.g., about welfare effects of wage or price changes) may well be different. For example, when H affects utility directly, the "value" (marginal utility) of leisure is no longer measured by the wage. (See M. B. Johnson, 1966; Kraus, 1979.)

The slope of the post-tax budget line will become increasingly flat as hours of work increase if the tax system (or transfer benefit system) is "progressive," that is, if the marginal rate of taxation (or benefit reduction) rises with income, and hence with hours of work. (For more on such questions, see Chapter 6.)

In another interesting modification of the simple model, the wage rate W is assumed to be endogenous – to depend on the individual's choices rather than being given as an inalterable fact of life. Roughly speaking, models of this kind fall into two categories: *hours* models, in which W is a function of the number of hours worked, and *job* models, in which W depends on attributes of the job as such.

One simple justification for a functional dependence of W on H in hours models derives from the notion that workers may have to get "warmed up" at the start of each working day and may become fatigued later on, so that average and marginal rates of pay diverge. (For example, see Barzel, 1973; Cohen and Stafford, 1974; Owen, 1969. Pencavel, 1977, considers such effects in the context of piece-work and other payment systems.) Alternatively, various fixed or quasi-fixed costs of employment that employers must initially bear (for example, time required for calling roll or handing out assignments) may make marginal productivity net of such costs a function of hours worked even if gross marginal productivity is constant. (See, for example, Larson, 1979; H. Rosen, 1976b.)

In job models, W is a function of various attributes of the workplace itself. For example, Lewis (1957) observes that individuals may consume leisure and market goods at the workplace (via coffee breaks, lush carpets, air conditioning, and the like); see also Cohen and Stafford (1974), Duncan and Stafford (1980), and Sattinger (1977). Unless this kind of consumption contributes directly to employee productivity and hence to the employer's revenues, employees will have to pay for such consumption. They may do so directly (e.g., employees who belong to a company swimming club may have to pay membership fees) or indirectly, in the form of wages that are lower than would otherwise be the case. For example, Klemesrud (1981, p. 17) quotes the actress Britt Ekland, who played Mary Goodnight in a James Bond film, *The Man with the Golden Gun*, about the experience: ". . . it was one of the happiest films I've ever made. You're treated like gold. You get to go to spectacular locations and you stay in the best hotels. I later realized that maybe one of the reasons you get those sort of things was because your salary was never high.''

In a rather more formal analysis, Tinbergen (1956) considers a model in which different jobs have different attributes and in which workers maximize utility by choosing the "optimal" job subject to the constraint that the wage depends on the attributes (and hence on the actual job) chosen. Although Tinbergen assumes that each job requires the same number of hours of work, it is a simple matter, at least in conceptual terms, to extend the model to treat hours of work as a choice variable along with other job attributes. In effect, jobs would then be viewed as bundles of attributes, hours of work requirements, and rates of pay.

The main empirical complication raised by such models is that, in the setting they describe, observed combinations of rates of pay and hours of work no longer describe a labor supply schedule but rather a labor supply—wage rate locus. A labor supply schedule is supposed to show how much labor a given individual would supply at different wage rates, other things being equal. A labor supply—wage rate locus only describes the labor supply—wage rate combinations a given individual would choose in conjunction with the other attributes of various jobs, and these other attributes certainly need not stay the same from one job to another. In principle, one could derive a true labor supply schedule from a labor supply—wage rate locus by controlling for differences in the other attributes of different jobs; but in practice, this is likely to be hard to do. (See Atrostic, 1982, for an empirical study that estimates labor supply schedules using a data set that provides detailed information on job characteristics.)

Such models also introduce a theoretical complication: In general, when both W and H are choice variables, the individual's optimization problem involves an awkward form of convexity – so that his labor supply schedule may not be continuous. In technical terms, this means that the sufficiency condition for a constrained maximum of the concave utility function may no longer be guaranteed; in geometrical terms, it means that the individual's budget constraint may itself be convex, like his indifference curves. If so, then there may be not one but several points of budget line—indifference curve tangency. This means that (i) there may be multiple optima, only one of which truly yields maximum utility, and (ii) small changes in the individual's budget line may generate

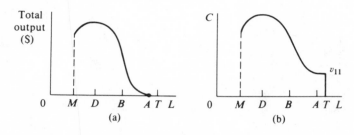

Figure 1.6.   Warm-up and fatigue effects

large, discontinuous jumps in labor supply or consumption
behavior.

A simple example of this is presented in panels (a) and (b) of
Figure 1.6 for an hours model of labor supply with "fatigue" and
"warm-up" effects. Panel (a) shows the worker's total output at
different levels of labor supply (leisure) per period. If there are no
fixed or quasi-fixed labor input costs, then the individual's marginal
product at any point on the curve is given by the slope of the line
tangent to the curve at that point. As shown in Figure 1.6(b), this
and the value of V can be used to construct the worker's budget line,
analogous to $Tv_{11}f_{11}$ of Figure 1.3. In Figure 1.6(b), warm-up effects
dominate at low values of H (as between T and B), and then fatigue
effects gradually take over. Note that, in such circumstances, a rise
in property income V will lead to several income and substitution
effects: It will change the number of hours worked via the usual
income effect, but this in turn will usually alter the (endogenous)
value of the marginal wage rate facing the individual, giving rise to
another income effect and to a substitution effect, which will
prompt further changes in labor supply and so forth. For more on
such models, see Barzel (1973), Cohen and Stafford (1974), Metcalf,
Nickell, and Richardson (1977), Owen (1969, especially pp. 29–37,
103–5, and 110–12), Pencavel (1977), Rosen (1976b), and Weiss
(1972).

The model can also easily be modified to incorporate the effects
of time and money costs associated with working. First, consider the
case of money costs of work, shown in Figure 1.7. If the individual
chooses not to work, he will be able to consume v units of the consumer good C, where $v = V/P$, property income in real terms. On

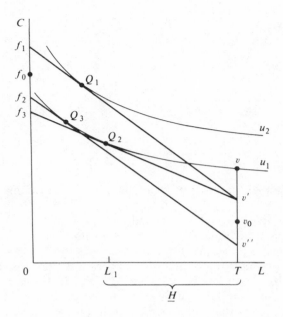

Figure 1.7.   Labor supply with money costs of working

the other hand, if he decides to work, he will have to spend an amount $v - v'$ on market goods (for example, for commuting). Hence, the individual in effect chooses between the point v (the "no-work" point) and any point along the budget line $v'f_1$. Now assume, as Figure 1.7 does, that the individual finds that working is better than not working when the budget line poses these two alternatives in this way. Then the individual will be in equilibrium at a point such as Q_1. As long as the money cost of working is $v - v'$, the individual will work provided the wage goes no lower than the slope of the line $v'f_3$: The slope of this line is, of course, his reservation wage, because working – that is, being at Q_2 – is no better than not working – that is, being at the no-work point v – when the wage implies a budget line of $v'f_3$ for people who work.

Next, suppose that money costs of working increase, from $v - v'$ to $v - v_0$. This will shift the individual's budget line from $v'f_1$ to v_0f_0, but it will not change the wage rate. Hence, the rise in money costs of working has a pure income effect: Provided leisure is a normal

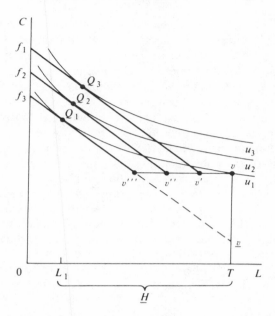

Figure 1.8. Labor supply with time costs of working

good, the individual will work more and consume less leisure. However, if money costs of working rise still further, the individual will cease working altogether, since being at Q_3 on the budget line $v''f_2$ is no better than not working at all (that is, being at the point v) – indifference curve u_1 includes both points. In sum, a rise in money costs of working makes some individuals less likely to work (that is, pushes them toward a point such as Q_3); but if someone does work, such an increase will increase his labor supply and reduce his leisure time.

Next consider the case of time costs of work, shown in Figure 1.8. If the individual chooses not to work, he can again have v units of C; and now suppose that, if he does work, he will have to "spend" v – v' hours simply getting to work. Hence, his budget line is $vv'f_1$ if he works, where the length of the flat segment $v'v$ measures the amount of the time cost of working. In general, a rise in such time costs will reduce *both* leisure time *and* labor supply. To see this, note from Figure 1.8 that a rise in the time cost of working – that is, an increase in the length of the "time cost" segment of his budget line from $v'v$ to, say, $v''v$ – has two important consequences. First, it reduces "full income," that is, his maximum earning power – measured by the height of the budget line on the C axis. Second, the rise in the time cost of working also reduces total time available for *either* leisure *or* work, so long as the individual continues to work. If consumption and leisure are both normal goods, then the individual will adjust to the reduction in full income (from $0f_1$ to $0f_2$) in part by reducing his leisure time and in part by reducing his consumption spending; and the decrease in consumption spending must mean that there is a decrease in wage income, and hence in labor supply.

Thus, an increase in the time cost of working will reduce the labor supplied by persons who work. Such an increase will also make some individuals stop working altogether: For example, from Figure 1.8, it is evident that a rise in time costs to v''' – v will induce the individual to stop working, since working at the wage rate implied by budget line $vv'''f_3$ – that is, being at the point Q_1 – is no better than not working at all (that is, being at the point v). (For details on time and money costs of working, see Cogan, 1980b; Heckman, 1974a.)

When there are fixed time or money costs of work, labor supply schedules look rather different from the ones implied by the very simplest static model discussed earlier. In the simplest model, individuals gradually reduce their labor supply to zero as the wage falls to the reservation level w_R; on the other hand, in "fixed-costs" models, the labor supply schedule is discontinuous and individuals who work will supply at least some fairly large minimum number of hours if they work at all. The reason for this is clear: When there are fixed costs, it makes no sense to work unless one works at least enough to recover the required outlay on fixed costs. Hence, in such fixed-costs models, people who work jump into the job market with both feet and work at least some fairly large minimum number of hours $\underline{H}$ if they work at all; and as shown in Figure 1.9, labor supply schedules start not at the vertical axis but to the right of it. In this setting, the reservation wage is still the wage at which the individual is indifferent between working and not working. However, in the simple model, a rise in the wage to a value above the reservation level will produce a gradual rise in labor supply from zero to somewhat larger values, whereas here a rise in the wage to a value above the reservation level will produce a discontinuous jump in labor supply,

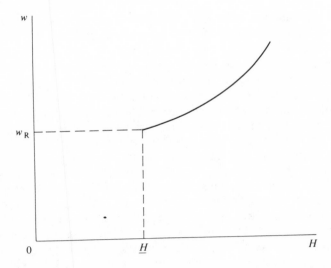

Figure 1.9. Labor supply schedule in fixed-costs models

all the way from zero to at least $\underline{H}$. (Compare Figure 1.5 with Figure 1.9.) Now, most observed labor supply distributions are characterized by (i) numerous observations at $H = 0$, (ii) numerous observations at or above some fairly large minimum positive value, and (iii) only small numbers of observations in between zero and the minimum amount that most persons seem to supply. That this is so suggests that fixed-costs models of labor supply may offer important insights into the determinants of work behavior.[13] However, it is important to keep in mind that time and money costs do not have quite the same effects on behavior. Increases in either kind of cost will induce some people to stop working and will reduce the leisure

---

[13] The simple analyses implicit in Figures 1.7 and 1.8 can be extended and elaborated in a variety of ways. First, both time and money costs of working are endogenously and interdependently determined (and will typically be functions of the wage rate, property income, etc.): For example, depending on my wage rate and property income, I may choose either to live within a central city close to my work or to commute to work (by bus, car, train, etc.) by trading off time and money costs of commuting. (See Cogan, 1980b; Wales, 1978.) Second, both time and goods used for work (e.g., commuting time, bus rides, choice of residence) may affect utility directly. (See Wales, 1978.)

time of persons who work; but increases in time costs will *decrease* the labor supply of working persons, whereas increases in money costs will *increase* it.

Models of this kind are also interesting for purposes of analyzing questions of economic and social policy. Chase (1967, esp. p. 179) uses the simple model in an analysis of optimal economic growth. As a second example, consider proposals for subsidies to reduce the cost of child care, such as a subsidy to all single parents who are at work (and assume that the number of children in the care of these parents is not affected by the subsidy!). This amounts to a reduction in the money cost of working. By this analysis, such a subsidy would increase the number of single parents who work, but it would also reduce the labor supply of some single parents who already work. Applications to more complicated child-care subsidy schemes (e.g., earnings-related subsidies that are available to two-parent families only when both parents work) and to other issues (e.g., the effect on labor supply of a rise in urban transit fares) may be made in a like manner; for example, see Heckman (1974a).

Thus, the simple labor supply model can yield a rich set of behavioral predictions and implications – particularly when it is made somewhat less simple. Much recent work on labor supply has been aimed at modifying and extending the model – for example, to allow for the impact of family membership on labor supply, to introduce risk into the simple model, or to add both a past and a future to the essentially timeless world of Figures 1.1–1.9. Of course, empirical verification of the model, with or without extensions, is critically important: No model is of much interest if its central predictions fail to survive a confrontation with data. Accordingly, in the following chapters, I will consider both elaborations and reformulations of the simple analysis outlined earlier and empirical tests of a variety of labor supply models, both simple and not so simple.

2

Extensions of the simple short-run model of labor supply

In this chapter, I consider four important reformulations of the simple model discussed in Chapter 1. Each reformulation modifies that model by introducing new assumptions about the nature of the utility function or about the constraints subject to which the individual maximizes utility.

2.1. Labor supply of family members

At one time or another, three main kinds of models of the relation between family membership and labor supply have attracted attention in the literature.[1] In order of chronological

[1] Although restricted to questions about the effect of family status on labor supply, this section raises a much broader issue: Are individuals affected not only by the behavior of others in their family but also by the behavior of persons outside the family, in the rest of the economy? This notion has received a fair measure of attention in studies focused on consumption spending, for example, see Anderson (1974), Cazenave and Morrison (1973), Cichetti and Smith (1973), Duesenberry (1949), Kalman (1968), Leibenstein (1950, 1974), Pollak (1976), and, of course, Veblen (1934). The idea that labor supply decisions are interdependent (for example, the idea that my labor supply can be affected by the wage that you earn, my notion of what some reference group earns, or the wage settlement that some reference group gets) has attracted attention since at least Keynes (1936, especially p. 14) and is implicit in various analyses that were directly concerned with other questions (e.g., Burton, 1977; Eckstein and Wilson, 1962; Shulenberger, 1978). (See Annable, 1977, 1980, and Trevithick, 1976, for macroeconomic applications of this notion, and Doeringer and Piore, 1971, for microeconomic applications.) In general, however, this notion has not been analyzed extensively, and its potential implications remain largely unexplored. See Easterlin (1968), Morgan (1968), and Winston (1965a) for discus-

appearance, the first of these, which might be called the *male chauvinist* model, is the simplest. In this analysis, the wife views her husband's earnings as a kind of property income (and so, in effect, regards her husband as a kind of income-producing asset) when she makes labor supply decisions, whereas the husband decides on his labor supply without reference to his wife's labor supply decisions, solely on the basis of his own wage and the family's actual property income. The male chauvinist model therefore differs from the simple model of Chapter 1 only with respect to its treatment of the labor supply of wives, and then only because the V relevant to the wife is assumed to include the husband's earned income as well as property income as such.[2]

The second model to appear in the literature might be called the *family utility–family budget constraint* model. Here the utility that is maximized is total *family* utility, assumed to depend on total family consumption, C, and on the leisure times of each of the family's members, $L_1, L_2, \ldots, L_n$, where n refers to the nth family member. The family is assumed to pool the total earnings of its different members (and thus, implicitly, its consumption spending), so that utility is maximized subject to a family budget constraint. This states that total family expenditures per period must equal total family income per period – consisting of property income V and the sum of the earnings of its individual members, $\Sigma_i W_i H_i$, where W_i is the wage rate and H_i the hours of work of the ith family member.[3]

This model is implicit in Samuelson's (1956) paper; developed in the first instance by Kosters (1966), it has proved to be by far the

---

sions of interdependent labor supply decisions and Hamermesh (1975) for a useful formal analysis.

[2] For examples of the use of the male chauvinist model, see Barth (1967), Bowen and Finegan (1965, 1966, 1969), Parker and Shaw (1968), and Tella, Tella, and Green (1971).

[3] Thus, the general family utility function is written as $u = u(L_1, \ldots, L_m, C_1, \ldots, C_n)$, where C_i is consumption by the family of the ith consumer good and L_j is the leisure time of the jth family member, whereas the family budget constraint is written as $\Sigma_i P_i C_i = \Sigma_j W_j H_j + V$, where H_j is the labor supply of the jth family member. (Note, however, that if all P_i's stay in the same proportion, one may use the composite commodity theorem to aggregate the C's into a composite good, C.) For a geometric presentation of the two-person family analogous to the geometric discussion in Chapter 1 of the one-person "family," see MacRae and Yezer (1976).

most popular treatment of family labor supply behavior.[4] One important reason for this popularity is that the model fits neatly within the familiar treatment of consumer choice developed by Slutsky, Hicks, Allen, and others and long enshrined in textbooks. Thus, all the familiar comparative statics results derived from the consumer behavior model without labor supply and from the model of an individual person who chooses between a single consumption good C and leisure time L, carry over to this more general treatment with little or no modification. (See, for example, Abbott and Ashenfelter, 1976; Ashenfelter and Heckman, 1974.)

To see just how simply and easily the family utility–family budget constraint model fits into the framework of the simple model, suppose that all family members' wage rates rise by the same percentage and that the prices of all consumer goods stay the same. Then, since the prices of all members' leisure times have remained in the same relation to each other (and similarly for all consumer goods), one may invoke Hicks' composite commodity theorem and treat the aggregate of family members' leisure times and the aggregate of the family's consumption expenditures as two composite commodities – which may be labeled L and C, respectively, just as in Chapter 1. Of course, as indicated in Chapter 1, the fact that these two goods, L and C, are composites means that they must be interpreted as expenditure for the goods included within them. Provided that this reinterpretation is adhered to, however, one may proceed as before. Thus, it is straightforward to show that if, say, property income V increases and if the leisure times of each of the family members are normal goods, then the family's L will increase; further, since L is expenditure on (that is, earnings forgone for) total family leisure, the rise in family L implies that total family earnings fall. Likewise, if the family moves from a point such as Q_{A1} to Q_{A2} in Figure 1.4 when the wage rates of each of its members rise by the same proportion, then composite or family L has increased as a result of the wage increase. An "income-

[4] The model has since been used, sometimes with extensions and elaborations, by Bloch (1973), Bognanno, Hixson, and Jeffers (1974), Ashenfelter and Heckman (1974), Cohen, Rea, and Lerman (1970), Fisher (1971), Gramm (1974, 1975), Greenberg and Kosters (1973), Hall (1973), Hill (1971b, 1973), Kosters (1969), Kraft (1973), and Olsen (1977), among others.

compensated" equiproportionate rise in all members' wage rates would always reduce composite L and increase composite C (that is, would cause a shift from I_A to Q_{A2} in Figure 1.4); moreover, because this change in wage rates increases consumption expenditure, total family earnings must increase due to the substitution effect of this rise in wage rates.

Although the family utility–family budget constraint model fits comfortably into the simple framework, this model nevertheless broadens the simple analysis in several important respects. Most important, as Ashenfelter and Heckman (1974), Cohen, Rea, and Lerman (1970), Kniesner (1976a) and Kosters (1966, 1969), have stressed, in this model there are not one but two substitution effects that are relevant to the labor supply of any given family member. First, there is the substitution effect on the family member's labor supply of an increase in the family member's own wage – the *own-substitution effect*. Second, there is also the effect on the family member's labor supply of an income-compensated rise in the wage of some *other* family member – the *cross-substitution effect* – where, in this case, the income compensation involved is a change in property income that, when combined with the rise in the wage of the other family member, keeps the family at the same utility it initially enjoyed. The cross-substitution effect of a rise in family member i's wage on family member j's labor supply is positive or negative depending on whether the leisure times of i and j are complements or substitutes; regardless of the sign of these cross-substitution effects, the structure of the model is such that they will always be equal.[5] Thus, as Ashenfelter and Heckman (1974, p. 75), put it, the model implies that "an income compensated change in the

---

[5] Roughly speaking, this is because the cross-substitution effect of a rise in family member i's wage on family member j's leisure time is proportional to (and has the same sign as) the change in the marginal utility of j's leisure to the family with respect to a change in i's leisure time. In terms of the family utility function of note 3, this quantity is simply $\partial^2 u / \partial L_i \partial L_j$. Moreover, if the utility function is "well behaved" and is twice continuously differentiable, $\partial^2 u / \partial L_i \partial L_j = \partial^2 u / \partial L_j \partial L_i$, which in turn implies that the cross-substitution effects will be equal. (See H. A. J. Green, 1971, pp. 306–12; Cohen, Rea, and Lerman, 1970, pp. 184–6.) By definition, if the cross-substitution effect entails a rise in j's leisure when i's wage rises, then j's leisure and i's leisure are said to be substitutes; and if the cross-substitution effect of a rise in i's wage is a fall in j's leisure, then the two leisure times are said to be complements.

husband's wage rate has the same effect on the wife's work effort as an income compensated change in the wife's rate has on the husband's work effort.'' However, the gross or total effect of a rise in i's wage on j's labor supply need not equal the total effect of a rise in j's wage on i's labor supply; this is because the income effects on the two family members need not be equal.

Finally, as Cohen, Rea, and Lerman (1970, p. 186) and Ashenfelter and Heckman (1974) point out, if the cross-substitution effects are zero for all family members, then the only effect on one member's labor supply of a rise in another member's wage is a pure income effect. If so, then, at least for graphical purposes, the family utility–family budget constraint model for a given individual reduces to the simple model of Chapter 1 and depicted graphically there (see in particular Figures 1.3 and 1.4). The only difference is that in this case the V relevant to any given family member includes not only property income as such but also the earnings of all other family members.[6] Perhaps not surprisingly, this version of the model (with all cross-substitution terms assumed equal to zero) is the most popular variant of the model; for examples, see Bognanno,

---

[6] Also, regardless of whether the cross-substitution effects are zero or nonzero, the family's demand functions for each C_i and each L_j will be homogeneous of degree zero in property income, all wage rates and all prices. Thus, if cross-substitution effects are not zero, the family's demand functions for any C_i and any L_j are

$$C_i = C_i[(W_1/P_k), \ldots, (W_m/P_k), (P_1/P_k), \ldots, (P_n/P_k), (V/P_k)]$$
$$L_j = L_j[(W_1/P_k), \ldots, (W_m/P_k), (P_1/P_k), \ldots, (P_n/P_k), (V/P_k)]$$

where P_k is the price of any arbitrary consumer good C_k. If cross-substitution effects between family members' leisure times are all zero, then each L_j demand function simplifies to

$$L_j = L_j[(P_1/P_k), \ldots, (P_n/P_k), W_j, (V + \sum_{i \neq j} W_i H_i)/P_k]$$

Note that if all consumer goods prices stay in the same proportion, then each relative price ratio P_i/P_k is constant and can be dropped from explicit representation in the L_j functions, thereby simplifying those functions still further. It is interesting to note that the expression just given suggests that, whether or not it is consistent with behavior in the real world, the male chauvinist model does not seem to be consistent with the logic of utility maximization. The family utility model implies that ''other family members' earnings,'' $\sum_{i \neq j} W_i H_i$, appears along with V in *each* family member's demand-for-leisure function L_j, but the male chauvinist model implies that this is true only for the wife's function.

Hixson, and Jeffers (1974), Cohen, Rea, and Lerman (1970), and Fisher (1971).

Regardless of specific assumptions about the cross-substitution effects, however, the family utility–family budget constraint model in effect assumes that the family as a whole derives utility from consumption as a whole. This in turn means that the distribution of the family's total consumption to its different members cannot affect the total level of family utility. This may make sense for consumer goods that are "public goods" with respect to the family (such as heating and lighting), but it is obviously questionable as regards the many consumer goods that are "private goods" with respect to the family (such as food). (For more on such issues, see Pfouts, 1955.) Likewise, the model is silent as to the process that actually generates the "household" preference structure that reacts to prices and wages and, in so doing, determines the labor supplied by each of its members. For example, there is no indication of the way in which the family determines its marginal utility for the leisure or non-market time of the husband or of the wife.

Partly as a consequence of these considerations, a variety of new models have appeared recently. The models in this third group differ from one another in many respects, but they are alike in emphasizing the individual (rather than "the family") as an important decision maker, even in a family context. Leuthold (1968) introduced what might be called the *individual utility–family budget constraint* model, later used by Ashworth and Ulph (1981b). In this approach, each individual family member maximizes his or her own individual utility – which, for a given individual, is a function of family consumption and of the individual's own leisure time – subject to a family budget constraint. Hence, family resources and family consumption are pooled, as before, but now individuals maximize their own individual utility.

In inspecting this kind of model, the economist sometimes asks himself what actual family members often ask themselves: When everyone "does his own thing," is there any guarantee that the household will be stable? In other words, the husband's and wife's consumption and labor supply decisions may be inconsistent, in the sense that the husband (wife) will base his (her) labor supply decision H_m (H_f) on an incorrect value of the wife's (husband's) labor supply, and hence of total family consumption. Analysis of this

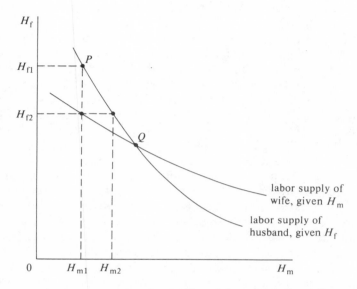

Figure 2.1. Husband and wife as labor supply duopolists

question is formally similar to the use of "reaction curves" in models of duopolists, each of which is trying to maximize individual profit and can affect the other's market (see Allen, 1938, pp. 200–4). Analogous reaction curves for husband and wife in a two-person individual utility–family budget constraint model are shown in Figure 2.1. The two reaction curves intersect at Q. Thus, Q is the only place where the two family members' actions are consistent with each other (i.e., provide total earnings just sufficient to permit the purchase of the amount of C that both spouses have taken for granted in deciding on their individual labor supplies). At other points, supplies will be inconsistent. For example, at P, where the wife's labor supply is H_{f1}, the husband will supply H_{m1}, but this leads the wife to reduce her supply to H_{f2}; this in turn induces the husband to increase his supply to H_{m2}, and so on. Evidently, this process of reaction will be stable (that is, will ultimately lead to Q) if and only if the slope of the husband's reaction curve in the $H_m H_f$ plane exceeds that of the wife's. A sufficient condition for this to be true is that consumer goods are normal goods for both spouses. (If only this were sufficient to ensure household stability in the more general sense!)

As the foregoing suggests, some of the implications of the individual utility–family budget constraint model are quite different from those of the more widely used family utility–family budget constraint model. As another example, in the individual utilities model there are no intrafamily cross-substitution effects. Cross-substitution effects (of a change in i's wage on j's labor supply) arise in the family utility model due to the common utility function; in the individual utilities model, there are instead what may be called *indirect income effects*. These arise because – despite the fact that individuals maximize individual utilities – consumption and earnings are pooled. Thus, as Figure 2.1 suggests, a change in one individual's behavior (which changes total family earnings) has an indirect or feedback effect on other family members' decisions via its impact on total family earnings available for consumption. For example, when, say, the husband's wage rises, there are the usual income and own-substitution effects on the husband and also – since family earning power increases – an income effect on the wife. However, there is also an indirect income effect on the wife's labor supply due to the rise in the husband's wage, because the husband's substitution effect induces him to work more, thereby raising family income still more. If the wife regards her own leisure as a normal good, this must raise the wife's leisure and reduce her labor supply. In the conventional model, this secondary effect on the wife attributable to the husband's own-substitution effect would be called a cross-substitution effect; here, since there is no single family utility function, it seems more appropriate to call it an indirect income effect. It is interesting to note that whereas the family utility model entails equal cross-substitution effects of indeterminate sign,[7] the analogous indirect income effects on labor supply in the individual utilities model are necessarily negative (provided leisure is a normal good for each spouse), but not necessarily equal.

"Bargaining" models of family members' behavior are another version of the individual utilities approach; for examples of this kind of analysis, see Horney and McElroy (1978), Manser and Brown (1979, 1980), and McElroy and Horney (1981). The main

---

[7] In particular, see note 5.

idea here is that the husband and wife arrive at decisions about labor supply and consumption spending through a complex process of bargaining. As in the individual utility model, there are indirect income effects *rather than* cross-substitution effects in such bargaining models; and such indirect income effects need *not* be equal for husband and wife. Another interesting empirical implication of bargaining models arises from the fact that, in such a process of bargaining, changes in the distribution to its different members of the household's total income or consumption spending will usually affect the utilities and behavior of those members. In the mainstream family utility model, the effect on a given partner's labor supply of a change in property income will be the same, regardless of whether it is property income received by the wife or the husband: Precisely because the model assumes that all such income is pooled, it makes no difference who actually receives it. On the other hand, when the two spouses bargain, this will not usually be the case. Rather, differences in the distribution by recipient (husband or wife) of a given total amount of property income may lead to differences in the bargaining strengths of the two partners, and hence to changes in their behavior. What was once the basis of dozens of Victorian novels may form the basis for new economic models of household behavior!

As all this suggests, marital status and labor supply are closely related. Indeed, a change in marital status is often tantamount to − and accompanied by − a change in labor supply; and in a fundamental sense marital status and labor supply may be determined jointly, through a process of optimization more general than any described above. Some work on this issue has begun (see, for example, Becker, 1974, 1981), but to date no fully developed model of this kind exists.

The relevance of such issues to empirical and public policy questions is, of course, considerable. For example, the relation between marital status and labor supply, especially among women, is longstanding and extremely strong; an understanding of the structural determinants of this relation would be most useful for analyzing current employment patterns and, perhaps, also for forecasting future trends. It is often said that current tax laws discourage labor force participation of married women (see, e.g., Boskin, 1974), and widely publicized stories of "tax divorces"[8] suggest that in some instances causation runs from labor supply to marital status, rather than the reverse, as usually assumed. As a final example of unsettled questions in this general area, consider the occasional practice of including "family variables" (e.g., for marital status, number of children, and the like) in earnings or market wage functions used to examine questions of wage determination or male–female pay differences. (For example, see Mincer and Polachek, 1974, 1978.) In and of themselves, such variables may constitute little more than crude proxy measures of family membership and, therefore, of the determinants of *reservation*, not *market*, wages. If so, then it is hardly surprising that such variables usually prove to be strongly correlated with market wages; after all, individuals participate in the job market only if their market wage exceeds their reservation wage. By the same token (and for the same reason), however, it is not obvious that estimates of *market* wage functions in which such variables appear have much to do with market wages or their determinants *per se*. (For example, see Heckman, 1976c, Trussell and Abowd, 1980.)

2.2.   Labor supply and the allocation of time

The models discussed in the previous section treat all time not devoted to market work as leisure and are silent about the amount of leisure time required to consume different amounts of different consumer goods. To some extent, this "problem" is merely semantic: Nothing is changed if one recognizes that the L of the previous sections is not always "leisure" time and instead refers to it as "nonwork" time. Something more important, however, is at issue. For models such as those previously discussed also imply that families act as if the consumption of market goods entailed only a monetary cost equal to the unit price of the good in question and as if consumption were an end in and of itself. Housewives (and house husbands), customers of fast-food restaurants, suburbanites attending Broadway plays, and families deciding between buying a washing machine and using a launderette may well ask: Can models of this kind really be used to analyze such leisure time (or nonwork time) behavior satisfactorily? On the other hand, analysts familiar

---

[8] See *New York Times* (1979).

with the considerable generality of the conventional model ask a somewhat different question: Will alternative models of the demand for different kinds of leisure (or nonwork) time really help explain labor supply more satisfactorily?

Theoretical and empirical work based on traditional models of consumer behavior and labor supply such as the one presented in Chapter 1 has usually ignored such issues. In contrast, Becker (1965) and Mincer (1962, 1963) have reformulated the traditional model in order to confront these issues directly.[9] In Becker's (1965) seminal paper on the subject, the fundamental objects of choice – the things on which utility depends directly – are not various kinds of market goods and services and leisure time but rather "commodities" or "activities," Z_i. The individual not only consumes these Z_i but also "produces" them, using "inputs" – his own time and market goods and services – via "household production functions."[10] So now utility is given by $u = u(Z_1, \ldots, Z_o)$, where any Z_i is given by the household production function $Z_i = Z_i(L_i, C_{1i}, \ldots, C_{ni})$, L_i is the amount of leisure or nonmarket time devoted to production of activity i, and C_{ji} is the amount of the jth consumer good devoted to production of activity i.

Clearly, the production of Z_i entails not only a direct or money cost (that is, purchases of the market goods used to produce Z_i) but also an indirect or forgone-earnings cost (because time must be

[9] Their work has since been extended by Altman and Barro (1971), Boskin (1974), Fisher (1971), Ghez and Becker (1975), Gronau (1973a–c), Landsberger (1971, 1973), Leibowitz (1974), Owen (1969, 1971), and Smith (1973). For a simple graphical exposition, see Sharir (1975). Becker was concerned with a single individual in his initial paper (1965) but has since applied the notion to the behavior of family members (1974, 1975a). For applications that focus on consumption expenditure rather than labor supply, see DeSerpa (1971), Fan (1972), Lancaster (1966), Mabry (1970, 1971), Michael and Becker (1973), Muth (1966), and Ng (1971). For critiques, see Barnett (1977) and Pollak and Wachter (1974); for a Marxist perspective, see Himmelweit and Mohun (1977).

[10] The "household production function" concept seems to have originated with Becker (1965); see also Muth (1966). Somewhat earlier, Mincer stressed the importance of nonmarket work (1962) and the role of time both in nonmarket work and as an indirect cost of consumption (1963). Becker (1977) and Olsen (1976) have recently extended the list of inputs into the production functions to include effort, the idea being that the individual allocates not only a fixed total amount of available time but also a fixed total amount of effort to market work and to production of various activities in the home.

diverted from market production of market goods for employers –
that is, from work – to nonmarket production of Z_i).[11] The analysis
therefore highlights both the fact that "consumption" (in other
words, production and enjoyment of the Z_i) takes time, and the fact
that leisure time is often simply a different kind of work, performed
at home rather than for an employer.[12] Indeed, many discussions of
the Becker–Mincer time allocation model abandon all reference to
leisure as such, and refer to nonmarket work (or, more generally,
nonmarket time) instead.[13]

This kind of analysis has proven quite useful in studies of the
allocation of time to alternative kinds of *nonmarket* production (see
Gronau, 1977). However, its value for analyses of labor supply –
market production – is less obvious. For in the time allocation
model as in conventional models, one's choice of inputs L and C still
depends on wages and prices. In particular, the L_i and each C_{ji} used
in production of the commodity Z_i are still chosen so as to maximize
a utility function subject to the usual budget constraint; and utility
still depends on L_i and C_{ji}, via the household production functions,
Z_i ( ). In other words, the time allocation model's building blocks
are the utility and household production functions,

$$u(Z_1, \ldots, Z_o) \quad \text{and} \quad Z_i = Z_i(L_i, C_{1i}, \ldots, C_{ni})$$

[11] Becker (1965) also suggests that leisure time and the consumption of market goods
may have an effect on productivity directly. For more on the notion that consumption of goods and leisure may be productive, see Cohen and Stafford (1974),
Conant (1963), Heavy (1971), Leveson (1967), Meissner (1971), and Yotopoulos
(1965).

[12] This results in sometimes novel interpretations of the conventional model. For
example, suppose commodities that are inferior (whose consumption will fall as
income rises), such as "loafing," require relatively much time and relatively few
goods, whereas commodities that are normal (whose consumption will rise as income
rises), such as boating, require relatively little time and relatively many goods. Then,
as income rises, with the wage and all prices constant, the individual will engage in less
of the inferior activities and more of the normal activities. In reducing inferior (and
time-consuming) activities, he may end up working more, even though he increases
his consumption of normal (but not highly time-consuming) activities. Thus, as in the
conventional model, the income effect is of indeterminate sign; but the reason *why*
the income effect on labor supply might be negative seems more plausible in the context of the time allocation model than in the conventional model.

[13] Of course, the model includes pure leisure – activities that require no goods, such
as loafing or sunbathing naked – as a special case.

respectively. However, one can always substitute the second of these expressions, for Z_i, into the first, for utility, and, thus, write utility as a function of the leisure times and consumer goods devoted to different activities.

The utility function then becomes

$$u[Z_1(L_1, C_{11}, \ldots, C_{n1}), \ldots, Z_o(L_o, C_{1o}, \ldots, C_{no})]$$

Moreover, the opportunity cost of an hour of the individual's time is always W in *any* nonmarket activity, and the price of a unit of the jth consumption good is always P_j in *any* nonmarket activity. So, one may invoke the composite commodity theorem and aggregate the leisure times devoted to the various activities into a composite good called leisure, and aggregate the amounts of the jth consumption good devoted to the various activities into a composite called C_j. (For good measure, one can then aggregate these C_j aggregates into a composite called C.) The result will be a utility function giving utility as a function of composite L and composite C – exactly as in the conventional model. The main difference is that, in the conventional model, one can consider only the behavior of composite leisure, $L = \Sigma_i L_i$, whereas in the time allocation model one can also consider allocation of this composite to the different activities Z_i.

However, most propositions about the individual's labor supply, $H = T - \Sigma_i L_i = T - L$, that are implied by the time allocation approach will also be found in the conventional approach; in this respect, the former says little that is not implied by the latter.[14] In particular, the optimal L and C may still be written as in Chapter 1 – that is, as homogeneous-of-degree-zero functions of prices, wages, and property income. The notion that consumption of market goods C entails time or forgone-earnings costs as well as direct or money costs is already embedded in the conventional model of Chapter 1, since the demand function for any consumer good C_j implied by that model includes the wage rate W as well as the prices

---

[14] Becker appears to think that this is not the case; for example, he suggests that, in the time allocation model, the substitution effect on labor supply of a rise in the wage could be either positive (as must always be the case in the conventional model) *or* negative. (See Becker, 1965, esp. p. 505.) However, as the discussion in the text indicates, this is not correct; see, for example, Atkinson and Stern (1981), who show that the substitution effect must indeed always be positive in the time allocation model, as in the conventional model.

of all consumer goods in the list of determinants of the demand for C_j.[15] Likewise, the notion that one uses market goods with one's leisure time is already reflected in the conventional model, because the model's demand function for L includes the prices of all consumer goods as well as the wage rate W in the list of determinants of the demand for L.

The importance of the time allocation model is therefore twofold. First, it provides a convenient and highly flexible framework for analyzing a variety of questions about the *division* of total leisure or nonmarket time L into various different uses, such as recreation, fertility, child-rearing, cooking at home versus eating out, driving to work versus taking public transportation, and so on. The conventional model of Chapter 1 was not designed, and therefore cannot be used, to address questions of this kind. Second, the time allocation model also highlights the fact that one's demand for consumer goods depends on one's wage rate as well as on the prices of consumer goods; and the fact that one's demand for leisure (and hence one's labor supply) depends on the prices of consumer goods as well as on one's wage rate. Here, the conventional model has exactly the same implications – although, in practice, these implications have usually been ignored.

This being the case, it appears that the most interesting – and certainly the most novel – applications of time allocation models are likely to be (indeed, have been) concerned with the allocation of total leisure time to various different nonmarket uses.[16] So long as one keeps in mind the full set of implications of the conventional model, the conventional model seems adequate for analyzing questions about market time (and therefore the total amount of nonmarket or leisure time) as such. Here, although the time allocation model often says some things more clearly or in a more striking

---

[15] Until quite recently, empirical studies of expenditure on different consumer goods did in fact ignore the wage rate as a determinant of such expenditure. However, as Abbott and Ashenfelter (1976, pp. 392–3) point out, the conditions under which this is appropriate in the conventional model are rather special.

[16] For applications of the time allocation model to questions about leisure time that are often provocative and sometimes highly amusing, see Linder (1971) and the symposium on his book in Schelling, ed. (1973). For an application of the model to "growth accounting" and to measurement of changes in total "economic welfare," see Nordhaus and Tobin (1972).

manner, it usually does not say much that is new.[17] For this reason, having noted the main message of such models with respect to labor supply as such, I will pass on to other topics.

2.3.   Dimensions of labor supply: hours, weeks, years, lifetimes

The preceding discussion ignored a basic issue about which the conventional static model is silent: What is the time period to which the model refers – a day, a week, a year, or some other unit of time? In practice, empirical research on the conventional model has used data on whatever time period was actually measured in the data base being used, but of course this simply begs the question.

The different dimensions of labor supply obviously are not completely interchangeable or equivalent; for example, most people would not be indifferent between working 100 hours per week for 20 weeks out of the year and working 40 hours per week for 50 weeks out of the year, even though each of these yields the "standard workyear" of 2,000 hours. Hanoch (1980a) addresses these questions explicitly, starting from the premise that weeks of work and hours of work per week are *imperfect substitutes* – or, equivalently, that leisure hours during nonworking weeks, L_n, and leisure hours during working weeks, L_w, are separate arguments in the individual's utility function. By definition, an individual's annual leisure hours are $L = L_n + L_w$; but whereas in the conventional

---

[17] In other more subtle respects, the model may eventually prove to be quite useful. First, as suggested earlier (see note 12), the model provides a coherent and fairly detailed framework – very much absent from the stark and highly abstract conventional model – within which a variety of phenomena can be analyzed. For example, improved "household technology" (better stoves, refrigerators, etc.) has led to improved "household productivity" and thus, presumably, to changes in labor supply. (See Long, 1958, Chap. 7.) It is not obvious how such improvements could be represented within the conventional model, but in the time allocation model it would be natural to treat such developments as "technical progress" that alters the household production functions. Second, when wedded to *other* refinements of the conventional model, the time allocation model may provide a richer set of hypotheses about labor supply. For example, see Atkinson and Stern (1981), who consider the case where individuals' utilities are directly affected by their labor supply, and Gramm (1974, 1975), who considers the relation between nonmarket and market work. Finally, the time allocation model may lead to improved specifications for the functional form of empirical labor supply relations; for example, see Wales and Woodland (1977).

model utility depends on L, in Hanoch's approach L_n and L_w appear separately in the utility function.

Of course, any leisure hour, regardless of when it is consumed, always involves the same opportunity cost, W. So the composite commodity theorem applies here just as it does in time allocation models (which are of course also about the allocation of leisure time – to different activities, rather than to working and nonworking weeks during the year). One may therefore aggregate L_n and L_w, and the fact that they have the same price, W, means that the relevant composite commodity is simply L (or, more precisely, WL). In other words, like the time allocation model, the L_n, L_w model differs from the conventional model primarily with respect to predictions about the composition (rather than the total amount) of the composite good known as leisure. In each case, a simple test of the model would be to see whether the different components of the composite (in the time allocation model, the allocations of total leisure time to different activities; in the L_n, L_w model, the allocations of total leisure time to working and nonworking weeks) are perfect substitutes.

If L_n and L_w are not perfect substitutes, then, as Hanoch (1980a, p. 141) notes, "caution should . . . be exercised in analyzing and interpreting equations estimated with [weekly hours of work] as the dependent variable, and the annual magnitudes [annual workhours] and [annual workweeks] should be used as the labor supply variables in the specification of new models." This is because, at least in Hanoch's formulation, functions for hours of work per week are simply ratios of the functions for hours of work per year and weeks of work per year and, as such, have no obvious or direct interpretation in terms of, say, income and substitution effects. Of course, this is an automatic consequence of the particular way in which utility is specified: as a function of the number of nonworking weeks (that is, of L_n) and leisure during workweeks (that is, of L_w). Thus, suppose individuals regard the number of nonworking weeks and the amount of leisure per workweek as the relevant choice variables for utility maximization. Then the annual workhours function is the product of the two supply functions that are directly implied by the model. In this case, it is the annual hours function that has no clear underlying behavioral interpretation.

Thus, the general problem remains: The conventional model of labor supply does not specify the dimension(s) of the time period considered, and it is difficult to specify the relevant time period on an a priori basis. As the basis for such a specification, it is tempting to draw an analogy with Marshall's "short period," and to define the time period considered by the conventional model as the length of time during which the relevant stock variables – notably, the wage rate (considered as an index of human capital) and property income (considered as an index of physical capital) – are constant. This addresses at least some of the important conceptual issues, but it also begs some important questions. For example, it of course does not provide an unambiguous or straightforward operational definition of the short period that is suitable for empirical analysis. Moreover, even if an operational definition of this kind could readily be established, the conventional model would still seem incomplete. For as it stands, it says nothing about the determinants of such behavior as saving or human capital investment that change the relevant stock variables and carry the individual from the "short period" into the "long period." For example, one can certainly include a variable V in the individual's budget constraint for the short period, with V defined as property income net of savings (where negative savings denote debt repayments); for details, see Chapter 5. However, in this kind of setting the budget "constraint" is simply an accounting identity, and the value of V that appears within it is a choice variable. It would still be necessary to develop a coherent story about the determinants of each period's V.[18]

Of course, this means that the conventional model must be made dynamic; and that its simple story about what determines choices and equilibrium at a given moment must be supplemented by a story about how equilibrium changes over time and about how today's choices change tomorrow's equilibrium. I will consider these questions in Chapter 5.

2.4. The discontinuous budget line: nontangencies, rationing, unemployment, and "disequilibrium"

Although the models discussed so far differ in various ways, they all assume that the individual decision maker faces a

---

[18] For simple extensions of the static model to multiple time periods, see Lluch (1973), Phlips (1978), and Chapter 5.

"well-behaved" – that is, a *continuous* – budget line. In such a setting, utility maximization usually[19] leads to a "tangency equilibrium," at which the individual's highest attainable indifference curve is tangent to the (continuous) budget line. In the presence of a discontinuous budget line, however, utility maximization usually will not entail such tangency. Why might budget lines be discontinuous, and how does such discontinuity affect labor supply decisions?

Discontinuous budget lines may arise for a variety of reasons. For example, a firm may find that production is most efficient when its employees are organized into teams or work on an assembly line (Deardorff and Stafford, 1976). In turn, this will usually require that the workers all be at work at the same time and for the same length of time. If such considerations set extremely rigid limits on the length of the working day at the firm, then the firm may adopt a "take-it-or-leave-it" labor supply regime, whereunder persons who work at the firm must work a standard workday, workweek, and so forth. If so, and if the individual has no alternatives (a matter that I consider later), then the individual's budget line shrinks to just two points: a "take-it" point, denoting the income that he can earn and the hours he must work per period if he accepts the firm's offer, and a "leave-it" point, that is, a no-work point, showing the income he can have if he does not work (e.g., v_{11} in Figure 1.2). More generally, if efficient production permits some flexibility in hours of work per period, then firms will offer a take-it *range* of hours (e.g., between 20 and 40 hours per week). Either way, the budget line is no longer continuous for hours of work between zero and T hours per period.

Factors peculiar to the individual supplier of labor (rather than to his employer) are a second reason why the budget line may be discontinuous. For example, an individual's health may prevent him from working more than $\bar{H}$ hours per period (Parsons, 1977). In this case, the individual's budget line will be continuous between zero

---

[19] One important exception is the corner solution (e.g., in terms of Figure 1.3, the individual with indifference curve u_1 will be at a corner solution when the real wage is w_{31}, and u_1 will not be tangent to the budget line $f_{31}v_{11}$); however, note that $H = 0$ at corner solutions. As discussed in Chapter 6, nontangencies with positive hours of work can arise if, due to taxes, the budget line is continuous but kinky (i.e., is composed of several connected line segments, associated with different marginal tax rates).

and $\overline{H}$ hours per period but for all intents and purposes will simply not exist beyond $\overline{H}$ hours.

Unemployment is a third reason why budget lines may be discontinuous. In the simple model, there is no such thing as unemployment: Individuals are perfectly mobile and perfectly informed about the availability of offers, so that, as soon as the individual decides he wants to work, he can get an offer at the going wage. (Moreover, competition and job switching by perfectly mobile and perfectly informed individuals would ensure that the going wage would be the same at all firms.) In more elaborate models, individuals are imperfectly mobile and imperfectly informed and so may not be able to generate offers immediately (and may not be able to take up offers even when they get them). Of course, the fact that an individual is unemployed on any given day (and thus finds that his hours of work on that day are constrained to be zero)[20] may be of little or no consequence. For example, a worker who would freely choose to work only 100 days a year is not likely to feel seriously inconvenienced if he is unemployed for exactly one day out of the year. Thus, the impact of unemployment on the budget line is more subtle than one might initially imagine: In effect, it sets an upper limit on the number of hours that the individual can work in a given period, thereby truncating the budget line at some maximum number of hours of work per period $\overline{H}$. In such a setting, the budget line is discontinuous at $\overline{H}$ hours even though it is continuous for hours of work between zero and $\overline{H}$.

As explained in more detail below, when the budget line is discontinuous, the (C, L) point that a utility-maximizing individual chooses may be one at which his highest attainable indifference curve is *not* tangent to the (discontinuous) budget line. Recent work on behavior under these conditions can be divided in two: Some of this work in effect treats such nontangencies as disequilibria, whereas other work treats them as equilibrium points.[21]

---

[20] However, note that not all unemployed persons are constrained to have zero hours of work. The worker who gets a job offer but rejects it in order to look for a better one will typically be counted as unemployed in official statistics but of course is not constrained to have hours of work equal to zero.

[21] In general terms, equilibrium is simply a state of affairs in which there is no automatic tendency for things to change. As the discussion of Figure 2.2 suggests, individuals confronted with a discontinuous budget line reach a point on such a line that

First, consider disequilibrium analyses. These start from the premise that discontinuous budget lines of the kind previously described impose a real constraint on the number of hours that individuals may work per period, so that such individuals are, in effect, "rationed" with respect to labor supply.[22] To analyze labor supply decisions under such "rationing," it is convenient to start with the simplest case: a take-it-or-leave-it regime in which all persons who work must work exactly H_R hours, the labor supply ration.[23]

is optimal at least in the sense that they are better off at that point than they are at any other point *on the same budget line.* This being so, it would seem that such a point is an equilibrium point, not a disequilibrium point. However, as emphasized later, the point chosen is usually one at which the marginal rate of substitution MU_L/MU_C and the real wage W/P are not equal; and in such circumstances the individual would desire to change C and L until MU_L/MU_C and W/P were equal. In this sense, there is an automatic tendency for things to change and so such points may be called disequilibrium points. However, as noted later, whether the individual will ever be *able* to change in the direction he desires is a different question.

[22] For general discussions of behavior under rationing, see Tobin and Houthakker (1951) and Tobin (1952). Note that, in at least one important respect, labor supply rationing differs from "conventional" rationing of, say, food in wartime. Under conventional rationing, persons who do not want to consume all of their food ration at prevailing prices may be able to arrange direct trades with persons who find the ration insufficient. (See Radford's, 1945, classic account of how persons in a prisoner-of-war camp developed a remarkably complex exchange economy organized around trading "surplus" rations of food, cigarettes, etc., that they received in Red Cross parcels.) Alternatively, persons may be able to sell surplus rations – that is, the difference between their ration and the amount they actually want to consume – in an illegal "black," or legal "white," market to persons who want to consume more than the rationed amount. However, under labor supply rationing, it is usually difficult for persons who want to work less than the rationed amount of labor supply at the prevailing wage rate to "trade" or "sell" their surplus labor supply to persons who want to work more than the rationed amount.

[23] Much of the original work on labor supply rationing was concerned with such regimes; for an excellent survey, see Perlman (1969). Moses (1962), Mossin and Bronfenbrenner (1967), Perlman (1966, 1968b), and Wilensky (1963) base their discussions on the simple model of Chapter 1 as modified to allow for the rationing of hours of work. Sherman and Willett (1972) examine such topics in the context of the Becker (1965) time allocation model, as discussed in the present chapter. Ashworth, McGlone, and Ulph (1977), Bienefield (1969), Bosworth and Dawkins (1980), Dankert (1962), Deardorff and Stafford (1976), Dickinson (1975), Meyers (1965), Moffitt (1982), Owen (1979), Powell (1979), Shishko and Rostker (1976), and Whybrew (1968) give particular attention to aspects of take-it-or-leave-it regimes and to questions about overtime, shift working, and the standard workweek. Mabry (1969) considers salaried professionals' supply decisions under such regimes. S. G. Allen (1981) discusses worker absenteeism; Ehrenberg (1970) considers the implications of overtime and absenteeism for employers.

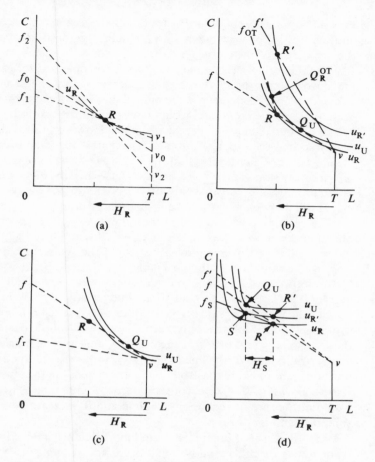

Figure 2.2. Labor supply rationing; overemployment; nonparticipation; underemployment

Suppose first that the money wage is W_0, property income is V_0, and the price level is P. Then the real wage is $w_0 = W_0/P$, equal to the slope of the line from v_0 to f_0 in Figure 2.2(a), and real property income is $v_0 = V_0/P$, equal to the height of the line from T to v_0 in Figure 2.2(a). In the absence of any rationing, the individual can pick any point on the dashed budget line Tv_0f_0. However, under a take-it-or-leave-it regime, the budget line shrinks to only two points:

the take-it point R, entailing H_R hours of work at the real wage w_0, and the leave-it or no-work point v_0, entailing zero hours of work (i.e., rejection of the employer's offer).

When the real wage is w_0 and real property income is v_0, the rationing of work opportunities has no particular importance: The dashed budget line $Tv_0 f_0$ is tangent to the individual's indifference curve u_R at point R, so the individual would have chosen the take-it point R even if the budget line had been continuous. However, this is clearly a very special case. For example, suppose next that real property income is the higher level v_1 and the real wage is the lower level w_1 (given by the slope of the line from v_1 to f_1). When the budget line is discontinuous and consists only of the points R and v_1, the individual will pick R and work since R yields more utility than v_1. However, at real wage w_1 and real property income v_1, R is a point of nontangency and – at least in this analysis – disequilibrium. That is, the individual is "overemployed" at R, in the sense that, at real wage w_1, he would desire (but is unable) to reduce his hours of work below the rationed amount H_R. (This is because, at R, the individual has $MU_L / MU_C > w_1$, so that if the budget line $Tv_1 f_1$ were continuous, he would increase his leisure time and reduce both his consumption and his labor supply.) Just the reverse will be true when the individual's real property income is v_2 and his real wage is w_2 (equal to the slope of the line from v_2 to f_2 in Figure 2.2(a)). In this third case, the individual will be "underemployed," in the sense that if the budget line $Tv_2 f_2$ were continuous, he would prefer R to v_2 but would also desire to reduce leisure time and to increase both consumption and labor supply.

Panels (b) – (d) of Figure 2.2 permit more detailed analysis of the labor supply of underemployed and overemployed persons.[24] First, consider panel (b), showing an overemployed person. Possibly this individual could move at least partway toward Q_U (which he would

---

[24] Panel (a) of Figure 2.2 indicates that an individual with given tastes may be underemployed, overemployed, or fully employed depending on the values of W, V, and P that confront him, that is, panel (a) shows how variations in the budget line may produce different behavior for a given indifference curve. Panels (b)–(d) show that, by the same token, differences in tastes may affect whether different individuals who face the same values of W, P, and V will be underemployed, overemployed, or fully employed, that is, these panels all depict the same budget line Tvf and display different indifference curves.

choose if the budget line Tvf were continuous) from R (the rationed amount that he chooses under a take-it-or-leave-it regime) by engaging in absenteeism. (The extent to which he will be able to do so will depend on how strictly his employer enforces the terms of the take-it-or-leave-it regime.) On the other hand, his employer might act as a discriminating monopsonist with respect to the individual's workhours – by offering an overtime wage, paid only for hours worked in *excess* of H_R, equal to the slope of the line from R to f_{OT}. If so, then the individual may find himself at a point of tangency equilibrium at Q_R^{OT}. Changes in the base wage rate – that is, in the slope of the line from v to f – might also reduce absenteeism, but at a much greater cost. This is because introduction of an overtime wage rate will have a relatively small income effect (since it will apply only to hours worked in excess of H_R), whereas a change in the "basic" wage will have a much larger income effect (since it will apply to all hours worked).

For the most part, however, conventional income and substitution effects are not particularly relevant to analysis of the overemployed individual's labor supply. For example, in terms of Figure 2.2(b), suppose that the real wage w were raised to a new level w' (given by the slope of the line from v to f') with no change in the rationed level of hours H_R. The new take-it point R' would be preferred to the leave-it point v, so the individual would move from R to R'. Cursory and simpleminded comparison of the "before" point R and the "after" point R' would seem to suggest that the income and substitution effects of the rise in the wage from w to w' have exactly offset each other – when in fact the real reason why labor supply remains unchanged at H_R is simply that the employer has not changed the standard workweek. (See section 3.4 for further discussion of this point.)

Likewise, analysis of the determinants of labor force participation becomes more complicated once one introduces the notion of labor supply rationing. This is illustrated in Figure 2.2(c). The individual shown there would choose point Q_U if he faced a continuous budget line like Tvf. However, if confronted with a take-it-or-leave-it regime requiring him to choose between points R and v, he would prefer v: At R, he would be overemployed to such an extent that he would actually be better off not working at all. Thus, unrationed persons will always supply some labor so long as the wage exceeds the reservation level (= the slope of the line from v to f_R in panel (c)). In contrast, labor supply under rationing depends not only on whether the wage exceeds this reservation level but also on the amount of the labor supply ration.

Next, consider panel (d), which depicts an underemployed person.[25] If he were unrationed and faced a continuous budget line like Tvf, he would pick Q_U, an unrationed labor supply tangency equilibrium. Under a take-it-or-leave-it regime, however, the individual picks R instead of v. This individual is therefore underemployed; he would be willing to work at a second job (to moonlight or, alternatively, work overtime, in excess of the standard workweek H_R), even if the wage rate were somewhat lower than the one he gets at his first job. (For example, if his first job put him at R with real wage w, he would supply H_S hours to a second job paying a real wage w_S, where w_S is equal to the slope of the dashed line from R to f_S, even though w_S is less than w.)

Like the individuals shown in panels (b) and (c), the individual shown in panel (d) is not at a tangency equilibrium when he is rationed at R with wage w (equal to the slope of the line from v to f). Here, too, then, conventional income and substitution effects on leisure have little or no direct relevance to analyzing behavior. For example, an increase in the rationed amount of employment H_R will increase this individual's hours of work even if the wage is unchanged. Note also that if the wage were to rise from w to w', this individual would use all of the resulting increase in potential earnings from work to purchase more consumer goods:[26] This individual is underemployed and so would not desire to use any of this rise in

[25] Note that nothing in the model indicates the form in which this underemployment will occur. In the sense used here, an individual suffers "underemployment" either (i) if he is continuously employed but works a smaller number of hours than he desires to work at the prevailing wage rate or (ii) if he is employed some of the time but without work the rest of the time that he would desire to work at the prevailing wage rate. For a variety of reasons, discussions of this second kind of underemployment have attracted particular interest. For general discussions of underemployed individuals, see Ashenfelter (1978a,b, 1980a) and Ashenfelter and Ham (1979).

[26] Here, "rise in potential earnings" is simply $(w' - w)H_R$, the rise in earnings that the individual would enjoy were he to continue working H_R hours. In the absence of rationing, the income effect of the wage increase would prompt the individual to reduce his hours below H_R, that is, to "purchase" some additional leisure time using part of this increase in potential earnings.

potential earnings to obtain more leisure. Likewise, an increase in the rationed number of workhours would result in more consumption spending even if the wage did not change. Thus, in the presence of labor supply rationing, consumption spending depends only on *total income* and does *not* depend on wage rates except to the extent that a change in wage rates changes total income.

This contrasts sharply with the conventional consumption function $C = C(W/P, V/P)$ implied by the simple neoclassical microeconomic model of Chapter 1. However, it is quite similar in spirit to the simple Keynesian macroeconomic consumption function $C = C(Y/P)$, where Y/P is total real income, with $Y/P = (W/P)\overline{H} + (V/P)$, and where $\overline{H}$ is a *fixed* amount of hours of work (which in this setting may be taken to be the equivalent of H_R). An obvious corollary to this is that, in the presence of un(der)employment and an hours constraint, a decrease in the real wage (e.g., from w' back to w) will reduce total income and hence consumption spending – and therefore, in Keynesian macroeconomic terms, will also reduce the level of aggregate demand.[27]

The simple analysis of labor supply rationing presented here can be extended and refined in various ways. For example, Ashenfelter (1980a) and Ham (1982) develop models of rationing in which individuals who want to work face not a rationed or take-it *point* but rather a rationed *line segment* such as $R_L R_U$ in Figure 2.3. Thus, in this more general version of the rationing model, labor supply may not exceed H_U or be less than H_L but may be anything in between.

A second refinement, considered by Ashenfelter (1980a), Blundell and Walker (1982), Deaton and Muellbauer (1981), Kniesner (1976a), Parsons (1977), and Ransom (1982), among others, generalizes the earlier analysis to the case of a family that has m members and that purchases n consumption goods. In this setting, the fact

---

[27] See Ashenfelter (1980a), Barro and Grossman (1971, 1974), and Clower (1965). As shown in Figure 2.2(d), the consumption function implied by the rationed labor supply model is not truly Keynesian. For one thing, since *all* of the rise in income attributable to a wage increase is used for increased consumption spending, the simple rationed labor supply model implies that the marginal propensity to consume is unity, not less than unity as in conventional Keynesian treatments. However, this is simply because the model ignores savings; a more elaborate treatment that allows for savings would conform much more closely with the conventional Keynesian consumption function.

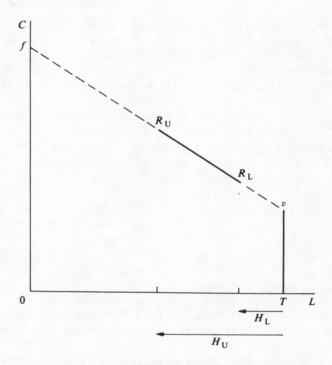

Figure 2.3.   General model of labor supply rationing

that the labor supply of a given family member i is rationed will affect both the labor supplies of other unrationed family members and the family's consumption of each distinct consumer good.[28]

As noted earlier, labor supply rationing may affect not only labor supply behavior (e.g., causing labor supply responses to wage changes to differ from those that would be implied by conventional

---

[28] In the analyses of Kniesner and of Blundell and Walker, family member i is at a "corner" and therefore is rationed in the sense that "desired" leisure time exceeds total available time per period T, that is, family member i is at a point of nontangency like the one shown in Figure 1.3 involving indifference curve u_1 and budget line $Tv_{11}f_{31}$. In Parsons' analysis, family member i is rationed because he is unable to work more than some number of hours $\bar{H}$ per period due to ill health. In Ashenfelter's analysis, family member i is rationed in the sense that an exogenously imposed and unanticipated spell of unemployment prevents him from working more than some number of hours $\bar{H}$ per period.

income and substitution effects) but also consumption behavior (e.g., causing consumption spending to differ from the level that would be implied by the "simple model consumption function" and to resemble closely the behavior implied by a Keynesian consumption function). (See Ashenfelter, 1980a; Barro and Grossman, 1971, 1976; Howard, 1977; MacKay and Whitney, 1980; Neary and Roberts, 1980.) The reverse is also true: That is, consumption rationing may affect not only consumption behavior but also labor supply behavior. (For example, in various East European countries, the quantities of various consumer goods provided by state agencies are strictly less than the amounts that consumers want to buy at the prices that the agencies charge. This consumption rationing may in turn affect work incentives and labor supply, for example, see Barro and Grossman, 1974.)

In general, then, constraints affecting one aspect of an individual's behavior will also affect other aspects of that individual's behavior. A third line of development of the notion of rationing consists of working out a fully parallel analysis of how rationing and other similar constraints affect various aspects of the behavior of *other* agents – notably firms – and of merging these essentially microlevel treatments of the behavior of different kinds of agents into a macrolevel treatment of the behavior of the economy as a whole.[29] (For example, see Barro and Grossman, 1971, 1976;

---

[29] For example, suppose that foreign countries' demands for U.S. exports fall (and that this decline is both unanticipated by and exogenous to agents in the U.S. economy). U.S. firms will then feel "sales constrained," which will in turn affect their employment decisions, leading to layoffs. Workers then become "labor supply constrained" and so reduce their consumption spending – which in turn reduces product demand, further reinforcing the sales constraint facing firms. So employment falls; wages fall too, as workers bid down wages in an attempt to regain their jobs. However, at least for a time, this attempt may be unsuccessful, for even if wages fall substantially, firms will not increase their hiring at all: they are sales constrained, and so there is little point in hiring workers to produce additional output when there is little chance that the output can be sold. (This is particularly so when the product cannot be stored.) Of course, the decline in real labor costs will also reduce the price level; and this will increase the real value of assets like cash that are denominated in nominal, or money, terms. This will stimulate demand for output via a "real balance," "Pigou," or "real wealth" effect. (See, in particular, Barro and Grossman, 1971, 1976.) However, the fall in the price level may also result in bankruptcies and thus further *reductions* in demand. (See Arrow and Hahn, 1971, esp. pp. 354–63.) As Keynes (1936, p. 264) put it: "Indeed if the fall in wages and prices

Clower, 1965; Futia, 1977; Howard, 1977; Portes and Muellbauer, 1978; Varian, 1977.)

In all of these models, budget line discontinuities represent real, and exogenous, constraints on the ability of individuals to supply labor and lead to disequilibria – at least in the sense that rationed persons find that their (discontinuous) budget line is usually not tangent to their highest attainable indifference curve. Rather, they find that their marginal rate of substitution MU_L / MU_C is less (or greater) than their real wage W/P, so that, in the absence of rationing, they would desire to increase (or reduce) their labor supply from its current level.

Is this kind of situation really a disequilibrium, and is such rationing really an exogenous constraint on choice? Not necessarily. In equilibrium analyses of the discontinuous budget line, such situations are in fact equilibria that may well be a *result* of voluntary choices rather than a *constraint* on choice – despite outward appearances to the contrary.

The basic idea underlying such analyses is simple. If large numbers of individuals were really "rationed," in the sense just mentioned, then they would have an incentive to seek – and firms would have an incentive to offer – more, and different, wage hours packages. Such packages would permit "true" equilibria (at which neither firms nor individuals would have any reason to attempt further modifications or adjustments to the existing set of wage hours packages). In this view, the fact (if it is a fact) that many individuals face discontinuous budget lines and are not at "tangency equilibria" simply means that any tangency equilibria on continuous budget lines that are available (or could be arranged) are less attractive than nontangencies on discontinuous budget lines. To maintain otherwise, in this view, is to assert that both firms and individuals correctly perceive that there are potential "gains from

---

goes far, the embarrassment of those entrepreneurs who are heavily indebted may soon reach the point of insolvency – with severely adverse effects on Investment" (and, one may add, on other components of demand and on employment as well). Of course, it is natural to regard this process of feedback (in which rationed behavior in one part of the macroeconomy affects behavior of other agents elsewhere in the economy) as the familiar Keynesian multiplier process. (For example, see Barro and Grossman, 1971, 1976; Portes and Muellbauer, 1978.) For a critique of this kind of analysis, see Peisa (1977).

trade" but nevertheless fail to do anything to realize such gains.[30] Although such nontangency solutions do not entail equality between the marginal rate of substitution and the real wage, they are nevertheless equilibria in any meaningful sense of the term.

Thus, to put the point somewhat crudely, individuals will not, in this view, submit forever to constraints on their ability to supply labor unless no better alternative is available. Moreover, although this argument, taken literally, applies only to persons employed under take-it-or-leave-it labor supply regimes, it applies with equal force to other similar situations that appear to involve "constraints" on choice – for example, regimes with "compulsory" overtime and regimes in which persons receive an annual salary payment that is "independent" of hours of work. In the former case, overtime is compulsory only if one agrees to work under the regime that requires such overtime; in the latter case, pay is independent of hours of work only if one assumes that no alternatives (with different salaries and *implied* requirements about "normal" or "expected" hours of work) are available. Nor are such arrangements, even for the individuals who accept them, fixed for all time: Unions renegotiate compulsory overtime provisions, and the implicit number of normal hours that employers expect salaried employees to work can also change.

For example, consider Figure 2.4, which shows alternatives available to employees at a firm that, given the way production is currently organized, can either (i) allow employees to vary their hours of work at will along the continuous budget line vf at a rather low real wage w_1 (equal to the slope of vf) or (ii) require all employees to work exactly H_R hours per period in return for real earnings of C_R (i.e., for an implied real wage w_3, equal to the slope of the line between v and point a_3, where w_3 is appreciably greater than w_1).[31] The individual with indifference curves u_1 and u_R will

---

[30] See Kniesner (1980b) and Grossman (1981) for a clear statement of this view. There are potential "gains from trade" in the sense that, as indicated in note 21, persons facing discontinuous budget lines usually have MU_L/MU_C less than (*or* greater than) W/P. This means that they stand to gain by trading an hour of leisure for W/P worth of consumer goods (or by trading W/P worth of consumer goods for an hour of leisure).

[31] In other words, production is simply much more efficient, in a technological sense, when everyone works exactly H_R hours per period than it is when everyone is free to

obviously find that the latter regime is more attractive than the former. Moreover, the fact that this individual is not at a tangency equilibrium with a continuous budget line at point a_3 does not, in this view, mean that he is in disequilibrium. The alternative to the point a_3 is the continuous budget line Tvf, and all points on vf are markedly less desirable than a_3: In other words, at a_3, no further gains from trade remain to be exploited.

To date, most equilibrium analyses of the discontinuous budget line of this kind are based either on the notion of compensating wage differentials or on the notion of the optimal employment contract. (In either case, the principal reason for discontinuity in the budget constraint is usually assumed to be unemployment.) In models of compensating wage differentials, firms with lower-than-average levels of rationed hours, H_R, or greater-than-average variability in hours over time offer prospective employees wage premia, designed to compensate them for such differentials in opportunities for work. (See, for example, Abowd and Ashenfelter, 1979, 1981; Deardorff and Stafford, 1976.) For example, in terms of Figure 2.4, the continuous budget line vf may be taken to represent an unrationed job that pays a real wage w_1 and permits employees to vary their hours of work at will. Because the indifference curve that contains the point a_0 must lie below the indifference curve u_1, it follows that an individual with convex indifference curves and real property income v will always prefer this unrationed job to a rationed job that pays the *same* real wage w_1 but in which he may work no more than H_R hours per period (e.g., because the rationed job is one with frequent layoffs). In order to attract workers, the rationed job will therefore have to pay a wage greater than w_2. This is because w_2 (equal to the slope of the line between v and a_2) is the lowest wage that the rationed job could pay that would leave the individual indifferent between the rationed job and the unrationed job, when the latter

choose his own hours of work. Note that all this takes as given "the way production is currently organized" and alternative technologies might have different implications about the magnitude of the optimal work requirement H_R and the implied wage w_3. For example, new computer technology, such as the so-called office of the future, may permit substantially greater flexibility in both the timing and duration of the work day than is currently feasible. Note also that the high wages that may be required in order to make fixed work requirements attractive to employees may also eventually induce development of new technology that permits more flexibility in work requirements.

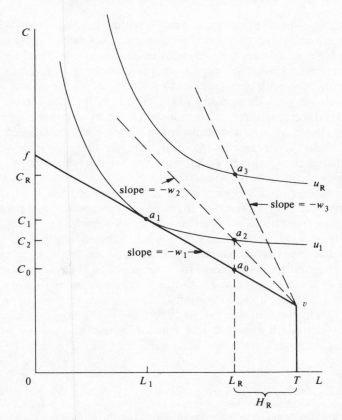

Figure 2.4. Equilibrium model of discontinuous budget line

pays w_1. The difference between w_2 and the unrationed wage w_1 is thus a compensating differential, since it compensates the individual for the difference in hours of work per period between the two jobs.[32]

---

[32] This differential is a "mean compensation," made for differences in *levels* of average hours of work. However, as Abowd and Ashenfelter (1979, 1981) note, jobs may also differ in terms of the *variability* of hours of work, and this will also generate a compensating wage differential. (See also Eden, 1980, who shows that when two income streams are subject to different degrees of random variation the riskier or more variable stream will, in equilibrium, have a higher expected present value. Eden

At least within the compensating differentials model developed by Abowd and Ashenfelter (1979, 1981), the existence of potential gains from trade due to differential employment opportunities in different jobs gives rise only to compensating wage differentials: Differences in work opportunities (e.g., in H_R values) from one job to another do not change. In this limited sense, it is still correct to say that the discontinuity of the budget line under a rationed regime of this kind is an exogenous constraint – *once the individual elects to work under such a regime.* (However, note also that individuals can still change their hours of work by changing regimes and that wages adjust to compensate individuals to the extent that different regimes offer different work opportunities.) A natural extension of this approach, of course, would be to see whether the existence of potential gains from trade will lead to adjustments in the discontinuity itself (e.g., in H_R values), as well as to adjustments in wages.

To date, most optimal employment contract models – the second kind of equilibrium analysis of the discontinuous budget line – have not been directly concerned with questions about hours of work as such (or about the joint determination of wages and of hours of work).[33] However, in many respects such models have an important, if indirect, bearing on just this kind of issue. The question with which such models are immediately concerned is a simple one: When

and Pakes, 1979, present empirical tests of this proposition.) As Abowd and Ashenfelter point out, the ideas of a "mean compensation" and a "variance compensation" are both due to Adam Smith. Writing on the extent and variability of employment opportunities for masons and bricklayers, Smith commented: "What he earns, therefore, must not only maintain him while he is idle, but make him some compensation for those anxious and desponding moments which the thought of so precarious a situation must sometimes occasion" (Smith, 1776, Book I, Chap. X).

[33] This is, both optimal employment contract models and compensating-differentials models implicitly assume that "a job is a job is a job" – in other words, that *when they are employed* persons work a given and fixed number of hours. However, it appears that this assumption is largely one of convenience and no major conclusions would be changed were one to allow for variability and choice of labor supply during periods of employment. (For caveats on this point, see Azariadis, 1981, esp. p. 230; Baily, 1977; and R. J. Gordon, 1976.) Moreover, although each kind of model ignores the possibility of variation in labor supply during periods of employment, each model focuses explicitly on the extent to which periods of employment alternate with periods of unemployment. In this longer-run sense, both kinds of models have much to say about variation in labor supply.

firms experience price changes due to cyclical changes in product demand, what will they do about the wages they pay and the number of workers they employ? At first glance, the answer to this question would seem to be obvious: A decline (increase) in product price will shift all firms' demand-for-labor schedules down and to the left (up and to the right), resulting in a decline (increase) in wages. This "variable-wage" solution thus entails (i) different wages at different stages of the business cycle (e.g., a wage w_H when demand is "high" and a wage w_L when demand is "low," with $w_H > w_L$) and (ii) "full employment," in the sense that workers are free to work as many hours as they choose at the prevailing wage.[34]

However, this variable-wage solution exposes workers to substantial fluctuations in wages – which is another way of saying that, under such a solution, there may be potential gains from trade (that is, from working out alternative ways to cope with cyclical fluctuations in product prices and, hence, employment demand). Indeed, Azariadis (1975, 1976, 1981), Baily (1974, 1977), Barro (1977), Bryant (1978), Calvo and Phelps (1977), Feldstein (1976), D. Gordon (1974), Grossman (1977, 1978, 1981), Hall (1980a), Hall and Lillien (1979), Polemarchakis (1979), Polemarchakis and Weiss (1978), and others have argued that, in some circumstances, both workers and the firm may therefore be better off by arranging a "fixed-wage" solution than they would be under the variable-wage solution previously described.[35] Under such a fixed-wage solution, the firm adjusts to fluctuations in demand by resorting to layoffs when demand is low (and to recalls when demand is high) but pays the same fixed wage w_F regardless of demand conditions. Thus, the fixed-wage solution entails (i) a fixed wage, w_F, and (ii) unemployment during periods of low demand, summarized by a layoff probability λ (meaning that λ percent of the firm's work force will be idle – that is, constrained to have $H = 0$ – when demand is low).

---

[34] Thus, the firm's employment adjusts to demand changes via the effect of wage changes on labor supply. (For example, provided a decline in the wage to w_L during periods of low demand reduces hours of work or induces some persons to leave the labor force, labor supply falls to a level equal to the firm's lower level of labor demand, and similarly for periods of high demand.)

[35] For details, see, for example, Azariadis (1981), whose presentation is particularly straightforward and clear-cut. For a critique of optimal employment contract models, see Pissarides (1979).

Such a fixed-wage solution entails a discontinuous budget line[36] but may nevertheless be superior to the variable-wage solution, which entails a continuous budget line. Moreover, under the fixed-wage solution, both wages and employment opportunities differ from what they would be under the variable-wage solution: The fixed-wage wage w_F will generally lie in between the "low-demand" and "high-demand" wages w_L and w_H that are paid under the variable-wage solution; and, of course, the variable-wage solution provides for a continuous budget line and full employment, whereas the fixed-wage solution entails a discontinuous budget line and lay-offs and unemployment (during periods of low demand). Hence, in these analyses, *both* wages *and* work opportunities (that is, budget lines) adjust in response to perceived gains from trade.

Both in models of compensating wage differentials and in models of optimal employment contracts, then, budget line discontinuities do not really impose constraints on choices. Rather, such discontinuities are a *consequence* of choices. In other words, workers and firms freely arrive at arrangements that exploit perceived opportunities for gains from trade, resulting in budget lines that, although discontinuous, nevertheless provide opportunities for work that are superior to (or at least no less good than) the ones afforded by continuous budget lines.[37]

---

[36] To see this, let H_F be the number of hours that a worker would want to work if confronted with a *continuous* budget line paying a wage w_F; and note that, when demand conditions are low, the fixed-wage solution implies that any given worker will be unemployed, with $H = 0$, some λ percent of the time. On average, then, when demand conditions are low, each worker will expect to work $(1 - \lambda)H_F$ hours, whereas when demand conditions are high each worker will work H_F hours. Suppose further (simply for illustration) that demand conditions are low 50 percent of the time and high the rest of the time. Then, in the long run, a worker who can choose his hours of work *when he is able to work* in effect faces a budget line that has a slope of w_F and is (i) continuous for hours of work in between zero and $\overline{H}$ and (ii) discontinuous (indeed, nonexistent) for hours of work beyond $\overline{H}$, where $\overline{H} \equiv 0.5 H_F + 0.5[(1 - \lambda)H_F] = (1 - 0.5\lambda)H_F$.

[37] That is, the real constraint on choice arises from factors that cause variations in demand that are both unanticipated by and cannot be controlled by either workers or firms: changes in the weather, monetary disturbances, shifts in the pattern or level of demand, and so on. "Optimal" employment contracts are optimal in the sense that they are the best that firms and workers can do to mitigate the consequences of such variations in demand; but such optimal employment contracts are obviously not necessarily ideal, a point that some discussion of such models (both by proponents

Moreover, in both kinds of models, the question of whether or not "unemployment" is "voluntary" is largely semantic, with rather little relevance for normative judgments or policymaking. For example, under a fixed-wage optimal employment contract, low demand will result in some λ percent of a firm's workers being laid off – that is, constrained to have hours of work $H = 0$ – even though they are willing to supply some positive number of hours of work H_F at the wage rate w_F that is paid to the workers who are still employed. Likewise, workers who work in a rationed job (e.g., construction workers or longshoremen) are not able to supply all of the hours they would like to supply at the wage paid to workers in that kind of job; and the difference between their actual hours and their desired hours may well take the form of unemployment (that is, periods during which hours are zero). Both kinds of workers can be said to be "involuntarily unemployed" (in the sense that, at given wage rates, they want to supply more hours than they are able to supply). Both kinds of workers will almost surely be counted as unemployed according to the definitions used in official government surveys (and be upset by their being unemployed). However, workers employed under an optimal employment contract are of course free to work instead at a firm that follows a variable-wage contract (and to suffer large wage declines during slumps); and workers in constrained or rationed jobs are of course free to work instead in unconstrained jobs (and to give up the compensating wage differentials they currently enjoy). In this ex ante sense, then, any unemployment that results from such decisions about what kind of job to accept is purely voluntary. As Feldstein (1976, p. 955) puts it, "any particular spell of unemployment may be both involuntary and loudly protested, even though the decision rule that led to the layoff may have been chosen by the employees" (and, one might add, even though the decision rule may have been better, or less bad, than any feasible alternative).

Thus, the idea that budget lines are discontinuous (in either an

and critics) seems to have overlooked. Finally, it is worth noting that such employment contracts may be either explicit and formal, or else implicit and unwritten. (In the latter case, firms keep to such agreements in order not to get a bad reputation among workers and, thus, to avoid difficulties in recruiting employees.) See Martin (1977) for discussion of formal and informal procedures governing layoffs and other kinds of terminations.

equilibrium or a disequilibrium sense) has a wide range of implications for analysis and policy, both at the microlevel (e.g., issues about compensating wage differentials and the length of the workday and the workweek) and at the macrolevel (e.g., issues about unemployment and wage rigidity). Not surprisingly, then, analyses of such discontinuities raise numerous issues that are subjects of controversy and debate. For example, what conditions are necessary and sufficient for the existence of layoff unemployment or fixed-wage employment contracts (Mortensen, 1978)? Do such conditions include greater risk aversion on the part of workers than on the part of firms, a positive value of leisure (or payment of unemployment insurance benefit) during times of unemployment, or something else? (See Azariadis, 1977, 1981; R. J. Gordon, 1976, 1977.) Do propositions derived from simple models with discontinuous budget lines change once one allows for worker heterogeneity (Grossman, 1978, 1981) or for variable hours of work while at work (Azariadis, 1975; Feldstein, 1974a)? Similarly, optimal employment contract models typically assume that there is a quasi-permanent relationship between workers and "their" firm (e.g., because it is difficult or costly for workers to change firms) and that workers are able to monitor and, thus, in effect, to enforce the terms of the arrangement, explicit or implicit, that they reach with their firm. However, do the results of such models change once one allows for turnover and for the fact that workers search for jobs at other firms and quit into unemployment or to accept work at other firms (Akerlof and Miyazaki, 1980; Hall, 1980a)?[38] Is

---

[38] The notion of job search raises questions of a fundamentally dynamic nature that are more or less ignored in optimal employment and other discontinuous budget line models. For example, simple optimal employment contract models assume that suppliers of labor act as if life were a sequence of single periods like the "single period" to which the simple one-period labor supply model of Chapter 1 refers. Although some periods differ from others (due to fluctuations in demand), and whereas agents are aware of this and, accordingly, act to reach arrangements that minimize the consequences of these differences between periods, agents are assumed to act as if they had neither a past nor a future in all other respects. (For example, they usually are assumed not to save.) In contrast, in job search models, agents *do* have a past and a future and in any given period make decisions with an eye to their future consequences. For example, individuals weigh the current cost of devoting time to job search (in the form of reduced earnings or leisure in the current period) against the expected future benefits (in the form of a greater probability of getting a job and/or a better wage in the future). For more on such dynamic models, see Section 5.3.

unemployment still voluntary (at least in the ex ante sense previously used) if workers are not perfectly informed about firms' behavior or if it is costly to monitor compliance with (or enforce the terms of) implicit arrangements about layoffs that accompany compensating differentials or fixed-wage implicit contracts (Eaton and Quandt, 1980)? Will fixed-wage optimal employment contracts, or employment arrangements with compensating wage differentials, always involve layoffs during recessions, or could such contracts sometimes take other forms, such as (i) pure "spot" market arrangements, with wages *and* employment adjusting to demand and price changes, or (ii) "guaranteed income" contracts, with fixed wages and *no* layoffs (Akerlof and Miyazaki, 1980; Azariadis, 1981; Hashimoto and Yu, 1980; Markusen, 1979)?

Many of these analytical questions are still controversial. (See Mortensen, 1978, for a thorough discussion of many of these issues.) Moreover, empirical work on employment contract and similar models at both the macrolevel (Eaton and Quandt, 1980; Rosen and Quandt, 1978) and at the microlevel (Abowd and Ashenfelter, 1979, 1981; Ashenfelter and Ham, 1979; Ham, 1982) is still in its early stages. Finally, the policy implications of such models have not yet been fully worked out. For example, the fact that unemployment is voluntary in equilibrium models of the discontinuous budget line simply means that, faced with forces over which they have no control (e.g., the existing state of technology, fluctuations in demand), firms and workers try to make arrangements to mitigate the impact of such forces on their earnings, profits, and so forth. However, this does not necessarily mean that government policies to mitigate the impact of such forces are unnecessary or undesirable, if (and this is a separate, and equally important, analytical question) such policies can be effective (Baily, 1981; Grossman, 1981).

Finally, it is worth emphasizing that, whether or not such budget line discontinuities are constraints on or the result of choices, such discontinuities complicate the task of estimating income and substitution effects. For example, in terms of Figure 2.4, an individual who would choose point a_1 at wage w_1 on a continuous budget line would be just as well off at point a_2 with an hours constraint H_R and wage w_2. Presumably, then, a random sample of workers will contain both some individuals at points like a_1 and some individuals at points like a_2. However, since a_2 is not a point of tangency, the labor supply difference $(L_1 - L_R)$ associated with the wage difference $(w_1 - w_2)$ is clearly not the sum of a conventional income and a conventional substitution effect. Moreover, if there were no constraints on hours of work, then an individual at point a_2 would choose a point involving more than H_R hours of work if he could earn a wage of w_2 (note that, at a_2, the marginal rate of substitution is smaller than w_2). Thus, ignoring the fact that a_2 is not a point of tangency will exaggerate the extent to which an uncompensated wage increase (with no constraints on hours of work) would reduce hours of work. Indeed, it is entirely possible that an individual with real property income v who had no constraints on hours of work would choose to work more hours at wage w_2 than he would at wage w_1. (In other words, the indifference curve that is tangent to the dashed line that passes through points v and a_2 could easily be tangent to that line at a level of leisure below L_1.) If so, then ignoring budget line discontinuities could result in the conclusion that the supply of labor falls as the wage increases, even though, in the absence of budget line discontinuities, the supply of labor would *rise* as the wage rises.

3

Empirical studies of static labor supply models: introduction, with a summary of "first-generation" results

Empirical studies of static labor supply models are of interest for at least four reasons. First, they may be used to test the predictions and implications of theoretical models: For example, is the own-substitution effect of a wage increase on labor supply positive? Second, such studies may provide information on the signs and magnitudes of effects about which theoretical models make no a priori predictions: For example, is leisure a normal good, and is the labor supply schedule backward bending? Third, such studies may shed light on a variety of important labor market developments, such as the phenomenal increase in labor force participation of women (particularly married women) in the past quarter century or the apparent constancy over the past four decades of the length of the average workweek. Fourth, empirical studies are an important tool for evaluation of proposed government policies: For example, will tax cuts or transfer program increases affect work effort, and, if so, by how much?

In principle, empirical analysis of labor supply models is straightforward. One adopts a specification for the labor supply function, collects data for a sample of observations (e.g., individuals) on the variables that appear in the function, and then computes the regression of labor supply on those variables. However, the actual history of empirical work on static labor supply models is much more complicated than this abstract outline suggests. "First-generation" empirical studies of labor supply, most of which appeared in the 1960s and early 1970s, usually used simple methodology and – as the discussion of the results of these studies in Section 3.4 indicates – often raised more questions than they answered. Gradually, two things became apparent. First, many of the problems encountered in these first-generation studies were interrelated. For example, first-generation researchers wrestled with (i) the fact that data on wage rates are almost never available for persons who are not working, (ii) the question of whether to include or exclude persons who are not working when fitting a labor supply regression, and (iii) the question of whether a simple linear function can adequately represent labor supply behavior, especially when labor supply can never be *less* than zero and when many individuals' labor supplies are *exactly* zero. Thus, problems of (i) measurement, (ii) sample selection, and (iii) functional form are often intimately connected. Second, particularly because they were so closely related, these problems had to be confronted using not only a unified and sophisticated theoretical methodology but also improved econometric techniques specifically designed to suit that methodology.

These concerns fostered a number of "second-generation" studies, which date from the mid-1970s and which directly address some of the problems that were glossed over or left unresolved in first-generation research. These studies are the subject of Chapter 4.

3.1.   Econometric specification

As Abbott and Ashenfelter (1976, p. 396) note, there are essentially three different ways to specify a labor supply function. First, one may adopt an explicit direct utility function and then solve the first-order conditions for a maximum, to obtain demand functions for leisure time, L, and a composite consumer good, C. (For examples of studies that take this approach, see Hurd, 1978; Leuthold, 1968.) For example, suppose that the individual's utility function is

(3.1) $u = C^{\alpha}L^{\beta}$

and is maximized subject to the budget constraint

(3.2) $PC = W(1 - L) + V$

As before, C is defined as the amount of a (composite) consumer good that sells for a price of P per unit; L is now the *fraction* of available time per period devoted to leisure, and similarly for H, labor supply, so that now $H + L = 1$; W is the wage rate per period; and V is property income per period. As noted in Chapter 1, if the individual works, then two first-order conditions for maximum utility are satisfied. First, the budget constraint (3.2) holds; and, second, the individual's indifference curve is tangent to his budget line – or, in algebraic terms, his marginal rate of substitution, M, is equal to the real wage, W/P. Now, the marginal rate of substitution is defined as $M \equiv (\partial u/\partial L)/(\partial u/\partial C)$. So, use (3.1) to calculate M and use the second of the two first-order conditions to equate M with W/P. This yields

$$(3.3) \quad (\beta/L)/(\alpha/C) = W/P$$

for an individual who works. Now, (3.2) and (3.3) constitute two equations in the worker's two decision variables, L and C. Solve them, and then use the fact that $H^* = 1 - L^*$, to obtain

$$(3.4) \quad H^* = 1 - b - b(V/W)$$
$$(3.5) \quad C^* = (1 - b)[(W + V)/P] \quad \text{where } b \equiv \beta/(\alpha + \beta)$$

which give the individual's *desired* levels of H and C, H^* and C^*, when the utility function is (3.1).

The second method of specification is to adopt a particular form for a function other than the direct utility function that is nevertheless related to the direct utility function. Thus, Heckman, Killingsworth, and MaCurdy (1981) discuss labor supply functions that are derived from specifications of the marginal rate of substitution function. Likewise, Dickinson (1980) discusses labor supply functions implied by different versions of the expenditure function (which gives the minimum expenditure required, at given W, V, and P, to attain a fixed level of utility $\bar{u}$). Other researchers (e.g., Burtless and Hausman, 1978; Wales and Woodland, 1976, 1977) derive labor supply models by specifying an indirect utility function and then using Roy's Identity to derive functions for C^* and L^*.[1]

---

[1] Any one of these four functions – utility, marginal rate of substitution, expenditure, or indirect utility – implies a particular form for the other three. For example, the marginal rate of substitution function implied by the utility function (3.1) is $M = (\beta/\alpha)(C/L)$, as indicated by (3.3). Likewise, when the utility function is (3.1), then the minimum amount of real expenditure on goods and leisure $X = (PC + WL)/P = C + (W/P)L$ required to attain a given level of utility $\bar{u}$ is given by the expenditure function $X = (\alpha + \beta)\beta^{-1}(\beta/\alpha)^{\alpha/(\alpha+\beta)}(W/P)^{\beta/(\alpha+\beta)}\bar{u}^{1/(\alpha+\beta)}$. (To derive

For example, suppose one analyzes labor supply by starting with an indirect utility function in which maximum utility (that is, utility maximized subject to (3.2) and expressed as a function of W, V, and P) is assumed to be given by

$$(3.6) \quad u^* = (a/b)(V/P)^b + (c/d)(W/P)^d$$

Now, by Roy's Identity (see Chapter 1), the utility-maximizing values of H and C are given by $H^* = (\partial u^*/\partial W)/(\partial u^*/\partial V)$ and $C^* = -(\partial u^*/\partial P)/(\partial u^*/\partial V)$. Hence, when the indirect utility function is (3.6), the individual's desired H and C are

$$(3.7) \quad H^* = (c/a)(V/W)(W/P)^d (V/P)^{-b}$$
$$= (c/a)(W/P)^{d-1}(V/P)^{1-b}$$
$$(3.8) \quad C^* = (V/P) + (c/a)(W/P)^d (V/P)^{1+b}$$

Finally, under the third approach – followed in most first-generation studies – one simply adopts, a priori, either (i) a set of "approximate functions" giving H^* and C^* as functions of W, V, and P or (ii) a set of finite approximations to differentials of functions for desired levels of H and C, expressing *changes* in H^* and C^* as functions of *changes* in W, V, and P. (For an example of (i), see Lau, Lin, and Yotopoulos, 1978; for examples of (ii), see Ashenfelter and Heckman, 1973; Barnett, 1981. These studies are considerably more thorough than most other works of the same kind.) Such functions for levels of (or changes in) C^* and H^* will look like the functions given earlier, that is, like (3.4) and (3.5) or (3.7) and (3.8). However, the coefficients in approximation functions do not necessarily have an immediate interpretation in terms of utility or indirect utility function parameters, whereas those of equations (3.4) and (3.5) and (3.7) and (3.8) do. (Deaton and

---

this, set u equal to $\bar{u}$ in (3.1), solve (3.1) and (3.3) for L and C and use the definition $X = C + (W/P)L$.) Finally, when the utility function is (3.1), so that optimal C and H are given by (3.4) and (3.5), use the relation $L^* = 1 - H^*$ and substitute (3.4) and (3.5) into (3.1) to derive the indirect utility function implied by (3.1), $u^* = (1-b)^\alpha b^\beta [(W+V)/P]^\alpha [1 + (V/W)]^\beta$. In principle, then, choosing which of these four functions to use in deriving a labor supply specification is largely a matter of taste, although in particular cases there may be important practical advantages in working with one particular one of these functions rather than any of the other three. See Brown and Deaton (1972) and Deaton (1974, 1981) for discussion of the implications of a variety of functional forms for these functions.

Mueilbauer, 1981, discuss the preference structures implied by commonly used approximation functions for labor supply, in which labor supply is expressed as a linear function of the wage and property income.)

Needless to say, labor supply is the focus of interest here; consumption is at best of secondary importance (though it may well be much more important in other contexts, or to other researchers). Nevertheless, it is important to note that the way in which one treats different kinds of consumption spending may have an important bearing on the way one analyzes labor supply, and even on the validity of analyses of labor supply. In particular, if one can aggregate all consumer goods into a single Hicksian composite commodity C, then one can express labor supply as a function of the real wage W/P and the real value of property income V/P, where the price P is the price of any arbitrarily selected good that is part of the composite good C. The previous discussion, of course, is based on just this assumption. However, recall from Chapter 1 that this aggregation is appropriate only if the prices of all consumer goods stay in the same proportion to each other. In some cases, this requirement is in fact satisfied. For example, in an analysis of the labor supply of a cross section of persons in a fairly compact geographic area, such as a city or a county, it would usually seem reasonable to assume that relative prices P_i/P_j of any pair of consumption goods C_i and C_j will be more or less the same at all points (neighborhoods, cities) within that area: indeed, all price *levels* will be more or less the same. If so, then it is not even necessary to deflate the nominal quantities W and V by the price level P: Since P is the same for all observations, such deflation simply changes units of measurement. Indeed, most studies of labor supply neglect the price(s) of consumption goods (and the demand for consumption goods) entirely, apparently on the grounds (or in the hope!) that relative prices are, indeed, roughly constant.

However, this assumption of roughly constant relative consumption goods prices (and, hence, lumping all consumption goods into a single composite) may be much less appropriate in an analysis of persons in a broad geographic area (e.g., a state or a country) or in an analysis of time-series data. At a minimum, one would usually want to deflate W and V by regional or annual general price indices to allow for regional or time-series differences in the price level. (For example, see Boskin, 1973; Hall, 1973; Schultz, 1980.) However, that still requires the assumption of constant *relative* prices, and relative prices may not be constant. For example, the price of fuel relative to shelter is not necessarily the same in California as it is in Maine, and it has certainly not remained constant through time.

In cases such as these – that is, when the prerequisites of the composite commodity theorem are not satisfied – it is necessary to find an alternative justification for labor supply functions that omit variables for the prices of various consumer goods. A necessary and sufficient condition for ignoring such consumer goods prices in a labor supply function is the assumption of a weakly separable utility function. "Weak separability" means that the function giving utility explicitly as a function of leisure and each of the n distinct consumer goods, $u = u(C_1, C_2, \ldots, C_n, L)$ may be written as $u = z[c(C_1, C_2, \ldots, C_n), L]$, where the function $c(C_1, C_2, \ldots, C_n)$ is linearly homogeneous in its arguments (Abbott and Ashenfelter, 1976, p. 392; Barnett, 1979a, p. 543). Unfortunately, weak separability turns out to have some rather restrictive empirical implications. For example, it implies that if leisure and some consumer good C_i are both normal goods, then C_i is necessarily a substitute for leisure (in the sense that an income-compensated rise in W (in P_i) will always increase consumption of good C_i (of leisure)), even though it is not hard to think of various "recreation" goods that are both normal and *complementary* to leisure (Owen, 1971).

Accordingly, a number of studies have considered the entire system of demand functions (for leisure, consumption good C_1, consumption good C_2, . . . , etc.); each such demand function (including the leisure demand function) includes not only V and W but also all consumption goods prices, $P_1, P_2, \ldots, P_n$ among its arguments. (For surveys, see Barten, 1977; Brown and Deaton, 1972. For examples, see Abbott and Ashenfelter, 1976, 1979; Atkinson and Stern, 1981; Barnett, 1979a, 1981; Blundell, 1980; Darrough, 1977; Keller, 1977; Kiefer, 1976, 1977.)

There remain two final questions about specification – ones that were largely overlooked in first-generation studies.

First, even though they are based on the simplest possible underlying labor supply model and the simplest possible budget constraint, (3.2), equations such as (3.4) and (3.7) are not a complete model of labor supply. To see this, consider (3.4) by way of example

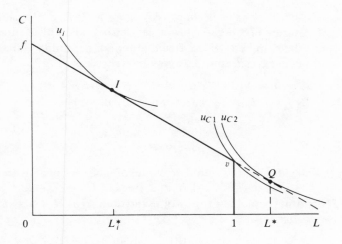

Figure 3.1.   Corner and interior solutions

(the argument is more or less the same for (3.7) and for approximation functions). Now, (3.4) is derived on the assumption that the
individual works and thus has $M = W/P$. However, the individual
will work and have $M = W/P$ *only* if his real wage W/P exceeds his
reservation wage $M_{L=1}$, where $M_{L=1}$ is the value of M when $L = 1$
and $H = 0$. As such, (3.4) ignores values of W/P that are below the
reservation wage – in other words, (3.4) says nothing about what
happens if the demand for leisure (desired leisure, $L*$) exceeds total
available time and therefore cannot be completely satisfied.

A situation of this kind is represented by the point Q in Figure 3.1:
At real wage w (equal to the slope of budget line $1\,vf$), the individual
with indifference curves u_{C1} and u_{C2} attains a point of tangency at Q
and has leisure demand, $L*$, in excess of total available time. Of
course, what happens in this case is obvious: Since the individual
cannot satisfy all of his demand for leisure $L*$, his actual leisure time
L will equal unity (1) and will exhaust all available time. Thus, the
individual will be at a corner equilibrium at v. As noted in Chapter 1,
$W \le M_{L=1}$ at corner equilibria. Moreover, when the utility function
is (3.1), the function for the marginal rate of substitution M is
simply $M = \beta C/\alpha L$. Hence, when the utility function is (3.1), the
reservation wage – that is, the value of M when $L = 1$, $H = 0$, and

$PC = V + WH = V -$ is simply $M_{L=1} = \beta V/\alpha P$. So let *actual* hours of leisure be L and, as before, let *desired* hours of leisure be L^*. Then, the complete leisure demand model for utility function (3.1) and budget constraint (3.2) may be written as

$$L^* = b + b(V/W) \quad \text{where} \quad b \equiv \beta/(\alpha + \beta)$$
$$L = L^* \qquad \text{if and only if}$$
$$W/P > M_{L=1} = \beta V/\alpha P$$
$$L = 1 \qquad \text{if and only if}$$
$$W/P \leq M_{L=1} = \beta V/\alpha P$$

By the same token, the complete model of labor supply – with H^* denoting desired hours of work (and defined as $H^* = 1 - L^*$), and with H denoting actual hours of work (and defined as $H = 1 - L$) – may be written as

$$(3.9) \qquad H^* = 1 - b - b(V/W) \quad \text{where} \quad b \equiv \beta/(\alpha + \beta)$$
$$(3.10) \qquad H = H^* \qquad \text{if and only if}$$
$$W/P > M_{L=1} = \beta V/\alpha P$$
$$(3.11) \qquad H = 0 \qquad \text{if and only if}$$
$$W/P \leq M_{L=1} = \beta V/\alpha P$$

(3.10) and (3.11) show what actual labor supply, H, will be when the individual must obey the constraint that $H + L$ must be unity – that is, can take up (exactly) 100 percent of total available time per period. (3.9) shows the "desired" level of labor supply, that is, the labor supply the individual would desire to have if it were possible to equate M and W/P – in other words, to reach a tangency – without regard for this constraint. In some cases, as for the individual with indifference curve u_i in Figure 3.1, L^* is a positive fraction, and therefore $H^* = 1 - L^*$ is also a positive fraction. Here, the constraint $H + L = 1$ has no particular importance. However, in other cases, for example, the individual with indifference curves u_{C1} and u_{C2} in Figure 3.1, L^* exceeds unity and so H^* is negative. In such cases, the constraint does become important, as implied by (3.11).

Second, thus far, this discussion of labor supply models has been concerned with a given individual, but empirical studies use data on different individuals. Now, as noted in Chapter 1, different individuals may supply very different amounts of labor even if they receive the same property income (V/P) and can earn the same wage (W/P). (Recall Figure 1.4.) Because such persons face the same budget constraint, these labor supply differences are necessarily due to utility function differences – differences in tastes for work.[2] In terms of the present discussion, this means that different individuals may have different values for the parameter $b \equiv \beta/(\alpha + \beta)$ – that is, for the utility function parameters α and β in (3.1).

To some extent, these parameter differences may be associated with age, sex, race, and other *observed* variables. Thus, investigators often consider data on individuals who are alike in terms of these factors (or else, in many cases, add "demographic variables" reflecting these factors to "basic" labor supply functions such as (3.12)). (For a thorough discussion of the use of such variables, see Pollak and Wales, 1980, 1981.)

However, even persons in the same age–sex–race group who have the same V/P and the same W/P may have different labor supplies – again, due to differences in tastes for work. Moreover, almost by definition, many of the factors that may be related to tastes for work are unmeasured in any data set. These unmeasured factors – more generally, factors that are known to the individual who actually supplies labor but are not known to or observed by the researcher – are represented by a so-called error term, ϵ, denoting the impact of these unmeasured variables on labor supply.[3] It is conventional to assume that ϵ is a "mean-zero random variable," that is, has a mean

---

[2] Of course, such labor supply differences might also be due to errors in the measurement of H, W/P, or V/P – that is, persons might appear to face identical constraints (because their measured W/P and V/P values are the same) but in fact face different constraints (because the seeming equality of these variables is due only to errors of measurement); and persons who face identical budget constraints may appear to supply different H simply because their measured H values differ even though in fact their actual H values are identical. Finally, persons with identical W/P and V/P values might still face different budget constraints due to other, unobserved, factors (e.g., when one individual must "pay" a time or money cost in order to work, whereas the other does not).

[3] In particular, ϵ may arise from unobserved components on *either* side of labor supply functions such as (3.12). On the one hand, the measure of labor supply available to the investigator, $\widetilde{H}$, may differ from the amount of labor actually supplied by the individual, H, due to a measurement error m. (Hence $\widetilde{H} - H = m$.) Whenever H is replaced with $\widetilde{H}$ in empirical studies, the error term ϵ includes the amount of measurement error m. On the other hand, omitted right-hand-side variables – that is, factors other than W/P and V/P that affect labor supply but for which the investigator has no measures – or errors in the measurement of included right-hand-side variables are also usually taken to be included within, and to give rise to, ϵ.

of zero and is uncorrelated with the included right-hand-side variables (W/P, V/P, etc.) in the group of individuals for whom the labor supply function is to be estimated.

In most studies, the factors comprehended within ϵ are assumed to enter additively into the labor supply function; roughly speaking, this amounts to an assumption that such factors affect the intercept of the labor supply schedule but not its slope. Of course, particularly if one thinks of taste differences as differences in utility function parameters, it would make sense to treat labor supply slope parameters (e.g., income and substitution effects) as functions of unobservables as well as of observable (e.g., demographic) characteristics (Burtless and Hausman, 1978; Dickinson, 1975). Although some studies do in fact treat such parameters as functions of unobservables (see, in particular, Burtless and Hausman, 1978), most studies rely on a maintained hypothesis that unobservables are purely additive.[4]

Thus, to get a "complete" (though still very simple) *empirical* labor supply function for desired hours of work, H^*, one typically adds an ϵ term to (3.9). This yields

$$H^* = 1 - \beta - \beta(V/W) + \epsilon$$

Now, for purposes of empirical work, investigators must use data on *actual* labor supply, H: Data on *desired* labor supply, H^*, are usually not available whenever $W \leq M_{L=1}$, that is, whenever individuals do not work (and so have actual labor supply, H, equal to zero). To write functions for actual hours of work that are analogous to (3.10) and (3.11), proceed as before by observing that actual and desired hours of work are equal whenever desired hours of work are positive and otherwise actual hours of work are zero. The complete *empirical* labor supply model – written in terms of

[4] On the whole, first-generation research had little to say about the nature and sources of ϵ; in contrast, as will become evident in Chapter 4, consideration of such questions about ϵ is an important aspect of second-generation work. Finally, both first- and second-generation research typically assume that ϵ is a *normally distributed* mean-zero random variable. This assumption is convenient (which helps account for its widespread use), but it is not always essential, particularly in first-generation work.

actual hours of work, H, for purposes of econometric estimation – is therefore[5]

$$(3.12) \quad H^* = b_0 + b_1 X_1 + \epsilon \qquad \text{where} \quad b_0 = 1 - b, b_1 = b,$$
$$\text{and} \quad X_1 = -V/W$$

$$(3.13) \quad H = b_0 + b_1 X_1 + \epsilon \qquad \text{if and only if}$$
$$b_0 + b_1 X_1 + \epsilon > 0$$

$$(3.14) \quad H = 0 \qquad \text{if and only if}$$
$$b_0 + b_1 X_1 + \epsilon \leq 0$$

To see this in graphical terms, consider Figure 3.2, where dots show the *desired* labor supplies, H^*, of different individuals (all of whom have the same V value) as computed from the function for desired labor supply, (3.12). Curve *def* shows the desired labor supply of an individual whose value of ϵ is zero (i.e., whose unmeasured tastes for work are neither negative nor positive). The value of ϵ for any individual whose dot lies above or below *def* is given by the vertical distance between his particular "dot" and the line *def*. Broken line 0*ef* shows the *actual* labor supply of an individual whose value of ϵ is zero. Note that the actual and desired labor supply schedules for an individual with $\epsilon = 0$ coincide when (and only when) the real wage W/P exceeds the reservation wage $M_{L=1} = \beta V/\alpha P$. Note also that actual labor supply H is zero (whereas desired labor supply H^* is negative) whenever the reservation wage exceeds the real wage.

Thus, the dot for the *actual* labor supply of any individual whose desired labor supply is negative (and whose actual labor supply is therefore zero) will lie on the horizontal axis, whereas the dot for the *actual* labor supply of any individual whose desired labor supply is positive (and whose actual labor supply is therefore equal to the desired level) will coincide with the dot denoting his desired

---

[5] Note that the condition $b_0 + b_1 X_1 + \epsilon > 0$ has behavioral content. It is equivalent to the condition $1 - b - b(V/W) + \epsilon = [\alpha - \beta(V/W) + (\alpha + \beta)\epsilon]/(\alpha + \beta) > 0$, or, after simplifying, to $W/P > \beta V/[\alpha + (\alpha + \beta)\epsilon]P$. If ϵ were always zero, as in a purely deterministic model, the right-hand side of this inequality would be the reservation wage $M_{L+1} + \beta V/\alpha P$, calculated in the usual way from the utility function (3.1). The condition $b_0 + b_1 X_1 + \epsilon > 0$ in the empirical labor supply model therefore amounts to a statement that reservation wages depend not only on real property income V/P and on utility function parameters α and b but also on unobservable or random factors ϵ.

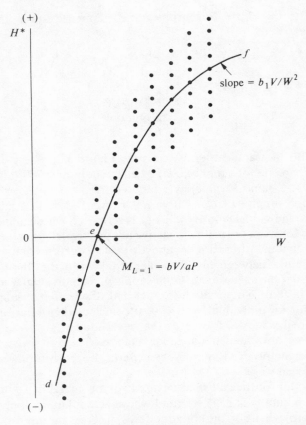

Figure 3.2.   Graph of labor supply function $H^* = b_0 + b_1 X_1 + \epsilon$ for persons with fixed V

supply. Finally, the slope of the line *ef* shows how an individual who has a specific, fixed, value of ϵ will respond to a change in the wage whenever the wage exceeds the reservation level. From (3.12) or (3.13), this slope is simply $\partial H^*/\partial W = b_1 (\partial X_1/\partial W) = bV/W^2$ and depends on the utility function parameter $b \equiv \beta/(\alpha + \beta)$.

3.2.   **Sample selection**
Randomly selected samples taken from the entire popula-tion are sometimes used in estimating labor supply functions, but in

many cases either choice or necessity dictates that something other than a pure random sample be used. Sometimes, the investigator wants to study only the labor supply behavior of a population subgroup, for example, poor people, married women, teenagers, or men. In other cases, data are available only for a particular population subgroup. (For example, certain kinds of survey data sets refer only to persons below the "poverty" level of income, wage data are usually available only for persons currently at work, and so on.) No particular difficulties arise if the subgroup is selected according to wholly exogenous factors, such as age, sex, or race, that are determined outside the model of labor supply behavior. However, if the subgroup is selected according to endogenous factors – that is, factors that may be determined along with labor supply, such as current earnings or current income – then a variety of complications may arise.

The basic reason why these complications arise is that when a sample is selected on the basis of endogenous factors the error term ϵ may not be a mean-zero random variable in the resulting *sample* even if it is a mean-zero random variable in the population as a whole. As a result, direct application of simple regression methods such as ordinary least squares (OLS) may be inappropriate – for such methods provide valid results only if ϵ *is* a mean-zero random variable within the sample. Rather, simple regression estimates will suffer from what is known as *sample selection* (or *selectivity*) *bias*.

For an intuitive understanding of the essentials of the problem, suppose one were to estimate the labor supply function (3.12) using a sample limited to workers – that is, persons with $H > 0$. From the discussion in the previous section, this means that the sample is limited to persons who, in terms of Figure 3.2, have data points that lie above the horizontal axis (and have $H^* > 0$). All data points on or below the axis are excluded from the analysis, since these refer to nonworkers. Now, roughly speaking, simple regression methods entail drawing a line that, at each value of the independent variable(s), will lie in the middle of the scatter of data points being analyzed. Obviously, fitting a regression line to the *complete* scatter of points shown in Figure 3.2 would yield the true labor supply schedule, *def*: At each value of W, *def* does indeed lie in the middle of the scatter of data points.[6] But ignoring all points in Figure 3.2 that lie on or below the horizontal axis – looking only at workers – must necessarily result in a regression line, *xyz*, that will lie above the true schedule, *def*. (See Figure 3.3.) Thus, the regression line derived from data for the working subpopulation will provide statistically biased and inconsistent measures of structural labor supply parameters. For example, note from Figure 3.3 that the regression line *xyz* implies both that (i) the reservation wage (that is, the point at which the supply schedule cuts the *W* axis) is lower and (ii) the slope of the regression line is flatter than the slope of the true labor supply schedule *def*.

The source of the problem is obvious. Within the sample of workers, ϵ is not a mean-zero random variable, even though it is a mean-zero random variable in the population as a whole. In particular, within the sample of workers, the average value of ϵ tends to be positive. (Indeed, it would be somewhat surprising if one did not find that tastes for work, ϵ, were higher, on average, in a sample of workers than in the general population.) Because the sample is limited to persons who work, observations with small or negative ϵ values will generally lie below the horizontal axis, implying $H^* < 0$ and $H = 0$. Such observations will therefore be excluded from the sample to be analyzed.

Moreover, within the sample of workers, ϵ will be negatively correlated with *W*: As *W* increases, an observation can have a smaller, or more negative, value of ϵ and yet still lie above the horizontal axis (and, therefore, can still qualify for inclusion in the sample to be analyzed). Because ϵ is positive on average within the sample, the regression line *xyz* constructed for the sample will lie above the true schedule *def*: The regression method assumes (incorrectly, in this case) that ϵ has a mean of zero in the sample of workers; thus, at any given value of *W*, the regression line for the sample will lie above the "true" schedule by an amount equal to the actual mean of ϵ in the sample at that value of *W*. Further, since (the mean of) ϵ is nega-

---

[6] Since *def* is a curve, it may sound strange to speak of fitting a straight line to the scatter of data points. However, note that (3.15) is indeed linear in X_1 ($= V/W$) and that *def* is a curve only because the variable on the horizontal axis, *W*, is in the denominator of the expression for X_1. If (3.15) were plotted with *H* on the vertical and X_1 on the horizontal axis, then of course the scatter of data points would imply a straight-line regression "line."

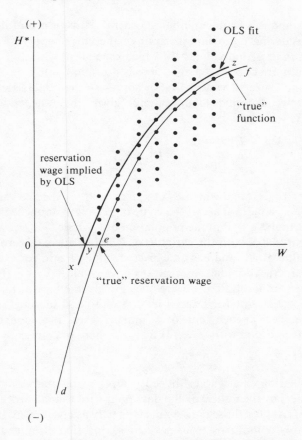

Figure 3.3. OLS fit to labor supply function $H^* = b_0 + b_1 X_1 + \epsilon$ shown in Figure 3.2, when sample restricted to persons who work

tively correlated with W in the sample of workers, this discrepancy between the regression line for the sample and the true labor supply schedule will fall as W rises and will rise as W falls. Hence, the regression line xyz will be flatter than the true labor supply schedule def.[7]

---

[7] This discussion may leave the impression that one way to avoid the problems that arise when nonworkers are excluded from the estimation sample is to include nonworkers. This is one possible solution, but it is not a simple one to implement. First,

To understand this problem in more general terms, it is useful to start by considering regression analysis of the labor supply of an entire *population* of individuals (in which case all observations in the population are considered and there is no sampling). Now, by definition, the expected value of labor supply in the population – more precisely, expected labor supply, given the independent variable(s) X_1 – is equal to

$$(3.15)\quad E[H \mid X_1] = E[b_0 + b_1 X_1 + \epsilon \mid X_1]$$
$$= b_0 + b_1 X_1 + E[\epsilon \mid X_1]$$
$$= b_0 + b_1 X_1 + K_P$$

where $K_P \equiv E[\epsilon \mid X_1]$ and where $E[x \mid y]$ means "the expected value of x, given (i.e., conditional on) the value of y." Now, suppose that one assumes that $K_P = 0$ in the population as a whole. This means that ϵ is uncorrelated with the variable(s) X_1, has a mean of zero at any given value of X_1, and has an expected value of zero for every observation in the population with any given value of X_1. (For example, the ϵ values in Figure 3.2, which are given by the distance between any given dot for desired labor supply and the line *def*, average out to zero at each value of X_1 and are, therefore, independent of – uncorrelated with – X_1.) If $K_P = 0$, then, of course,

$$(3.16)\quad E[H \mid X_1] = b_0 + b_1 X_1$$

for the population as a whole. Indeed, simple regression assumes that, regardless of the nature of the data points to be analyzed, the value of $E[H \mid X_1]$ for those data points is exactly as given by (3.16). (This is simply a more rigorous way of saying that "regression methods draw a line through the middle of the scatter of data points to be analyzed.") In particular, if one has data on the desired labor supplies H^* of all individuals of a population, and if $E[\epsilon \mid X_1] = 0$ within that population, then one can obtain unbiased and consistent

---

data on the desired (as opposed to actual) labor supplies of nonworkers are not available – in contrast with workers, for whom actual labor supply is nonzero and equals desired labor supply. In order to include nonworkers, then, one would have to obtain measures of nonworkers' desired labor supplies. Further, one would have to obtain measures of the wages that nonworkers could earn were they to work – and, in general, such measures are not available for nonworkers precisely because they are not working.

estimates of the labor supply parameters b_0 and b_1 by using simple regression methods.

Next, however, consider application of simple regression to a sample of individuals *selected from* a population in which $E[\epsilon \mid X_1]$ = 0. This involves using a *sample selection rule*, that is, a set of criteria that determine which observations in the population will (or will not) be included in the sample to be analyzed. In its essentials, any sample selection rule takes the following form:

> *Sample selection rule*: Include an observation i in the sample to be analyzed, if and only if $S_i > C_i$, where S_i is the value of a sample selection variable, and C_i is a particular cutoff value.[8]

(For example, if S_i refers to hours of work and C_i is always zero for all observations, then the selection rule "include if and only if $S > C$" simply means "include only individuals who work.")

Now, by definition, expected labor supply for a sample selected according to a sample selection rule – that is, expected labor supply, given X_1 *and* that each observation in the sample satisfies the conditions set out in the selection rule – may be written as

$$(3.17) \quad E[H \mid X_1, \text{sample selection rule}]$$
$$= E[b_0 + b_1X_1 + \epsilon \mid X_1, S > C]$$
$$= b_0 + b_1X_1 + E[\epsilon \mid X_1, S > C] = b_0 + b_1X_1 + K_S$$

where $K_S \equiv E[\epsilon \mid X_1, S > C]$. Note that $K_S \equiv E[\epsilon \mid X_1, S > C]$ will be equal to $E[\epsilon \mid X_1]$, which is in turn equal to zero (by assumption) for all observations in the population, *only* if S and ϵ are independent, or, in other words, only if S is exogenous to labor supply in the sense that S is uncorrelated with the labor supply error term ϵ. If so, then $E[H \mid X_1, \text{sample selection rule}] = b_0 + b_1X_1$, exactly as assumed in simple least-squares regression; and simple regression estimates of b_0 and b_1 will be unbiased and consistent so long as $E[\epsilon \mid X_1] = 0$ in the underlying population. On the other hand,

---

[8] Note that the condition $S_i > C_i$ can be generalized to a set of conditions referring to numerous sample selection variables S_{1i} through S_{si} and corresponding cutoff values C_{1i} through C_{si}, respectively. (Thus, one could select a sample containing only people age 45 or more *and* earning income of $10,000 or more.) Likewise, the "greater than" condition is inessential; for example, if S_i is defined as the *negative* of income, whereas C_i is set at − 5,000, then the rule "select if and only if $S_i > C_i$" entails selecting only persons with incomes *below* $5,000.

suppose that S and ϵ are not independent, or, in other words, that S is endogenous to labor supply (in the sense that S is correlated with the labor supply error term). In this case, K_S will be nonzero even if $E[\epsilon \mid X_1] = 0$ in the underlying population. (For example, if S and ϵ are positively correlated, then K_S will be positive.) Simple regression nevertheless assumes that $K_S = 0$ and hence omits the nonzero variable K_S from (3.17); in this case, then, simple regression estimates of b_0 and b_1 will be biased and inconsistent.

Several examples help to illustrate this basic point. First, suppose one selects a regression sample on a purely random basis, so that the sample selection variable S is a randomly assigned number.[9] In this case, then, S is necessarily uncorrelated with ϵ, so that K_S is zero. In other words, if S is a random number (which means that S is uncorrelated with ϵ), then $E[\epsilon \mid X_1, S > C] = E[\epsilon \mid X_1]$; and, by assumption, $E[\epsilon \mid X_1] = 0$ for (each and every observation in) the population. Here, then, application of least squares is entirely appropriate.

Next, suppose that the sample selection variable S is some variable that is exogenous to labor supply, in the sense that this S is uncorrelated with ϵ. (Examples of exogenous S variables might be age, sex, or race; increases in ϵ cannot be associated with increases in any of these variables, since they are all fixed.) For example, suppose that S refers to age and that C is 44 for all observations, so that the selection rule is "select if and only if the observation is older than 44 years of age." This kind of selection is certainly not "random"; indeed, it is highly "systematic" and "nonrandom," in the ordinary language sense. However, this kind of selection is nevertheless random *with respect to labor supply*, in the sense that such an S is uncorrelated with the labor supply error term ϵ and is therefore exogenous to labor supply. Thus, for this kind of selection rule as for random selection, $E[\epsilon \mid X_1, S > C] = E[\epsilon \mid X_1]$; and, by assumption, $E[\epsilon \mid X_1] = 0$ for (each and every observation in) the population. Again, then, application of least squares is entirely appropriate.

---

[9] For example, suppose one randomly assigns, to each observation, one of a set of randomly chosen numbers taken from a table of random normal numbers with mean zero and unit standard deviation. The number thus assigned to any observation i would be called S_i. About 15.87 percent of all observations will have S values in excess of 1.0; thus, for example, one could select a random sample of about 15.87 percent of the entire population of observations by selecting if and only if $S_i > 1.0$.

Finally, however, suppose that the sample selection variable S is endogenous to labor supply, in the sense that S is correlated with the labor supply error term ϵ. As one example of this kind of S, suppose that $S = H$ and $C = 0$. Here the selection rule will select only persons who are working. In this case, it is obvious that $K_S = E[\epsilon \mid X_1, H > 0] = E[\epsilon \mid X_1, \epsilon > -(b_0 + b_1X_1)]$ will be nonzero (unless $-(b_0 + b_1X_1) = -\infty$!), even if $E[\epsilon \mid X_1] = 0$ for each observation in the population: A rule that selects only observations with ϵ values that exceed $-(b_0 + b_1X_1)$ is obviously a rule that excludes observations with "small" ϵ values, meaning that, on the average, the ϵ values *within* the sample will be positive. Thus, as implied earlier, in this case application of least squares will result in biased estimates of the labor supply parameters b_0 and b_1. (For a clear and relatively nontechnical discussion of this case, see Layard, Barton, and Zabalza, 1980.)

More subtle examples of selection rules involving an endogenous S (that is, an S that is correlated with the labor supply error term ϵ) include the following:[10]

[10] For example, of the studies in Cain and Watts (1973b), all but the work by Hall (1973) use samples restricted to workers; Rosen (1978) considers only families in which both husband and wife work; Wales and Woodland (1976) consider only families in which both husband and wife work more than 400 hours per year; most of the studies in Brown (1981) are restricted to persons who work at least 8 hours per week. (Dickinson, 1979, and Wales, 1978, restrict their samples to families in which the husband works and the wife does not.) Among others, Hill (1973), Kalachek and Raines (1970), and Leuthold (1968) use samples restricted to persons (or families) with incomes below an upper limit, e.g., the "poverty line." (See Cain and Watts, 1973a, for discussion of the effects of this particular selection rule.) Boskin (1973), Garfinkel (1973a), Greenberg and Kosters (1973), Hall (1973), and Wales and Woodland (1976), among others, analyze samples limited to persons who do not receive transfer payments. Almost all of the studies in Smith (1980c), and in Cain and Watts (1973b), analyze samples selected according to marital status. Dickinson (1979), Wales (1978), and Wales and Woodland (1976) limit analyses to persons whose labor supply is not "constrained" (where one is defined to be constrained if he is unable to change his hours of work and says he would like to be able to do so). Needless to say, the problem of sample selection bias may arise whenever a sample is selected on the basis of an endogenous variable and is by no means peculiar to analysis of labor supply. Cain (1976, pp. 1246–7) and Heckman (1976a, 1979) discuss the use of samples selected on the basis of occupational status to analyze questions about the impact of education on earnings; Bloom and Killingsworth (1982) discuss selection bias in the context of studies of pay discrimination.

(i) S refers to "income" and C is some dollar amount (so that the selection rule means "select only persons who receive more than $\$C$ in income")

(ii) S refers to "amount of transfer payments received," and C is some dollar amount (so that the selection rule means "select only persons who receive more than $\$C$ in transfer benefits")

(iii) S refers to "marital status," coded "1" for married persons and "0" for nonmarried persons, and C is set at 1 for all observations (so that the selection rule means "select only married persons")

(iv) S refers to "hours of work are not constrained," coded "1" for persons who say they are either free to change their hours of work at will or else are not free to do so but are happy to work the hours they actually work and "0" otherwise, and C is set at 1 for all observations (so that the selection rule means "select only 'unconstrained' persons")

In cases of this kind, S may be regarded as a function of observed variables Z and unmeasured variables v, that is, $S = aZ + v$. For example, unlike age, sex, and race, variables such as income, transfer benefit receipts, and even marital status and "facing an hours 'constraint'" are to some extent choice variables, determined by functional relationships of some kind. Thus, when one selects a sample on the basis of an S of this kind, the K_S of (3.17) is given by $K_S = E[\epsilon \mid X_1, v > C - aZ]$. If v is uncorrelated with ϵ, then $K_S = 0$ and application of least squares remains appropriate provided $E[\epsilon \mid X_1] = 0$ in the population. However, v may well be correlated with ϵ – that is, unmeasured factors that affect income, receipt of transfer benefits, marital status, or "being 'constrained'" (motivation, willingness to work, etc.) may be correlated with unmeasured factors that affect labor supply. If so, then K_S will not be zero within a sample selected on the basis of such an S, even if $E[\epsilon \mid X_1] = 0$ in the population as a whole. Rather, if v and ϵ are positively (negatively) correlated, then K_S will be positive (negative). In either instance, simple regression analysis, which assumes that (3.16) is appropriate to a sample selected on the basis of such an S, omits the nonzero variable K_S and thus will generate biased and inconsistent estimates of the labor supply parameters b_0 and b_1. (See Heckman, 1976c, 1979.)

Of course, it is one thing to observe that selection bias *may* arise, and quite another to demonstrate that (i) such selection bias *does* arise (e.g., that the v and ϵ of the earlier discussion are in fact correlated) and (ii) the *magnitude* of this bias is sufficiently substantial to be worth worrying about. For example, if restricting an estimation sample to married persons results in a simple regression estimate of b_1 in (3.15) that is always 0.00001 percent smaller than the true value, even in large samples, then the least squares estimate of b_1 is certainly biased and inconsistent – but no one would care very much. However, some recent evidence suggests that the bias and inconsistency introduced by some selection rules may be considerable; I will say more about this in Chapter 4.

3.3. Problems of measurement

Having adopted a specification and selected a sample, the researcher must next obtain measures of the variables such as W, V, and H that appear in the labor supply function. As will become clear presently, this raises several issues of measurement – ones that are often closely related to questions of specification and sample selection.

Measurement of the wage variable

Most empirical studies define the W of expressions such as (3.12) as the current wage rate and obtain measures of W that are derived from one or more of the following components: E_H, earnings per hour; E_W, earnings in the week referenced by the survey being undertaken to collect data: H_W, hours worked during the survey week; E_A, earnings in the year before the survey week; S_A, weeks worked during the year before the survey week. Time-series analyses sometimes use E_F, earnings of year-round, full-time workers, or W_A, a measure of average hourly earnings of workers. Typically, studies drawing on such variables construct measures of the current wage using one of the following definitions: $W_1 = E_W/H_W$, $W_2 = E_A/S_A H_W$, $W_3 = E_W$, $W_4 = E_A/S_A$, $W_5 = E_H$, $W_6 = E_F$, or $W_7 = W_A$.

Each of these measures suffers from one or more defects. First, the dependent variable, H, and W_1, W_2, and W_4 may be definitionally related, because the denominator of each of these measures is constructed using a measure of labor supply. Hence, any errors in the measurement of labor supply will be duplicated in the constructed measure of W, which will give rise to a spurious correlation – due only to errors of measurement – between measured W and measured H. (See Borjas, 1980; Hall, 1973.) Second, W_1, W_2, and

W_3 refer, in whole or in part, to the experience of just one week and thus to a time period that may differ from the one to which the dependent variable refers. Third, W_2 is constructed from components that refer to different time periods (years in the numerator, years and weeks in the denominator). Fourth, some or all of the components used to construct these wage measures may be expressed not as actual numbers but rather as categories (e.g., S_A may be measured only as being between 40 and 47 weeks). Most researchers simply "guesstimate" the actual number associated with being in categories of this kind, and this introduces imprecision into variables constructed from such measures (e.g., W_4). Finally, all of these wage measures ignore nonpecuniary components of pay and are expressed in nominal (W) rather than real (W/P) terms.[11]

In addition to these problems, which are all more or less questions of measurement per se, attempts to derive a satisfactory wage measure must also confront an important analytical issue: All of the wage measures previously discussed are measures of an *average* of *earnings*, defined in various ways, but in general what is in fact required is a measure of the *marginal* wage *rate*.

For example, consider two situations in which marginal wage rates and average hourly earnings differ, as shown in Figure 3.4(a) and (b). Figure 3.4(a) refers to a case discussed briefly in Chapter 1, in which earnings for an additional hour of work depend on the number of hours already worked because of warm-up or fatigue effects. The individual shown in Figure 3.4(a) has v in real property income and takes $1 - L_x$ hours to get warmed up at work. After that, earnings change with hours of work as shown by the curve xf. If this individual chooses to work $1 - L_a$ hours, that is, locates at point a, then he acts *as if* the real wage were w_a (equal in absolute value to the slope of the line $v_a a$, which is tangent to xf at point a) and *as if* real property income were v_a (which is the height of the line $v_a a$ at $L = 1$). Thus, the marginal wage rate at point a is w_a. Note that average hourly earnings at point a, equal to the slope of the line from v to a, are less than w_a.[12]

[11] Recall the discussion earlier in this chapter about the role of consumer goods prices in labor supply functions.
[12] That is, earnings at a are equal to total income in real terms, C_a, minus property income in real terms, v; whereas hours worked are $1 - L_a$. So earnings per hour of work at a are $(C_a - v)/(1 - L_a)$ = the slope of the line from v to a.

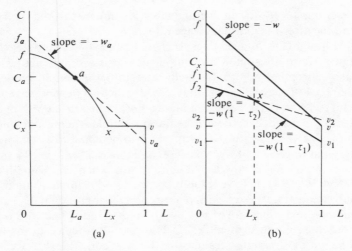

Figure 3.4. Average and marginal wages with warm-up and fatigue effects, and under progressive tax system

In Figure 3.4(b), average and marginal wages diverge for a different reason. In this example, the individual receives real property income of v and earns a gross real wage of w per hour worked (equal to the absolute value of the slope of the line vf). However, the individual must also pay taxes on total income (property income plus earnings). Specifically, when total income is C_x or less in real terms, the individual must pay taxes at the rate of $100\tau_1$ percent; further, any income received in excess of C_x is taxed at a marginal rate of $100\tau_2$ percent. Thus, the pre-tax budget line is $1vf$, but the post-tax budget line is $1v_1xf_2$. Since expenditures on C are made from after-tax income, the budget line relevant to decision making is the latter, not the former. (Note that the vertical distance between the two budget lines is equal to the total amount of tax paid.) The post-tax budget constraint entails after-tax property income of $v_1 = v(1 - \tau_1)$. For hours worked in between zero and $1 - L_x$ hours, the after-tax wage rate is $w(1 - \tau_1)$, equal in absolute value to the slope of v_1x. For hours worked beyond $1 - L_x$, the after-tax wage rate is $w(1 - \tau_2)$, equal in absolute value to the slope of xf_2. Moreover, whenever the individual works beyond $1 - L_x$ hours – that is, locates somewhere on segment xf_2 of the post-tax budget constraint $1v_1xf_2$ – then average after-tax hourly earnings is larger than the after-tax marginal wage rate.[13]

Although the budget lines $1vxf$ in Figure 3.4(a) and $1v_1xf_2$ in Figure 3.4(b) are somewhat complicated, it is a simple matter – at least conceptually – to fit such cases into the simple model of Chapter 1. To see this, note that, for all practical purposes, an individual who works at point *a* in Figure 3.4(a) when faced with budget line $1vxf$ behaves exactly *as if* he faced a simple straight-line budget constraint $1v_aaf_a$, with real property income equal to v_a and a real marginal wage rate of w_a. Likewise, an individual who works somewhere along segment v_1x in Figure 3.4(b) when confronted with budget line $1v_1xf_2$ behaves exactly *as if* he faced a simple straight-line budget constraint $1v_1xf_1$ with real property income equal to v_1 and a real marginal wage rate of $w(1 - \tau_1)$; and an individual who works somewhere along segment xf_2 in Figure 3.4(b) behaves exactly *as if* he faced a simple straight-line budget constraint $1v_2xf_2$ with real property income equal to v_2 and a real marginal wage rate of $w(1 - \tau_2)$.

This suggests that cases with complicated budget constraints can be simplified by "linearization" – that is, by converting such constraints into their straight-line equivalents – at each individual's equilibrium point. In Figure 3.4(a), this would mean deriving measures of v_a and w_a for all individuals (who may, of course, have different equilibrium points, or (w_a, v_a) combinations) and then treating these two magnitudes as the V and W of the standard labor supply model. In Figure 3.4(b), this would mean using $w(1 - \tau_1)$ and v_1 as the relevant W and V for all individuals on line segment v_1x, and using $w(1 - \tau_2)$ and v_2 as the relevant W and V for all individuals on line segment xf_2. (Note that, as mentioned earlier, the *marginal* wage – not average hourly earnings – is used in all these cases.) Having computed such linearized measures of W and V, one would then proceed *as if* the budget constraint were of the simple straight-line variety – that is, *as if*, after linearization, the model

[13] Real after-tax income (property income plus earnings) at any point on xf_2 is equal to the amount of consumption expenditure implied by that point; real after-tax property income is v_1. Therefore, for any given point on xf_2, real after-tax earnings per hour worked are given by the slope of the line drawn from v_1 to that point. This is always larger than the slope of xf_2 itself ($= w(1 - \tau_2)$, the real after-tax wage along xf_2).

were the simple one described in Chapter 1. (See Chapter 6 for further discussion of this point.)

In theoretical terms, this "linearized budget constraint" approach is simple and straightforward. From an empirical standpoint, however, it raises several difficult issues. First, note that linearized W and V depend on actual hours worked.[14] Because the ϵ term in the empirical labor supply function affects hours worked and, therefore, linearized W and V, these linearized budget constraint variables are necessarily correlated with ϵ. This renders OLS unsuitable for purposes of estimation: The validity of OLS requires that ϵ be uncorrelated with the variables on the right-hand side of the labor supply function, including linearized W and V. A method that recognizes the simultaneity between ϵ and linearized W and V must be used instead.[15] Second, in many cases it may be quite difficult to construct accurate measures of linearized W and V. For example, many researchers use published statutory tax rates to determine applicable marginal rates of taxation (e.g., τ_2, which is required to compute $w(1 - \tau_2)$). However, *actual* marginal rates of tax often differ from statutory rates, due to underreporting or concealment of income by individuals and to the exercise of administrative discretion by tax-collecting agencies. (For more on this point, see Chapter 4.)

A different kind of wage-measurement problem arises from the fact that wages usually cannot be observed at all for persons who are not employed. As previously explained, the problem cannot be solved by applying OLS to an estimation sample restricted to persons who *are* employed (and whose wages are, therefore, observed). Rather than do this, some researchers have used an "imputed wage." To derive an imputed wage, one first uses data on

---

[14] For example, in Figure 3.4(a), when the location of the point a changes (i.e., when hours worked changes), the slope of the line tangent to a will change and so will the marginal wage. Likewise, in Figure 3.4(b), the real after-tax wage will be $w(1 - \tau_1)$ if the individual chooses to work less than $1 - L_x$ hours, whereas it will be $w(1 - \tau_2)$ if the individual chooses to work $1 - L_x$ hours or more.

[15] For example, one could use instrumental variables measures of linearized W and V rather than their actual values. In practice, however, most empirical studies use actual values of linearized W and V. For example, see Boskin (1973), Dickinson (1979), Hall (1973), Leuthold (1978b), Rosen (1976a, 1978), and Wales and Woodland (1976).

a sample of working individuals to estimate the parameters of a wage function, such as

(3.18) $W = \mathbf{X}\gamma + \omega$

where W is the wage rate, $\mathbf{X}$ is a vector of personal characteristics (age, years of work experience, sex, etc.), and ω is the error term in the wage function. One then uses the wage function OLS parameter estimates $\hat{\gamma}$ to compute a "predicted" or "imputed" wage rate, $\hat{W} = \mathbf{X}\hat{\gamma}$, either for (i) *all* individuals, working or not, or (ii) non-workers only. Under variant (i), $\hat{W}$ is used as the measure of W for all persons in estimating the labor supply function (e.g., (3.12)). Under variant (ii), one uses an individual's actual W in (3.12) if actual W is available and uses $\hat{W}$ otherwise.

Under either of these two variants, it is possible to include all individuals, employed or not, in the sample to be used to estimate the labor supply function. Moreover, it is often asserted, the imputed wage serves as a kind of instrumental variable: Although it doubtless measures the true wage with some error, there is probably no correlation between such measurement errors and errors in the measurement of H – a correlation that is certain to arise when one uses such measures of W as W_1, W_2, or W_4.[16]

However, there is a potential difficulty inherent in the imputed wage procedure: Imputed wages are derived from estimates of (3.18) computed for a sample restricted to workers. As the earlier discussion of selection bias suggests, the error term ω in (3.18) may not be a mean-zero random variable in a sample *restricted to workers* even if it is a mean-zero random variable in the population as a whole. For example, it seems at least possible that, on average, persons who

---

[16] For a particularly sophisticated procedure for wage imputation, see Aigner (1974). For examples of studies that use imputed wages, see Boskin (1973), Bloch (1973), Hall (1973), Kalachek and Raines (1970), and T. P. Schultz (1980). J. Smith (1973) apparently imputes a wage to married women solely on the basis of the average wage of employed married women by husband's age. Kosters (1966, 1969) imputes solely on the basis of the wife's schooling and size of place of residence. Ironically, Boskin (1973) and Hall (1973) use their imputed wage measure to compute the labor *supply* variable (by taking the ratio of reported earnings to the imputed wage) used in their regressions. As Greenberg (1972) notes, this procedure reintroduces the correlated errors-in-variables bias that arises when W is measured using W_1, W_2 or W_4 and that might otherwise be avoided by use of a linearized wage.

work are persons with above-average ω values – that is, persons who got above-average wage offers, other things (the **X**) being equal. Thus, imputed-wage measures of W may suffer from sample selection bias, and so OLS estimates of labor supply functions in which imputed-wage measures of W are used may be biased as well. (I will consider this question in more detail in Chapter 4.)

Thus far, this discussion has been concerned with different ways of measuring the current wage. A final issue is concerned with a basic conceptual point: Should one actually use *any* measure of the *current* wage as the W of labor supply equations such as (3.12)? In particular, some researchers argue that it is important to distinguish between "permanent" and "transitory" components of the wage and to use a measure of the permanent wage (or perhaps measures of both the permanent and transitory components of the current wage) in the labor supply equation rather than a measure of the current wage as such. (For example, see Kalachek, Mellow, and Raines, 1978.)

Reduced to its essentials, this is an argument that labor supply behavior should be analyzed using a long-run dynamic model, rather than a simple static model, such as the one presented in Chapter 1. It would therefore seem natural to distinguish between permanent and transitory components of the wage by developing a formal dynamic model in which this question can be analyzed explicitly. (Indeed, most work aimed at introducing notions about permanent and transitory components of the wage has been somewhat disappointing largely because most such research has been based more on ad hoc theorizing than on formal dynamic models.) Accordingly, I postpone a detailed discussion of such issues until Chapter 5.

Measurement of the property income variable

Persons receive income from many sources other than employment, and this poses various difficulties for researchers trying to measure V, property (or "nonemployment" or "nonlabor") income.

First, should the measure of V include only money income, or should it also include the estimated money value of the stream of nonmoney services received from physical assets, such as housing and other durables? In principle, the latter seems the correct approach, but it entails considerable conceptual and practical difficulties and has been adopted in only a few empirical studies.[17] Most measures of V refer to money flows only.

Second, some kinds of income, although not derived from employment, are nevertheless employment related and are certainly not property income (i.e., exogenous) in the usual sense. Work-related transfer payments (and possibly even gifts and other remittances) are in general inversely related to income and hence to labor supply. Because transfer payments may be regarded as a form of ("reverse") taxation, this leads the researcher directly back to the earlier discussion of the relation between labor supply and tax and transfer systems. (For further details, see Chapter 6.) In practice, most first-generation research either (i) eliminated transfer recipients from the sample used to estimate the labor supply function, (ii) distinguished between transfer income and other forms of nonemployment income by treating each as a separate independent variable in the labor supply function, (iii) included all transfer payments in the measure of V used in the labor supply function, (iv) excluded all transfer payments from the measure of V used in the labor supply function, or (v) specified a separate function for the amount of work-related transfers and estimated it jointly with the supply function.[18]

---

[17] Notable exceptions are Bloch (1973), Boskin (1973), Fleisher, Parsons, and Porter (1973), Greenberg (1971), Greenberg and Kosters (1973), and Hall (1973). Indeed, when Bloch omitted the imputed value of home ownership from his measure of V, the estimates he obtained implied that leisure is an inferior good.

[18] Those who eliminate all recipients of work-related transfers include Ashenfelter and Heckman (1973), Boskin (1973), Garfinkel (1973a), Greenberg (1971), Greenberg and Kosters (1973), Hall (1973), H. Rosen (1976a, b, 1978), and Wales and Woodland (1976). Hill (1973) and J. Smith (1973) use two variables to measure V; one refers to the amount of transfer payments, whereas the other refers to other kinds of nonemployment income. Becker (1975c), Cohen, Rea, and Lerman (1970), Hanoch (1980b), and Rosen and Welch (1971), include such transfers as part of V. Kalachek and Raines (1970), Kalachek, Raines, and Mellow (1978), and T. P. Schultz (1980) include transfer recipients as part of their sample and exclude work-related transfer payments from their measure of V; however, Kalachek and Raines (1970) use several dummy variables indicating residence of recipients in states whose transfer programs have varying standards of provision and eligibility. Fleisher, Parsons, and Porter (1973, esp. Appendix 8-D) sometimes include and exclude transfers from V and argue forcefully that Rosen and Welch (1971) found "evidence" of strong income effects mainly because their estimates − based on the *inclusion* of transfers in their measure

Method (i) of course involves use of a sample selection rule. As discussed earlier estimates derived from this method may therefore be biased unless the impact of the selection rule on the ϵ term within the sample used in estimation is reflected in the estimation technique used. Methods (ii) and (iii) include an endogenous variable – the amount of transfer payments – on the right-hand side of the supply function and thus require use of an estimation technique that recognizes this endogeneity. Method (iv) may be regarded as an attempt to estimate a reduced-form version of the system considered under method (v).[19] Under either procedure, the main problem that arises is that it is difficult to specify the nature of the budget constraint when that constraint contains kinks and convexities. (Note, for example, the "kink point" x in Figure 3.4(b) induced by a tax system. Similar kinks occur in the presence of a transfer payment system.)

Various other components of V may also be endogenous to labor supply. For example, as noted in Chapter 2 (see in particular note 6), if one assumes that all intrafamily cross-substitution effects on labor supply in the conventional family labor supply model are zero, then the V variable relevant to a given family member i, $V_i = V + \Sigma_{j \neq i} W_j H_j$, includes not only property income as such (V) but also the earnings of all *other* family members j. However, V_i is necessarily correlated with i's error term, ϵ_i. To see this, simply note that an increase in ϵ_i entails an increase in i's labor supply and hence in i's earnings, other things being equal. This will increase augmented V, V_j, for all other family members j (because i's earnings appear in augmented V for those other members) and will therefore affect their labor supplies. In turn, this change in the labor supplied by

---

of V – are biased. Finegan (1962b), Kehrer (1976), Maurizi (1966), McGuire and Rapping (1968, 1970), Owen (1969, 1971), Vahovich (1977), and Winston (1966) do not use a measure of V. Altman and Barro (1971), Benham (1971), Bognanno, Hixson, and Jeffers (1974), and Finegan (1962b) use husband's income as a proxy measure of V in studies of married women; Cogan (1980b, 1981) uses husband's earnings. Cogan (1980a), Gramm (1974, 1975), and Heckman (1974c, 1976c, 1980) use net worth (that is, the *level* of property) in place of V (= income *from* property).

[19] One technical difficulty with method (iv) is that, because it is a reduced-form equation, it yields estimates that confound tax function parameters and behavioral (i.e., utility function) parameters. This makes it difficult to retrieve pure income and substitution effects.

other family members will affect *their* earnings and, thus, i's augmented V – implying a correlation between ϵ_i and V_i.

To address this problem, one can either use an estimation technique that recognizes the endogeneity of V_i or else revert to the alternative (and more general) version of the family labor supply model, in which cross-substitution effects are not constrained to be zero. However, estimation of the more general version of the model requires data on the wage rates of all family members – yet many family members may not be at work, giving rise to one of the wage measurement problems previously discussed. In practice, most studies of the augmented V version of the family labor supply model have used OLS.[20] Most work on the more general version of the model has been based on samples restricted to families in which all members (e.g., both husband and wife) are at work, which may involve selection bias. (See note 10.)

Finally, several recent studies suggest that actual property income as such is also endogenous to the labor supply decision – that is, that ϵ is correlated with property income per se. Fleisher, Parsons, and Porter (1973) argue that individuals whose current assets differ from some desired long-run level will change their labor supply (and hence draw down on, or else add to, their current stock of assets) to reach this desired level. Thus, measures of i's *current* property income may include a disequilibrium component that may be correlated with ϵ: In other words, in this view, *both H and V* are the result of *current* choices, so that to include the latter in an OLS regression for the former may result in biased estimates. Greenberg and Kosters (1973) provide an alternative rationale for essentially the same conclusion. In their view, cross-sectional variation in values of V, even when V is simply property income as such, is partly a result of differences in individual "tastes for asset accumulation," differences that are probably correlated with "tastes for market work" and thus with ϵ.

Underlying both these views is a more basic idea discussed in greater detail in Chapter 5: accumulation of property, and thus the current level of property income V, is the result of a process of dynamic utility optimization in which labor supply plays an impor-

[20] For example, see Atkinson and Stern (1981), Cohen, Rea, and Lerman (1970), Greenhalgh (1980) and Hanoch (1980b).

tant role; in particular, both property income and labor supply may be jointly determined. If so, then one needs an explicitly dynamic treatment of this process.

Measurement of the labor supply variable

Can labor supply functions, such as (3.13), be applied indiscriminately to a variety of different measures of labor supply? A priori, this would not seem likely. However, as Cain and Watts (1973a, Table 9.3) indicate, researchers have used at least 18 distinct measures of labor supply. These measures fall into two main categories: "participation" variables and "time" variables.

The nature of the participation measure used in different labor supply studies[21] depends on the nature of the data being used. In microlevel cross-section data, such variables are dichotomous, equal to unity if the individual is in the labor force (or, in some research, if the individual is employed) and zero otherwise. In aggregate cross-section or time-series data, participation is usually the labor force participation rate (or, in some work, the employment–population ratio) for the observation (SMSA, year, etc.) in question.[22]

As noted in Chapter 1, both participation and hours of work are determined simultaneously: If one works, then hours of work are necessarily positive (and vice versa); if one does not work, then hours of work are necessarily zero (and vice versa). However, one cannot usually use results from analyses of participation to draw inferences about, say, income and substitution effects on hours of work. For example, the probability that a given individual will work (participate) must always be positively related to the real wage, other things being equal – but there is no a priori reason to suppose that the *number* of hours a given worker works will necessarily be positively related to the real wage. In general, therefore, one cannot use

---

[21] Used by, for example, Ashenfelter and Heckman (1974), Benham (1971), Bishop (1973), Bowen and Finegan (1969), Cain (1966), Greenhalgh (1977, 1979), Joshi et al. (1981), Mincer (1962), and Theeuwes (1981). For discussions of participation, see Bowers (1975), Hughes (1972), Hunter (1970), Mincer (1966), and Parnes (1970).

[22] Of course, participation and employment are not necessarily identical: Some labor force participants are unemployed. Nevertheless, many studies of participation proceed as if the dichotomy "is or is not a labor force participant" were synonymous with the dichotomy "is or is not employed."

exactly the same model in exactly the same way to analyze different dimensions of labor supply, such as participation and hours of work. Some of the first-generation literature erred in this respect – for example, in using results derived from empirical studies of participation measures of labor supply to discuss "income" and "substitution" effects, which are relevant to time measures rather than to participation per se.[23]

Deriving time measures of labor supply is often difficult. In part, this is because available data sets do not always contain direct measures of hours worked except over short (and, thus, possibly quite unrepresentative) spans of time, for example, hours worked during a particular week. Thus, measures of labor supply, like measures of the wage rate, are frequently derived, rather than direct. For example, some studies define labor supply per year to be equal to (i) weeks worked in the year prior to the date of the survey that gathered the data used in the study, multiplied by hours worked during the survey week (or, alternatively, hours "usually" worked per week),[24] or (ii) labor earnings for the year prior to the survey, divided by a measure of the wage rate (e.g., the amount that a survey respondent says he "usually" earns per hour of work).[25]

On the other hand, even when they can be measured precisely, *measured* hours of work do not always correspond to hours actually spent *at* work. For example, Heckman (1980, p. 224) notes that the weeks worked variable usually used in deriving a measure of annual hours of work (by multiplying weeks worked by hours worked in a given week) generally means "weeks employed," which include both vacation time and time spent sick. The use of such measures will therefore overstate the amount of actual work, create the statistical illusion of a standard workweek and workyear, and considerably understate the true sample variation in labor supply. Further,

[23] See Ben-Porath (1973), Heckman, Killingsworth, and MaCurdy (1981), and Lewis (1972) on this point.

[24] For example, see Greenberg and Kosters (1973), Heckman (1976c), Leuthold (1978b), H. Rosen (1976b), Rosen and Welch (1971), T. P. Schultz (1980), and Tella, Tella and Green (1971). Kalachek, Mellow and Raines (1978, p. 358) use the product of weeks worked and usual hours worked per week on the grounds that a measure of this kind "minimizes the importance of temporary disturbances." (Curiously, one of the major objectives of their study is to see whether transitory and permanent wage changes result in different labor supply responses.)

[25] For example, see Boskin (1973), Hall (1973), and Heckman (1980).

some time spent *at* work may not correspond to time spent actually *working*. (See note 2 of Chapter 2.)

The mere fact that recorded hours of work do not always measure actual hours of work correctly is of no particular concern: After all, the error term ϵ in the labor supply equation certainly includes, among other things, errors in measurement of the dependent variable. Although such a measurement error reduces the efficiency of the estimates of labor supply parameters, no problem of bias or inconsistency need arise – *unless* this measurement error is nonrandom. The problem is that such measurement error may not be random – for example, vacation time, time devoted to coffee breaks, and the like may be correlated with W and V.

Somewhat similar problems arise when one attempts to estimate the labor supply model in the presence of take-it-or-leave-it regimes or unemployment. In this case, if one assumes that desired hours of work are not the same as hours actually spent working, then the error term ϵ includes, among other things, the difference between actual hours of work ($= H$) and desired hours of work ($= H^*$, the labor supply variable with which the model is concerned). If discrepancies between actual and desired hours of work are random, no problems of bias arise. However, these discrepancies – and thus the ϵ term in the labor supply function – may well be correlated with, say, W – for example, recall the discussion of compensating wage differentials models in Chapter 2. (See Heckman, Killingsworth, and MaCurdy, 1981, pp. 112–9, for further discussion.)

In an attempt to avoid the problems of bias and inconsistency that can arise in this case, some researchers construct a measure of desired hours of work (that is, of the H^* with which the model is concerned) by adding actual hours and search time (i.e., hours spent unemployed and looking for work).[26] However, it is not clear that search time accurately measures the difference between actual and

---

[26] For example, see Cohen, Rea, and Lerman (1970), Greenberg (1971), Greenberg and Kosters (1973), Hill (1973), Kalachek, Mellow, and Raines (1978), Kalachek and Raines (1970), Leuthold (1978b), and J. Smith (1973). Bloch (1973), Boskin (1973), and Kalachek, Mellow, and Raines (1978) find that using measures of desired rather than actual hours of work does not alter labor supply parameters estimates appreciably, though Kalachek, Mellow, and Raines add that using desired rather than actual H makes their estimated labor supply schedule start to bend backward at lower wage rates.

desired labor supply as such; for example, see Greenberg (1972) and Fleisher, Parsons, and Porter (1973). On the other hand, it is not obvious that actual and desired labor supply are always equal (recall the discussion of budget line discontinuities in Chapter 2). Here, as in several other cases cited in this chapter, the task is to develop formal models that explicitly represent such phenomena, rather than to resort to ad hoc procedures with little or no analytical foundation.

3.4.   Results of first-generation studies

With the rather depressing catalog of problems of Section 3.3 as prologue, I now consider the results of first-generation studies of static labor supply models. In the main, these studies used OLS to get estimates of labor supply functions of which the following are simple prototypes:

$$(3.19) \quad H = a + bW + cV + \epsilon$$

$$(3.20) \quad H_i = a_i + \sum_{j=1}^{m} b_{ij} W_j + c_i V + \epsilon_i$$

$$(3.21) \quad H_i = a_i + b_i W_i + c_i \left(V + \sum_{j \neq i} W_j H_j \right) + \epsilon_i$$

(3.19) refers to a given individual; (3.20) and (3.21) refer to family members. (3.20) refers to family member i (in an m-member family); cross-substitution effects are not constrained to equal zero, so that the wages W_j of other family members affect i's labor supply along with V, total *family* property income. (3.21) assumes that intrafamily cross-substitution effects are zero, so that i's labor supply depends on i's wages and on augmented property income V_i (that is, the sum of V and the earnings of all other family members).

Lest it seem that first-generation studies were based on very simple methodology indeed, it is worth emphasizing that equations (3.19)–(3.21) are simple prototypes, *not* actual estimating equations. In particular, many first-generation studies include numerous additional control variables (e.g., for age, race, and the like) over and beyond the wage rate and property income variables shown in equations (3.19)–(3.21), and few such studies are based on linear functional forms as simple as the ones used in (3.19)–(3.21). Moreover, various first-generation studies, notably "demand system" studies,[27] have derived estimating equations from explicitly specified utility (or marginal rate of substitution, indirect utility, etc.) functions, and not infrequently use techniques other than least squares (such as maximum likelihood).

Thus, first-generation work is certainly not all of a piece. However, as noted earlier, studies of this kind usually have two features in common: In general, questions about corner solutions are ignored; and, typically, so are questions about the error term in the labor supply function (and related issues, e.g., about selection bias).

Second-generation work – which focused on these (and other) issues to a much greater extent – is the subject of Chapter 4. In the present section, I summarize the results of first-generation work, concentrating on the main labor supply elasticities: The gross ("uncompensated") elasticity of labor supply with respect to the wage, own- and cross- (or intrafamily) substitution ("compensated") elasticities of labor supply with respect to the wage, and the elasticity of labor supply with respect to property income. In general, labor supply refers to hours of work (usually per year) rather than to participation. Most of the elasticities discussed in this section are given by the authors cited and are evaluated at sample means. (In some cases, I have calculated the elasticities myself by using information given by the author of a given study or by making interpolations.) Obviously, all figures should be regarded as approximate. This is particularly true when, as is often the case, a given study presents a variety of different results for a given labor supply elasticity, based on different sample selection criteria, independent variables, and the like.[28] Two particular caveats seem worth particular emphasis. First, all results can be quite sensitive to

[27] Roughly speaking, such studies are of two kinds. One is concerned with family labor supply decisions, and, therefore, the demand system considered in this kind of study consists of a leisure demand (or labor supply) function for the husband, a leisure demand (or labor supply) function for the wife, and a consumer goods demand function for the family. The second kind of study is concerned with a demand system consisting of a leisure demand (or labor supply) function and two or more demand functions for different kinds of consumer goods. For examples of the former, see Ashworth and Ulph (1981b), H. Rosen (1978) and Wales and Woodland (1976, 1977). For examples of the latter, see Abbott and Ashenfelter (1976, 1979), Barnett (1979a, 1981), and Kiefer (1976, 1977).

[28] For other summaries of first-generation studies of labor supply, see Borjas and Heckman (1979), Cain and Watts (1973a), Keeley (1981), and Killingsworth (1981).

differences in sample selection rules, in procedures for measuring variables such as W, V, and H and in equation specification. Second, even if two different studies yield *exactly* the same point estimate of a particular labor supply response they may nevertheless imply quite different values for the relevant *elasticity* of response if the mean values of the relevant variables differ across the two studies.[29] (In other words, in the regression function $Y = Xb + e$, the effect on Y of a unit change in X is equal to b, but the elasticity of Y with respect to X evaluated at the means $\overline{Y}$ and $\overline{X}$ of these two variables is $b\overline{Y}/\overline{X}$. So even if the two studies yield essentially the same value of b, they may nevertheless imply quite different elasticities if the means $\overline{Y}$ and $\overline{X}$ are different.)

Gross wage elasticity of labor supply

To compute the gross or "uncompensated" wage elasticity of labor supply, take the first derivative of the labor supply function for a given individual with respect to the individual's own wage and write the result in elasticity form, as $(\partial H/\partial W)/(W/H)$. The main "stylized fact" or empirical regularity that emerges from consideration of the uncompensated own-wage elasticity in first-generation studies is that male labor supply is much less sensitive to wage changes than is female labor supply. Indeed, the male labor supply schedule appears to be gently backward bending with respect to the wage, whereas the female schedule, according to most first-generation studies, is strongly positive sloped.

However, there is rather little agreement on the magnitude of the uncompensated elasticity, for either men or women. Most measures of the male gross wage elasticity lie somewhere in between 0.000 and −0.400; results of this kind appear in studies of aggregate (e.g., industrial or occupational) cross sections, aggregate time-series data, and microlevel cross sections.[30] However, some microlevel

---

[29] For a detailed and instructive sensitivity analysis of the impact of alternative selection rules, measures of W, V and H, and so forth on labor supply results for prime-age males, see DaVanzo, DeTray, and Greenberg (1973, 1976).

[30] Aggregate cross-section studies include Altman and Barro (1971), Ashenfelter and Heckman (1974), Benham (1971), Finegan (1962b), Metcalf, Nickell, and Richardson (1977), and S. Rosen (1969). Aggregate time-series studies include Holmes (1972), Lucas and Rapping (1970), Mosbaek (1959), and Owen (1969). Owen includes a price of leisure time variable (constructed so as to reflect the cost of recreation goods and

studies find significant positive elasticities for males: Some of the results of Kalachek and Raines (1970) imply an elasticity between about 0.050 and 0.300. Hall (1973), Rosen and Welch (1971), and Wales (1973) also obtain positive elasticities for some subgroups in the male population.[31]

This wide range of estimates for men is the result of a variety of factors: the use of different samples (selected according to quite different selection rules), different measures of the dependent and independent variables, and the like. In no small way, however, it is a simple consequence of the large number of first-generation studies of male labor supply, which in turn is due to one happy aspect of male labor supply behavior: Because male participation rates are typically well above 0.50 and in many cases are close to unity, it is possible to obtain measures of labor supply and wage rates for most observations in most samples of adult men.

In contrast, participation rates for a variety of different groups of females (e.g., married women or women aged 25–34) have typically not been much more than 0.50 or 0.60 – and in some cases appreciably less – until fairly recently. This posed various difficult questions (e.g., about sample selection bias and measurement of wage rates for nonworkers) to which first-generation methodology had no ready answers. Hence, there are many fewer first-generation studies of female labor supply than there are first-generation studies of male labor supply.[32]

Most gross wage elasticities obtained in such studies of females are positive and fairly large. However, the range of estimates for the uncompensated own-wage elasticity for women is, if anything,

services) in an attempt to incorporate Becker's (1965) time allocation construct in the labor supply function. Most first-generation work is based on microlevel cross-section data. For example, see Cohen, Rea, and Lerman (1970), Greenberg (1971), Greenberg and Kosters (1973), Kosters (1966, 1969), Leuthold (1968), and the studies in Cain and Watts (1973b).

[31] Hill, Wales, and Rosen and Welch use specifications that permit the labor supply function to bend backward. Some of their observations lie on the positive-sloped part of the schedule, whereas others are on the backward-bending part.

[32] In no small way, second-generation methodology is the result of attempts to address problems associated with the analysis of female labor supply (see Smith, 1980a). Although this methodology can readily be applied to the analysis of male labor supply, there are many fewer second-generation studies of male labor supply than there are second-generation studies of female labor supply.

larger than the range of estimates for men: between about 0.200 and 0.900 in most aggregative cross section and microlevel cross-section studies of female labor supply.[33] Although the *number* of first-generation studies of female labor supply is somewhat smaller than the number of such studies of male labor supply, the problems that typically arise in studies of female labor supply are – as just implied – more serious, and the variety of attempted solutions to those problems has been considerable. That the range of estimates for female wage elasticities is likewise greater is, therefore, not very surprising.

Finally – and, again, perhaps not surprisingly, given the wide variation in estimates of male and female elasticities – the range of estimates of the gross wage elasticity of labor supply for the total labor force (males and females combined) is also quite large. Winston's (1966) OLS study of an international cross section produced estimates between -0.05 and -0.11, but the range of aggregate time-series estimates for U.S. data is larger. For example, Mosbaek's (1959) OLS results generally suggest that the elasticity is negative, but Lucas and Rapping (1970), who use two-stage least squares, get a short-run elasticity between 1.35 and 1.58. Their long-run elasticity is between approximately zero (if an assets variable is omitted from the supply function) and 1.12 (if one is included). Holmes's (1972) OLS study implies a reverse-L-shaped Keynesian supply schedule, with near-infinite elasticity at a wage "floor" and a near-zero elasticity at higher wage levels.

Because virtually all standard macroeconomics texts draw the aggregate labor supply schedule with a positive slope with respect to the wage, it may seem surprising that, as indicated earlier, the male labor supply elasticity with respect to the wage is generally negative. However, it is possible that this seeming contradiction is more apparent than real. First, the aggregate supply schedule obviously refers to the total of male and female labor supply, and the female schedule, according to most first-generation results, is strongly positive sloped. (This conclusion is reinforced and strengthened by the results of second-generation studies, as will become evident in

---

[33] For example, see Hall (1973) and Kalachek and Raines (1970). However, Leuthold's study (1968) implies an elasticity of about -0.067, and Boskin (1973) obtains elasticities as large as 1.60 for some groups of women.

Chapter 4.) Second, although the aggregate supply schedule in macroeconomics texts refers to the way in which a wage increase changes total labor supply – including not only the supply of persons already working but also persons who were not originally at work but enter the market due to the wage increase – many first-generation studies are based on samples that are restricted to persons who are working. Even if one ignores issues of selection bias, therefore, these studies refer only to the relation between wages and the labor supply of persons who are already at work. Finally, most first-generation studies of labor supply are based on microlevel cross-section data on individuals at a given point in time, whereas the aggregate labor supply schedule in macroeconomics texts refers to behavior in short-run (that is, business cycle) time-series. The question of whether cross-section studies and time-series studies of a given phenomenon really refer to the same kind of behavior is a standard, and much debated, one in many contexts. In the present case, there is some reason to doubt whether cross-section results can be directly applied to questions about time-series behavior, or vice versa. For example, cross-section differences between different individuals might primarily be the result of long-run factors (e.g., permanent differences in wage rates, asset levels, and property income flows), whereas time-series variation in aggregate data might primarily be the result of short-run or business cycle factors (e.g., cyclical movements in wage rates, asset levels, and property income flows). If so, then it would hardly be surprising if cross-section and time-series results seemed quite different.[34]

[34] As this implies, it may be that the time-series response of labor supply to a wage change will be larger and more positive than the cross-section response. If time-series fluctuations in wages are more or less accurately anticipated, then the income effect of such wage changes will be minimal (because they will not cause individuals to revise their view of their long-run "well-offness" to any major extent; rather, such changes – if correctly anticipated – will by definition be just what was expected). However, as noted in Chapter 5, such changes will still have an "efficiency effect" on labor supply: Simple considerations of efficiency will prompt the individual to work more in periods when work is well paid and less in periods when work is not well paid, *ceteris paribus*. If so, then one might find sharp positive responses to wage increases in short-run time-series data and much smaller or even negative responses in long-run time-series or cross-sectional data. (See Bailey, 1954, 1962, p. 34; Barzel and McDonald, 1973, pp. 627–8; Ehrenberg and Smith, 1982, pp. 164–6; Friedman, 1949.) The results of Lucas and Rapping (1970) are roughly consistent with this notion. Their short-run wage elasticity is larger than their long-run elasticity and

Own- and cross-substitution elasticities of labor supply

Substitution elasticities refer to substitution ("compensated") effects of wage changes measured in elasticity form. As noted in Chapter 1, a substitution effect refers to the effect of a wage change with property income adjusted so as to keep utility constant – in other words, the effect of an "income-compensated" wage change. Refer to the substitution effect on individual i's labor supply, H_i, of a unit change in individual j's wage, W_j, as $S_{W_j}(H_i)$, and note that the total effect on H_i of a unit change in W_j, $\partial H_i / \partial W_j$, may be written as the sum of this substitution effect and of the income effect of the change in W_j on H_i. Now, the income effect on i's labor supply of a unit change in j's wage may, in turn, be written as the product of (i) the response of i's labor supply to a unit change in (property) income and (ii) the increase in income that would occur, ceteris paribus, when j's wage changes. The first of these components is simply $\partial H_i / \partial V$. Since a unit increase in j's wage will entail a unit increase in income for *each* of the H_j hours worked by j, the second of these components is simply H_j. Thus, write the total change in i's labor supply in response to a unit change in j's wage as the sum of the substitution effect and the income effect, to obtain

$$\partial H_i / \partial W_j = S_{W_j}(H_i) + H_j(\partial H_i / \partial V)$$

The substitution effect $S_{W_j}(H_i)$ may, therefore, be computed as the difference between the total effect, $\partial H_i / \partial W_j$, and the income effect, $H_j(\partial H_i / \partial V)$. (Note that, when i's hours of work are zero and i's wage is equal to the reservation level, a rise in i's wage entails only a pure own-substitution effect on i's labor supply: In this case, the income effect of the wage increase is zero – note that $H = 0$ at the reservation wage – and the compensated and uncompensated effects of the wage increase are equal.) The total effect may be computed by taking the partial derivative of the function for H_i with respect to W_j, as noted earlier; the income effect may be computed similarly, by taking the partial derivative of the function for H_i with respect to V. For example, in (3.20), the substitution effect is simply $S_{W_j}(H_i) = b_{ij} - c_i H_j$. Since this refers to the income-compensated effect on

appreciably larger than the elasticity found in most cross-section studies. However, questions about reconciling results obtained in time-series and cross-section studies have not been explored thoroughly in either first- or second-generation work. See also Chapter 5, note 4, p. 216.

i's labor supply of a unit change in j's wage, it is, of course, a cross- or intrafamily substitution effect. The own-substitution effect – the income-compensated effect on i's labor supply of a change in i's own wage – is, however, computed in just the same manner: This is simply $S_{W_i}(H_i) = b_{ii} - c_i H_i$. (By the same token, the own-substitution effect in (3.19) would be calculated as $b - cH$.) Note that all cross-substitution effects in (3.21) are zero: That is, in (3.21), $S_{W_j}(H_i) = (\partial H_i / \partial W_j) - H_j(\partial H_i / \partial V) = c_i H_j - c_i H_j = 0$.

The standard simple model of static labor supply does not predict the sign of the gross wage elasticity, but it does imply (i) "nega- tivity," that is, that the income-compensated own-wage elasticity of labor supply $S_{W_i}(H_i) W_i / H_i$ must be positive; and (ii) "symmetry," that is, that income-compensated cross-substitution effects $S_{W_i}(H_j)$ and $S_{W_j}(H_i)$ must be equal.[35] Most studies for which the own- substitution elasticity of labor supply has been calculated do, in fact, find that it is positive. For males, the own-substitution elasticity $S_{W_i}(H_i) W_i / H_i$ is usually between about 0.000 and 0.360 (for example, see Bloch, 1973). However, some estimates are well outside this range. For example, Hill (1973) obtains elasticities between about 0.470 and 0.560, although these results are derived from samples restricted to whites and blacks, respectively, whose income is below the poverty line. Kalachek and Raines (1970), who also analyze a poverty sample, obtain estimated elasticities for men between about 0.800 and 0.960. On the other hand, a number of studies imply, at least for some samples, that the own-substitution elasticity for male labor supply is small and negative.[36]

To some extent, the variation in these estimates may be the result of misspecification, measurement problems, and the like. For example, inclusion of work-related transfer payments in the mea- sure of V in equations such as (3.19)–(3.21) is likely to induce a

---

[35] "Negativity" means that the income-compensated own-wage elasticity of *leisure demand* is negative (which means that the compensated wage elasticity of labor supply is positive). Note that symmetry refers to the absolute magnitudes of cross- substitution *effects* $S_{W_i}(H_j)$ and $S_{W_j}(H_i)$ and not to the cross-substitution *elasticities* $S_{W_i}(H_j) W_i / H_j$ and $S_{W_j}(H_i) W_j / H_i$.

[36] For example, see Boskin (1973), Cohen, Rea, and Lerman (1970), Fleisher, Parsons, and Porter (1973), Garfinkel (1973a), Hall (1973, esp. for nonwhites), Kosters (1966, 1969), Leuthold (1968), S. Rosen (1969), and (for some rural males) Rosen and Welch (1971).

spurious negative relation between measured V and hours of work H and, therefore, produce a negative bias in OLS estimates of the parameter c (or c_i). If so, then the derived value of the own-substitution elasticity $(b_{ii} - c_i H_i) W_i / H_i$ will be biased in a positive direction. On the other hand, use of constructed measures of the wage rate such as W_1, W_2, or W_4 that are essentially ratios of earnings to labor supply may entail a spurious inverse relation between labor supply and the measure of W, attributable to errors in measurement of H that are repeated in the denominator of measured W. This may bias the estimate of b (or b_i) in equations (3.19)–(3.21) downward and thus produce a negative value for the own-substitution elasticity.

Of course, the fact that estimates of the own-substitution elasticity are not always positive may simply mean that the simple static labor supply model has been tested and found wanting. On the other hand, the fact that most such estimates are positive, as implied by the simple model, is not necessarily comforting. As Cain and Watts (1973a, p. 331) note, this may simply raise

> the nagging possibility that most investigators . . . have learned their theory well, have a prior belief in [these] qualitative characteristics of labor supply, and continue to permute samples, variables and functional forms until they obtain results they can be comfortable with . . .
> [This] should be kept in mind as a qualification against interpreting [the usual] conformity [of estimates with theoretical predictions] as yet another thoroughly independent confirmation of standard theory.

Estimates in first-generation work of the own-substitution elasticity for female labor supply – like those of the female gross elasticity – are few and far between. Most are significantly positive and range between about 0.100 and 2.000.[37] The main "nagging possibility" of concern here is that most such estimates are derived from samples restricted to working women, that is, women for whom $H > 0$. If only because a substantial fraction of the total female

---

[37] See Boskin (1973), Hall (1973), Kalachek and Raines (1970), and Leuthold (1968). Kalachek and Raines get negative substitution elasticities for weeks per year and hours per week. Only after they add the substitution elasticity for labor force participation does the "total" substitution elasticity – for participation, weeks given participation and hours given weeks worked – become positive.

population is excluded by such a selection rule, the possibility for sample selection bias in the estimation of labor supply parameters for women is evident.

Finally, estimates of intrafamily or cross-substitution elasticities are very rare. Here, one can find positive, negative, and zero estimates. Moreover, in most cases, symmetry – that is, equality of the absolute magnitudes $S_{W_j}(H_i)$ and $S_{W_i}(H_j)$ – is resoundingly rejected. On the whole, most first-generation results imply that the cross-substitution elasticity for the husband's labor supply is not significantly different from zero, whereas the comparable elasticity for the wife's labor supply is usually significantly positive and in between 0.000 and 0.400.[38] Ashenfelter and Heckman (1974) test for symmetry and are unable to reject the hypothesis that the cross-substitution effects $S_{W_j}(H_i)$ and $S_{W_i}(H_j)$ are both zero and not significantly different from each other. However, these results are based on regressions in which labor supply is defined as labor force participation rather than hours of work. Thus, they do not in fact provide a direct test of the theoretical prediction of symmetry (since the theory's prediction is couched in terms of hours of work, rather than participation), and in any event their results are not comparable to results in which labor supply is defined as hours of work. (See McElroy, 1981, for further discussion of estimates of intrafamily cross-substitution effects.)

Property income elasticity of labor supply

Standard theory is silent about the sign of the elasticity of labor supply with respect to property income. However, it seems reasonable to suppose that leisure is a normal good and, thus, that this elasticity – $(\partial H / \partial V) V/H$ – will be negative.[39] In the main, first-generation studies appear to confirm this conjecture, although –

---

[38] For example, see Bloch (1973), Hill (1973), Kalachek and Raines (1970), Kosters (1966, 1969), and Olsen (1977), who all obtain results in which these two magnitudes are quite different. When computed using the standard expression, given in the text, for the cross-substitution elasticity, Leuthold's (1968) results also imply quite different cross-substitution elasticities for husband and wife. However, as noted in Chapter 2, her individual utility–family budget constraint model does not imply, a priori, that such cross-substitution effects (or elasticities) will be equal.

[39] The elasticity can be calculated directly from equations such as (3.19)–(3.21). Specifically, $(\partial H / \partial V)$ is equal to the parameter c in (3.19) and is equal to the para-

particularly in recent work – not with much regularity. For males, the estimated income elasticity is usually weak, negative, and in between 0.000 and – 0.160, but in some work it is not significantly different from zero.[40] On the other hand, Kalachek and Raines (1970) obtain an elasticity as large as – 0.330. For women, the estimated income elasticity is generally negative and much greater, in absolute value, than the male elasticity. In general, the range of estimates for women is in between about – 0.100 and – 0.200. Again, however, some studies get a much larger absolute figure, whereas others find elasticities that are not significantly different from zero for some female subgroups.[41] The main caveat that must be borne in mind with respect to these results for women is that they are in almost all cases derived from samples restricted to women who work.

Results of recent studies: a summary

To round out the previous general discussion of first-generation work, in Tables 3.1–3.5, I summarize a number of recent

---

meter c_i in (3.20) or (3.21). Finally, note that, by the standard decomposition of the total effect of a change in family member j's wage on family member i's labor supply,

$$(\partial H_i/\partial W_j)(W_j/H_i) = S_{W_j}(H_i)(W_j/H_i) + H_j(\partial H_i/\partial V)(W_j/H_i)$$

The second term on the right-hand side of this expression may be rewritten as $(\partial H_i/\partial V)(H_j W_j/H_i)$ or, when $i = j$, as $(\partial H_i/\partial V) W_i$; it is sometimes called the *total income* elasticity. (Abbott and Ashenfelter, 1976, refer to its complement, $(\partial L_i/\partial V) W_i$, as the "marginal propensity to consume unearned income.") Thus, the gross (uncompensated) wage elasticity is equal, by definition, to the sum of the substitution (compensated) wage elasticity and the total income elasticity; however, note that the total income elasticity is not the same as the property income elasticity even when $i = j$.

[40] For example, Ashenfelter and Heckman (1973), Bloch (1973), Cohen, Rea, and Lerman (1970), Greenberg (1971), Greenberg and Kosters (1973), Hall (1973), Hill (1973), Rosen and Welch (1971), and Wales (1973) all obtain elasticities that, in general, fall in between 0.000 and – 0.160. For exceptions, see Boskin (1973), Garfinkel (1973a), Kosters (1966, 1969), Leuthold (1968) and S. Rosen (1969), who find approximately zero elasticities.

[41] See Cohen, Rea, and Lerman (1970), Hall (1973), and Leuthold (1968) for elasticities between about – 0.100 and – 0.200. Kalachek and Raines (1970) get estimates between – 0.410 and – 0.750. Boskin (1973) and Hall (1973) get elasticities that are approximately equal to zero. Bloch's (1973) results, based on an hours-of-work regression, imply that the income elasticity for females is quite small (about – 0.03), but statistically significant.

Table 3.1. *Characteristics of first-generation studies summarized in Tables 3.2–3.5*

Study	Characteristics of sample	Construction of measures of H, W, V
Abbott & Ashenfelter (1976)	Aggregate time series for United States, 1929–67 (fits labor supply function as part of system of commodity demand functions)	H = hours of work per employee per year W = total private sector wage and salary bill ÷ total hours worked in private sector × [1 − (personal taxes paid/personal income)] V = total consumption expenditure − total earnings
Abbott & Ashenfelter (1979)	Same as Abbott & Ashenfelter (1976)	Same as Abbott & Ashenfelter (1976) but with data errors in series of consumer goods prices corrected
Ashenfelter & Heckman (1973)	Married white men, with positive H, nonworking spouse, not receiving transfers – SEO	H = annual earnings ÷ normal hourly wage W = normal hourly wage V = rent, dividends, interest income, royalties, private-transfer receipts, alimony
Ashworth & Ulph (1981b)	Married couples in which each spouse works ≥8 hours per week and no other family member works (fits family labor supply models) – BMRBS	For husband's H, W: same as Brown, Levin, & Ulph (1976, 1981) For wife: H = hours of work per week W = earnings ÷ H, corrected for taxes (linearized) V = net nonemployment income, including transfers, corrected for taxes (linearized)

111

Table 3.1. *(cont.)*

Study	Characteristics of sample	Construction of measures of H, W, V
Atkinson & Stern (1980)	Household heads earning between £0.85 and £3.00/hour, age 18–64, not self-employed, in full-time employment (fits labor supply function as part of system of commodity demand functions) – 1973 FES	H = normal hours per week W = normal earnings per week $\div$ H V = total income (including social security benefits) – husband's earnings
Atkinson & Stern (1981)	Same as Atkinson & Stern (1980)	Same as Atkinson & Stern (1980), but series on consumer goods purchases do not include certain purchases (e.g., purchases on credit)
Atrostic (1982)	Employed married white male twins who have served in armed forces – National Academy of Sciences–National Research Council Twin Registry	H = annual hours worked W = either (i) as reported by respondent or (ii) earnings $\div$ H V = reported nonlabor income + other family members' earnings
Barnett (1979b, 1981)	Aggregate times series for United States, 1890–1941 and 1946–55 (fits leisure demand function as part of system of commodity demand functions)	L = index of leisure hours per capita W = earnings per fulltime equivalent employee, corrected for unemployment V = full income, corrected for unemployment (= goods expenditure + expenditure on leisure evaluated at W)
Boskin (1973)	Persons in 12 large metropolitan areas, not in school, disabled, in family receiving $\geq$ \$1,000 in self-	H = annual earnings $\div$ W W = imputed wage per hour (calculated by auxiliary regression) deflated by cost-

112

of-living index for area of residence and corrected for Federal marginal tax rate (linearized)

V = full income, corrected for tax liability (= goods expenditure + expenditure on leisure evaluated at W) (linearized)

H = hours of work per week

W = marginal net wage (wage at second job, if constrained on first job; or lower of the wages on two jobs, otherwise), inclusive of overtime premium (if any) and corrected for marginal tax rate (linearized)

V = net nonemployment income, including earnings of other family members and transfers, but excluding own earnings and corrected for taxes (linearized) (separate variable for actual net nonemployment income also included)

L = index of leisure consumption per capita
W = index of current wage rate
V = mean wealth per capita

H = hours of work per year (1969–72 average)

W = marginal wage rate, corrected for marginal tax rate (linearized) (1969–72 average)

V = nonwage income corrected for taxes (linearized) (1969–72 average)

---

employment income or any income from public assistance – SEO

Brown, Levin, & Ulph (1976, 1981)
Married working men, working ≥ 8 hours per week, salaried, no family members other than wife work – BMRBS

Darrough (1977)
Aggregate time series for Japan, 1946–72

Dickinson (1979)
White married men age 25–60, employed in each of the years 1969–72, not farmers or proprietors and free to vary hours (or, if not, satisfied with present hours), no second job, nonworking wife, has nonzero marginal wage rate – PSID

Table 3.1. *(cont.)*

Study	Characteristics of sample	Construction of measures of H, W, V
Fleisher, Parsons, & Porter (1973)	Urban married men age 45–59, employed with earnings in 1965–66 – NLS	H = weeks worked × usual hours worked per week W = annual earnings ÷ H V = net family *assets* (NB: *not* property income), excluding consumer durables
Garfinkel (1973a)	Married men age 25–61 not enrolled in school or disabled, not self-employed or in armed forces, not transfer or pension recipients, worked in previous year and in survey week – SEO	H = weeks worked + weeks looking for work W = earnings last week ÷ hours worked last week V = interest, dividends, rent, Social Security, and other nonemployment income
Gayer (1977)	Adult family heads and spouses, including nonworkers – SM	H = hours worked in survey week × 52 W = earnings in prior month ÷ (4.29 × hours worked in survey week), corrected for taxes (linearized) (imputed, using regression, for nonworkers) V = property income + government and private transfer payments
Glaister, McGlone, & Ruffell (1981)	Persons working ≥ 8 hours per week, with no family members working other than spouse – BMRBS	H = hours of work per week W = hourly wage, inclusive of overtime premium (if any), corrected for taxes (linearized) V = nonemployment income + other family members' earnings, corrected for taxes (linearized)

114

Gramm (1974)	Married women teachers, substitute teachers and nonworking teachers living in Chicago, 1970	L = total nonmarket time per week (nonworkers' L set at 168 (?)) W = earnings per year V = estimated total value of household assets
Gramm (1975)	Same as Gramm (1974)	H = fraction of full-time workload worked in 1969 (1,600 hours defined as full-time) W = annual earnings for persons working full-time (for substitutes, earnings if worked all day every day) V = estimated total value of household assets
Greenhalgh (1980)	Married working women, not in families with "complex tax schedules for low incomes" – 1971 GHS	H = annual hours worked W = imputed wage rate, gross of tax V = family income, net of tax, exclusive of wife's earnings (tax computed as if wife had no earnings)
Hall (1973)	Same as Boskin (1973), except as follows: includes only persons in 12 largest SMSA's, includes all households except those in highest wage rate and full income classes – SEO	Same as Boskin (1973)
Hill (1973)	Family heads age 25–54 in which husband and/or wife worked at least one week in 1966 as private wage earner, not self-employed, total income of family below poverty line – SEO	H = weeks worked per year × F, where F = 40 if primarily full-time worker during year and F = 30 if primarily part-time worker W = annual earnings ÷ hours worked per year V = total income other than earnings (including transfer payments)

Table 3.1. *(cont.)*

Study	Characteristics of sample	Construction of measures of H, W, V
Kiefer (1976, 1977) Lau, Lin, & Yotopoulos (1978)	Same as Abbott & Ashenfelter (1976) Pooled data for averages of eight agricultural regions in Taiwan, 1968–9	Same as Abbott & Ashenfelter (1976) H = regional average labor time of family, in days per year W = price of leisure V = total income − expenditures (including imputed expenditures on leisure)
Layard (1978)	Married employed men age 25–55 – 1974 GHS	H = hours worked per week W = gross annual earnings ÷ {weeks worked per year × [normal hours per week + (1.25 × overtime hours)]}, imputed using regression and linearized at standard tax rate V = rent, interest, and dividends + value of house + family allowance − mortgage interest, linearized at standard tax rate
Leuthold (1978b)	Married employed women age 30–44 with spouse present – NLS	H = usual hours worked per week × weeks employed or looking for work W = after-tax usual hourly wage V = after-tax nonwork income (from rent, dividends, or business or profession)

116

Masters & Garfinkel (1977)	Married persons age 25–54, not self-employed or enrolled in school or in armed forces, worked during previous year – SEO	H = weeks working or looking for work during year × 40 (if normally worked full-time) or 20 (if voluntarily worked part-time)
		W = imputed wage, derived from regression for ratio of normal weekly earnings to actual hours worked during survey week
		V = interest, dividend, rent, pension, and Social Security income, exclusive of transfer payments
Phlips (1978)	Aggregate time series for United States, 1938–67	H = as in Abbott & Ashenfelter (1976)
		W = as in Abbott & Ashenfelter (1976)
		V = wealth
H. Rosen (1976a)	White married women age 30–44, not in families receiving public assistance – NLS	H = annual hours worked (= usual weekly hours × weeks worked in year) or hours worked per week (nonworkers' H set at zero)
		W = imputed wage, derived from regression for actual hourly wage rate, linearized at marginal tax rate applicable to earnings when wife does not work
		V = gross other family income (linearized)
H. Rosen (1978)	Black and white married couples in which wife was age 30–44, both spouses worked, neither spouse self-employed or transfer recipient, gross family income ≥\$1,000 – NLS	H = annual hours worked
		W = linearized wage, evaluated at marginal tax rate applicable when wife works 500 hours per year and husband works 1,500 hours per year
		V = unearned income (linearized)

117

Table 3.1. *(cont.)*

Study	Characteristics of sample	Construction of measures of H, W, V
Wales & Woodland (1976)	Married persons, not transfer recipients, husband and wife both worked ≥400 hours in year, able to vary hours of work (or satisfied with present level of hours of work), head does not hold second job or get income from overtime, bonuses, or commissions – PSID	L = 8,760 – hours worked in 1971 W = money income from work ÷ hours worked in 1971 (linearized at actual marginal tax rate) V = nonemployment income (linearized)
Wales & Woodland (1977)	Same as Wales & Woodland (1976)	Same as Wales & Woodland (1976)

Note: Unless otherwise noted, all data refer to the United States. BMRBS, British Market Research Bureau survey (U.K.); FES, Family Expenditure Survey (U.K.); GHS, General Household Survey (U.K.); NLS, National Longitudinal Survey; PSID, Panel Study of Income Dynamics; SEO, Survey of Economic Opportunity; SM, Survey of Manpower (Israel).

Table 3.2. *Labor supply elasticity estimates for men*

Study	Wage elasticity		Total income elasticity
	Uncompensated	Compensated	
Ashenfelter & Heckman (1973)	−0.15	0.12	−0.27
Atrostic (1982)			
Controlling for job characteristics			
Homothetic translog (OLS)	−0.05	−0.11	0.06
Homothetic translog demand system	0.25	1.26	−1.01
Basic translog demand system	0.34	0.97	−0.63
Boskin (1973)			
Whites	−0.29	0.12	−0.41
Blacks	−0.20	0.00	−0.20
Fleisher, Parsons, & Porter (1973)			
All	−0.19	0.04	−0.23
Excluding transfer recipients	−0.27	−0.19	−0.08
Garfinkel (1973a)	≈ 0	≈ 0	≈ 0
Greenberg & Kosters (1973)	−0.09	0.20	−0.29
Hall (1973)			
Whites	−0.18 to −0.45	0.06	−0.24 to −0.51
Nonwhites	−0.22 to −0.38	−0.10	−0.12 to −0.28
Hill (1973)			
Whites below poverty line	−0.21	0.47	−0.68
Blacks below poverty line	−0.08	0.27	−0.35
Whites above poverty line	−0.34	0.52	−0.86
Blacks above poverty line	−0.32	0.56	−0.88

Table 3.2. *(cont.)*

| Study | Wage elasticity | | Total income elasticity |
	Uncompensated	Compensated	
Kniesner (1976a)			
With working wife	−0.17	−0.16	−0.01
With nonworking wife	−0.06	< 0	< 0
Wales & Woodland (1976)	−0.11 to −0.12	n.a.	< 0
Wales & Woodland (1977)			
With children	−0.22 to −0.27	n.a.	n.a.
Without children	0.00 to −0.07	n.a.	n.a.
Masters & Garfinkel (1977)	0.04	0.08	−0.04
H. Rosen (1978)			
Stone–Geary utility	−0.02	1.00	−1.02
CES utility	−0.42	0.14	−0.55
Dickinson (1979)	−0.09 to −0.12	0.14 to 0.38	−0.26 to −0.49
Brown, Levin, & Ulph (1976, 1981)[a]			
All	−0.11 to −0.26	0.16 to 0.22	−0.30 to −0.46
Nonworking wife	−0.09 to −0.31	0.22 to 0.47	−0.35 to −0.73
Layard (1978)[a]			
Single-equation model	−0.13	−0.08	−0.05
Husband–wife model	−0.12	−0.09	−0.03

Atkinson & Stern (1980)[a]			
LES model	−0.15	−0.21	0.06
LES with time allocation model	−0.16	−0.09	−0.07
Atkinson & Stern (1981)[a]			
Single-equation model	−0.15	−0.16	0.01
LES model	−0.21	−0.29	0.08
Stone–Geary utility	−0.23	−0.30	0.07
Ashworth & Ulph (1981b)[a]			
Family utility–family budget constraint model	−0.03	2.17	−2.21
Individual utility–family budget constraint model	−1.00	0.47	−1.47
Glaister, McGlone, & Ruffell (1981)[a]	−0.02	−0.06	0.04
Gayer (1977) ("family heads")[b]	−0.45	−0.27	−0.18

Note: Unless otherwise noted, all estimates refer to data for United States.

n.a., not available.

[a] Refers to data for United Kingdom.

[b] Refers to data for Israel.

Table 3.3. *Labor supply elasticity estimates for women*

| Study | Wage elasticity | | Total income elasticity |
	Uncompensated	Compensated	
Boskin (1973)			
Whites	0.19	0.29	−0.10
Blacks	0.70	0.77	−0.07
Hall (1973)			
Whites	4.60	2.50	2.10
Blacks	1.66	0.26	1.40
Gramm (1974)	0.85	0.85	≈ 0
Gramm (1975)	0.68	0.68	≈ 0
Wales & Woodland (1976)	0.01 to −0.02	n.a.	< 0
Wales & Woodland (1977)			
With children	−0.03 to −0.35	n.a.	n.a.
Without children	0.20 to 0.27	n.a.	n.a.
Masters & Garfinkel (1977)	0.43	0.49	−0.06
H. Rosen (1976a)			
Hours per year	1.90	n.a.	n.a.
Hours per week	1.30	n.a.	n.a.
H. Rosen (1978)			
Stone–Geary utility	1.06	1.53	−0.47
CES utility	−0.16	0.26	−0.42
Leuthold (1978b)			
Whites	0.05 to 0.16	0.06 to 0.18	n.a.
Blacks	0.10 to 0.13	0.09 to 0.13	n.a.

Layard (1978)[a]	0.66	0.84	−0.19
Greenhalgh (1980)[a]			
All	0.72	0.80	−0.08
Paying standard rate of tax	0.64	0.72	−0.08
Ashworth & Ulph (1981b)[a]			
Family utility–family budget constraint model	−1.18	−1.14	−0.04
Individual utility–family budget constraint model	−4.46	−5.02	0.56
Glaister, McGlone & Ruffell (1981)[a]	0.09	0.09	0.00
Gayer (1977) ("spouses")[b]	−0.50	−0.27	−0.23

Note: Unless otherwise noted, all estimates refer to data for United States.

n.a., not available.

[a] Refers to data for United Kingdom.

[b] Refers to data for Israel.

Table 3.4.   *Intrafamily cross-substitution elasticities*

	Elasticity with respect to spouse's wage	
Study	Uncompensated	Compensated
Gramm (1974)		
Wives	− 0.25	− 0.25
Gramm (1975)		
Wives	− 0.17	− 0.17
Wales & Woodland (1976)		
Husbands	0.21 to 0.23	n.a.
Wives	0.02 to − 0.06	n.a.
Wales & Woodland (1977)		
Families with children		
Husbands	0.13 to − 0.01	n.a.
Wives	0.14 to − 0.41	n.a.
Families without children		
Husbands	0.17 to 0.22	n.a.
Wives	0.13 to 0.39	n.a.
Rosen (1978)		
Stone−Geary utility		
Husbands	− 0.83	− 0.39
Wives	− 1.96	− 0.89
CES utility		
Husbands	− 0.30	− 0.06
Wives	− 1.11	− 0.14
Layard (1978)[a]		
Single-equation model		
Wives	− 0.10	− 0.09
Husband−wife model		
Husbands	− 0.06	− 0.05
Wives	− 0.40	− 0.79
Ashworth & Ulph (1981b)[a]		
Family utility−family budget constraint model		
Husbands	− 0.16	0.75
Wives	1.73	1.81
Individual utility−family budget constraint model		
Husbands	0.87	1.48
Wives	5.05	6.41

Note: Unless otherwise noted, all estimates refer to data for United States.
n.a., not available.
[a] Refers to data for United Kingdom.

Table 3.5. *Labor supply elasticity estimates for aggregate labor supply*

| | Wage elasticity | | Total income |
Study	Uncompensated	Compensated	elasticity
Abbott & Ashenfelter (1976)			
Rotterdam model	−0.14	0.03	−0.17
Separable Rotterdam model	−0.07	0.08	−0.15
Linear model	−0.08	0.04	−0.12
Addilog model	1.07	0.37	0.70
Abbott & Ashenfelter (1979)			
Rotterdam model	−0.14	0.03	−0.17
Separable Rotterdam model	−0.07	0.08	−0.15
Linear model	−0.07	0.06	−0.13
Addilog model	0.88	0.27	0.61
Kiefer (1976) (translog model)	−0.05	−0.85	0.80
Kiefer (1977) (Rotterdam model)			
Least-squares estimates	−0.19	−0.01	−0.18
Bayesian estimates	−0.19	0.00	−0.18
Phlips (1978)			
Short run	−0.09	0.04	−0.13
Long run	−0.09	0.14	−0.23
Barnett (1979a)	n.a.[a]	−0.11[a]	0.28[a, b]
Darrough (1977)[c]	−0.33[a]	−7.62[a]	−0.37[a, b]
Lau, Lin, & Yotopoulos (1978)[d]	0.17	0.89	−0.72

Note: Unless otherwise noted, all estimates refer to data for United States.
[a] Dependent variable is demand for leisure (not labor supply).
[b] Elasticity with respect to wealth (not total income elasticity).
[c] Refers to data for Japan.
[d] Refers to data for Taiwan.

studies. (For analogous tables summarizing earlier work, see Borjas and Heckman, 1979; Cain and Watts, 1973a; Killingsworth, 1981.) As in the previous discussion, labor supply in these tables refers to hours of work (usually per year) rather than to participation; moreover, although many of the results shown in the tables are taken from the studies cited (and most are evaluated at actual sample means), in some cases I have had to calculate the elasticities myself by using information given in the study in question or by making informed guesses. Thus, as before, all numerical entries in the tables should be regarded as approximate, and most results will be sensitive to differences in procedures, values of sample means, and the like.

Some of the main features of these studies are summarized in Table 3.1. Tables 3.2 and 3.3 present results on own-wage and income elasticities of labor supply for men and women, respectively; Table 3.4 presents results on cross-wage elasticities for husbands and wives. Finally, Table 3.5 presents results on aggregate labor supply (usually measured as hours of work per worker, representing an average for both sexes combined), obtained from aggregate time-series data.[42] As implied by the previous general discussion, some of the results shown in Tables 3.2–3.5 are anomalous. In particular, compensated wage elasticities are not infrequently negative and property income elasticities are often negative but very small or else

[42] Analyses of aggregate time-series data must confront at least two issues that do not arise in the context of analyses of microdata of the kind summarized in Tables 3.2–3.4: aggregation and simultaneity. The aggregation problem is concerned with whether analyses of aggregate data (e.g., on mean hours worked, mean wage rates, and the like) provide useful information about the behavior of "representative" individuals or households; Barnett (1979a, b, 1981) and Muellbauer (1981), among others, have discussed conditions under which one may use household commodity demand and labor supply functions to derive specifications suitable for aggregate data which, when estimated, permit meaningful inferences about behavioral responses (e.g., income and substitution effects for representative individuals or households). The simultaneity problem arises from the fact that, in an aggregate or macrodata context, the "independent" variables in the various behavioral relations to be estimated (e.g., commodity demand and labor supply functions) are not in fact independent (that is, exogenous) but rather are determined *along with* the "dependent" variables of the model (e.g., commodity demands and labor supply) as part of aggregate equilibrium. (For example, in the aggregate, both labor supply and the wage rate are determined by the intersection of workers' supply schedules and firms' demand schedules; see Feldstein, 1968; Rayner, 1969.) Thus, at the aggregate level, the error term and the independent variables will generally be correlated. (For example, suppose the error term in the aggregate labor supply equation increases, thereby increasing aggregate labor supply. Other things being equal, this will reduce the equilibrium wage rate, meaning that the aggregate labor supply error term will be correlated with the market wage rate. In contrast, microdata refer to individual workers who – in the absence of any warm-up or fatigue or other, similar, effects of the kind discussed in Chapter 1 – may generally be taken to be price-takers, unable to affect the wage they can earn. In that case, causation runs from the wage to labor supply but *not* vice versa – although, as noted in Chapter 4, the wage and labor supply may still be correlated in microdata if unobservables that affect the wage are correlated with unobservables that affect labor supply.) Despite this simultaneity, most studies of aggregate data proceed as if the wage rate (and other independent variables, e.g., commodity prices) were in fact independent of the error term. (Two exceptions are the studies by Lucas and Rapping, 1970, and S. Rosen, 1969.)

positive – especially for men. It is possible that these peculiarities are simply the result of some of the problems previously noted, such as sample selection bias. However, at least in the case of men, sample selection bias may not explain very many of the oddities shown in Table 3.1, since many of the studies cited in that table include virtually all working men, and a high fraction of all men work. An alternative explanation of the negative compensated wage elasticities and near-zero property income elasticities for men has to do with the notion of the discontinuous budget line (recall Section 2.4). For example, if hours of work are rationed (either as the result of voluntary choice, or in the form of a constraint on choice), then, as implied by Figure 2.4, one will generally observe (i) little or no association between labor supply and property income (because the rationed level of hours of work is invariant with respect to such factors) and (ii) a negative relation between hours of work and wage rates (see, in particular, points a_1 and a_2 in Figure 2.4). In terms of estimated labor supply parameters, then, one would expect to find (i) a negative gross (uncompensated) relation between hours of work and wage rates; (ii) a weak relation between hours of work and "exogenous" income, V; and – since the substitution (compensated) wage elasticity is usually calculated as the difference between the gross elasticity and a multiple of the property income elasticity – (iii) negative *calculated* values of the net (compensated) relation between hours of work and wage rates. Of course, this "explanation" fails to explain why these phenomena are not observed for working women as well as for working men. To say that men have a greater commitment to the labor force than women, on average, may provide part of the answer but begs several important questions (e.g., why are working women less "committed to work," on average, than working men?) and ignores the fact that important subgroups of women seem to be highly committed to work.

3.5.   First-generation studies: summary and conclusions

To sum up: Whether expressed in terms of gross wage elasticities, own-substitution elasticities, cross-substitution elasticities, or property income elasticities, most first-generation studies imply that women are more "sensitive" than men – at least as far as labor supply is concerned! On the whole, these studies also suggest that leisure is a normal good, both for men and for women, and an income-compensated increase in one's own wage will increase one's labor supply. However, the theoretical prediction of symmetry does not survive the few confrontations with data to which it has been subjected; and *negative* compensated wage elasticities of labor supply are not exactly unheard of. All in all, then, use of results of first-generation studies to support basic propositions of the simple static labor supply model is not to be recommended to those whose main concern is peace of mind.

Using the results of labor supply models to analyze the effects of policy is also hazardous. In large measure, this is because – as Tables 3.1–3.3 and the discussion in the previous section indicate – the range of estimates for any given labor supply elasticity is usually quite substantial. For example, in discussing the practical meaning of this range of variation, Cain and Watts (1973a, p. 339) point out that simulation of the effects of negative income tax schemes using estimated elasticities such as the ones discussed earlier would imply a reduction in labor supply of the working poor by anything between 4 and 46 percent, depending on just which set of estimates is used. For policy purposes, this range of estimates is simply too wide to be of much practical value.

However, there is no reason why one should give all studies equal weight in attempting to determine the relevant empirical range of labor supply elasticities, evaluating the usefulness of such estimates for simulations and other policy discussions, or computing the likely effect of proposed policy measures. For example, Borjas and Heckman (1979, esp. pp. 329–31) argue that one should ignore altogether the results of several studies[43] all of which suffer from one or more of the following defects: use of poverty samples restricted to persons whose income is below the poverty line, inclusion of work-related transfer payments in the measure of V, and use of measures of W that are definitionally related to labor supply. After eliminating one other study on the grounds that the measure of H used in it is seriously defective,[44] Borjas and Heckman find that the range of

[43] Hill (1973), Kalachek and Raines (1970), and Rosen and Welch (1971).
[44] Masters and Garfinkel (1977). They use a constructed measure of "normal" labor supply, equal to 40 × weeks worked for individuals who said they normally work, or would like to work, "full-time" and equal to 20 × weeks worked for individuals who said they normally work, or would like to work, "part-time."

estimated gross own-wage elasticities for prime-age males in the remaining studies they consider is quite small: between -0.07 and -0.19. Similarly, the range of estimated own-substitution elasticities narrows to between 0.04 and 0.20. The range of likely effects of a negative income tax scheme on prime-age male labor supply implied by these labor supply elasticities is likewise small: The studies that remain imply a reduction in labor supply of between 8 and 15 percent.

The motivation for, and merits of, such "selective evaluations" of labor supply results is clear. However, there is also a danger. Even for a given data base – but particularly as regards comparisons of studies using different data bases – it is difficult to say a priori just how sensitive a given parameter estimate will be to various kinds of errors, or to specify a priori the extent to which such errors may simply offset each other. There is, thus, a temptation – understandable, but probably unwarranted – to conclude that errors in a given study have had serious consequences from the fact that the study's estimates seem out of line with those obtained in other work. Absent additional information, this is probably the best one can hope to do. However, there remains the risk that selective evaluations of this kind will give a seal of approval to studies that imply a fairly narrow range of estimated elasticities simply because one observes a fairly narrow range of estimates in those studies. Besides, intuitive attempts to feel one's way past possible errors in first-generation studies are a poor substitute for second-generation attempts to surmount these errors. Such attempts stand a better chance of generating new knowledge (and they may well attract a higher level of grant support). With this survey of first-generation results as prologue, I will, therefore, turn next to the methodology and results of second-generation studies.

4

Second-generation studies of static labor supply models: methodology and empirical results

As noted in Chapter 3, the results of first-generation empirical studies of static labor supply models were somewhat disappointing. First, at times they provided only weak evidence in support of certain basic theoretical notions underlying the simple static model. Second, they appeared to provide evidence *against* certain other propositions underlying that model. Third, the range of estimates yielded by such studies was too wide to be of much use for purposes of analysis or policy. In principle, one could react in two different (but not mutually exclusive) ways to this body of work. On the one hand, one might conclude that the simple static labor supply model is inadequate and proceed to develop and analyze more elaborate models. On the other hand, one might also (or instead) conclude that the simple techniques used in first-generation work were not well suited to analysis of even the simple labor supply model and proceed to develop and use more elaborate empirical techniques.

These concerns have fostered a growing body of "second-generation" labor supply research. This literature differs from first-generation work in several respects: specification, estimation technique, and the range of models considered.

1. *Specification*. First-generation empirical studies were chiefly concerned with estimating the parameters of ad hoc labor supply functions, such as (3.19)–(3.21), that were not derived from a formal model of utility maximization subject to constraints. Different aspects of labor supply (e.g., participation vs. hours of work) were dealt with in a piecemeal manner. On the other hand, second-

generation work typically is concerned with estimating the parameters of labor supply functions generated by maximizing an explicitly specified utility function (or an explicitly specified function for some other utility-related index of behavior, such as the marginal rate of substitution function) subject to explicitly specified budget constraints. As such work has emphasized, different aspects of labor supply (e.g., participation and hours of work) are closely related; in most cases, they cannot sensibly be considered independently of one another.

2. *Estimation.* As noted in Chapter 3, most first-generation research either ignored or else dealt in an ad hoc fashion with a variety of problems of estimation (e.g., the fact that wage data are missing for nonworkers and the question of whether to exclude or include nonworkers from the sample used to estimate the labor supply function). In contrast, second-generation research tackled these problems head-on. In particular, as second-generation research has emphasized, these problems are not simply quirks or oddities but are fundamentally linked to other aspects of labor supply: For example, the reason why wage data are not available for nonworkers is, of course, that nonworkers are not supplying labor! As such, problems of this kind are really part of the subject being studied, and in formulating econometric models of labor supply, one must recognize that they exist. To ignore such problems – that is, to treat them only as annoying data flukes with no implications about behavior – may result not merely in lost information about some aspects of labor supply but also in biased estimates of the parameters that govern labor supply.

3. *Modeling.* Most first-generation research was concerned with the very simple static labor model of Chapter 1 (or with its extension to an *n*-person family, discussed in Chapter 2). For the most part, taxes, costs of labor market entry, questions about dynamic behavior and other complications were ignored. In contrast, second-generation research has begun to introduce complexities of this kind into the simple model, making it richer and, at least potentially, more relevant, particularly for purposes of analysis and policy.

In this chapter, I summarize the main analytical and empirical results of second-generation research on static labor supply models. (I discuss dynamic labor supply models in Chapter 5.) I start by reviewing the simple static labor supply model and by describing the general principles underlying the kinds of econometric techniques used in second-generation work for estimating such a model. Next, I survey specific procedures used in actual second-generation studies. The chapter concludes with a summary of empirical findings of second-generation work. As will quickly become apparent – particularly in the final section – the second-generation literature has certainly not yet provided answers to all of the questions about labor supply that have been noted in previous chapters. It has, however, provided a solid analytical framework that can be used to get such answers.

4.1.   The static labor supply model revisited

To understand the fundamentals of the second-generation approach, it is useful to start by considering again the simple static labor supply model discussed at the beginning of Chapter 3. In that model, utility, given by the function $u = C^\alpha L^\beta$, is maximized subject to the budget constraint $WH + V = PC$. To simplify the exposition, redefine W and V to be the real wage and the real level of property income, respectively (so that P may be dropped from the discussion). Now, as noted in Chapter 3, if the individual's utility function is $u = C^\alpha L^\beta$, then the function for his marginal rate of substitution, M, and the value of his reservation wage, M^*, are given by

$$M = [b/(1 - b)]C/L = [b/(1 - b)](WH + V)/(1 - H)$$
$$M^* = M_{L=1} = [b/(1 - b)]V$$

respectively, where $b = \beta/(\alpha + \beta)$. Moreover, the individual will work if the wage he can earn, W, exceeds the value of his reservation wage, M^*:

$$H > 0 \quad \text{if and only if} \quad W > M^*,$$

that is, if and only if $W > [b/(1 - b)]V$. Finally, if the individual does work (and thus is at a point of indifference curve–budget line tangency, such as the point I in Figure 3.1), then his wage rate W and his marginal rate of substitution M are equal at his particular level of hours of work. Because M is a function of hours of work H, this means that the actual value of labor supply in this case is determined by the condition $W = M$, that is, by solving the relation

$$W = [b/(1 - b)](WH + V)/(1 - H)$$

for H. This yields the labor supply function

$$H = \frac{1 - b}{W} \left[W - \frac{b}{1 - b} V \right]$$
$$= 1 - b - b(V/W)$$

Thus, this simple model provides both an account of participation (that is, the decision to work or not to work) and an account of hours of work. Indeed, it emphasizes that both the participation decision and the choice of hours of work are inextricably intertwined, since both are the result of the same maximizing behavior and of the same parameters.

Of course, this simple theoretical model is not an empirical model suitable for econometric estimation, since it ignores the fact that individuals differ not only in terms of observable variables (i.e., V and W) but also in terms of unobservables (i.e., the ϵ or random error term of (3.12)). A key insight of second-generation research is that such unobservables, like observable variables, play a part in labor supply decisions and appropriate specification of empirical labor supply functions requires not only specification of the role of observable variables but also careful specification of the way in which unobservables affect labor supply decisions.

To see this point clearly, it is useful to consider a generalization of the earlier simple labor supply model to include an unobservable error term e (so as to make the model suitable for application to a population of different individuals). Specifically, let the utility function be given by

(4.1) $\quad u = [W(H + e) + V]^\alpha [1 - (H + e)]^\beta$

where e is an unobservable error term that varies from one person to another and that may be interpreted as a "taste shifter," that is, as representing interpersonal differences in tastes. (In particular, note that (4.1) implies that persons with different values of e will not derive the same enjoyment from given amounts of $C = WH + V$ and of $L = 1 - H$, even if their wage rates and property incomes are the same.) The marginal rate of substitution function implied by this utility function is

(4.2) $\quad M = (\partial u/\partial L)/(\partial u/\partial C)$
$\quad\quad = [b/(1 - b)] [W(H + e) + V]/[1 - (H + e)]$

where $b = \beta/(\alpha + \beta)$. The reservation wage is

(4.3) $M^* = [b/(1 - b)] (eW + V)/(1 - e)$

Thus, an individual with a given value of e will work if and only if $W > M^*$, or, by (4.3), if and only if

(4.4) $-e > \dfrac{-(1 - b)}{W} \left[W - \dfrac{b}{1 - b} V \right]$

Thus,

(4.5) $H > 0$ if and only if $\epsilon_H > -[(1 - b) - b(V/W)]$
(4.6) $H = 0$ if and only if $\epsilon_H \leq -[(1 - b) - b(V/W)]$

where $\epsilon_H = -e$. Moreover, if such an individual does work, his hours of work are determined by the condition $W = M$, that is, by solving the relation

(4.7) $W = [b/(1 - b)] \dfrac{W(H + e) + V}{1 - (H + e)}$

for H. This yields the empirical labor supply function

(4.8) $H = \dfrac{1 - b}{W} \left[W - \dfrac{b}{1 - b} V \right] - e$

or, equivalently,

(4.9) $H = (1 - b) - b(V/W) + \epsilon_H$ where $\epsilon_H = -e$.

More generally, let utility be a function of C, L and unobservables summarized by an error term, such as $u = u(C, L, e)$. Then the marginal rate of substitution function and the reservation wage for an individual with a particular e are

$$M = (\partial u/\partial L)/(\partial u/\partial C) = M(C, L, e)$$
$$= M(WH + V, 1 - H, e)$$
$$M^* = M(V, 1, e)$$

respectively. The individual will work if and only if $W > M(V, 1, e)$; and the hours of work of any individual who works are defined by the relation $W = M(WH + V, 1 - H, e)$ and thus may be obtained by solving this relation for H. (Of course, per the discussion at the beginning of Chapter 3, similar procedures can be used if the model is specified in terms of other utility-related functions, such as the indirect utility function.)

In and of itself, (4.9) is not much different from the sort of labor supply function used in much first-generation work (for example, see equations (3.19)–(3.21)). At first glance, therefore, it might seem that nothing new has emerged from this exercise. However, as this exercise indicates, (4.9) is far from the whole story about labor supply; and, taken together, equations (4.1)–(4.9) say more about labor supply than do the labor supply functions used in first-generation research. First, equations (4.1)–(4.9) emphasize a crucial threshold condition: Individual i will work if (4.5) is satisfied and will not work if (4.6) is satisfied. (In behavioral terms, this means that an individual with given V and W will work only if his tastes for work, as summarized by the magnitude of ϵ_H, are sufficiently great – bigger than the quantity $-[(1 - b) - b(V/W)]$.) Second, the model highlights the fact that *the* labor supply function is really *two* functions: One, (4.9), applies if and only if $W > M^*$, that is, if (4.5) holds; the other is simply the function "$H = 0$" and applies if and only if (4.6) is satisfied. Third, examination of the labor supply function(s) for hours of work and the threshold condition for the choice of whether or not to work makes it clear that the same observable variables, unobservable random terms, and parameters affect both kinds of decisions.

First-generation empirical labor supply functions generally ignore all these considerations; in contrast, second-generation estimation procedures bring them to the forefront. In the next two sections, I will describe general principles of estimation and, then, specific applications of these general principles as used in second-generation work.

4.2. Second-generation estimation techniques: general principles

To understand the basic ideas that underlie estimation procedures used in second-generation empirical work, it is helpful to assume that measures of the wage rate W are available for all individuals in the population, including nonworkers. (In the next section, I will consider techniques designed for the more complicated but unfortunately also more realistic case in which wage data are available only for workers.)

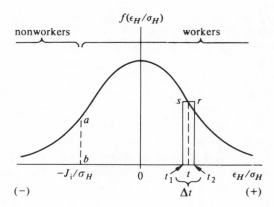

Figure 4.1. Illustration of probit analysis of participation

As noted earlier, *labor supply* means both participation and hours of work. Begin by considering empirical analysis of participation – that is, of being, or not being, employed.[1] Equations (4.5) and (4.6) highlight a crucial threshold condition, stating that individual i will work if and only if $\epsilon_{Hi} > -J_i$, where $J_i \equiv [(1 - b) - b(V_i/W_i)]$ and an i subscript denotes i's value of a particular variable. This simply means that i will work if and only if his wage exceeds his reservation wage; it also means that, given W_i and V_i, the value of ϵ_{Hi} – i's taste for work – determines whether i works.

To proceed further, it is necessary to make an assumption of some kind about the distribution of tastes for work – that is, of ϵ_H – in the population. Not infrequently, it is both highly convenient and quite reasonable to assume that ϵ_H has a mean of zero and is normally distributed in the population as a whole.[2] If so, then the transformed

---

[1] Of course, participation (being in the labor force) is not always the same as employment: Some labor force participants are unemployed. If all unemployment is, in effect, a form of leisure time (see Lucas and Rapping, 1970, who take essentially this view), then these two notions may be treated interchangeably; otherwise, as indicated in Chapter 1's discussion of unemployment, a quite different model may be required. Nevertheless, I follow virtually all of the second-generation literature in equating participation and employment – with the obvious caveat that work on a model that permits one to distinguish between these two notions deserves a high priority for future research. (See Sec. 5.3 for further discussion.)

[2] For useful discussions of the standard normal distribution, see Mood, Graybill, and Boes (1974), Theil (1978), and Wonnacott and Wonnacott (1977). Although the

variable ϵ_{Hi}/σ_H has a mean of zero and follows the standard normal distribution, where σ_H is the standard deviation of ϵ_{Hi} in the population. This is shown in Figure 4.1, which plots the probability density $f(\epsilon_{Hi}/\sigma_H)$ of the standardized variable ϵ_{Hi}/σ_H for each value of ϵ_{Hi}/σ_H. Since the mean of ϵ_{Hi} is zero (by assumption), the curve is centered at zero.

A researcher can never be sure whether an individual with particular values of V and W will or will not work. That depends on ϵ_H as well as on V and W; and ϵ_H, unlike V and W, is not known to a researcher. However, given an assumption (such as the one of "normality" just introduced) about how ϵ_H is distributed in the population, it is possible to derive an expression for the *probability* that such an individual will (or will not) work. In particular, the height of the curve in Figure 4.1 at any value of ϵ_{Hi}/σ_H, such as t in Figure 4.1, is equal to the probability density of ϵ_{Hi}/σ_H at that value, namely $f(t)$.

Consequently, the probability that a given individual i will work is given by[3]

---

assumption of normality is almost always used, it is important to note that one could instead assume that ϵ_H follows some other distribution and that virtually all of the principles applicable to the case of normality also apply when a different distribution is assumed.

[3] To see this, note that $f(t)$ is approximately equal to the ratio of (i) the probability that ϵ_{Hi}/σ_H will lie within the upper and lower limits t_2 and t_1 of a small interval that includes the value t to (ii) the size of that small interval, $t_2 - t_1$. For short, let Δt denote the quantity $t_2 - t_1$. Then, in more formal language,

$$f(t) = \lim_{t_2 - t_1 \to 0} \frac{\Pr[t_2 > (\epsilon_{Hi}/\sigma_H) > t_1]}{t_2 - t_1} = \lim_{\Delta t \to 0} \frac{\Pr[t_2 > (\epsilon_{Hi}/\sigma_H) > t_1]}{\Delta t}$$

Thus, for example, the probability that the value of ϵ_{Hi}/σ_H will lie somewhere in between t_1 and t_2 in Figure 4.1 is closely approximated by the product of (i) the height of the curve in the vicinity of point t, namely $f(t)$, and (ii) the distance $\Delta t = t_2 - t_1$ — that is, by the area of the "skinny rectangle," $t_1 t_2 rs$. In other words,

$$\Pr[t_2 > (\epsilon_{Hi}/\sigma_H) > t_1] \simeq f(t) \, \Delta t$$

where $f(t)$ is the height of $t_1 t_2 rs$ and Δt is its base. By extension, then, the probability that ϵ_{Hi}/σ_H will exceed $- J_i/\sigma_H$ may be approximated by adding the areas of all the many skinny rectangles similar to $t_1 t_2 rs$ that one could construct under the curve and to the right of ab. (Note that this sum of the areas is equal to the probability that someone will work if his value of $- J_i/\sigma_H$ is equal to the value associated with the line ab in Figure 4.1.) Of course, this is simply the entire area under the curve and to the

(4.10) $\Pr[i \text{ works}] = \Pr[\epsilon_{Hi}/\sigma_H > -J_i/\sigma_H]$

$$= \int_{-J_i/\sigma_H}^{\infty} f(t) \, dt$$

$$= 1 - F(-J_i/\sigma_H)$$

where $J_i = 1 - b - b(V_i/W_i)$, f = standard normal density function, and F = standard normal cumulative density function.

In sum, the probability that someone will work, when his value of $-J_i/\sigma_H$ is equal to the amount associated with the line *ab*, is given by the area under the curve in Figure 4.1 to the right of *ab*. (Similarly, the probability that such an individual will not work is given by the area under the curve to the left of *ab*.) By extension, suppose one were to consider a large number of persons all of whom had a value of $-J_i/\sigma_H$ equal to the amount associated with the line *ab*: The proportion of such persons who would not work is given by the area under the curve to the left of *ab*, whereas the proportion of such persons who would work is given by the area under the curve to the right of *ab*. Note that if the coefficient b is positive and if W_i increases, then $-J_i/\sigma_H$ will fall and the threshold line *ab* will shift to the left, implying a reduced probability of not working and an increased probability of working for any given individual (and a reduced proportion not working and an increased proportion work-

right of *ab*. Readers familiar with the normal distribution and with integral calculus will recognize that this is just what (4.10) says. Readers *not* familiar with the normal distribution or integral calculus may find it reassuring to learn that (4.10) is just another way of saying that the probability that a given individual will work (when his value of $-J_i/\sigma_H$ is equal to the one implied by *ab*) may be found by determining the area under the curve in Figure 4.1 to the right of *ab*. In particular, the symbol $\int_{-J_i/\sigma_H}^{+\infty}$ means "add up, starting at $-J_i/\sigma_H$ and continuing all the way out to plus infinity," whereas the term $f(t)\, dt$ in effect refers to the area of each of the skinny rectangles like $t_1 t_2 rs$ that one can construct for all possible values of t to the right of the line *ab*. That is, $f(t)$ is the height of a rectangle of this kind, whereas dt is its base. (Use of dt here instead of Δt means that the bases of all such rectangles are infinitesimally small.) Finally, as its name implies, the *cumulative density function F* is a shorthand way of referring to a "sum of skinny rectangles" (that is, densities). In particular, $F(-J_i/\sigma_H)$ is a shorthand way of writing the area under the curve to the *left* of the line *ab*, that is, of writing the quantity $\int_{-\infty}^{-J_i/\sigma_H} f(t)\, dt$. Because the curve is symmetric, the quantity $1 - F(-J_i/\sigma_H)$ – that is, the area to the *right* of the line *ab* – is equal to the quantity $\int_{-J_i/\sigma_H}^{+\infty} f(t)\, dt$.

ing among a group of individuals). Similarly, if $b>0$ and V_i increases, then $-J_i/\sigma_H$ will rise and the threshold line ab will shift to the right, implying an increased probability of not working and a decreased probability of working for any given individual (and an increased proportion not working and a decreased proportion working among a group of individuals).[4]

Finally, the assumption that ϵ_{Hi} is a normally distributed random variable leads directly to an empirical participation equation, whose parameters may be estimated by the method of maximum likelihood. Under the assumptions outlined earlier, one may use (4.5) and (4.6) to write the likelihood function[5] for a sample of persons who are either employed or not employed as

---

[4] Note also that when J_i is negative and large in absolute value, the crucial "threshold" value $-J_i/\sigma_H$ will be positive and large, the threshold line ab will lie well to the right of the center of the normal distribution curve in Figure 4.1, and only a small proportion of individuals with that value of J_i will work. (Equivalently, the probability that any given individual with that J_i will work will be very low.) Such individuals will all have very strong tastes for work, that is, positive and very large values of ϵ_H. This is directly related to the notion of sample selection bias: Other things being equal, restricting empirical analysis to persons who work may result in a sample in which ϵ_H does not have a mean of zero even if ϵ_H does have a mean of zero in the total population.

[5] For useful introductions to the notion of a likelihood function and of maximum-likelihood estimation, see Kmenta (1971) and Theil (1978). Readers unfamiliar with these concepts may find the following highly intuitive explanation helpful. The probability that some individual i will work is $1 - F[-(1 - b)^* + b^*(V_i/W_i)]$, or, for short, $1 - F(i)$, where $F(i)$ is some fraction (e.g., 0.333 or 0.924) that depends on V_i, W_i, and the parameters b^* and $(1 - b)^*$, which, so far, are unknown. Similarly, the probability that some other individual j will work may be written $1 - F(j)$, where, again, j is shorthand for what appears inside the parentheses of the F function. So long as these two probabilities are independent, the probability that *both i and j* will work is therefore $[1 - F(i)][1 - F(j)]$ – just as the probability that one will get two heads in two successive independent flips of a coin is $0.5 \times 0.5 = 0.25$ (provided the coin is "fair," i.e., comes up heads 50 percent of the time). By extension, then, consider a group of N total individuals, in which the first k are working, whereas the rest (individuals $k + 1$ through N) are not. The probability – or likelihood – that one will observe all these individuals doing what they are actually doing is equal to

$$\prod_{i=1}^{k} [1 - F(i)] \cdot \prod_{j=k+1}^{N} F(j)$$

Because individuals 1 through k are in the set E of employed persons, whereas individuals $k + 1$ through N are in the set $\overline{E}$ of persons who are not working, this is the

(4.11) $l = \prod\limits_{i \in E} \{1 - F[-(1 - b)^* + b^*(V_i/W_i)]\}$

$\times \prod\limits_{i \in \overline{E}} F[-(1 - b)^* + b^*(V_i/W_i)]$

where

E = the set of persons who are employed
$\overline{E}$ = the set of persons who are not employed
$b^* = b/\sigma_H$
$(1 - b)^* = (1 - b)/\sigma_H$

This is the standard probit equation, whose parameters b^* and $(1 - b)^*$ may be estimated by maximizing the likelihood function (4.11) (or its logarithm) with respect to b^* and $(1 - b)^*$.

Next, consider the empirical analysis of hours of work, that is, estimation of (4.9). Maximimum-likelihood probit estimates of b^* and $(1 - b)^*$ provide complete information[6] on the parameters that govern labor supply: Since they are equal, by definition, to b/σ_H and $(1 - b)/\sigma_H$, respectively, it follows that they imply that $\sigma_H = 1/[b^* + (1 - b)^*]$ and that $b = b^*/[b^* + (1 - b)^*]$. However, they are derived in a manner that ignores an important source of information on labor supply, since probit makes no use of data on *hours* of work as such. (Note that the likelihood function (4.11) uses information on V, W, and the fact that given individuals are or are not working but does not use any data on H for persons who do work.) If wage

same as (4.11) in the text. Of course, so far, the parameters $(1 - b)^*$ and b^* are unknown; how may they be computed? The natural answer is: Find the values of $(1 - b)^*$ and b^* that *maximize* this likelihood (or, equivalently, that maximize the value of l in (4.11)), since these l-maximizing values are the ones that make it most likely to observe what actually *has* been observed (i.e., the numbers of persons working or not working). Finally, although the task of actually finding values of $(1 - b)^*$ and b^* that maximize l might seem forbidding, modern high-speed computers can be (and have been) programmed to tackle this job in a few seconds.

[6] Readers familiar with probit analysis of the participation decision may find this puzzling, since, in general, probit analysis does *not* provide estimates of *all* the parameters that govern labor supply. For example, if the hours equation were generalized to read $H = a + b(V/W)$, then probit analysis would provide estimates of a/σ_H and of b/σ_H only; thus, these probit estimates would be proportional to the parameters a and b, but it would not be possible to use them to determine the actual values of a and b as such. However, in this particular model the intercept a and the slope b have to add up to unity, making it possible to use probit estimates of $(1 - b)^*$ and b^* in (4.11) to derive estimates of the underlying parameters b and σ_H.

data are available for all individuals (nonworkers as well as workers), then there are several alternative ways to use this information on hours of work.

One approach is to apply Tobit analysis directly to (4.5), (4.6), and (4.9). Tobit analysis is a form of regression analysis that is adapted to a situation ignored in conventional OLS regression: the case in which the dependent variable can never be less than some minimum amount (or, alternatively, greater than some maximum amount). (See Amemiya, 1973, Tobin, 1958.) In the present case, there is a lower limit of zero on the dependent variable H_i. To see how the Tobit likelihood function is derived, first note from (4.10) that the probability that an individual with wage W_i and property income V_i will not be working (and so will have $H_i = 0$) is

$$\Pr[i \text{ does not work}] = F(-J_i/\sigma_H)$$

As far as persons who work are concerned, note that, by the definition of a conditional probability, the probability that individual i works H_i hours *and* that this amount H_i is positive may be written as

$$\Pr[i \text{ works } H_i \text{ hours and } H_i > 0]$$
$$= \Pr[i \text{ works } H_i \text{ hours} \mid H_i > 0] \cdot \Pr[H_i > 0]$$

Thus the probability that individual i works H_i hours, given that he works at all (i.e., has $H_i > 0$), may be written as

$$\Pr[i \text{ works } H_i \text{ hours} \mid H_i > 0]$$
$$= \Pr[i \text{ works } H_i \text{ hours and } H_i > 0]/\Pr[H_i > 0]$$

Moreover, $\Pr[H_i > 0]$ is simply $1 - F(-J_i/\sigma_H)$, whereas the probability (more precisely, probability density) of observing i working exactly H_i hours is $f(\epsilon_{Hi}/\sigma_H)/\sigma_H$. It follows that the likelihood function for the entire sample of N observations, consisting of the set E of workers and the set $\overline{E}$ of nonworkers, is

$$(4.12) \quad l = \prod_{i \in E} f(\epsilon_{Hi}/\sigma_H)/\sigma_H \prod_{i \in \overline{E}} F(-J_i/\sigma_H)$$

where

$$\epsilon_{Hi} = H_i - [(1 - b) - b(V_i/W_i)]$$
$$-J_i = -[(1 - b) - b(V_i/W_i)]$$

which is a Tobit likelihood function. The parameters b and σ_H may be estimated by maximizing (4.12), or its logarithm, with respect to those parameters.

Note that the first part of the right-hand side of (4.12) refers to persons who are working, whereas the second part refers to persons who are not working. The first part is identical to the likelihood function that is implicit in a conventional OLS regression, whereas the second resembles part of the probit likelihood function (4.11). In this sense, Tobit analysis is a combination of regression and probit (indeed, Tobit is sometimes called "Tobin's probit"[7]): it uses all observations, on both workers and nonworkers; it recognizes that (except for unmeasured factors ϵ_H) the same variables W and V and the same parameters b and σ_H generate the labor supply (meaning both participation and hours of work) of all persons; and it uses all available data (i.e., not only data on who does or does not work but also data on the amount of labor supplied by those persons who do work). Evidently, if everyone in the population works, then the set of nonworkers $\overline{E}$ is empty and the second part of the Tobit likelihood function (4.12) disappears. In this case, applying conventional OLS regression to estimation of the hours-of-work parameters b and σ_H will yield unbiased estimates. However, if some persons do not work, then the Tobit likelihood function is more appropriate than OLS, since Tobit distinguishes between participation (via the probit part of (4.12)) and hours of work (via the regression part of (4.12)), whereas OLS does not. Indeed, estimation using Tobit not only provides estimates of b and σ_H, and thus a means of describing hours of work H (e.g., via equation (4.9)), it also, and at the same time, provides an analysis of the determinants of the decision to work or not to work. This is because once Tobit estimates of b and σ_H are available, they can be used in conjunction with expressions (4.5) and (4.6) to derive the probability that a given individual, with given values of V and W, will or will not work.[8]

---

[7] The etymology of the term *Tobit* is unclear. However, Herman Wouk, the novelist, was a classmate of Tobin in naval officer training school during World War II and went on to create a midshipman named "Tobit" in his best-seller, *The Caine Mutiny*.

[8] For example, suppose that the Tobit estimates of b^* and $(1 - b)^*$ imply that $b = 0.75$ and that $\sigma_H = 0.25$. Then, by (4.5), the probability that an individual with a wage of 5 and property income of 1 will work is simply the probability that the standard normal random variable $\epsilon_{H\,i}/\sigma_H$ will exceed the value of $-[(1 - b) - b(V/W)]/\sigma_H = -J_i/\sigma_H = -0.40$. As shown in tables of areas of the standard

Although Tobit is thus quite useful for analyzing labor supply, it is by no means the only procedure suitable for empirical studies of this kind. A second procedure for estimating labor supply function parameters, which may be called *selection bias-corrected regression*, also uses regression analysis and probit analysis – like Tobit – but does so in a somewhat different way. Moreover, this second procedure involves a somewhat different underlying specification of the determinants of hours of work and of the participation decision. As such, consideration of this second procedure (and a comparison between it and Tobit) is quite useful, not merely for understanding some of the complexities of estimation procedures but also for understanding a number of important substantive issues and controversies discussed in greater detail later in this chapter.

The point of departure for selection bias-corrected regression is the notion that, when one considers workers *only*, the expected value of hours of work for individual *i*, *given that* individual *i* works, is

$$
\begin{aligned}
E[H_i \,|\, i \text{ works}] &= E[(1 - b) - b(V_i/W_i) + \epsilon_{Hi} \,|\, \epsilon_{Hi} > -J_i] \\
&= 1 - b - b(V_i/W_i) \\
&\quad + E[\epsilon_{Hi} \,|\, (\epsilon_{Hi}/\sigma_H) > -J_i/\sigma_H] \\
&= 1 - b - b(V_i/W_i) + K_i
\end{aligned}
$$

where

$$
\begin{aligned}
K_i &= E[\epsilon_{Hi} \,|\, (\epsilon_{Hi}/\sigma_H) > -J_i/\sigma_H] \\
J_i &= 1 - b - b(V_i/W_i)
\end{aligned}
$$

K_i is the conditional mean of ϵ_{Hi}, that is, the mean of expected value of ϵ_{Hi} *given that* ϵ_{Hi} is at least as large as *i*'s value of $-J_i$. Now, if ϵ_{Hi} is a normally distributed mean-zero random variable with a standard deviation equal to σ_H, then it can be shown that[9]

$$
K_i = \sigma_H \lambda_i
$$

where $\lambda_i = f(-J_i/\sigma_H)/[1 - F(-J_i/\sigma_H)]$. OLS regression based on data on H, W, and V for a sample of workers (persons for whom

---

normal distribution, this probability (in other words, the area under the curve and to the right of $-J_i/\sigma_H$, when $-J_i/\sigma_H$ is set at -0.40) is equal to about 0.6554.

[9] See Heckman (1976c, 1979, 1980), Johnson and Kotz (1972), and Mood, Graybill, and Boes (1974).

$\epsilon_{Hi}/\sigma_H > -J_i/\sigma_H$) entails regressing H_i on the variable $X_{1i} = V_i/W_i$ but *not* on the variable K_i. In effect, then, OLS regression proceeds on the erroneous assumption that the conditional mean of ϵ_{Hi} in the sample of workers is zero and thus omits the variable K_i. This is why OLS regression estimates of (4.9), if based on samples restricted to workers, will be biased. (See Heckman, 1976c, 1979, 1980.) However, by the same token, this analysis suggests that it *is* possible to obtain consistent estimates of the parameters of (4.9) even when the sample *is* restricted to workers – *provided* one includes a measure of K_i (or, equivalently, from the aforementioned, a measure of λ_i) in the regression. To do so, one would first obtain probit estimates of the parameters of (4.11) and use these estimates to compute measures of $f(-J_i/\sigma_H)$, $1 - F(-J_i/\sigma_H)$ and thus their ratio λ_i for all observations – workers and nonworkers alike. One would then take data on the H_i, W_i, V_i, and λ_i of workers only and obtain estimates of the selection bias-corrected regression equation

$$(4.13) \quad H_i = 1 - b - b(V_i/W_i) + a\widetilde{\lambda}_i + v_{Hi}$$

where

$\widetilde{\lambda}_i$ = a measure of the "selection bias" variable λ_i, derived from estimated parameters of a "first-stage" probit equation (4.11)

v_{Hi} = a mean-zero random error term[10]

and where, from the aforementioned, a regression estimate of the parameter a in (4.13) should be interpreted as an estimate of the parameter σ_H. Inclusion of the selection bias variable $\widetilde{\lambda}_i$ takes account of the fact that K_i – the mean of the error term ϵ_{Hi} – is not a mean-zero random variable when the estimation sample is restricted to persons who work.

Like Tobit estimation, selection bias-corrected regression uses both probit and regression methods: probit, to derive a measure of

---

[10] The error term v_H appears in (4.13) both because λ_i is an *estimate*, derived from *estimated* probit coefficients, of the actual value of the selectivity bias variable λ_i, and also because the *actual* value of hours of work, H, is not always equal to its *expected* value, $E[H]$. Heckman (1976c, 1979) and Wales and Woodland (1980) discuss the derivation of v_H and point out that it is heteroskedastic, which means that conventional OLS estimates of (4.13) will be inefficient.

λ_i; regression, to obtain estimates of the parameters b and σ_H once the selection bias variable λ_i is added to the hours of work function (4.9). Thus, like Tobit estimation, this procedure explicitly takes account of the fact that *labor supply* refers to two intimately connected relationships: a work–not work function, based on a comparison between the wage and the reservation wage, and an hours of work function. In the case of Tobit, that is, (4.12), these two functions are estimated simultaneously; in the present case, they are estimated in a two-step procedure. Note from (4.10) that, if *all* individuals have a probability of working equal to unity, then K_i is simply the mean of the *entire* distribution of ϵ_{Hi} (rather than the mean of only those ϵ_{Hi} values that lie above $-J_i$) – so that K_i, and thus λ_i, is zero in this case. Again, then, restricting an estimation sample to workers only and using OLS does not entail any selection bias problem when – but *only* when – everyone in the relevant population works.

Although selection bias-corrected regression and Tobit are similar in these important respects, they differ in another, equally important, way. The reason is that, in the case of selection bias-corrected regression, the parameters that determine participation – the "work/don't work" decision – will *not* necessarily be equal to the parameters that determine hours of work for people who participate, whereas in the case of Tobit these two sets of parameters are treated (and estimated) as identical. To see why, note first that the selection bias-corrected regression method entails computing both (i) probit estimates of the parameters b^* and $(1 - b)^*$ in the probit likelihood function (4.11) and (ii) regression estimates of the parameters b and σ_H (or, equivalently, a) in the selection bias-corrected regression equation (4.13). Moreover, as indicated earlier, the probit estimates of b^* and $(1 - b)^*$ may be used to derive one set of estimates of b and σ_H, whereas the estimated parameters of the regression equation (4.13) provide a *second* set of estimates. Of course, these two sets of estimates should be identical, *if* the simple model embodied in equations (4.1)–(4.9) is correct. However, nothing about the two-stage selection bias-corrected regression procedure serves to *constrain* the two sets of estimates to be equal to each other. Rather, unless one explicitly imposes such a constraint, the procedure permits the two sets of estimates to differ. In contrast, Tobit analysis in effect computes both a probit and a regression at the same time (rather than in two distinct and independent steps), and so provides one and only one set of estimates of b and σ_H.

This being the case, it might seem that the two-stage procedure of computing first a probit and then a selection bias-corrected regression simply provides one set of estimates too many. The temptation is to conclude that it makes just as much (if not more) sense simply to compute only the first stage probit equation or, alternatively, to stick with Tobit. However, the fact that probit together with selection bias-corrected regression provides two estimates of the labor supply parameters b and σ_H may be more than a nuisance or an embarrassment. Indeed, it may be quite useful as a simple test of the possibility that the labor supply function may *not* be as specified by equations (4.1)–(4.9), and in particular as a test of the possibility that the labor supply schedule is discontinuous.

To see this, let $\hat{b}_1$ and $\hat{b}_2$ stand for the estimates of b derived, respectively, from the first (probit) stage of the procedure and from the second (selection bias-corrected regression) stage and assume that $\hat{b}_1 > \hat{b}_2$. Now note from (4.5) and (4.11) that $\hat{b}_1$ may be used to define the conditions under which an "average" member of the population (someone whose $\epsilon_{Hi} = 0$) will work: He will work if $W > [\hat{b}_1/(1 - \hat{b}_1)] V$ and otherwise will not. Thus, in terms of Figure 4.2, an average person whose W lies to the right (left) of the vertical line bc will (will not) work. Next, note from (4.9) and (4.13) that $\hat{b}_2$ may be used to draw the labor supply schedule for an individual with a given value of ϵ_{Hi} and V at alternative values of W. In particular, (4.9) and (4.13) imply that labor supply for an average person who works will move along the line acd as the wage rate changes (with V staying the same); acd runs into the W axis at the point $[\hat{b}_2/(1 - \hat{b}_2)] V$. However, the first stage or probit estimate $\hat{b}_1$ implies that this individual will actually work only if his wage exceeds $[\hat{b}_1/(1 - \hat{b}_1)] V$, which is *greater* than $[\hat{b}_2/(1 - \hat{b}_2)] V$. In other words, taken together, the first- and second-stage results derived under this procedure imply that labor supply is discontinuous, in the sense that hours of work will be (i) zero for wage rates below $[\hat{b}_1/(1 - \hat{b}_1)] V$ and (ii) *at least* H_0 for wage rates in excess of $[\hat{b}_1/(1 - \hat{b}_1)] V$.[11]

[11] Of course, all this assumes that $\hat{b}_1 > \hat{b}_2$. If the two estimates are equal, then (in terms of Figure 4.2) the line bc crosses the W axis at the point a, and the labor supply schedule is continuous. Although it seems logically possible to have $\hat{b}_1 < \hat{b}_2$, this is

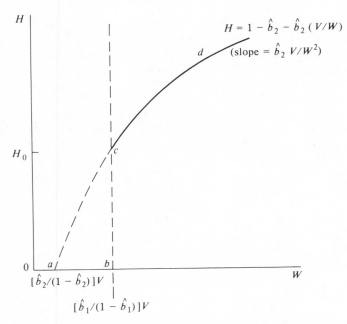

Figure 4.2. Example of discontinuous labor supply schedule implied by selection bias-corrected regression results

Thus, Tobit and selection bias-corrected regression may provide quite different results. The former in effect assumes that the labor supply schedule is continuous, in the sense of Figure 1.5. The latter allows for the possibility that the labor supply schedule may be discontinuous. (More or less equivalently, use of probit together with selection bias-corrected regression permits a simple empirical test of the hypothesis that the labor supply schedule is discontinuous, whereas Tobit cannot be used for this purpose.) On the other hand, each procedure provides a means for considering both the work/don't work and hours of work dimensions of labor supply,

empirically implausible, because this would mean that the reservation wage implied by the probit results is *less* than the lowest wage at which, according to the hours-of-work function estimates, individuals supply labor. A result of this kind would constitute strong evidence against the model! For further cautionary remarks on methods that test for discontinuities in supply, see Section 4.6.

and consideration of either procedure serves to underline a basic point: Ignoring one or the other of these dimensions, as in first-generation work, may result in biased estimates of the parameters that effect both dimensions of labor supply.

Thus far, I have assumed, mainly in order to simplify the exposition, that wage data are available for all individuals, whether working or not. However, in applying the principles previously described in specific studies, second-generation researchers have had to contend with the fact that, ordinarily, wage data are available for workers only.

At least in conceptual terms, allowing for this additional complication is straightforward. (I will describe several specific solutions in the next section.) First, the threshold conditions (4.5) and (4.6) now define not only (i) the probability that a given individual will work, and thus have a positive labor supply, but also (ii) the probability that available data will contain information on the wage that any given individual earns (or is capable of earning). Second, whereas data on nonworking individuals typically will not contain information on the wages that such individuals earn (or are capable of earning), such data typically will contain information for these individuals on the values of variables such as education, age, and so forth, that, according to economic theory, are structural determinants of wage rates. Finally, data on working individuals typically will contain not only information on such wage variables (education, age, and the like) but also on actual wages. This suggests that, by extension of the procedures outlined in the previous section, it may be possible to derive an appropriate *imputed* wage even for nonworking individuals and then to proceed to analyze labor supply on more or less the same lines as described earlier.

In particular, assume – as is done in most second-generation studies – that, in the population as a whole, the wage rate that a given individual i earns (or is capable of earning) is given by a wage function $W_i = W(\mathbf{X}_i, \epsilon_{Wi})$, where $\mathbf{X}_i$ is a vector of observed "wage variables" (education, age, etc.), whose nature is dictated by an economic model of wage determination (e.g., a human capital model such as that of Mincer, 1974) and that can be observed for all individuals, and ϵ_{Wi} is a mean-zero random error term representing the effects of unobserved factors ("motivation," "innate ability," etc.) on wages. Next, let individual i's marginal rate of substitution be given by the general function $M_i = M(W_iH_i + V_i, 1 - H_i, \mathbf{Z}_i, \epsilon_{Mi})$, where $\mathbf{Z}$ is a vector of observable variables believed to represent factors associated with tastes and ϵ_M is an unobserved mean-zero random error term referring to unobservable taste factors. The W_i that appears in this function may be replaced by $W(\mathbf{X}_i, \epsilon_{Wi})$, yielding

$$M_i = M[W(\mathbf{X}_i, \epsilon_{Wi})H_i + V_i, 1 - H_i, \mathbf{Z}_i, \epsilon_{Mi}]$$

As before, the reservation wage M^* is the value of M when $H = 0$, so i's reservation wage may (still) be written as $M_i^* = M(V_i, 1, \mathbf{Z}_i, \epsilon_{Mi})$. Similarly, the individual will (will not) work if W exceeds (is less than) M^*; note also that W will (will not) be observed if the individual does (does not) work. Finally, as before, if the individual does work, his hours of work may be found by determining the value of H_i that satisfies the condition

$$W(\mathbf{X}_i, \epsilon_{Wi}) = M[W(\mathbf{X}_i, \epsilon_{Wi})H_i + V_i, 1 - H_i, \mathbf{Z}_i, \epsilon_{Mi}]$$

Although relatively simple to describe, this approach to specifying the labor supply function is likely to prove rather messy and inconvenient in most applications. This is because, except in special cases, the function for H_i derived by solving the above expression for H_i will be highly nonlinear not only in observable variables (the $\mathbf{X}_i$ and $\mathbf{Z}_i$) but also in the unobservable random terms (ϵ_{Wi} and ϵ_{Mi}). If so, then the function for H_i will usually be rather difficult to estimate using most standard econometric procedures for estimating a regression function. This is because, for the most part, such procedures rely on the assumption that the function to be estimated is additive in the unobservable random term(s) – in other words, that the unobservable term(s) in such a function are simply added onto the rest of that function.

In consequence, most second-generation research has proceeded by making the function for W_i linear in the $\mathbf{X}_i$, and by making the function for M_i linear in the wage, W_i, hours of work, H_i, property income, V_i, and other characteristics $\mathbf{Z}_i$ and unobservables ϵ_{Mi} and ϵ_{Wi}. Thus, the basic building blocks of such research are usually linear functions, such as

(4.14) $W_i = \gamma \mathbf{X}_i + \epsilon_{Wi}$
(4.15) $M_i^* = a_M^* + c_M^* V_i + \mathbf{d}_M^* \mathbf{Z}_i + \epsilon_{Mi}^*$

(4.16) $M_i = a_M + b_{1M}W_i + b_{2M}H_i + c_M V_i + \mathbf{d}_M \mathbf{Z}_i + \epsilon_{Mi}$

(4.17) $H_i = a_H + b_H W_i + c_H V_i + \mathbf{d}_H \mathbf{Z}_i + \epsilon_{Hi}$

for the wage rate, reservation wage, marginal rate of substitution, and hours of work, respectively.

4.3.   Applications to the simple labor supply model

I now consider various second-generation procedures for estimating simple labor supply functions, such as (4.17). (I will discuss applications to more complicated models in Sections 4.4 and 4.5.) I have summarized procedures that figure prominently in second-generation empirical studies[12] in Table 4.1; the reader may find it useful to refer to this from time to time as the exposition progresses.

If only for purposes of comparison, a number of second-generation studies include results based on *Procedure I* or *Procedure II*, because one or the other of these is usually used in first-generation research. Procedure I consists of two steps: First, estimate the wage equation (4.14) by least squares using data on workers only, and use the least-squares parameter estimates $\hat{\gamma}$ and data on the independent variables $\mathbf{X}$ to derive an imputed wage $\hat{W}$ for all persons, working or not; second, estimate the hours equation (4.17) by ordinary least squares using data on all individuals, using $\hat{W}$ in place of W and setting the hours of nonworkers at zero. Procedure II consists of just one step: Estimate the hours equation (4.17) by least squares using data on working individuals only. (Sometimes, however, this procedure uses an imputed wage $\hat{W}$, derived as under Procedure I, in place of W on the right-hand side of (4.17).)

However, as noted before, neither procedure is likely to produce unbiased estimates of the hours function's parameters. Procedure I is based on a misspecification, since it in effect assumes that a function such as (4.17) refers to the labor supply of all persons, rather than only to the supply of persons with positive H. Procedure II will suffer from selection bias, since persons with $H = 0$ are excluded from estimation.

---

[12] A number of different techniques that have been proposed apparently have not (yet) been used in empirical work. See Wales and Woodland (1980) for discussion of some of these methods.

Table 4.1. *Alternative procedures for estimating static labor supply models*

Procedure	Stage(s) and equation(s) estimated	Estimation technique	Sample used	Remarks
I	1. (4.14)	OLS	Workers only	Estimates of (4.14) used to derive a $\hat{W}$ for all persons (including nonworkers)
	2. (4.17)	OLS	All persons	H of nonworkers set at zero; uses $\hat{W}$ derived from Stage 1
II	1. (4.17)	OLS	Workers only	A $\hat{W}$ (computed as in Procedure I) sometimes used instead of W
III	1. (4.14)	OLS	Workers only	Estimates of (4.14) used to derive a $\hat{W}$ for all persons (including nonworkers)
	2. (4.12)	Tobit	All persons	Uses $\hat{W}$ derived from Stage 1
IV	1. (4.14)	OLS	Workers only	
	2. (4.24)	OLS	All persons	H of nonworkers set at zero
V	1. (4.26)	Tobit	All persons	Estimates of (4.26) used to derive a $\tilde{\lambda}$
	2. (4.18)	OLS, GLS, etc.	Workers only	Uses $\tilde{\lambda}$ derived from Stage 1 in selection bias-corrected regression
VI	1. (4.27)	Heckit (FIML)	All persons	
VII	1. (4.28)	probit	All persons	Estimates of (4.28) used to derive a $\tilde{\lambda}$
	2. (4.29)	OLS, GLS, etc.	Workers only	Uses $\tilde{\lambda}$ derived from Stage 1 in selection bias-corrected regression
	3. (4.30)	OLS, GLS, etc.	Workers only	Uses $\tilde{\lambda}$ derived from Stage 1 in selection bias-corrected regression
VIII	1. (4.28)	Probit	All persons	Estimates of (4.28) used to derive a $\tilde{\lambda}$
	2. (4.29)	OLS, GLS, etc.	Workers only	Uses $\tilde{\lambda}$ derived from Stage 1 in selection bias-corrected regression; estimates of (4.29) used to derive a $\hat{W}$
	3. (4.31)	OLS, GLS, etc.	Workers only	Uses $\tilde{\lambda}$ derived from Stage 1 and $\hat{W}$ derived from Stage 2 in selection bias-corrected regression

As suggested earlier, the Tobit technique provides a means of addressing both difficulties. However, the Tobit likelihood function (4.12) cannot be used when data on the wage rates of nonworkers (persons in set $\overline{E}$ of (4.12)) are not available. *Procedure III* is an attempt at finding a simple remedy for this problem within the context of Tobit: First derive imputed wages $\hat{W}$ from least-squares estimates of (4.14), as under Procedure I; then, use these imputed wages $\hat{W}$ in place of W in (4.12).

Unfortunately, there is a potential selectivity bias problem with Procedure III, because the imputed wage derived under this procedure is based on least-squares regression estimates of (4.14) for data on workers only. To see this, note that, by (4.14) and (4.17), the expected value of the wage in a group of workers is

$$(4.18) \quad E[W_i \,|\, H_i > 0] = E[\gamma \mathbf{X}_i + \epsilon_{Wi} \,|\, \epsilon_{Hi} > -J_i]$$
$$= \gamma \mathbf{X}_i + E[\epsilon_{Wi} \,|\, \epsilon_{Hi}/\sigma_H > (-J_i/\sigma_H)]$$
$$= \gamma \mathbf{X}_i + (\sigma_{WH}/\sigma_H)\lambda_i$$

where

$$\lambda_i = f(-J_i/\sigma_H)/[1 - F(-J_i/\sigma_H)]$$
$$J_i = a_H + b_H W_i + c_H V_i + \mathbf{d}_H \mathbf{X}_i$$
$$\sigma_{WH} = E(\epsilon_{Hi}\epsilon_{Wi}) = \text{covariance between } \epsilon_{Hi} \text{ and } \epsilon_{Wi}$$
$$\sigma_H = \text{standard deviation of } H$$

provided both ϵ_{Hi} and ϵ_{Wi} are jointly normally distributed. (For example, see Heckman, 1976c, pp. 478–479.) Hence, unless ϵ_{Hi} and ϵ_{Wi} are uncorrelated, so that $\sigma_{WH} = 0$, least-squares estimates $\hat{\gamma}$ of the parameters of the wage function will suffer from sample selection bias. Another consequence of a correlation between ϵ_W and ϵ_H is less obvious, but potentially just as serious: Such a correlation would present difficulties for estimation of labor supply models, such as equation (4.17), even if data on actual wage rates W were available for *all* individuals. This is because, in this case, ϵ_H cannot be assumed to be uncorrelated with the right-hand-side variables in (4.17). Rather, if ϵ_H is correlated with ϵ_W, it is necessarily correlated with W itself as well. In other words, in this sense, W is endogenous.

The notion that ϵ_H and ϵ_W are correlated is certainly not far-fetched. It simply means that there is a correlation between unmeasured factors (tastes for work?), ϵ_H, that affect labor supply and unmeasured factors (productivity? motivation?), ϵ_W, that affect wage rates. For example, suppose that persons who work many hours tend also to be persons with high wage rates, *other things being equal* (where the "other things" in question refer to all other *measured* characteristics of individuals, such as V and the observed variables in the wage function, $\mathbf{X}$). If so, then $\sigma_{WH} > 0$. Of course, it is just as easy to describe circumstances in which the covariance σ_{WH} would be negative. Either way, W must be regarded as endogenous – as correlated with ϵ_H.

If so, then *neither* use of imputed wage data derived from least-squares regression *nor* use of *actual* wage data (if they were somehow available for all individuals) will yield consistent estimates of the labor supply model under any of the procedures described thus far, since all these procedures require, for one reason or another, that W be exogenous (or, equivalently, that σ_{WH} be zero).

To tackle this difficulty, Heckman (1974c, 1976c) begins by adopting a convenient "proportionality" hypothesis: the market wage is given by (4.14); the reservation wage is given by (4.15); hours of work are (i) proportional to the difference between W and M^* whenever the former exceeds the latter and (ii) zero otherwise.[13] This leads to the model

(4.19) $\quad W_i = \gamma \mathbf{X}_i + \epsilon_{Wi}$

(4.20) $\quad M_i^* = a_M^* + c_M^* V_i + \mathbf{d}_M^* \mathbf{Z}_i + \epsilon_{Mi}^*$

(4.21) $\quad H_i = b(W_i - M_i^*) = a + bW_i + cV_i + \mathbf{dZ}_i - b\epsilon_{Mi}^*$
$\qquad\qquad$ if and only if $\quad W_i > M_i^*$

(4.22) $\quad H_i = 0 \qquad$ if and only if $\quad W_i \leq M_i^*$

where $a = -ba_M^*$, $c = -bc_M^*$, $\mathbf{d} = -b\mathbf{d}_M^*$. The participation equation implied by equations (4.19)–(4.22) is

$$
\begin{aligned}
\Pr[i \text{ works}] &= \Pr[W_i > M_i^*] \\
&= \Pr[\gamma \mathbf{X}_i + \epsilon_{Wi} > a_M^* + c_M^* V_i + \mathbf{d}_M^* \mathbf{Z}_i + \epsilon_{Mi}^*] \\
&= \Pr[\epsilon_{Wi} - \epsilon_{Mi}^* > -J_i]
\end{aligned}
$$

where $J_i = \gamma \mathbf{X}_i - (a_M^* + c_M^* V_i + \mathbf{d}_M^* \mathbf{Z}_i)$. Now define $\epsilon_{Di} \equiv (\epsilon_{Wi} - \epsilon_{Mi}^*)$. Since ϵ_{Di} is the difference between two normally distributed

---

[13] Actually, Heckman formulates the model in terms of the *logarithm* of W and the *logarithm* of M, as do a variety of other researchers, such as Cogan (1980b, 1981) and Nakamura and Nakamura (1981). For a generalization based on suggestions by Heckman (1974c), see Trussell and Abowd (1980).

random variables with variances σ_W^2 and σ_M^2 and with a covariance σ_{WM} (which may or may not be zero), ϵ_{Di} is also a mean-zero normally distributed random variable, with a variance σ_D^2 equal to $\sigma_D^2 = \sigma_W^2 + \sigma_M^2 - 2\sigma_{WM}$. Thus, as before, the empirical parameters governing participation may be estimated using probit – that is, the likelihood function for a sample composed of a set E of workers and a set $\overline{E}$ of nonworkers is

$$(4.23) \quad l = \prod_{i \in E} [1 - F(-J_i/\sigma_D)] \cdot \prod_{i \in \overline{E}} F(-J_i/\sigma_D)$$

where $J_i = \gamma \mathbf{X}_i - a_M^* - c_M^* V_i - \mathbf{d}_M^* \mathbf{Z}_i$. As regards analysis of hours of work, note that one may substitute (4.19) into (4.21) to obtain

$$(4.24) \quad H_i = a + b\gamma \mathbf{X}_i + cV_i + \mathbf{dZ}_i + b\epsilon_{Di}$$
$$\text{if and only if} \quad a + b\gamma \mathbf{X}_i + cV_i + \mathbf{dZ}_i + b\epsilon_{Di} > 0$$
$$(4.25) \quad H_i = 0$$
$$\text{if and only if} \quad a + b\gamma \mathbf{X}_i + cV_i + \mathbf{dZ}_i + b\epsilon_{Di} \leq 0$$

where $a = -ba_M^*$, $c = -bc_M^*$, $\mathbf{d} = -b\mathbf{d}_M^*$. Thus, this approach "substitutes out" W, which is endogenous and for which data are usually available only for workers, by replacing W with the right-hand side of (4.14). As a result, the right-hand side of (4.24) is a reduced-form equation, since its right-hand side contains only variables that are exogenous.[14] (Note that the variables on the right-

---

[14] Note that (4.24) raises a potential problem of identification, in the sense that it may not be possible to derive an estimate of the key labor supply parameter b (that is, to "identify" b from estimates of (4.24)). To see this, note that $\mathbf{X}_i$ and $\mathbf{Z}_i$ are *vectors* of variables, so that, in (4.24) $b\gamma \mathbf{X}_i$ and $\mathbf{dZ}_i$ are shorthand expressions for $b\gamma_1 X_{1i} + b\gamma_2 X_{2i} + b\gamma_3 X_{3i} + \ldots$ and for $d_1 Z_{1i} + d_2 Z_{2i} + d_3 Z_{3i} + \ldots$, respectively, where X_{1i} is i's value for variable X_1 (e.g., years of work experience), Z_{2i} is i's value for variable Z_2 (e.g., number of dependents), and so forth. Now, if the vector $\mathbf{X}_i$ and the vector $\mathbf{Z}_i$ contain elements in common (e.g., if the variable "age" appears in both the wage function and the hours function), then the coefficient on each such common element in a least-squares regression will be equal to, for example, $b\gamma_j + d_j$, where j refers to the particular variable that is common to both vectors. The question, then, is whether it is possible to recover estimates – to identify – b and each γ_j and each d_j. Because each γ_j is a parameter in the wage equation, it is clear that one will have to estimate the parameters of the wage equation as well as the parameters of (4.24) in order to recover estimates of b and all of the γ_j and d_j. Moreover, although necessary, estimation of the wage equation in and of itself is not sufficient for identification; other conditions must be satisfied as well. Most second-generation research has relied on a procedure that is sufficient for identification: to include one variable in the wage

hand side of (4.24) are usually measured for *all* persons,[15] in contrast with the W on the right-hand side of conventional labor supply functions such as (4.17).

At first glance, it might therefore seem that (4.24) can be estimated using least squares and data on the entire population – nonworkers as well as workers. For future reference, I will refer to the procedure of deriving estimates of (4.24) using least squares and data on the entire population (with the labor supply of each nonworker set at zero) as *Procedure IV*. However, note that this procedure still suffers from a defect: (4.24) refers to workers only (that is, to persons for whom the right-hand side of (4.24) is positive). Unless all persons in the population work, applying (4.24) to the entire population entails a misspecification (as under Procedure I), but applying this procedure to workers only will entail selection bias (as under Procedure II).

One solution to this problem is based on the fact that the error term ϵ_{Di} in equations (4.24) and (4.25) is a normally distributed mean-zero random variable and the dependent variable H_i can never be less than zero. This implies that one can estimate the parameters of equations (4.24) and (4.25) by maximizing an appropriately modified[16] version of the Tobit likelihood function (4.12), that is, by maximizing

$$(4.26) \quad l = \prod_{i \in E} f(b\epsilon_{Di}/b\sigma_D)/b\sigma_D \cdot \prod_{i \in \bar{E}} F(-J_i/\sigma_D)$$

where

$$b\epsilon_{Di} = H_i - bJ_i$$
$$J_i = \gamma \mathbf{X}_i - (a_M^* + c_M^* V_i + \mathbf{d}_M^* \mathbf{Z}_i)$$

with respect to the parameters a_M^*, c_M^*, $\mathbf{d}_M^*$, γ, b, and σ_D. Once these parameters have been estimated, they can then be used to derive an

equation vector $\mathbf{X}_i$ that is *not* included in the hours equation (or marginal rate of substitution equation, etc.) vector $\mathbf{Z}_i$. For further discussion of this point, see Heckman (1974c, 1979) and note 17.

[15] For example, such variables include education, age, sex, race, years of work experience, and so on, which are frequently (though not always) measured for all individuals in a data set, whether or not they are currently working.

[16] Note that the actual Tobit expression (4.12) contains an error term ϵ_H, whereas in equations (4.24) and (4.25) the error term $b\epsilon_D$ is actually the product of an error term and one of the hours-of-work function parameters.

expression for the probability that an individual with given $\mathbf{X}_i$, $\mathbf{Z}_i$, and V_i will work and, thus, to derive a measure of the selection bias variable λ for each individual (in just the same way that the parameters of (4.12) permit one to construct an expression for the probability that an individual with given W_i, $\mathbf{Z}_i$, and V_i will work and, thus, to obtain a measure of λ for each individual), using the definition $\lambda_i = f(-J_i/\sigma_D)/[1 - F(-J_i/\sigma_D)]$. One can then proceed to second-stage estimation of a wage function, making the appropriate correction for possible selection bias, by fitting a selection bias-corrected wage function (using least squares, generalized least squares, etc.) to data on workers only.[17] For future reference, I will refer to this two-stage procedure as *Procedure V*.

Procedure V gets around the fact that equations (4.21) and (4.22) have a right-hand-side endogenous variable, W, by fitting *reduced-form* equations (4.24) and (4.25) using Tobit. An alternative to Procedure V is, of course, to extend Tobit to a system of simultaneous equations, that is, to the equation system (4.19)–(4.22), using full-information maximum likelihood (FIML). This is the basis of *Procedure VI*, proposed by Heckman (1974c), which is in effect *Heckman's Tobit* or, more familiarly, *Heckit*. To see how Heckit extends Tobit to a simultaneous equations setting, note that the error term in the hours equation (4.21) is $\epsilon_{Di} = \epsilon_{Wi} - \epsilon_{Mi}$, whereas the error term in the wage equation (4.19) is ϵ_{Wi}. If ϵ_M and ϵ_W are jointly normally distributed and have a covariance of σ_{WM}, then ϵ_D and ϵ_W are *also* jointly normally distributed and have a covariance of

---

[17] Recall from note 14 and inspection of equations (4.24)–(4.26) that if the vector $\mathbf{X}_i$ and the vector $\mathbf{Z}_i$ contain elements in common, then the coefficient on any such common element (e.g., a variable measuring age) will be equal to $b\gamma_j + d_j$, where j denotes a particular variable that is common to both vectors. How can one use these estimates to recover estimates of b, each γ_j, and each d_j? In most second-generation research, the wage equation vector $\mathbf{X}_i$ includes one (and only one) variable that is *not* included in the hours equation vector $\mathbf{Z}_i$. In this case, the Tobit coefficient on that variable is equal to $b\gamma_j$, and it remains to get estimates of b and γ_j separately. To do so, simply get the second-stage (wage equation) estimate of γ_j and divide it into the Tobit coefficient on the same variable, $b\gamma_j$, to get the implied Tobit estimate of b. Now that b has been determined, one can use the other second-stage (wage equation) estimates of the parameter vector γ along with the implied Tobit estimate of b to get the implied Tobit estimates of all the elements of the parameter vector $\mathbf{d}$. Similar solutions to the identification problem may be used in the context of the other procedures described here.

$\sigma_{DW} = \sigma_W^2 - \sigma_{WM}$. This leads to the following likelihood function for the wage rates, hours of work, and participation of the entire population of N persons, of whom some are in the set E of workers and the rest are in the set $\overline{E}$ of nonworkers:

$$(4.27) \quad l = \prod_{i \in E} j(b\epsilon_{Di}/b\sigma_D, \epsilon_{Wi}/\sigma_W) \cdot \prod_{i \in \overline{E}} F(-J_i/\sigma_D)$$

where

j = probability density function of two joint normal random variables[18]

$$b\epsilon_{Di} = H_i - bJ_i$$
$$J_i = \gamma \mathbf{X}_i - (a_M^* + c_M^* V_i + \mathbf{d}_M^* \mathbf{Z}_i)$$
$$\epsilon_{Wi} = W_i - \gamma \mathbf{X}_i$$

The most obvious difference between Tobit, (4.12), and Heckit, (4.27), is that the latter treats W and H as simultaneously determined due to the possible correlation between ϵ_W and ϵ_M, whereas the former treats W as strictly exogenous. Hence, the part of the Tobit likelihood function (4.12) that is concerned with workers is based on a univariate normal distribution (f), whereas the part of the Heckit likelihood function that is concerned with workers is based on a bivariate or joint normal distribution (j). Unlike Tobit estimation using (4.26), Heckit estimation using (4.27) exploits all available data on wage rates W and hours of work H for workers (persons in set E).

4.4. Applications to discontinuous labor supply schedules

All of the procedures in the previous section involve an important assumption: that labor supply falls *continuously* to zero in response to, say, changes in W or V. (For example, (4.17) obviously makes this assumption, and so does Heckman's proportionality hypothesis, as reflected in, e.g., (4.21).) This section is concerned with methods for estimating discontinuous labor supply schedules – that is, with procedures that allow for the possibility that the lowest number of hours that a worker will work may be substantially in excess of zero.

---

[18] For discussion of the bivariate or joint normal distribution and its properties, see Hoel (1971, pp. 151–57) and Mood, Graybill, and Boes (1974).

To see the basic idea underlying such techniques, recall the discussion of selection bias-corrected regression as applied to equation (4.13), and note a key distinction between the procedure used in that case and Procedures I–VI. Procedures I–VI all tie the participation decision and the hours of work decision very tightly together: in Procedures I, II, and IV, by simply classifying persons with zero hours of work as nonworkers and by adopting a specification that implicitly assumes that hours may fall continuously to zero; in Procedures III, V, and VI, by assuming explicitly that the fraction of available time devoted to labor supply varies continuously between unity and zero, and that the smallest number of hours any worker will work is (just above) zero.

In contrast, as emphasized in Figure 4.2, application of selection bias-corrected regression to equation (4.13) involved a much less stringent set of assumptions about the labor supply schedule. In particular, this procedure involved first calculating a probit, (4.11), for the probability of being a worker and then calculating a selection bias-corrected regression for the hours worked by workers – *without*, however, imposing any requirement or making any assumption that the lower limit on the hours worked by workers is zero. Thus, as noted in the discussion of Figure 4.2, this approach allows for the possibility of a discontinuous labor supply schedule.

One way to implement this approach using general functional forms, such as those given by equations (4.14)–(4.17), is to use a three-stage method that I will call *Procedure VII*: First, fit a probit for the probability of working, and use the coefficient estimates to form a measure of λ for each observation; second, use data on λ and on the variables $\mathbf{X}$ for workers to estimate the parameters of the wage equation (4.14) via selection bias-corrected regression; third, use selection bias-corrected regression to fit the reduced-form equation for the hours worked by persons who work (obtained by substituting the right-hand side of (4.14) for W into (4.17)). In Procedure VII, the probability of participation is simply the probability that $W_i > M_i^*$, so, by (4.14) and (4.15), the first stage consists of maximizing the probit likelihood function

$$(4.28) \quad l = \prod_{i \in E} [1 - F(-J_i/\sigma_D)] \cdot \prod_{i \in \bar{E}} F(-J_i/\sigma_D)$$

where

$$J_i = \gamma \mathbf{X}_i - (a_M^* + c_M^* V_i + \mathbf{d}_M^* \mathbf{Z}_i)$$
$$\epsilon_D = \epsilon_{Wi} - \epsilon_{Mi}^*$$

with respect to the parameters γ/σ_D, a_M^*/σ_D, c_M^*/σ_D, and $\mathbf{d}_M^*/\sigma_D$. Then, use the estimated parameters to form a measure of λ_i, call it $\widetilde{\lambda}_i$, computed as $f(-J_i/\sigma_D)/[1 - F(-J_i/\sigma_D)]$, where $-J_i/\sigma_D$ should be computed using the probit parameter estimates. Second, use $\widetilde{\lambda}_i$ and data on the $\mathbf{X}_i$ to compute a selection bias-corrected regression for the wage using data on workers, which, by (4.14) and (4.18), is

(4.29) $\quad W_i = \gamma \mathbf{X}_i + z\widetilde{\lambda}_i + v_i$

where $v_i =$ a mean-zero random error term and, in the present context, the estimate of the parameter z should be interpreted as an estimate of the ratio σ_{WD}/σ_D, where σ_{WD} is the covariance between ϵ_{Wi} and ϵ_{Di} ($= \epsilon_{Wi} - \epsilon_{Mi}^*$).

Next, note that (4.14) and (4.17) imply that the function for hours of work may be written as

$$H_i = a_H + b_H \gamma \mathbf{X}_i + c_H V_i + \mathbf{d}_H \mathbf{Z}_i + (\epsilon_{Hi} + b_H \epsilon_{Wi})$$

Thus, the *expected* value of hours worked *among people who work* may be written as

$$
\begin{aligned}
E[H_i \mid W_i > M_i^*] &= E[H_i \mid (\epsilon_{Di}/\sigma_D) \overset{\cdot}{>} (-J_i/\sigma_D)] \\
&= a_H + b_H \gamma \mathbf{X}_i + c_H V_i + \mathbf{d}_H \mathbf{Z}_i \\
&\quad + E[\epsilon_{Hi} + b_H \epsilon_{Wi} \mid (\epsilon_{Di}/\sigma_D) > (-J_i/\sigma_D)] \\
&= a_H + b_H \gamma \mathbf{X}_i + c_H V_i + \mathbf{d}_H \mathbf{Z}_i \\
&\quad + [(\sigma_{HD}/\sigma_D) + b_H(\sigma_{WD}/\sigma_D)]\lambda_i
\end{aligned}
$$

where

$$\sigma_{HD} = \text{covariance between } \epsilon_{Hi} \text{ and } \epsilon_{Di} \, (= \epsilon_{Wi} - \epsilon_{Mi}^*)$$
$$\sigma_{WD} = \text{covariance between } \epsilon_{Wi} \text{ and } \epsilon_{Di} \, (= \epsilon_{Wi} - \epsilon_{Mi}^*)$$
$$\lambda_i = f(-J_i/\sigma_D)/[1 - F(-J_i/\sigma_D)]$$
$$J_i = \gamma \mathbf{X}_i - (a_M^* + c_M^* V_i + \mathbf{d}_M^* \mathbf{Z}_i)$$

Hence, the third stage of Procedure VII is to estimate a selection bias-corrected regression, that is, to fit

(4.30) $\quad H_i = a_H + b_H \gamma \mathbf{X}_i + c_H V_i + \mathbf{d}_H \mathbf{Z}_i + \delta \widetilde{\lambda}_i + v_i$

to data on persons who work (and who therefore have $W_i > M_i^*$).
Note from the aforementioned that the estimate of the parameter δ
in (4.30) should be interpreted as an estimate of the quantity
$[(\sigma_{HD}/\sigma_D) + b_H(\sigma_{WD}/\sigma_D)]$. In principle, the results that will be
obtained under this procedure will be the same as those obtained
under a procedure that assumes a continuous labor supply schedule
(e.g., Procedure VI) *only* if the parameters of the marginal rate of
substitution function are identical to the corresponding parameters
of the hours of work function – that is, only if $a_M^* = a_H$, $c_M^* = c_H$,
and $\mathbf{d}_M^* = \mathbf{d}_H$. In this case, equations (4.14)–(4.17) do indeed imply
that H will fall continuously to zero as W and V change. In all other
cases, however, there is the possibility that the empirical labor
supply schedule will be discontinuous, as in the example shown in
Figure 4.2.

A slightly different approach to estimating a discontinuous hours
of work function, which I shall call *Procedure VIII*, differs from
Procedure VII only at the third stage: Rather than get around the
problem of an endogenous W by fitting a reduced form (as in Procedure VII's (4.30)), Procedure VIII instead uses an instrumental-
variables measure of W (that is, an imputed wage), derived from the
second-stage estimates of the wage function for workers, (4.29).
That is, in the third stage of Procedure VIII, one uses selection bias-
corrected regression to fit

(4.31) $H_i = a_H + b_H \hat{W}_i + c_H V_i + \mathbf{d}_H \mathbf{Z}_i + \delta \widetilde{\lambda}_i + v_i$

to data on persons who work. The $\hat{W}_i$ in this expression is computed
as $\hat{W}_i = \hat{\gamma} \mathbf{X}_i$, where the $\hat{\gamma}$ are the estimated parameters of (4.29).
(Thus, (4.31) is analytically identical to (4.30). In particular, the
estimate of δ in (4.31) has exactly the same interpretation as the
estimate of δ in (4.30), namely, $[(\sigma_{HD}/\sigma_D) + b_H(\sigma_{WD}/\sigma_D)]$. The difference is that (4.31) estimates b_H directly and requires estimation of
the selection bias-corrected wage equation (4.29) *first*; whereas
(4.30) is a selection bias-corrected reduced-form equation that
estimates $b_H \gamma$ and thus requires estimation of (4.29) as a *second* step
for identification of b_H as such.) Unlike the imputed wages used in
first-generation work, the $\hat{W}$ in (4.31) is corrected for possible selectivity bias: $\hat{\gamma} X_i$ is an unbiased estimate of the wage that someone
with characteristics X_i in the population can earn, on average, and

$\hat{\gamma} X_i + \hat{z} \tilde{\lambda}_i$ is an unbiased estimate of the wage that a *worker* with characteristics X_i earns (recall that (4.31) and (4.30) are fitted to data on workers).

Although they permit a researcher to judge the magnitude of possible labor supply discontinuities, Procedures VII and VIII are a "black box," since they provide no insight into the factors that give rise to those discontinuities. Description of the factors underlying discontinuity requires a structural model in which such factors are represented explicitly. To see how such a model can be constructed, it is helpful to use the so-called indirect utility function u^* and to consider discontinuities associated with fixed costs of labor market entry, as described in Chapter 1.

The indirect utility function gives *maximum* (or *maximized*) utility u^* as a function of tastes (i.e., a random term), exogenous characteristics, and the key pecuniary variables – the wage rate, prices, and property income – that determine the nature of the constraints on the individual's ability to maximize utility. (Recall the discussion in Chapter 1.) Similarly, actual utility u depends not only on consumption C and leisure time L but also on unmeasured taste factors, which I will write as ϵ. As before, define both the wage and property income to be measured in real terms, so that prices do not need to be included explicitly in the discussion. Then, for empirical purposes, $u^* = u^*(W, V, \epsilon)$ and $u = u(C, L, \epsilon)$. In the *absence* of fixed costs, the individual will (will not) work if and only if $u^*(W, V, \epsilon)$ is greater (equal to or less) than $u(V, 1, \epsilon)$.

On the other hand, as implied in Chapter 1 (see in particular the discussion of Figures 1.7 and 1.8), introducing fixed costs of labor market entry has essentially the same effect on the individual's decision *to work or not to work* as does reducing his property income by some amount f, regardless of whether the fixed costs in question refer to fixed time *or* money costs of labor market entry. In other words, someone with property income V who is willing to work at wage rate W in the presence of time *or* money costs of work whose *monetary equivalent* is some amount f is, in effect, on a budget line with a slope equal to W and with "adjusted property income" equal to $V - f$. In this respect, the only difference between fixed time and fixed money costs of work has to do with the underlying determinants of f. In the case of fixed money costs, f is, of course, the actual amount of such costs (of, e.g., bus tickets, tools, uniforms, etc.). In the case of fixed *time* costs, however, f is the money equivalent of the amount of *time*, t_c, that the individual loses (and cannot use for work or leisure) when he decides to work; in other words, in this case, f is equal to $t_c W$. Hence, in the case of fixed money costs, f may be independent of W, whereas in the case of fixed time costs, f is necessarily a function of W.[19]

To see how one may specify an empirical model with fixed costs of labor market entry, first consider the case of fixed money costs. Individual i will work if and only if the maximum utility attainable when he works (that is, by earning wage rate W_i, receiving $V_i - f_i$ in property income *net* of fixed costs of working) is better than the utility attainable when he does not work (that is, when property income and thus consumption is V_i, no money costs of working must be borne and $L_i = 1$). Utility in either state depends on unobservable taste factors, ϵ_i, as well as on observable factors. Thus, the probability that individual i will work is given by

$$\Pr[i \text{ works}] = \Pr[u^*(W_i, V_i - f_i, \epsilon_i) > u(V_i, 1, \epsilon_i)]$$

After explicitly specifying the functions u^* and u, one can then rearrange the inequality $u^*(W, V - f, \epsilon) > u(V, 1, \epsilon)$ so as to put ϵ *alone* on the left-hand side. The right-hand side of this "rearranged" inequality will obviously contain terms involving W, V, and f – call it simply $z(W, V, f)$. So, the earlier expression for i's probability of working may then be expressed in general terms as

$$\Pr[i \text{ works}] = \Pr[\epsilon_i > z(W_i, V_i, f_i)]$$

If ϵ is assumed to be a normally distributed mean-zero random variable, then the empirical participation equation corresponding to the earlier expression is a probit function. (Note that estimation of such a function would require data on W_i for all individuals, including

---

[19] In principle, the value of f can be compued by projecting the individual's budget line back to the point where $L = 1$ and taking the difference between the height of that line at $L = 1$ and the value of v. As Cogan (1980b) observes, the value of f is in effect the result of optimizing decisions (about the optimal commuting mode, the optimal set of purchases required for work, etc.) and so itself is a function of variables, such as W, V, and so forth. This is particularly evident from Figure 1.8, where, even holding V constant, the magnitude of fixed costs in dollar equivalents, $f(= v - \underline{v})$, will depend on W (i.e., on the slope of the budget line $v'''f_3$).

nonworkers, and also the assumption that W_i is uncorrelated with the error term ϵ.)

To analyze hours of work under this approach, note that, by Roy's Identity (see Chapter 1), hours of work for persons who work are given by

$$H_i = [\partial u^*(W_i, V_i - f_i, \epsilon_i)/\partial W_i]/[\partial u^*(W_i, V_i - f_i, \epsilon_i)/\partial V_i]$$

To simplify notation a bit, rewrite this as $H_i = H_i(W_i, V_i - f_i, \epsilon_i)$. Thus, the complete model of labor supply under fixed costs (of either kind) would consist of a participation equation and a pair of equations for hours of work, that is,

(4.32) $\quad \Pr[i \text{ works}] = \Pr[\epsilon_i > z(W_i, V_i, f_i)]$

$\qquad H_i = H_i(W_i, V_i - f_i, \epsilon_i) \qquad$ if and only if

(4.33) $\qquad\qquad\qquad\qquad\qquad\qquad \epsilon_i > z(W_i, V_i, f_i)$

$\qquad H_i = 0 \qquad\qquad\qquad\qquad$ if and only if

$\qquad\qquad\qquad\qquad\qquad\qquad \epsilon_i \leq z(W_i, V_i, f_i)$

For future reference, I shall refer to this version of the fixed-costs model as the *indirect utility – no-work utility* approach, since the focal point of the estimation procedure involves comparing u when the individual does not work with u^* when the individual does work.

For alternative (but very similar) routes to essentially the same empirical fixed-costs labor supply model, note that the reservation wage is always, by definition, the value of W at which an individual would be indifferent between working and not working – that is, at which the maximum utility attainable through working is just the same as the utility associated with not working. In the present model, the reservation wage, which I shall write as $W_{H=H_0}$, is the value of W that satisfies the relation

$$u^*(W, V - f, \epsilon) = u(V, 1, \epsilon)$$

Whenever $W > W_{H=H_0}$, the individual will work, whereas otherwise he will not – exactly as in the simple labor supply model. Moreover, as noted in Chapter 1, Roy's Identity implies that the labor supply of an individual who works and who has a wage equal to $W_{H=H_0}$ and property income equal to $V - f$ is given by

(4.34) $\quad H_0 = [\partial u^*(W_{H=H_0}, V - f, \epsilon)/\partial W]$

$\qquad\qquad \div [\partial u^*(W_{H=H_0}, V - f, \epsilon)/\partial V]$

– again, exactly the same as in the simple model, at least in formal terms. There is, however, one difference: In the simple model, both f and H_0 are zero, whereas in the fixed-costs model both f and H_0 are positive (see, in particular, Figure 4.2). Now, H_0 is "minimum" hours of work; for wage levels in excess of $W_{H=H_0}$ hours of work will exceed H_0, but they may still be derived by replacing $W_{H=H_0}$ in (4.34) with the relevant value of W, that is,

$$(4.35) \quad H = [\partial u^*(W, V - f, \epsilon)/\partial W]/[(\partial u^*(W, V - f, \epsilon)/\partial V]$$

Again, then, the analysis provides (i) an expression for the hours of work for persons who work, (4.35), and (ii) a formal statement of the conditions under which a given individual will or will not work (that is, a comparison between W and $W_{H=H_0}$ or, alternatively, a comparison between H and H_0). This leads to two more ways to derive the empirical model of labor supply with fixed costs.

One derivation takes the comparison between the wage and the reservation wage as its focal point. To outline the basic components of this model, note that, in principle, one can solve (4.32)–(4.33) to derive an expression for the reservation wage $W_{H=H_0}$ in terms of V, f, and ϵ. Call this expression the *reservation wage equation*, and write it as $W_{H=H_0} = W_{H=H_0}(V, f, \epsilon)$; in this sense, an individual i will work if and only if $W > W_{H=H_0}(V, f, \epsilon)$. Now rearrange this inequality so as to put ϵ on the left-hand side; the right-hand side will contain terms involving W, V, and f. Write the right-hand side in very general form as $w(W, V, f)$ and note that the rearranged inequality simply means that individual i will work if and only if $\epsilon > w(W, V, f)$. This "market wage–reservation wage" version of the fixed-costs model therefore implies that labor supply behavior is described by an expression for participation and two expressions for hours of work per se, namely,

$$(4.36) \quad \Pr[i \text{ works}] = \Pr[\epsilon_i > w(W_i, V_i, f_i)]$$

$$(4.37) \quad H_i = H_i(W_i, V_i - f_i, \epsilon_i) \quad \text{if and only if}$$
$$\epsilon_i > w(W_i, V_i, f_i)$$

$$(4.38) \quad H_i = 0 \quad \text{if and only if}$$
$$\epsilon_i \le w(W_i, V_i, f_i)$$

respectively.

Finally, consider another derivation of the model, formulated in terms of a comparison between actual hours of work H and minimum hours H_0. To derive an expression for participation for the model, note that one can solve (4.34) to obtain an expression for minimum hours of work in terms of W, V, f, and ϵ. Call this expression the *minimum hours* equation, and write it as $H_0 = H_0(W, V, f, \epsilon)$. Thus, in terms of the aforementioned, an individual i will work if and only if $H > H_0(W_i, V_i, f_i, \epsilon_i)$. Now rearrange this inequality so as to put ϵ on the left-hand side and write the right-hand side of the rearranged inequality in general form as $h(W, V, f)$; hence individual i will work if and only if $\epsilon_i > h(W_i, V_i, f_i)$. Thus, the "actual hours–minimum hours" version of the fixed-costs model would consist of a participation equation and two equations for hours of work, namely,

(4.39) $\Pr[i \text{ works}] = \Pr[\epsilon_i > h(W_i, V_i, f_i)]$

(4.40) $H_i = H_i(W_i, V_i - f_i, \epsilon_i)$ if and only if
$$\epsilon_i > h(W_i, V_i, f_i)$$

(4.41) $H_i = 0$ if and only if
$$\epsilon_i \leq h(W_i, V_i, f_i)$$

As a glance at equations (4.32)–(4.33), (4.36)–(4.38), and (4.39)–(4.41) readily confirms, these three ways of writing the model of labor supply in the presence of fixed money costs of labor market entry differ *only* in terms of the manner in which they are derived: Regardless of whether one thinks of the participation decision in terms of comparisons between u^* and u, between W and $W_{H=H_0}$, or between H and H_0, the eventual result is the same in each case.

Now consider how to derive a model of labor supply in the presence of fixed *time* costs of labor market entry. As noted earlier, expressions for the probability that a given individual i will work, such as (4.32), (4.36), or (4.39), apply equally well to the fixed-time-costs case as to the fixed-money-costs case. However, as indicated in Chapter 1, the impact of fixed time costs on *hours of work* is quite different from the impact of fixed money costs: An increase in the amount of fixed money costs of market entry will increase the hours worked by people who work, but an increase in the amount of fixed time costs will reduce hours worked by workers (provided consumption and leisure are normal goods). The reason is simple: When fixed time costs increase, someone who works has less time available for work *or* leisure and, in effect, suffers a loss in full income. If both consumption and leisure are normal goods, such an individual will react to this reduction in full income by reducing both leisure and consumption – and the fact that consumption falls means that earnings, and thus labor supply, will also fall. Consequently, as far as effects on hours of work are concerned, changes in fixed money costs are equivalent to changes in property income (in the opposite direction), but changes in fixed time costs are not: Expressions such as (4.33), (4.37), and (4.40), therefore, do not apply to the case of fixed time costs.

Fortunately, however, it is relatively simple to modify the models (4.32)–(4.33), (4.36)–(4.38), and (4.39)–(4.41) to allow for fixed time (as opposed to fixed money) costs. One way is to treat V_i and f_i ($= t_c W$, in the fixed-time-cost case) as *separate* arguments in expressions such as (4.33), (4.37), and (4.40) rather than to combine them as a single argument, $V_i - f_i$. Combining them into a single argument constrains the effect of a rise in f_i (e.g., via a rise in t_c) to be the same as the effect of a fall in V_i, whereas treating V_i and f_i as separate arguments does not. An even more straightforward modification, however, is to treat *leisure time* rather than *labor supply* as the dependent variable in expressions such as (4.33), (4.37), or (4.40). This is because, as indicated in Chapter 1, a rise in either kind of fixed cost will certainly reduce leisure time, just as a decrease in property income will do.

Having derived a specification for labor supply under either kind of fixed costs, one must then consider three other questions. First, the earlier discussion has assumed that the wage rate W is uncorrelated with the error term ϵ and that wage data are available for all individuals – workers and nonworkers alike. If either of these two conditions is not satisfied, it would be necessary to add a wage equation such as (4.14) to the model to be estimated and then proceed in a manner similar to the one described earlier. Second, one must make some specific assumptions about functional forms – for example, one must specify the utility function (or the indirect utility function or the minimum-hours equation) explicitly.[20] Third, since data on

---

[20] Thus, although the models (4.32)–(4.33), (4.36)–(4.38), and (4.39)–(4.41) are all identical in principle, they need not be equal or identical in practice. For example, if the utility function u is specified as linear in ϵ, then, in general, the function for the reservation wage $W_{H=H_0}$ (and the function for minimum hours H_0) will not be linear in ϵ, and vice versa.

the amount of "fixed costs in dollar equivalents," f_i, for different individuals are rarely available, one must decide how to measure (or what to do with expressions involving) f_i.

For example, Hausman (1980) estimates the no-work utility –indirect utility version of the fixed-costs model by (i) adopting a specific functional form for the labor supply function and then deriving the direct and indirect utility functions implied by that labor supply function and (ii) assuming that f is an *exact* function involving estimable parameters and observed variables but *no* stochastic term. He uses a utility function that has a particularly convenient property: Not only utility, u, but also indirect utility, u^*, and their difference $u^* - u$ are all monotonic functions of the unmeasured taste component of utility, ϵ. Together with the assumption that f depends on observed variables only, this leads to a relatively simple model in which all equations – for participation and hours of work – can be written explicitly in terms of the parameters of the utility function, the parameters of the f function, and observable variables. Thus, Hausman's approach explicitly recognizes that there are numerous across-equation restrictions in the model (4.32)–(4.33) – that is, that these equations have numerous parameters in common. Indeed, it turns out that it is possible to use the model to estimate all labor supply parameters (including, e.g., substitution effects on hours of work H) using data on participation *only* – that is, without using any data on the number of hours worked by people who work.

Of course, one pays a price for this remarkable result. First, ignoring available data on hours of work wastes information, and so the resulting estimates are less efficient than they would be were data on H used in estimation. Second, it is necessary to adopt a quite specific (and, therefore, somewhat arbitrary) utility function, and (at least to keep the analysis simple) to assume that no unmeasured factors affect f. Heckman (1974a) proceeds in a somewhat similar fashion. He estimates a version of the market wage–reservation wage formulation of the fixed-costs model and treats f as a stochastic function (i.e., allows for the possibility that unobservable factors affect f). However, a fully general treatment of the stochastic structure of this model – to allow for correlation between the unobservables that affect W, f, and the reservation wage $W_{H=H_0}$ – raises severe computational problems, so Heckman instead assumes a priori that the unobservables that affect f are uncorrelated with the unobservables that affect W and $W_{H=H_0}$.

Due at least in part (or so it seems) to these considerations, Cogan (1980b, 1981) and Hanoch (1980b) adopt general a priori specifications for the models (4.36)–(4.38) and (4.39)–(4.41), respectively. Largely because their functions for actual hours, minimum hours, and the reservation wage are not based on an explicit utility function, their approach is less restrictive than Hausman's but, by the same token, also less tightly specified: In particular, they ignore any restrictions implied by utility maximization (e.g., that some of the parameters in their H, H_0, and $W_{H=H_0}$ functions might be the same). (However, they do note that it is possible to use the H_0 and H functions to derive an expression for $W_{H=H_0}$, i.e., that these three functions are not completely independent.)

4.5.   Applications to labor supply models with taxes

In the absence of taxes, the fundamentals of the labor supply decision are easy to describe. Whether or not there are any fixed costs of labor market entry, the individual chooses between a no-work point and the best possible point along a *single* budget line segment (which may or may not contain the no-work point). In contrast, when the individual pays taxes or receives transfer payments, the budget line consists of several different segments, each associated with a different marginal tax rate, except when taxes are strictly proportional or "lump sum." (For example, recall Figure 3.4(b).) In this setting, the labor supply decision is, therefore, not simply a question of choosing between not working and working, but, rather, a question of choosing between not working, working on budget line segment 1 at the net or post-tax wage $W(1 - \tau_1)$, working on budget line segment 2 at the net wage $W(1 - \tau_2)$, and so forth, where τ_j is the marginal tax rate relevant to the jth budget line segment.

In principle, then, one can extend the empirical framework described earlier to cover the case of labor supply in the presence of taxation (Hausman, 1979). In order to perform a satisfactory analysis of labor supply in the presence of taxes, however, the researcher has to know the particular budget line segment, and thus the particular marginal tax rate, that each individual in the data set to be studied has chosen. This introduces two complications not present in simpler models. First, available data on hours of work may measure the hours that some individuals actually work with error. If so, then such data do not always correctly indicate the specific budget line segment that a particular individual has chosen. Second, data on the marginal tax rates actually paid by individuals are rarely if ever available, and for a variety of reasons – legal tax avoidance, illegal tax evasion, or the exercise of discretion by agencies that administer the tax laws – one cannot always be sure that individuals actually pay taxes (or have their transfer benefits reduced) at the statutory marginal rate. If so, then, even if data on hours of work always correctly measure the hours actually worked by individuals, such data will not always correctly indicate the marginal tax rates actually paid by individuals who supply given amounts of labor.

The first of these difficulties raises some interesting technical questions about estimation technique that have already received some attention in the second-generation literature; for example, see Burtless and Hausman (1978), Hausman (1980), Heckman, Killingsworth, and MaCurdy (1981), Heckman and MaCurdy (1981) and Wales and Woodland (1979). The second of these difficulties raises some very important substantive questions, for example, about the actual (as opposed to the intended) consequences of tax laws and the extent of tax avoidance and tax evasion. (For discussion of tax avoidance and tax evasion, see Andersen, 1977; Baldry, 1979; Cowell, 1981b; Heckman, 1981; Isachsen and Strøm, 1980; Pencavel, 1979; Sandmo, 1981. For discussion of "transfer evasion" – concealment of income to avoid reductions in one's transfer benefits – and the exercise of discretion by agencies responsible for transfer payments, see Greenberg, Moffitt, and Friedmann, 1981; Heffernan, 1973; Lurie, 1974; Rowlatt, 1972.) The implications of tax avoidance and tax evasion for estimation of labor supply functions have been largely ignored. One implication is decidedly unsettling: When expenditures on some goods and services (housing, medical care, etc.) are tax deductible – so that their purchase entails legal tax avoidance – whereas other expenditures are not, individuals in different tax brackets are confronted with different marginal prices for the same bundle of goods. Thus, use of the composite commodity theorem to justify aggregating all consumer goods into a single composite (whose price is taken to be the same for all individuals) is no longer appropriate (Heckman, 1981).

However, my purpose here is to provide a general outline of methods for analyzing labor supply under taxation, not a detailed description of particular techniques used in specific cases. Accordingly, in what follows, I shall be concerned with empirical analysis when the composite commodity theorem remains applicable and when available data on hours of work not only correctly measure the actual number of hours worked by all individuals who work but also are sufficient to permit one to determine (e.g., from published tax tables)[21] the tax rates that all individuals actually pay. (See Heckman, 1981; Heckman, Killingsworth, and MaCurdy, 1981; and Heckman and MaCurdy, 1981; for discussions of techniques suitable for more complex cases.)

To derive a model for analyzing labor supply under taxation subject to these assumptions, it is useful to begin by examining Figure 4.3, which reproduces most of Figure 3.4(b). The individual's indifference curves are strictly convex (that is, the slope of a given indifference curve increases in absolute value as hours of work increase), whereas the budget constraint $1v_1xf_2$ is concave. It follows that one can describe labor supply decisions in terms of either (i) comparisons of indirect utility functions or (ii) comparisons between after-tax marginal wage rates and marginal rates of substitution, at different segments of the budget line.

For example, to describe these decisions in terms of marginal rate of substitution–marginal wage rate comparisons, let the marginal rate of substitution M at any given combination of C and L be a function $M(C, L, \epsilon)$ of C, L and unmeasured taste factors ϵ. Now, note that the individual will not work at all if and only if $M(v_1, 1, \epsilon)$ – his reservation wage – exceeds or equals the after-tax marginal wage rate at v_1, $w(1 - \tau_1)$. Thus,

(4.42) $M(v_1, 1, \epsilon) \geq w(1 - \tau_1)$ if and only if $H = 0$

---

[21] In other words, I assume that there is sufficient information to permit a researcher to fill out a complete tax return for each individual in the researcher's data base and, thus, to compute the rate of tax that applies, at the margin, to each such individual. In most actual studies, this is done by assuming, for example, that each individual in the data base files jointly with his or her spouse, takes the standard deduction, and so forth.

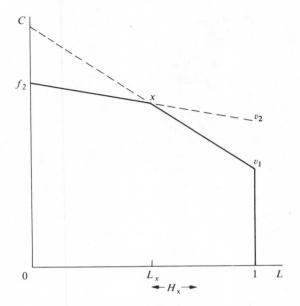

Figure 4.3.   Labor supply under taxation

Likewise, the individual will work in between zero and $H_x = 1 - L_x$ hours (that is, will pick some point on the interior of budget line segment $v_1 x$) if and only if two conditions are satisfied. First, the inequality in (4.42) must obviously be reversed. Second, the individual's marginal rate of substitution at point x (that is, the slope, evaluated at x, of the indifference curve that passes through point x) is greater than $w(1 - \tau_1)$, the after-tax wage rate along segment $v_1 x$. Thus,

$$(4.43) \quad M[v_1 + (1 - \tau_1)wH_x, L_x, \epsilon] > w(1 - \tau_1) > M(v_1, 1, \epsilon)$$

if and only if $0 < H < H_x$.

Next, the individual will work exactly H_x hours – that is, will work at the kink point x – if and only if his marginal rate of substitution at x is not only (i) no greater than the marginal wage rate along $v_1 x$, $w(1 - \tau_1)$ but also (ii) no smaller than the marginal wage rate along the second segment of the budget line ($x f_2$), $w(1 - \tau_2)$. (Also, it must, of course, still be the case that the inequality in (4.42) is reversed.) Thus,

(4.44) $w(1 - \tau_1) > M(v_1, 1, \epsilon)$ and
$$w(1 - \tau_1) \geq M[v_1 + (1 - \tau_1)wH_x, L_x, \epsilon] \geq w(1 - \tau_2)$$

if and only if $H = H_x$. (Obviously, at least one of the equal to or greater than signs in (4.44) will be a strictly greater than sign in actuality. In other words, the slope at point x of an indifference curve that touches the budget line only at point x must either be (i) equal to the slope of v_1x and, thus, greater than the slope of xf_2; (ii) equal to the slope of xf_2 and, thus, less than the slope of v_1x; or (iii) greater than the slope of xf_2 and also less than the slope of v_1x.)

Finally, the individual will work more than H_x hours – that is, will work somewhere along the interior of the second budget line segment, xf_2 – if and only if the inequality (4.44) is reversed *and* provided his marginal rate of substitution at point x is smaller than the after-tax marginal wage rate along xf_2, $w(1 - \tau_2)$. That is,

(4.45) $w(1 - \tau_1) > M(v_1, 1, \epsilon)$ and
$$w(1 - \tau_2) > M[v_1 + (1 - \tau_1)wH_x, L_x, \epsilon]$$

if and only if $H > H_x$.

Once one adopts a specific form for the marginal rate of substitution function M, one can translate the earlier general analysis into a form suitable for econometric estimation. For example, suppose that one specifies the M function as

(4.46) $M = m_0 + m_1 C + m_2 L + \epsilon_M$

Then conditions (4.42)–(4.45) may be rewritten as follows:

(4.47) $\epsilon_M > (1 - \tau_1)w - J_1$ if and only if $H = 0$

where $J_1 = m_0 + m_1 v_1 + m_2$.

(4.48) $(1 - \tau_1)w - J_1 > \epsilon_M > (1 - \tau_1)w - J_2$
                  if and only if $0 < H < H_x$

where $J_2 = J_1 + m_1(1 - \tau_1)wH_x - m_2(1 - L_x) > J_1$.

(4.49) $(1 - \tau_1)w - J_2 \geq \epsilon_M \geq (1 - \tau_2)w - J_2$
                  if and only if $H = H_x$

(4.50) $(1 - \tau_1)w - J_2 > \epsilon_M$ if and only if $H_x < H$

Note that J_2 is larger than J_1, τ_2 is larger than τ_1, and, in the context of this model, ϵ_M may be interpreted as the individual's taste for leisure.[22] Thus, other things (namely, w and v) being equal, the individual will not work at all if his taste for leisure, ϵ_M, is very large. If ϵ_M is somewhat smaller (in between $(1 - \tau_1)w - J_1$ and $(1 - \tau_1)w - J_2$), then he will work more than zero hours but less than H_x hours. If ϵ_M is smaller still (in between $(1 - \tau_1)w - J_2$ and $(1 - \tau_2)w - J_2$), then he will work exactly H_x hours. Finally, if ϵ_M is extremely small (less than $(1 - \tau_2)w - J_2$), then he will work more than H_x hours.

If ϵ_M is assumed to be a mean-zero random variable that follows the normal distribution and has a standard deviation of σ_M, then this analysis can be expressed in graphical terms very similar to those given in Figure 4.1. This is shown in Figure 4.4, which plots the standardized random variable ϵ_M/σ_M and identifies the key "thresholds" highlighted in equations (4.47)–(4.50). This makes it clear that empirical analysis of labor supply under taxation may be regarded as a generalization of the simple model to allow for multiple thresholds – one for not working versus working along segment v_1x, shown as ab in Figure 4.4; a second, for working along v_1x versus working at x, shown as cd in Figure 4.4; and a third, for working at x versus working along xf_2, shown as ef in Figure 4.4. With given w and v and given tax rates τ_1 and τ_2, the individual's labor supply depends on his taste for leisure, ϵ_M, and in particular on how strong this taste for leisure is relative to the thresholds associated with working at different segments of the budget line or at the kink point x.

---

[22] In other words, suppose, for example, that an individual's ϵ_M were to increase. By (4.46), the marginal rate of substitution M and thus the reservation wage M^* increase when ϵ_M increases, reducing both the probability that the individual will work and the hours the individual will work when he or she works. The M function given by (4.46) has one other property worth noting at this point. Consumption at any equilibrium point may be written as $C = v_p + (1 - \tau_p)wH$, where v_p is linearized property income at the equilibrium point p and τ_p is the marginal rate of tax at p. Now replace C in (4.46) with this expression and totally differentiate with respect to H, to obtain $dM/dH = m_1(1 - \tau_p)w - m_2$ (because $dL/dH = -1$). Because M increases as H increases (because indifference curves are convex), it follows that $m_1(1 - \tau_p)w - m_2$ is positive for all τ_p. This turns out to mean that the quantity J_2 is larger than the quantity J_1 (see text).

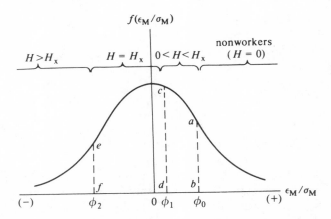

Figure 4.4. Ordered-probit analysis of labor supply under taxation

In view of this, and, in particular, given the obvious similarity between Figures 4.1 and 4.4, it comes as no surprise to see that the likelihood function for participation in the model of labor supply with taxes is also a generalization of the analogous function in the simple model. Specifically, when there are data on N total individuals of whom some are in a set $\overline{E}$ of nonworkers, some are in a set E_1 of persons working along segment $v_1 x$ of the budget line, some are in a set E_x of persons working at the kink point x, and the rest are in a set E_2 of persons working along segment $x f_2$ of the budget line, then the generalized probit likelihood function for this sample is

$$(4.51) \quad l = \prod_{i \in \overline{E}} F(-\phi_0) \cdot \prod_{i \in E} [F(-\phi_1) - F(-\phi_0)]$$
$$\times \prod_{i \in E_x} [F(-\phi_2) - F(-\phi_1)] \cdot \prod_{i \in E_2} [1 - F(-\phi_2)]$$

where

$$\phi_0 = [(1 - \tau_1)w - J_1]/\sigma_M$$
$$\phi_1 = [(1 - \tau_1)w - J_2]/\sigma_M$$
$$\phi_2 = [(1 - \tau_2)w - J_2]/\sigma_M$$

Note that the model implies that the value of ϵ_M for persons in each of the sets $\overline{E}, E_1, E_x$, and E_2 can be ordered relative to the value of ϵ_M

for persons in the other sets. Naturally enough, therefore, this is known as an *ordered probit* function. (See Amemiya, 1975, 1981. Moffitt, 1979b, smoothes the budget constraint to analyze labor supply using ordinary or two-outcome probit. Zabalza, 1983, takes an approach that is very similar to the one described here.)

Finally, consider the analysis of hours of work, H. It is interesting to note that one can identify and estimate *all* the parameters of the marginal rate of substitution function by maximizing the ordered-probit likelihood function (4.51). Thus, it is possible to derive all parameters of direct relevance to hours of work without actually using any data on hours of work as such: All that is required is information to identify the hours-of-work *category* ($H = 0, 0 < H < H_x, H = H_x$, or $H > H_x$) to which each individual in the sample belongs. (For example, see Hausman, 1980, and Zabalza, 1983.) However, data on actual hours of work add considerable information and, hence, improve efficiency of estimation. To use this information, note, first, that one can derive an expression for hours of work on a given segment of the budget constraint by using Roy's Identity or, alternatively, by equating the marginal rate of substitution on that segment with the after-tax marginal wage rate on that segment and then solving for H. For example, when the M function is (4.46), someone who works along segment $v_1 x$ of the budget constraint has $w(1 - \tau_1) = m_0 + m_1[v_1 + w(1 - \tau_1)H] + m_2(1 - H) + \epsilon_M$, whereas someone who works along segment xf_2 of the budget constraint has $w(1 - \tau_2) = m_0 + m_1[v_2 + w(1 - \tau_2)H] + m_2(1 - H) + \epsilon_M$. Accordingly, hours of work H are given by

$$(4.52) \quad H = [(1 - \tau_s)w - m_0 - m_1 v_s - m_2 - \epsilon_M]/z_s$$

where $z_s = m_1 w(1 - \tau_s) - m_2$ and where s subscripts refer to budget line segment s ($= 1$, for segment $v_1 x$, or $= 2$, for segment xf_2).

It remains to introduce the hours-of-work function (4.52) into the empirical labor supply model. As one example, consider an equation similar to the one used by Pellechio (1979), which amounts to a generalization of selectivity bias-corrected regression for labor supply. First, note that expected hours of work in the population are given by

(4.53) $E[H] = \Pr[H = 0]\cdot 0$
$+ \Pr[0 < H < H_x]E[H \,|\, 0 < H < H_x]$
$+ \Pr[H = H_x]H_x$
$+ \Pr[H > H_x]E[H \,|\, H > H_x]$

Next, note that $E[H | 0 < H < H_x]$ and $E[H | H > H_x]$ may be written as $E[H \,|\, \text{segment} = 1]$ and $E[H \,|\, \text{segment} = 2]$, respectively, where "segment" refers to a segment of the budget line $v_1 x f_2$ (either $v_1 x$, segment 1, or $x f_2$, segment 2). Moreover, note that

(4.54) $E[H \,|\, \text{segment} = s]$
$= \{[(1 - \tau_s)w - m_0 - m_1 v_s - m_2]/z_s\}$
$- E[\epsilon_M/z_s \,|\, \text{segment} = s]$

(4.55) $E[\epsilon_M/z_1 \,|\, \text{segment} = 1] = E[\epsilon_M/z_1 \,|\, \phi_0 > \epsilon_M/\sigma_M > \phi_1]$
$= g_1 \lambda_1$

where

$\lambda_1 = [f(-\phi_1) - f(-\phi_0)]/[F(-\phi_1) - F(-\phi_0)]$
$g_1 = \sigma_M/z_1$

(4.56) $E[\epsilon_M/z_2 \,|\, \text{segment} = 2] = E[\epsilon_M/z_2 \,|\, \phi_2 > \epsilon_M/\sigma_M] = g_2 \lambda_2$

where

$\lambda_2 = f(-\phi_2)/[1 - F(-\phi_2)]$
$g_2 = \sigma_M/z_2$

Finally, note that (4.51) gives the probability that the individual will work zero hours, H_x hours, or on either of the two segments of the budget line. Accordingly, use (4.51) and (4.54)–(4.56) to rewrite $E[H]$ as given by (4.53), and then let $H = E[H] + v_H$, where v_H is an error term (reflecting differences between $E[H]$ and H), to obtain

(4.57) $H = [F(-\phi_1) - F(-\phi_0)]$
$\times \{[(1 - \tau_1)w - m_0 - m_1 v_1 - m_2]/z_1\} + g_1 \lambda_1$
$+ [F(-\phi_2) - F(-\phi_1)]H_x$
$+ [1 - F(-\phi_2)]$
$\times \{[(1 - \tau_2)w - m_0 - m_1 v_2 - m_2]/z_2\} + g_2 \lambda_2$
$+ v_H$

The similarity between (4.57) and the analogous expression for "simple regression with selection bias correction" is evident. The main difference is that (4.57) is quite nonlinear in the parameters, and also includes two selection bias variables (λ_1 and λ_2, referring to persons on each of the two segments of the budget constraint that involve work).

Of course, relying on after-tax marginal wage rate versus marginal rate of substitution comparisons is only one way to specify the labor supply function in the presence of taxes. One could instead work with, say, an explicit utility function or an explicit indirect utility function. (For examples, see Burtless and Hausman, 1978; Hausman, 1980, 1981a; Wales and Woodland, 1979.) Thus, for example, a model based on a specific indirect utility function would attack participation decisions by deriving expressions giving the range of values of the error term in the indirect utility function that imply nonparticipation, working along the first segment of the budget line, working at the first kink point of the budget line, and so forth, for all segments and all kink points. The limits of these ranges are thresholds, analogous to those previously discussed, and may be used in an ordered probit analysis similar in nature to that previously described. Functions for hours of work along any given budget line segment can be derived using Roy's Identity. Again, then, the basic approach is the same: to analyze both discrete choices (nonparticipation or working at any given kink point or along any given budget line segment) and continuous choices (that is, hours of work), using concepts that are firmly grounded in basic theoretical models (e.g., wage–marginal rate of substitution comparisons, Roy's Identity, and the like).

Procedures of this kind (and similar procedures, such as estimation of (4.51) or (4.57)) in effect locate the individual's optimum by checking the entire budget constraint, including both flat segments and kink points. As such, I shall refer to such procedures as examples of the complete budget constraint (cbc) approach. Describing this way of locating the individual's optimum – a simple process of checking utility (or the marginal rate of substitution, etc.) at each point on the budget constraint – is straightforward in a conceptual sense. Implementing it can be difficult, for at least three reasons. First, individual preferences (e.g., the utility or marginal rate of substitution function) may include an error term, reflecting unmeasured variables. Second, data on *observed* hours of work may also include an error term, reflecting errors or failure of optimization and/or simple errors of measurement, that is, desired and observed hours may differ due to unobservable factors. Third, the budget constraint (e.g., the wage rate and/or the marginal tax rate) may be measured with error. Allowing for all three sources of error in implementing the cbc approach is certainly possible (Heckman and MaCurdy, 1981), but as a practical matter this is enough to give even the most seasoned econometrician a few desponding moments. As noted in Section 4.6 (see particularly Table 4.3), studies that use cbc have allowed for only one, or at most two, of these three kinds of unobservables (sources of error).

An alternative to the cbc approach is, of course, the much simpler linearized budget constraint (lbc) procedure. Provided the budget constraint is smoothly concave (as would be the case under a smoothly increasing marginal tax rate), it is straightforward to replace W and V with their linearized counterparts, $\hat{W}$ and $\hat{V}$. (Recall the discussion of Figure 3.4(b) and see Section 6.1, especially the discussion of (6.7), for further details.) In most cases, the transformed labor supply equation is estimated using OLS. However, in general, this is appropriate only if there are no disturbances in the labor supply function and no errors in measured hours data. Otherwise, it is necessary to instrument the $\hat{W}$ and $\hat{V}$ variables in order to obtain consistent parameter estimates. Fortunately, this is not particularly difficult, even though it has been done only infrequently (see Johnson and Pencavel, 1982a,b; Layard, Barton, and Zabalza, 1980).

If the lbc approach is so simple (at least when compared with the cbc approach), why bother with the cbc approach? The answer is that lbc is not universally applicable. In most real-world tax systems, the budget constraint is not smoothly concave; rather, it contains kink points and – particularly once one introduces transfers – may include regions of convexity. When there are kink points, the marginal wage $\hat{W}$ is undefined; when the budget constraint contains convex regions, it may be tangent to the individual's (convex) indifference curve at more than one point, and a given indifference curve–budget line tangency point may not be the optimum. The obvious solution to *these* problems is to check the entire budget constraint for the true optimum level of labor supply; but that leads directly back to the cbc approach.

As in many other settings, then, in this case "you pays your money" (if only for large amounts of computer time) "and you takes your choice" – between a variety of compromises. Heckman (1981) suggests that lbc may be more robust, in actual applications, than cbc, which involves more structure and requires more information. Unfortunately, the available evidence (discussed in Section 4.6) on this issue is scanty, if only because there currently exist few direct comparisons, conducted using the same data set, between cbc and lbc. Detailed sensitivity analyses similar to those undertaken for first-generation work (DaVanzo, DeTray, and Greenberg, 1973, 1976) may help provide some of the answers.

4.6. Results of second-generation labor supply studies

I now consider empirical findings of second-generation studies of labor supply. These results furnish evidence on several questions of empirical interest on which first-generation work is either silent or else not very informative. First, both for general analytical purposes and for specific policy decisions (e.g., concerning taxes or transfer programs), it is important to know whether time and money costs of participation in the labor force make for substantial discontinuity in labor supply schedules. If so, then, at least in some circumstances, small changes in wage rates or other determinants of labor supply, such as transfer payments or tax rates, could lead to quite large changes in labor supply.

Second, *in principle*, estimates of labor supply parameters based on second-generation methodology are preferable to OLS estimates, since the latter may suffer from one or more forms of bias. But *in practice*, it is not obvious that different estimation techniques must necessarily yield substantially different results. If biases in OLS estimates are of relatively minor magnitude, then, as a practical matter, there is not much reason to abandon OLS estimation, even if its theoretical purity leaves something to be desired. On the other hand, if the magnitude of OLS biases is substantial, then the case for alternative estimation techniques is considerably stronger.

Finally, if estimates based on second-generation methodology are accepted as unbiased, and if they differ markedly from those obtained in conventional work, then one other important issue arises: what do the new estimates imply about labor supply behavior, including, in particular, the magnitudes of wage, income, and substitution elasticities?

Discussion of these issues raises questions of interpretation and comparison; I will consider such questions next. I will then compare the results of first- and second-generation studies, focusing on whether parameter estimates are sensitive to alternative estimation techniques. I will conclude by discussing evidence on the importance of discontinuities in labor supply schedules and on procedures for analyzing labor supply in the presence of taxation.

Comparability and interpretation of parameter estimates

In principle, estimates of the parameters of labor supply models provide information on one or more of a number of somewhat different aspects of labor supply:

(i) the structural labor supply schedule, that is, the hours of work supplied by a given individual at alternative values of variables, such as the wage, property income, and so forth;

(ii) labor force participation, that is, the decision of an individual to have positive or zero hours of work at alternative values of variables, such as the wage or property income (which, in mathematical terms, may be written as $\Pr[H > 0]$);

(iii) the labor supply of workers, that is, the mean hours of work of all persons who have positive hours of work (which, in mathematical terms, may be written as $E[H \mid H > 0]$); and

(iv) total labor supply, that is, the mean hours of work of all persons, including both those with positive and those with zero hours of work (which, in mathematical terms, may be written as $E[H]$).

These four concepts are illustrated in Figure 4.5, which makes plain the fact that they are closely related. (See Heckman, Killingsworth, and MaCurdy, 1981, and Schultz, 1980, for further discussion of these concepts and their interrelation.) In Figure 4.5, dots represent levels of desired labor supply for different individuals all of whom have the same property income (V) and who are alike in terms of all other *observed* determinants of labor supply except the wage rate (W). The fact that, at any given wage rate, different individuals supply different quantities of labor indicates that these individuals differ in terms of unobservable characteristics (e.g., tastes), ϵ. Dots that lie below the W axis refer to individuals such as the one at point Q in Figure 3.1 (note that the actual labor supply of any individual such as this one will be zero). The line $a'bc$ represents levels of desired labor supply for an individual whose taste variable ϵ is equal to zero. (Thus, the vertical distance between any given dot

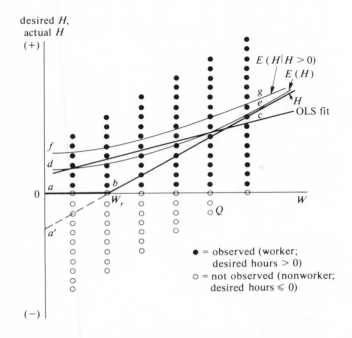

Figure 4.5. Alternative dimensions of labor supply

and the line $a'bc$ is the value of ϵ for the individual to whom that dot refers.) The broken line abc represents the structural labor supply schedule for an individual whose taste variable ϵ is equal to zero. Note that abc implies that this individual's actual labor supply is zero for all wage rates below the reservation level W_r, and that below W_r his desired supply, given by the line ba', is negative.

Property income and other observed characteristics determine each individual's reservation wage. (Thus, provided leisure is a normal good, an increase in property income would raise the reservation wage of an individual with $\epsilon = 0$, thereby shifting $a'bc$ up, reducing the length of the line segment ab, and shifting W_r to the left.) Income and substitution effects determine how each individual changes his labor supply in response to changes in the wage rate, that is, determine the slope of the line bc. Thus, estimates of the slope and intercept (or, equivalently, of the slope and location of the point *b*) of the structural labor supply schedule may be used to derive measures of income and substitution effects for someone with a *given* value of the unobservable taste variable ϵ.

Analyses of labor force participation in effect locate the wage level at which an individual's actual labor supply switches from zero to some positive amount (or, equivalently, examine the fraction of desired labor supply dots that lie above the *W* axis), the way in which a change in a variable such as *W* will change this fraction and the determinants of the point *b*. Analyses of the labor supply of workers are concerned with the average value of *H* for the dots that lie above the *W* axis and with the way in which this average changes when variables such as *W* change. Finally, analyses of total labor supply are concerned with the average value of *H* associated with all the dots shown in Figure 4.5 (note that all dots on or below the *W* axis have an *H* value of zero) and with the way in which this average value changes when variables such as *W* change.

As explained in previous sections, some of the procedures summarized in Table 4.1 may produce biased estimates of the parameters of the structural labor supply schedule *abc*, and thus of income effects and compensated and uncompensated wage effects. However, it need not follow that these procedures must also yield seriously biased estimates of relations that refer to the other three aspects of labor supply or that the biases are always in the same direction and of the same size. For example, Procedure I may produce a regression line like the one labeled "OLS fit" in Figure 4.5. That line is clearly a badly biased approximation to the labor supply schedule *abc*, but over most of its range it fits the labor supply of workers schedule $E[H \mid H > 0]$ rather well, and except for an approximately constant difference (i.e., a downward-biased intercept) also fits the total labor supply schedule $E[H]$ fairly satisfactorily. Thus, a badly biased method like Procedure I may turn out to be fairly useful for some purposes, even if it is seriously defective for others.

First, consider Procedure II. Most first-generation work treated estimates based on this method as estimates of the structural labor supply schedule. As noted earlier, however, such estimates are derived from least-squares regression for workers only; they may therefore produce biased measures of income and substitution effects. However, estimates obtained using Procedure II might instead be interpreted as approximations of the parameters that govern the labor supply of working persons – that is, $E[H \mid H > 0]$. If so, then elasticities derived from such estimates may be interpreted as approximations of the changes in the average labor supply of working persons that will be associated with changes in variables, such as the wage or property income. Such coefficients do not provide direct information on the behavior of total labor supply, that is, on the average supply of all persons (including persons whose labor supply is zero). However, some authors supplement their Procedure II estimates with estimates of a probability-of-working function (that is, with an analysis of participation), compute the elasticity of this probability with respect to W, V, and the like, and then add this elasticity to the elasticity derived using Procedure II. The result is then interpreted as the elasticity of total labor supply with respect to the variable in question.[23]

Next, consider Procedures I and IV. In most first-generation work, estimates derived under these procedures (particularly Procedure I) were interpreted as measures of structural labor supply parameters. Of course, the functions used in these procedures misspecify the complete supply function, since they assume that, say, a change in W will *always* affect H, even though in fact a change in W will affect H only when $W > M^*$; estimates derived from these procedures may therefore provide biased measures of income and substitution effects. However, estimates derived using either of these two methods might instead be treated as approximations of the parameters that govern total labor supply, $E[H]$. If so, then an elasticity derived under either procedure may be interpreted as an approximation to the elasticity of total labor supply $E[H]$ with respect to a given variable (the wage rate, property income, etc.). Note also that, at least in principle, one could fit a probability-of-working function and then *subtract* elasticities derived from this function from elasticities for total labor supply to yield elasticities of labor supply for working persons (that is, for $E[H \mid H > 0]$).

Next, consider Procedures III, V, and VI, all of which use Tobit or Tobit-like techniques. The estimated coefficients of functions for desired hours of work in these models may be used directly in calculating structural income, substitution, and own-wage elastici-

---

[23] For example, see Boskin (1973) and Kalachek and Raines (1970).

ties of labor supply. Moreover, these coefficients may be used to calculate participation probabilities for each observation, $P(H > 0)$ (for example, recall the discussion of (4.26)), and also to compute measures of $E[H | H > 0]$ and of $E[H]$. (For example, see Heckman, Killingsworth, and MaCurdy, 1981.)

Finally, consider Procedures VII and VIII. Here, estimated coefficients refer to the desired hours of work of given individuals and so may be used directly in calculating structural income, substitution, and own-wage elasticities: That is, when V changes while everything else (including taste factors embodied in λ) is held constant, the effect on the (desired) hours of work of a given individual is given by the coefficient on V in (4.30) or (4.31), and similarly for other variables. To derive effects of changes in given variables on participation, one may use the probit estimates of (4.28). Effects on the labor supply of working persons of changes in any given variable Z may be computed from (4.30) or (4.31) as $(\partial H / \partial Z) + [(\partial H / \partial \lambda) (\partial \lambda / \partial Z)]$, that is, as the sum of (i) the "direct" or "structural" effect of Z on H, $\partial H / \partial Z$, and (ii) the "indirect" or "taste" effect of Z on H that arises by virtue of the association between Z and the error term (or, equivalently, between Z and λ) within a sample of working persons, $[(\partial H / \partial \lambda) (\partial \lambda / \partial Z)]$. Effects on total labor supply may be computed using (4.28) and either (4.30) or (4.31) together: Estimates of (4.28) provide a measure of the probability $P(H > 0)$ that an individual will work, whereas, as just noted, (4.30) or (4.31), as appropriate, can be used to measure the hours worked by people who work $E[H | H > 0]$. Total labor supply may be written as $E[H] = P(H > 0)E[H | H > 0]$, and so changes in total labor supply with respect to any variable Z may be computed as

$$dE[H]/dZ = d\{P(H > 0)E[H | H > 0]\}/dZ$$
$$= E[H | H > 0] [\partial P(H > 0)/\partial Z]$$
$$+ P(H > 0)\{(\partial H/\partial Z) + [(\partial H/\partial \lambda) (\partial \lambda/\partial Z)]\}$$

that is, as the sum of (i) the change in labor supply stemming from the change in participation caused by the change in Z and (ii) the change in labor supply stemming from the change in hours worked by workers caused by the change in Z.

Comparison of estimates

With these conceptual preliminaries out of the way, I now consider estimates of the various dimensions of labor supply that have been obtained in second-generation studies, focusing on hours of work. Characteristics of the studies discussed here are summarized in Table 4.2, whereas the results themselves are set out in Tables 4.3–4.5. As in Chapter 3 (recall in particular Section 3.4), I have sometimes had to calculate the elasticities set out in Tables 4.3–4.5 using sample means provided by authors or (in some cases) informed guesses. Thus, the same caveats and cautionary remarks apply to these tables as apply to Tables 3.2–3.5.

Structural elasticities. Table 4.3 presents a number of estimates of structural elasticities derived in second-generation research: uncompensated and compensated (substitution) wage effects and the "total-income" effect (i.e., the difference between the uncompensated and compensated wage elasticity).

As implied in Table 4.3, and as will be discussed, the results of these second-generation studies are certainly not all of a piece: There are a number of anomalies, outliers, and the like. However, examination of these results reveals a number of patterns and "stylized facts," some of which differ from those in first-generation work.

First, although there are relatively few second-generation studies of male labor supply, the available results confirm the notion that male labor supply is considerably less sensitive to wage rates, property income, and the like than female labor supply. For example, most of the second-generation results for men imply that the gross wage elasticity is between -0.20 and 0.14. (The female gross wage elasticity is usually at least 0.60, and is often much higher.) Discarding studies with negative *compensated* elasticities narrows the range of *uncompensated* elasticities for U.S. men to -0.03 to 0.14.

As far as female labor supply is concerned, second-generation estimation methods that assume a continuous supply schedule (i.e., Procedures III, V, and VI) typically produce greater female labor supply elasticities than do second-generation techniques that allow for a discontinuous labor supply schedule (i.e., Procedures VII and VIII), whereas first-generation techniques (i.e., Procedures I and II)

Table 4.2. *Summary of data used in second-generation studies*

Study	Characteristics of sample	Construction of measures of *H*, *W*, *V*
Ashworth & Ulph (1981a)	Same as Brown, Levin, & Ulph (1976, 1981) (see Table 3.1), except individuals with second job excluded if either (i) gross wage on second job > overtime rate on first job or (ii) did not want to work more overtime on first job than actually worked	Same as Brown, Levin, & Ulph (1976, 1981) (see Table 3.1), except that *V* defined as net family income excluding own earnings
Blundell & Walker (1982)	Husbands, wives both of whom work, husband a manual worker, total weekly expenditures between £35 and £55 – FES	H = hours of work per week W = earnings ÷ H^a V = unearned income^{a,b}
Burtless & Hausman (1978)	Black husbands (otherwise, same as Hausman, 1980), excluding nonworkers	H = average of hours worked per week during first, fourth, and seventh surveys conducted during experiment W = hourly wage[b] V = nonwage income[b]
Cogan (1980a)	White wives age 30–44 – NLS	H = annual hours of work[b] W = hourly wage[b] V = husband's annual income
Cogan (1980b)	White wives not in school, disabled or retired, self and spouse not self-employed or farmer – PSID	H = annual hours of work[b] W = hourly wage[b] V = husband's earnings
Cogan (1981)	White wives age 30–44, self and spouse not self-employed or farmer – NLS	H = usual weekly hours × weeks worked in prior year W = earnings in prior year ÷ hours worked in prior year

Study	Sample	Variables
Dooley (1982)	Wives age 30–54 – USC	V = husband's earnings H = hours worked in survey week × weeks worked in prior year W = earnings ÷ H V = other income exclusive of earnings of family members self-employment income, Social Security, and public assistance benefits (separate variables included for husband's predicted income and actual – predicted husband's income)
Franz & Kawasaki (1981)	Married women – M	H = hours worked in survey week W = hourly wage[b] V = income of husband
Franz (1981) Ham (1982)	Same as Franz & Kawasaki (1981) Men age 25–50 in 1967, not retired during 1967–74 – PSID	Same as Franz & Kawasaki (1981) H = annual hours worked[b] W = predicted value of prior year's earnings ÷ prior year's H, derived from selection bias-corrected regression V = unearned income, including imputed rental income
Hanoch (1980b)	White wives, husband a wage earner and nonfarmer – SEO	H = hours worked in survey week × weeks worked in prior year W = earnings in survey week ÷ hours worked in survey week V = husband's earnings + property income + transfer payments + other regular nonwage income

Table 4.2. (cont.)

Study	Characteristics of sample	Construction of measures of H, W, V
Hausman (1980)	Black female household heads in Gary Income Maintenance Experiment, observed during experiment (households with preexperiment income > 2.4 times poverty line were excluded from experiment)	H = 1 if worked during middle 2 years of experiment, = 0 otherwise W = hourly wage[b] V = nonlabor income[b]
Hausman (1981a)	Husbands age 25–55, not self-employed, farmers, or disabled; wives of these husbands; female household heads – PSID	H = annual hours worked[b] W = hourly wage[b] V = imputed return to financial assets
Hausman & Wise (1976)	Husbands in New Jersey–Pennsylvania Income Maintenance Experiment, observed during experiment (households with preexperiment income > 1.5 times poverty line were excluded from experiment)	H = average of weekly hours worked recorded during 12 quarterly surveys conducted during experiment, × weeks worked in year prior to experiment W = earnings ÷ hours worked during weeks covered in second through fifth surveys during experiment[c] V = family income excluding wage income of husband[c]
Hausman & Wise (1977)	Same as Hausman & Wise (1976), except that data refer to year prior to experiment	H = earnings during year prior to experiment ÷ W W = average of earnings ÷ hours worked during weeks covered in second through fifth surveys conducted during experiment

Study	Sample	Variable definitions
Heckman (1976c)	White wives age 30–44 – NLS	V = family income (including imputed asset income) excluding wage income of husband
Heckman (1980)	White wives age 30–44, husband not farmer – NLS	H = weeks worked × average hours worked per week W = usual wage V = assets[b] H = annual earnings ÷ W W = usual hourly wage V = assets[b]
Layard, Barton, & Zabalza (1980)	Wives age ≤60, not self-employed – GHS	H = annual weeks worked × usual weekly hours W = predicted value of annual earnings ÷ H, derived from OLS wage regression[a] V = net annual unearned income, including imputed rent, interest and dividends (husband's W, derived as for wife's W, included as separate variable)[a]
Nakamura, Nakamura, & Cullen (1979)	Wives with no nonrelatives in household – CC	H = hours worked in survey week × weeks worked in prior year W = annual earnings ÷ H V = husband's earnings + asset income
Nakamura & Nakamura (1981)	Wives – CC, USC	H = hours worked in survey week × weeks worked in prior year W = annual earnings ÷ H[a] V = husband's earnings + asset income[d]

Table 4.2. (cont.)

Study	Characteristics of sample	Construction of measures of H, W, V
Ransom (1982)	Husbands age 30–50, wives (no self-employment or piecework income for either spouse) – PSID	H = hours of work per week W = either usual wage (husbands) or predicted wage, derived from selection bias-corrected wage equation (wives)[a] V = after-tax income other than earnings[a]
H. Rosen (1976b)	White wives age 30–44, not receiving public assistance – NLS	H = hours of work per year[b] W = reported compensation ÷ period of time over which compensation paid[c] V = gross family income excluding wife's earnings[c]
Ruffell (1981)	Same as Glaister, McGlone, & Ruffell (1981) (see Table 3.1)	Same as Glaister, McGlone, & Ruffell (1981) (see Table 3.1)
Schultz (1980)	Wives, husband not full-time student or in armed forces – SEO	H = hours worked last week × weeks worked last year W = last week's earnings ÷ last week's hours of work, adjusted for regional cost-of-living differences[a] V = nonemployment income
Trussell & Abowd (1980)	Wives age 25–45 who between age 12 and 30 delivered at least one child – NSFG	H = annual hours of work[b] W = hourly wage[b] V = other family income[b]

Wales (1978) Husbands working ≥400 hours per year, free to work desired hours of work, not holding second job, not farmer, not receiving overtime/ bonuses/welfare, living in detached one-family dwelling, drives car to work, wife not working – PSID

H = annual hours of work
W = earnings ÷ H^a
V = residual (difference between expenditure and earnings)

Wales & Woodland (1979)
Zabalza (1983) Same as Wales (1978)

Wives age <60, not self-employed, with working husband age <65 and not self-employed – GHS

Same as Wales (1978)
H = hours worked in survey week (in intervals, according to marginal tax rate value)
W = hourly earnings
V = husband's earnings + unearned family income

Note: CC, Census of Canada, Statistics Canada; FES, Family Expenditure Survey, Office of Population Censuses and Surveys, United Kingdom; GHS, General Household Survey, Office of Population Censuses and Surveys, United Kingdom; M, Microcensus, Statistiches Bundesamt, Federal Republic of Germany; NLS, National Longitudinal Survey, Center for Human Resource Research, Ohio State University; NSFG, National Survey of Family Growth, National Center for Health Statistics; PSID, Panel Study of Income Dynamics, Survey Research Center, University of Michigan; SEO, Survey of Economic Opportunity, Office of Economic Opportunity; USC, U. S. Census, Bureau of the Census, Department of Commerce.

[a]Budget line linearized at equilibrium hours of work, equilibrium marginal tax rate.
[b]Not otherwise defined.
[c]Budget line linearized at standard level of hours of work, marginal tax rate applicable to income at standard level of hours of work.
[d]Taxes payable at zero hours of work subtracted from value of variable.

191

produce elasticities that are smaller than those derived under either kind of second-generation methodology.[24] (See, in particular, the results of Cogan, 1980a, and Schultz, 1980, on this point.) For example, as noted in Chapter 3, most first-generation estimates of the female gross own-wage elasticity are in between 0.1 and 0.9, whereas second-generation continuous-schedule methods shown in Table 4.3 often yield estimates in excess of 2.0, and most second-generation discontinuous-schedule procedures yield elasticities between about 0.6 and 1.1.[25]

Although the second-generation studies shown in Table 4.3 seem fairly consistent in these respects, they differ markedly in others. For example, Schultz (1980), who uses Procedure III (thereby assuming a continuous supply schedule), reports wage elasticities for women that are much lower than those obtained by Hanoch (1980b) and Heckman (1980), both of whom allow for discontinuity. However, Schultz's wage elasticities are fairly similar to those obtained by Cogan (1980b, 1981), who also allows for discontinuity. As noted in Table 4.2, these four studies use somewhat different data and quite different measures of "exogenous income" (the V of the previous discussion); perhaps these differences account for the differences in their results. Note also that Hausman's results in 1981a imply total-income elasticities for women that are much greater, in absolute value, than those obtained in most other second-generation work. However, a possible reason for this is that Hausman constrains the income effect to be negative (as do a few other studies, e.g., ones that rely on a CES direct utility function).

The most striking anomaly, however, is the set of results of Nakamura, Nakamura, and Cullen (1979, for Canadian women) and Nakamura and Nakamura (1981, for both Canadian and U.S.

[24] Procedure IV is hard to categorize. It recognizes the endogeneity of W but fits the (reduced-form) hours of work equation using least squares. Although Heckman (1976c, 1980) calls it a "conventional" regression procedure, first-generation research appears never to have used it.

[25] Thus, these patterns are very much in keeping with the findings of Wales and Woodland (1980). They perform not an empirical study but a simulation study, aimed at seeing how well different techniques succeed at estimating *known* parameters when applied to "synthetic" data constructed using those parameters and using randomly generated numbers. They find that, in general, second-generation techniques do much better at this task and that least-squares procedures typically produce downward-biased estimates of structural parameters.

Table 4.3. *Estimated elasticities for hours worked by given individuals in second-generation studies*

Study	Sample, procedure used	Wage elasticity		Total-income elasticity
		Uncompensated	Compensated	
Estimates for men				
Hausman & Wise (1976)	Husbands – lbc-s corrected for truncation of sample to families in poverty (constant elasticity lsf)	0.14	n.a.	−0.02[a]
Hausman & Wise (1977)	Husbands – corrected for truncation of sample to families in poverty (constant elasticity lsf)	0.09	0.11	−0.01
Ham (1982)	Men age 25–50 – 2SLS			
	Full sample	−0.16	−0.05	−0.11
	Subsample with H unconstrained	−0.14	−0.08	−0.06
	Subsample with H unconstrained (corrected for selection bias)	−0.14	−0.06	−0.08
Ransom (1982)	Husbands age 30–50 – ML, lbc (quadratic family duf)			
	Wife's $H > 0$	0.00 to 0.04	0.08 to 0.09	−0.05 to −0.08
	Wife's $H = 0$	−0.03 to 0.05	0.19 to 0.24	−0.20 to −0.21
Wales (1978)	Husbands – ML, fc (generalized Cobb–Douglas iuf)	−0.20	n.a.	−0.12
Burtless & Hausman (1978)	Black husbands – ML, fc, and cbc (ep, eh) (constant elasticity lsf)	0.00	n.a.	−0.05[a]
Wales & Woodland (1979)	Husbands – ML (CES duf)			
	Lbc	0.06	0.77	−0.70
	Cbc (eh)	0.14	0.84	−0.70

193

Table 4.3. *(cont.)*

Study	Sample, procedure used	Wage elasticity		Total-income elasticity
		Uncompensated	Compensated	
Hausman (1981a)	Husbands – ML, fc, and cbc (ep, eh) (linear lsf)	0.00 to 0.03	0.95 to 1.00	– 0.95 to – 1.03
Blundell & Walker (1982)	U.K. husbands – ML, lbc (family ds using Gpf, corrected for selection bias in requiring wife's $H > 0$)	– 0.23	0.13	– 0.36
Ashworth & Ulph (1981a)	U.K. husbands <65			
	OLS – lbc (quadratic lsf)	– 0.00 to 0.06	0.15 to 0.31	– 0.09 to – 0.31
	ML – lbc			
	CES iuf	– 0.13	0.23	– 0.36
	restricted generalized CES iuf	– 0.38	0.19	– 0.57
	generalized CES iuf	– 0.38	0.19	– 0.57
	ML – cbc (eh)			
	CES iuf	– 0.07	0.50	– 0.57
	restricted generalized CES iuf	– 0.16	0.48	– 0.64
	generalized CES iuf	– 0.33	0.29	– 0.62
Ruffell (1981)	U.K. husbands <65 (quadratic lsf)			
	OLS – lbc	– 0.07	0.09	– 0.16
	ML – cbc (eh)	– 0.07	0.04	– 0.11
	MD – cbc (eh, eb)	– 0.05	0.03	– 0.08
Estimates for women				
Heckman (1976c)	White women age 30–44			
	Procedure IV	1.46	1.48	– 0.02
	Procedure VI	4.31	4.35	– 0.04

Cogan (1980a)	White women age 30–44			
	Procedure II	1.14	1.17	−0.03
	Procedure III	3.50	3.60	−0.10
	Procedure VI	2.83	2.91	−0.09
Schultz (1980)	White women age 35–44 (lbc)			
	Procedure I	0.16	0.21	−0.05
	Procedure II	0.13	0.19	−0.05
	Procedure III	0.65	0.83	−0.18
	Black women age 35–44 (lbc)			
	Procedure I	0.60	0.34	0.26
	Procedure II	0.42	0.41	0.01
	Procedure III	1.04	0.56	0.48
Trussell & Abowd (1980)	White women age 25–45			
	Procedure VI	4.50	n.a.	−0.41[a]
	Black women age 25–45			
	Procedure VI	2.93	n.a.	≈0[a]
Heckman (1980)	White women age 30–44			
	Procedure IV	2.26	2.26	≈0
	Procedure VII	1.47	1.47	≈0
	Procedure IV[b]	14.79	14.79	≈0
	Procedure VII[b]	6.62	6.62	≈0
	Procedure V[b,c]	4.47	4.47	≈0
Hanoch (1980b)	White women age 30–44			
	Procedure VIII (market wage–reservation wage version of discontinuous-hours model)			
	– with no "corner" in weeks worked	0.64	0.81	−0.17
	– with "corner" in weeks worked	0.42	0.54	−0.13

Table 4.3. *(cont.)*

Study	Sample, procedure used	Wage elasticity		Total-income elasticity
		Uncompensated	Compensated	
Cogan (1980b)	White women age 30–44			
	Procedure VI	2.45	2.64	−0.19
	Desired hours–reservation hours version of discontinuous-hours model			
	– OLS	0.89	0.93	−0.04
	– Procedure VII	1.14	1.19	−0.05
Cogan (1981)	White women age 30–44			
	Procedure VI	2.10	2.18	−0.08
	Procedure VII (desired hours–reservation hours version of discontinuous-hours model)	0.65	0.68	−0.03
Nakamura, Nakamura, & Cullen (1979)	Canadian wives – Procedure VIII			
	Age 30–34	−0.17	0.00	−0.17
	Age 35–39	−0.20	−0.16	−0.04
	Age 40–44	−0.32	−0.26	−0.06
Nakamura & Nakamura (1981)	Wives – Procedure VIII, lbc			
	Canada			
	Age 30–34	−0.24	0.11	−0.36
	Age 35–39	−0.17	−0.12	−0.05
	Age 40–44	−0.05	0.14	−0.19
	U.S.			
	Age 30–34	−0.27	0.23	−0.50

Study		Col 1	Col 2	Col 3
	Age 35–39	−0.31	−0.12	−0.19
	Age 40–44	−0.09	0.18	−0.27
Dooley (1982)	Wives – Procedure VII			
	Whites			
	Age 30–34	3.66	4.14	−0.48
	Age 35–39	15.24	15.35	−0.11
	Age 40–44	4.28	4.73	−0.45
	Blacks			
	Age 30–34	0.67	1.01	−0.35
	Age 35–39	−0.34	−0.17	−0.17
	Age 40–44	−0.89	−1.06	0.18
Ransom (1982)	Wives, husband age 30 – 50 – ML, lbc (quadratic family duf)	0.40 to 0.42	0.46 to 0.50	−0.05 to −0.09
Hausman (1980)	Black household heads – ML, fc, cbc (ep, eh) (linear lsf)	0.05	0.16	−0.11
Hausman (1981a)	ML, fc, cbc (ep, eh) (linear lsf)			
	Wives	0.91 to 1.00	0.44 to 0.50	−0.45 to −0.47
	Female household heads	0.46 to 0.53	0.58 to 0.77	−0.12 to −0.24
Layard, Barton, & Zabalza (1980)	U.K. wives age ≤60			
	No allowance for taxes			
	Procedure I (evaluated at overall means)	0.43	0.49	−0.06
	Procedure II (evaluated at workers' means)	0.08	0.09	−0.02
	Procedure III			
	evaluated at overall means	0.78	0.97	−0.19
	evaluated at workers' means	0.44	0.63	−0.19
	Lbc (eh, eb)			
	Procedure II (evaluated at workers' means)	0.06	0.06	−0.01

Table 4.3. *(cont.)*

Study	Sample, procedure used	Wage elasticity		Total-income elasticity
		Uncompensated	Compensated	
Blundell & Walker (1982)	U.K. wives – ML, lbc (family ds using Gpf, corrected for selection bias in requiring wife's $H > 0$)			
	Husband's H unrationed			
	No children	0.43	0.65	– 0.22
	One child	0.10	0.32	– 0.22
	Two children	– 0.19	0.03	– 0.22
	Husband's H rationed			
	No children	0.64	0.83	– 0.19
	One child	0.09	0.28	– 0.19
	Two children	– 0.30	– 0.11	– 0.19
Zabalza (1983)	U.K. wives ≤ 60 – ML (ordered probit analysis), cbc (ep) (CES duf)	1.59	1.82	– 0.23
Ashworth & Ulph (1981a)	U.K. wives, husband <65 OLS – lbc (quadratic lsf)			
	ML – lbc	– 0.09 to – 0.21	– 0.04 to – 0.23	0.02 to – 0.05
	CES iuf	– 0.19	0.29	– 0.48
	Restricted generalized CES iuf	0.21	0.30	– 0.09
	Generalized CES iuf	0.12	0.26	– 0.14
	ML – cbc (eh)			
	CES iuf	0.63	0.84	– 0.21
	Restricted generalized CES iuf	0.57	0.81	– 0.24
	Generalized CES iuf	0.32	0.55	– 0.23

Ruffell (1981) — U.K. wives, husband <65 (quadratic lsf)			
OLS – lbc	−0.00	0.04	−0.04
ML – cbc (eh)	0.43	0.51	−0.08
MD – cbc (eh, eb)	0.72	0.77	−0.05
Franz & Kawasaki (1981) West German wives Procedure VII	1.08	1.28	−0.20
Franz (1981) West German wives Modified Procedure VII[a]	1.37	1.66	−0.29

Note: All elasticities refer to hours of work per year. n.a., not available (not enough information available to permit derivation of elasticity). Total-income elasticity is defined as $W(\partial H/\partial V)$, equal to the difference between the uncompensated and compensated wage elasticities of hours of work. Estimation technique: OLS, ordinary least squares estimation; 2SLS, two-stage least squares estimation; ML, maximum likelihood estimation; MD, minimum distance estimation. Basis of specification: Gpf, Gorman polar form of expenditure function; duf, direct utility function; iuf, indirect utility function; ds, demand system; lsf, labor supply function; fc, allowance for fixed costs of working. Treatment of taxes: lbc, linearized budget constraint; lbc-s, linearized budget constraint, evaluated at standard level of hours of work; cbc, complete budget constraint. Error structure in cbc models: ep, variation (error term) in preferences (e.g., utility or marginal rate of substitution function); eh, errors (of optimization or measurement) in hours of work; eb, errors of measurement of budget constraint (e.g., wage rate or marginal tax rate).

[a] Elasticity of hours of work with respect to property income, $(\partial H/\partial V)/(V/H)$.

[b] Uses an instrumental variable for years of work experience in wage equation, to correct for possible endogeneity of this variable.

[c] No Stage 2 (wage equation) results available; wage elasticity computed using Stage 2 results obtained under Procedure VII instead.

[d] Reduced form hours equation estimated by Tobit; wage equation estimated as under Procedure VII.

women): In contrast with virtually all other first- *and* second-generation research, their Procedure VIII results based on Census data imply uncompensated wage elasticities for female hours of work that are *negative* (and in most cases both statistically significant at reasonable levels and fairly large in absolute value). One possible reason for this is that Nakamura, Nakamura, and Cullen do not include educational attainment in their specification of the labor supply schedule. (Most other research suggests that years of schooling is significantly associated with hours of work, even when the wage – and thus schooling's effect on the wage – is held constant. This might occur if, for example, educational attainment were positively associated with nonpecuniary compensation – better working conditions, etc.) Indeed, Dooley (1982), who does include education in the labor supply function, gets positive (and implausibly large) estimates in his study of Census data. Another possible reason for the negative elasticities of Nakamura, Nakamura, and Cullen is that, in contrast with most other second-generation work, Nakamura, Nakamura, and Cullen do not include a measure of actual work experience in their specification of the wage function or the probability-of-working function.[26] (Note that,

---

[26] Nakamura, Nakamura, and Cullen (1979) use Canadian (and, in 1981, also U.S.) Census data, which do not contain measures of women's actual work experience. (Most other second-generation research uses data such as the National Longitudinal Survey that do contain such measures.) Since they therefore cannot include a work experience variable in their wage equation (as in most other second-generation research), they instead include two proxy variables – age *at first marriage* and number of children age 6 or less – and fit their wage equation using data on women within specified age ranges (e.g., age 30–34, 35–39, etc.). However, it is possible that, even within a particular age range, the two proxy variables they use do not reflect actual work experience, or even current age, very well. Their wage equation also includes a variable J_a that is intended to measure the opportunity for jobs in the individual's area of residence a; J_a is calculated as $\Sigma_o f_o E_{ao}/P_{fa}$, where o refers to occupational category (managerial, clerical, etc.), f is the proportion of national employment in that category that is female, E is total employment (men and women) in the occupation in area a, and P is the population of women age 15 or over residing in the area. Thus, J_a may in effect be a crude measure of the probability of being employed (and thus an imperfect substitute for the selectivity variable λ); to the extent that occupation and wage rates go together, it may also be endogenous. Finally, although Nakamura, Nakamura, and Cullen (1979) and Nakamura and Nakamura (1981) offer several explanations for why their results differ so sharply from those of others, none seems particularly persuasive. For example, although they distinguish between participation and hours of work and allow for possible discontinuities in the supply

in second-generation procedures such as their Procedure VIII, these functions are closely connected with the hours-of-work function, so that errors of specification in the former may have important consequences on estimation of the latter.)

Alternative estimates for total labor supply. Both the analyses just presented and the limited empirical evidence summarized in Table 4.3 seem to suggest that first-generation methods may not yield satisfactory estimates of structural labor supply parameters. However, as suggested earlier, it is possible that the results of first-generation procedures may constitute approximations of different kinds of parameters (even if first-generation research rarely took them as such): For example, Procedure II results may in effect approximate the labor supply of workers, $E[H \mid H > 0]$, Procedure I results may in effect approximate total labor supply, $E[H]$, and so on.

There is not much evidence on this point, but what is available – some of which appears in Table 4.4 – lends some support to this notion, though not in a particularly conclusive fashion. For example, Schultz (1980) finds that, considered as approximations to the elasticity of total labor supply, Procedure II results are fairly close to those obtained using Procedure III. (In results not shown in Table 4.4., Schultz also finds that conventional total labor supply elasticities, computed as the sum of elasticities derived from two separate procedures – a logit analysis of the probability of working and Procedure I or II estimates of the hours worked by persons at work – are very close to the total-hours elasticities implied by his

schedule (Nakamura and Nakamura, 1981, p. 478), numerous other second-generation studies also do so (and all of those find positive, not negative, wage elasticities for women). Likewise, although they point out that the work experience variables used in wage functions in most other studies may be endogenous (Nakamura and Nakamura, 1981, p. 480) and this may overstate the wage elasticity of female labor supply, Heckman (1980) finds that his estimated wage elasticities are *particularly* large when he uses an instrumental variables procedure to correct for such endogeneity. Further, although they include a detailed array of variables in their hours equation to "control for child status" (Nakamura and Nakamura, 1981, p. 478), unlike most other second-generation work, they also include a child status variable in their *wage* equation. Hence, their wage equation may really be a hybrid of labor supply (reservation wage) and labor demand (market wage) factors rather than a wage equation as such.

Table 4.4.   *Estimated elasticities for total labor supply*

Study	Sample, procedure used	Wage	Exogenous income
		\multicolumn{2}{c}{Elasticity}	
Rosen (1976b)	White women age 30–44		
	Procedure I	1.60	n.a.
	Procedure III	2.20	n.a.
Schultz (1980)	White women age 35–44		
	Procedure I	0.16	– 0.12
	Procedure III	0.25	– 0.02
	Black women age 35–44		
	Procedure I	0.60	0.02
	Procedure III	0.59	0.02
Hanoch (1980b)	White women age 30–44		
	Procedure VIII	1.44	– 0.92
Zabalza (1983)	U.K. women age < 60		
	ML – ordered probit analysis		
	of CES duf (cbc, ep)	2.00	– 0.18

Note: All figures are elasticities of hours of work per year with respect to indicated variable and refer to change in hours of work, on average, in the population as a whole, including both workers and persons initially not working. n.a., not available (not enough information available to permit derivation of elasticity). (Also see notes to Table 4.3.)

Procedure III results.)[27] The wage elasticity estimates of H. Rosen (1976b) and Hanoch (1980b), and Hanoch's estimated income elasticity, are considerably larger than Schultz's estimates. However, as noted in Table 4.2, these authors use somewhat different data and different measures of exogenous income. It is, thus, not surprising that their estimates differ – though just what accounts for the magnitude of the differences is hard to say.

[27] Note that this means only that the two sets of elasticities are close to each other when they are evaluated at sample means. As Schultz (1980) points out, they diverge to the left or to the right of the sample means, as shown in Figure 4.5. (See also the concluding comments in Tobin, 1958.) The point is that although ordinary least squares is the best *linear* estimator of a given conditional function (e.g., hours of work, conditional on positive hours of work), other estimators – including, of course, nonlinear ones – may be superior to ordinary least squares.

Table 4.5. *Values of desired and reservation hours of work* (H *and* H₀) *implied by selected second-generation studies*

		Implied value of:	
Study	Group considered	Desired hours (H)	Reservation hours (H_0)
Hanoch (1980b)	Married women 30–44		
	Workers	1,099	820
Heckman (1980)	Married women 30–44		
	Workers	1,427	1,383
	Nonworkers	1,289	1,300
Cogan (1980b)	Married women		
	Workers	1,361	1,126
	Nonworkers	1,101	1,143
Cogan (1981)	Married women 30–44		
	Workers	1,418	1,257
	Nonworkers	1,145	1,318

Note: All figures are for hours of work per year and are derived using estimated coefficients and mean values of all variables for the indicated group (workers or nonworkers).

Discontinuities in the supply schedule. Most research that explicitly considers discontinuity in the supply schedule appears to suggest that such discontinuity is substantial; Table 4.5 summarizes the implications of several of these studies regarding the "point of discontinuity," that is, the minimum or reservation level of hours. On this point the studies seem to have remarkably similar implications. For example, Hanoch (1980b) finds that, for workers, actual hours of work H are on average only about a third greater than the level of reservation hours H_0; Cogan (1980b, 1981) and Heckman (1980) get rather similar results.

Of course, the fact that a model that allows for discontinuity produces estimates of this kind is not necessarily conclusive proof that the labor supply schedule is actually discontinuous (even if such estimates are entirely consistent with this view). For example, it may simply be the case that the labor supply schedule is continuous but changes slope considerably (so that, within the range of wage rates earned by most working persons, the slope is much flatter than it is at lower wage rates), as shown in Figure 4.6. In other words, one can

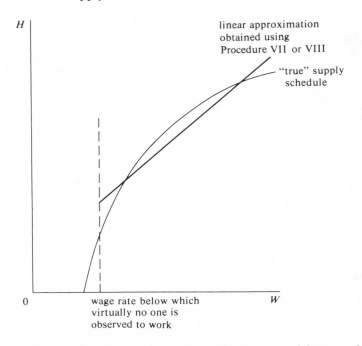

Figure 4.6. Labor supply discontinuity versus labor supply nonlinearity

in some circumstances interpret an hours-of-work function such as (4.30) (in the case of Procedure VII) or (4.31) (in the case of Procedure VIII) not as a discontinuous labor supply schedule but rather as a simple linear approximation (within the relevant range of wage rates) to a curvilinear but continuous schedule. (For further discussion of this issue, see Heckman, 1980; Cogan, 1980b, 1981.)

Methods for analyzing taxation. Finally, what do the estimates shown in Table 4.3 suggest about the effects of adopting the lbc versus the cbc approach? Unfortunately, not much. Of the cbc studies of U.S. data, Wales and Woodland (1979) assume a CES direct utility function, thereby forcing the estimated total-income elasticity to be negative; the other U.S. cbc studies (Burtless and Hausman, 1978; Hausman, 1980, 1981a) impose a negative total-income elasticity directly, in estimation. Likewise, Zabalza's (1983) cbc study of U.K. data assumes a CES direct utility function. Although these cbc studies' results certainly differ from those obtained in roughly comparable lbc studies, it is, therefore, difficult to tell how much of the difference is due to treatment of the budget constraint and how much is due to enforcing a negative total-income elasticity. Finally, the cbc studies by Ashworth and Ulph (1981a) and Ruffell (1981) of U.K. data use samples restricted to persons working at least eight hours per week but do not correct for the potential selection bias involved in this restriction.

4.7. Second-generation studies: summary and conclusions

Having struggled through probits, Tobits, fixed costs, sample truncation, and other second-generation topics, the reader may well wonder whether it has all been worthwhile and, more generally, whether the money and time that have been devoted to second-generation research have resulted in anything useful.

From a purely empirical standpoint, the cynic might well say, "Not much." Second-generation research indicates that structural responses (income and substitution effects) are considerably greater for women than for men, but this simply confirms first-generation findings. If first-generation results provide a dauntingly wide range of estimates of such responses, however, the same is pretty much true of second-generation work. As a simpleminded example of this problem, note that the second-generation work reported in Table 4.3 provides estimates of the uncompensated wage elasticity of female labor supply of anywhere between -0.89 and $+15.24$. This is not quite so bad as to merit Johnson's caustic remark (1976, p. 107, note 9) about the elasticity of substitution in production, "In recent years, economists have narrowed its value down to a range between zero and infinity," but it certainly comes close.

Of course, second-generation work is not all concerned with exactly the same set of people and, as implied by Table 4.2, second-generation work that does analyze exactly the same set of people (e.g., married white women age 30–44) does not always do so in exactly the same way. That there are differences, even substantial ones, between one set of results and another in *either* first- *or* second-generation work is therefore hardly very surprising. In this regard, it is particularly important to recall the caveat noted several times already: Most of the elasticities reported in Table 4.3 (like most of the elasticities reported in Table 3.2) are not fixed numbers but rather are functions of, for example, the mean values of variables, such as the wage rate and the level of labor supply – variables that are often defined and measured quite differently in different studies. Thus, comparisons across studies are inherently rather hazardous. Comparisons of this kind might be considerably easier to make if authors were to make it standard operating procedure to provide mean values (and, perhaps, standard deviations and interquartile ranges) of all of the variables used in their studies; unfortunately, however, not all authors do so.

Although second-generation research has certainly not succeeded in pinning down structural labor supply response elasticities any more precisely than first-generation research, it has nevertheless been productive in other more subtle ways. First, as Table 4.3 indicates, this work suggests that female labor supply responses are somewhat larger than was apparent in first-generation research. (Although hardly copper bottomed, this conclusion is on at least somewhat firmer footing than are conclusions about the precise magnitude of such responses. This is because, as indicated in Table 4.3, many second-generation studies provide not only second-generation but also first-generation estimates for the *same* sample. Thus, whereas comparisons of results across studies are not always convincing, comparisons of results for given studies are often fairly illuminating.)

Second, and perhaps most important, whereas second-generation research has hardly provided firm empirical findings, it has at least provided a much more solid analytical framework for use in deriving empirical findings. (Indeed, part of the reason why the range of results in second-generation research is as large as it is is probably that the researcher now has a variety of different models and procedures from which to choose, and so can analyze labor supply with or without fixed costs of labor market entry, with or without correction for taxes, etc.) Ten years of research – starting with the discussion of sample truncation by Cain and Watts (1973a), sample selectivity by Gronau (1974) and Lewis (1974), and Heckman's seminal paper on participation and hours of work (1974b) – is not a very long time in the life of a discipline; the most interesting work, and more precise empirical answers, are yet to come.

5

Dynamic labor supply models

In this chapter, I will consider theoretical and empirical analyses of labor supply in a dynamic setting. Such analyses have attracted increasing attention in recent years; it is not hard to see why. First, analyzing the ways in which decisions are taken with an eye to the future, and in which the consequences of decisions are distributed through time, is an exciting and demanding intellectual enterprise. Second, dynamic labor supply models are a response to an important empirical challenge: to develop a coherent story that can explain and illuminate a wide variety of "stylized empirical facts" about the lifecycle behavior of men and women that appear with surprising regularity in a variety of different kinds of data. Such stylized facts about the life cycle include the following:

1. In general, data for men suggest that the time profiles of labor supply or market time, wage rates (earnings per hour of market time), and earnings per year are all concave. That is, each of these variables tends to rise rapidly early in life but rises much more slowly in middle age. Indeed, both annual hours of work and annual earnings typically decline, among men, as the age of retirement approaches, with the peak in annual hours of work preceding the peak in annual earnings. On the other hand, wage rates – earnings per hour of market work – do not seem to decline, or, if they do fall, decrease only slightly at the end of working life. Thus, the decline in annual earnings that usually occurs toward the end of working life is apparently due primarily to a decline in hours of work per year rather than to a decline in wage rates.

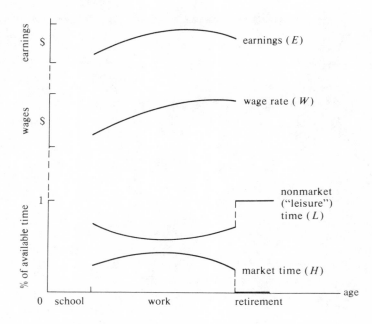

Figure 5.1.   Stylized facts about the life cycle

2. The typical man spends the first part of his life in school, often starting to work while still attending school; after leaving school (usually after the minimum school-leaving age), he generally works more or less continuously until retirement; once he retires, he usually remains out of the labor force until death.

3. The typical woman alternates, or "cycles," between working in the home and working in the market after leaving school. However, many women who have left school either work more or less continuously until retirement or else spend little or no time in the labor force. (See Heckman, 1978a; Heckman and Willis, 1977, 1979; and Mincer and Ofek, 1979, for a summary of some of the evidence on this issue.)

Figure 5.1 is a stylized representation of the first two of these empirical regularities.[1] Much has been done to develop models of

---

[1] For empirical evidence underlying these stylized facts about the life cycle, see the age–earnings, age–wage, and other profiles presented by Becker (1975c, pp. 85–92), Ghez (1975, pp. 58–60), Heckman (1976a, pp. 248–9), Mincer (1974, pp. 66–9, 71),

labor supply dynamics and to advance understanding of the processes that generate these empirical regularities. However, there is still no single coherent model that predicts all of them; much remains to be done. In the present chapter, I will discuss recent developments in the analysis of dynamic labor supply models, starting with a general overview of such models and then turning to a more detailed discussion of theoretical and empirical analyses of two main kinds of dynamic models of labor supply. In the first, wages are exogenous, whereas property income (the V of the previous chapters) is endogenous; in the second, both wages and property income are endogenous.

5.1. Dynamic labor supply models: an overview

The simplest way to extend the simple one-period labor supply model of Chapter 1 to multiple periods – to make that static model dynamic – is to treat leisure at any two different dates as two different goods (and similarly for consumption). Thus, at the most general level, one would specify the function for multiple period or lifetime utility, U, as

$$(5.1) \quad U = U[C(0), L(0), C(1), L(1), \ldots, C(T), L(T)]$$

where $L(t)$ is leisure during period t, $C(t)$ is consumption during period t, and the individual's lifetime starts at $t = 0$ and ends at $t = T$. (Compare (5.1) with equation (1.1).)

The next step is to specify the dynamic or lifetime budget constraint subject to which lifetime utility, U, is maximized. In many dynamic labor supply models, it is assumed that credit markets are perfect, so that the individual may save or borrow at an exogenously given market rate of interest r subject to the requirement that he must at least "break even" (have a positive or zero net worth, Z) at the end of his life. Let $Z(0)$ denote the level of net worth that the individual possesses at the start of "life" (i.e., as of $t = 0$, which

---

and J. P. Smith (1977b, pp. 213–16, 218–19, 220–4). It is worth emphasizing that this is *stylized* evidence on life cycle behavior, since nearly all of the empirical profiles presented by these authors trace earnings, wages, and the like for "synthetic cohorts" of different individuals at different ages at the *same* point in time (that is, as observed in a cross section "snapshot") rather than for a true cohort (i.e., a panel or longitudinal data set) of the same individuals over time. (For discussion of synthetic cohort data, see Section 5.4.)

could of course mean the start of his "life" as an economic agent rather than his date of birth as such). Then the individual's net worth Z will change over time according to the relation

(5.2) $Z(t + 1) - Z(t) = rZ(t) + W(t) H(t) - P(t) C(t)$

with $Z(0) = Z_0$, an exogenously given constant, and subject to the requirement that $Z(T + 1) \geq 0$, where $Z(t)$, $W(t)$, and $P(t)$ refer, respectively, to the individual's net worth and to the wage rate and price level as of time t. Note that $rZ(t)$ is equivalent to the V of the static model, since it represents interest earnings on the individual's net worth as of t, and that (5.2) is therefore identical to the budget constraint of the static model (see equation (1.2)) save in one important respect: $Z(t + 1) - Z(t)$, the *change* in the individual's net worth between t and $t + 1$, need not be zero. Rather, if the right-hand side of (5.2) is positive – meaning that the individual's income $rZ(t) + W(t) H(t)$ exceeds his expenditures on consumption goods $P(t) C(t)$ – then the individual is saving (adding to his net worth), whereas if the right-hand side of (5.2) is negative – meaning that the individual's income is less than his consumption spending – then he is borrowing or dissaving (reducing his net worth). Either way, (5.2) indicates that property or assets, Z, can be accumulated (or "decumulated") over time and therefore that, in a life cycle framework, property *income $rZ(t)$* is a choice variable, because it is a result of prior decisions to borrow, save, and so forth that affect today's net worth $Z(t)$. (See Cotterman, 1981; and J.P. Smith, 1977a, b, 1980b.)[2]

---

[2] Some attempts to introduce dynamic considerations into the static models of previous chapters modify such models even less than do equations (5.1)–(5.2). For example, Pfouts (1960) simply adds savings, S, to both the single-period utility function and the single-period budget constraint. Thus, under his formulation, in each period the individual maximizes $u = u(C, L, S)$ subject to the constraint $PC + S = WH + V$, where V = property income = rZ, r is the rate of interest, and Z is the current stock of assets. This kind of model is a substantial simplification of the dynamic models discussed in this chapter, but its implications are not entirely appealing. For example, it ignores the fact that savings are undertaken to permit consumption of leisure and consumer goods (including bequests as a special kind of consumer good) in the future; and it implies that changes in the interest rate r affect consumption, leisure, labor supply, and savings via a pure income effect (and then only because a change in r leads to a change in V, $= rZ$). Faurot and Sellon (1981) use a variant of the Pfouts model in which an exogenous increase in assets Z translates dollar for dollar into an increase in savings and, therefore, has *no* effect on current

The reason why the individual must have a nonnegative net worth when he dies (that is, have $Z(T + 1) \geq 0$) is simple: By definition, a world of perfect credit markets is one in which the individual must be able to repay all loans by the time he dies. Moreover, if the individual does not desire to leave bequests, inheritances, and so forth to other persons when he dies, there is no reason for him to have a *positive* net worth when he dies (that is, have $Z(T + 1) > 0$): After all, "you can't take it with you." To simplify the analysis, I shall therefore assume that the individual does not, in fact, want to make any bequests upon death. Under this assumption, the weak inequality $Z(T + 1) \geq 0$ in (5.2) becomes an equality, $Z(T + 1) = 0$. Using the fact that $L(t) = 1 - H(t)$ for all t, one may therefore rewrite (5.2) to read as follows:

$$(5.3) \quad (1 + r)Z(0) + \sum_{t=0}^{T} (1 + r)^{-t} W(t)$$
$$= \sum_{t=0}^{T} (1 + r)^{-t} [W(t)L(t) + P(t)C(t)]$$

where, to repeat, I have assumed there are no bequests, implying that $Z(T + 1) = 0$.

Several features of the lifetime budget constraint embodied in (5.3) are worth emphasizing at this point. First, following Ghez and Becker (1975), one may refer to the left-hand side of this expression as *full wealth*, since it is equal to the present value of the wealth that the individual would accumulate were he (i) to devote all available

labor supply or consumption spending. Phlips (1978) assumes that the individual maximizes the single-period utility function $u = u(C, L, M)$ subject to the single-period budget constraint $PC + P_M M = WH + V$, where M is the individual's stock of nominal cash balances and P_M is the price (or opportunity cost) of holding money balances. (In turn, P_M depends on the rate of interest.) Although superficially very similar to Pfout's model, Phlips' model is in fact quite different. First, Phlips assumes explicitly that saving (that is, accumulation of interest-bearing assets) is zero in each period, as in most static models. Second, Phlips treats the stock of money – a *non*-interest-bearing asset – as a "good" with a *convenience yield*. Hence, Phlips' approach in effect is to add an equation for the transactions demand for money balances to the conventional static model's demand functions for consumer goods and leisure time. (See Arrow and Hahn, 1971, p. 358, for a model with many of the same features.) As Phlips (1978, p. 1027) recognizes, "a fully satisfactory treatment of [consumer durable goods], money and wealth would require an intertemporal approach . . . rather than the myopic instantaneous maximization behavior" that he assumes; the same remarks apply to the Pfouts and Faurot–Sellon models.

time each period to working (that is, set $L(t) = 0$ for all t) and (ii) to bank, and thus earn interest on, all his earnings in each period (that is, set $C(t) = 0$ for all t). As such, full wealth is the *maximum* present value of the level of wealth attainable by the individual. Second, one may also say that the individual "spends" his full wealth on streams of leisure and consumer goods whose total cost – equal to the right-hand side of (5.3) – cannot exceed his full wealth. The similarity between the dynamic model's full wealth and the static model's full income ($V + W$) is obvious; so is the similarity between the dynamic model's expenditure stream $\Sigma_{t=0}^{T} (1 + r)^{-t}$ $[W(t)L(t) + P(t)C(t)]$ and the static model's expenditure amount $WL + PC$. Finally, note from (5.3) that, viewed from the perspective of the present (time $t = 0$), leisure consumed during period t has a "price" equal to $w(t) \equiv (1 + r)^{-t} W(t)$, whereas a unit of the consumer good consumed during period t has a "price" equal to $p(t) \equiv (1 + r)^{-t} P(t)$.

At least in formal terms, then, the dynamic model consisting of equations (5.1)–(5.3) is strikingly similar to the simple static model of Chapter 1. In the simple static model, the individual chooses a *pair* of goods L and C with prices W and P, respectively, so as to maximize utility (which is a function of the amounts of the two goods chosen) subject to the constraint imposed by his level of full income, $V + W$. In the general dynamic model, the individual selects a *set* of goods $L(0)$, $C(0)$, $L(1)$, $C(1)$, . . . , $L(T)$, $C(T)$, with prices $w(0)$, $p(0)$, $w(1)$, $p(1)$, . . . , $w(T)$, $p(T)$, subject to the constraint imposed by his level of full wealth, $Z(0) + \Sigma_{t=0}^{T} w(t)$. (See Diewert, 1974.) In either case, analysis is concerned chiefly with (i) the nature of equilibrium – either "static equilibrium" or "dynamic equilibrium" – and (ii) displacements from equilibrium – either "comparative statics" or "comparative dynamics."

Thus, static equilibrium is concerned with the *levels* of C and L that the individual will select in response to given *values* of W, P, and V – that is, with the determinants of points such as Q in Figure 1.3. By analogy, dynamic equilibrium is concerned with *sets* of levels of C and L *over time* – in other words, with the *time profiles* of C and L – that the individual will select in response to a *set* of values (time profiles) for W and P and a value of initial net worth $Z(0)$. In other words, dynamic equilibrium is concerned with how points such as Q will move over time as the wage rate and the price level change over time, or, equivalently, with the shape of, for example, labor supply profiles such as the one shown in Figure 5.1.

By the same token, comparative statics is concerned with how *levels* of C and L will change in response to changes in the values of W, P, and V – that is, with shifts in points such as Q in Figure 1.3. Analogously, comparative dynamics is concerned with how the *time profiles* of C and L will change in response to changes in the time profiles of wages or prices, or changes in initial net worth. Thus, comparative dynamics is concerned with (i) how differences across individuals in initial net worth or in wage or price profiles will lead to differences in time profiles for labor supply like the one shown in Figure 5.1 and (ii) how changes in a given individual's initial net worth or in his wage or price profiles will affect his labor supply profile.

Viewed in these terms, then, the general dynamic model of labor supply fits quite neatly into the analytical framework presented in previous chapters, even though that framework was purely "static": In large measure, all that has changed is the number of choice variables, and many of the analytical tools that are convenient for static analysis remain useful in a dynamic context. For example, consider the comparative dynamics effect of an increase in $Z(0)$. Provided consumption and leisure at all points in the life cycle are normal goods, both $C(t)$ and $L(t)$ for all t will rise in response to the increase in $Z(0)$ – an "income effect" (more precisely, an "initial wealth effect"). Similarly, consider the comparative dynamics effect of a rise in leisure's price at time t, $w(t)$, coupled with a simultaneous adjustment in initial assets $Z(0)$ that keeps lifetime utility U unchanged. Then $L(t)$ will fall in response to this "income-compensated" (more precisely, "initial-wealth-compensated") rise in its own price – an own-substitution effect. Finally, by analogy with the family labor supply model of Chapter 2, consider the comparative dynamics effect of an income-compensated (or initial-wealth-compensated) rise in $w(t)$ on leisure at time t', $L(t')$, where $t' \neq t$: This is a cross-substitution effect, one that will be positive or negative depending on whether $L(t)$ and $L(t')$ are net substitutes or net complements. Note also that the cross-substitution effect on $L(t)$ of a rise in $w(t')$ will be equal to the cross-substitution effect on $L(t')$ of a rise in $w(t)$: provided one replaces "husband" with t and "wife" with t', Chapter 2's static analysis of a decision-making unit concerned with numerous persons carries over completely to the present dynamic case of a decision-making unit concerned with numerous periods.

Despite the formal similarity between static and dynamic labor supply models, however, the latter are both more complex, from an analytical standpoint, and potentially more useful and comprehensive, from an empirical standpoint. For example, as noted in Chapter 1, analysis of equilibrium in a static labor supply model yields little or nothing in the way of empirical implications; rather, empirical work on static models is almost entirely a matter of deriving and testing various comparative statics propositions (e.g., about the signs and magnitudes of income and substitution effects). In contrast, in dynamic models even the analysis of equilibrium can yield a set of predictions about the (equilibrium) behavior of labor supply, earnings, consumption, and so forth over time – that is, about the shape of the profiles shown in Figure 5.1.

The main ideas underlying much work in this area emerge from consideration of two models, both of which are relatively straightforward extensions of the simple static model of Chapter 1: first, a dynamic model in which savings and financial assets are endogenous, whereas wages are exogenous; and, second, a model in which both financial assets and wages are endogenous. In what follows, I will discuss each of these in turn, focusing on their implications for labor supply, wages and earnings. I shall for the most part assume an environment of perfect information and perfect certainty, mainly in order to simplify the exposition.[3]

5.2.   Dynamic labor supply models with exogenous wages: theory

I will start by considering the first kind of dynamic labor supply model, in which wages in each period are exogenously given, whereas savings, borrowing, and, thus, the individual's financial asset holdings are endogenous.

---

[3] Hence, for the most part I ignore (i) dynamic models of labor supply and related behavior under risk, uncertainty, and imperfect information and (ii) variables other than wages, labor supply, and earnings (e.g., consumption, savings, asset holdings, family size, and number of children, etc.). For more on (i) see Section 5.3. For more on (ii), see Ghez and Becker (1975), Heckman (1974b), Kasper (1966), and Landsberger and Passy (1973).

Overview

To begin, it is useful to discuss briefly and intuitively the main ideas underlying the dynamic equilibrium and comparative dynamics of such models, which, for ease of reference, I shall call *exogenous wage models*.

Dynamic equilibrium. By definition, the optimum in a dynamic labor supply model with exogenous wages is a set of *equilibrium time profiles* for labor supply and consumption determined for a given value of initial wealth or net worth, $Z(0)$, and for given values – time profiles – of wages and prices $W(t)$ and $P(t)$ for all periods t.

How, then, will equilibrium labor supply behave over the life cycle? It is natural to suppose that simple efficiency considerations would dictate that the individual will work the most during periods when the wage (the opportunity cost of leisure) is highest. As Weiss (1972, p. 1297; see also Ghez and Becker, 1975, p. 12) puts it:

> Work is allocated according to lifetime wage
> differentials. There is a *positive* association between
> changes in wages and changes in hours of worked. The
> "dynamic" effect of a wage increase is clearly less
> ambiguous than its "static" effect. The reason for this
> difference is the separation of consumption and
> production [i.e., work] decisions due to the existence of
> savings. Efficiency requires the transfer of effort to
> periods with high earning capacity.

However, as Weiss (1972, see pp. 1297–9) goes on to show, this does not quite tell the whole story: Two other motives also affect the shape of the equilibrium labor supply profile. On the one hand, the fact that the individual may invest his earnings at compound interest will induce him to work relatively much at first, bank his earnings, and reduce his labor supply with advancing age, provided leisure is a normal good. On the other hand, "future effort seems less painful when viewed from the present" (p. 1297) – that is, in more formal terms, the individual has a positive subjective rate of time preference, ρ, and, other things being equal, would prefer to enjoy leisure now rather than later. Provided leisure is a normal good, this will induce the individual to work relatively little at first and to postpone devoting greater amounts of time to market work for as long as possible – meaning that labor supply will tend to rise as time passes.

Hence, the behavior of labor supply over time in a dynamic equilibrium is the net result of three forces: an "efficiency" effect, making individuals work more in periods when the wage is higher; an "interest rate" effect, making individuals work much at first, and less later on; and a "time preference" effect, making individuals work little at first, and more later on. In particular:

(i)   The *efficiency effect* on labor supply is proportional to the size of the rate of change in the wage. Specifically, other things being equal, the rate of change of labor supply over time due to the efficiency effect will be positive (negative) when the rate of change in the wage is positive (negative) and will be larger (smaller) in absolute value whenever the rate of change in the wage is larger (smaller) in absolute value.[4]

(ii) The *interest rate effect* on labor supply is proportional to the negative of the rate of interest, $-r$, whereas the *time preference effect* on labor supply is proportional to the subjective rate of time preference, ρ. Moreover, these two effects can be collapsed into a single *time effect* that is proportional to the difference between ρ and r. Specifically, other things being equal, the rate of change of labor supply over time due to the time effect, that is, the net result of the interest rate and time preference effects, will be positive or negative depending on whether $\rho - r$ is positive or negative, provided leisure is a normal good.

---

[4] This positive relation, *ceteris paribus*, between the wage rate and labor supply over time is sometimes called the *intertemporal substitution effect*, since it refers to the fact that, other things being equal, the individual will work most in periods when the wage is high and least when the wage is low – thereby consuming leisure by substituting "cheap time" for "expensive time" *over* time. However, lest this terminology lead to confusion, several points deserve emphasis. First, the intertemporal substitution effect is only one of three distinct determinants of life cycle equilibrium dynamics, the other two being the interest rate and time preference effects. Movements along a given labor supply profile are the net result of all three effects, not just of the intertemporal substitution (i.e., efficiency) effect. Second, the intertemporal substitution effect is not a "substitution effect" in the sense used in this chapter (or, for that matter, in the sense used in previous chapters). Rather, I use "substitution effect" in a dynamic context to refer to a *shift* in the labor supply *profile*; whereas the intertemporal substitution effect refers to (one aspect of) movements *along* a *given* labor supply profile. Third, the efficiency (or intertemporal substitution) effect determines an individual's labor supply response to a perfectly anticipated real wage change due to, e.g., business cycle factors. Hence it may be useful for understanding the time-series response of labor supply to wage changes. However, both the empirical magnitude of this effect and its implications for macroeconomic analysis

Thus, for example, if $\rho = r$ (so that the time preference and interest rate effects exactly offset each other), then H and W will always move in the same direction over the life cycle as the individual fulfills his equilibrium plan over time. On the other hand, if, for example, $\rho < r$, then H and W may move in opposite directions for at least part of the life cycle. In particular, suppose both that (i) $\rho < r$ and (ii) the wage rises rapidly early in the life cycle but rises slowly later on. Then early in the life cycle both the wage and hours of work will rise; but later on hours of work will peak and then start to fall, whereas wages will go on increasing (though at a slower rate).[5] Because earnings are just the product of the wage and hours of work, it follows that earnings will also increase early in the life cycle but will fall later on – *and* that the peak in annual earnings will come after the peak in hours of work. (See Heckman, 1974b, for further discussion.)

Thus, dynamic equilibrium in simple models such as this one can easily generate the empirically observed patterns of life cycle behavior shown in Figure 5.1. This is a striking illustration of the potential empirical power of such models and suggests strongly that the payoff to refinements of such models may be considerable.

Finally, just as the optimum in the static model may entail a "corner solution" at which $H = 0$ (for example, recall the discussion of Figure 3.1 in Chapter 3), the optimum in a dynamic model may entail a corner solution in which hours of work during one *or more* periods will be zero. Roughly speaking, hours of work will be zero at any moment in the life cycle when the wage rate is sufficiently low – lower than the minimum or reservation wage level required to induce the individual to participate. Thus, the previous discussion of course applies only to periods during which the wage rate exceeds the reservation level; for example, hours of work will remain at zero even if the wage is rising rapidly so long as the wage *level* remains below the reservation level.

---

are topics of considerable controversy: See Altonji (1982, 1983), Clark and Summers (1982), Hall (1980b), Lucas and Rapping (1970), and Chap. 3, n. 34, pp. 105–6.

[5] In other words, suppose that $(\rho - r)$ is negative (so that the time effect on hours of work is negative) and that the wage rate rises rapidly over time early in the life cycle, and slowly later on. Then, early (late) in the life cycle, the efficiency effect will exceed (be less than) the time effect and so hours of work will rise (fall) over time early (late) in the life cycle.

Comparative dynamics. As previously implied, the comparative dynamics properties of dynamic labor supply models depend on the relative magnitudes of dynamic income (more precisely, wealth), own-substitution, and cross-substitution effects. However, the magnitudes and even the directions of these effects depend crucially on the extent to which changes in exogenous variables (e.g., the wage rate) in a given period t are anticipated. (Of course, such effects will also depend on whether the individual is or is not at a "corner" during part of the life cycle, i.e., has $H = 0$ over some interval of time. If so, then changes in the wage profile, initial assets, and the like need not have *any* effect on labor supply during periods when the wage rate is well below the reservation level, although such changes may still have effects on labor supply during other periods. This qualification should be kept in mind in all of what follows.)

First, consider the effect of an unanticipated increase in initial net worth (due to a windfall gain, e.g., an unexpected lump-sum transfer payment from the government). Provided consumption and leisure at all dates are normal goods, this will increase consumption and leisure at all dates. By extension, suppose that the individual suddenly learns at time 0 that at time $t^* > 0$ he will receive a previously unexpected lump sum transfer payment Λ. The present value of this payment is $(1 + r)^{-t^*} \Lambda$; its impact on consumption and leisure at all dates will be identical to the effect of a lump-sum transfer of $(1 + r)^{-t^*} \Lambda$ paid to the individual at time 0. On the other hand, if the individual already knows at time 0 that he will receive such a lump-sum payment at time t^*, his behavior at t^* (and at every other date) will not change further when he actually receives the payment at t^*: Nothing will have happened that the individual did not expect would happen when, at time 0, he formulated his life cycle optimization strategy. In other words, his actual behavior at t^* will differ from the behavior that, at time 0, he planned for t^* *only* if the payment that he gets at t^* comes as a complete surprise to him.

Next, consider the effect of an increase in the wage the individual can earn at time t, $W(t)$, on both (i) labor supply at the same date, $H(t)$, and (ii) labor supply at *other* dates, $H(t')$, where $t' \neq t$. If the individual knows at time 0 that the wage at t will "increase" (relative to the wage in the previous period), this knowledge will already have been built into the plan he formulates, at time 0, for supplying labor at time t, time t', and every other date: This kind of wage increase is fully anticipated and so does not cause labor supply at time t (or any other date) to differ in the slightest from the level that the individual originally planned to supply at time t when, at time 0, he formulated his life cycle plan.

On the other hand, suppose the increase in $W(t)$ comes as a complete surprise to the individual – in other words, suppose that, as period t begins, the actual value of $W(t)$ turns out to be larger than the value the individual expected to prevail at t when, at time 0, he formulated his life cycle plan. In this case, there will be both wealth and substitution effects on labor supply at t and all future periods. On the one hand, the increase in the wage (relative to the initially anticipated level) raises the individual's full wealth; provided leisure is a normal good at all dates, this will reduce labor supply at all dates via a wealth effect. On the other hand, the wage increase makes leisure at time t more expensive, and makes leisure at *other* dates $t' \neq t$ relatively less expensive, than the individual thought would be the case when, at time 0, he formulated his life cycle plan. This will raise labor supply and reduce leisure time at time t, via an own-substitution effect, and will raise or reduce leisure time at other dates $t' \neq t$, via a cross-substitution effect, depending on whether leisure at time t' is a net substitute or a net complement for leisure at time t.

In sum, the distinction between "anticipated" and "unanticipated" changes in wage rates, prices, or initial assets is very important. Labor supply responses to the former constitute *movements along* a *given* labor supply time profile (e.g., the one shown in Figure 5.1) whose analysis is a matter of dynamic equilibrium. Labor supply responses to unanticipated changes, however, constitute *shifts of* the labor supply time profile itself whose analysis is a matter of comparative dynamics. It is only the latter kind of change, and *not* the former, that may be treated in terms of income (more precisely, wealth) and substitution effects. There are two reasons for this. First, by analogy with discussions of static models, it is natural to think of income and substitution effects only in the context of changes in (displacements from) equilibria. Second, it would hardly make sense to use income and substitution effects to analyze *both* kinds of changes in labor supply – dynamic equilibrium changes that go on over time in fulfillment of a given lifetime equilibrium plan as the individual moves along a given labor supply profile and comparative dynamics changes that occur in response to unanticipated shifts in exogenous factors and that are manifested via shifts in the labor supply profile itself. (See MaCurdy, 1981a, pp. 1072–4, and especially note 19.)

Finally, note that comparative dynamics refers not only to shifts in profiles facing a given individual but also to *differences* in profiles facing *different* individuals. Thus, the previous discussion applies just as much to the latter case as to the former one. For example, suppose individual A faces a wage profile that is uniformly higher than the wage profile facing individual B. Then the difference between the labor supply of A and of B at any date t may be decomposed into (i) a positive own-substitution effect, arising from the fact that A's wage at t is higher than B's wage; (ii) a cross-substitution effect, arising from the fact that A's wages at all dates $t' \neq t$ are higher than B's, which will be positive (negative) if leisure times at different dates are complements (substitutes); and (iii) a wealth effect, arising from the fact that A's full wealth or potential lifetime earnings exceeds B's, which will be negative provided leisure at all dates is a normal good. By the composite commodity theorem, if A's wages are higher than B's by the same proportion at all dates, one can also say that "composite leisure" will be lower, and, therefore, lifetime *earnings* will be higher, for A than for B.

A formal model

To see these concepts more clearly, it is useful to set down the notions previously introduced in a formal model. In doing so, a number of simplifying assumptions are virtually indispensable: Otherwise, the task of deriving unambiguous results can become quite difficult. Two assumptions are particularly helpful: intertemporal separability of the utility function U and an "interior solution" (i.e., no corners).

Intertemporal separability. Suppose one were to adopt the very general lifetime utility function (5.1), and suppose that T is reasonably large, as in the case of someone who is now age 21 and who confidently (!) expects to die at age 70. Then there are a total of 50 own-substitution effects and a total of $(50^2 - 50)/2 = 1225$ cross-substitution effects to contend with! (See note 16.) To simplify, I will therefore follow most of the previous literature by specializing the general lifetime utility function given by (5.1) to one that is separable in time. This means that the marginal utility of consumption or of leisure consumed at any time t is independent of the amount of the consumer good and the amount of leisure consumed at all other dates $t' \neq t$. For many purposes, this assumption of "intertemporal separability" (strictly speaking, "intertemporal additive separability") is fairly innocuous.[6] However, in certain respects, this assumption entails some fairly specific implications about behavior. In particular, if one also assumes that leisure time at any given date is a normal good, then intertemporal separability implies that leisure times at different dates are net substitutes. In other words, intertemporal separability combined with normality of leisure time implies that all cross-substitution effects of wage rate changes on hours of work are negative – that a rise in the wage rate at some time t, accompanied by a reduction in initial assets that keeps lifetime utility constant, will always *increase* leisure time (and reduce labor supply) at all *other* dates $t' \neq t$. (See Brown and Deaton, 1972, pp. 1165–7; and Deaton, 1974.)

The main advantage of the assumption of intertemporal separability is that it permits one to treat the life cycle as a sequence of individual periods, so that lifetime utility may be found by simply adding up the utilities received within each of the individual periods. This raises a subsidiary, but not unimportant, issue: whether to describe lifetimes as a sequence of periods each of which takes up a discrete span of time (i.e., to develop a discrete-time model) or to describe lifetimes as a sequence of instants each of which takes up an infinitesimally small span of time (i.e., to develop a continuous-time model). To some extent, this choice is simply a matter of taste. However, in the present setting, a variety of results are more easily

---

[6] For criticism and discussion of the assumption of intertemporal separability, see Hadley and Kemp (1971, pp. 361–2), Heckman, (1971, esp. pp. 6–8; 1976a, p. 230), Hicks (1965, p. 261), and Strotz (1956, 1957, 1959). Note also that one can assume that lifetime utility is a function of the terminal stock of assets, $Z(T + 1)$, either through a separate function $B[Z(T + 1)]$ or as an additional argument in an "inseparable" function such as (5.1). The idea here is that the individual may desire to make bequests or else intends to retire at T and desires to accumulate financial wealth for consumption during retirement. (For discussion, see Heckman, 1976b.)

derived in the context of a continuous-time model than in the context of a discrete time model. (See Tintner, 1938, for fully parallel analyses of consumer behavior – which do not, however, consider leisure or labor supply – using both discrete-time and continuous-time models.) In what follows, I therefore use the former kind of approach rather than the latter.

An interior solution. I shall also assume that the lifetime equilibrium does not involve any corners and is therefore an interior solution, involving positive labor supply $H(t)$ at all ages t. As an analytical assumption, this is reasonably innocuous, *provided* one keeps in mind the caveats noted earlier about how conclusions about dynamic equilibrium and comparative dynamics must be modified when the life cycle includes corners at one or more points in time. (As an empirical assumption, however, this may be much less innocuous; recall the discussion of specification and selection bias problems of Chapter 4.)

Accordingly, ignore corners, treat the life cycle as a continuous sequence of infinitesimally small instants, and write the individual's lifetime utility U as the "sum" (more precisely, the integral) of utilities received at each distinct instant in the life cycle. Let the instantaneous utility function – that is, the utility derived from consumption of consumer goods and leisure, $C(t)$ and $L(t)$, as of time t – be $u(t) = u[C(t), L(t)]$. If the life cycle begins at time $t = 0$ and ends at time $t = T$, and if the individual's subjective rate of time preference is ρ, then U, the (present value of the) individual's lifetime utility, is given by

$$(5.4) \quad U = \int_0^T e^{-\rho t} u[C(t), L(t)] \, dt$$

where the fact that leisure time $L(t)$ and hours of work $H(t)$ exhaust total available time each period means that $L(t) = 1 - H(t)$.

The instantaneous utility function $u(t)$ is assumed to be "well behaved." This means, for example, that the marginal utility of consumer goods at any moment t is positive but diminishes with the amount of $C(t)$, and likewise for leisure time. Thus,

$$u_C(t) > 0, \quad u_L(t) > 0, \quad u_{CC}(t) < 0, \quad u_{LL}(t) < 0$$

where $u_i(t)$ is the partial derivative of $u(t)$ with respect to i ($= C(t)$ or $L(t)$)) and $u_{ij}(t)$ is the partial derivative of $u_i(t)$ with respect to j ($= C(t)$ or $L(t)$)). A well-behaved utility function is also strictly concave. Among other things, this means that, at any moment t, indifference curves showing the combinations of $C(t)$ and $L(t)$ that yield the same instantaneous utility $u(t)$ are strictly convex, so that

$$\Delta(t) \equiv u_{CC}(t)u_{LL}(t) - u_{CL}(t)u_{LC}(t) > 0$$

Finally, suppose – just for the moment – that the life cycle consisted of only one period and that the individual were forced to pick $C(t)$ and $L(t)$ so as to maximize *single-period* utility $u(t)$ (rather than lifetime utility U), subject to the conventional *single-period* constraint $P(t)C(t) = W(t)H(t) + V(t)$, where $V(t)$ is the amount of exogenous income received by the individual during period t. Then it can be shown[7] that the income effect on i ($= C(t)$ or $L(t)$) of a change in $V(t)$ is proportional to $Y_{iV}(t)$, where

$$Y_{CV}(t) \equiv - [u_C(t)u_{LL}(t) - u_L(t)u_{CL}(t)]/\Delta(t)$$
$$Y_{LV}(t) \equiv - [u_L(t)u_{CC}(t) - u_C(t)u_{LC}(t)]/\Delta(t)$$

and that the substitution effect on i of a change in its price, k ($= P(t)$ or $W(t)$) is proportional to $S_{ik}(t)$, where

$$S_{CP}(t) \equiv u_C(t)u_{LL}(t)/\Delta(t)$$
$$S_{LW}(t) \equiv u_L(t)u_{CC}(t)/\Delta(t)$$

Of course, the model to be developed here refers to lifetime optimization – that is, to maximizing U, as given by (5.4), but, as will become clear shortly, single-period income and substitution effects are relevant to lifetime optimization as well as to single-period optimization.

Having described lifetime utility, now consider the lifetime constraint subject to which lifetime utility is maximized. If – as I shall assume, mainly in order to simplify the exposition – the individual does not desire to leave any bequests, then he has no reason to end his life with a positive net worth. Accordingly, in terms of the present continuous-time model, the lifetime budget constraint amounts to a requirement that net worth at death, $Z(T)$, must be

---

[7] For example, see Cohen, Rea, and Lerman (1970, pp. 184–6).

zero.[8] Accordingly, continuous-time versions of equations (5.2) and (5.3), which are for the discrete-time case, may be written as

(5.5) $\dot{Z}(t) = rZ(t) + W(t)H(t) - P(t)C(t)$

with $Z(0) = Z_0$, an exogenous constant, and $Z(T) = 0$ and

(5.6) $Z(0) + \int_0^T e^{-rt}[W(t)H(t) - P(t)C(t)]\, dt = 0$

where a dot over any variable indicates differentiation of that variable with respect to time (so that, for any variable θ, $\dot{\theta} \equiv d\theta/dt$).

One may, therefore, write the individual's decision problem – to maximize U subject to the constraints (5.5) and (5.6) – in formal terms as

(5.7) $\max\limits_{[C(t),\,H(t),\,\mu]} \left(\int_0^T e^{-\rho t} u[C(t), 1 - H(t)]\, dt + \mu\{Z(0) \right.$
$$\left. + \int_0^T e^{-rt}[W(t)H(t) - P(t)C(t)]\, dt\} \right)$$

where μ, which will be discussed in detail later, may be interpreted as the marginal utility of initial financial wealth $Z(0)$ or, equivalently, as the imputed value ("shadow price") of initial wealth.

In order to solve this optimization problem, the individual will have to trade off the marginal cost and marginal benefit of changes in his labor supply and consumption spending at each moment t. If (as I have assumed) there are no corners, then two of the necessary conditions for a maximum are

(5.8) $e^{-\rho t} u_C[C(t), 1 - H(t)] = e^{-rt} P(t)\mu$
(5.9) $e^{-\rho t} u_L[C(t), 1 - H(t)] = e^{-rt} W(t)\mu$

where the left-hand sides of these equations represent the marginal benefits of increases in consumption and leisure time, respectively, whereas the right-hand sides give the marginal costs of such increases. Finally, a third necessary condition for an optimum is, of course, that the individual must satisfy the lifetime budget constraint, that is, must choose $C(t)$ and $H(t)$ for all t so as to

---

[8] It is straightforward to allow for bequests, at the price of some additional complication of the analysis. (For example, see Heckman, 1976b, and note 6.)

satisfy not only (5.8) and (5.9) but also the intertemporal budget constraint

$$(5.10) \quad Z(0) + \int_0^T e^{-rt} [W(t)H(t) - P(t)C(t)] \, dt = 0$$

In effect, these first-order or necessary conditions for a maximum – equations (5.8)–(5.10) – constitute three equations in three unknowns: $H(t)$, $C(t)$, and μ. Provided the instantaneous utility function $u(t)$ is well behaved, in the sense previously defined, the first-order conditions uniquely determine μ and (for all t) the values of $C(t)$ and $H(t)$. (Thus, the first-order conditions (5.8)–(5.10) are not only necessary but also sufficient for a unique solution to the individual's optimization problem.)

To understand this optimization process in intuitive terms, note that, in order to optimize correctly, the individual must determine not only the "right" values for $C(t)$ and $H(t)$ – for all t – but also the "right" value for μ, the marginal utility or imputed value of initial assets. Indeed, as will become apparent later, unless the individual determines the right value for μ – that is, determines just how much his initial stock of assets is "worth" to him – he will not be able to pick the right values for $C(t)$ and $H(t)$: For example, someone who imputes too low a value to his initial assets $Z(0)$ (picks too low a value for μ) will act as if he were better off than he actually is, will work too little and consume too much, and will thereby end up with $Z(T) < 0$.

Now that the model has been set up, it may be used to analyze both the dynamic equilibrium and the comparative dynamics of the individual to whom it refers. To see the distinction between these two concepts, consider Figure 5.2. As previously noted, the individual formulates an equilibrium lifetime plan – consisting of an optimal (utility-maximizing) value of μ and of optimal values of the $H(t)$ and $C(t)$ for all t – subject to an exogenously given value of $Z(0)$ and to exogenously given time profiles of $W(t)$ and $P(t)$. For example, suppose the individual is faced with the wage profile *abcde* in Figure 5.2 (and with a particular value of $Z(0)$ and a particular price profile, neither of which is shown in Figure 5.2 in order to avoid clutter). In response to these "givens," the individual settles on a utility-maximizing or equilibrium *lifetime plan* consisting of three elements: a particular value of μ, a particular time profile for

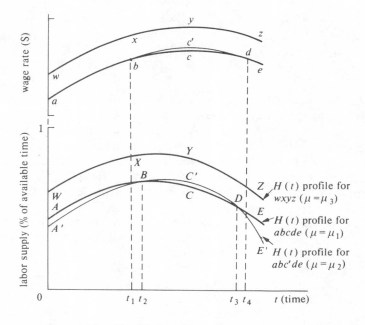

Figure 5.2.   Equilibrium dynamics and comparative dynamics in exogenous wage life cycle model

consumption $\dot{C}(t)$, and a particular time profile for labor supply $H(t)$. Suppose that the time profile that he chooses for labor supply is the one labeled *ABCDE* in Figure 5.2. (The time profile for consumption that he chooses at the same time is not shown, again in order to avoid clutter.) This means that, as time passes – that is, as the individual moves in an "easterly" direction – he will not only (i) move along the wage profile *abcde* but also (ii) move along the labor supply profile *ABCDE* (and also, of course, along the consumption profile that he has chosen). The changes in $H(t)$ that occur over time – that is, as a result of the passage of time, during which the wage $W(t)$ is of course also changing – as the individual follows *ABCDE* represent the fulfillment of his equilibrium plan, that is, his dynamic equilibrium. Note that μ does *not* change over time due to the mere passage of time as such. Rather, since μ is *part* of the individual's equilibrium plan, it will change only if his equilibrium plan changes (due, e.g., to a change in the exogenously given wage profile).

Now suppose that, just prior to embarking on this lifetime plan, the individual learns that his wage rate will follow the time path *abc'de* rather than the path *abcde* that is the basis of the equilibrium time path for labor supply *ABCDE*. What will happen?

Clearly, the individual's equilibrium – meaning not only the time paths for $C(t)$ and $H(t)$ but also the μ that he will select – will change. In general, both $C(t)$ and $H(t)$ at *each* date t will change even though, as shown in Figure 5.2, the time path of wage rates *abc'de* deviates from the time path of wage rates *abcde* only between time t_1 and time t_4. (To understand why, see the formal discussion of comparative dynamics later in this section.) Let the new labor supply path be $A'BC'DE'$. Differences between the $H(t)$ values implied by the two paths *ABCDE* and $A'BC'DE'$ at any given date t are a question of comparative dynamics – that is, refer to how $H(t)$ will change in response to exogenous changes in the time paths of (exogenous) variables such as $W(t)$. Such differences in $H(t)$ values at given t along the two paths may be regarded as the result of two factors. First, the shift in the wage profile to *abc'de* from *abcde* would change labor supply even if μ remained the same. Second, however, the shift in the wage profile leads to a change in μ, the value the individual imputes to his initial asset stock $Z(0)$, and this prompts a further change in labor supply.

Of course, the new equilibrium time profile of labor supply $A'BC'DE'$ does not differ very much from the initial profile *ABCDE*. This is because the wage profile *abc'de* relevant to the new equilibrium does not differ very much from the wage profile *abcde* of the initial equilibrium. In a loose sense, then, the value of μ relevant to the new equilibrium – call it μ_2 – does not differ very much from the one relevant to the initial equilibrium – call it μ_1. However, if the wage profile differs markedly from the initial one, *abcde*, then the new labor supply profile will differ markedly from *ABCDE* and the new value of μ will differ markedly from the initial one. For example, a new wage profile like *wxyz* will be associated with a new value of μ – call it μ_3 – and a new time profile for labor supply – call it *WXYZ* – that could be quite different from the ones associated with the initial equilibrium.

With this as prologue, I now consider both dynamic equilibrium and comparative dynamics in more detail.

Dynamic equilibrium. To describe the individual's dynamic equilibrium – changes in $C(t)$ and $H(t)$ that occur simply as a result of the passage of time, as the individual fulfills his equilibrium plan – rearrange (5.8) and (5.9) and differentiate them totally with respect to time (t), to obtain

(5.11) $u_{CC}(t)\dot{C}(t) - u_{CL}(t)\dot{H}(t) = \dot{A}_1(t)$
(5.12) $u_{LC}(t)\dot{C}(t) - u_{LL}(t)\dot{H}(t) = \dot{A}_2(t)$

where

$$A_1(t) = e^{(\rho - r)t} P(t)\mu$$
$$A_2(t) = e^{(\rho - r)t} W(t)\mu$$

where, as before, a dot over a variable denotes its rate of change over time.

Now, the mere passage of time as such does not change μ: Rather, μ remains the same so long as the individual's lifetime equilibrium proceeds "on schedule," as wages change over time in the manner implied by the wage profile used in determining μ (e.g., *abcde* in Figure 5.2). Hence, the fact that μ does not change as the individual's equilibrium unfolds over time means that

$$\dot{A}_1(t) \equiv dA_1(t)/dt = \{(\rho - r) + [\dot{P}(t)/P(t)]\}A_1(t)$$
$$\dot{A}_2(t) \equiv dA_2(t)/dt = \{(\rho - r) + [\dot{W}(t)/W(t)]\}A_2(t)$$

where $A_1(t)$ and $A_2(t)$ are defined as in equations (5.11) and (5.12). Thus, (5.8)–(5.12) imply that, as time passes with μ remaining the same, the rates of change of $C(t)$ and $H(t)$ over time are given by

(5.13) $\dot{C}(t) = S_{CP}(t) [\dot{P}(t)/P(t)] - [u_L(t)u_{CL}(t)/\Delta(t)]$
            $\times [\dot{W}(t)/W(t)] - Y_{CV}(t) (\rho - r)$
(5.14) $\dot{H}(t) = [u_C(t)u_{CL}(t)/\Delta(t)] [\dot{P}(t)/P(t)]$
            $- S_{LW}(t) [\dot{W}(t)/\dot{W}(t)] + Y_{LV}(t) (\rho - r)$

respectively.

Note that if leisure is a normal good in the single-period sense previously defined, then $Y_{LV} > 0$; that if consumption is likewise a normal good, then $Y_{CV} > 0$; and that both S_{CP} and S_{LW} are negative. Thus, for example, (5.14) implies that if prices are stable over time (so that $\dot{P}(t)/P(t) = 0$ for all t), then

$$\dot{H}(t) = -S_{LW}(t)[\dot{W}(t)/W(t)] + Y_{LV}(t)(\rho - r)$$

This is the result derived by Weiss (1972) and discussed in some detail earlier (see pp. 215–17). The first term on the right-hand side of the above expression is the efficiency effect; the second is the time effect.

Finally, as suggested earlier, intertemporal changes in $H(t)$ – that is, $\dot{H}(t)$ – that occur as part of the individual's equilibrium dynamics are simply an aspect of the individual's *lifetime equilibrium*. As such, it is somewhat nonsensical to think of $\dot{H}(t)$ as the net outcome of "income" (or wealth) and "substitution" effects, for such effects refer to *changes* in an equilibrium, whereas the $\dot{H}(t)$ discussed here *is* (part of) an equilibrium. It is certainly true, as just shown, that the equilibrium association between wage changes over time and hours of work changes over time can be written using expressions proportional to "one-period" income and substitution effects. In particular, when the wage changes over time by some percentage w, the accompanying equilibrium change in hours of work over time will equal $\dot{H}(t) = -S_{LW}(t)w + Y_{LV}(t)(\rho - r)$. However, it is more appropriate to refer to the first component of this expression as an efficiency effect and to the second as a time effect (where the latter is the sum of the time preference and interest rate effects previously discussed) than to call them substitution and income effects, respectively. Substitution and income (more precisely, wealth) effects arise only when the individual's lifetime equilibrium *changes* as a result of changes in the exogenous variables – $Z(0)$ or the time profiles of wages $W(t)$ or prices $P(t)$ – that determine that equilibrium; such changes have to do with questions of comparative dynamics, that is, changes or differences in equilibrium profiles.[9]

---

[9] In this rather technical respect, the remarks of Ghez and Becker (1975, p. 12) in their important work are somewhat misleading. They write: "Since we assume that time can be allocated only to market or consumption activities, hours spent in the market, i.e., hours of 'work,' would be positively related to the wage rate over the life cycle. They would rise as long as the wage rate rose and fall when the wage rate fell . . . . In our analysis there is no income or wealth effect because all changes in wealth are perfectly foreseen [since they are the basis of the individual's lifetime optimization strategy]. Hence a rise in wage rates with age generates only substitution effects, and the supply curve of labor would be positively sloped." (A footnote adds: "This conclusion is not a negation of the observation that a parametric shift in the wage

Comparative dynamics. Accordingly, now suppose that $Z(0)$ or the time profile of prices or of wages changes, and ask how such changes will alter the individual's equilibrium time profiles of $H(t)$ and $C(t)$ as of any moment t.

As stressed earlier, such exogenous shifts will change all aspects of the individual's equilibrium, including not only the time profiles of labor supply and consumption but also μ, the value he imputes to his initial stock of assets. For example, intuition suggests that if the entire time profile of wage rates shifts upward, implying higher wages throughout the life cycle, then the individual will be "better off" and will therefore impute a *lower* implicit value to his initial assets: Since he now expects to enjoy higher wages, he does not "need" his initial assets to the extent he did before and so can feel freer about spending them. This change in μ will, in turn, be accompanied by further changes in $C(t)$ and $L(t)$ (or $H(t)$).

To make this intuition more precise, rearrange and then differentiate totally equations (5.8) and (5.9), with t kept constant, to obtain

(5.15) $u_{CC}(t)\, dC(t) - u_{CL}(t)\, dH(t) = dA_1(t)$
(5.16) $u_{LC}(t)\, dC(t) - u_{LL}(t)\, dH(t) = dA_2(t)$

where $A_1(t)$ and $A_2(t)$ are as defined in (5.11) and (5.12). Note also that, for any *given* t,

$$dA_1(t) = e^{(\rho - r)t} [P(t)\, d\mu + \mu dP(t)]$$
$$dA_2(t) = e^{(\rho - r)t} [W(t)\, d\mu + \mu dW(t)]$$

profile generates both income and substitution effects.") However, there are several difficulties with this interpretation. First, the assumption that "time can be allocated only to market or consumption [leisure] activities" is not sufficient to guarantee that "hours spent in the market . . . would be positively related to the wage rate." Two other conditions must also be satisfied: (i) as Ghez and Becker themselves show, the subjective rate of time preference ρ and the rate of interest r must be equal; and (ii) as Blinder and Weiss (1976, p. 457) show, the individual must equate the opportunity cost of time to the potential wage R, that is, to the amount he could earn if all his market time were devoted to market work, leaving no time for learning on the job. If either of these two conditions is not met, then wages and hours of work may move inversely at different points in the life cycle. (See, e.g., Blinder and Weiss, 1976, p. 463, and the discussion in Section 5.5.) Second, as noted in the text, even if these two conditions are satisfied, it makes sense to interpret a change in labor supply over time in terms of income and substitution effects only if the change is induced by a change in some exogenous factor, e.g., "a parametric shift in the wage profile."

In this case, then, equations (5.8) and (5.9) and (5.15) and (5.16) imply that, when μ, $W(t)$, and $P(t)$ change, the individual's consumption and labor supply in a given period t will change by the amounts

$$(5.17) \quad dC(t) = S_{CP}(t) \, [dP(t)/P(t)] \; - \; Y_{CV}(t) \, (d\mu/\mu)$$
$$- \; [u_L(t)u_{CL}(t)/\Delta(t)] \, [dW(t)/W(t)]$$
$$(5.18) \quad dH(t) = - \; S_{LW}(t) \, [dW(t)/W(t)] \; + \; Y_{LV}(t) \, (d\mu/\mu)$$
$$+ \; [u_C(t)u_{LC}(t)/\Delta(t)] \, [dP(t)/P(t)]$$

respectively. In other words, for example, (5.18) means that $H(t)$ will be larger than would otherwise be the case if (i) $W(t)$ is larger, other things (meaning μ and $P(t)$) being equal; or if (ii) μ is larger, other things (meaning $W(t)$ and $P(t)$) being equal. A larger $P(t)$ will make $H(t)$ larger or smaller than would otherwise be the case depending on whether $u_{LC}(t)$ is positive or negative, other things (meaning μ and $W(t)$) being equal. (Similar conclusions can be derived for $C(t)$ using (5.17).)

Of course, as noted above, μ – like $H(t)$ and $C(t)$ – is endogenous. Like $H(t)$ and $C(t)$, it will, therefore, change whenever initial wealth or the wage or price profile changes. Equations (5.17) and (5.18) provide two of the equations needed to solve for the three unknowns $d\mu$, $dH(t)$, and $dC(t)$ in terms of $dZ(0)$, $dW(t)$, and $dP(t)$; the third comes from total differentiation of the budget constraint, (5.10):

$$(5.19) \quad dZ(0) + \int_0^T e^{-rt} \, [W(t) \, dH(t) \; + \; dW(t)H(t)$$
$$- \; P(t) \, dC(t) \; - \; dP(t) \, C(t)] \, dt = 0$$

Solving the equation system (5.17)–(5.19) would seem to be a rather forbidding task. Fortunately, however, the solution turns out to be relatively simple provided one proceeds in two stages. In the first, one uses (5.17) and (5.18) to derive "direct" effects on $H(t)$ and $C(t)$ of changes in $Z(0)$, $W(t)$, and $H(t)$ *with μ held constant*. In the second stage, one determines how these "direct" or "μ-constant" changes in $H(t)$ and $C(t)$ will (have to) lead to changes in μ in order to ensure that (5.19) is satisfied, thereby inducing further "indirect" (or "μ-variable") effects on $H(t)$ and $C(t)$.

Thus, one may decompose the total change in $H(t)$ that occurs in response to a change in some exogenous factor ($Z(0)$, $W(t)$, or $P(t)$) into two effects: a "μ-constant" change and a "μ-variable" change. It is tempting to treat these as equivalent to, respectively, the conventional substitution and full wealth effects discussed earlier in this chapter. However, the conventional substitution effect is a "U-constant" change – that is, a change in $H(t)$ caused by a change in an exogenous factor accompanied by a change in full wealth that keeps the *level of lifetime utility U* constant – whereas the "μ-constant" change in $H(t)$ refers to a change in $H(t)$ caused by a change in an exogenous factor accompanied by a change in full wealth that keeps the *marginal utility of initial wealth μ* constant. Thus, in general, the μ-constant effect on $H(t)$ of a change in $W(t)$ or $P(t)$ is not the same as the substitution (that is, U-constant) effect on $H(t)$ of a change in $W(t)$ or $P(t)$. Similarly, the μ-variable effect on $H(t)$ of a change in $W(t)$ or $P(t)$ is generally not the same as the full wealth (that is, U-variable) effect on $H(t)$ of a change in $W(t)$ or $P(t)$. (Of course, both the substitution and μ-constant effects on $H(t)$ of a change in initial assets $Z(0)$ are zero. For further discussion, see MaCurdy, 1981a, pp. 1072–4.)

With these preliminaries out of the way, it remains to examine μ-constant and μ-variable effects in more detail. First, consider μ-constant effects of wage changes on labor supply. Even with μ held constant, a change in the wage at some date t^* resulting from a change in the time profile of wages will affect labor supply at time t^*, $H(t^*)$: In other words, by (5.18),

$$(5.20) \quad \partial H(t^*)/\partial W(t^*) \big|_{\bar{\mu}} = - S_{LW}(t^*)/W(t^*)$$

Now consider indirect or μ-variable effects. With μ held constant, the only effect on $H(t^*)$ of a wage profile change that alters $W(t^*)$ will be the one given by (5.20). Similarly, with μ held constant, the only effect on $C(t^*)$ of a wage profile change that alters $W(t^*)$ will be

$$(5.21) \quad \partial C(t^*)/\partial W(t^*) \big|_{\bar{\mu}} = - u_L(t^*)u_{CL}(t^*)/\Delta(t^*)W(t^*)$$

However, will such a change in the wage profile leave μ unchanged? Certainly not. To see this, note that such a change in the wage profile will turn the equality (5.10) into an inequality. In particular, unless μ changes, a wage profile shift in which only the wage at t^*,

$W(t^*)$, changes will alter both consumption and labor supply at t^* while leaving consumption and labor supply at all other dates unchanged. Accordingly, until μ changes, the only effect of such a wage profile shift on (5.10) will be a change in the particular component inside the integral in that expression that pertains to time t^*. Specifically, the integral will change by an amount $d\xi/dW(t^*)$, where

$$(5.22) \quad d\xi/dW(t^*) = e^{-rt^*}\{H(t^*) + W(t^*)[\partial H(t^*)/\partial W(t^*)]$$
$$- P(t^*)[\partial C(t^*)/\partial W(t^*)]\}$$
$$= e^{-rt^*}[H(t^*) + Y_{LV}(t^*)]$$

Provided leisure is a normal good (in the one-period sense given earlier), $d\xi/dW(t^*) > 0$. This means that, unless μ changes, the first-order condition (5.10) will be violated – in other words, unless μ changes, the individual will end his life with a positive net worth, violating (5.19). Since he does not desire to leave any bequests, and since "you can't take it with you," this cannot be optimal; he can increase lifetime utility by, in effect, "spending" this "excess net worth" before he dies – by having more C, more L, or both. In other words, now that the wage profile has shifted upward (in the sense that the wage rate at one particular date t^* is now higher), the individual need not place such a high implicit value on his initial stock of wealth, $Z(0)$; he can "afford" to let μ fall in response to this shift in the wage profile.

To see that μ will indeed fall (rather than rise) as a result of this increase in the wage profile, note from (5.17) and (5.18) that the changes in consumption and hours of work at *any* date t as a result of a reduction in μ are

$$(5.23) \quad \partial C(t)/-\partial\mu = Y_{CV}(t)/\mu > 0$$
$$(5.24) \quad \partial H(t)/-\partial\mu = -Y_{LV}(t)/\mu < 0$$

respectively, provided $C(t)$ and $L(t)$ are both normal goods. Hence, as intuition suggests, when the individual reduces μ he simultaneously reduces his labor supply and increases his consumption spending at each date t, thereby reducing the value of $W(t)H(t) - P(t)C(t)$ at each date t. This offsets the *increase* in the value of $Z(T)$ that occurs as a result of the upward shift in the wage profile (more precisely, the exogenous increase in $W(t^*)$) and means that the individual will no longer have a positive net worth at time T. In other words,

(5.25) $\partial\mu / \partial W(t^*) < 0$

Similar reasoning leads to the conclusion that an increase in initial wealth will reduce the imputed (shadow) value of such wealth:

(5.26) $\partial\mu / \partial Z(0) < 0$

The effect on μ of a shift in the time profile of the price level is more complicated. To see this, note that, unless μ changes, a price level profile shift in which only the price level at time t^*, $P(t^*)$, changes will alter both consumption and labor supply at t^* while leaving consumption and labor supply at all other dates unaffected. Accordingly, until μ changes, the integral in (5.10) will change by an amount $d\xi / dP(t^*)$, where

$$
\begin{aligned}
d\xi / dP(t^*) &= e^{-rt^*} \{ W(t^*) [\partial H(t^*)/\partial P(t^*)] - C(t^*) \\
&\quad - P(t^*) [\partial C(t^*)/\partial P(t^*)] \} \\
&= e^{-rt^*} [- C(t^*) + Y_{CV}(t^*)]
\end{aligned}
$$

whose sign cannot be determined a priori.[10] Thus, the net impact on of an increase in $P(t^*)$, other things being equal, depends on the magnitude of Y_{CV} and on C itself as of t^*:

(5.27) $\partial\mu / \partial P(t^*) \gtrless 0$ as $C(t^*) - Y_{CV}(t^*) \gtrless 0$

Now, (5.25) implies that

---

[10] The first term inside the square brackets in the expression in the text, $- C(t^*)$, miight be called the direct effect of the shift in the price level: A rise in the price level at t^* makes it more expensive to maintain the originally planned level of consumption spending at t^*, $C(t^*)$. Other things being equal, this will tend to make $Z(T)$ negative and, thus, to raise μ – that is, to make the individual act as if his initial asset endowment $Z(0)$ were more "valuable," and thereby spend it less freely. The second term inside the square brackets, $Y_{CV}(t^*)$, might be called the induced effect of the shift in the price level. It serves to reduce μ: Other things (including μ) being equal, a rise in $P(t^*)$ reduces consumption spending, by (5.17), and this will tend to make $Z(T)$ *positive*. Hence the induced effect of the rise in $P(t^*)$ makes the individual act as if his initial asset endowment $Z(0)$ were less valuable, prompting him to spend it more readily. Consequently, the net impact on μ of an increase in $P(t^*)$ depends on whether the direct effect of the increase is stronger or weaker than its induced effect.

$$(5.28) \quad dH(t^*)/dW(t^*) = [\partial H(t^*)/\partial W(t^*)]\,|_{\bar{\mu}}$$
$$+ [\partial H(t^*)/\partial \mu][\partial \mu/\partial W(t^*)]$$
$$= -[S_{LW}(t^*)/W(t^*)]$$
$$+ [Y_{LV}(t^*)/\mu][\partial \mu/\partial W(t^*)]$$

In intuitive terms, this simply means that an exogenous increase in the wage profile that takes the form of an increase in the wage at a particular date t^* has two effects on labor supply at t^*: It has a direct effect on H even with μ held constant (the first term on the right-hand side of (5.28)), which prompts a reduction in leisure time and an increase in labor supply at t^*; and it also changes μ, leading to a further indirect effect (the second term) that induces an increase in leisure time and a decrease in labor supply at t^* provided leisure is a normal good.

Next, note that an exogenous increase in $W(t^*)$, other things being equal, will also affect labor supply at other dates $t \neq t^*$. Unless the increase in $W(t^*)$ is accompanied by a change in the wage at other dates, it will not have a direct (that is, μ-constant) effect on labor supply at any time t other than t^*: By (5.18), $\partial H(t)/\partial W(t^*)\,|_{\bar{\mu}}$ = 0 for $t \neq t^*$. However, an exogenous increase in $W(t^*)$ will still have an indirect or μ-variable effect on $H(t)$, because it will change μ. In other words, for $t \neq t^*$,

$$(5.29) \quad dH(t)/dW(t^*) = [\partial H(t)/\partial W(t^*)]\,|_{\bar{\mu}}$$
$$+ [\partial H(t)/\partial \mu][\partial \mu/\partial W(t^*)]$$
$$= 0 + [\partial H(t)/\partial \mu][\partial \mu/\partial W(t^*)]$$
$$= [Y_{LV}(t)/\mu][\partial \mu/\partial W(t^*)]$$

This set of results – equations (5.28) and (5.29) – explains why a shift in the wage profile from *abcde* to *abc'de*, as shown in Figure 5.2, will induce a comparative dynamics shift in the hours-of-work profile from *ABCDE* to one resembling *A'BC'DE'*. The reason is simple: The shift in the wage profile changes wage rates *only* between time t_1 and time t_4, so it leads to work-increasing μ-constant effects only between t_1 and t_4. However, the shift in the wage profile also changes μ and thereby leads to work-reducing μ-variable effects for *all* t between 0 and T. Clearly, then, labor supply between $t = 0$ and $t = t_1$ will fall and so will labor supply between $t = t_4$ and $t = T$. At dates in between t_1 and t_4, the impact on labor supply depends on whether the μ-variable effect is stronger or weaker than the

μ-constant effect. (The labor supply profile $A'BC'DE'$ is drawn on the assumption that the μ-variable effect is stronger than the μ-constant effect between t_1 and t_2, weaker than the μ-constant effect between t_2 and t_3, and stronger after t_3.)

If the *entire* wage profile shifts upward, implying higher wages at all points in the life cycle, then the resulting change in labor supply at any given date t will be determined by both a μ-variable and a μ-constant effect. An example of this kind of shift in the wage profile is the change from *abcde* to *wxyz* in Figure 5.2, with a resulting shift in the time profile of labor supply from *ABCDE* to *WXYZ*. (In drawing *WXYZ* as shown in Figure 5.2, I have of course assumed, simply for purposes of illustration, that the μ-constant effect of the shift in the wage profile from *abcde* to *wxyz* is stronger than its wealth effect at *all* dates t.)

Finally, note that the dynamic labor supply function, like the simple static labor supply function in Chapter 1, possesses the "no money illusion" property, that is, is homogeneous of degree zero in assets, wages, and prices taken together. To see this, observe that if initial assets $Z(0)$ and *all* wages and prices are increased or decreased by the same percentage, the individual will not need to change either $C(t)$ or $H(t)$ at any t in order to continue to satisfy (5.10).

An example

As a means of illustrating the results previously discussed, the following simple example may be useful. Assume that the instantaneous utility function $u(t)$ is given by $u(t) = \alpha \ln C(t) + \beta \ln L(t)$; note that, under this assumption, $u_C(t) = \alpha/C(t)$ and $u_L(t) = \beta/L(t)$; and recall that $W(t)H(t) = W(t) - W(t)L(t)$. Substitute these expressions into equations (5.8)–(5.10) and rearrange terms to obtain

(5.30) $P(t)\,C(t) = \alpha e^{-(\rho - r)t}/\mu$

(5.31) $W(t)\,L(t) = \beta e^{-(\rho - r)t}/\mu$

(5.32) $Z(0) + \displaystyle\int_0^T e^{-rt}\,W(t)\,dt$

$$= \int_0^T e^{-rt}\,[\,W(t)L(t) + P(t)C(t)\,]\,dt$$

Now substitute (5.30) and (5.31) into (5.32) to obtain

$$(5.33) \quad Z(0) + \int_0^T e^{-rt} W(t)\, dt = \int_0^T e^{-rt}[(\alpha + \beta)e^{-(\rho - r)t}/\mu]dt$$

$$= [(\alpha + \beta)/\mu] \int_0^T e^{-\rho t}\, dt$$

$$= [(\alpha + \beta)/\mu][(1 - e^{-\rho T})/\rho]$$

so that

$$(5.34) \quad \mu = [(\alpha + \beta)(1 - e^{-\rho T})/\rho]/[Z(0) + \int_0^T e^{-rt} W(t)\, dt]$$

Note that μ will not change provided neither $Z(0)$ nor the wage that can be earned at any given moment t, $W(t)$, changes. This means that the mere passage of time as such will not change μ: It is independent of t.

For ease of reference, define the numerator and denominator of the right-hand side of (5.34) as

$$\nu \equiv (\alpha + \beta)(1 - e^{-rT})/\rho$$
$$\Phi \equiv Z(0) + \int_0^T e^{-rt} W(t)\, dt$$

respectively, and note that Φ is full wealth. Next, note that[11]

$$(5.35) \quad \partial\mu/\partial Z(0) = -\mu/\Phi < 0$$
$$(5.36) \quad \partial\mu/\partial W(t) = -\mu e^{-rt}/\Phi < 0$$
$$(5.37) \quad \partial\mu/\partial P(t) = 0$$

It follows that

$$(5.38) \quad C(t) = \alpha\Phi e^{-(\rho-r)t}/\nu P(t)$$
$$(5.39) \quad L(t) = \beta\Phi e^{-(\rho-r)t}/\nu W(t)$$

Note also that the difference between the individual's earnings $W(t)H(t)$ and his consumption spending $P(t)C(t)$ at any date t is given by $-V(t)$, where

$$(5.40) \quad -V(t) = W(t)H(t) - P(t)C(t)$$
$$= W(t) - W(t)L(t) - P(t)C(t)$$
$$= W(t) - [(\alpha + \beta)\Phi/\nu]e^{-(\rho-r)t}$$

[11] To understand (5.37), note that, when the instantaneous utility function is as specified here, it turns out that the quantity $Y_{CV}(t)$ is always equal to the value of $C(t)$. By (5.27), then, in this special case, $\partial\mu/\partial P(t) = 0$ for all t.

Now consider equilibrium dynamics questions. The mere passage of time as such does not change μ, so, by equations (5.13), (5.14), (5.38), and (5.39), as the individual proceeds over time along *given* equilibrium paths for consumption and hours of leisure, C and L will change over time according to the relations

(5.41) $\dot{C}(t)/C(t) = \{(r - \rho) - [\dot{P}(t)/P(t)]\}$
(5.42) $\dot{L}(t)/L(t) = \{(r - \rho) - [\dot{W}(t)/W(t)]\}$

respectively.

Next, consider comparative dynamics questions. First, suppose that $Z(0)$ changes unexpectedly by an amount $dZ(0)$. Since μ is a function of $Z(0)$, it follows that

(5.43) $dC(t)/dZ(0) = C(t)/\Phi > 0$
(5.44) $dH(t)/dZ(0) = -dL(t)/dZ(0) = -L(t)/\Phi < 0$

Next, suppose that the wage at some particular date t^*, $W(t^*)$, changes unexpectedly by an amount $dW(t^*)$. (That is, suppose there is an unanticipated upward shift in the wage profile as of t^* by an amount $dW(t^*)$.) Since μ is a function of the wage profile, it follows that

(5.45) $dC(t)/dW(t^*) = e^{-rt^*}C(t)/\Phi > 0$ $(t \neq t^*)$
(5.46) $dC(t^*)/dW(t^*) = e^{-rt^*}C(t^*)/\Phi > 0$
(5.47) $dH(t)/dW(t^*) = -dL(t)/dW(t^*)$
$= -e^{-rt^*}L(t)/\Phi < 0$ $(t \neq t^*)$
(5.48) $dH(t^*)/dW(t^*) = -dL(t^*)/dW(t^*)$
$= L(t^*)[W(t^*)^{-1} - (e^{-rt^*}/\Phi)]$

Finally, suppose that the price level at some particular date t^* changes unexpectedly by an amount $dP(t^*)$. (That is, suppose there is an unanticipated upward shift in the price profile as of t^* by an amount $dP(t^*)$.) Since μ is independent of the price level, it follows that

(5.49) $dC(t)/dP(t^*) = 0$ $(t \neq t^*)$
(5.50) $dC(t^*)/dP(t^*) = -C(t^*)/P(t^*) < 0$
(5.51) $dH(t)/dP(t^*) = -dL(t)/dP(t^*) = 0$ (all t)

Note that (5.50) implies that the price elasticity of demand for consumption goods is equal to -1 in this model, which explains why μ

is independent of the price level at all dates t under the particular specification of the instantaneous utility function adopted here: That is, other things (*including* μ) being equal, a rise in the price level of any given percentage results in an equal percentage decrease in consumption, so consumption *spending* $P(t)C(t)$ is on balance unchanged after the price increase even without a change in μ. The budget constraint is still satisfied; there is no need to change μ. Hence, if he has the particular instantaneous utility function assumed here, the individual's sole response to a price increase in period t will be a decrease in consumption in the same period that keeps consumption spending constant; he will change neither his labor supply profile nor μ.

5.3.   Risk and uncertainty

Individuals can never be (and, more to the point, never *are*) completely certain about the future. Nevertheless, the discussion thus far has ignored risk and uncertainty, and so has most of the literature on labor supply. To be sure, models of job search and imperfect information are explicitly concerned with uncertainty about future wage rates and employment prospects. However, such models typically assume that labor supply is fixed and that individuals maximize the expected present value of earnings rather than the expected present value of utility. (For example, see Lippman and McCall, 1976a, b.)

The essentials of the labor supply decision in the presence of uncertainty about wage rates are easily understood in the context of a simple discrete-time model with two periods: the present, period 0; and the future, period 1. The individual knows the current wage rate $W(0)$ but is uncertain about the wage $W(1)$ that he will receive in the future.[12] This uncertainty is embodied in an assumption that the

[12] Researchers have sometimes analyzed the effect of uncertainty on labor supply in the context of a one-period model. For example, Hartley and Revankar (1974) consider the consequences of uncertainty about being unemployed. In effect, they assume that individuals learn at the beginning of the period whether they are employed, know with certainty the wage they will get if they are employed, and make their labor supply decisions given their employment status and (if employed) their wage rates. However, as Sjoquist (1976) points out, if one also assumes that individuals in this environment maximize expected utility, then changes in the probability of *being* employed today obviously have no effect on labor supply *if* employed today. That is, labor supply of employed persons who maximize expected utility in the

individual acts as if $W(1)$ could take on any of a variety of values as given by a known probability density function $f[W(1)]$, with a minimum value of W_a and a maximum of W_b. Thus, the kind of uncertainty considered here (and in most other discussions of wage rate uncertainty) is a situation in which the individual does not know in period 0 what the value of period 1's wage will be but does know (or acts as if he were completely certain about) the nature of the probability density function of period 1's wage. In Knight's (1921) terminology, this is a situation involving *risk*. (Knight uses *uncertainty* to refer to a setting in which the individual not only (i) does not know what future wages will be but also (ii) does not know, or act as if he knew, the probability density function of the future wage rate.)

In virtually all other important respects, the model is the same as

presence of this kind of uncertainty does not differ at all from labor supply in the absence of uncertainty. In order to obtain a nonzero effect of a change in today's employment probability on today's labor supply of an expected utility maximizer, it is necessary to introduce one of a variety of somewhat dubious assumptions. For example, Sjoquist (1976) in effect assumes that the individual must decide at the beginning of the period how many hours he will work without knowing whether he will be paid for his work; here, then, "unemployment" simply means that the individual learns at the end of the period that he will not be paid for the hours he has worked. Not surprisingly, an increase in the probability of this kind of unemployment (that is, in the probability of not being paid for work one has performed) reduces labor supply. Yaniv (1979) modifies Sjoquist's model to allow for unemployment compensation payable to persons who become "unemployed" (in Sjoquist's sense), with the amount of the payment being proportional to the earnings that the unemployed person would have received had he instead been "employed" (that is, paid for his work). Labor supply will *increase* in response to an increase in the probability of this kind of unemployment: In effect, the individual insures against not being paid by supplying more hours, thereby raising the amount of "unemployment compensation" he will receive if he is not paid.

In contrast with these analyses of employment uncertainty, Block and Heineke (1973), Cowell (1981a, b), and Eaton and Rosen (1980b) use single-period models to analyze uncertainty about wage rates. In one important respect, these models are similar to the one Sjoquist uses: In each case, one in effect assumes that the individual must decide at the beginning of the period how many hours he will work but does not learn until the end of the period what wage he will be paid for his work. In this kind of setting, an increase in uncertainty about wage rates leads both to effects that resemble conventional income effects and to effects that resemble conventional substitution effects. (Block and Heineke, 1973, p. 383, call them *uncertainty income effects* and *uncertainty substitution effects*, respectively.)

one of behavior under certainty. Utility within each period t is given by a well-behaved single-period utility function $u(t) = u[C(t), L(t)]$, $t = 0$ or 1; lifetime utility (that is, utility over the two periods combined) is the sum of utilities in the two periods, with future utility discounted at the subjective rate of time preference ρ. Manipulation of equation (5.2) for the case $T = 1$ yields expressions for consumption in each of the two periods:

$$(5.52) \quad C(0) = (1 + r)\,[Z(0)/P(0)]$$
$$+ \,[W(0)/P(0)]H(0) - [Z(1)/P(0)]$$
$$(5.53) \quad C(1) = (1 + r)\,[Z(1)/P(1)] + [W(1)/P(1)]H(1)$$

(Note that this assumes that the individual makes no bequests, so that $Z(2) = 0$.) Assets as of period 0, $Z(0)$, are exogenously given; once both $H(0)$ and $Z(1)$ (the assets the individual decides during period 0 to take with him into period 1) are determined, $C(0)$ is determined. Likewise, as of period 1, $Z(1)$ is fixed (it was determined during period 0), so once $H(1)$ is determined, $C(1)$ is also determined.

The main difficulty with all one-period models of this kind is that uncertainty is essentially a problem about what the *future* will bring, so that careful analysis of uncertainty requires a model with at least two periods: the present *and* "the future." Eaton and Rosen (1980b, p. 366) offer a rationale for treating wage rate uncertainty in a one-period context: As they point out, "workers who contract to work at fixed money wages do not know the effect that changes in consumer prices will have on their real wages during the contract period" and so are subject to uncertainty about *real* wage rates during the contract period. However, there are two difficulties with this argument. First, it is prices, not nominal wages, that are uncertain in this case; and although uncertainty about nominal wages entails uncertainty about real wages but not real property income or real assets, uncertainty about prices entails uncertainty about both real wages and real property income (and real assets): Price uncertainty and real wage uncertainty are not synonymous. Second, even if price uncertainty and real wage uncertainty were synonymous (as Eaton and Rosen implicitly assume), the individual may be able to change his consumption and/or labor supply *within* the "contract period," that is, the contract period may contain more than one decision-making period. Thus, here, and in other one-period models, collapsing both the present and future decision-making periods into a single period results in a model that may at best be no more than an imperfect metaphor for an intertemporal model. Moreover, the empirical implications of one-period models are rather restrictive. Such models ignore changes in current savings as a means of adjusting to changes in uncertainty about the future and imply that changes in tomorrow's employment probability or in expectations about tomorrow's wage rate will have no effect on today's labor supply.

As soon as period 1 begins, the individual will know the wage rate $W(1)$ that he can earn and, by (5.53), he will then pick $H(1)$ to maximize $u(1)$ subject to the constraints imposed by the wage $W(1)$ that he can actually earn and by the savings decision he made in period 0, as embodied in $Z(1)$. Thus, during period 1, behavior is just as described in a conventional static one-period labor supply model: As soon as period 1 begins, there is no future.

However, as of period 0, the individual does have a future – or, rather, many different possible futures, one for each possible value of $W(1)$. If there were no uncertainty about $W(1)$, then the future and the future wage would be known quantities, and so the individual could proceed now – in the present period, period 0 – to select values of $Z(1)$, $H(0)$, and $H(1)$ that maximize lifetime utility. However, in the presence of uncertainty about $W(1)$, the individual cannot now decide what $H(1)$ will be. At the moment, he knows only that he *will* know what $W(1)$ will be when period 1 begins, and he realizes that today's choice of $Z(1)$ will become tomorrow's constraint. So the individual must make decisions today, during period 0, taking into account not only the effect of today's decisions on current utility $u(0)$, which can be calculated with certainty, but also their effect on future utility $u(1)$. The latter is uncertain and can be evaluated only by working out both (i) the *nature* of each possible future contingency (e.g., the way in which today's choice of $Z(1)$ will affect the utility attainable during period 1 at each of the possible future wage rates $W(1)$ that one *might* receive) and (ii) the *probability* of each such contingency (e.g., does it seem more likely that the future wage will be high or low?).

With this as background, modifying the dynamic model of previous sections of this chapter to introduce uncertainty (that is, Knightian risk) is relatively straightforward. It is particularly helpful to view decision making in the kind of risky environment considered here as a two-stage process. In the first stage, the individual works out a *set* of *contingency plans* for the future. These describe what optimal labor supply will be (given today's choice of $Z(1)$) for each alternative possible future wage rate and, thus, what maximum utility will be (during period 1 only) under each such contingency. In the second stage, the individual works backward from the future to the present and decides what he will actually do in the present, taking into account (i) the impact of his actions on utility enjoyed during period 0, (ii) the impact of his actions on maximum utility attainable during period 1 under each contingency that may arise, and (iii) the probability of each such contingency. (This way of working out the individual's optimization problem is an application of dynamic programming. See Arrow and Kurz, 1970, esp. Chap. 2, and Dixit, 1976, esp. Chap. 10, for expositions of dynamic programming; and see Samuelson, 1969, for an application to questions involving risk.) I first consider the individual's current (as of period 0) equilibrium, and then consider changes in this equilibrium.

Equilibrium

As just noted, when period 1 begins, the individual's problem will be the standard one-period static labor supply problem: to maximize period 1's utility $u(1)$ subject to the budget constraint (5.53), i.e., to find *maximum* period 1 utility $U^*(1)$, where

$$(5.54) \quad U^*(1) = \max_{\{H(1)\}} u\left[(1 + r) \frac{Z(1)}{P(1)} + \frac{W(1)}{P(1)} H(1), 1 - H(1)\right]$$

where both $Z(1)$ and $W(1)$ are taken as given (as of period 1). On the assumption of an interior solution, the first-order condition for this maximization problem is

$$(5.55) \quad u_C(1) [W(1)/P(1)] - u_L(1) = 0$$

where concavity of the single-period utility function u ensures that the labor supply value $H(1)$ that satisfies (5.55) also solves the maximization problem (5.54).

To see how changes in $Z(1)$ and $W(1)$ affect labor supply $H(1)$, differentiate (5.55) and rearrange terms to obtain

$$(5.56) \quad dH(1) = \frac{1 + r}{P(1)} \frac{y_L(1)}{\gamma(1)} dZ(1) + \frac{1}{P(1)} \frac{w_H(1)}{-\gamma(1)} dW(1)$$

where

$$\gamma(1) \equiv u_{CC}(1) [W(1)/P(1)]^2$$
$$- 2u_{CL}(1) [W(1)/P(1)] + u_{LL}(1) < 0$$
$$y_L(1) \equiv - u_{CC}(1) [W(1)/P(1)] + u_{CL}(1)$$
$$w_H(1) \equiv u_C(1) - H(1)y_L(1)$$

and where $\gamma(1) < 0$ by (5.55) (which implies that $W(1)/P(1) = u_L(1)/u_C(1)$) and by concavity of the single-period utility function u. The income effect on labor supply of an increase in assets, $(1 + r)y_L(1)/P(1)\gamma(1)$, is negative provided leisure is a normal good. Thus, if leisure is statically normal (that is, normal in the static one period sense) then $y_L(1)$ is positive, and vice versa. The income effect on labor supply of an increase in the wage rate, $H(1)y_L(1)/P(1)\gamma(1)$, is proportional to the income effect of an increase in assets, where $H(1)/(1 + r)$ is the factor of proportionality, and is also negative provided leisure is statically normal. The substitution effect on labor supply of an increase in the wage rate, $u_C(1)/ - \gamma(1)P(1)$, is always positive by concavity of the single-period utility function u. If the substitution effect of a wage increase outweighs (is outweighed by) the income effect, then the labor supply schedule may be called *statically positive (negative) sloped*.

Before moving backward in time to the second stage of the individual's decision-making process and to a complete description of his equilibrium, it is helpful to work out how changes in $Z(1)$ and in $W(1)$ affect *maximum* utility in period 1, $U^*(1)$. To do so, treat $H(1)$ as a function of $Z(1)$ and $W(1)$ and totally differentiate $U^*(1)$, taking care to note that since $H(1)$ is a function of $Z(1)$ and $W(1)$, equation (5.55) always holds whenever $u(1)$ is at a maximum and $H(1)$ always changes in response to changes in $Z(1)$ and $W(1)$ in the manner specified by (5.56). Total differentiation yields

$$dU^*(1) = u_C(1) \frac{1 + r}{P(1)} dZ(1) + u_C(1) \frac{H(1)}{P(1)} dW(1)$$

$$+ \left[u_C(1) \frac{W(1)}{P(1)} - u_L(1) \right] dH(1)$$

$$= u_C(1) \frac{1 + r}{P(1)} dZ(1) + u_C(1) \frac{H(1)}{P(1)} dW(1)$$

Thus,

(5.57) $dU^*(1)/dZ(1) = u_C(1)(1 + r)/P(1) > 0$

(5.58) $dU^*(1)/dW(1) = u_C(1)H(1)/P(1) > 0$

So the maximum utility attainable in period 1 will be higher when either the level of assets $Z(1)$ or the wage rate $W(1)$ is higher. Now, as noted in Chapter 1, another name for maximized utility – for the utility function when its arguments are the *optimal* levels of C and

L, treated as functions of Z and W – is the indirect utility function. In view of this, it should come as no surprise that equations (5.57) and (5.58) lead immediately to Roy's Identity (Roy, 1947), discussed in Chapter 1. To see this, recall that in the present setting the analog to the property income, V, of the simple model of Chapter 1 is the quantity $(1 + r)Z(1)$: Since the individual has no future and makes no bequests, he devotes all of his assets $Z(1)$ and asset income $rZ(1)$ to consumption during period 1. By (5.57), then, $dU^*(1)/d[(1 + r)Z(1)] = u_C(1)/P(1)$ so equations (5.57) and (5.58) imply that

(5.59) $\quad H(1) = \{dU^*(1)/dW(1)\}/\{dU^*(1)/d[(1 + r)Z(1)]\}$

which is Roy's Identity: Labor supply is equal to the ratio of (i) the effect on maximized utility of an increase in the wage to (ii) the effect on maximized utility of an increase in exogenous "income" available for consumption (which in this case is $(1 + r)Z(1)$).

Now, (5.57) is an expression for the marginal (maximum) utility of assets. To see how this marginal utility changes when either the asset level or the wage changes, differentiate (5.57) and rearrange terms using (5.55) and (5.56) to obtain

$$d[dU^*(1)/dZ(1)] = \frac{1 + r}{P(1)} \left\{ \frac{1 + r}{P(1)} \frac{\Delta(1)}{\gamma(1)} \, dZ(1) \right.$$
$$\left. + \frac{1}{P(1)} \left[u_{CC}(1)H(1) + y_L(1) \frac{w_H(1)}{\gamma(1)} \right] dW(1) \right\}$$
$$= \frac{1 + r}{[P(1)]^2} \frac{1}{\gamma(1)} \{(1 + r)\Delta(1) \, dZ(1)$$
$$+ [\Delta(1)H(1) + y_L(1)u_C(1)] \, dW(1)\}$$

where $\Delta(1) \equiv u_{CC}(1)u_{LL}(1) - [u_{CL}(1)]^2 > 0$ and where $\Delta(1) > 0$ by concavity of the utility function u. Thus,

(5.60) $\quad \dfrac{d^2U^*(1)}{dZ(1)^2} = \left[\dfrac{1 + r}{P(1)} \right]^2 \dfrac{\Delta(1)}{\gamma(1)} < 0$

(5.61) $\quad \dfrac{d^2U^*(1)}{dW(1)dZ(1)} = \dfrac{1 + r}{[P(1)]^2} \dfrac{1}{\gamma(1)} [\Delta(1)H(1) + y_L(1)u_C(1)]$

So this implies diminishing marginal (maximum) utility of assets as assets rise. Provided leisure is statically normal, so that $y_L(1) > 0$, the marginal utility of assets also falls as the wage rate rises. In other words, other things being equal, the gain in (maximum) utility attainable in period 1 that would occur if one dollar more in assets became available during period 1 will be small if the amount of assets is already high or (provided leisure is statically normal) if the wage rate is high.

These results have crucial implications for decisions made during period 0, when the individual is uncertain about period 1's wage. For example, intuition suggests that someone who expects that tomorrow's wage will be high will be likely to save relatively little today (that is, will be likely to make $Z(1)$ relatively small) – because, as (5.61) indicates, the marginal utility of assets tomorrow will be relatively low if tomorrow's wage is high.

To make this and similar intuitive statements more precise, note that the individual's problem *in period 0* is to maximize the *expected* value of *lifetime* utility (meaning periods 0 and 1 taken together). (See Schoemaker, 1982, for discussion of the notion of expected utility maximization.) In other words, he must find $E\{U^*(0)\}$, the expected maximum value of lifetime utility, which is given by

$$(5.62) \quad E\{U^*(0)\} = \max_{\{H(0), Z(1)\}} \left\{ u\left[(1+r)\frac{Z(0)}{P(0)} + \frac{W(0)}{P(0)}H(0)\right.\right.$$
$$\left.\left. -\frac{Z(1)}{P(0)}, 1 - H(0)\right] + (1+\rho)^{-1}E\{U^*(1)\} \right\}$$

where

$$E\{U^*(1)\} = \int_{W_a}^{W_b} U^*(1)f[W(1)]\, dW(1)$$
$$= \int_{W_a}^{W_b} \max_{H(1)} u\left[(1+r)\frac{Z(1)}{P(1)} + \frac{W(1)}{P(1)}H(1), 1 - H(1)\right]$$
$$\times f[W(1)]\, dW(1)$$

where $E\{ \ \}$, the expectations operator, denotes the expected value of the expression inside the curly braces. Although this expression for $E\{U^*(0)\}$ may look unfamiliar, its meaning should be plain. It is the maximized sum of today's utility $u[C(0), L(0)]$ and *expected* maximum future utility $E\{U^*(1)\}$ (discounted at the subjective rate of time preference ρ). In turn, because actual future utility depends on the actual future wage $W(1)$, maximum future utility expected as of period 0 is a kind of weighted sum of all possible values of (maximized) utility attainable during period 1, where the weights are in effect the probabilities of the different values that $W(1)$ may take on. (More precisely, $E\{U^*(1)\}$ is a weighted integral of $U^*(1)$ values, where the weights are the densities of the distribution of $W(1)$.)

On the assumption of an interior solution, the first-order conditions for the maximization problem posed by (5.62) are

$$-u_C(0) [P(0)]^{-1} + (1 + \rho)^{-1} [dE\{U^*(1)\}/dZ(1)] = 0$$
$$u_C(0) [W(0)/P(0)] - u_L(0) = 0$$

By (5.57), these expressions may be written as

$$(5.63) \quad -u_C(0) [P(0)]^{-1} + \left[\frac{1 + r}{1 + \rho}\right] E\{u_C(1)\} [P(1)]^{-1} = 0$$
$$(5.64) \quad u_C(0) [W(0)/P(0)] - u_L(0) = 0$$

where $E\{u_C(1)\}$ is the expected value of the marginal utility of consumption during period 1, that is,

$$E\{u_C(1)\} = \int_{W_a}^{W_b} u_C \left[(1 + r) \frac{Z(1)}{P(1)} + \frac{W(1)}{P(1)} H(1), 1 - H(1)\right]$$
$$\times f[W(1)] \, dW(1)$$

(In other words, $u_C(1)$, like $U^*(1)$, depends in part on the future wage $W(1)$ and is not known with certainty as of period 0. So $E\{u_C(1)\}$ is a probability-weighted sum – strictly speaking, a probability density-weighted integral – of the different possible $u_C(1)$ values.)

At first glance, the first-order conditions (5.63) and (5.64) seem to suggest that behavior in the presence of uncertainty is qualitatively not very different from behavior in a world of perfect certainty. Equation (5.64) indicates that, though wages are uncertain, the individual still chooses his current hours of work $H(0)$ by comparing his marginal rate of substitution $u_L(0)/u_C(0)$ with the current real wage $W(0)/P(0)$ – just as he would do in a world of certainty. Likewise, equation (5.63) shows that the individual makes savings and borrowing decisions in a risky environment in just the same way that he would in a world of perfect certainty: by comparing the disutility of spending one dollar less on consumer goods today, $u_C(0)/P(0)$, with the utility of having one dollar more in assets tomorrow (inclusive of accrued interest at rate r and net of discounting at the subjective rate of time preference ρ), $[(1 + r)/(1 + \rho)]E\{u_C(1)\}/P(1)$.

Finally, manipulation of equations (5.63) and (5.64), which refer to a risky world, leads to expressions that closely resemble equations (5.8) and (5.9), which refer to a world of certainty. To see this, note first that an extra one dollar in assets available now (as of the initial period, period 0) can be used either for current consumption or for savings. If used for current consumption, one dollar in extra assets will raise current utility by the amount $u_C(0)/P(0)$; if used for savings, one dollar in extra assets will raise future utility by the expected amount $[(1 + r)/(1 + \rho)]E\{u_C(1)\}/P(1)$ after allowance for accrued interest (at the market rate r) and time preference (at the subjective rate ρ). Moreover, by (5.63), these two amounts are equal. Thus, $u_C(0)/P(0)$ – which I will denote by μ_0 – is the shadow or implicit value of initial assets. Next, note that equations (5.63) and (5.64) can be written as follows:

$$(5.65) \qquad u_C(0) = P(0)\mu_0$$
$$(5.66) \qquad E\{u_C(1)\} = [(1 + \rho)/(1 + r)]P(1)\mu_0$$
$$(5.67) \qquad u_L(0) = W(0)\mu_0$$

The resemblance between equations (5.65)–(5.67) and equations (5.8) and (5.9) is considerable, particularly when one notes that the quantity $(1 + \rho)/(1 + r)$ is the discrete-time equivalent of the quantity $e^{(\rho - r)t}$ when t is set equal to unity (so as to refer to "period 1").

Thus, regardless of whether the future is risky or certain, the individual makes the same kinds of trade-offs in deciding about labor supply, consumption, and savings; and it is possible to write the individual's current consumption and labor supply decisions as functions of the subjective rate of time preference, the interest rate, the current price level, the current wage rate, and the shadow value of an additional dollar of assets. As MaCurdy (in press) observes, this has an important implication for empirical work: It means that empirical specifications for current labor supply $H(0)$ derived under the assumption of perfect certainty carry over almost completely, and with only minor modification, to a world of wage uncertainty.

However, the fact that behavior in the presence of wage uncertainty is qualitatively very similar to behavior under perfect certainty does not mean that the *amounts* of labor supply and consumption in all periods (or in any period) will be the same in the presence of wage uncertainty as they would be in the absence of such uncertainty. If the future is uncertain, then, as the first-order conditions (5.63) and (5.64) indicate, the individual compares the disutility of spending one dollar less on consumption today with the *expected* utility of having one dollar more in assets tomorrow − or, equivalently, with the *expected value* of the marginal utility of future consumption, $E\{u_C(1)\}$. In general, then, the amount of assets that the individual facing an uncertain future will actually carry with him into the future will differ from the amount that he would choose if he were certain of earning a wage equal to the expected (mean) value of the wage rate in the uncertain future that actually awaits him. For exactly the same reasons, labor supply in an uncertain world will in general differ from labor supply in a world of perfect certainty, even if the expected (mean) value of the wage rate in the uncertain world is the same as the actual wage rate that prevails in the certain world.

Moreover, in a world of certainty, one can express decisions not only during period 0 but during each and every subsequent period in terms of the shadow price of *initial* assets (provided there are no parametric shifts, e.g., in the wage profile), whereas, in contrast, in a world of uncertainty one cannot. To see this, note first that equations (5.8) and (5.9), which refer to a world of certainty, can be written as

(5.68) $u_C(0) = P(0)\mu = P(0)\mu_0$

(5.69) $u_C(1) = \dfrac{1 + \rho}{1 + r} P(1)\mu = P(1)\mu_1$

(5.70) $u_L(0) = W(0)\mu = W(0)\mu_0$

(5.71) $u_L(1) = \dfrac{1 + \rho}{1 + r} W(1)\mu = W(1)\mu_1$

where

$$\mu_1 = \dfrac{1 + \rho}{1 + r} \mu_0$$
$$\mu_0 = \mu$$

after one rearranges terms and replaces the quantity $e^{(\rho-r)t}$ with its discrete-time equivalent, $[(1 + \rho)/(1 + r)]^t$, and sets t at either 0 or 1. Here, then, $\mu_t (= u_C(t)/P(t))$, $t > 0$, is an exact function of $\mu_0 = \mu$, the marginal utility or shadow price of initial (as of period 0) assets; and so all decisions at all dates can be written in terms of μ_0, without reference to μ_t at any future date $t > 0$.

This is not the case in a risky world. True, equations (5.55), (5.63), and (5.64), which refer to the risky world, can be written as

(5.72) $\qquad u_C(0) = P(0)\mu_0$

(5.73) $\quad E\{u_C(1)\} = \dfrac{1 + \rho}{1 + r} \, P(1)\mu_0$

(5.74) $\qquad u_C(1) = P(1)\mu_1$

(5.75) $\qquad u_L(0) = W(0)\mu_0$

(5.76) $\qquad u_L(1) = W(1)\mu_1$

where $\mu_t \equiv u_C(t)/P(t)$, $t = 0, 1$. However, this means that one can write μ_t, $t > 0$, as an exact function of μ_0 only if $E\{u_C(1)\}$ turns out to be equal to $u_C(1)$. In other words, roughly speaking, in an uncertain world, decisions at all dates can be written in terms of the shadow price of initial assets $\mu_0 = \mu$ only if what the individual *expects* (during the current period) the value of $u_C(1)$ will be turns out to coincide with the *actual* value (in the future) of $u_C(1)$. If not – if the individual's expectations do not turn out to be exactly correct, in this sense – then the relation between μ_t ($t > 0$) and μ_0 will contain at least some random (nonsystematic) elements, making it impossible to express future behavior solely in terms of μ_0, without reference to μ_t. That this is so should not be surprising. As (5.61) indicates, the marginal utility or shadow price of assets at any date depends in part on the wage at that date – and, in an uncertain world, one's actual future wage is a random variable, meaning that μ_t is also a random variable rather than an exact function of μ_0.

Changes in equilibrium

To derive further results, it is necessary to determine how changes in exogenous factors lead to changes $dZ(1)$ and $dH(0)$ in the equilibrium values of the individual's two current-period decision variables. Before one plunges into this question, however, it is important to understand both the meaning of $dZ(1)$ and $dH(0)$ and the meaning of the exogenous changes that generate these behavioral responses.

The meaning of the change $dH(0)$ is obvious enough: It is a change in the individual's current labor supply. The meaning of the change $dZ(1)$ is more subtle. This denotes a change in the level of assets that the individual decides, during period 0, to carry with him into period 1. Although certainly correct, this definition of $dZ(1)$ is quite a mouthful. Fortunately, however, one can be equally accurate and less verbose if one refers to $dZ(1)$ as the change in the individual's *current savings*. To see this, note that, by definition, the individual's savings during period 0 is simply the net change in his asset holdings between period 0 and period 1, $Z(1) - Z(0)$. Since $Z(0)$ is exogenously given as of the start of period 0, a positive (negative) $dZ(1)$ denotes an increase (decrease) in savings and vice versa. To avoid confusion, however, it is important to keep in mind that savings represents an *addition* to assets rather than the *level* of assets, even though savings is often used colloquially in the latter sense. (For example, we often use "my savings" to mean "the balance in my savings account" – in other words, the amount of assets I own – even though, strictly speaking, savings represent *additions* to savings accounts and other forms of wealth.)

Now consider the exogenous changes that set these behavioral responses in motion. Changes in initial assets $Z(0)$ and in the current wage $W(0)$ may be represented in the usual way, as changes of amounts $dZ(0)$ and $dW(0)$, respectively. On the other hand, the future wage rate $W(1)$ is not a single number, like $Z(0)$ or $W(0)$. Rather, $W(1)$ is a random variable whose value is unknown at present (as of period 0) and which could take on any of a variety of different values according to the probability density function $f[W(1)]$. Accordingly, the notion of a change in the future wage rate should in fact refer to a change in the *distribution* of the future wage rate. In most of the literature, two kinds of distributional changes are singled out for detailed examination: a ceteris paribus change in the mean of the distribution; and a ceteris paribus change in the variance of the distribution. (For example, see Block and Heineke, 1972, 1973; Eaton and Rosen, 1980a, b.)

The first kind of change in the $W(1)$ distribution simply shifts the entire distribution up or down by the same amount. This kind of change does not make the future more or less uncertain (that is, it does not widen or narrow the range of possible future wage rate values), but it does make the future either brighter or gloomier (that is, it raises or reduces the expected future wage rate). The second kind of change expands or contracts the entire future wage distribution without affecting its central tendency (that is, its mean). This second kind of change, therefore, makes the future either more or less uncertain but does not make the future wage outlook either brighter or gloomier.

To see in formal terms what each of these two kinds of changes amounts to, let μ_W denote the mean or expected value, and σ_W^2 the variance, of the distribution of $W(1)$. By definition,

$$\mu_W \equiv E\{W(1)\} = \int_{W_a}^{W_b} W(1)f[W(1)] \, dW(1)$$

$$\sigma_W^2 \equiv E\{[W(1) - \mu_W]^2\}$$

Next, define a new variable, $W(1)'$, as follows:

$$W(1)' = vW(1) + m$$

Since $W(1)$ is a random variable, $W(1)'$ is also a random variable. The mean and variance of the $W(1)'$ distribution are, respectively,

$$E\{W(1)'\} = \int_{W_a}^{W_b} [vW(1) + m]f[W(1)] \, dW(1) = v\mu_W + m$$

$$E\{([vW(1) + m] - [v\mu_W + m])^2\} = E\{[vW(1) - v\mu_W]^2\}$$
$$= v^2\sigma_W^2$$

Of course, when $v = 1$ and $m = 0$, the distributions of $W(1)'$ and $W(1)$ are identical: They will differ (in particular, the means and/or variances of the two distributions will differ) only if, starting at $v = 1$ and $m = 0$, one changes v by some amount dv and changes m by some amount dm. Inspection of the expressions for the mean and variance of $W(1)'$ shows that changing the mean *without* changing the variance entails keeping v fixed (at 1) while changing m by some amount dm. Specifically, a variance–constant change in the mean of the $W(1)'$ distribution is one in which dv and dm satisfy

$$dE\{W(1)'\} = d[v\mu_W + m] = \mu_W \, dv + dm \neq 0$$
$$dE\{([vW(1) + m] - [v\mu_W + m])^2\} = 2v \, \sigma_W^2 \, dv = 0$$

So this kind of distributional change is one in which m changes but v does not, that is, in which $dv = 0$ and $dm \neq 0$. On the other hand, a mean-constant change in the variance of the $W(1)'$ distribution is one that satisfies the two conditions

$$\mu_W \, dv + dm = 0$$
$$2v \, \sigma_W^2 \, dv \neq 0$$

So this kind of distributional change is one in which both v and m change, with the change in m offsetting the impact of the change in v on the *mean* of the distribution, that is, $dv \neq 0$ and $dm = -\mu_W \, dv$.

With these conceptual preliminaries out of the way, it is now possible to analyze how changes in exogenous factors will affect current choices. To simplify exposition, I will ignore changes in interest rates and in the price level, and will set $P(t) = 1$ in both periods. To allow for changes in the distribution of future wage rates, I will replace $W(1)$ in equations (5.63) and (5.64) with $W(1)' = vW(1) + m$, with v and m initially set at 1 and 0, respectively. Now totally differentiate equations (5.63) and (5.64) with respect to $H(0)$, $Z(1)$, $Z(0)$, $W(0)$, m, and v and rearrange terms, using (5.61). This yields

$$(5.77) \quad \left[u_{CC}(0) + \frac{(1 + r)^2}{1 + \rho} E\left\{ \frac{\Delta(1)}{\gamma(1)} \right\} \right] dZ(1) + y_L(0) \, dH(0)$$
$$= (1 + r)u_{CC}(0)dZ(0) + u_{CC}(0)H(0) \, dW(0)$$
$$- \frac{1 + r}{1 + \rho} E\left\{ \frac{[H(1)\Delta(1) + y_L(1)u_C(1)]}{\gamma(1)} \right\} dm$$
$$- \frac{1 + r}{1 + \rho} E\left\{ \frac{[H(1)\Delta(1) + y_L(1)u_C(1)] W(1)}{\gamma(1)} \right\} dv$$

$$(5.78) \quad y_L(0) \, dZ(1) + \gamma(0) \, dH(0)$$
$$= (1 + r)y_L(0) \, dZ(0) - w_H(0) \, dW(0)$$

These are two simultaneous equations expressing the two unknowns $dH(0)$ and $dZ(1)$ in terms of changes in $Z(0)$, $W(0)$, m, and v. Solving these equations for $dH(0)$, one derives an expression for $dH(0)$ in terms of $dZ(0)$, $dW(0)$, dm, and dv; and similarly for $dZ(1)$. Finally, by taking the expression for $dH(0)$ or $dZ(1)$ and setting all but one (say, $dZ(0)$) of the changes in the exogenous variables at zero, one obtains an expression for the change in $H(0)$ or $Z(1)$ when that one exogenous variable changes, ceteris paribus, and similarly for ceteris paribus changes in each of the other exogenous variables.

Thus, it is straightforward to derive results about the effects on

$H(0)$ and $Z(1)$ of changes in initial assets $Z(0)$ and the initial wage rate $W(0)$. The wealth effect of an increase in either $Z(0)$ or $W(0)$ will always increase $Z(1)$ and will reduce $H(0)$ provided leisure is statically normal. Likewise, an increase in $W(0)$ will always have a positive cross-substitution effect on $Z(1)$ and a positive own-substitution effect on $H(0)$. Rather than provide a full derivation of these results, however, I will leave this task for the interested reader and will instead focus on the impact of changes in the mean or the variance of the distribution of future wage rates.

First, consider the effects on current behavior of a variance–constant increase in the mean of the distribution of future wage rates, as embodied in a positive value of dm and a zero value of dv. Other things being equal (that is, with $dW(0) = dZ(0) = 0$), such a change makes the future brighter without making it more or less uncertain. Solve equations (5.77) and (5.78) for this case to obtain

$$(5.79) \quad \frac{dZ(1)}{dm} = -\frac{1 + r}{1 + \rho} \frac{\gamma(0)}{\Gamma} E\left\{ \frac{[H(1)\Delta(1) + y_L(1)u_C(1)]}{\gamma(1)} \right\}$$

$$(5.80) \quad \frac{dH(0)}{dm} = -\frac{y_L(0)}{\gamma(0)} \frac{dZ(1)}{dm}$$

where

$$\Gamma \equiv \Delta(0) + \frac{(1 + r)^2}{1 + \rho} E\left\{ \frac{\Delta(1)}{\gamma(1)} \right\} \gamma(0)$$

Note that, provided leisure is statically normal (so that $y_L(1) > 0$), the quantity $[H(1)\Delta(1) + y_L(1)u_C(1)]/\gamma(1)$ is always negative. Hence, the expected value of this quantity is always negative also. By concavity of preferences, $\Delta(t) > 0$ and $\gamma(t) < 0$, $t = 0$ or 1; hence, $E\{\Delta(1)/\gamma(1)\} < 0$ and $\Gamma > 0$. Thus, provided leisure is statically normal, a uniform improvement in the outlook for future wages will unambiguously prompt the individual to reduce both his current savings and his current hours of work.

Now consider the effects on current behavior of a mean-constant increase in the variance of the distribution of future wage rates, as embodied in a positive value of dv and a (negative) value of dm equal to $-\mu_W\,dv$. This kind of change makes the future more uncertain without making it any brighter or gloomier (in terms of the individual's future wage prospects). Since in this case $dm = -\mu_W\,dv$, the terms involving dm and dv on the right-hand side of (5.77) combine to form a single term,

$$-\frac{1 + r}{1 + \rho} E\left\{ \frac{[H(1)\Delta(1) + y_L(1)u_C(1)][W(1) - \mu_W]}{\gamma(1)} \right\}.$$

The expected-value component of this term can be written somewhat more compactly as $\text{cov}\{[H(1)\Delta(1) + y_L(1)u_C(1)]/\gamma(1), W(1)\}$, where $\text{cov}[x, y]$ is the covariance between the variables x and y. To see this, note that, by the definition of the covariance between any two random variables x and y,

$$\begin{aligned}
\text{cov}[x, y] &\equiv E\{[x - \mu_x][y - \mu_y]\} \\
&= E\{xy\} - \mu_x E\{y\} - \mu_y E\{x\} + \mu_x\mu_y \\
&= E\{xy\} - \mu_x\mu_y \\
&= E\{xy\} - \mu_y E\{x\} = E\{x[y - \mu_y]\}
\end{aligned}$$

where μ_i, $i = x$ or y, is the mean (expected value) of variable i. (For example, see Wonnacott and Wonnacott, 1977, pp. 122–4.) Note that if x and y tend to move in the same direction – that is, if y is usually above (below) its average or mean value μ_y whenever x is above (below) its mean value μ_x, and vice versa – then $\text{cov}[x, y]$ will be positive. Likewise, if x and y tend to move in opposite directions, then $\text{cov}[x, y]$ will be negative.

Accordingly, solving equations (5.77) and (5.78) in this case yields

$$(5.81) \quad \left.\frac{dZ(1)}{dv}\right|_{dm = -\mu_W dv} = -\frac{1 + r}{1 + \rho} \frac{\gamma(0)}{\Gamma} \text{cov}\{[H(1)\Delta(1) + y_L(1)u_C(1)]/\gamma(1), W(1)\}$$

$$(5.82) \quad \left.\frac{dH(0)}{dv}\right|_{dm = -\mu_W dv} = -\frac{y_L(0)}{\gamma(0)} \cdot \left.\frac{dZ(1)}{dv}\right|_{dm = -\mu_W dv}$$

(Recall that $\Gamma > 0$.) These expressions resemble equations (5.79) and (5.80), except that equations (5.79) and (5.80) contain a term involving the *expected value* of $[H(1)\Delta(1) + y_L(1)u_C(1)]/\gamma(1)$, whereas equations (5.81) and (5.82) contain a term involving the *covariance between* this quantity and $W(1)$.

Thus, the sign of each of the changes given by equations (5.81) and (5.82) depends on the sign of the covariance term. In turn, the sign of the covariance term depends on whether $[H(1)\Delta(1) +$

$y_L(1)u_C(1)]/\gamma(1)$ increases or decreases when the wage $W(1)$ increases. Now, $[H(1)\Delta(1) + y_L(1)u_C(1)]/\gamma(1)$ depends on first- and second-order partial derivatives of the single-period utility function (e.g., $u_C(1)$ and $u_{CC}(1)$). So changes in this quantity depend on second- and *third*-order partial derivatives of the utility function (e.g., $u_{CC}(1)$ and $u_{CCC}(1)$). In other words, one can determine the sign of the covariance term in equations (5.81) and (5.82) and, thus, the signs of the changes given by these expressions only by making some assumptions about the signs and relative magnitudes of second- and third-order partial derivatives of the single-period utility function $u(C, L)$. Simply assuming concavity of the utility function is not enough, since that involves restrictions only on the signs and relative magnitudes of the utility function's first- and second-order partial derivatives.

In deciding just what assumptions to make about third-order partial derivatives, a number of researchers have drawn on work by Pratt (1964), who developed indexes of absolute and proportionate *risk aversion*. (See also subsequent work by Diamond and Stiglitz, 1974; Rothschild and Stiglitz, 1970, 1971.) Pratt analyzed behavior toward risk when utility is a function $u°$ of consumption *only*, so that $u° = u°(C)$, and when the risk involved is either (i) an uncertain *amount* z_A that is added to, or (ii) an uncertain *proportion* z_P that is multiplied times, an initial sum x. This makes actual consumption either $x + z_A$ or xz_P, respectively, where $z_i (i = $ A or P) is a random variable with a probability density function $f(z_i)$. To measure aversion to the riskiness of z_i, Pratt considered the absolute risk premium π_A that makes the utility of receiving the amount $x + E\{z_A\} - \pi_A$ with certainty equal to the *expected* utility of receiving the uncertain amount $x + z_A$ and considered the proportionate risk premium π_P that makes the utility of receiving the amount $E\{xz_P\} - \pi_P$ with certainty equal to the *expected* utility of receiving the *uncertain* amount xz_P. Thus, the risk premia π_A and π_P are numbers that satisfy the relations

(5.83) $u°[x + E\{z_A\} - \pi_A] = E\{u°[x + z_A]\}$
(5.84) $u°[E\{xz_P\} - \pi_P] = E\{u°[xz_P]\}$

respectively. Clearly, an individual for whom π_A (π_P) is relatively large derives relatively low utility from the situation involving absolute risk, $E\{u°[x + z_A]\}$ (from the situation involving proportionate risk, $E\{u°[xz_P]\}$), and may, therefore, be said to be *highly adverse* to absolute (proportionate) risk. Pratt went on to show that the size of the absolute risk premium π_A is directly proportional to $r_A(x) \equiv -u°_{CC}/u°_C$, where $u°_C$ and $u°_{CC}$ are the first and second derivatives of the utility function $u°(C)$ with respect to its single argument, C, and where $r_A(x)$ is called the *index of absolute risk aversion*. Similarly, Pratt showed the size of the proportionate risk premium π_P is directly proportional to $r_P(x) \equiv -xu°_{CC}/u°_C$, where $r_P(x)$ is called the *index of proportionate (or relative) risk aversion*. The higher $r_A(x)$ $(r_P(x))$ at any given value of x, the higher the absolute (proportionate) risk premium and, thus, the higher the degree of absolute (proportionate) risk aversion.

Of course, in general, the absolute or proportionate risk premium is not a constant number; rather, it will depend on x (that is, on consumption in the absence of any risky opportunities). Specifically, absolute risk aversion may be said to be increasing, constant, or decreasing depending on whether $dr_A(x)/dx$ is positive, zero, or negative: In other words,

$$(5.85) \quad \text{absolute risk aversion is} \begin{bmatrix} \text{increasing} \\ \text{constant} \\ \text{decreasing} \end{bmatrix}$$

$$\text{as} \quad dr_A(x)/dx = -[u°_C u°_{CCC} - (u°_{CC})^2 (u°_C)^{-2}](u°_C)^{-2} \begin{bmatrix} > \\ = \\ < \end{bmatrix} 0$$

Similarly,

$$(5.86) \quad \text{proportionate risk aversion is} \begin{bmatrix} \text{increasing} \\ \text{constant} \\ \text{decreasing} \end{bmatrix}$$

$$\text{as} \quad dr_P(x)/dx = -u°_{CC}(u°_C)^{-1} - x[u°_C u°_{CCC} - (u°_{CC})^2](u°_C)^{-2} \begin{bmatrix} > \\ = \\ < \end{bmatrix} 0$$

Thus, an assumption about the behavior of the intensity of risk aversion as x changes has implications about the signs and relative magnitudes of the derivatives of the single-argument utility function $u°$. For example, both Arrow (1963) and Pratt (1964) argue that absolute risk aversion can reasonably be assumed to be a decreasing function of x. Roughly speaking, this means that absolute risk-bearing is a "normal good" or, equivalently, that one would be more likely to accept an absolute risk (z_A) when one has \$1 million than when one has only \$10,000. By (5.85), decreasing absolute risk aversion in the sense of Pratt implies both that $u_C^\circ u_{CCC}^\circ > (u_{CC}^\circ)^2$ and, therefore (because $u_C^\circ > 0$ always), that $u_{CCC}^\circ > 0$.

The simplest way to extend this analysis to the case of the two-argument utility function $u = u(C, L)$ is to define indexes

$$R_A(C, L) = -u_{CC}(C, L)/u_C(C, L)$$
$$R_P(C, L) = -Cu_{CC}(C, L)/u_C(C, L)$$

and then to assume something about the partial derivatives of one or the other of these indexes with respect to C, L or both C and L. For example, Block and Heineke (1973, p. 378) assume that $R_A(C, L)$ is a decreasing function of C and is independent of L, that is, that

$$\partial R_A(C, L)/\partial C = -[u_C u_{CCC} - (u_{CC})^2](u_C)^{-2} < 0$$
$$\partial R_A(C, L)/\partial L = -[u_C u_{CCL} - u_{CC}u_{LC}](u_C)^{-2} = 0$$

Likewise, Eaton and Rosen (1980b, p. 367) assume that $R_P(C, L)$ is constant with respect to C, implying that $u_C u_{CCC} - (u_{CC})^2 = -u_C u_{CC}/C$.

This way of using Pratt's risk aversion indexes certainly generates implications about the signs and relative magnitudes of the partial derivatives of the two-argument utility function $u(C, L)$ that can be used to draw conclusions about the impact of, for example, greater wage uncertainty. (For example, see Block and Heineke, 1973; Cowell, 1981a, b; Eaton and Rosen, 1980b.) However, R_A and R_P do not have much to do with risk aversion in the case of the two-argument utility function and neither do assumptions about the behavior of these two indexes: The analogy between them and Pratt's indexes is imperfect. In Pratt's analysis, the utility function has a single argument that may be called *consumption* or *money*, and there is a single source of risk: risk in the amount of consumption or money that the individual can enjoy. Pratt's risk aversion indexes r_A and r_P may, therefore, accurately (if long-windedly) be called *indexes of absolute and proportionate money risk aversion* in the case of a single-argument utility function. However, when the individual maximizes a two-argument utility function $u = u(C, L)$ subject to a budget constraint $(1 + r)Z + WH = PC$ (as in the "period 1" of the model of this section), then there are, of course, two arguments in the utility function rather than one and – provided the individual is able to choose his own hours of work – there are three sources of risk: in the interest rate, in the wage rate, and in the price level.

Generalizing Pratt's (1964) analysis to cover this case is, therefore, not a question of simply using his risk aversion indexes without essential modification but rather of extending his treatment of risk premia so as to make it applicable to a different setting. For example, when the wage rate is random, one may define a wage rate risk premium π_W that makes the utility of being able to earn the wage rate $E\{W\}$ – π_W with certainty equal to the *expected* utility of earning the *uncertain* wage rate W, where W is a random variable with a probability density function $f(W)$. Since $L = 1 - H$, the wage rate risk premium π_W is, therefore, the number that satisfies the relation

(5.87) $u\{(Z/P) + [(E\{W\} - \pi_W)/P]H, 1 - H\}$
$= E\{u[(Z/P) + (W/P)H, 1 - H]\}$

One would then derive a measure of wage rate risk aversion in the case of a two-argument utility function by finding an index – written in terms of derivatives of the utility function u – that is functionally related (e.g., proportional) to π_W. Measures of interest rate and price risk aversion may be derived in an analogous manner. (See Kihlstrom and Mirman, 1974, for a generalization of Pratt's analysis to the case in which the utility function has more than one argument, and Abowd and Ashenfelter, 1979, who extend Pratt's analysis by deriving an expression for the compensating wage differential or hours of work risk premium π_H that employers will have to pay workers when *hours of work* are subject to risk – random variation – due to layoffs, bad weather, and the like.)

As applied to the present setting, the point of departure for an analysis of this kind is the fact that the wage premium π_W that satisfies (5.87) can be written as

(5.88) $\pi_W = \dfrac{\sigma_W^2}{2} \left[-\dfrac{1}{H} \dfrac{w_H}{-\gamma} + \dfrac{1}{U_C^*} \dfrac{y_L U_C^* + H\Delta}{-\gamma} \right]$

where the second term inside the parentheses is positive provided leisure is statically normal; where all terms refer to *maximized* utility; and where all terms are evaluated with W set at its mean, μ_W.

(See Killingsworth, 1982b.) Note that $w_H/-\gamma$ is the slope of the static one-period labor supply schedule. Now assume the following:

(i)   The slope of the labor supply schedule is positive and diminishing with respect to the wage rate (positive but diminishing marginal responsiveness of labor supply to the wage rate).

(ii) The individual's behavior exhibits constant or decreasing aversion to wage risk, in the sense that π_W is either the same or smaller at high mean wage levels μ_W than at low mean wage levels.

Assumption (i) implies that, as the wage rises, the first term inside the parentheses in (5.88), which is negative, *rises* in algebraic value, making π_W *bigger*, other things being equal. Equation (5.61) implies that $1/U_C^*$ also rises as the wage rises; and this, too, makes π_W bigger, other things being equal. (In other words, (5.61) implies that the maximum marginal utility of assets, which is proportional to U_C^*, is smaller at higher wage levels.) However, assumption (ii) implies that, on balance, π_W is either constant or decreasing with respect to the wage rate – which means that the second term inside the parentheses in (5.88), which is positive-signed, must *fall* as wages rise. The negative of this second term, therefore, *rises* in algebraic value as wages rise; in other words, assumptions (i) and (ii), together with (5.61), imply that

(5.89) $\mathrm{cov}\{[H(1)\Delta(1) + y_L(1)u_C(1)]/\gamma(1), W(1)\} > 0$

Now consider equations (5.81) and (5.82) again. If the covariance term is indeed positive, then equations (5.81) and (5.82) imply that when the wage outlook becomes more uncertain, the individual will increase *both* his labor supply *and* his savings in the current period.

The assumptions that underlie these conclusions seem fairly reasonable: constant or decreasing aversion to wage risk (in the sense that $d\pi_W/dW \leq 0$), positive but diminishing responsiveness of labor supply to the wage rate, and static normality of leisure. However, these assumptions are obviously somewhat arbitrary; and if, say, the labor supply schedule is backward bending, then (5.89) does not necessarily hold even if the individual exhibits constant or decreasing aversion to wage risk. The main conclusion that one can derive from equations (5.81) and (5.82) that does not require *any* assumptions about the slope of the labor supply schedule or about risk aversion is that an increase in wage uncertainty will lead to changes in both current savings and current labor supply in the *same direction*: If today's savings rise (fall) in response to an increase in future wage uncertainty – that is, in response to a mean-constant increase in the variance of future wages – then today's labor supply will rise (fall) as well, and vice versa. As indicated in the discussion of equations (5.79) and (5.80), the same is true of the individual's response to an improvement in future wage prospects, that is, to a variance–constant increase in the expected value of future wages.

Extensions

Although the discussion so far in this section has been concerned exclusively with risky *wages*, it is a relatively simple matter to extend the model to allow for risky *employment prospects*. As a first step, one might simply assume that the individual has a probability η of being employed in period 1 and, thus, will be unemployed with probability $1 - \eta$. If he is in fact unemployed in period 1, then his hours of work $H(1)$ are necessarily zero, so his utility during period 1 will be $u[Z(1)/P(1), 1]$ with certainty. If he is employed in period 1, his utility during period 1 is uncertain (because it depends on the wage rate $W(1)$ he actually gets) but is equal in expected value to the quantity $E\{U^*(1)\}$ defined in (5.62). Thus, in the presence of risky employment opportunities as well as risky wages, the individual's problem is to find

$$
\begin{aligned}
E\{U^*(0)\} = \max_{\{H(0), Z(1)\}} \Big\{ & u\Big[(1 + r)\,\frac{Z(0)}{P(0)} \\
& + \frac{W(0)}{P(0)}\,H(0) - \frac{Z(1)}{P(0)},\, 1 - H(0)\Big] \\
& + (1 + \rho)^{-1}(1 - \eta)u[Z(1)/P(1), 1] \\
& + (1 + \rho)^{-1}\eta E\{U^*(1)\} \Big\}
\end{aligned}
$$

This modifies (5.62) in only one respect: There is now one additional exogenous factor, the employment probability η, that can affect the individual's behavior. Deriving the response of current savings and current labor supply to changes in η is straightforward, since it involves just the same kind of analysis used in this section.

A second, much more challenging modification of (5.62) is to introduce η *and* to assume that η is a function of time the individual allocates to job search during period 0, $S(0)$. Thus, leisure time becomes $1 - H(0) - S(0)$, and η becomes $\eta[S(0)]$; one might reasonably assume that $\eta' > 0$ and that $\eta'' < 0$, that is, that there are positive but diminishing returns to job search.

Unfortunately, a "job search" model of this kind raises a technical, but potentially quite important, problem: in this case, satisfying the first-order conditions for a maximum of expected lifetime utility $E\{U^*(0)\}$ does not necessarily guarantee an optimum. In technical terms, this means that expected lifetime utility is not necessarily jointly concave in the individual's three decision variables, $H(0)$, $Z(1)$, and $S(0)$. Concavity of the single-period utility function in its two arguments C and L ensures that lifetime utility is jointly concave in $H(0)$ and $Z(1)$. Likewise, concavity of the single-period utility function in leisure time $L(0)$ ($= 1 - H(0) - S(0)$) and the assumption of positive but diminishing returns to search time $S(0)$ ensures that lifetime utility is also concave in $S(0)$. However, when η is a concave function of search time and future utility is a concave function of savings $Z(1)$ (recall (5.60)), expected future utility is the *product* of two concave functions; and, in general, the product of two concave functions is not *itself* concave. Thus, expected future utility may not be jointly concave in $Z(1)$, $H(0)$, and $S(0)$ taken together. This means that there may be more than one ($Z(1)$, $H(0)$, $S(0)$) point that satisfies the applicable first-order conditions for maximizing lifetime utility. If several points do in fact satisfy the first-order conditions, then some may *not* entail the true maximum value of lifetime utility. On the other hand, it may be possible to attain the true maximum at more than one ($Z(1)$, $H(0)$, $S(0)$) point.

In view of this, it is not surprising that the analysis of job search with endogenous labor supply (or, equivalently, of labor supply with endogenous job search) is in its infancy. Most job search models avoid the difficulties noted here by making labor supply fixed. Alternatively, Burdett and Mortensen (1978) assume that the individual is free to vary labor supply but does not save or borrow and is obliged in *each period t* to satisfy the *static* budget constraint $rZ(t) + W(t)H(t) = P(t)C(t)$. This simplifies the task of analysis greatly: It makes lifetime utility jointly concave in the individual's two remaining decision variables, $H(0)$ and $S(0)$. However, it also imposes some important restrictions on the model's empirical relevance, since it rules out savings as a possible mode of response to changes in future labor market prospects.

Indeed, perhaps the most interesting issue raised by the job search model with endogenous labor supply is precisely its nonconcavity. Here, as in other settings, the essential *practical* implication of nonconcavity is that small changes in certain parameters may generate large and discontinuous changes in decision variables, including, of course, labor supply. For example, as noted in Chapter 1, a small change in time or money costs of labor market entry may entail a large and discontinuous shift in labor supply from some large positive amount to zero or the reverse. The job search model outlined here may, therefore, provide another explanation for the seeming discontinuity of observed labor supply behavior – that is, numerous observations clustered at zero, numerous observations with hours of work at or in excess of some large positive amount and relatively few observations in between. For example, a change in the offered wage may induce the individual to reduce $S(0)$ from a large positive amount to zero and to increase $H(0)$ from zero to a large positive amount – to stop full-time search and start full-time work.

5.4. Dynamic labor supply models with exogenous wages: empirical analysis

Empirical analysis of dynamic labor supply models, like empirical analysis of static models, rests (or, at least, ought to rest) on specifications that link observed behavior to a reasonably explicit and formal utility function (or to some other utility-related function, such as the marginal rate of substitution function, the indirect utility function, etc.). In the dynamic case, the question of specification raises many of the issues noted in the previous section: Is it reasonably innocuous to assume that the lifetime utility function is intertemporally separable (i.e., resembles (5.4) rather than (5.1)) and, thus, that all leisure times at different dates are net substitutes? To what extent is it possible to estimate the parameters that affect life cycle – that is, dynamic – behavior using cross-section data, that is, observations on different individuals' behavior at a single point in time? How can one make an empirical distinction between movements *along* life cycle profiles and shifts *of* life cycle profiles? To what extent is it necessary to modify specifications derived under the assumption of perfect foresight (which implies that labor supply at any date t can be expressed in terms of μ, the *initial* shadow price of assets) in order to make them applicable to an environment of risk and uncertainty?

After considering these and other questions of specification, I will briefly discuss problems of data and measurement of variables, including, in particular, attempts to decompose wage rates into "permanent" and "transitory" components. I will then summarize the results of a number of recent empirical studies of dynamic labor supply.

Specification

As noted later, there are a variety of different ways to manipulate dynamic exogenous wage labor supply models so as to derive a specification, suitable for econometric estimation, of a dynamic labor supply function. In many cases, the result is an expression that is strikingly similar to a static labor supply function.

For example, suppose one assumes that the dynamic utility function is not separable in time and that the individual enjoys perfect foresight. In this case, the dynamic labor supply function is analogous to the static labor supply function of a family member: In a static setting, a family member's labor supply is a function of the family's property income and of the wage rates of all family members; in a dynamic setting, the individual's current labor supply is a function of the individual's initial assets (or, alternatively, of his current level of assets) and the wage rates that will prevail at every different date. In other words, one can convert the static family labor supply function to a dynamic function by simply changing subscripts (from i, for family member i, to t, for period t) and by replacing property income V with either initial assets $Z(0)$ or current assets $Z(t)$. The only essential difference is that although property income V is exogenous in the static case, current assets $Z(t)$ are endogenous in the dynamic case.

On the other hand, suppose one assumes that the dynamic utility function is separable in time and that the individual enjoys perfect foresight. In this case, one can view the life cycle as a sequence of individual periods and, in formal terms, behavior in each of these periods strongly resembles behavior in the simple static one-period model of Chapter 1. In particular, intertemporal separability implies that the marginal rate of substitution $m(t)$ during each life cycle period t depends only on current consumption $C(t)$ and current leisure time $L(t)$, that is, $m(t) = m[C(t), L(t)]$, and is equated to the current real wage rate $W(t)/P(t)$. Of course, exactly the same condition holds in the simple static model. Moreover, at each point in the life cycle, the individual's consumption spending $P(t)C(t)$ and earnings $W(t)H(t)$ satisfy the accounting identity $V(t) + W(t)H(t) = P(t)C(t)$, where $V(t)$ is property income *net of* increases or decreases in the individual's level of assets $Z(t)$. These two facts about behavior under intertemporal separability mean that one can derive a function for current labor supply by using the conditions $m[C(t), L(t)] = W(t)/P(t)$ and $V(t) + W(t)H(t) = P(t)C(t)$, very much as one would do in the static case. Once again, the main difference is that, in the static case, property income V is exogenous and no saving or borrowing occurs, whereas in the dynamic case, the individual may save and borrow so that $V(t)$ is endogenous. (Alternatively, one may say that, since $V(t)$ is endogenous, $H(t)$ and $C(t)$ need not be related in any simple way, as they would be in a static model in which choice of H is tantamount to choice of C.)

Before considering ways of deriving a dynamic labor supply specification, however, it is important to note that estimation of a dynamic exogenous wage model may also require estimation (and, thus, specification) of a dynamic *wage* function.

This is so for three main reasons. First, the fact that exogenous wage dynamic labor supply models treat wage rates as exogenous in *analytical* terms (i.e., treat wages as independent of the individual's choices) does not necessarily mean that wage rates should be assumed to be exogenous in *statistical* terms (i.e., should be assumed to be uncorrelated with unobservable factors that affect labor supply). Rather, wage rates may well be statistically endogenous (i.e., correlated with the error term of the dynamic labor supply function). This being the case, it is necessary to consider explicitly the purely statistical endogeneity of wage rates over the life cycle – to decide on a set of instruments for wage rates or to specify a formal functional relation between the wage at any given date and the individual's characteristics at that date – even though wage rates are assumed exogenous in an analytical sense.

Second, the fact that wage rates of persons who are not at work are not observed raises issues of selection bias. In general, avoiding selection bias in estimating the parameters of a dynamic labor supply model means specifying and estimating the determinants of the decision to work – and, thus, specification of an important determinant of the decision to work: the wage offer. (For discussion of selection bias problems in a dynamic context, see Heckman and MaCurdy, 1980.)

These two reasons for specifying a wage equation as part of a dynamic labor supply model should sound familiar: They simply extend, to a dynamic setting, the same considerations that underlie the case for specifying a wage equation as part of a static labor supply model (recall the discussion in Chapter 4). A third reason, however, is peculiar to dynamic models: the inevitability of gaps in data on life cycle wage profiles. At least in principle, estimation and interpretation of a dynamic exogenous wage model of labor supply may require data on wages over the *entire* life cycle – yet, in practice, investigators typically have access to data for, at best, only a rather small portion of any individual's entire life cycle. This means that, in the usual case, investigators have data on only a portion of the lifetime wage profile of any given individual – even an individual who works more or less continuously.

For all of these reasons, researchers not infrequently estimate a dynamic wage equation along with a dynamic labor supply equation, even if the latter is the relationship of primary interest. As a fairly general dynamic wage equation, MaCurdy (1981a) proposes the following function that is quadratic in age (t), with an intercept and slope coefficients that depend on age-invariant characteristics of individuals:

$$(5.90) \quad \ln W(t) = a_0 + a_1 t + a_2 t^2 + w$$

where $a_j = \mathbf{Y}'\mathbf{b}_j$; $j = 0, 1, 2$; $\mathbf{Y}$ is a vector of observable characteristics; t is age; the $\mathbf{b}_j$ are vectors of parameters; and w is a random error term representing the effects of unobservables.

As noted later, wage functions such as (5.90) can be used to correct for the three problems just mentioned – statistical endogeneity of the wage rate, selection bias, and gaps in life cycle wage data – and, thus, to permit more reliable estimation of life cycle labor supply functions. It remains to be seen how one might specify life cycle labor supply functions per se. The procedures that will be considered here are the "brute force" method, the DMRS method, the "two-stage" method, and the COLISPIA method.

Brute force. The logic underlying the brute force procedure is simple and straightforward. Under this method, the dynamic labor supply function is specified as[13]

(5.91) $H(t) = H_t[Z(0)/P(0), W(0)/P(0), W(1)/P(0), \ldots ,$
$W(T)/P(0), P(1)/P(0), \ldots , P(T)/P(0)]$

It is important to note that expressions such as (5.91) are valid labor supply functions regardless of whether one assumes that the utility function is (as in (5.4)) or is not (as in (5.1)) separable over time. In the case of an inseparable utility function, note from the previous discussion that one may always treat the life cycle optimization problem as equivalent to a static problem in which the individual chooses goods $C(0), L(0), C(1), L(1), \ldots , C(T), L(T)$, with prices $p(0), w(0), p(1), w(1), \ldots , p(T), w(T)$, where $p(t) \equiv (1 + r)^{-t} P(t)$ and $w(t) \equiv (1 + r)^{-t} W(t)$. Note also that, in general, *each* of the goods (both C and L for all t) is a function of the prices w and p of *all* of the goods [14] (and also, of course, of real initial assets, $Z(0)/P(0)$). On the other hand, in the case of a separable utility utility function such as (5.4), note from the previous discussion (e.g., equations (5.8)–(5.10)) that labor supply and consumption at any date t depend directly on the wage rate and the price level

[13] As noted earlier, labor supply (and consumption) at any date is homogeneous of degree zero in initial assets and all wage rates and price levels. Accordingly, one may normalize by, for example, dividing initial assets and all wage rates and price levels by the price level at any arbitrarily selected date, such as $P(0)$. Note also that, as (5.91) implies, there is a function, such as (5.91), for *each* date's labor supply *and* for *each* date's consumption, just as, for example, the family utility–family budget constraint model of Chapter 2 generates a function for family consumption and for each family member's labor supply.

[14] Recall, for example, that the static family utility–family budget constraint model generates labor supply functions in which *each* family member's labor supply is a function of the family's property income and of the wage rates of *each* of the other family members.

at that date, and also on μ; and that, in turn, μ is a function of initial assets $Z(0)$ and of wage rates and prices at all dates. Thus, (5.91) holds whether or not the utility function is separable in time. The main consequence of using or eschewing the assumption of separability is that under inseparability signs of all intertemporal cross-substitution effects are unrestricted, whereas under separability these effects are constrained to be negative (i.e., leisure times at different dates are assumed to be net substitutes).[15]

Although it is straightforward to specify relations such as (5.91), it is sometimes difficult to estimate them. First, if one assumes that the utility function underlying (5.91) is inseparable, then estimating functions such as (5.91) requires estimation of an extremely large number of parameters.[16] (Of course, as Diewert, 1974, points out, one can reduce the magnitude of this problem considerably by, for example, assuming that some of the parameters are equal to others and by assuming that some of the other parameters are equal to zero.) Second, regardless of whether the utility function is assumed to be separable or inseparable, estimating functions such as (5.91) require data on initial assets and on wages and prices at *every* point in the life cycle. Different authors have attempted to solve this problem in different ways. For example, Diewert (1974) treats the

[15] Under the assumption of perfect foresight, each individual knows exactly what his wage rate at t' (and at every other date) will be, and the wage changes that occur *over time* do not change full wealth or generate substitution effects. Thus, it may seem strange to read that an increase in the wage at some time t' will have a cross-substitution effect on labor supply at $t \neq t'$.) However, note that empirical analysis is concerned with *different* persons and that differences in the labor supplies of two persons that are associated with *differences* in their wage rates can of course be interpreted in terms of wealth and own- and cross-substitution effects.

[16] To see this, think of the life cycle as a total of $T + 1$ distinct periods of finite length starting at $t = 0$ and ending at $t = T$. (Thus, for the moment, use a discrete-time model of the life cycle.) Then the matrix of own- and cross-substitution terms involving labor supply has $T + 1$ rows and $T + 1$ columns, one for each period, making a total of $(T + 1)^2$ own- and cross-substitution terms for labor supply (or, equivalently, leisure time). $T + 1$ of these are own-substitution terms, leaving $(T + 1)^2 - (T + 1)$ cross-substitution terms. By symmetry, the cross-substitution effect on leisure (labor supply) at any time t of a rise in the wage at any other time t' ($t' \neq t$) is equal to the cross-substitution effect on leisure (labor supply) at t' of a rise in the wage at t; hence there are $[(T + 1)^2 - (T + 1)]/2$ *distinct* cross-substitution terms involving labor supply. For large T (e.g., a life cycle that begins at age 21 and ends at age 70), the number of terms to be estimated can be very large indeed.

U.S. *economy* as a "representative individual" and treats aggregate time-series data on the average wage rate as the equivalent of (or as analogous to) a wage profile, that is, data on the $W(t)$ of (5.91). On the other hand, Heckman (1971) develops a wage function similar in spirit to (5.90) and uses predicted wages derived from this function as measures of the $W(t)$ that appear in (5.91).

Most alternatives to the brute force approach rely on a separable utility function: as will be seen shortly, assuming separability can reduce substantially some of the problems that arise in estimation of a dynamic life cycle model, even if it does not dispose of such problems entirely.

DMRS. The DMRS approach – DMRS being an abbreviation for *dynamic marginal rate of substitution* – is based on the fact that, *if* the utility function is intertemporally separable, then $m(t)$ – the marginal rate of substitution at time t – is a function of $C(t)$ and $L(t)$ but *not* of consumption or leisure at *other* dates. Thus, given an expression for $m(t)$, one may immediately derive an expression for $C(t)$ and $L(t)$, and thus $H(t)$, in terms of the real wage $W(t)/P(t)$. (See MaCurdy, 1981b, for an application of this method.)

For example, suppose one specifies the marginal rate of substitution using the log–linear function

(5.92) $\ln m(t) = \alpha_C \ln C(t) + \alpha_L \ln L(t) + \mathbf{X}(t)'\gamma + \epsilon(t)$

where $\mathbf{X}(t)$ is a vector of observed characteristics (age, sex, race, schooling, etc.) that may affect $\ln m(t)$, and $\epsilon(t)$ is a random term representing unobservable factors (e.g., tastes) that may affect $\ln m(t)$. (Note that (5.92) assumes a separable utility function: otherwise, $\ln m(t)$ would depend also on C and L at all other dates $t' \neq t$ as well as on $C(t)$ and $L(t)$.) Then, from the aforementioned,

(5.93) $\ln [W(t)/P(t)] = \mathbf{X}(t)'\gamma + \alpha_C \ln C(t) + \alpha_L \ln L(t)$
$\qquad\qquad\qquad + \epsilon(t)$

Of course, neither $C(t)$ nor $L(t)$ is exogenous; rather, both are choice variables and so are endogenous. Accordingly, (5.93) should be estimated not by OLS, which ignores this endogeneity but rather by a technique such as two-stage least squares (2SLS) that takes account of such endogeneity. Thus, as Heckman (1974a, esp. note

15) and MaCurdy (1981b) note, the investigator who uses the DMRS approach needs data on hours of work $H(t)$, consumption $C(t)$, characteristics $X(t)$, *and* a valid set of instruments (for use in 2SLS estimation). However, it is interesting to note that, at least in principle, one can use the DMRS method even if the only available data are for a single cross section: In a life cycle setting, behavior observed at a given point t (that is, in a single cross-section "snapshot") is still the result of dynamic or life cycle forces, and so data on behavior at that date can be used to estimate some of the parameters (α_C, α_L, etc.) that govern dynamic behavior. Of course, if panel or longitudinal data, which track a group of individuals over time, are available, so much the better. However, although such data may be quite valuable, access to such data is not strictly necessary for implementation of the DMRS approach.

Although the DMRS method is certainly much simpler to use than the brute force method, its scope is much more limited. First, DMRS entails the assumption that consumption and leisure at dates other than t do not affect $m(t)$. Second, although estimates of (5.93) certainly provide estimates of the parameters of the marginal rate of substitution function (e.g., α_C, α_L, and γ), these are not sufficient to provide a complete characterization of the dynamic equilibrium of a representative individual: It is also necessary to have an estimate of (or an a priori assumption about) the value of $\rho - r$. Finally, the DMRS approach also provides little useful information about the comparative dynamics of a representative individual. This is because estimates of functions based on this approach (e.g., of (5.93)) do not show, and cannot be used to determine, how differences across individuals in life cycle wage profiles will lead to differences in μ, and hence to differences in life cycle labor supply profiles.

The two-stage method. In a single-period model, the budget constraint may be written as $-V = WH - PC$, where V is exogenous, whereas in a dynamic exogenous wage model the budget constraint may be written as $\dot{Z}(t) - rZ(t) = W(t)H(t) - P(t)C(t)$, where both $\dot{Z}(t)$ and $rZ(t)$ are endogenous. However, one may nevertheless split life cycle decision making into two stages: In the first stage, the individual chooses the optimal value of net property income (that is, property income net of savings $\dot{Z}(t)$), which I will write as $V(t) \equiv rZ(t) - \dot{Z}(t)$, for each t; in the second stage, he then chooses $H(t)$ and $C(t)$ subject to his first-stage choice of $V(t)$, that is, subject to the constraint $-V(t) = W(t)H(t) - P(t)C(t)$. At least in formal terms, the second stage of this process closely resembles decision making in a simple one-period labor supply model, despite the fact that in several important respects the two models are of course quite different.

Both the similarities and the differences are most easily seen as follows: In the static one-period case, the labor supply function is $H = H(W/P, V/P)$ with both W/P and V/P exogenously given, whereas in the dynamic case the labor supply function may be written as $H(t) = H[W(t)/P(t), V(t)/P(t)]$ with $W(t)/P(t)$ treated as exogenous but with $V(t)/P(t)$ treated as endogenous due to the fact that both components of $V(t)$ – savings or borrowing $\dot{Z}(t)$ and property income $rZ(t)$ – are the result of life cycle choices. However, the effect on $H(t)$ of a rise in $V(t)/P(t)$ in the dynamic model is the same as the effect on H of a rise in V/P in the static model. (For further discussion of this point, see MaCurdy, 1981b.)

It is simple to show that one can indeed split life cycle decision making into these two stages (i.e., choice of $V(t)$ and then choice of $C(t)$ and $H(t)$ given choice of $V(t)$). Note from the definition $V(t) \equiv rZ(t) - \dot{Z}(t)$ that one may rewrite equations (5.5) and (5.6) to read

$$-V(t) = W(t)H(t) - P(t)C(t)$$
$$Z(0) - \int_0^T e^{-rt} V(t)\, dt = 0$$

Thus, one may rewrite the individual's maximization problem, (5.7), as

$$(5.94) \quad \max_{[C(t), H(t), V(t), \lambda(t), \mu]} \left(\int_0^T e^{-\rho t} u[C(t), 1 - H(t)]\, dt \right.$$
$$+ \lambda(t) [V(t) + W(t)H(t) - P(t)C(t)]$$
$$\left. + \mu \left[Z(0) - \int_0^T e^{-rt} V(t)\, dt \right] \right)$$

where μ is the marginal utility or implicit (shadow) value of initial assets $Z(0)$, as before, and $\lambda(t)$ is the marginal utility or implicit (shadow) value as of time t of net property income $V(t)$. The first-order conditions for a maximum are

(5.95) $e^{-\rho t} u_C(t) = \lambda(t) P(t)$

(5.96) $e^{-\rho t} u_L(t) = \lambda(t) W(t)$

(5.97) $\lambda(t) = e^{-rt} \mu$

(5.98) $V(t) + W(t) H(t) - P(t) C(t) = 0$

(5.99) $Z(0) - \int_0^T e^{-rt} V(t)\, dt = 0$

Next, note that, by (5.97) one may replace $\lambda(t)$ in (5.95) and (5.96) with $e^{-rt}\mu$, drop (5.97) from the first-order conditions (5.95)–(5.99), and use (5.98) to replace $V(t)$ in (5.99) with $-[W(t)H(t) - P(t)C(t)]$, which leads back to equations (5.8)–(5.10). Thus, equations (5.95)–(5.99) are identical to equations (5.8)–(5.10) and refer to exactly the same optimization problem; they differ from each other only in that they describe the problem in slightly different ways. Note also that (5.95), (5.96), and (5.98) show that one may think of the individual as equating the marginal rate of substitution to the real wage – setting $u_C(t)/u_L(t) = W(t)/P(t)$ – subject to the requirement $-V(t) = W(t)H(t) - P(t)C(t)$. Of course, provided one interprets $V(t)$ as analogous to the V of the one-period model of Chapter 1, this description of life cycle optimization is identical to the description of static optimization presented in Chapter 1.

To see how one may implement the two-stage approach, let the instantaneous utility function $u(t)$ be given by $u(t) = \alpha \ln C(t) + \beta \ln L(t)$. By equations (5.30), (5.31), and (5.97), then,

$$P(t) C(t) = \alpha e^{-(\rho - r)t}/\mu$$
$$W(t) L(t) = \beta e^{-(\rho - r)t}/\mu$$

and, by (5.40),

$$-V(t) = W(t) - [e^{-(\rho - r)t}(\alpha + \beta)/\mu]$$

so that

$$C(t) = [\alpha/(\alpha + \beta)] [W(t) + V(t)]/P(t)$$
$$L(t) = [\beta/(\alpha + \beta)] [W(t) + V(t)]/W(t)$$

Finally, introduce random terms $\epsilon_C(t)$ and $\epsilon_H(t)$ and assume that they represent unobserved factors that have additive effects on $C(t)$ and $H(t)$. Then the empirical dynamic consumption and labor supply functions implied by this model are

(5.100) $C(t) = a[W(t)/P(t)] + a[V(t)/P(t)] + \epsilon_C(t)$
(5.101) $H(t) = 1 - b - b[V(t)/W(t)] + \epsilon_H(t)$

where $a \equiv \alpha/(\alpha + \beta)$ and $b \equiv \beta/(\alpha + \beta)$. Equations (5.100) and (5.101) are identical to the functions that would be generated by a *static* model of an individual who chooses $C(t)$ and $H(t)$ (or $L(t)$) so as to maximize a *single-period* utility function $u(t) = \alpha \ln C(t) + \beta \ln L(t)$ subject to a *single-period* constraint $- V(t) = W(t)H(t) - P(t)C(t)$, with $V(t)$ treated as exogenously given.

Of course, in the dynamic setting considered here, $V(t) \equiv rZ(t) - \dot{Z}(t)$ is a choice variable rather than an exogenous constraint: Its two components, property income $rZ(t)$ and savings $\dot{Z}(t)$, depend on the individual's past and present choices. There is no *theoretical* reason why adjusted property income $V(t)$, property income $rZ(t)$, the current level of assets $Z(t)$ or savings $\dot{Z}(t)$ must be excluded from the dynamic labor supply function. However, if unmeasured factors that affect savings decisions and, thus, property income (and current asset levels) are correlated with the error term in the labor supply function, then including $V(t)$, $rZ(t)$, $Z(t)$, or $\dot{Z}(t)$ in the labor supply equation may lead to *empirical* problems. (See Cotterman, 1981; Fleisher, Parsons, and Porter, 1973; Greenberg, 1971; Greenberg and Kosters, 1973; J. P. Smith, 1977a, b, 1980b.) One way to address such problems is to use instrumental variables techniques. Another is to derive an explicit expression for $V(t)$ as a function of exogenous variables only. (For example, for the particular log–linear utility function discussed in the previous example, (5.40) is just such an expression.) Then one can estimate equations (5.100) and (5.101) *and* the parameters of the $V(t)$ function together. Note also that, at least in principle, one can use the two-stage procedure – like the DMRS procedure – to fit a dynamic labor supply function even if the only data available are for a single cross section: As in the case of DMRS, longitudinal or panel data are certainly helpful for estimation using the two-stage procedure, but such data are not an indispensable necessity.

Finally, note that, like the DMRS method, the two-stage method entails the assumption that $m(t)$ depends only on consumption and leisure at t (and not at other dates) and that estimates derived under this method are not sufficient to characterize the life cycle completely. As in the DMRS case, it is necessary to obtain an estimate (or a guesstimate) of the magnitude of $(\rho - r)$; this, together with estimates of the parameters of the "first-stage" functions (e.g., relations such as equations (5.100) and (5.101), can then be used to derive dynamic equilibrium effects of intertemporal changes in wage rates. In addition, the two-stage approach, like the DMRS approach, provides little or no useful information on comparative dynamics, for example, on how differences across individuals in life cycle wage profiles will lead to differences in μ, and hence to differences in life cycle labor supply profiles.

COLISPIA. A final method for specifying the dynamic labor supply function when wages are exogenous is based on the fact, noted earlier, that the marginal utility or shadow price of initial assets μ is constant over the individual's lifetime – *provided* he remains in his initial equilibrium. Hence, I call this the COLISPIA method, since it is based on the assumption of "constant lifetime shadow price of initial assets."

To see how one uses the COLISPIA approach to specify the dynamic labor supply function, recall that one can solve for $C(t)$ and $H(t)$ as functions of $W(t)$, $P(t)$, time (that is, t), and μ; and μ in effect summarizes all of the information pertinent to the individual's lifetime equilibrium: That is, μ is a function of the initial stock of assets and of the time profiles of the wage rate and the price level over the individual's entire life cycle. In general terms, then, one may solve equations (5.8)–(5.10) for $H(t)$ and $C(t)$ to obtain

$$C(t) = C[e^{(\rho - r)t}\mu P(t), e^{(\rho - r)t}\mu W(t)]$$
$$H(t) = H[e^{(\rho - r)t}\mu P(t), e^{(\rho - r)t}\mu W(t)]$$

By adopting an explicit specification for the instantaneous utility function $u(t)$, one can give explicit functional forms for these two expressions. For example, suppose one specifies $u(t)$ as $u(t) = A(t)C(t)^\alpha L(t)^\beta$, where $A(t)$ is a function of the individual's characteristics (observables such as sex, age, race, etc., and unobservable taste factors). Then equations (5.8) and (5.9) become

$$\alpha A(t)C(t)^{\alpha - 1} L(t)^\beta = e^{(\rho - r)t}\mu P(t)$$
$$\beta A(t)C(t)^\alpha L(t)^{\beta - 1} = e^{(\rho - r)t}\mu W(t)$$

Take logarithms of both sides of these expressions and rearrange terms to solve for $\ln C(t)$ and $\ln L(t)$:

$$\ln C(t) = \kappa_C + [\ln A(t)/\Delta] - [(\rho - r)/\Delta]t$$
$$- [(1 - \beta)/\Delta] \ln P(t) - (\beta/\Delta) \ln W(t) - (\ln \mu/\Delta)$$
$$\ln L(t) = \kappa_L + [\ln A(t)/\Delta] - [(\rho - r/\Delta]t$$
$$- (\alpha/\Delta) \ln P(t) - [(1 - \alpha)/\Delta] \ln W(t) - (\ln \mu/\Delta)$$

where

$$\Delta \equiv 1 - \alpha - \beta$$
$$\kappa_C \equiv [(1 - \beta)/\Delta] \ln \alpha + (\beta/\Delta) \ln \beta$$
$$\kappa_L \equiv [(1 - \alpha)/\Delta] \ln \beta + (\alpha/\Delta) \ln \alpha$$

Finally, suppose that $\ln A(t)$ is given by $\ln A(t) = \mathbf{X}(t)'\gamma + \epsilon(t)$, where $\mathbf{X}$ is a vector of observable characteristics and $\epsilon(t)$ is an unobservable random term. Then the expressions immediately above become

(5.102) $\quad \ln C(t) = \kappa_C + \mathbf{X}(t)'\gamma^* - [(\rho - r)/\Delta]t$
$$- [(1 - \beta)/\Delta] \ln P(t) - (\beta/\Delta) \ln W(t)$$
$$- (\ln \mu/\Delta) + \epsilon^*(t)$$
(5.103) $\quad \ln L(t) = \kappa_L + \mathbf{X}(t)'\gamma^* - [(\rho - r)/\Delta]t$
$$- (\alpha/\Delta) \ln P(t) - [(1 - \alpha)/\Delta] \ln W(t)$$
$$- (\ln \mu/\Delta) + \epsilon^*(t)$$

where

$$\epsilon^*(t) = \epsilon(t)/\Delta$$
$$\gamma^* = \gamma/\Delta$$

Of course, $\ln \mu$ usually cannot be observed. It is tempting to treat it as an unobservable random variable similar in nature to $\epsilon^*(t)$ and, thus, to lump it into the error term of these regression equations. However, this would be incorrect: Since μ is a *function* of the wage and price profiles, it is necessarily correlated with $W(t)$ and $P(t)$.

What is to be done? One relatively simple solution is the one proposed and implemented by Ashenfelter and Ham (1979), Heckman and MaCurdy (1980) and MaCurdy (1981a): to treat μ (or its logarithm) as an individual-specific constant term or fixed effect. For example, if one has observations on the labor supply, consumption spending, and so forth of all individuals at two different dates t and t', then one can simply take the difference between each individual's $\ln L(t')$ and his $\ln L(t)$ as given by (5.103), thereby eliminating the unobserved constant term (ln μ/Δ), which varies across individuals but is fixed over time for any *given* individual (*provided* each individual remains in his original equilibrium lifetime plan).

As an alternative – one that is particularly useful when three or more observations on each individual are available for three or more dates – one can estimate regression functions, such as (5.103), by adding dummy variables (one for each individual appearing in the data) to the set of variables already in (5.103). Under the hypothesis that all individuals enjoy perfect foresight (so that no one's value of (ln μ/Δ) need ever be revised due to unanticipated changes in the wage or price profiles), the coefficient on such a dummy variable for a particular individual is an unbiased estimate of the value of (ln μ/Δ) for that individual. (The other parameter estimates are likewise unbiased.) Thus, panel data – at least two different observations, for at least two different dates, for each of the individuals in the data set – are essential to the COLISPIA procedure, unlike, for example, either the DMRS or the two-stage procedure. It is worth noting that the relevant fixed effect (that is, (ln μ/Δ) or its analog) may not always appear in the dynamic labor supply function in simple linear form, as in (5.103); this depends on the functional form one chooses for the utility function. (See Ashenfelter and Ham, 1979, esp. pp. S113–4, for a model in which the fixed effect in the labor supply function is nonlinear, requiring a fairly sophisticated strategy for estimation.)

Estimates of expressions such as (5.102) and (5.103), of course, provide measures of utility function parameters (e.g., the α and β of equations (5.102) and (5.103)) and also of the magnitude of $\rho - r$. Hence, they may be used to describe the dynamic equilibrium of a representative individual. In and of themselves, estimates of expressions such as (5.102) and (5.103) are not sufficient to provide a complete description of the comparative dynamics of a representative individual. Evaluation of comparative dynamics requires estimation of the relation between μ and exogenous variables, such as initial assets, wage rates, and the like. Accordingly, Heckman and MaCurdy (1980) and MaCurdy (1981a) regress *estimates* of each individual's value of ln μ, obtained from estimation of equations such as (5.102) and (5.103), on a set of exogenous variables. For example, as applied to equations (5.102) and (5.103), MaCurdy's

(1981a) approach would entail assuming that each individual's value of $(\ln \mu/\Delta)$ may be approximated by a linear function of a vector of his measured characteristics $\mathbf{X}$, the value of his $\ln W(t)$ at each age t, the value of his initial wealth $Z(0)$, and a random term v representing unobserved characteristics, as follows:

$$(\ln \mu/\Delta) = \mathbf{X}'\phi + \sum_{t=0}^{T} \kappa_t \ln W(t) + \zeta Z(0) + v$$

Now insert (5.90) into this expression, to obtain

(5.104) $(\ln \mu/\Delta) = \mathbf{X}'\phi + a_0 \bar{\kappa}_0 + a_1 \bar{\kappa}_1 + a_2 \bar{\kappa}_2 + \zeta Z(0) + \bar{v}$

where

$$\bar{v} \equiv v + w\left(\sum_{t=0}^{T} \kappa_t \right)$$

$$\bar{\kappa}_j \equiv \sum_{t=0}^{T} t^j \kappa_t, \qquad j = 0, 1, 2$$

and where a_j $(j = 0, 1, 2)$ is as defined in equation (5.90). Note that, as the dependent variable in (5.104), one would use *estimates* of individuals' $(\ln \mu/\Delta)$ as derived from econometric results for (5.102) and (5.103).

Two features of (5.104) deserve mention. First, (5.104) and (5.90) imply that a unit increase in the intercept term in the coefficient $a_0 = \mathbf{Y}' \mathbf{b}_0$ is the equivalent of a unit increase in the natural logarithm (or, approximately, a 100 percent increase in the *value*) of *all* wages, that is, represents a shift in the entire wage profile facing the individual, and the parameter $\bar{\kappa}_0$ measures the extent to which such a shift in the wage profile affects $(\ln \mu/\Delta)$ and, thus, by equations (5.102) and (5.103), leisure time at each date. Hence, $\bar{\kappa}_0$ is an empirical measure of the μ-variable effect of such a shift in the entire wage profile on leisure time (measured in units of natural logarithms). (Note also from (5.103) that the μ-constant effect on $\ln L(t)$ of such a profile shift is given by the coefficient on $\ln W(t)$ in the dynamic labor supply function, that is, by the estimate of $-(1 - \alpha)/\Delta$.) Second, although the formal model of dynamic labor supply decisions presented in the previous section ignored bequests, the present method for estimating the determinants of μ does not. In other words, rather than make the analytically convenient, but empirically dubious, assumption that individuals' valuation of initial assets is just low enough to result in their having a net worth of exactly zero at time T, the empirical treatment of μ implicit in (5.104) makes no such assumption. Instead, other things being equal, a high estimated value of μ (or of (ln μ/Δ)) may be regarded as a strong taste for asset accumulation and, hence, for bequests.

Risk and uncertainty. All of these procedures for specifying the dynamic labor supply function assume perfect foresight and complete certainty. However, it is fairly straightforward to allow for risk and uncertainty, at least if one assumes that the utility function is separable in time. For example, as noted in Section 5.3, the individual equates the current marginal rate of substitution $m(t)$ to the current real wage $W(t)/P(t)$ even when future wage rates are uncertain. Also, current earnings and current consumption still obey the relation $V(t) + W(t)H(t) = P(t)C(t)$, where $V(t)$ is property income net of changes in assets, even when future wages are uncertain; after all, this relation is just an accounting identity. Thus, specifications based on either the DMRS method or the two-stage method apply just as much to a risky world as they do to a world of perfect certainty.

Specifications based on the COLISPIA approach under the assumption of perfect certainty require some modification before they can be taken to apply to a risky world, however. As noted just earlier, the assumption of perfect certainty means that one can write labor supply decisions at *all* dates in terms of the *initial* (as of time $t = 0$) shadow price of assets, μ. In contrast, as noted in Section 5.3, one cannot do so when the future is uncertain. In this case, the shadow price variable that is relevant to decisions at time t is $\mu_t \equiv u_C(t)/P(t)$, the shadow price of assets *as of* time t; and μ_t cannot be written as an exact function of the shadow price of *initial* assets, μ_0 ($= \mu$), alone. However, the difference between μ_t and μ_{t-1} depends on the discrepancy between the expected (as of period $t - 1$) and actual (as of period t) marginal utility of consumption during period t. For example, equations (5.72)–(5.76) can be generalized to yield

$$\mu_t - [(1 + \rho)/(1 + r)]\mu_{t-1} = [E\{u_C(t)\} - u_C(t)]/P(t)$$

So long as these discrepancies are random, one can, therefore, modify the perfect-foresight interpretation of μ as an individual-specific fixed effect by treating each period's μ_t as an individual-specific time-varying effect that is serially correlated, changing over time according to a relation such as

$$\mu_t = s\mu_{t-1} + z(t)$$

where $z(t)$ is a random variable that reflects discrepancies between expected and actual values of the marginal utility of consumption as of period t, and s, the serial correlation coefficient, is a parameter.

Sample selection and measurement of variables

For the most part, problems of sample selection and of measurement of variables are the same in the case of empirical studies of dynamic labor supply models as they are in the case of empirical studies of static labor supply models. Since these issues have already been discussed in Chapter 3, there is no need to go over them again. However, a few problems are peculiar to dynamic models. These include the following.

Initial wealth and property income. As noted in the discussion earlier in this section of the two-stage method of specifying dynamic labor supply models, property income $rZ(t)$, current assets $Z(t)$, and savings $\dot{Z}(t)$ are endogenous in a life cycle context. Inclusion of such variables in the labor supply function may cause statistical bias if unmeasured factors that affect these variables are correlated with the labor supply error term. Thus, in contrast with most specifications of the static labor supply function, empirical specifications of the dynamic labor supply function often do not include a property income or current assets variable. (For example, see (5.103).) Initial wealth, $Z(0)$, often takes the place of property income or current wealth in dynamic labor supply models (for example, see (5.104)). However, data on $Z(0)$ may be hard to come by. *Provided* one assumes that the utility function is separable, dynamic models such as the ones described above may be interpreted as a description of individuals who remaximize utility at each date over (the rest of) their time horizon; one may therefore treat time 0 as the present period (or, more generally, as the first year covered by the data, when the data are longitudinal) and, thus, interpret $Z(0)$ as *current* net worth. (See Cotterman, 1981.) Alternatively, MaCurdy (1981a) suggests using a function that expresses actual initial wealth (e.g., net worth at age 18) as a function of observed variables, such as the current level of property income.

Consumption. Some empirical specifications of the dynamic labor supply function require data on consumption, the variable $C(t)$ of the previous discussion. (For example, see (5.93), derived under the DMRS specification approach.) Now, the $C(t)$ of such models refers to a flow of consumption *services* rather than to a flow of consumption *expenditures*. The service flow of nondurable goods may reasonably be taken to be equivalent to real expenditures on such goods, but the services yielded by durable goods are a function of the total stock of such durables and may be greater or less than the amount of *expenditure* on such goods. In principle, then, the $C(t)$ of the analyses presented earlier should be defined as

$$(5.105) \quad C(t) = C_n(t) + r_D(t)D(t)$$

where $C_n(t)$ is expenditure on nondurable goods as of t, $D(t)$ is the stock of durable goods possessed at t, and $r_D(t)$ is the service yield or implicit rental rate on durables at t.[17]

Taxes, transfers, and fixed costs. To a surprising extent, the analysis of taxes, transfers, and fixed costs in static labor supply models of Chapter 4 carries over to the dynamic case – *provided* one is careful to draw the analogy between the static case and the dynamic case in an appropriate manner. In either case, the notion of the linearized budget constraint provides important insights that are useful both for theoretical analysis and econometric estimation.

First, consider analysis of taxes and transfers. In the static case, one may write the static labor supply function as $H = H(\hat{W}, \hat{V})$, where $\hat{W}$ is the after-tax wage rate and $\hat{V}$ is adjusted property income, calculated by extending the budget line segment that the individual chooses back to where $L = 1$.[18] Note that both $\hat{W}$ and $\hat{V}$ are endogenous, since they both depend on the value of the marginal

---

[17] Of course, $r_D(t)$ cannot be observed directly; rather, it must either be treated as a parameter or else guesstimated. For example, MaCurdy (1981b) assumes that $r_D(t) = 0.1$ for all t.

[18] For example, recall the discussion of Figure 4.3 in Chapter 4.

rate of tax τ at the individual's equilibrium, which, in turn, depends on his labor supply.

It is straightforward to extend this to the dynamic case. First, consider a simple tax system that levies *lump-sum* taxes, and let $\Lambda(t)$ denote the amount of the lump-sum tax that must be paid at age t. The fact that individuals may save and borrow (and may therefore move earnings, income, and liabilities either forward or backward in time) means that, with perfect foresight, such a tax liability payable at t is the equivalent of a liability of $e^{-rt}\Lambda(t)$ that is payable at time 0. Thus, someone confronted with such a tax system in effect starts the life cycle with net initial assets $\hat{Z}(0)$, where $\hat{Z}(0) = Z(0) - \int_0^T e^{-rt}\Lambda(t)\,dt$. In other words, a lump-sum tax system alters the effective level of $Z(0)$. By extension, a tax system that levies taxes on the basis of earnings or income (i.e., earnings plus asset income) will not only alter the effective level of initial assets but will also change the reward for an additional hour of work and the return on an additional dollar of asset income. When the marginal tax rate on earnings at time t is $\tau_E(t)$ and the marginal tax rate on asset income at time t is $\tau_Z(t)$, the net wage rate is $\hat{W}(t) \equiv [1 - \tau_E(t)]W(t)$, whereas the net interest rate is $\hat{r}(t) \equiv [1 - \tau_Z(t)]r$. Accordingly, in the presence of taxation, one may describe dynamic labor supply decisions as choices made subject to a "linearized lifetime budget constraint" that expresses the stream of leisure and consumption the individual can enjoy over his lifetime as a function of effective initial assets $\hat{Z}(0)$, the time profile of the price level $P(t)$, and the time profiles of the net wage rate $\hat{W}(t)$ and the net interest rate $\hat{r}(t)$; note that, in general, $\hat{Z}(0)$ will be a function of the parameters of the tax system. (I will defer further discussion of the lifetime budget constraint under taxation until Chapter 6.)

To complete the analogy between the static case and the dynamic case, note that the dynamic model's variables $\hat{Z}(0)$, $\hat{W}(t)$, and $\hat{r}(t)$, like the static model's variables $\hat{V}$ and $\hat{W}$, are endogenous: They depend on, for example, marginal tax rates, which depend on income, which in turn depends on labor supply. (See MaCurdy, 1981b, and Chapter 6 for further discussion.) Note also that transfer payments may be regarded as negative tax liabilities, so that, at this level of generality, the previous discussion applies to transfers as well as to taxation.

282   *Labor supply*

Next consider analysis of fixed costs of labor market entry in the dynamic case. More or less by definition, such fixed costs do not affect wages, but they do reduce the net earnings that can be obtained from work. In the static case, someone who chooses to work in the presence of fixed costs that are equivalent to a reduction of f in his property income V acts as if he faced a wage rate of W and net property income equal to $\hat{V} \equiv V - f$. (Recall the discussion of Chapter 4.) In the dynamic case, the fact that individuals may save and borrow means that a fixed cost of amount $f(t)$ that is incurred at time t is the equivalent of a fixed cost of $e^{-rt}f(t)$ incurred at time 0. It follows that, in the presence of fixed costs of working, one may describe dynamic labor supply decisions as choices made subject to a linearized lifetime budget constraint that is determined by the wage profile and by "adjusted initial assets" $\hat{Z}(0)$, where $\hat{Z}(0)$ is defined as $\hat{Z}(0) \equiv Z(0) - \int_0^T e^{-rt}f(t)\delta(t)\,dt$, where $\delta(t)$ is a dummy variable equal to unity if the individual does work at time t (and so incurs the fixed cost $f(t)$) and equal to zero otherwise. To complete the analogy between the static case and the dynamic case, note that the dynamic model variable $\hat{Z}(0)$, like the static model variable $\hat{V}$, is endogenous, since it depends on labor supply decisions (e.g., on whether $\delta(t)$ is zero or unity).

Synthetic cohort data. Recent work on dynamic exogenous wage empirical labor supply models has been based largely on microdata (i.e., single cross sections or panels on a group of individual people). However, much of the early work on such models used "synthetic cohort" data, which are *averages* of data on individuals arranged by age so as to yield a "synthetic life cycle" or "synthetic cohort." (For example, see Becker, 1975c; Smith, 1977a, b, 1980b.) To construct such data, one selects a group of individuals (e.g., all individuals in a random population sample, all individuals residing in a particular state, all individuals with exactly 12 years of schooling, etc.) from a particular cross section (e.g., a Census sample); splits the group up according to age; and then computes the mean wage rate, mean labor supply, and so forth of the individuals in each such age category. The result is a set of pseudoprofiles giving labor supply, wage rates, and so forth at each different age (e.g., age 18 through age 65 inclusive).

Such data may then be used in estimating the parameters of dynamic labor supply functions, such as the ones described earlier. For example, Becker (1975c) and Smith (1977a, b, 1980b) use such data in regressing labor supply (or leisure time) on the wage rate, age (that is, t), and various taste variables (all of which are assumed to be exogenous). As MaCurdy (1981a) notes, provided one assumes that μ is constant (apart from random variation) across all age groups, this amounts to estimation of a COLISPIA version of the dynamic labor supply function in which the estimate of the intercept term may be treated as an estimate of the mean value of μ (or some quantity related to μ, such as the term $\kappa_L - (\ln \mu/\Delta)$ in (5.104)) across all age groups.[19]

Regressions of this kind require data on only one synthetic cohort (e.g., data for the mean wage rate and mean labor supply, by age, for persons with 12 years of schooling). By extension, one can derive such data for a large number of synthetic cohorts (e.g., get mean values of the wage rate, labor supply, etc., by age for persons in each of the approximately 300 Standard Metropolitan Statistical Areas in the U.S.), thereby resulting in a large number of observations with data on mean labor supply at each age, $H(t)$, and wage rates at *all* ages, $W(0)$, $W(1)$, $W(2)$, . . . , $W(T)$. One can then use these data to fit a brute force specification, such as

$$(5.106) \quad H_i(t) = b_t + \sum_{j=0}^{T} b_{tj} W_i(j) + \epsilon_i(t)$$

where i refers to the ith synthetic cohort (e.g., to the ith SMSA), $H_i(t)$ refers to the mean value of labor supply among persons who are t years old and are in the ith synthetic cohort, $W_i(t)$ refers to the mean value of the wage rate of persons who are t years old and are in the ith synthetic cohort, and $\epsilon_i(t)$ is an error term. The parameter b_t is an intercept term, whereas b_{tj} ($j = 0, 1, . . . , T$) is the slope coefficient on the variable $W(j)$.[20]

---

[19] Note that if vintage effects are "smooth," then they will be absorbed into the coefficient on the variable for age (t) in labor supply or leisure time functions, such as (5.103), meaning that this coefficient will measure not only interest rate and time preference effects related to ρ and r, but also vintage effects.

[20] As written, (5.106) does not include an initial assets variable; one can certainly include a variable of this kind, although it is not entirely obvious what to use. (For example, one could simply use a measure of the initial assets of persons in the ith

Use of synthetic cohort data is certainly not without its attractions, particularly as a means of estimating brute force specifications of the dynamic labor supply function.[21] However, use of such data also raises a number of important questions. First, synthetic cohort data confound the effects of time (that is, aging) per se with the effects of "vintage." Because such data refer to individuals observed at a given moment in time (e.g., the 1980 Census), differences in age in such data are necessarily differences in vintage as well: Someone 50 years old in 1980 comes from the 1930 (i.e., Depression-era) "vintage," someone 20 years old in 1980 comes from the 1960 (i.e., Vietnam war-era) "vintage," and so on. Thus, in order to accept estimates of life cycle labor supply parameters derived from such data, one must be willing to assume, for example, that, if faced with the same initial wealth, wage profile, and so forth, a representative individual of the 1960 vintage would behave in exactly the same way in the year 2010 as a representative individual of the 1930 vintage behaved in 1980.

Second, synthetic cohort data may also be subject to various kinds of selection biases, arising from the manner in which they were constructed. To see this, note that synthetic cohort data derived from, for example, the 1980 Census on the value of $W(t)$ at different t represent means of wage rates of individuals at different ages who were working during 1980. Because the fraction of persons

---

cohort who are "0" years old, e.g., 18 years old, if 18 is deemed to be the start of the life cycle. Alternatively, *if* one is willing to assume that initial assets are uncorrelated with wage rates, one could simply allow $Z(0)$ to be absorbed into the error term $\epsilon_i(t)$.) One can also add a vector of taste variables (denoting race, sex, years of schooling completed as of $t = 0$, etc.) to (5.106). Finally, note that (5.106) is really a *system* of $T + 1$ equations, one for each period between the start of the life cycle at $t = 0$ and its end at $t = T$. Each cohort contributes a total of $T + 1$ observations (one for each age), but each equation in the system denoted by (5.106) contains $T + 2$ parameters to be estimated (an intercept, b_t, and $T + 1$ slope parameters, b_{tj}). Estimation of all of the parameters is possible only if one can obtain data on a large number of synthetic cohorts (so as to make the number of observations, that is, synthetic cohorts, sufficiently larger than the number of parameters to be estimated).

[21] At least in general terms, the brute force specification (5.91) does not assume anything in particular about cross-substitution terms, and, as such, its estimation (e.g., estimation of (5.106)) requires estimation of a very large number of parameters. (Recall note 16.) However, if one can obtain data for numerous synthetic cohorts, one will have more observations than there are parameters to be estimated, that is, a reasonably large number of degrees of freedom. (Recall note 20.)

who work is never unity, this raises conventional static selection bias problems of the kind discussed in Chapter 4. However, synthetic cohort data may also raise questions of possible "dynamic" selection bias. The reason is that the proportion of persons at work is typically rather low both at young and old ages – so that the mean value of $W(t)$ derived by averaging wages among those who are working may refer to quite unrepresentative segments of the total *population* of persons with low or high t. In turn, this may mean that such synthetic cohort or pseudoprofile data may give a distorted impression of the *actual* life cycle profiles of the wage rates of any given set of persons. The same is, of course, true as regards synthetic cohort data on $H(t)$.[22]

Permanent and transitory wages. All of the specification procedures discussed earlier in this section generate regression functions in which the *current* wage rate $W(t)$ is one of the independent variables. However, a number of researchers have suggested that including the current wage rate in the dynamic labor supply function may not yield meaningful results. (For example, see Kalachek, Mellow, and Raines, 1978, p. 357.) Instead, they argue, it is desirable, or even essential, to analyze labor supply by decomposing the observed current wage rate $W(t)$ into two components – a transitory wage, $w(t)$, and a permanent wage, W^*, with $W(t) = W^* + w(t)$ – in much the same way that Friedman (1957) distinguished between transitory and permanent *income* in his classic analysis of consumption.

Starting from this common premise, researchers who distinguish between transitory and permanent wages have then gone in two different directions. In one view, which I will call *PT-1* for short, it is possible to decompose the current wage $W(t)$ into two components,

<hr>

[22] Measurement of the $H(t)$ values for a synthetic cohort raises problems similar to those encountered in first-generation work on static models. In the present case, the problem is to decide how to compute average $H(t)$ for each t. Excluding persons with zero hours of work from the group used to compute average $H(t)$ engenders a form of selection bias. Including them involves a misspecification, since, as in the case of static models, labor supply functions such as (5.91), (5.93), (5.103), and so on are applicable only for persons with positive $H(t)$, that is, only if, for example, the marginal rate of substitution at zero hours of work exceeds the wage rate. See Heckman and MaCurdy (1980) for further discussion of, and a solution to, selection bias problems in the context of dynamic labor supply models.

the permanent wage W^* and the transitory wage $w(t)$, such that labor supply does respond to changes in W^* but does not respond at all to changes in $w(t)$ as such. (For example, see Kalachek and Raines, 1970; Watts, Poirier, and Mallar, 1977.) Thus, according to this view, if one were to include appropriately measured variables W^* and $w(t)$ in a regression equation such as

$$H(t) = b_0 + b_P W^* + b_T w(t) + \text{other variables} + \text{error}$$

then one should obtain both (i) an estimate of b_T that will be zero (that is, not statistically different from zero) and (ii) an estimate of b_P that will in general be nonzero (though of indeterminate sign). PT-1, therefore, implies that, with only slight modifications, Friedman's work on consumption – in which consumption depends only on permanent income and not on transitory income – carries over to the analysis of labor supply.[23]

In the second view, which I will call *PT-2* for short, a change in the permanent wage is by definition a change in lifetime earnings prospects, while a change in the transitory wage is by definition a change in current earnings prospects with no change in lifetime earnings

[23] Mincer (1962) seems to have been the first researcher to apply Friedman's work to the analysis of labor supply. However, what Mincer did (in analyzing the labor force participation of married women) was to divide the *income of other family members*, rather than the wage rate, into permanent and transitory components. Kalachek and Raines (1970, pp. 160–1) seem to have been among the first to distinguish between transitory and permanent wage components, adopting a fairly specific version of the PT-1 hypothesis given in the text: "the labor supply response of the semiskilled worker who fulfills the company's manhours expectations cannot be attributed . . . to his current wage, but rather to the average expected wage discounted over his planning horizon." Other researchers have preferred using a measure of the permanent wage to using the current wage but have been less specific about b_T than Kalachek and Raines. For example, Watts, Poirier, and Mallar (1977, p. 52) argue that, in estimating "average labor supply behavior over substantial periods of time," it is "appropriate to use [wage and income] variables which reflect average circumstances" in order to "develop estimates of wage rates or income that are less affected by simple measurement errors or actual but transitory fluctuations." The idea that wage data may be subject to "simple measurement errors" raises a purely econometric issue, the well-known problem of errors in the variables. (For example, see Kmenta, 1971, pp. 307–9.) What is novel here is the notion that observed wage changes may also include "actual but transitory fluctuations" and the implication that labor supply may not respond to such wage changes in the same way that it would to "nontransitory" or "permanent" wage changes; this raises the analytical issue considered in the text.

prospects. Consequently, according to this view, a change in the permanent wage is a shift in the wage profile itself and will have opposite-signed substitution and wealth effects (or, alternatively, μ-constant and μ-variable effects) on labor supply. On the other hand, a change in the transitory wage is either (i) a movement *along* a given wage profile or (ii) a change *in* the wage profile that does not alter lifetime earnings prospects. As such, a change in the transitory wage will have either (i) an efficiency effect *only* or (ii) a pure substitution effect *only*, leading in either case to a change in labor supply in the same direction as the (transitory) wage change. (See Kalachek, Mellow, and Raines, 1978, p. 357, and Lillard, 1978, p. 369, for statements of this kind.) Thus, PT-2 implies that fitting a regression for $H(t)$ such as the one discussed immediately above should produce both (i) a *positive* estimate of b_T and (ii) an estimate of b_P that will be either negative or else positive but smaller than the estimate of b_T.

Of course, in other contexts, "permanent" and "transitory" are sometimes used to describe the *duration* of a shift in the wage profile or, equivalently, to describe the *length* of the segment of the wage profile that is affected by some exogenous event. For example, the shift in the (after-tax) wage profile caused by a structural (and thus, presumably, long run) reform of the tax laws could be called a permanent change in the wage (or in the wage profile); the shift in the wage profile caused by a sudden influx of temporary immigrant workers could be called a transitory change in the wage (or in the wage profile); and so on. (For example, see Heckman, 1978b, and Metcalf, 1973, 1974, who discuss the effects on current labor supply of temporary, that is, experimental, and permanent negative income tax programs.) The labor supply effects of transitory or permanent wage changes in this duration-of-shift sense, which I will call *DS* for short, depend on substitution and wealth (or, alternatively, μ-constant and μ-variable) effects whose magnitudes and net impact can only be determined empirically. Proponents of both the PT-1 and the PT-2 views would argue that this kind of empirical determination requires an empirical distinction between W^* and $w(t)$. In the PT-1 view, this is because labor supply responds to W^* but not $w(t)$. In the PT-2 view, this is because both transitory and permanent wage changes, in the DS sense, entail changes in lifetime earnings prospects (that is, changes in W^*) that should not be confounded with changes in $w(t)$, that is, movements along or movements of the wage profile that do not entail changes in lifetime prospects.

As this brief discussion indicates, researchers who attempt to decompose wage changes into permanent and transitory components in the sense of either PT-1 or PT-2 are certainly focusing on an important idea: Labor supply may not respond in exactly the same way to different *kinds* of wage changes. Moreover, analysis of this issue would appear to be an important prerequisite for analyses of the effects of wage profile shifts of different durations (in other words, DS-oriented analyses). Accordingly, the basic questions to consider are the following: First, how should the permanent wage (defined in the PT-1 or PT-2 sense) be measured? Second, is either the PT-1 or the PT-2 view about the signs and magnitudes of the coefficients b_P and b_T in fact correct?

Begin by considering how to devise an empirical measure of the permanent wage, W^*. (Once this has been derived, the transitory wage $w(t)$ can be calculated as the difference between the current wage $W(t)$ and W^*, i.e., $w(t) = W(t) - W^*$.) The most natural measure of the permanent wage – one that, as noted later, is very similar to Friedman's (1957) theoretical measure of permanent income – is the amount that would be paid out between time $t = 0$ and time $t = T$ pursuant to an annuity with a present value equal to the present value of maximum potential lifetime earnings. Now, the present value of maximum potential lifetime earnings, E, is simply the present value of the individual's wage profile evaluated at $H(t) = 1$ for all t (recall that $H(t)$ is the fraction of available time devoted to work). In other words,

$$E = \int_0^T e^{-rt} W(t)\, dt$$

Thus, the permanent wage W^* is implicitly defined by the relation

$$E = \int_0^T e^{-rt} W^*\, dt = W^* \int_0^T e^{-rt}\, dt = W^*/r^*$$

so that

$$W^* = r^* [\int_0^T e^{-rt} W(t)\, dt] = r^* E$$

where

$$r^* \equiv r/[1 - e^{-rT}]$$

Thus, W^* is the return, paid out at interest rate r^*, on one's lifetime earning power E. (When $T = \infty$, $r^* = r$; in other words, r is the interest rate implicit in a perpetuity or consol with a present value of E that pays the amount W^* forever. Since $T < \infty$, meaning that the payment W^* ends at time T, the interest rate here that exhausts the present value amount E is the somewhat larger finite-life-corrected quantity r^*.) Note that W^* is a function of the interest rate and the wage profile (that is, the sequence of $W(t)$ values) only. Thus, W^* is independent of all other aspects of behavior, such as actual labor supply and consumption decisions, the subjective rate of time preference, utility function parameters, and so forth.

Of course, as a practical matter, it is not possible to measure W^* in precisely this manner: Available data do not provide observations on all $W(t)$ values in any individual's lifetime wage profile. Accordingly, it is necessary to use something less than the entire wage profile in deriving an empirical measure of W^*. However, it is important to note that most researchers who have derived empirical measures of W^* (e.g., Kalachek, Mellow, and Raines, 1978; Kalachek and Raines, 1970; Kalachek, Raines, and Larson, 1979; Lillard, 1978; Watts, Poirier, and Mallar, 1977) have done so on the basis of regression analyses of the behavior of wages over time (in other words, analyses of the shape and position of *segments* of the wage profile) without reference to anything else. Accordingly, the permanent wage variable used in such studies is either an approximation to the W^* of this discussion or else is related (e.g., proportional) to it.

Unfortunately, however, neither empirical approximations to W^* nor theoretical distinctions of this kind between the permanent wage and the transitory wage are of much value for the analysis of labor supply (Heckman and MaCurdy, 1980). Except in special cases, labor supply at time t *will* change whenever the transitory wage at time t (or any empirical approximation to it) changes: The PT-1 analogy with Friedman's distinction between permanent and transitory income is invalid. Likewise, except in special cases, the idea that one can summarize the entire wage profile by a single number, W^*, is incorrect: The PT-2 notion that permanent wage changes do entail wealth (or μ-variable) effects whereas transitory wage changes do not is in error.

To understand why, it is useful to start by considering Friedman's permanent income hypothesis. Reduced to its essentials, Friedman's analysis is a special case of the problem summarized by (5.7) above in which labor supply is fixed at some number of hours $\overline{H}$ throughout the life cycle. Since labor supply (and, thus, leisure time) is fixed, consumption is the only argument in the utility function over which the individual has any discretion, so the decision problem for such an individual is a rather simple one: to maximize lifetime utility by choosing the optimal level of consumption for each moment t, subject to the constraints imposed by the exogenously given levels of r, $Z(0)$, $\overline{H}$, and the life cycle wage profile.

Three key ideas underlie the permanent income hypothesis, as applied to this model. First, the present value of the individual's lifetime *income* stream (inclusive of his initial level of wealth) is given by Z^*, where

$$Z^* = Z(0) + \int_0^T e^{-rt} W(t) \overline{H} \, dt$$

and the present value of the individual's lifetime *earnings* stream is given by $\overline{E}$, where

$$\overline{E} = \int_0^T e^{-rt} W(t) \overline{H} \, dt$$

Hence, $Z^* = Z(0) + \overline{E}$. Second, let *permanent income* refer to the amount that would be paid out between time $t = 0$ and time $t = T$ pursuant to an annuity with a present value of Z^*. Then permanent income, Y^*, is implicitly defined by the relation

$$(5.107) \quad Z^* = \int_0^T e^{-rt} Y^* \, dt$$

so that

$$(5.108) \quad \begin{aligned} Y^* &= r^* Z^* \\ &= r^* Z(0) + r^* \overline{E} \end{aligned}$$

where $r^* = r/(1 - e^{-rT})$. *Transitory income*, which I will write as $y(t)$, may then be defined as the difference between actual income $Y(t) \equiv rZ(t) + W(t)\overline{H}$ and permanent income Y^*, that is,

(5.109) $Y(t) = Y^* + y(t)$

Analogously, one may write

(5.110) $\qquad \overline{E} = \displaystyle\int_0^T e^{-rt} W^* \overline{H} \, dt$

(5.111) $\quad W^* = r^* \overline{E} / \overline{H}$

(5.112) $\quad W(t) = W^* + w(t)$

where W^* is the *permanent wage*, $w(t)$ is the *transitory wage*, and the observed wage $W(t)$ is therefore taken to be the sum of its "permanent" and "transitory" components. Note also that

(5.113) $Y^* = r^* Z(0) + W^* \overline{H}$

Hence, permanent income is equal to the sum of income from initial wealth, $r^* Z(0)$, and permanent earnings, $W^* \overline{H}$.

The third point – Friedman's key insight – is that consumption at any moment t depends only on time and on the two components of Y^*, permanent property income and permanent earnings, but is entirely independent of transitory income $y(t)$ and the transitory wage $w(t)$.

The basic reason for this is that, in the special case Friedman considers, hours of work are fixed. This assumption has several very important implications. First, it means that changes in wage rates and changes in both actual *and* potential earnings are always in direct proportion to each other (where $\overline{H}$ is the factor of proportionality). Second, since there can be no substitution between C and L, it means that changes in (permanent) wage rates *do* have μ-variable effects but do *not* have μ-constant effects on C. (Of course, it also means that changes in wage rates do not affect H or L at all.) Finally, it means that one can collapse the entire wage profile into a single wealth or permanent income variable Z^* or Y^*. So long as the price of consumer goods $P(t)$ remains constant over the life cycle, this implies that one can write consumption as a function of time and wealth alone (or as a function of time and permanent income alone, or as a function of time, initial wealth, and the permanent wage alone). In more formal terms,

(5.114) $C(t) = g(r^*Z^*, t) = g(Y^*, t) = g[r^*Z(0) + W^*\overline{H}, t]$

where $\partial C(t)/\partial w(t) = \partial C(t)/\partial y(t) = 0$.

Consequently, any change in the wage profile that leaves Z^* (and, thus, Y^* and W^*) unchanged will have no effect on $C(t)$ at *any* given date t, even if such a change in the wage profile alters the values of $w(t)$ *and* $y(t)$ at *all* dates t. Evidently, then, Y^* (or Z^*) is intimately connected with μ, the shadow value of initial assets; indeed, when labor supply is fixed, μ will remain the same so long as Z^* remains the same.

To derive these propositions rigorously, note that, once one assumes that H (and, therefore L) is fixed over the life cycle, some of the first-order conditions (5.8)–(5.10) for a maximum of lifetime utility must be modified. In particular, (5.8) remains unchanged, but (5.9) is no longer relevant (because, by assumption, L cannot be varied) and the $H(t)$ in (5.10) must be replaced with $\overline{H}$. Moreover, terms involving the cross-partial derivatives $u_{CL}(t)$ and $u_{LC}(t)$ disappear from all derivations based on the first-order conditions (again, because L cannot be varied). Accordingly, if one assumes (mainly in order to simplify exposition) that the price of C is constant over the life cycle, then (5.13) and (5.17), both of which are derived from the first-order conditions (5.8) and (5.9), reduce to

(5.115) $\dot{C}(t) = -Y_{CV}(t)(\rho - r)$
(5.116) $dC(t) = -Y_{CV}(t)(d\mu/\mu)$

respectively.

Now, (5.115) implies that the behavior of $C(t)$ over time in the individual's dynamic equilibrium, as given by the sign of $\dot{C}(t)$, is independent of $W(t)$. Further, (5.116) implies that the comparative dynamics of the individual's consumption decisions are such that changes in $W(t)$ will affect $C(t)$ through, and *only* through, induced changes in μ. In particular, use (5.107)–(5.112) to rewrite the version of (5.10) that is relevant to this case to obtain

(5.117) $Z^* = \int_0^T e^{-rt}P(t)C(t)\,dt$

or, equivalently,

$$(5.118) \quad Z(0) + (W^*\overline{H}/r^*) = \int_0^T e^{-rt} P(t) C(t) \, dt$$

By (5.116), changes in the wage profile will affect $C(t)$ only to the extent that they affect μ. However, (5.118) implies that any change in the wage profile that does not affect the permanent wage W^* will keep the left-hand side of (5.118) unchanged. In turn, this means that a change in the wage profile that keeps W^* constant will leave μ and, therefore, consumption at all dates unchanged, regardless of how the change in the wage profile alters either $y(t)$ or $w(t)$ at any particular date.

Specifically, when labor supply is fixed, μ is inversely related to $Z^* = Z(0) + (W^*\overline{H}/r^*)$, provided consumption is a normal good (i.e., provided $Y_{CV}(t) > 0$). To see why, note that if W^* or $Z(0)$ (and, therefore, Z^*) rises, then, by (5.118), someone who does not change $C(t)$ will end life with a positive net worth, violating the lifetime budget constraint's requirement that $Z(T) = 0$. To satisfy this requirement,[24] someone who regards consumption as a normal good will reduce μ: As (5.116) indicates, a reduction in μ will raise consumption at each age t, thereby increasing the right-hand side of (5.118) to equal the new, higher, level of the left-hand side. Hence, one may write $\mu = \mu(Z^*) = \mu[Z(0) + (W^*\overline{H}^*r^*)]$, with $\mu' < 0$. In other words, in the special fixed-labor-supply case Friedman considers, Z^* or Y^* is a measure of and is inversely related to μ; these variables are essentially equivalent.

However, none of these conclusions carries over to the case in which labor supply and leisure time are choice variables. The basic reason for this is that, if leisure is a choice variable, then (i) changes in the wage profile will generally have *both* μ-variable *and* μ-constant effects on *both* consumption *and* labor supply, *regardless* of whether the change in the wage profile affects the permanent wage, and (ii) there need no longer be a simple one-to-one correspondence between μ and either permanent income Y^* or the

---

[24] Recall that the individual will in fact want to have $Z(T) = 0$: having $Z(T) > 0$ will certainly permit him to break even, but, since (by assumption) he does not desire to make bequests, will not give him as much utility as he could enjoy were he to spend all his earnings and assets by time T.

permanent wage W^*, as was true in Friedman's fixed-labor-supply case.

To put this in formal terms, let full wealth Z^* in a world of endogenous labor supply be defined as previously, but with earning power evaluated at $H(t) = 1$ rather than at $H(t) = \overline{H}$. So Z^* is now

$$Z^* = Z(0) + \int_0^T e^{-rt} W(t)\, dt$$

Similarly, define the permanent wage so as to evaluate potential earnings at $H(t) = 1$ rather than at $H(t) = \overline{H}$, and likewise for permanent income, transitory income, and so forth. Then, provided one remembers to set $\overline{H}$ at unity, equations (5.107)–(5.112) carry over without further modification to the endogenous labor supply case (after all, they are simply definitions). Next, note from (5.22) that when the wage rates at two different dates t_1 and t_2 change by amounts $dW(t_1)$ and $dW(t_2)$, respectively, the integral in (5.10) will change by an amount $d\xi_{12}$, where

$$d\xi_{12} = e^{-rt_1} [H(t_1) + Y_{LV}(t_1)]\, dW(t_1)$$
$$+ e^{-rt_2} [H(t_2) + Y_{LV}(t_2)]\, dW(t_2)$$

Now suppose that this change in the wage profile (that is, in both $W(t_1)$ and $W(t_2)$) does not change the permanent wage, W^*. By the definition of W^* given by (5.107)–(5.112), this means that, when $\overline{H} = 1$, $e^{-rt_1} dW(t_1) = -e^{-rt_2} dW(t_2)$ or, equivalently, $dW(t_2) = e^{-r(t_1 - t_2)} dW(t_1)$. Now substitute this into the expression for $d\xi_{12}$ and then rearrange terms to obtain an expression for $d\xi_{12}\,|\,_{\overline{W}^*}$, that is, for the amount by which the integral in (5.10) will change when $W(t_1)$ and $W(t_2)$ are changed, while W^* is kept constant. This is

$$d\xi_{12}\,|\,_{\overline{W}^*} = e^{-rt_1} \{[H(t_1) + Y_{LV}(t_1)]$$
$$- [H(t_2) + Y_{LV}(t_2)]\}\, dW(t_1)$$

Except in special cases (e.g., in which H, L, and C are the same at time t_1 as at time t_2), this expression is nonzero.[25] If it is positive

<hr>

[25] Note that the model summarized by equations (5.30)–(5.51) is an example of just such a special case: Under the utility function assumed for that model, it turns out that $Y_{CV}(t) = L(t)$ for all t, so that in this case $d\xi_{12}\,|\,_{\overline{W}^*}$ is in fact equal to zero. Note also from (5.34) that, in this case, one can indeed write μ as a simple function of the

(negative), then the individual will end up with positive (negative) net worth at T unless he changes μ, meaning that μ will fall (rise) in response to this shift in the wage profile – even though the profile shift leaves the permanent wage, W^*, *unchanged*.

This means that, in general, a change in the wage profile will change μ and will therefore have a μ-variable effect on labor supply (and on consumption) at *all* dates, even if this profile change does *not* affect the permanent wage, W^*, as defined by (5.107)–(5.112). In contrast with Friedman's fixed-labor-supply case, then, there is now no simple one-to-one relation between W^* and μ; there is no way to summarize the entire wage profile by a single number such as W^*. Thus, the main hypothesis of PT-1, that $b_T = 0$, has little or no analytical foundation: Wage changes that keep W^* the same – in other words, so-called transitory wage changes – will, in general, affect labor supply. Also, note that equations (5.17)–(5.19) imply that a change in the wage profile will have μ-constant effects on both hours of work and consumption even if the wage profile shift does not affect W^*. The extent to which the μ-variable effects of such a profile shift will offset or reinforce these μ-constant effects depends in part on the sign of $d\xi_{12} \mid \overline{w^*}$, which, of course, is indeterminate a priori. So there is also no analytical basis for the main PT-2 hypotheses[26] about b_T: that the estimate of b_T will be positive and will exceed the algebraic value of the estimate of b_P. (Note that all this assumes that W^* can actually be measured. As noted earlier, the absence of complete data on wages over the life cycle forces researchers to use approximations to W^*; and there is little or no reason to suppose that the behavior of such approximations to W^* or to its complement, the transitory wage $w(t)$, will correspond to the empirical predictions of either PT-1 or PT-2 any better than would exact measures of W^* and $w(t)$.)

All this raises the fundamental question underlying the difficulties just mentioned: Is there *any* definition of the permanent wage that permits an empirical distinction between shifts of the wage profile

---

wage profile and thus as a function of W^* – that, in this case, any change in the wage profile that keeps W^* (as defined by equations (5.107) – (5.112)) unchanged will not change μ. The main reason for this is that the utility function that is the basis for equations (5.30)–(5.51) is separable in C and L as well as in time.

[26] For example, see the studies by Kalachek, Mellow, and Raines (1978) and Lillard (1978).

and movements along it? As just noted, defining a permanent wage using only the wage profile itself, as in the case of the W^* of the earlier discussion, does not in fact facilitate this kind of empirical distinction. However, an alternative concept that can be used to make just this kind of distinction is μ, the shadow value of initial assets. In particular, as MaCurdy (1981a) points out, when labor supply is a choice variable, it is μ itself that is analogous to Friedman's Y^* (or Z^*). Moreover, as (5.18) indicates, a rise in a given $W(t)$ that is accompanied by changes in the wage profile (that is, by changes in wages at other dates) that keep μ constant, thereby setting $d\mu$ at zero, will certainly have only a positive μ-constant effect on labor supply at time t; and an increase in a given $W(t)$ that is *not* accompanied by changes in the wage profile that keep μ constant will have both a positive μ-constant effect and also (via an induced change in μ, of the kind discussed earlier) a negative μ-variable effect on labor supply at time t. The first kind of wage change may certainly be called a transitory wage change, whereas the second may certainly be called a permanent wage change.

Under this definition of permanent and transitory wage changes, it is neither necessary nor sufficient to define or measure a permanent wage rate such as the W^* of the earlier discussion. In particular, in contrast with W^*, μ is a function not only of the wage profile but also of initial assets and the individual's preference structure (and, thus, of his chosen levels of consumption and labor supply at all dates t). Moreover, all that is required for implementation of this kind of permanent wage concept is estimation of the labor supply function using a COLISPIA specification, in which the only wage data required are data on current wage rates $W(t)$. Finally, estimates of the parameters that determine labor supply that have been derived from such specifications can be used to analyze the effects of permanent (long run) and temporary (transitory or short run) shifts in the wage profile – that is, to examine permanent and transitory wage changes defined in the DS sense.

Empirical estimates of dynamic labor supply functions

I now consider empirical estimates of the parameters of dynamic exogenous wage labor supply functions, as summarized in Table 5.1. In most cases, such estimates have been used only to derive measures of the efficiency effect of a wage change on labor supply, or leisure, over time as the individual moves along a *given* labor supply (or leisure) profile, with μ constant, in fulfillment of a *given* dynamic equilibrium plan. For the most part, therefore, the entries in Table 5.1 refer to this particular kind of wage effect (and are net of time preference and interest rate effects that *also* occur over time as the individual proceeds along a given labor supply or leisure profile). However, in a few cases noted in Table 5.1, authors have also (or instead) used estimates of the parameters of a dynamic labor supply model to measure the extent to which a *shift* in the wage profile leads to a *shift of* the labor supply (or leisure) profile, for example, have sought to measure comparative dynamics effects of wage changes, inclusive of the labor supply effects of changes in μ that are induced by such wage changes. Finally, in most cases the studies noted in Table 5.1 have described such wage effects (either efficiency or comparative dynamics effects) on leisure time rather than on labor supply; accordingly, entries in the last column of the table refer to the elasticity of leisure time (rather than labor supply) with respect to either kind of wage change.

The number of dynamic labor supply studies is too small to permit more than the most guarded inferences about empirical magnitudes, but a few tentative conclusions do seem warranted. First, elasticities derived from synthetic cohort data are usually smaller than elasticities derived from microdata (for example, compare the results derived for women from J. P. Smith's studies, 1977a, b, 1980b, with those derived for women by Heckman and MaCurdy, in press). Second, the efficiency effect of a wage increase on leisure time is generally negative, as implied by analytical models of the kind discussed earlier.[27] Finally, the efficiency effect among men is generally rather small: between 0 and about -0.15. (MaCurdy's, 1981b, results, which refer to data on the Seattle–Denver Income Maintenance Experiment, are a notable exception to this generalization.)

5.5. Human capital: labor supply with endogenous wages

In the model of the previous section, decisions to supply labor depend not only on wages, prices, and initial assets $Z(0)$ but also on preferences for the present over the future and on the opportunity cost of "jam today" (that is, on ρ and r). This is because that

---

[27] For example, see (5.14).

Table 5.1. *Summary of results of empirical studies of dynamic labor supply models*

Study	Specification procedure	Sample and data used	Type of effect measured	Magnitude of effect (expressed as an elasticity)
Male labor supply				
Becker (1975c)	COLISPIA	Synthetic cohort data from 1960 U.S. Census 1/1000 sample	Efficiency effect on $L(t)$ of change in $W(t)$ White men Black men	 −0.08 −0.01
Smith (1977a, b, 1980b)	COLISPIA	Synthetic cohort data from 1967 NLS	Efficiency effect on $L(t)$ of change in $W(t)$ White men Black men	 −0.10 −0.06
Lillard (1978)	Ad hoc	White household heads age 18–58 in 1967 – PSID for 1967–73	Elasticity of $L(t)$ with respect to transitory wage (= efficiency effect on $L(t)$ of change in $W(t)$ (?)) Elasticity of $L(t)$ with respect to permanent wage (= comparative dynamics effect on $L(t)$ of change in $W(t)$ (?))	0.06 0.06
Kalachek, Mellow, & Raines (1978)	Ad hoc	Men age 45–59 in 1966 – NLS for 1967	Elasticity of $L(t)$ with respect to transitory wage (= efficiency effect on	

			L(t) of change in W(t)) (?))	>0
Kalachek, Raines, & Larson (1979)	Ad hoc	Men age 45–59 in 1966 – NLS for 1966, 1969, and 1973	Elasticity of L(t) with respect to permanent wage (= comparative dynamics effect on L(t) of change in W(t) (?))	<0
			Elasticity of L(t) with respect to transitory wage (= efficiency effect on L(t) of change in W(t) (?))	>0
			Elasticity of L(t) with respect to permanent wage (= comparative dynamics effect on L(t) of change in W(t) (?))	−0.01 to −0.07
Ashenfelter & Ham (1979)	COLISPIA	White men age 25–50 in 1967 – PSID for 1967–74	Efficiency effect on L(t) of change in W(t)	−0.13 to −0.12
MaCurdy (1981a)	COLISPIA	White married men age 25–48 in 1967 – PSID for 1967–75	Efficiency effect on L(t) of change in W(t)	−0.40 to −0.12
			Comparative dynamics effect on L(t) of change in W(t)	−0.07
			Comparative dynamics effect on L(t) of equiproportionate change in all wages	≈0

Table 5.1. *(cont.)*

Study	Specification procedure	Sample and data used	Type of effect measured	Magnitude of effect (expressed as an elasticity)
MaCurdy (1981b)	DMRS	Men age 25–60 in 1971 – SDIME for 1972–75	Efficiency effect on $L(t)$ of change in $W(t)$ Controls in SDIME Full SDIME sample	−1.90 −0.79
Altonji (1983)	COLISPIA, DMRS	Husbands age 25–48 in 1967, worked 1967–78 – PSID for 1967–78	Efficiency effect on $H(t)$ of change in $W(t)$	0.10 to 0.35
Female labor supply				
Smith (1977a, b, 1980b)	COLISPIA	Synthetic cohort data from 1967 SEO	Efficiency effect on $L(t)$ of change in $W(t)$ White women Black women	−0.04 −0.04
Heckman & MaCurdy (1980)	COLISPIA	White married women age 30–65 in 1968 – PSID for 1968–75	Efficiency effect on $L(t)$ of change with $W(t)$ (constrained, in estimation, to be ≤ −1)	−1.00
Heckman & MaCurdy (in press)	COLISPIA	White married women age 30–65 in 1968 – PSID for 1968–75	Efficiency effect on $L(t)$ of change in $W(t)$ (value not constrained in estimation)	−0.41
Altonji (1983)	DMRS	Wives of husbands in Altonji (1983) study of males – PSID for 1967–78	Efficiency effect on $H(t)$ of change in $W(t)$	0.80 to 1.00

Aggregate time series

Lucas & Rapping (1970)	COLISPIA	U.S. aggregate time series, 1930–65	Elasticity of $L(t)$ with respect to transitory wage (= efficiency effect on $L(t)$ of change in $W(t)$ (?))	− 0.50
			Elasticity of $L(t)$ with respect to permanent wage (= comparative dynamics effect on $L(t)$ of change in $W(t)$ (?))	$\simeq 0$
Diewert (1974)	Brute force	U.S. aggregate time series, 1946–65	Comparative dynamics effect on $L(t)$ of equiproportionate change in all wages	0.25
Hall (1980b)	COLISPIA	U.S. aggregate time series, IQ 1949–IIIQ 1978	Efficiency effect on $H(t)$ of change in $W(t)$	0.44 to 0.49
Altonji (1982)	COLISPIA, RE	U.S. aggregate time series	Efficiency effect on $H(t)$ of change in $W(t)$:	
			1931–76	− 1.15 to − 1.89
			1948–76	− 1.38 to − 1.64

Note: Ad hoc specification: Labor supply function is not specified in terms of a formal model of utility maximization. The wage variable in the labor supply function is decomposed into permanent and transitory components; accordingly, the labor supply function might be interpreted as similar, at least in spirit, to a COLISPIA-style specification. However, the ad hoc specification does not include age (t) as an independent variable, whereas the COLISPIA specification does. NLS, National Longitudinal Survey; SDIME, Seattle–Denver Income Maintenance Experiment; PSID, Panel Study of Income Dynamics; SEO, Survey of Economic Opportunity. RE = rational expectations, $L(t)$ = current labor supply, $H(t)$ = current leisure time, $W(t)$ = current wage rate.

301

model extends the simple model of Chapter 1 to allow for the possibility that individuals may transfer earnings from work either forward (by saving) or backward (by borrowing) over time, that is, for the accumulation of financial wealth. One of the most rapidly growing areas of work on labor supply extends this still further by allowing for endogenous wages and for the accumulation of *human* wealth, or "human capital."

The basic idea underlying such human capital models of labor supply is that much "wealth" – that is, a stock of something or other, such as health, children, knowledge, and so forth – is embodied in individual people or families, cannot be disposed of or sold to others (since slavery is illegal), can usually be acquired only at a cost (e.g., outlays for physician services, tuition charges, earnings and leisure time that must be forgone, etc.), and yields a flow of services (greater vitality, happiness, productivity in the market or in the home, etc.) over the individual's, or family's, lifetime.[28] The basic problem in a "human capital" analysis of dynamic labor supply behavior, then, is to see how an individual will allocate his time and initial endowments of both financial *and* human wealth so as to maximize lifetime utility, subject to constraints on the amount of time available per period and on his ability to accumulate *each* kind of wealth.[29]

[28] Although the present discussion is concerned mainly with labor supply, wages, and earnings over the life cycle, it is worth noting that the general concept of human capital has been applied to a great variety of topics (e.g., the demand for health care, fertility, child-rearing) and serves as a useful unifying concept for analysis of a broad range of questions about life cycle behavior. See Becker (1975b, 1975c), Mincer (1970), T. W. Schultz (1961, 1962, 1971, 1972), and Thurow (1970) for discussions of work in this general area and Kiker (1966) for a discussion of the history of the concept of human capital.

[29] Many models of human capital accumulation assume that the individual seeks to maximize the present value of lifetime *earnings*, and that market time is fixed at a given constant amount each period (either because of institutional constraints or because an income-maximizing individual would allow himself only the bare minimum amount of leisure time consistent with the goal of maximizing earnings). For example, see Ben-Porath (1967, 1970), Haley (1973, 1976), W. T. Johnson (1970), S. Rosen (1975, 1976), Sheshinski (1968), von Weiszäcker (1967), and Wallace and Ihnen (1975). The assumption that market time (labor supply) is fixed simplifies the task of analysis considerably, and work on these simplified models has played an important part in the literature on human capital. (Indeed, most utility maximization models of human capital accumulation are fairly direct descendants of these income maximization models; see particularly Heckman, 1976b.) Nevertheless, since they

These general notions are quite straightforward, but making them operational sometimes is not. To simplify the discussion, I restrict my attention to forms of human capital, K, such as schooling, formal and informal on-the-job training, and work experience that affect *market productivity* and, thus, wages.[30] Even with this simplification, however, the way in which one specifies a life cycle model with endogenous wages depends on the way one answers two closely related questions: What is the nature of human capital, and how do individuals accumulate it? As a result, several different (though not necessarily incompatible) formulations of the human capital model of dynamic labor supply have appeared in the literature: the "job choice" formulation, the "time allocation" formulation, and the "learning-by-doing" formulation.

Each of these analyses assumes that time is allocated between leisure and the market sector and that human capital, K, is positively related to market productivity, R, that is, that

$$(5.119) \quad R(t) = \phi[K(t)]$$

where ϕ is either linear or strictly concave in K, reflecting an assumption that human capital has either constant or diminishing returns in market production. Each version of the human capital model also assumes that the stock of human capital at any moment in time is given by a stock-flow relationship, analogous to (5.2) and (5.3) for financial wealth, such as

$$(5.120) \quad K(t + 1) = K(t) - \delta K(t) + k(t)$$

where $K(t)$ is the stock of human capital at t, δ is the percentage rate of "depreciation" or obsolescence of human capital per period, and $k(t)$ is the amount of gross investment in new human capital during period t.[31] However, although similar in these respects, these three

obviously have nothing to say about labor supply, I shall ignore such models in what follows, focusing instead on models of utility maximization in which leisure and labor supply are endogenous.

[30] A closely related area of inquiry concerns activities that increase the yield or rental per unit of productivity. For example, in a world of imperfect markets, expenditures for job search or migration may increase the return one earns on one's existing stock of human capital.

[31] Note that equations (5.119) and (5.120) implicitly assume that there is one kind of human capital or, equivalently, that all forms of human capital are, in effect, perfect

alternative treatments of human capital and its relation to labor supply differ in others.

The job choice formulation

In this approach, utility-maximizing individuals allocate time between leisure and the market and also choose between different jobs with different opportunities for *training and earning*.[32] For example, one could choose a job that is "all work," with no training content whatever; attend school, which almost by definition is usually a "job" that is "all training" and does not as such involve any work; or take other kinds of jobs (e.g., an apprenticeship or a "junior" position) that typically involve both work and training. In other words, as Becker (1975b, esp. pp. 16–37) and S. Rosen (1972a) put it, individuals "invest" by deciding to take one of a wide variety of jobs at firms that not only purchase labor services – market work – but also sell training opportunities.[33] (In this framework, schools are "firms" that sell training but purchase little or no labor from those buying the training.) Consequently, the wage the individual receives per hour spent at the firm, W, will be negatively related to the "training content" of the job he has chosen, F,

substitutes. One could certainly expand equations (5.119) and (5.120) to allow for numerous types of imperfectly substitutable human capitals, for example, by letting (5.119) become $R(t) = \phi[K_1(t), K_2(t), \ldots, K_k(t)]$, where $K_i(t)$ is the *i*th type of human capital and by letting (5.120) become a set of k equations, one for each of the k total types of human capitals. I will not pursue this refinement here. (See Fisher, 1968, 1971, Chap. 2; Weiss, 1971.)

[32] For example, see Becker (1975c), Blinder and Weiss (1976), and S. Rosen (1972a).

[33] This implies that the training is "general," that is, raises the worker's marginal product in many firms besides the one providing it. In a competitive economy, the worker receives all the benefits of general training, since he can always get a job elsewhere once he gets such training if his present firm does not raise his wage up to the level of his now-higher post-training marginal productivity. Firms, then, receive none of this benefit and are willing to provide training of this kind only if the worker pays the cost, which – since training will raise his future productivity and, thus, future wages – he may be willing to do. If training is "specific," that is, raises the worker's marginal product only in the firm providing it, both the firm (which must pay at least some of the cost) and the worker (whose productivity will be higher within the firm than elsewhere) have a stake in staying together and so will tend to share both the costs and the benefits of specific training. (See Becker, 1975b, pp. 19–37.) In the training models discussed here, specific training is ignored; for a discussion of specific training in which market time is assumed fixed, see Nickell (1976).

whereas his human capital investment in any period, k, will be positively related to this "training content." In more formal terms, then,

(5.121) $k(t) = j[F(t)K(t)H(t)]$, with $j(0) = 0, j' > 0$
(5.122) $W(t) = g[F(t)]R(t)$, with $g(0) = 1, g' < 0$,
$$g'' \leq 0$$

(5.123) $E(t) = W(t)H(t) = g[F(t)]R(t)H(t)$

where $k(t)$ is gross investment in human capital in period t; $W(t)$ is earnings per hour spent at the firm during period t; $E(t)$ is total earnings during period t; and $F(t)$, an index of the training content of the job held during period t, ranges between 1 (the case of a job that is all training) and 0 (the case of a job that is all work). Note that $k = 0$ both for people who devote all their time to leisure (have $H = 0$) and for people who take jobs with no training content (have $F = 0$), FK is a measure of the amount of market productivity devoted to accumulating human capital (rather than to actual market work) per unit of market time, H, that FKH measures the total amount of investment undertaken, and $j(FKH)$ measures the resulting gross increment in human capital. (Hence, j is increasing in its argument, FKH.) The g function is assumed to be either linear or strictly concave in F, reflecting an assumption of either constant or increasing "marginal cost of training content."[34] Note also that (5.122) implies that $g(F)$ measures the fraction of market productivity R actually realized (via wages) at work, that is, $g(F) = W/R$.

The time allocation formulation

In this second version of the human capital model of life cycle labor supply, which is similar (though not identical) to the job choice approach, the individual divides his time between leisure and the market and chooses not the kind of job at which to work but, rather, how to allocate his total market time H between working and training (or "investing").[35] Thus, labor supply or market time, that is, the fraction of total available time devoted to the market, $H(t)$,

[34] Blinder and Weiss (1976) and S. Rosen (1972a) make $g(F)$ concave. In most other work, it is assumed to be linear, that is, $g(F) = 1 - F$.
[35] This is the approach taken by Ghez and Becker (1975), Heckman (1976a, b), and Ryder, Stafford, and Stephan (1976), among others.

consists of a portion devoted to market production, $M(t)$, and a portion devoted to investment, $I(t)$, so that $H(t) + L(t) = 1$ and $H(t) = M(t) + I(t)$. Individuals who attend school full time are said to devote all market time to investment (and thus have $M(t) = 0$ and $H(t) = I(t)$); individuals who combine school and a part-time job, or who have left school but train on the job, in effect have both positive I and positive M; and so on.[36]

In this second version of the human capital model, the k function in (5.120) is a human capital production function, giving the amount of gross increment to the human capital stock that the individual "produces" using investment time, I, and other inputs;[37] earnings are simply the product of market productivity, R, and time spent in actual market production, M; and the wage (i.e., earnings per hour spent *at* work) is the ratio of earnings to time spent *at* work, H. Thus, in formal terms,

$$(5.124) \quad k(t) = n[I(t), K(t)],$$
$$\text{with} \quad n(0, K(t)) = 0,$$
$$n_i > 0, \quad n_{ii} < 0, \quad i = I, K$$
$$(5.125) \quad W(t) = R(t)M(t)/H(t)$$
$$(5.126) \quad E(t) = R(t)M(t)$$

Gross investments k are zero when no time is devoted to investment, so that $n[0, K(t)] = 0$; inclusion of K among the arguments of the n function means that human capital is "self-productive," that is, that having knowledge makes it easier to acquire still more knowledge. The worker's output in the firm per period is simply $R(t)M(t)$; since a portion of the individual's labor supply H is spent getting training rather than working, not all time spent *at* work (H) is actually devoted *to* work (M). Hence W, the wage the worker actually gets per hour spent at work, is only MR/H, which is less

[36] Of course, in modern industrial settings, the term *investment time* may often be a figure of speech rather than something that can readily be measured. Some on-the-job training is highly formal and takes place in classrooms, but much of it is highly informal: workers observe other workers, get pointers from co-workers and supervisors, and so forth. The basic notion is that, in on-the-job training, the ratio I/H measures the "training content" of each hour spent at the workplace. Hours of work H can certainly be measured directly, but in many cases I cannot.

[37] Some authors, such as Ghez and Becker (1975) and Heckman (1976b), allow for other inputs, such as purchased goods and services (tuition, books, materials, and the like). I shall not pursue these complications here.

than R (his actual productivity per hour in market work) whenever $M < H$.

These two versions of the human capital model are by no means incompatible. For example, both imply that, when the worker invests, the wage (W) is less than his actual market productivity (R) and when the worker invests, time spent at the firm (H) exceeds the amount of time actually devoted to work as such (M). (This has a number of important implications for empirical studies of dynamic labor supply; see Section 5.7.) Moreover, if one assumes that the $g(F)$ function of (5.122) is simply $g(F) = 1 - F$ and specifies the n function of (5.124) as $n(I, K) = n(IK)$, then the F of the job choice model is equivalent to the ratio I/H in the time allocation model and the two "different" versions of the human capital analysis of dynamic labor supply reduce to exactly the same thing: The fraction of market productivity R that is forgone for investment, F, and the fraction of market time devoted to investment, I/H, are identical.[38] To be sure, one model interprets investment in terms of a fraction of market productivity R not realized in the market (i.e., as a choice of job), whereas the other interprets it in terms of an amount of market time not used for work (i.e., as an allocation of market time). However, in both models, there is a trade-off between current and future earning power, in the sense that both models imply that an individual cannot have higher future earning power (that is, have $k(t) > 0$) without simultaneously having lower current earning power (that is, have $W(t) < R(t)$). I shall refer to models in which this is true as *training models*; thus, in this sense, both the job choice model and the time allocation model of human capital accumulation are training models.

The learning-by-doing formulation

In contrast, in the third version of the process of human capital accumulation, which I call the notion of *experience* or *learning by doing*, someone who spends more time in the market, and thus has higher current earnings, necessarily also invests more as well.[39] That is, people are assumed to learn from experience and, in

---

[38] This is the most popular kind of training model, for example, see Heckman (1976a, b) and Ryder, Stafford, and Stephan (1976).

[39] For models of learning by doing (or "experience"), which have received much less attention in the literature than models of training, see Fisher (1971, Chap. 2), Heckman (1971), Killingsworth (1982a), and Weiss (1972).

particular, to learn about market activities – to learn how to work and how to learn – by engaging in market activities; and the amount they learn is assumed to be directly related to the amount of time they devote to market activities. (See Arrow's, 1962, seminal paper, and also Flueckiger, 1976.) Thus, in the learning-by-doing approach, market activity entails joint production: Learning is an inevitable by-product of work. (See S. Rosen, 1972b, in which all such learning is assumed to be specific to the firm in which it took place.) At the most general level, then, in the learning-by-doing model, the analog to equations (5.121)–(5.123) or (5.124)–(5.126) is

$$(5.127) \quad k(t) = x[H(t), K(t)],$$
$$\text{with} \quad x[0, K(t)] = 0,$$
$$x_i > 0, \quad x_{ii} < 0, \quad i = H, K$$
$$(5.128) \quad W(t) = R(t)$$
$$(5.129) \quad E(t) = W(t)H(t) = R(t)H(t)$$

In other words, in this view, experience or learning by doing "is an unavoidable joint product with goods production" (Eckaus, 1963, p. 504). Thus, as equations (5.127)–(5.129) imply, the accumulation of "experience" necessarily – by definition – entails an increase *both* in current *and* in future earning power. In particular, note that (5.127) and (5.128) imply that one can accumulate human capital (have $k(t) > 0$) without suffering *any* reduction in current earnings per hour, that is, without having to reduce earnings per hour of market time, $W(t)$, to a level less than current market productivity, $R(t)$. In contrast, both training models imply that this is not possible (note in particular equations (5.122) and (5.125)).

This being the case, learning by doing may sound too good to be true. Indeed, many writers are highly skeptical of the distinction between training and learning by doing and argue that the latter is in fact no different from the former. For example, Becker (1975c, p. 55) notes that differential opportunities for "costless" learning (that is, for having positive $k(t)$ with no reduction in $W(t)$ to a level below $R(t)$) would create a clear incentive for some persons to leave (enter) jobs with low (high) learning opportunities, which, in turn, would lead to precisely the kinds of investment-related wage differentials that are implicit in equations (5.122) and (5.125), that is, in training models. (See Mincer, 1974, pp. 65 and 132, for similar comments.)

However, none of this implies that the *worst* opportunity for (e.g., job involving) learning by doing entails no learning at all, as is implied in training models (in which the gross amount of investment, expressed either as F or as I, is entirely subject to individual choice and can be reduced to zero). On this point, Psacharopoulos and Layard (1979, p. 489) ask:

> Is costless learning impossible? For this to be the case there must always exist a job at which no learning occurs and at which we could currently produce more (net) than in any job where we can learn anything. There need not actually be anybody doing this job, though in a perfect market it would be surprising if someone were not doing it . . . . We have spent some years trying to think what this job is . . . . But we have found it impossible to think of any such job.

The core of the notion of learning by doing, then, is that even the job with the least learning involves *some* learning per hour spent at the job and that, therefore, people can learn more, even at this job, if they are willing to spend more time doing it. Nor is it really correct to say that this learning is entirely costless. True, in a world of learning by doing, the individual can both accumulate human capital (have $k(t) > 0$) and enjoy positive earnings (have $E(t) > 0$) without having to accept a wage $W(t)$ that is less than the full amount of his current market productivity $R(t)$. However, these highly desirable benefits are not costless: They come about only if the individual is willing to sacrifice some leisure (that is, have $H(t) > 0$ and, thus, have $L(t) < 1$), and can be increased only if leisure is reduced.

In sum, training and learning by doing refer to essentially different and distinct phenomena. On the other hand, training and learning by doing are by no means incompatible. To see this, consider the general model

(5.130) $\quad k(t) = k[I(t), H(t), K(t)],$

where

$$k_i > 0, \quad i = I, H, K, \quad \text{and}$$
$$k(t) > 0 \quad \text{if} \quad H(t) \geq I(t) > 0 \quad \text{or if} \quad H(t) > I(t) = 0,$$
$$k(t) = 0 \quad \text{otherwise}$$

(5.131) $\quad W(t) = W[I(t), R(t)],$

where

$$W_I < 0, \qquad W_R > 0, \quad \text{and}$$
$$W = 0 \quad \text{if} \quad I(t) = H(t), \qquad W = R(t) \quad \text{if} \quad I(t) = 0$$

(5.132) $E(t) = W(t)H(t)$

where $I(t)$ is always in the range $[0, H(t)]$. In the pure learning-by-doing case, $I(t)$ is fixed (e.g., at zero), whereas in the pure training case, the $k(t)$ function specializes to (5.121) or (5.124) rather than (5.130). (See Killingsworth, 1982a, for further discussion.)

5.6. **Dynamic labor supply models with endogenous wages: theory**

With these preliminaries out of the way, I now discuss what each kind of human capital model implies about labor supply, wages, and earnings over time.

First, consider pure training models. To see what such models imply about dynamic equilibrium, it is useful to start by working out the way in which investment in training will change over time. If such investment is ever "profitable," then it is likely to be particularly profitable early in life: At that point, current earning opportunities (and hence the forgone-earnings cost of investing) are relatively low, whereas many years remain for the individual to reap the benefits of such investment. If so, then, in general,[40] investment in training will be large early in life, and so market productivity R will rise relatively rapidly early in life.

As each year goes by, however, less and less time remains before retirement, so that the individual has less and less time in which to recoup the benefits of additional investment. Moreover, the forgone-earnings cost of additional investments rises because market productivity R – that is, the individual's potential earning power – rises as a direct consequence of previous investment. If training decays rapidly (that is, if δ is large), then there may be some point in postponing some investment until later in life. Hence, some

---

[40] In order to provide a coherent intuitive account of the main implications of the rather complicated models considered here, it is sometimes necessary to sacrifice rigor and to gloss over various details. Words such as "typically" and "generally" are intended to put the reader on notice that, when they appear, I am in fact sacrificing rigor and sweeping relatively minor details to one side.

training models imply that investment in "time-equivalent units" (either FH or I) may rise early in the life cycle. However, close to retirement, the payoff to additional investment is very small and the cost is very great, and so purely pecuniary motives will eventually dictate that little or no further investment should be undertaken.

This proposition on the time profile of investment has direct implications for the shape of the time profiles of market productivity, market time, earnings per hour, and annual earnings over the life cycle. Although investment may rise early in the life cycle, it ultimately must fall; hence market productivity (the "potential wage"), R, rises at first but must ultimately start to fall as gross investment $k(t)$ finally drops below the level required to offset depreciation $\delta K(t)$. (See equations (5.119) and (5.120).) The wage rate (earnings per hour of market time), W, will behave in roughly the same way. To see this, note from (5.121)–(5.126) that W is directly related to R but inversely related to investment (that is, to I or F). In general, investment falls more or less monotonically (except perhaps during the first part of the life cycle), whereas, as just noted, R rises during the early stage of the life cycle but then falls. If so, then W must rise early in the life cycle and then fall; moreover, it must peak after R peaks, since the effect of the decline in investment (that is, in either F or I) will be to increase W for a time even when R is no longer increasing.

Moreover, since R typically has an inverse-U-shaped time profile that peaks before W does, the profile of labor supply, H, will *also* be shaped roughly like an inverted U. (However, if $r > \rho$, then the peak in labor supply will come earlier in the life cycle than the peak in R, and therefore before the peak in hourly earnings, W.) This is because, more or less as in the exogenous wage model of the previous section, the relationship between H and R is the net outcome of the tug-of-war of a set of opposing effects. On the one hand, if $r > \rho$, then the market opportunity cost of jam today, r, is high relative to the individual's subjective assessment of the painfulness of future effort in relation to current effort, ρ. On balance, then, this time effect spurs the individual to work much at first, bank much of his earnings, and reduce his labor supply as he gets older. On the other hand, the rational allocation of effort dictates that the individual consume less leisure (and spend more time in the market) when the opportunity cost of leisure, which is either related to or else identical to R, is greater. Other things being equal, this efficiency effect spurs the individual to spend more time in the market when R is high and, thus, to increase labor supply H as R rises due to human capital accumulation.

So long as R grows rapidly early in the life cycle, the efficiency effect dominates the time effect (i.e., the sum of the interest rate and time preference effects) at first. Hence, market time H rises early in the life cycle. However, the rate of growth of R will eventually taper off because investment (I or F) eventually falls. As R grows more slowly, the efficiency effect ultimately gets weaker than the time effect. In consequence, market time H ultimately falls in the later stages of the life cycle.

Indeed, it turns out that the sign of the change in hours of work in the time allocation model of investment in training, in which the wage rate is endogenous, is given by

$$(5.133) \quad \dot{H}(t) = -S_{LW}(t)\,[\dot{R}(t)/R(t)] + Y_{LV}(t)\,(\rho - r)$$

where S_{LW} and Y_{LV} are as defined in Section 5.2, and $\dot{R}(t)/R(t)$ is the percentage rate of change over time of R, market productivity (the potential wage). (The first term in this expression is the efficiency effect, whereas the second is the time effect.) The resemblance between this expression and the comparable expression for the sign of the change in hours of work over time in the simple exogenous wage model of Section 5.2, (5.14), is striking. (Remember that P is fixed here.) It is even more striking when one recognizes that, in the exogenous wage model, R (the potential wage) and W (earnings per hour of time spent at work) are the same (because no investment in training takes place).[41]

***

[41] Thus, Ghez and Becker (1975, p. 22) conclude that "the question of whether these [life cycle] paths [of variables such as labor supply] are rising or falling as the wage rate is rising or falling is completely independent of the reasons for changes in the wage rate," that is, is independent of whether R changes exogenously or endogenously. However, as Blinder and Weiss (1976, p. 457) point out, this is not necessarily so. When the potential wage R is endogenous, the total opportunity cost of leisure is given by the sum of (i) current earnings per unit of market time, W; and (ii) the present value of future benefits arising from investment on the job. In the job choice model, these two components sum to R, the potential wage, provided $g(F) = 1 - F$. However, when the $g(F)$ function is strictly concave in F, the two components of the opportunity cost of leisure sum to an amount that is strictly greater than W and

Finally, so long as W and H both rise at first and then fall, with the peak in H preceding the peak in W, current earnings $E = WH$ will also rise early in the life cycle and then, eventually, start to fall, peaking before the peak in W but after the peak in market time (labor supply), H. Hence, the age–earnings profile will also tend to be shaped like an inverted U, as shown in Figure 5.1.

In sum, the implications of training models accord fairly well with intuition, casual observation, and stylized empirical evidence on life cycle behavior. That a single model can more or less predict not only the shapes of the individual profiles shown in Figure 5.1 but also the interrelationships between them (e.g., the temporal order in which they will peak) gives some idea of the power and attraction of such models.

More elaborate training models have still richer empirical implications. For example, much of the training literature in effect assumes that both market time and investment time are positive up to the last moment of life.[42] Blinder and Weiss (1976) abandon this assumption and allow instead for corner solutions, that is, for the possibility that hours of market time H or investment (that is, I or F) may fall to zero at any point in the life cycle. They show that someone who starts life by attending school full time (has $F = 1$ at first) will usually then enter an on-the-job training stage of work and training (with $0 < F < 1$), followed by a period of pure work with no investment in training (so that $F = 0$ and $H > 0$), and then, finally, a retirement period (with $H = 0$). Similarly, Heckman (1976b)

that depends on F as well as on R. Hence $\dot{R}/R$ does not measure the rate of change of the total opportunity cost of leisure, and neither the Ghez–Becker argument nor Weiss's result (cited in the text) applies. However, it is interesting to note that, even in this case, the peak in labor supply H will precede the peak in the profile of the potential wage R (see Blinder and Weiss, 1976, pp. 465–6). Evidently, this particular result in training models is quite robust with respect to alternative assumptions about the way in which R is endogenous, about $g(F)$, and so forth.

[42] In some cases, researchers simply assume a priori that I (or, alternatively, F) will be positive throughout the life cycle except at the last instant. (For example, see Heckman, 1976b.) In other cases, researchers guarantee that I (or F) will be positive throughout the life cycle by introducing a very strong assumption about the accumulation of training: that training time I (or training content F) is infinitely "productive" at the margin when no training is currently being undertaken. (In terms of equations (5.121) and (5.124), this is an assumption that $j' \to \infty$ as $F \to 0$, or, alternatively, that $n_I \to \infty$ as $I \to 0$.) For example, see Ryder, Stafford, and Stephan (1976).

assumes, largely for analytical convenience, that I and M are both positive throughout the life cycle. However, if one allows for corner solutions in either I or M or both, then it can be shown that someone who starts the life cycle with a period of full-time schooling ($I = H$, $M = 0$) will follow one of only two types of life cycle paths. In the first, the period of full-time schooling will be followed by a period of on-the-job training (with I and M both positive), then by a period of pure work (with $I = 0$ and $M = H$), and, finally, by retirement (with $I = M = H = 0$ and $L = 1$), exactly as in the Blinder–Weiss model. In the second kind of path, the period of full-time schooling will be followed by a period of retirement ($L = 1$) lasting until the end of life. (See Killingsworth, 1982a.) The first of these patterns seems a reasonably good description of the life cycle behavior of many men; the second seems a not unreasonable approximation to the life cycle behavior of some – though hardly most – women.

Training models that allow for corner solutions (zero values for I, M, H, etc.) have one other interesting implication: cycling, that is, the recurrence of a particular life cycle stage (e.g., retirement or on-the-job training). In some cases, cycling involves alternation between pure work and on-the-job training; in others, such cycling can entail several retirement segments interspersed with segments of on-the-job training, pure work, and so forth. (See Blinder and Weiss, 1976; Driffill, 1980; Killingsworth, 1982a.) Now, as noted at the start of this chapter, many women appear to alternate between periods of positive market work and periods of zero market work. In terms of the models described here, this is a form of cycling. Theoretical training models with cycling have only begun to be explored thoroughly. However, it is clear that such models may provide insights into the dynamics of female labor supply, particularly once one explicitly allows for family interdependencies and fertility.

The literature on pure experience or pure learning-by-doing models such as the one embodied in equations (5.127)–(5.129) is much less developed than the literature on pure training models. Fisher (1971, Chap. 2) focuses on interpreting the first-order conditions in such experience models; Weiss (1972, pp. 1302–11) provides a thorough discussion of alternative possible empirical life cycle patterns that might arise under one particular specification of the x function of (5.127). The basic point that underlies both analyses is that, in a world in which all human capital accumulation occurs via learning by doing, the opportunity cost of leisure is always *greater* than market productivity, R: What one gives up in order to enjoy an extra hour of leisure is not just R, but R *plus* the implicit value of the experience one can gain (via learning by doing) by devoting the hour to market rather than nonmarket activities. (This implicit amount is the appropriately discounted stream of increments to future earnings that the individual will get by virtue of having had an extra hour's worth of experience, and thus extra human capital.) For this reason, changes in R do not necessarily imply changes in the opportunity cost of leisure and vice versa. Thus, market or nonleisure time, H, and the opportunity cost of leisure time will generally move in the same direction, ceteris paribus, but labor supply (H) and the wage (R) need not be related in any particular way. Indeed, the time profile of labor supply can take on a variety of different shapes, for example, monotonically increasing, monotonically decreasing, U shaped, or inverse-U shaped. (See Weiss, 1972, pp. 1304–6.)

Although Weiss's results are in part a result of his choice of form for the $k(t)$ function in (5.120), his analysis suggests that learning-by-doing models may be too general to be entirely satisfactory: Almost any kind of labor supply profile could be consistent with that model, making one wonder whether it has been formulated in a way that makes it refutable. To be sure, the predictions of pure training models are not nearly as sharp, in all cases, as the necessarily rather compact summary presented here would seem to suggest. However, such models do usually have somewhat sharper implications than do learning-by-doing models, particularly once one assumes that $r > \rho$.

On the other hand, training models are not entirely satisfactory either. Despite my repeated reference to what I have called *stylized facts* about the life cycle, the notion that the wage rate W falls towards the end of (e.g., at the very end of) the life cycle is not so much a stylized fact as a factoid or even a quasi-fact: Several studies suggest that earnings per hour of market time, W, rise monotonically over the entire life cycle.[43] However, training models imply

---

[43] For example, see Becker (1975c, p. 84) and Mincer (1974, esp. pp. 69, 71). Their data are based on a synthetic cohort rather than on actual life cycles (see note 1), but this complicates the issue. One difficulty with such synthetic cohort data is that persons from more recent cohorts (more recent vintages) may enjoy greater or lesser

that *W must* eventually fall, albeit at a later date in the life cycle than the point at which *R* begins to decline. If pure experience models are too general, this implication of pure training models may be too specific, and, thus, too easily refuted. Further work may help to clear up such questions and provide richer theoretical answers to Blaug's sharp criticism to the effect that models of human capital accumulation have not yet distinguished between training and learning by doing and have not yet shown the relative importance of each kind of accumulation.[44] (See Blaug, 1976, esp. p. 840.)

5.7.   **Dynamic labor supply models with endogenous wages: empirical analysis**

As indicated in Section 5.6, the qualitative predictions of endogenous wage life cycle models (e.g., training models) seem reasonably consistent with stylized lifetime profiles of wage rates, market time, and earnings. However, simple qualitative comparisons between the theoretical predictions of a model and stylized facts about actual behavior are not really a substitute for econometric estimation of the parameters of that model. Quantitative tests – estimation of, for example, the magnitudes of the efficiency and time effects previously discussed – are clearly more powerful than simple qualitative comparisons and are much more useful for analytical and policy questions.

Quantitative tests of endogenous wage models may be particularly important as a means of distinguishing between *rival* analyses of life cycle behavior. For example, in sharp contrast with training models, in which investment is a choice variable, one might assume (i) that individuals receive exogenously determined *b* units of human

productivity, ceteris paribus, than do persons from previous cohorts. Since synthetic cohorts are ones in which persons from recent vintages are young, whereas persons from previous vintages are older, synthetic cohort data may confound affects of age as such with effects of vintage. Thus, for example, age–wage profiles derived from synthetic cohorts may systematically understate or overstate the extent to which wages rise (or fall) with age over the life cycle for persons of the *same* vintage – even if one has already adjusted those wage profiles for the effects of exogenous dynamic factors, such as technical progress or inflation.

[44] For example, models in which one may accumulate human capital both through investment in training and through learning by doing seem to have more palatable implications than do models in which all accumulation occurs exclusively through one form rather than the other. See Killingsworth (1982a).

capital per period merely as the result of exogenous biopsychological development, maturation, and the like, and (ii) that gross of
depreciation, human capital growth occurs entirely as a result of this
wholly exogenous process. Under these assumptions, human capital
will grow over time according to the relation $K(t + 1) - K(t) = b - \delta K(t)$. If b is sufficiently large relative to $K(0)$, the individual's
initial endowment of human capital, then the time profile of K and
hence of the wage rate W will be shaped like an inverted U. If $r > \rho$
and if C and L are normal goods, then the individual's market time,
wage rate, and earnings will have time profiles like those shown in
Figure 5.1. In other words, each of two quite different rival models
– an exogenous wage model and an endogenous wage model – can
"fit" the stylized facts about life cycle behavior shown in Figure 5.1.
Only quantitative evaluation is likely to provide useful evidence on
the relative merits of each model, by, for example, providing measures of the relative importance of biopsychological factors and
investment in training in human capital accumulation.[45]

Unfortunately, a researcher who wants to estimate the parameters
of an endogenous wage life cycle model must confront a number of
difficult and interrelated problems that do not usually arise in other
settings:[46] problems of measurement, problems of specification and
estimation, and the problem of collective plausibility.

Measurement problems

In most cases, the variables of primary interest in
endogenous wage models (particularly training models) are not
directly observable. This makes it difficult both to (i) estimate the
parameters of such models and (ii) use parameter estimates, if they
can be obtained, to make quantitative statements about variables of
particular interest.

As an example of the first difficulty, recall from Section 5.6 that,
in training models, one can often[47] write time spent in the market,

---

[45] The lack of empirical tests of the relative importance of various alternative forms
of wage change (e.g., learning by doing vs. investment in training, endogenous vs.
exogenous) seems to be one of the main reasons why Blaug (1976, esp. pp. 836–40,
842–5) takes a "jaundiced view" of human capital models of the life cycle.

[46] One must also confront many of the problems noted in Chapters 3 and 4 (e.g.,
selectivity bias).

[47] Recall the previous discussion and, in particular, equation (5.133).

$H(t)$, as a function of the potential wage (market productivity), $R(t)$, and of time itself. Thus, provided one replaces $W(t)$ with $R(t)$, a function such as equation (5.103) applies equally well to an endogenous wage training model as to an exogenous wage model. However, when wages are endogenous, the potential wage, $R(t)$, cannot usually be observed. Rather, as (5.122) and (5.125) indicate, when individuals invest in training, the observed wage rate $W(t)$ – that is, earnings per hour spent *at* work – is less than the potential wage $R(t)$ by an amount that depends on $I(t)$ (or on $F(t)$, in the job choice formulation); and $I(t)$ is not observable. Hence, such a modified version of (5.103) cannot readily be estimated, since one of the independent variables, $R(t)$, is unobservable.

As an example of the second difficulty, note that the dependent variable in such a modified version of (5.103) would be either leisure time, $L(t)$, or hours spent *at* work, $H(t)$ and hours spent *at* work consist of hours devoted to investment, $I(t)$, and hours spent actually working, $M(t)$. Thus, even if it were possible to estimate the parameters of such a modified version of (5.103), the parameter estimates could be used to determine only, for example, the efficiency effect of a change in $R(t)$ on leisure or on hours spent *at* work. In and of themselves, the estimates could not be used to determine how a change in $R(t)$ leads to changes in hours spent actually working, $M(t)$, or in investment time, $I(t)$. Of course, one can certainly manipulate training models so as to derive specifications for both $I(t)$ and $M(t)$. Such specifications would express $I(t)$ and $M(t)$ as functions of, for example, market productivity, time, and so forth. Such specifications, however, cannot readily be estimated, because the dependent variables ($I(t)$ and $M(t)$) in these functional relationships are unobservable.

Specification and estimation

The fact that many of the variables in endogenous wage models are unobservable makes specifying and estimating such models rather difficult. One must not only manipulate the first-order conditions of such models so as to derive explicit functions for dependent variables that can be observed (e.g., earnings, $E(t)$; time spent at work, $H(t)$; the observed wage, $W(t)$); one must also make sure that such specifications express these dependent variables in terms of independent variables that are also observable. However, when wages are endogenous, the only observable independent variable is time, t, itself; and in many cases, writing an explicit specification for a dependent variable such as earnings or the observed wage as a function of time (i.e., age) turns out to require solving a complex set of differential or difference equations. Unfortunately, unless one imposes some quite stringent assumptions on, for example, the nature of the human capital production function, an analytically tractable solution to such equations may not exist; further, even if a solution does exist, it may be highly nonlinear in the parameters to be estimated. In such cases, the appropriate estimation technique is an iterative maximum-likelihood procedure; but a procedure of this kind can be very expensive to use and may converge at a local (rather than a global) maximum of the likelihood function.

Collective plausibility

Even if one can surmount the problems noted previously and is able to obtain estimates of the parameters of an endogenous wage model, such estimates cannot be called "good" or "plausible" unless they pass two tests: First, are they individually plausible; and, second, are they collectively plausible?

The first of these notions, *individual plausibility*, is the criterion usually applied to a parameter estimate: Does it have the "right" sign and is its magnitude roughly what one would expect a priori? The second, *collective plausibility*, refers to a somewhat different criterion: Does the *set* of estimates, taken together, generate a set of life cycle paths for the endogenous variables (earnings, hours spent at work, hours spent actually working, the observed wage rate, etc.) that are plausible on a priori grounds?

Of course, as just noted, if each of the endogenous variables could be measured, then one could jointly estimate equations for each of these variables as part of a simultaneous system, with appropriate across-equation constraints. The resulting parameter estimates would always be collectively plausible, that is, would fit the observed paths of the endogenous variables used in estimation of the equation system. Here the sole test of the plausibility of the estimates would be the usual one, individual plausibility. However, as previously indicated, the investigator is usually able to estimate functions for only a few of the endogenous variables, since most are unobserved. By construction, an estimated function for earnings (or hours spent at work, or the observed wage, etc.) will fit observed profiles for earnings (or hours spent at work, or the observed wage, etc.) reasonably well. However, even if each of the parameter estimates is individually plausible, in the sense just given, it does not follow that the set of parameter estimates will generate plausible profiles for the other endogenous variables of the model, those for which equations are not (because they cannot be) estimated.

In view of these difficulties, it is evident that empirical analysis of endogenous wage models of labor supply poses a considerable challenge to researchers. The fact that the results thus far are few and not very convincing should not, therefore, be entirely surprising. Since my focus here is on labor supply, I shall ignore studies that estimate the parameters of life cycle earnings profiles on the assumption that market time is fixed and the individual maximizes earnings. Instead, I will focus on two empirical studies by Heckman (1976a, b), who estimates training models of human capital accumulation in which labor supply over the life cycle is a choice variable.[48]

In the first study, Heckman (1976a) exploits the fact that, in the time allocation version of the training model, the potential wage R is simultaneously equal to both (i) the sum of initial productivity, $R(0)$, plus investments undertaken between time 0 and time t (net of depreciation) and (ii) the opportunity cost of time, which, in turn, is equal (in equilibrium) to the marginal benefit of current investment time (measured as the present value of future benefits attributable to current investment).[49]

---

[48] For reasons that will shortly become obvious, these two studies by Heckman appear to be the only two published efforts to estimate the parameters of a rigorously developed endogenous wage model of life cycle utility maximization. (For studies that estimate the parameters of life cycle earnings profiles on the assumption that individuals maximize the present value of their lifetime earnings stream, see Ben-Porath, 1970; Brown, 1976; Haley, 1976; Mincer, 1974.)

[49] Most readers will probably accept these notions as self-evident and will be willing to accept on faith the functional relations discussed later (equations (5.134)–(5.147)) that are derived from them. Other readers, however, may wonder – quite rightly – just how these relations are in fact derived. The answer is that they are based on optimal control theory, which is a particularly convenient way of analyzing optimization over time. (See the theoretical sections in Heckman's, 1976a, b, papers; see also Blinder and Weiss, 1976, and Weiss, 1972, which also use optimal control theory.) A

To give these general notions some specific content, Heckman assumes that $R(t) = K(t)$ for all t (so that market productivity and human capital are treated as equivalent) and that the general human capital production function of (5.124), $k(t)$, has a Cobb–Douglas functional form. Thus, in terms of (5.120), $K(t + 1) - K(t) = cI(t)^{\eta_1}K(t)^{\eta_2} - \delta K(t)$, or, in continuous time, $\dot{K}(t) = cI(t)^{\eta_1}K(t)^{\eta_2} - \delta K(t)$. The latter is a first-order nonlinear differential equation in $K(t)$, whose solution is

$$(5.134) \quad K(t) = e^{-\delta t}\left[K(0)^{1-\eta_2} + (1 - \eta_2) \int_0^t e^{(1-\eta_2)\delta\tau} cI(\tau)^{\eta_1} d\tau\right]^{1/(1-\eta_2)}$$

Next, the marginal benefit of investment time is simply the present value of the future stream of benefits associated with an increase in current investment time, $I(t)$. Heckman assumes that beyond time 0 (i.e., the first date to which the analysis is applicable) no corners occur, that is, that hours at work, H, hours of actual work, M, and hours of investment, I, are all positive between $t = 0$ and $t = T$. Under this assumption, the marginal benefit of investment time, $B(t)$, is given by[50]

formal exposition of optimal control theory is beyond the scope of this book; for an invaluable and admirably lucid introduction to the subject, see Arrow and Kurz (1970, Chap. 2). Sheshinski (1968) provides a very helpful example of the application of optimal control theory to a very simple model of investment in human capital in which the individual is assumed to maximize the present value of his lifetime earnings (rather than a lifetime utility function such as (5.1)). Takayama's (1974, Chap. 8) discussion of optimal control theory is detailed and includes numerous examples.

[50] The first term, in brackets, in this expression for $B(t)$ may be interpreted as the increase in $\dot{K}(t)$ associated with an increase in $I(t)$ – that is, the marginal productivity of investment time. The second term in curly braces may be interpreted as the future stream of benefits associated with having increased one's stock of human capital at time t. Roughly speaking, this depends on both hours of actual market work $M(s)$ and investment time $I(s)$ at all future dates $s > t$ (since having more human capital increases both one's ability to produce market goods and one's ability to undertake further investments in human capital). Since $M(s) + I(s) = H(s)$ for all s, it might therefore seem that the future benefit as of time s would depend only on $H(s)$, rather than on $H(s) - I(s)(1 - (\eta_1/\eta_2))$ as implied by the expression for $B(t)$. However, note that η_1 is the elasticity of human capital production $k(t)$ with respect to investment time $I(t)$, whereas η_2 is the elasticity of $k(t)$ with respect to the stock of human capital $K(t)$. If $\eta_1 = \eta_2$, then the future benefit of human capital at time s does indeed depend only on $H(s)$. Otherwise, human capital's benefit will be

$$B(t) = [c\eta_1 I(t)^{\eta_1 - 1} K(t)^{\eta_2}]$$
$$\times \left\{ \int_t^T e^{-(\delta + r)(\tau - t)} [H(\tau) - I(\tau)(1 - (\eta_1/\eta_2))] \, d\tau \right\}$$

In equilibrium, the marginal benefit of time $B(t)$ will equal the marginal cost of time; and in Heckman's model, the latter is equal to $R(t)$, the (maximum potential) productivity of a unit of time. Hence, in equilibrium, $R(t) = B(t)$; since $R(t)$ and $K(t)$ are taken to be synonymous, this yields

$$(5.135) \quad K(t) = \{c\eta_1 I(t)^{\eta_1 - 1} K(t)^{\eta_2}\}$$
$$\times \left\{ \int_t^T e^{-(\delta + r)(\tau - t)} \right.$$
$$\left. \times [H(\tau) - I(\tau)(1 - (\eta_1/\eta_2))] \, d\tau \right\}$$

To convert equations (5.134) and (5.135) to a form suitable for estimation, first rearrange them and take logarithms to obtain

$$(5.136) \quad \ln K(t) = [\ln c\eta_1/(1 - \eta_2)]$$
$$+ [(\eta_1 - 1)/(1 - \eta_2)] \ln I(t)$$
$$+ [1/(1 - \eta_2)] \ln \left\{ \int_t^T e^{-(\delta + r)(\tau - t)} \right.$$
$$\left. \times [H(\tau) - I(\tau)(1 - (\eta_1/\eta_2))] \, d\tau \right\}$$

greater or smaller than $H(s)$ depending on the sign of $1 - (\eta_1/\eta_2)$, which may be thought of as a "correction factor" that allows for the possible "nonneutrality" of human capital. To understand the meaning of nonneutrality, note that, under Heckman's assumptions, gross human capital output $k(t)$ is given by $k(t) = cI(t)^{\eta_1} K(t)^{\eta_2} = c[I(t)K(t)]^{\eta_1} K(t)^{\eta_2 - \eta_1}$, whereas output of market goods $E(t)$ is given by $E(t) = M(t)K(t)$. Thus, if the individual's stock of human capital rises by 1 percent, he can keep his earnings constant if he reduces $M(t)$ by 1 percent, whereas he can keep his gross human capital output constant if he reduces $I(t)$ by η_2/η_1 percent. Accordingly, when η_2 is greater (less) than η_1, human capital is said to be "biased" in favor of human capital production (market goods production), whereas if $\eta_2 = \eta_1$ human capital is said to be "neutral" or to "augment actual work time and investment time equally." Finally, because of depreciation, only $e^{-\delta(\tau - t)}$ of a unit of human capital created at time t will remain in existence at time $\tau > t$; and one dollar in income received at time $\tau > t$ is worth only $e^{-r(\tau - t)}$ of a dollar received today. Hence, the benefit as of time $\tau > t$ of a unit of human capital created at time t is discounted at the rate $e^{-(\delta + r)(\tau - t)}$.

(5.137) $\ln K(t) = -\delta t + [1/(1 - \eta_2)]$
$$+ [1/(1 - \eta_2)] \ln \left\{ K(0)^{1 - \eta_2} \right.$$
$$\left. + (1 - \eta_2) \int_0^T e^{(1 - \eta_2)\delta\tau} cI(\tau)^{\eta_1} d\tau \right\}$$

Now define $F(t) \equiv I(t)/H(t)$, where F is the fraction of time spent at work ($M(t)$) that is devoted to investment ($I(t)$). Hence

(5.138) $I(t) = F(t)H(t)$

Also, note from (5.125) and (5.138) that since $R(t) = K(t)$

(5.139) $\ln K(t) = \ln W(t) - \ln[1 - F(t)]$

Now use (5.138) and (5.139) to rewrite equations (5.136) and (5.137), and then add error terms $\epsilon_1(t)$ and $\epsilon_2(t)$ to obtain

(5.140) $\ln W(t) = [\ln c\eta_1/(1 - \eta_2)]$
$$+ [(\eta_1 - 1)/(1 - \eta_2)] \ln[F(t)H(t)]$$
$$+ [1/(1 - \eta_2)] \ln \left\{ \int_t^T e^{-(\delta + r)(\tau - t)} \right.$$
$$\left. \times H(\tau) [1 - F(\tau)(1 - (\eta_1/\eta_2))] dt \right\}$$
$$+ \ln[1 - F(t)] + \epsilon_1(t)$$

(5.141) $\ln W(t) = -\delta t + [1/(1 - \eta_2)]$
$$+ [1/(1 - \eta_2)] \ln \left\{ [W(0)(1 - F(0))]^{1 - \eta_2} \right.$$
$$\left. + (1 - \eta_2) \int_0^T e^{(1 - \eta_2)\delta\tau} c[F(\tau)H(\tau)]^{\eta_1} d\tau \right\}$$
$$+ \ln[1 - F(t)] + \epsilon_2(t)$$

Equations (5.140) and (5.141) are a two-equation simultaneous system that expresses the observed wage $W(t)$ (that is, earnings per hour spent at work) as a function of age (that is, t) and of present, past, and future values of (i) hours spent at work, $H(\tau)$, and (ii) the investment ratio, $F(\tau)$. In principle, then, one can use maximum-likelihood methods to estimate the parameters of equations (5.140) and (5.141) – the interest rate r, the depreciation rate δ, and the human capital production function parameters c, η_1, and η_2. However, the data required for such estimation substantially exceed what is usually available to an investigator: The investment ratio F is unobservable, and whereas the actual wage W and hours of work H are observable, no data set now in existence contains measures of W or H over any individual's entire life cycle – as is required for estimation of equations (5.140) and (5.141).

Heckman's solution to these two problems is as follows. First, he uses synthetic cohort data on hourly earnings and annual hours of work to develop measures of W and H at each age t. Second, in place of the unobservable variable F, Heckman uses a smooth logistic function of age, that is, assumes that $F(t)$ in equations (5.140) and (5.141) above may be replaced with

$$(5.142) \quad F(t) = \left[1 + \exp\left(\sum_{i=0}^{q} \alpha_i t^i \right) \right]^{-1}$$

This is a logistic function involving polynomials in age (t); for example, for $q = 2$, (5.142) involves an intercept term (α_0), a linear term in age (with slope α_1), and a quadratic term in age (with slope α_2). Note that this function constrains $F(t)$ to be a fraction at all ages t, in keeping with the definition of $F(t)$ as the fraction of market time devoted to investment rather than to actual work.[51]

Most of the estimated parameters of the system (5.140) and (5.141) have the "right" signs, and both the sign and magnitude of Heckman's estimate of the rate of depreciation of training (δ), 0.0016, seems not unreasonable. However, training is estimated to have negative self-productivity, in the sense that the estimate of η_2 is about -6.7 (and is different from zero at conventional levels of statistical significance). This means that "the accumulation of human capital *decreases* substantially the efficiency with which human capital can subsequently be produced" (T. P. Schultz, 1976, p. 263; emphasis original).

Such anomalies may be the result of various statistical difficulties. Heckman's synthetic cohort data may not adequately represent the behavior of any given individual, meaning that such data may not yield sensible parameter estimates even if the model embodied in equations (5.140) and (5.141) is an adequate characterization of life cycle behavior. Similarly, errors in measurement of hours at work,

[51] Note also that Heckman's approximation of the investment ratio $F(t)$, (5.142), is similar in spirit to Mincer's approximation of the same ratio (which Mincer calls k_t). The main difference is that Mincer (1974, esp. p. 85) assumes that the investment ratio falls either linearly or exponentially with age, whereas Heckman's approximation of the behavior of this ratio takes the more complicated logistic form given by (5.142).

H, in Heckman's data may not be independent of the errors ϵ_1 and ϵ_2 in the wage equations (5.140) and (5.141), meaning that maximum-likelihood estimates of the parameters of those equations will be biased.[52] Finally, although one must necessarily adopt some sort of assumption about the behavior of $F(t)$ at each age t (because $F(t)$ is unobservable), and although the particular assumption about $F(t)$ embodied in (5.142) is quite convenient from an econometric stand-point, there is no reason to suppose that (5.142) necessarily represents the actual behavior of $F(t)$ under utility maximization.

In his second study, Heckman (1976b) presents a more sophisticated but also more tractable training model, one that yields a somewhat simpler estimating equation in which all relationships can be derived in a fairly straightforward manner from principles of utility maximization – thereby eliminating the need for approximations such as (5.142). First, he assumes that instantaneous utility $u(t)$ is a function of consumption $C(t)$ and of augmented leisure $L(t)K(t)$ (that is, leisure as augmented by human capital – the idea being that human capital increases the productivity or enjoyment one derives from nonmarket time), according to the Cobb–Douglas function $u(t) = AC(t)^\alpha [L(t)K(t)]^\beta$. Next, the human capital production function is assumed to be $k(t) = c[I(t)K(t)]^\eta$, another Cobb–Douglas-type function. Further, Heckman assumes that there are no corners and, thus, H, I, *and* M are all positive over the age span (time 0 to time T) to which the model refers.

Under these assumptions, it turns out that augmented leisure time $L(t)K(t)$ (that is, leisure time as augmented by human capital) at any age t is equal to

(5.143) $\quad L(t)K(t)^{\cdot} = [\mu kAP(t)^\alpha e^{(\rho - r)t}]^\gamma$

where

$$\gamma \equiv -1/(1 - \alpha - \beta) \quad \text{and}$$
$$k \equiv \alpha^{-\alpha}\beta^{-(1-\alpha)}$$

and where μ is the marginal utility of initial assets $Z(0)$, as in the exogenous wage models discussed in Sections 5.2 and 5.4. Heckman

---

[52] Note that just the same kind of bias may arise in estimation of conventional static labor supply models, except that in that case the *dependent* variable is hours of work, whereas one of the *independent* variables is the wage rate. (Recall the discussion of Chapter 4 on this point.)

also shows that augmented investment time $I(t)K(t)$ (that is, investment time as augmented by human capital) at any age t is equal to

(5.144) $\quad I(t)K(t) = \{c\eta[1 - e^{(r+\delta)(t-T)}]/(r+\delta)\}^{1/(1+\eta)}$

where, as before, T is the individual's (economic) lifetime. Finally, human capital at any age t is equal to the level of the individual's initial stock of human capital plus investments made between time 0 and time t, net of depreciation, so that

(5.145) $\quad K(t) = e^{-\delta t} K(0) + \int_0^t e^{-\delta(t-\tau)} c[I(\tau)K(\tau)]^\eta \, d\tau$

By (5.126), earnings at age t, $E(t)$, is equal to $E(t) = M(t)R(t)$. Heckman next assumes that $K(t) = R(t)$ (hence, market productivity and human capital are again treated as equivalent). Together with the fact that $M(t) = 1 - L(t) - I(t)$, this implies that $E(t) = K(t) - L(t)K(t) - I(t)K(t)$. Finally, substitute equations (5.143)–(5.145) into this expression for earnings $E(t)$ and add an error term $\nu(t)$, to obtain the following econometric specification of the earnings function implied by the model

(5.146)
$$E(t) = e^{-\delta t} K(0) - [\mu k A P(t)^\alpha]^\gamma e^{[(\rho-r)/\gamma]t}$$
$$+ \int_0^t e^{-\delta(t-\tau)} c\{c\eta[1 - e^{(r+\delta)(\tau-T)}]/(r+\delta)\}^{\eta/(1-\eta)} \, d\tau$$
$$- \{c\eta[1 - e^{(r+\delta)(t-T)}]/(r+\delta)\}^{1/(1+\eta)} + \nu(t)$$

The only variables on the right-hand side of this expression are μ, age (that is, t), initial human capital $K(0)$ and the price level $P(t)$.[53] The parameters of the model are c, η, δ, A, α, β, ρ, and r.

---

[53] An important reason why it is possible to write earnings as a function of age, $P(t)$, $K(0)$, and μ only (rather than, as in the model of equations (5.140) and (5.141) as a function of age *and* all past, present, and future values of both H and F) is that in the present case Heckman assumes that human capital augments all three uses of time – leisure, $L(t)$; investment, $I(t)$; and market production, $M(t)$ – to the same extent. To see why the Heckman (1976b) model has this property, recall the discussion of note 50, and note that in this model the "production" of utility is given by $AC^\alpha(LK)^\beta$, whereas the production of human capital and market goods are given by $c(IK)^\eta$ and MK, respectively. Thus, a 1 percent increase in the stock of human capital K, coupled with 1 percent decreases in *each* use of time (L, I, and M), will keep the

Several features of (5.146) are particularly noteworthy. First, (5.146) is a function in which all variables, $E(t)$, μ, $K(0)$, $P(t)$, and age (t), either are observable or else are individual-specific fixed effects. Deriving a function of this kind from a life cycle model is no mean feat. (As inspection of equations (5.140) and (5.141) indicates, in some cases it is simply not possible, even after repeated substitution and manipulation, to derive such a function from an endogenous wage model.) Second, rather simple building blocks – Cobb–Douglas specifications of the utility and human capital production functions – lead to the rather complicated function (5.146); more elaborate functional forms for these basic building blocks typically lead to still more complex estimating equations (ones that, moreover, may have no closed-form solution). Finally, since $K(0)$ and μ are fixed for given individuals but vary from one individual to another, they may both be treated as individual-specific fixed effects. However, note that the impact of these fixed effects in (5.146) is more complicated than the impact of fixed effects in, for example, (5.103), in which the fixed effect (ln μ/Δ) is purely additive. In contrast, in (5.146) the fixed effect $K(0)$ is multiplied by the factor $e^{-\delta t}$, whereas the fixed effect μ is multiplied by the factor $[kAP(t)^\alpha]^\gamma e^{[(\rho - r)/\gamma]t}$. In this sense, then, the fixed effects in (5.146) are "multiplicative."

To estimate (5.146), Heckman uses synthetic cohort data constructed from the 1960 Census 1/1000 sample tapes for white men, grouped according to educational attainment. Since these data refer to a single year, the variable $P(t)$ may be treated as a constant; since such data are average values (of earnings, $E(t)$) for persons at each age t, Heckman treats both the $K(0)$ and the μ in (5.146) as constants (in other words, as average values of $K(0)$ and μ, respectively, among the individuals used in computing the synthetic cohort data) and thus as parameters to be estimated. This being the case, one may define $\tilde{\rho} \equiv (\rho - r)/\gamma$ and $\ell \equiv [\mu k AP(t)^\alpha]^\gamma$ and treat $K(0)$, $\tilde{\rho}$, and ℓ as parameters to be estimated. Accordingly, (5.146) becomes

amount of each kind of production unchanged. Further, it turns out that, when human capital is neutral, in this sense, with respect to the allocation of time, one can write LK as a function of μ, the price level, and age, and can write IK as a function of age (t) alone. Since one can write IK as a function of age alone, it follows that one can also write the current level of human capital as a function of the initial level $K(0)$ and age (see (5.145)). It is then possible to write earnings, $E = K - LK - IK$, as a function of μ, the price level, $K(0)$, and age.

(5.147)
$$E(t) = e^{-\delta t} K(0)$$
$$+ \int_0^t e^{-\delta(t-\tau)} c \{c\eta[1 - e^{(r+\delta)(\tau-T)}]/(r+\delta)\}^{\eta/(1-\eta)} d\tau$$
$$- \ell e^{\tilde{\rho} t} - \{c\eta[1 - e^{(r+\delta)(t-T)}]/(r+\delta)\}^{1/(1-\eta)}$$
$$+ \nu(t)$$

Note that the *only* independent variable in (5.147) is age,[54] t, and the parameters of (5.147) are c, η, δ, $K(0)$, ℓ, r, and $\tilde{\rho}$.

Heckman's results for three different sets of synthetic cohort data (classified by educational attainment) are given in Table 5.2. On the whole, the individual estimates seem fairly plausible. The human capital production function parameters c and η rise with schooling level, implying that persons with more formal education seem to be more efficient at producing human capital. Note that each estimate of η is less than unity, implying diminishing marginal productivity of augmented investment time, IK, in the production of human capital. The estimates of the depreciation rate δ seem plausible a priori (however, note that they are considerably higher than the estimate, 0.0016, that Heckman obtained in (1976a)).

Unfortunately, however, the estimates of the rate of interest, r, seem rather large, even when one takes into account the rather low asymptotic t-ratios associated with these estimates.[55] Thus, the individual plausibility of these particular estimates is somewhat doubtful. Moreover, my simulations of the life cycle profiles of H, W, and so forth implied by Heckman's estimates raise some doubts as to the collective plausibility of the estimates. Both for the synthetic high

---

[54] Thus, in estimating (5.147), one is in effect asking the data to identify and provide measures of seven parameters using only one independent variable. Even with the considerable nonlinearity of (5.147), this is not necessarily a simple task: As a practical matter, identifying parameters in this fashion may not be feasible even if identification is secured in a purely formal sense. (On this, see Heckman, 1976a, p. 246; T. P. Schultz, 1976.)

[55] A word of caution is in order here. Since the results shown in the table are based on synthetic cohort data, each set of results is based on a sample of about 45 data points (representing, e.g., mean earnings for persons with 12 years of schooling at age 21, 22, . . . , 65). The small-sample properties of the asymptotic t-statistics obtained in maximum-likelihood estimation are not well understood, and the degree of imprecision inherent in such estimation means that the computed magnitudes of these t-statistics may either under- or overstate the true magnitudes.

Table 5.2. *Estimates of parameters of Heckman (1976b) model
(asymptotic* t-*ratios in parentheses)*

Years of school	c	η	δ	$K(0)$	ℓ	r	$\tilde{\rho}$
12	14.5	0.509	0.047	5510.	574.	0.206	0.032
	(0.66)	(3.67)	(0.32)	(1.3)	(1.49)	(0.49)	(0.43)
13–16	17.3	0.520	0.037	8698.	3700.	0.196	0.027
	(0.69)	(7.31)	(0.41)	(0.31)	(0.13)	(0.32)	(0.28)
16	17.3	0.544	0.070	6341.	1170.	0.187	0.016
	(0.38)	(2.29)	(0.44)	(0.45)	(0.12)	(0.17)	(0.11)

school graduate and the synthetic college graduate, the simulated[56]
time profile of H implied by Heckman's estimates is inverse U
shaped, as in Figure 5.1. However, for the college graduate, H
declines with age starting in the early forties, whereas for the high
school graduate H declines with age starting in the early twenties.
Especially in the latter case, these turning points for hours *at* work,
H, occur earlier than those usually observed in simple scatter plots
of synthetic cohort data and almost certainly earlier than in actual
life cycles.

The tests of Heckman's model, (5.147), summarized in Table 5.2
are admittedly crude (Heckman, 1976b, p. S37). They are based on
synthetic cohort data rather than on data for actual individuals
(recall the special peculiarities of synthetic cohort data discussed in
Section 5.4). Also, Heckman derives (5.147), and hence estimates
the parameters of (5.147), under the assumption that individuals
work at all ages between time 0 and time T (recall the previous discussion of equations (5.143)–(5.145)). Hence, Heckman's specification ignores questions about labor force participation, selectivity

[56] To simulate the profile of H, note first that $H = 1 - (LK/K)$, where LK is given
by (5.143) and K is given by (5.145). This provides an expression for the value of H as
a function of age and the parameters of the model (c, η, δ, etc.). Accordingly, one
may insert the parameter estimates shown in the first row of the table into this
expression for H and calculate the value of H at age "0," at age "1," and so forth for
persons with 12 years of schooling. Similarly, one may use the parameter estimates
shown in the third row of the table to perform analogous calculations for persons
with 16 years of schooling.

bias, and the like. (Allowing explicitly for such phenomena and for other kinds of corners, such as investment time $I(t)$ falling to zero at some point prior to T, would result in a specification even more complex than (5.147).) However, the most noteworthy feature of the analysis is not that the tests presented in it are crude but rather that it shows that it is possible to derive empirical results of *any* kind from a formal and rigorous life cycle model with endogenous wages. In view of the difficulties noted earlier, this is no small achievement. Heckman's analysis is only a first step, but it is an important one.

6

Labor supply, taxes, and transfers

In this chapter, I discuss the labor supply effects of taxes and transfer payments. This topic is interesting and important because it raises a variety of challenging theoretical and empirical issues and is at the center of intense and sometimes emotional controversies about the role, scope, and consequences of an extensive and complex set of government programs. Moreover, for a variety of reasons – including, in particular, the ones just noted – in recent years government agencies and other bodies have provided extensive funding for research on the relation between labor supply, taxes, and transfers. Thus, economists have had strong pecuniary incentives (as well as strong intellectual incentives) to investigate such matters. It is no exaggeration to say, as Ashenfelter (1978c, p. 109) does, that "measuring labor supply behavior . . . is now big business and I can think of more than one organization whose capital value would shrink if the subject became moribund."

The first order of business in a discussion of taxes and transfers and their effects on labor supply should be to develop an analytical framework for use in theoretical and empirical inquiry. After setting up such a framework, I will then discuss the labor supply effects of five main kinds of tax and transfer programs: the income tax, cash transfer programs (including both programs now in existence and proposed negative income tax schemes), the Social Security system, in-kind transfer programs, and, finally, wage subsidy schemes.

331

6.1. Labor supply effects of taxes and transfers: analytical framework

To analyze the labor supply effects of taxes and transfers, it is necessary to begin by specifying how taxes and transfers affect both utility and the constraints subject to which utility is maximized. I will first discuss how taxes and transfers affect the budget constraint and then examine how they affect utility. I will conclude by discussing the concept of "excess burden" as it applies to taxes and transfers.

Taxes, transfers, and the budget constraint

As noted several times in previous chapters, it is often very convenient to analyze behavior in the presence of taxes or transfers using the notion of a "linearized budget constraint." (For example, see Section 3.3 and the discussion of Figure 3.4(b).) To keep otherwise-complicated issues relatively simple, it is also helpful to proceed in stages, first considering taxes and transfers in a static setting and then moving to the dynamic case.

The static case. In a static setting, the budget constraint in the absence of taxes and transfers is

$$(6.1) \quad V + WH = PC$$

where, as before, V is property income per period, W is the wage rate per period, H is the fraction of available time per period devoted to work, C is consumption per period of a composite commodity, and P is the price of a unit of C. It is straightforward to modify this constraint to allow for taxes. Taxes impose a liability Λ on the individual that, in most cases, is a function of property income V and of earnings E ($= WH$). Hence, in general,

$$(6.2) \quad \Lambda = \Lambda(V, E) \quad \text{where} \quad E = WH$$

so that, in the presence of taxes, the budget constraint becomes

$$(6.3) \quad V + WH - \Lambda(V, WH) = PC$$

Now, under most tax systems, one's tax liability increases with property income or earnings. Hence $\partial\Lambda/\partial V \equiv \tau_V > 0$ and $\partial\Lambda/\partial E \equiv \partial\Lambda/\partial(WH) \equiv \tau_E > 0$, where τ_V and τ_E may be defined as the marginal rate of tax on property income and earnings, respectively.

In most settings, both τ_V and τ_E are not only greater than zero but also less than unity, meaning that a one-dollar increase in property income or earnings will result in an increase of *less* than one dollar in one's tax liability Λ. Hence,

(6.4) $1 > \tau_i > 0, \qquad i = V, E$

Moreover, in many tax systems, marginal tax rates themselves depend on property income and on earnings, rising as property income or earnings rise. Hence, in fairly general terms, the tax liability or Λ function may be characterized by another property, namely

(6.5) $\partial^2\Lambda/\partial V^2 \equiv \tau_{VV} \geq 0, \quad \partial^2\Lambda/\partial E^2 \equiv \tau_{EE} \geq 0,$

$\partial^2\Lambda/\partial V\partial E = \partial^2\Lambda/\partial E\partial V \equiv \tau_{EV} \geq 0$

Note that, since earnings depend in part on labor supply, this means that, in many tax systems, marginal tax rates depend on labor supply.

Next, note that, when earnings are taxed, an additional hour of work raises not only earnings but also tax liabilities. So the *net* reward for an additional hour of work is given by

(6.6) $(\partial E/\partial H) - (\partial\Lambda/\partial H) = (\partial E/\partial H) - [(\partial\Lambda/\partial E)(\partial E/\partial H)]$
                    $= W - \tau_E W = \hat{W}$

where $\hat{W} \equiv (1 - \tau_E)W$. $\hat{W}$ is the net or marginal wage rate. In other words, in the presence of taxes, the reward for an additional hour of work is not the wage rate W, but only $\hat{W} = (1 - \tau_E)W$, where τ_E is the fraction of each wage dollar that the individual loses via the increase in his tax liability Λ that accompanies an increase in his earnings.

Now, the *real* net wage rate, $\hat{W}/P = (1 - \tau_E)W/P$, is the sacrifice that someone makes when he enjoys an additional hour of leisure rather than devote more time to work; and, in equilibrium, someone whose labor supply is positive equates the marginal rate of substitution to this quantity. Thus, $\hat{W}/P$ is the slope of the linearized budget constraint at the individual's labor supply optimum. To determine the position of the linearized budget constraint – that is, the level of the individual's adjusted property income $\hat{V}$ – note that $\hat{V}$ is implicitly defined by the relation $\hat{V} + \hat{W}H$ $= PC$ or, equivalently, $\hat{V} = PC - \hat{W}H$. To derive an explicit expression for $\hat{V}$, use (6.3) to eliminate PC, obtaining $\hat{V} = V + WH$ $- \Lambda - \hat{W}H$. Since $\hat{W} \equiv (1 - \tau_E) W$, it follows that $\hat{V} = V - (\Lambda - \tau_E WH)$. Thus, in the presence of taxes, the static linearized budget constraint may be written as

(6.7) $\hat{V} + \hat{W}H = PC$

where

$$\hat{W} \equiv (1 - \tau_E) W$$
$$\hat{V} \equiv V - (\Lambda - \tau_E WH)$$
$$\tau_E \equiv \partial\Lambda(V, WH)/\partial(WH)$$

In general, the marginal tax rate τ_E depends on earnings (see (6.5)) and, therefore, on labor supply. Thus, τ_E is endogenous to labor supply, and so are both $\hat{W}$ and $\hat{V}$.

So much for taxes and their effect on the static budget constraint. What about transfer payments? Transfer payments constitute a benefit, rather than a liability, for the individual; thus, whereas someone who pays taxes is said to have a positive value of Λ, someone who receives transfers may be said to have a negative value of Λ: Transfers are a negative tax. Moreover, the amount of transfer payments made to individuals (e.g., under "welfare" programs) is typically a function of property income and of earnings, rising when V or E falls and falling when V or E rises. Thus, in the case of transfers, the quantities $\partial\Lambda/\partial V \equiv \tau_V$ and $\partial\Lambda/\partial E \equiv \tau_E$ might be called the *marginal rate of transfer payment reduction* with respect to property income and earnings, respectively. A transfer recipient's (negative) value of Λ generally becomes "less negative" – that is, decreases in *absolute* value but rises in *algebraic* value – when either V or E increases. It follows that, in general, both the τ_V and the τ_E of transfer programs are positive, just as they are in tax laws. Hence, the τ_V and τ_E of transfer programs, like the τ_V and τ_E of tax laws, are marginal tax rates on property income and earnings, respectively: In effect, most transfer programs "tax" both property income and earnings, since an increase in either kind of income generally leads to a reduction in one's transfer payment. Further, an increase of one dollar in either kind of income typically reduces the transfer payment made to a transfer payment recipient by less than one dollar. Thus, the marginal tax rates of transfer programs, like the marginal tax rates of tax laws, are generally positive fractions, ones that may depend on property income and earnings (as in (6.5)). In sum, provided one thinks of transfers as *negative* taxes and, therefore, treats transfer payments as the equivalent of a negative value of Λ, equations (6.2)–(6.7) apply just as well to transfer payments as they do to tax laws.

The dynamic case. Now consider the dynamic case. In the absence of taxes and transfers, someone who does not desire to leave any bequests faces the dynamic or lifetime budget constraint

$$(6.8) \quad \dot{Z}(t) = rZ(t) + W(t)H(t) - P(t)C(t),$$

subject to $Z(0) = Z_0$, an exogenous constant, and $Z(T) = 0$. (Recall Chapter 5, including, in particular, the discussion of the fact that, in the absence of bequests, $Z(T) = 0$. All symbols are as defined in Chapter 5: Z is the current stock of assets, $\dot{Z}$ is the rate of change of Z over time, and r is the rate of interest.) In a dynamic setting, taxes and transfers affect the individual's ability to accumulate assets: Taxes are a liability that must be paid out of income $rZ(t) + W(t)H(t)$, whereas transfers are a *negative* "liability" that adds to income. Moreover, in a dynamic setting, taxes and transfers may depend not only on current property income and on current earnings but also on *past* levels of either kind of income and also on age, t, itself.[1] To simplify, however, I will restrict my attention to the simple case in which taxes and transfers depend only on age and on *current* property income and earnings (and do not depend on assets or on *past* levels of income of either kind). Thus, this simplified dynamic tax/transfer function is

$$(6.9) \quad \Lambda(t) = \Lambda[rZ(t), W(t)H(t), t]$$

and the dynamic budget constraint becomes

$$(6.10) \quad \dot{Z}(t) = rZ(t) + W(t)H(t) - P(t)C(t) - \Lambda(t)$$

---

[1] For example, in the U.S. tax system, some individuals may compute their tax liability for a given year by using "income-averaging," which in effect makes their current tax liability a complicated function of their incomes in previous years as well as in the current year.

subject to $Z(0) = Z_0$ and $Z(T) = 0$. In most cases, the dynamic tax/transfer function may be taken to have positive and nondecreasing marginal tax rates, that is,

(6.11) $1 > \partial\Lambda(t)/\partial[rZ(t)] \equiv \tau_V(t) > 0;$
         $1 > \partial\Lambda(t)/\partial[W(t)H(t)] \equiv \tau_E(t) > 0$

(6.12) $\tau_{ij}(t) \geq 0, \qquad i, j = E, V$

where the similarity between equations (6.11) and (6.12) and (6.4) and (6.5) is evident. Note that (6.9), (6.11), and (6.12) imply that marginal rates of tax may vary over time not only because rZ and WH may vary over time but also because marginal rates of tax may depend on age (that is, time) itself.[2]

As in the static case, the effect of an additional hour of work on current earnings *net* of tax/transfer liabilities ($= E'(t) \equiv E(t) - \Lambda(t) = W(t)H(t) - \Lambda[rZ(t), W(t)H(t), t]$) is given by

(6.13) $dE'(t)/dH(t) = W(t) - [\partial\Lambda(t)/\partial H(t)]$
         $= W(t) - \{\partial\Lambda(t)/\partial[W(t)H(t)]\}$
         $\times \{\partial[W(t)H(t)]/\partial H(t)\}$
         $= W(t) - \tau_E(t)W(t) = \widehat{W}(t)$

where $\widehat{W}(t) \equiv [1 - \tau_E(t)]W(t)$. Hence $\widehat{W}(t)$ is the net or marginal wage rate, analogous to the $\hat{W}$ of the static budget constraint. It measures the price of the individual's time, as of t, at the margin; in particular, someone whose labor supply at time t is positive equates the marginal rate of substitution at time t to the real net wage $\widehat{W}(t)/P(t) = [1 - \tau_E(t)]W(t)/P(t)$.

Similarly, the effect of an additional dollar of assets on asset income net of tax/transfer liabilities ($= V'(t) \equiv rZ(t) - \Lambda(t) = rZ(t) - \Lambda[rZ(t), W(t)H(t), t]$) is given by

(6.14) $dV'(t)/dZ(t) = r - [\partial\Lambda(t)/\partial Z(t)]$
         $= r - \{\partial\Lambda(t)/\partial[rZ(t)]\} \{\partial[rZ(t)]/\partial Z(t)\}$
         $= r - \tau_V(t)r = \hat{r}(t)$

[2] For example, in 1983, most working individuals age 61 or less paid a Social Security payroll tax of 6.7 percent on the first $35,700 of earnings, whereas working individuals age 65–69 who received Social Security benefits paid a tax of 6.7 percent on the first $35,700 of earnings *and* lost $0.50 in Social Security benefits for every dollar of earnings received in excess of $6,600. Hence, someone earning $7,000 pays a Social Security tax of $\tau_E = 0.067$ at age 60, but at age 66 a benefit recipient pays a Social Security tax of $\tau_E = 0.567$ on every dollar earned over $6,600.

where $r\hat{(t)} \equiv [1 - \tau_V(t)]r$. Thus, $r\hat{(t)}$ is the net or marginal interest rate. In general, the *net* interest rate $r\hat{(t)}$ will vary over time and be different at different ages even if the gross interest rate r is constant. This is because an individual may be in a different tax bracket (that is, may face a different marginal rate of tax $\tau_V(t)$ on asset income $rZ(t)$) at different dates.

In effect, $W\hat{(t)}$ and $r\hat{(t)}$ are "slopes" of the individual's dynamic linearized budget constraint at time t. To derive an adjusted initial wealth variable $Z\hat{(0)}$ that is analogous to the adjusted property income variable $\hat{V}$ of the static model – and, thus, to derive the position of the dynamic linearized budget constraint – note that one may rewrite (6.10) as

$$(6.15) \quad \dot{Z}(t) = r\hat{(t)}Z(t) + W\hat{(t)}H(t) - P(t)C(t) - V\hat{(t)}$$

where $V\hat{(t)} \equiv \Lambda(t) - \tau_V(t)rZ(t) - \tau_E(t)W(t)H(t)$. Next, note that, provided $Z(T) = 0$, as in the case of someone who does not desire to make any bequests, one may integrate (6.15), which is a first-order differential equation in $Z(t)$, to obtain

$$Z(t) = - \int_t^T e^{-\int_t^u r\hat{(s)}\,ds} [W\hat{(u)}H(u) - P(u)C(u) - V\hat{(u)}]\,du$$

Accordingly, rearrange terms and start at $t = 0$ to obtain

$$(6.16) \quad Z\hat{(0)} + \int_0^T e^{-\int_0^t r\hat{(s)}\,ds} [W\hat{(t)}H(t) - P(t)C(t)]\,dt = 0$$

where

$$r\hat{(t)} \equiv [1 - \tau_V(t)]r$$
$$W\hat{(t)} \equiv [1 - \tau_E(t)]W(t)$$
$$Z\hat{(0)} \equiv Z(0) - \int_0^T e^{-\int_0^t r\hat{(s)}\,ds} V\hat{(t)}\,dt$$

which is the dynamic linearized budget constraint. Finally, if the tax/transfer system does not tax property income at the margin – in other words, if the marginal rate of tax on property income $\tau_V(t)$ is zero – then (6.16) simplifies to

$$(6.17) \quad \widehat{Z(0)} + \int_0^T e^{-rt}[\widehat{W(t)}H(t) - P(t)C(t)]\,dt = 0$$

where

$$\widehat{W(t)} \equiv [1 - \tau_E(t)]W(t)$$

$$\widehat{Z(0)} \equiv Z(0) - \int_0^T e^{-rt}\widehat{V(t)}\,dt$$

$$\widehat{V(t)} \equiv \Lambda[rZ(t), W(t)H(t), t] - \tau_E(t)W(t)H(t)$$

Not surprisingly, the resemblance between (6.7), which applies to the static case, and (6.16) (or (6.17)), which applies to the dynamic case, is considerable. First, (6.16), like (6.7), applies just as much to transfers as it does to taxes, provided one treats transfers as negative tax liabilities and, thus, as the equivalent of a negative value of Λ. Second, both (6.16) and (6.7) highlight the parameters that are relevant to behavior *at the margin* (that is, the marginal wage and interest rates $\widehat{W(t)}$ and $\widehat{r(t)}$, in the dynamic case; or the marginal wage rate $\widehat{W}$, in the static case). Third, both (6.16) and (6.7) indicate that taxes and transfers shift the entire budget constraint, meaning that individuals act *as if* they made decisions based on an adjusted level of initial wealth $\widehat{Z(0)}$ (in the dynamic case) or an adjusted level of property income $\widehat{V}$ (in the static case) that is a function of tax/transfer liabilities and marginal tax rates; indeed, Hausman (1981a) refers to $\widehat{V}$ as "virtual [property] income." Finally, the marginal wage and interest rates and adjusted initial wealth in (6.16), like the marginal wage and adjusted property income in (6.7), are endogenous, since they depend on marginal tax rates at the individual's current optimum, that is, on his income and his current labor supply.

Concluding comments. Equations (6.7) and (6.16) (or (6.17)) show how taxes and transfers directly alter a given individual's budget constraint – by imposing a liability (positive, in the case of taxes; negative, in the case of transfers) on that individual. This liability or "direct" or "partial-equilibrium" effect on the budget constraint is certainly important, but it is not necessarily the whole story: Taxes and transfers may also have important indirect or "general-equilibrium" effects on the budget constraint. These arise for two main reasons.

First, to the extent that they affect labor supply, labor demand, savings, and capital formation in the aggregate, taxes and transfers will affect *gross* wage rates and interest rates (W, or $W(t)$ and r) and also property income (V or $rZ(t)$) as well as net or marginal wage rates and interest rates ($\hat{W}$, or $\hat{W}(t)$ and $\hat{r}(t)$). For example, if an increase in the income tax reduces labor supply, then gross wages will rise in response to the shortage of labor (the extent to which this will occur will depend on the elasticity of demand for labor). In turn, this will affect income from property, interest rates, and the like.

Second, once it collects resources via the tax system, government disposes of those resources somehow (e.g., destroys them, uses them to purchase bonds or bombs, to pay postal workers or presidents); and before it can disburse resources via the transfer system, government must first obtain those resources somehow (e.g., by levying taxes, by reducing expenditures on goods and services). The manner in which the resources collected via the tax system are disposed of, and the manner in which the resources required for transfer payments are obtained, may also affect labor supply, labor demand, savings, and capital formation, and thus gross wage rates, gross interest rates, property income, and the like.

Of course, in most cases, given *individuals* have no power to affect the structure of the tax/transfer system (i.e., the form of the tax/transfer function Λ) or to affect the equilibrium of the markets for labor, assets, and so forth, as summarized by the (equilibrium) values of W and V (in the static case) or $W(t)$ and r (in the dynamic case) that appear in the budget constraint.[3] Thus, labor supply functions based on specifications of the budget constraint such as (6.7) or (6.16) (or (6.17)) are perfectly adequate as representations of behavior in the presence of a *given* tax/transfer system and can be used in empirical work to derive meaningful estimates of income and substitution effects and the like.

On the other hand, labor supply functions based on specifications

---

[3] In other words, although one can obviously affect one's total tax liability (e.g., by deciding to work more or less), one generally cannot affect the tax laws or the rules subject to which the tax liability associated with a given level of labor supply is determined.

of the budget constraint such as (6.7) or (6.16) (or (6.17)) are not sufficient to permit one to make conclusions about, for example, how a *change* in the tax/transfer function would affect an individual's labor supply. The reason is simple. When the government changes the Λ function, this will, in general, change both tax receipts (or transfer payments) and the level of labor supply in the aggregate. The change in aggregate labor supply will affect gross wage rates (and, therefore, production and property income), leading to further effects on each individual's labor supply (and therefore on aggregate labor supply); what the government does to adjust to the change in its tax receipts (or transfer payments) will affect individuals', and, therefore, aggregate, labor supply as well. In other words, labor supply functions based on specifications of the budget constraint, such as (6.7) and (6.16) (or (6.17)), are necessary, but not sufficient, to permit one to work out the impact of a change in taxes on labor supply (either aggregate labor supply *or* any individual's labor supply). One also needs to know the parameters of labor demand functions and to work out how a tax change will disturb the labor market's supply–demand equilibrium, leading to changes in wage rates, interest rates, and so forth, and thus to further changes in equilibrium labor supply. (See Zeckhauser, 1977, for an interesting discussion of taxes in general equilibrium.)

Taxes, transfers, and the utility function

Taxes and transfers not only affect the budget constraint; they also affect utility.

The most obvious way in which taxes and transfers influence utility is via the liability effect previously mentioned: Taxes and transfers change the amount of resources available to the individual and will, therefore, prompt him to change his own behavior (e.g., his consumption spending and leisure time). Conventional utility functions of the kind used in previous chapters (e.g., (1.1) or (5.1) or (5.3)) specify the individual's utility as a function of certain aspects of his own behavior (in particular, his leisure time and consumption spending). If the liability effect of taxes and transfers were the only effect relevant to individual behavior, then such utility functions would be perfectly satisfactory for use in analyzing the effects of taxes and transfers.

However, as emphasized earlier, taxes and transfers affect not only the resources available to the individual, but also the resources available to the government. The way in which the government changes its behavior in response to the change in the amount of resources available to it may affect a given individual's utility, and, thus, his behavior, even if there is *no* liability effect and no change in his budget constraint. In other words, whereas "conventional" utility functions neglect the impact of the behavior of *others* on the utility (and, thus, the behavior) of a given individual – on the grounds (usually justified) that others' behavior is roughly constant – taxes and transfers inevitably are the cause of behavior that may affect any given individual indirectly even if he is not affected directly by the tax or transfer.

For example, suppose that the government taxes A, who lives in Maine, and uses the proceeds to build an airport in California near a vacation home owned by B. Even if these actions on the part of the government do not affect B's wage rate or property income, they may nevertheless affect B's behavior, including his consumption and labor supply. If the airport is noisy and is located right next to B's vacation home, it may reduce B's marginal rate of substitution (i.e., reduce the marginal utility of leisure, relative to the marginal utility of consumption goods, at B's current optimum). If the airport is a short distance from B's vacation home and makes it easier for B to get to his vacation home, however, it may increase B's marginal rate of substitution. In the first case, B may reduce his leisure time; in the second, he may increase it.

It is not hard to think of additional examples that make the same basic point: When transfers and taxes change, the resources available to the government change; and to the extent that the government responds to this change in the real resources available to it by altering its purchases of real goods and services, this may directly affect both the level of utility and the marginal rate of substitution between leisure and consumer goods of any given individual – even at *given* levels of consumption C and leisure L. This suggests that, to allow for this aspect of taxes and transfers, one might write the static utility function as

(6.18) $\quad u = u(C, L, G)$

where G is the amount of government purchases of real goods and services; and that one might write the dynamic utility function either as

(6.19) $U = U[C(0), L(0), G(0), \ldots, C(T), L(T), G(T)]$

in the intertemporally inseparable case, or as

(6.20) $U = \int_0^T e^{-\rho t} u[C(t), L(t), G(t)]\, dt$

in the intertemporally separable case, where $G(t)$ is the amount of government purchases of real goods and services at any time t.

Unfortunately, simply adding G to the relevant utility function does not quite complete the task of specifying how taxes and/or transfers affect utility: It is also necessary to say something about the extent to which a change in taxes and/or transfers will affect G and to specify how a change in G will affect the marginal rate of substitution (Winston, 1965b). The former is a question of modeling the behavior of the government; the latter is a question of specifying the properties of the individual's utility function. For example, consider the simple static model of labor supply in the presence of taxes and transfers formed by (6.4), (6.5), and (6.18). Provided he works, someone who maximizes utility as given by (6.18) subject to the budget constraint given by (6.4) and (6.5) will equate the marginal rate of substitution m to the real net wage $\hat{W}/P$ where, by (6.18) and the definition of m,

$$m = \frac{\partial u(C, L, G)/\partial L}{\partial u(C, L, G)/\partial C}$$

Note that, in general, m is not independent of G. Thus, in general, a change in taxes or transfers that leads to a change in G will affect the marginal rate of substitution m, and will, therefore, affect labor supply, even if it does *not* affect either the net wage $\hat{W}$ or adjusted property income $\hat{V}$. Thus, in analyzing the impact of a change in taxes or transfers on a given individual's behavior, one must not only say how this change will affect $\hat{W}$ and $\hat{V}$ but also say both how (i) the change in taxes or transfers will change government purchases G and (ii) the change in G will affect the marginal rate of substitution m.

This is obviously no simple task. Most of the literature has in fact assumed, implicitly or explicitly, that m is *independent* of government goods G – in other words, that the utility function is separable in G, on the one hand, and C and L, on the other. Under this separability assumption, (6.18)–(6.20) become

(6.21) $u = u[f(C, L), G]$

(6.22) $U = U\{g[C(0), L(0), \ldots, C(T), L(T)],$
$\qquad\qquad G(0), \ldots, G(T)\}$

(6.23) $U = \int_0^T e^{-\rho t} u[h(C(t), L(t)), G(t)] \, dt$

respectively. To see why the G-separability assumption simplifies matters considerably, note, for example, that the marginal rate of substitution function implicit in (6.21) is

$$m = \frac{\partial u / \partial L}{\partial u / \partial C} = \frac{[\partial u / \partial f][\partial f / \partial L]}{[\partial u / \partial f][\partial f / \partial C]} = \frac{\partial f(C, L)/\partial L}{\partial f(C, L)/\partial C}$$

so that, in (6.21), m is indeed independent of G. This being the case, it is no longer necessary to say anything further about either how (i) taxes or transfers affect G or (ii) a change in G, ceteris paribus, might affect labor supply. (Similar remarks apply to (6.22) and (6.23).) Accordingly, in what follows, I shall follow previous work by adopting utility functions such as (6.21)–(6.23) that are separable in G. However, such functions of course rest on a simplifying assumption – one that, in particular applications, may not necessarily be innocuous.

Excess burden and the design of optimal tax/transfer systems

Jean Baptiste Colbert, Louis XIV's celebrated finance minister, is said to have described the problem of choosing between different taxes as the art of "plucking the goose . . . while provoking the smallest possible amount of hissing."[4] Viewed in modern terms, Colbert's dictum raises two issues. First, once one takes into account the way in which government disposes of the taxes it collects, does taxation entail *any* "hissing" – that is,

---

[4] See *Forbes Magazine* (1972, p. 22). I thank Michael K. Taussig for this reference. Taussig emphasizes that, in Louis XIV's time, the hissing of some geese (e.g., the nobility) may have had more effect on the state's tax policy than that of other geese (e.g., the peasantry). Could the same be true today?

reduction in utility? Second, to the extent that taxation does involve some reduction in utility, how can the government minimize that reduction (provoke the "smallest possible amount of hissing")? It turns out that, under certain assumptions, income taxation will indeed reduce utility, relative to pure lump sum taxation, even after one takes into account the uses the government makes of the taxes it collects. This utility reduction is called the *excess burden* of the income tax. *Minimizing* the excess burden of income taxation is a question of the design of optimal income tax/transfer mechanisms.

First, consider analysis and measurement of the excess burden of an income tax using a simple static labor supply model. (Discussing excess burden in a dynamic setting is more cumbersome and raises few new points of principle.) Figure 6.1 shows an individual who, in the absence of any taxes, receives real property income of $V/P = v$ and earns a real wage of W/P. He, therefore, faces a budget line $1vc$. His pre-tax optimum, at point β, yields utility level u° and entails L_β hours of leisure and $H_\beta \equiv 1 - L_\beta$ hours of work. Since the indifference curve labeled u° in Figure 6.1 is associated with utility level u°, I shall refer to it as *indifference curve u°* in what follows.

Now suppose that the government desires to introduce an income tax, as embodied in a tax liability function such as (6.2). Of necessity, the government will have to spend (or otherwise dispose of) the taxes it collects, but it is convenient to analyze any such taxing-and-spending scheme in parts, examining first the income tax part and then the spending part. Accordingly, take up the income tax part as such, and assume – largely to simplify the exposition[5] – that the income tax imposes a liability on earnings only (and not on property income) at a constant marginal rate of tax τ_E. As implied by (6.7), this kind of income tax is equivalent to a reduction in the wage from W to $\hat{W}$, where $\hat{W} \equiv (1 - \tau_E)W$; hence, the tax shifts the

[5] By and large, most of the results derived here carry over, without substantial modification, to more complicated cases, for example, tax systems that tax property income as well as earnings, tax systems that involve progressively higher marginal rates of tax at higher levels of income, and so on. (To see why, note that virtually all of the discussion that follows requires only two key assumptions about the tax system: First, that the post-tax budget line, vbe, lies below the pre-tax budget line, vac, except possibly when hours worked are zero; and, second, that the tax system under consideration reduces the net wage from W to $\hat{W}$. If so, then vbe can be regarded as a linearization of the budget constraint, in the neighborhood of the individual's post-tax optimum, that the individual faces in his post-tax optimum.)

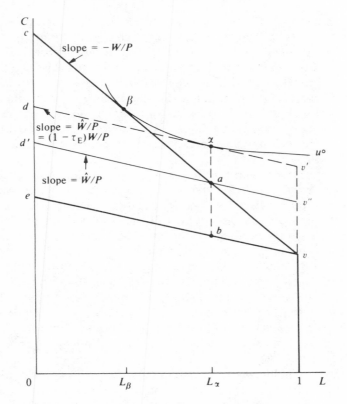

Figure 6.1.   Excess burden of an income tax

budget line from $1vc$ to $1ve$. The vertical distance between the lines vc and ve at any given level of labor supply or leisure time gives the amount of tax that the individual pays at that level of labor supply or leisure time.[6]

In response to this tax-induced change in his budget line from $1vc$ to $1ve$, the individual will move from his initial or pre-tax optimum,

---

[6] For example, when the individual works $H_\alpha \equiv 1 - L_\alpha$ hours, his gross income is $WH_\alpha + v$, equal to the vertical distance between L_α and a; but his net income is only $\hat{W}H_\alpha + v = (1 - \tau_E)WH_\alpha + v$, equal to the vertical distance between L_α and b. The amount of tax revenues at this point – that is the difference between his gross and his net income $WH_\alpha - (1 - \tau_E)WH_\alpha = \tau_E WH_\alpha$ – is, therefore, given by the distance between a and b.

β, to a new post-tax optimum at some point along the post-tax budget line $1ve$. Whether this new optimum involves more or less labor supply than β depends on whether the positive income effect of the tax on labor supply is stronger or weaker than the negative substitution effect. (As will become clear later, nothing in any of the analysis presented here assumes that the income effect is in fact greater or smaller than the substitution effect.) However, so long as the initial optimum point involves positive hours of work, it is clear that the new optimum point necessarily involves less utility than the initial point.[7]

Of course, this is not the end of the story: Having collected tax revenues from the individual, the government must *somehow* dispose of those revenues. Is it possible to do so in a manner that will leave the individual at least as well off as he was before introduction of the taxing-and-spending scheme – that is, to do so with the least amount of hissing? One kind of spending scheme that, if feasible, would put the individual back onto indifference curve $u°$ would be one involving a direct cash grant to the individual: This would leave the individual free to spend the grant on consumer goods or else – by forgoing earnings – on leisure time in whatever proportions he chose, with no interference from the government. However, how large a cash grant would be required to get the individual back to utility level $u°$? Evidently, as shown in Figure 6.1, the government's cash grant would have to be equal to the distance between α and b or, equivalently, between v and v', since it would take a cash grant this large to shift the individual's budget line from its post-tax level ve to a post-tax-*and*-spending level $v'd$ that would make utility level $u°$ attainable once again.

In effect, then, the *combined* impact of the tax *and* spending components of a tax-and-spending scheme that kept the individual as well off after its introduction as he was prior to its introduction

---

[7] After the income tax is introduced, consumption–leisure bundles within the triangle vce that were once attainable are no longer attainable: The tax part of the scheme forecloses many of the options that were previously open to the individual, including his initial equilibrium point β, without opening up any new ones. For this reason, the change in property income that is required to move the individual from the lower level of utility that he will enjoy at his optimum along the post-tax budget line vbe back to his initial utility level $u°$, $v'v$, is often called the *compensating variation* in property income. See Hausman (1981b), Hicks (1946, esp. pp. 40–41), and Zabalza (1982).

would simply be to pivot, or rotate, the individual's budget line in a counterclockwise direction around the indifference curve $u°$, that is, would be to shift the budget line from vc to $v'd$. This kind of rotation or pivoting will, of course, have a pure substitution effect on labor supply (because it amounts to a reduction in the net wage rate from W to $\hat{W} \equiv (1 - \tau_E) W$ coupled with a simultaneous adjustment in property income from v to v' that keeps the individual at the same indifference curve, $u°$).[8] In particular, the impact of this rotation depends *only* on the substitution effect (that is, on the curvature of the indifference curve $u°$) and on the magnitudes of W and τ_E. It does not depend in any way on the magnitude or even the sign of the income effect of the change in the wage from W to $\hat{W}$ that results from the tax part of the tax-and-spending scheme; and it also does not depend in any way on whether the optimum point the individual would choose on the post-tax budget line ve entails more or less labor supply than does his pre-tax equilibrium point β.

However, is a tax-and-spending scheme of this kind actually feasible? At the post-tax-and-spending equilibrium α, the tax revenues the government collects under the tax component of the scheme are equal to the distance ab in Figure 6.1. On the other hand, in order to keep the individual at $u°$, the spending component of the scheme must provide him with a cash grant or lump-sum transfer payment equal to αb, which exceeds tax revenues collected from the individual by the amount αa. In other words, this kind of tax-and-spending scheme is not feasible: Implementing it would require more revenues (to fulfill the spending component) than can actually be collected (under the tax component).[9] Given that it collects only ab in tax revenues from the individual, the most the government can afford to do is to return ab to the individual (in the form of a lump-sum or cash grant). As indicated in Figure 6.1, this means that, on balance, the individual's budget line will be shifted from $1vc$ to $1ve$ via the taxing component of the scheme and then from $1ve$ to $1v''d'$ via the spending component of a *feasible* scheme (one that does not involve grants in excess of tax revenues) – and that any point on

---

[8] Thus, the distance between v and v' is the compensating variation. (See note 7.)

[9] Of course, the government could certainly levy a tax, designed so as to raise a total of αb in revenue, on some *other* individual. However, this begs the question, since it would then be necessary to work out whether it would be possible to keep that second individual at *his* initial utility level.

$1v''d'$ entails less utility than his initial equilibrium point β. In order to get the individual back to u°, the government would need to find an additional αa for a further cash grant to the individual – an amount that of course exceeds what the government can actually collect.

This "excess amount" αa is usually called the *excess burden* of the income tax, since it is the amount by which a cash grant that would get the individual back to u° will have to exceed the revenues that can be collected from him. It is a measure of the welfare cost, or loss, of the income tax. It arises because the tax-and-spending scheme reduces incentives to work via a pure substitution effect that results from the decrease in the (net) wage from W to $\hat{W}$ that accompanies the cash grant-induced adjustment to income (which keeps the individual on u°): Basically, what happens is that the reduction in incentives to work makes it impossible for the government to collect enough in tax revenues to provide the cash grant the government must make to keep the individual at u°.

As previously indicated, the size of the excess burden depends directly on the size of the substitution effect of the tax-and-spending scheme (that is, the size of the change in hours of work between L_β and L_α). In turn, the scheme's substitution effect is simply the product of (i) the rate of change of labor supply with respect to an income-compensated (or "utility-held-constant") change in the wage rate, $(\partial H/\partial W)|_{u^\circ}$, and (ii) the *size* of the change in the (net) wage rate. Further, the latter quantity is simply $\hat{W} - W = -\tau_E W$. It follows that the size of the excess burden αa will be larger if the tax rate τ_E, the wage rate W or the substitution effect $(\partial H/\partial W)|_{u^\circ}$ is larger.[10] Moreover, as previously implied, the size of the excess

---

[10] The quantity $(\partial H/\partial W)|_{u^\circ}$ – in other words, the rate of change of labor supply with respect to an income-compensated increase in the wage rate – is what was called *the* substitution effect in previous chapters (e.g., Chapters 3 and 4). To see why excess burden is larger when *the* substitution effect, the marginal tax rate, and the gross wage rate are larger, consider Figure 6.1. The substitution effect of the tax-induced change in the (net) wage from W to $\hat{W}$ is equal to the distance between L_β and L_α. If the substitution effect were larger, other things being equal, then L_α would be larger than the amount shown in Figure 6.1 and the point α would be closer to v' (along the line $v'd$) than the point shown in Figure 6.1. (In other words, u° would be tangent to $v'd$ at a point closer to v' than the one shown in Figure 6.1.) If so, then, even though the total distance αb would remain the same with this larger substitution effect, the distance ab would be smaller and the distance αa – the excess burden – would be

burden has nothing to do with the size of the income effect of the tax (or even with whether leisure is a normal good). In particular, as Hausman (1980) has emphasized, even if an income tax does not change labor supply by very much, the excess burden of the tax (that is, its welfare cost) could still be sizable. For example, other things being equal, a large substitution effect $(\partial H/\partial W)|_{u^{\circ}}$ implies a large excess burden, but if the (positive-signed) income effect of the tax on labor supply is large enough to offset the (negative-signed) substitution effect and if the government does not in fact return any of the revenues it collects back to the individual (via a lump-sum grant or any other means), then on balance the tax need not change labor supply appreciably even though its excess burden is sizable.

These considerations lead directly to propositions about the design of optimal tax systems. In line with Colbert, the government's problem is to pick a tax system (for example, a marginal rate of tax) so as to maximize the combined utilities of its citizenry subject to a government budget constraint (stating that tax revenues must be at least as large as the amount the government desires to spend). (For example, see Mirrlees, 1971; Sadka, 1976a, b; Sandmo, 1976.) Equivalently, the government's task is to pick a tax system so as to minimize excess burden subject to a government budget constraint (for example, see Boskin and Sheshinski, 1979). Although a

larger. Hence, the larger the substitution effect (in other words, the flatter the indifference curve u°), the larger the size of the excess burden of the income tax, other things being equal. Similarly, note that if the marginal rate of tax on earnings τ_E were larger than the value implicit in Figure 6.1, then the post-"tax" (but pre-"spending") budget line vbe would be flatter than the one shown in Figure 6.1, and so would both the line $v''d'$ and the line $v'd$ (which, by construction, are parallel to vbe). Tangency of u° with the (now-flatter) line $v'd$ would occur at a point to the right of the present tangency point, α; and the new line ab would lie to the right of its present position. Thus, point a would lie closer to v than is the case in Figure 6.1. Moreover, since the slope of u° is smaller in absolute value at α than the slope of the pre-tax budget line vac, this means that the distance between the new point α and the new point a would be larger than the distance shown in Figure 6.1. Thus, the new value of αa would be larger than the old value: In other words, the larger the marginal rate of tax τ_E, the larger the excess burden of the income tax, other things being equal. Finally, note that an increase in the gross wage rate W – like an increase in τ_E – will make the slope of ve flatter *relative to* the slope of vc. Reasoning similar to that used just previously to analyze the relation between excess burden and τ_E, therefore, leads to the conclusion that excess burden will be larger, the larger is the gross wage rate W, other things being equal.

detailed review of propositions about optimal taxation is beyond the scope of this discussion, it is worth noting that, in most cases, studies of optimal taxation imply that tax systems with low marginal tax rates are more likely to satisfy Colbert's requirements – to minimize excess burden (or maximize the combined utilities of the citizenry) subject to the government's budget constraint – than are systems with high marginal tax rates. Given that excess burden increases as marginal tax rates increase, this proposition seems fairly self-evident. In principle, the optimal tax is a pure lump-sum tax combined with a pure lump-sum grant of equal size: Unlike the income tax of Figure 6.1, such a tax-and-spending scheme will of course keep the individual, on balance, at his original utility level (u°) – indeed, at his original equilibrium point (β) – with no excess burden at all.

However, it is important to note that these and similar propositions about excess burden and optimal taxation may be very sensitive to a number of important assumptions implicit in the results previously derived. First, many discussions of excess burden and optimal taxation ignore the general-equilibrium effects of taxes and transfers (e.g., the way in which such tax-and-spending schemes may affect *gross* wages W as well as net wages $\hat{W}$). In effect, such discussions assume that the individual shown in Figure 6.1 is the *only* individual affected by the tax-and-spending scheme and, there-fore, ignore the way in which induced labor supply changes will disturb labor market equilibrium and, thus, gross wage rates. (See Musgrave, 1959, pp. 140–59, for discussion of some of the general-equilibrium aspects of excess burden.) Second, many discussions of excess burden and, in particular, optimal taxation assume that all individuals in society have the same utility function or, more or less equivalently, that it is possible to make interpersonal utility comparisons. Third, "society" may value equalization of (post-tax) incomes as an end in and of itself, but most discussions of excess burden and optimal taxation in effect treat social welfare as the sum of individual utilities that depend only on consumption of a (composite) consumer good and leisure. Fourth, most discussions of excess burden ignore risk and uncertainty. However, as Eaton and Rosen (1980a–c) observe, if the wage rate (or the return to invest-ment in human capital) is risky, then the optimal tax may well involve some taxation of earnings. This is because taxation of earnings reduces the variance of earnings and thus "in effect acts as insurance – it lowers risk because the government shares in both losses and gains" (Eaton and Rosen, 1980a, p. 358). Although pure lump sum taxation entails no excess burden in the case of certainty, it does not reduce the variance of earnings when wages are uncertain. As such, it may not be the optimal tax in the presence of uncertainty.

Finally, discussions of excess burden and optimal taxation almost always assume that the spending part of the tax-and-spending scheme involves a lump-sum cash grant and, thus, increased spending by the individual on a (composite) consumer good and leisure. Hence, such discussions do not allow for "government goods" (for example, so-called public goods, such as the court system, police, firefighters, national defense, and the like).[11] In consequence, such discussions ignore the possibility that, in terms of Figure 6.1, even an amount of spending on government goods that is less than ab (=

---

[11] In other words, suppose the individual's utility depends not only on C and L but also on government goods, G. For simplicity, suppose further that utility is separable in G, as in (6.21). Then the curvature (that is, the marginal rate of substitution) of any indifference curve is independent of the size of G, but the *amount* of utility associated with any given (C, L) combination still depends on G: Specifically, if the marginal utility of G is positive, then any given (C, L) combination of course yields greater utility when G is large than it does when G is small. Now suppose the government introduces a tax on earnings of the kind shown in Figure 6.1 and uses the revenues derived from the tax to purchase more G. The (C, L) combinations now available to the individual are summarized by the line vbe, whereas the (C, L) combinations previously available to him are summarized by the line vc. The latter all involve less G than the former. Consequently, at least in principle, there is no reason why at least some of the (C, L) combinations on ve might yield more utility than any of the (C, L) combinations on vc, even though those on ve involve less C and/or less L than any of those on vc. Of course, one may well wonder why – if the individual values government goods so highly – the individual did not purchase more of them (and less C and/or L) when he faced the pre-tax budget line vc. One simple answer is that such government goods involve positive externalities and nonexcludability (meaning that the individual who pays for and consumes them cannot derive the full benefits of his purchase and consumption): For example, if I employ guards or firefighters to protect my house, my neighbor's house may be safer from criminals or fire than would otherwise be the case (and there may well be no practical way for me to change my neighbor for this benefit or, alternatively, to prevent him from deriving it). If so, I may tend to underconsume government goods relative to consumption C and leisure L (since these are, more or less by assumption, "private" goods – ones that involve no positive externalities).

tax revenues collected) might make the individual better off than a cash grant (and, thus, spending on the composite consumer good and on leisure) that is equal to αb.[12]

6.2.   Income taxes and labor supply

With the theoretical framework of Section 6.1 as background, I now consider the effect of income taxes on labor supply. To speak of *the* effect of income taxes on labor supply is somewhat misleading, however: As noted in Section 6.1, the effect of income taxes depends both on how the revenue raised via those taxes is used and on whether one uses a partial- or a general-equilibrium framework. To simplify matters, I shall follow most of the rest of the literature by using a partial-equilibrium framework (so that general-equilibrium effects on labor supply are ignored) and by assuming that, once it collects income taxes from individuals who pay income taxes, the government uses the proceeds to make transfers to other individuals. (This disposes of difficult issues that might arise were the government to use its tax revenues to purchase government goods; on this, see note 12.)

Theoretical issues

Although relatively straightforward in conceptual terms, theoretical analysis of the impact of taxes on labor supply – even

---

[12] This means that, on balance, the public may be better off after implementation of a government taxing-and-spending scheme than it was before implementation of such a scheme, even if the scheme involves an income tax. However, it does *not* mean that income taxation has no excess burden. To see this, note that one may analyze rival taxes using the notion of *differential incidence*, which refers to the difference in the effects of alternative tax measures that provide the same real amount of revenue and, thus, permit the same spending level by the government (Musgrave, 1959, pp. 211–13). Let utility in the absence of any taxing-and-spending scheme be u^a, and let the utility levels attainable under an income tax and a pure lump-sum tax that both raise the *same* amount of revenue be u^i and u^l, respectively. It is straightforward to show that, in the partial-equilibrium framework of Figure 6.1, $u^l - u^i > 0$, whether or not $u^i - u^a > 0$. (For example, see Musgrave, 1959, p. 144, and in particular his Figure 7–2, in which his "Product X" and "Product Y" may be interpreted as consumption and leisure, respectively.) Thus, in partial equilibrium, a taxing-and-spending scheme that relies on income taxation may raise public welfare, but lump-sum taxation can always do even better: Income taxation does entail an excess burden. (In other words, $u^i - u^a$ can certainly be positive, but $u^l - u^a$ always exceeds $u^i - u^a$ because $u^l - u^i > 0$.)

under the simplifying assumptions previously adopted – does not yield determinate conclusions: Rather, in most models, the effect of taxes depends on potentially offsetting effects whose magnitudes (and, thus, whose net impact on labor supply) cannot be determined *a priori*. For example, in a simple static world, such as the one shown in Figure 6.1, the effect on labor supply of levying a simple income tax on an individual (and using the revenue raised to make transfer payments to other individuals, thereby shifting the tax-paying individual's budget line from 1vc to 1ve) is theoretically indeterminate: The reduction in the (net) wage from W to $\hat{W}$ reduces the price of leisure at the margin, generating a negative substitution effect on labor supply; but the fact that the individual must now pay taxes, and therefore receives less income (net of tax) at any given level of labor supply, generates a positive income effect on labor supply (provided leisure is a normal good). Similarly, in a life cycle setting of perfect certainty, introducing a tax on earnings reduces adjusted initial wealth (the $\hat{Z(0)}$ of (6.16)), leading to a positive income effect on labor supply at all ages t; but the reduction in the adjusted or net wage rate (the $\hat{W(t)}$ of (6.16)) at all ages t that arises because earnings are subject to a positive marginal rate of tax $\tau_E(t)$ at all ages t leads to a negative substitution effect on labor supply at all ages t.[13] (Note that a change in the net wage at t, $W(t)$, will also affect labor supply $H(t')$ at all ages $t' \neq t$ via cross-substitution effects.)

Recent work (e.g., Axelsson, Jacobsson, and Löfgren, 1981; Ehrenberg and Smith, 1982, esp. pp. 151–3) extends an older literature (e.g., Bailey, 1954; Friedman, 1949) in arguing that the general-equilibrium effect of income taxation entails *only* a negative substitution effect on labor supply – that, in general equilibrium, the income effect of income taxation is zero. The reasoning behind this conclusion is simple. Once the government collects income tax revenue, it will have to return that revenue to households in *some* fashion (e.g., by introducing transfer payments, constructing public works, buying back government bonds, reducing other kinds of

---

[13] Note that if the tax system taxes *income* (including income from property) as well as *earnings*, the effects of the tax will be more complicated: As (6.15) and (6.16) indicate, such a tax also reduces the (net) interest rate from r to $\hat{r} \equiv (1 - \tau_V)r$, which will affect adjusted initial wealth $Z(0)$ and the difference $\hat{r} - \rho$ between $\hat{r}$, the (net) interest rate, and ρ, the subjective rate of time preference.

taxes). On balance, then, households cannot, and will not, have more or less real resources, in the aggregate, after the income tax is introduced than they did before the tax was introduced: The negative income effect on labor supply that occurs when the government returns the tax revenue to households *exactly* offsets the positive income effect on labor supply that occurs when the government collects those revenues. On the other hand, income taxation certainly reduces the net reward for an hour of work. So the only general-equilibrium or aggregate effect on labor supply of introducing an income tax will be a pure negative substitution effect. By extension, *raising* income tax rates necessarily reduces general-equilibrium labor supply; lowering tax rates necessarily raises general-equilibrium labor supply.

However, the assumptions under which this result is usually derived are rather stringent: a one-commodity world in which all households are identical and in which tax revenues are rebated to households in a pure lump-sum fashion. (For example, see Axelsson, Jacobsson, and Löfgren, 1981.) Edlefsen (1982) suggests that under only slightly more general assumptions, government taxing-and-spending programs will usually have nonzero income effects and, thus, that the net impact of such programs is indeterminate a priori. Ehrenberg and Smith (1982) add that, to the extent that such programs affect savings and capital formation, they may have a long-run impact on resources (and, thus, a long-run income effect) even if their short-run income effect is zero.

Some studies of the effects of income taxes on labor supply consider somewhat more sharply defined questions. One such question is the following: Relative to an income tax that is "less progressive" (i.e., entails either smaller tax liabilities, or a lower marginal tax rate, at given levels of income),[14] will a more "progressive" income tax that raises the same amount of revenue entail more, or less, labor supply? (See Allingham, 1972; Cassidy, 1970; Hemming, 1980; Kesselman, 1976.) Even here, however, the answer to such questions is often theoretically indeterminate and

---

[14] Various definitions of progressive tax are used in the literature. Some authors define *progressive* to mean "characterized by an increasing marginal rate of tax." Others define *progressive* to mean "characterized by an increasing average rate of tax." See Hemming (1980) for further discussion.

depends, for example, on whether the gross or uncompensated elasticity of labor supply with respect to the (net) wage rate is positive or negative.

Related to, but distinct from, these issues is the "Laffer curve" (Fullerton, 1982). The Laffer curve is a hypothesis about the relation between tax *revenues* and tax *rates*, according to which the graph of tax revenues against tax rates is shaped like an inverted "U": Successive increases in tax rates produce smaller and smaller increases in revenue and – beyond a certain critical tax rate – actually lead to lower revenue. It follows that, if the economy is operating to the right of the curve's maximum, the government can get higher tax revenues by reducing tax rates. (Some skeptics have dubbed this effect a "free lunch for the tax collector.") In one sense, the Laffer curve requires fewer assumptions than does the proposition that the income effect of taxing-and-spending policy is zero: The Laffer curve requires only that the income effect be weaker than the substitution effect. In another sense, however, the Laffer curve requires more than just an assumption that the net labor supply response to a taxing-and-spending measure is negative: An inverted-U-shaped Laffer curve requires an *increasing elasticity* of earnings (more generally, output or taxable income) with respect to tax rates, starting off at a value below unity in absolute value but exceeding unity in absolute value to the right of the curve's maximum.

Finally, the relation between taxes and investment in human capital is worth brief mention (if only because decisions to invest in human capital are, in effect, decisions to increase the quality or productivity of one's labor time). As Heckman (1976a) notes, introducing a simple proportional tax on income will increase investment in human capital in an environment of perfect capital markets and perfect certainty of the kind discussed in Chapter 5. This is so for two reasons. First, an income tax reduces the net interest rate (that is, reduces the value of $r(t)$ in (6.16)), which, therefore, reduces the cost of borrowing for purposes of investment. Second, forgone-earnings costs of investment are deductible (in the sense that they take the form of a reduction in observed earnings, the $W(t)H(t)$ of (6.16), which, provided taxes do in fact depend on

observed earnings, means a reduction in one's tax liability).[15] Eaton
and Rosen (1980a) add that, in an environment of wage uncertainty,
income taxation may encourage investment for a third reason:
Taxation reduces the variability in (net) wage rates and, thus, the
riskiness of wage-increasing human capital investments. (For
further discussion, see H. Rosen, 1980.)

Empirical issues

Empirical analysis of the labor supply effects of taxes is
particularly important because, as previously noted, theory offers
relatively little in the way of sharp a priori predictions about such
effects. Moreover, as H. Rosen (1976b, p. 503) notes, there has
been, historically, a "certain amount of skepticism [about] the
importance of taxes as a determinant of work effort" for at least
two reasons: First, it is sometimes argued that individuals simply do
not correctly perceive the marginal tax rate (and hence the discrepancy between the gross wage W and the net wage $\hat{W}$) confronting them; and, second, changes in the wage – in either the gross
or the net wage – are sometimes assumed not to have substantial
effects on labor supply in any case. (Note, however, that even if
empirical evidence were to show conclusively that the latter notion is
correct, such evidence, although important, would not necessarily
constitute evidence against any of the foregoing analysis. It might
simply mean that the substitution and income effects of a tax or
wage increase were approximately equal in absolute value, meaning
that such an increase would have no *net* effect on labor supply.

---

[15] Note that this ignores the role of investment goods and services (e.g., for tuition,
books, and the like) and assumes that the only cost of investment is a forgone-
earnings cost associated with diverting time from work to investment. Subject to a
number of exceptions, most outlays on investment goods and services are not tax
deductible (in particular, outlays of this kind generally cannot be deducted if they
qualify one for a profession or trade but usually *can* be deducted if they improve or
add to one's skills in the profession or trade one now works in). Thus, in general,
direct outlays on investment goods and services for formal schooling are generally not
deductible; this tends to discourage such investment. On the other hand, in most cases
individuals "pay" for investment goods and services used during formal or informal
on-the-job training by taking a reduction in earnings (rather than by making direct
money payments to their employer); in this case, such outlays do result in reductions
in observed earnings. Hence, the argument given in the text applies more to the case
of on-the-job training than to formal schooling.

Also, as noted in the discussion of excess burden in Section 6.1, the effect of a tax on labor supply as such is not necessarily the only, or even the most important, criterion to use in evaluating the tax for purposes of public policy.) The limited available evidence on labor supply effects of taxes tends to contradict both of these notions – though it is important to add that much of this evidence suffers from potentially serious methodological defects.

As regards the accuracy or inaccuracy of tax perceptions, H. Rosen (1976a, b) finds that married white women do appear to act as if they were confronted with a marginal tax rate that is about equal to the one they actually face – in other words, appear to perceive more or less correctly what their actual marginal tax rate is. To obtain this result, Rosen in effect modifies the usual linearized budget constraint model of static labor supply,

$$H = a + b\hat{W} + c\hat{V} + e$$

where

$$\hat{W} \equiv (1 - \tau_E)W$$
$$\hat{V} \equiv V + \tau_E W - \Lambda$$

derived from (6.7), by introducing a coefficient of tax perception, k. Thus, in general terms, Rosen's labor supply function is

$$
\begin{aligned}
H &= a + b(W - k\tau_E W) + c\hat{V} + e \\
&= a + bW - bk(\tau_E W) + c\hat{V} + e
\end{aligned}
$$

If k is close to zero, then individuals act as if they faced a marginal rate of tax that is approximately zero (even though their actual marginal rate of tax may be well above zero); if k is close to unity, then individuals act as if their marginal tax rate were in fact about the same as their actual marginal tax rate.[16] Rosen finds that most of

[16] However, note an inconsistency in Rosen's treatment of tax perceptions: If individuals do in fact act as if they faced a marginal tax rate of $k\tau_E$, where τ_E is the actual marginal tax rate and where k, the coefficient of tax perception, may or may not equal one, then they also act as if they receive property income of $\tilde{V} \equiv V - \Lambda + k\tau_E WH$ (calculated by projecting the line tangent to the individual's actual equilibrium, with slope equal to $\tilde{W} \equiv (1 - k\tau_E)W$, back to the point where $L = 1$). However, as indicated in the text, Rosen's model implies that individuals act as if property income were $\hat{V}$ rather than $\tilde{V}$ – in other words, that individuals may (if $k \neq 1$) incorrectly perceive the true marginal tax rate but correctly perceive the level of adjusted property income $\hat{V}$.

his estimates of k (measured by dividing the coefficient on the variable W in Rosen's expression for H into the coefficient on the variable $\tau_E W$) are in fact not significantly different from unity, in a statistical sense. (See Johnson and Pencavel, 1982b, for similar findings.) Rosen also finds that changes in the actual marginal tax rate τ_E generally lead to fairly sizable changes in labor supply. (For example, his estimates in 1976a imply that an increase of 0.1 in the marginal rate of tax would reduce the labor supply of a married white woman with a gross wage of $1.40 per hour in 1967 by between about 130 and 200 hours per year.) Similarly, Leuthold (1978a) presents evidence to the effect that labor force participation of married women, particularly blacks, is significantly reduced by increases in (marginal) tax rates. Leuthold (1978b) also derives results that imply that hours of work among married women are likewise significantly reduced by increases in (marginal) tax rates.

Such findings that higher tax rates appear to reduce both participation (that is, the probability of working) and hours worked by married women who work confirm simple intuition: Virtually all of the studies of married women reviewed in Chapters 3 and 4 suggest that married women's labor supply increases (often quite substantially) when wages increase; and a tax increase may be regarded as similar (though not necessarily identical) to a wage decrease.[17] Thus, given this evidence, one would certainly expect that labor

---

[17] However, recall the caveats and exceptions to this statement discussed earlier in this section (e.g., about general equilibrium effects, the fact that differences in the way government uses the tax revenue it collects may also lead to differences in labor supply, etc.). Leuthold (1978a, b) attempts to capture the general equilibrium effect of Social Security taxes on labor supply by setting the marginal tax rate on earnings payable under the Social Security system at double the marginal rate actually payable directly by individuals. (This is because the rate payable directly by employers is equal to the rate payable directly by individuals – so that, provided the Social Security tax is fully shifted to individuals, the effective marginal rate actually paid by individuals is double the rate at which they make direct payments under the Social Security tax scheme.) In all other respects, however, Leuthold's work and that of others is based on a partial-equilibrium framework in which general-equilibrium effects of the tax system on *gross* wages and property income are ignored. Strictly speaking, then, empirical findings about how a change in tax rates would affect labor supply show how the labor supply of a *single individual* would change were the tax system applicable to that *one* individual to be changed. Working out the aggregate effect of a change in the tax system requires a general-equilibrium framework, and, to my knowledge, nothing of this kind has yet been attempted in empirical studies.

supply of married women, measured either as participation or as hours of work, would fall in response to tax increases.[18] Hausman's (1981b) recent work provides additional evidence in support of this intuition and extends previous work to consider men. He presents simulations that imply that replacing the current progressive system of income taxation with a linear income tax would substantially reduce the excess burden of the income tax[19] and would raise hours of work considerably (e.g., by about 160 to 170 hours per year, for husbands, and by about 230 to 370 hours per year, for wives).

Although these tax effects on labor supply are large, they do not seem nearly large enough to support the notion that the U.S. economy is at present on the downward-sloping portion of its Laffer curve. Hausman (1981b, c) finds that cutting tax rates from their current levels would reduce tax revenues, in some cases by quite

[18] Hunt, DeLorme, and Hill (1981), like other researchers, find that an increase in the marginal tax rate will reduce the labor supply of married women, but their results also appear to suggest that a *rise* in the wage will *reduce* married women's labor supply. The reason for this anomalous finding may be that their labor supply function is misspecified: They regress hours of work on (i) the marginal tax rate, (ii) the *gross* wage rate, and (iii) other variables, rather than on the *net* wage rate ($\hat{W}$) and other variables.

[19] Hausman's results suggest that excess burden as a proportion of the total yield of the income tax is about 8.5 percent for husbands and about 18.4 percent for wives. H. Rosen (1978) gets rather different results. His calculations derived from estimates for a Stone–Geary utility function obtained by Abbott and Ashenfelter (1976) imply that excess burden is only about $6.05 per worker, or about 0.9 percent of total income tax revenues; his own results, derived from a Stone–Geary utility function fitted to data on a cross section of families, imply that excess burden is about 13 percent of total tax revenue versus only about 1.5 percent in results derived for the same cross section of families using a generalized CES family utility function. (Hausman corrects for corner solutions, that is, for nonworkers, whereas Rosen restricts his samples to families in which both husband and wife work without correcting for possible selection bias attendant upon this restriction. On the other hand, Hausman ignores intrafamily cross-substitution effects, whereas Rosen does not.) However, recall from Chapter 4 that although Hausman estimates the uncompensated wage effect on labor supply directly, he constrains the income effect to be negative. Now, many studies that present unconstrained estimates of the income effect find that the income effect is approximately zero. Thus, Hausman's procedure may overstate the *compensated* wage effect (that is, the substitution effect), because that is the difference between the uncompensated wage effect and the (negative) income effect. If so, then Hausman's results also overstate the tax system's excess burden, because excess burden varies directly with the substitution effect. See Heckman (1981) for further discussion.

sizable amounts. His findings are based on simulations within a partial-equilibrium framework, using parameter estimates derived from microdata; but Hausman adds that general equilibrium effects are very unlikely to be large enough to make revenue rise, on balance, in response to a tax rate cut. Fullerton's (1982) general-equilibrium simulations, based on an assumed aggregate wage-elasticity of labor supply of 0.15, lead to essentially similar conclusions: The U.S. economy is well to the left of the peak of its Laffer curve, which Fullerton estimates would occur at a marginal tax rate of about 0.80. However, Stuart (1981) considers Sweden, where effective marginal rates are in fact equal to about 0.80; he concludes – on the assumption that the aggregate wage elasticity is about 0.10 – that Sweden is indeed somewhat to the right of the peak of *its* Laffer curve.

6.3.   **Transfer payments and labor supply: introduction**

The most obvious difference between taxation and transfer payments is that, under taxation, one's tax liability – the Λ of expressions such as (6.3)–(6.5) (for the static case) or (6.9)–(6.12) and (6.16) (for the dynamic case) – is positive, whereas under transfers this liability is negative, that is, payments come from the government to the individual rather than the other way around. In most other respects, the Λ function for transfer payments is similar to the Λ function for tax payments. Just as individuals do not pay tax if their income is below a certain minimum "exclusion" level, so, too, individuals do not receive transfers if their income exceeds a certain maximum "break-even" level. A rise in income increases the algebraic magnitude of Λ in either case (that is, makes one's positive tax liability get bigger or makes one's negative transfer liability fall in absolute value). In some respects, however, taxes and transfers differ even in formal terms. For example, one normally pays one's tax liability to the state in cash, whereas, depending on the nature of the specific transfer program, the state may pay transfer benefits to individuals either in the form of cash *or* in the form of specific goods (i.e., require that the benefit can be spent only on certain particular commodities).

In this section, I will focus first on theoretical models of unrestricted income-related transfer schemes – ones whose benefits are paid out in the form of cash, and that may (at least in principle) be used for whatever purchases their recipients may desire.[20] In Sections 6.4 and 6.5, I will consider empirical studies of labor supply in the presence of negative income tax schemes, a particular kind of unrestricted income-related transfer mechanism to which much attention has been devoted in recent years. Section 6.6 discusses the Social Security system (a combination of a tax scheme *and* a transfer scheme) whereas Section 6.7 discusses restricted income-related transfer schemes (ones whose benefits may be used only for the purchase of certain specific goods)[21] and proposals for wage subsidies, that is, *wage rate*-related transfer schemes.

Models of labor supply and unrestricted income-related transfers

To develop models of labor supply in the presence of an unrestricted income-related transfer scheme, it is convenient to let B_Y (the transfer benefit) denote the value of $-\Lambda$ under the scheme (i.e., the absolute value of benefits paid under the scheme) and to use a simple version of the Λ function of equation (6.2) (and equation (6.9)):

(6.24) $\quad B_Y \equiv -\Lambda = G_Y - \tau_Y Y \qquad$ if $\quad Y \leq G_Y/\tau_Y$

(6.25) $\quad B_Y \equiv -\Lambda = 0 \qquad\qquad$ if $\quad Y > G_Y/\tau_Y$

where $Y \equiv WH + V$, $0 < \tau_Y < 1$ and $G_Y/\tau_Y \equiv Y_B$. Equations (6.24) and (6.25) define a simple negative income tax (NIT) plan that is a prototype of most of the NIT schemes considered in recent research.[22] (For example, see C. Green, 1968; Rees, 1974.) In a more

---

[20] For example, payments under the Aid to Families with Dependent Children (AFDC) program may generally be used for any expenditures that recipients may care to make, and similarly for payments under experimental negative income tax schemes (see Section 6.4). It is possible that caseworkers and other administrators may in fact exercise pressure on transfer recipients to spend their transfer payment in specific ways; however, one study of AFDC (Handler and Hollingsworth, 1971, esp. Chap. 4) finds little evidence that this is so.

[21] For example, Food Stamp program payments are subsidies that can only be used to purchase food, public housing is in effect a subsidy that can only be used for the rental of housing services, Medicaid program payments can be used only for medical care expenditures, and so on.

[22] Of course, other NIT schemes have sometimes been suggested. (See Boskin, 1967, 1969; Diamond, 1968; Friedman, 1962; C. Green, 1967; *Industrial Relations*, 1967;

general sense, however, equations (6.24) and (6.25) represent the basic structure of all unrestricted income-related transfer schemes: They supplement income whenever income falls below a certain break-even or poverty level Y_B but reduce the size of the supplement as income approaches that critical level. Equations (6.24) and (6.25) imply that the negative liability of – in other words, positive benefit paid to – the individual under the scheme, B_Y, is given by $B_Y = \tau_Y(Y_B - Y)$ if $Y \le Y_B$, and $B_Y = 0$ otherwise. Thus, for example, if Y_B is defined to be the poverty line level of income, then equations (6.24) and (6.25) imply that the aim of the subsidy is to make up τ_Y of the difference between an individual's (or a family's) income exclusive of the subsidy, Y, and the poverty line, whenever income is less than the poverty line. Accordingly, I shall refer to (6.24) and (6.25) in general terms as a hypothetical prototype transfer scheme, but it is worth noting at the outset that (6.24) and (6.25), or something similar, has actually been used on an experimental basis. (I say more about experimental NIT schemes in Sections 6.4 and 6.5.)

One feature of (6.24) and (6.25) turns out to be quite important for analysis: Individuals below the break-even level will receive payments under the transfer scheme even if their labor supply is in no way affected by introduction of such a scheme; but individuals whose income exceeds the break-even level prior to introduction of the scheme will have to reduce their labor supply in order to reduce income and thereby qualify for benefits. Consequently, it is important to distinguish between initially "above break-even" and initially "below break-even" individuals in any analysis of the impact of such a scheme, whether in a static or dynamic context.

1. Static models. First, consider the impact of the transfer scheme (6.24) and (6.25) in the simple static model of an individual's labor supply presented at the beginning of Chapter 1.

Kesselman, 1969a, b, 1973; Kesselman and Garfinkel, 1978; Kisker, 1967; Perlman, 1968a; Rein, 1973; and Tobin, 1964.) One popular variant of (6.24) and (6.25) is $B_Y = G_Y$ for $0 \le Y < Y_D$, $B_Y = G_Y - \tau_Y Y$ for $Y_D \le Y \le Y_B$ and $B_Y = 0$ for $Y > Y_B$, where Y_D is the income disregard level, that is, the maximum amount of income that one can earn before benefits are cut in response to increases in income. For an informative and detailed (but now somewhat outdated) review of the numerous components of the actual U.S. transfer system, see Subcommittee on Fiscal Policy (1972). Danziger, Haveman, and Plotnick (1981) survey studies of the effects of transfers on labor supply, savings, and income distribution.

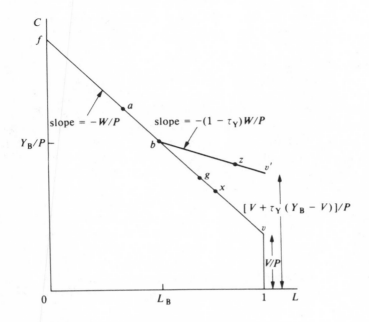

Figure 6.2.   Prototype transfer scheme

As in Chapter 1, assume that the individual initially earns a money wage of W, receives V dollars of exogenous (property) income per period, and pays a price P per unit of a composite consumer good C. To focus the analysis squarely on questions relating to the transfer scheme per se, ignore all other taxes and transfers.[23] Introducing the program embodied in (6.24) and (6.25) would change the individual's budget line from vf to $v'bf$, as shown in Figure 6.2. Note that the vertical distance between $v'b$ and vb at a given point z on $v'b$ measures the actual amount of benefit B_Y received by an individual who chooses that point, the vertical distance between z and the L axis measures the individual's gross income (earnings plus property

---

[23] Thus, the analysis now applies, at least in a literal sense, only to "working poor" persons who are *not* now receiving *other* subsidies (and who also are not now paying taxes); but note that most proposals for new transfer schemes involve *replacing* transfer programs now in existence with one such as (6.2).

income plus B_Y), and the difference between these two amounts is therefore the individual's income exclusive of the subsidy, Y, at point z.

Analysis of the labor supply effects of introducing the transfer scheme is straightforward, provided one distinguishes between persons who are initially above and persons who are initially below the break-even level. With respect to the latter group, direct application of the linearized budget constraint approach (see Chapter 4 and Section 6.1, esp. (6.7)) to Figure 6.2 suggests that introducing the scheme is similar to reducing the individual's wage and simultaneously raising exogenous income. In particular, reducing the wage rate (from W/P to $\hat{W}/P = (1 - \tau_Y) W/P < W/P$) has a negative substitution effect and, if leisure is a normal good, a positive income effect on labor supply. Raising exogenous income (from V/P to $\hat{V}/P = [V + B_Y + \tau_Y WH]/P = [V + \tau_Y(Y_B - V)]/P > V/P$) will have a negative income effect on labor supply, if leisure is a normal good. Moreover, on balance, the simultaneous change in the wage rate and in exogenous income leaves an individual who initially worked along segment vb with more total income at any given level of hours of work: That is, $v'b$ lies above vb. Thus, the positive "wage change" income effect is offset by a stronger negative "exogenous income" income effect. Both the substitution effect and the net income effect of the transfer scheme, therefore, reduce hours of work for an individual who worked along segment vb prior to introduction of the scheme: That is, someone initially at a point such as g on vb will always move to a point on $v'b$ that involves fewer hours of work than g. (Unless consumption, C, is an inferior good, the point on $v'b$ to which he will move will also involve more consumption than g.)

Next consider persons initially above the break-even level – that is, persons who initially were working along segment bf in Figure 6.2. Clearly, someone at a point such as a finds it superior to all other points along vf and will find points along $v'b$ superior to a only if his indifference curve at a is relatively flat. Of course, this is equivalent to saying that such an individual would never increase labor supply in response to introduction of the transfer scheme and would reduce it (by moving from a to a point on $v'b$) if and only if (i) his marginal rate of substitution of consumer goods for leisure changes relatively little as hours of work change, or, equivalently,

(ii) he treats consumer goods and leisure time as relatively close substitutes, or, still equivalently, (iii) his income-compensated wage elasticity of labor supply is relatively high.

In sum, in the simple static model of an individual's labor supply, a transfer scheme such as (6.24) and (6.25) will reduce the earnings and labor supply and will increase the leisure time of (i) all persons initially below the break-even level and (ii) those above break-even individuals whose own-wage income-compensated substitution elasticity is sufficiently high, relative to the break-even income level and the tax rate parameters of the program. Other persons – those initially above break-even with relatively low own-wage compensated substitution elasticities, and persons whose labor supply is initially zero – will not change their behavior.[24]

One final point deserves brief mention: An NIT may encourage risk-taking in the labor market, at least for persons initially below the break-even level of income. To see why, note that an NIT raises the incomes of such persons and also reduces the variance in their (net) wages. If risk-taking is a normal good, then inspection of (5.88) suggests that both NIT effects should make such persons less risk averse. (However, note that this ignores the reduction in the *level* of the net wage due to the NIT.) For further discussion and empirical evidence in support of this notion, see W. R. Johnson (1980).

Mutatis mutandis, the analysis can easily be extended to the conventional family utility–family budget constraint static model of the labor supply of family members outlined in Chapter 2. Family earnings is $E_F \equiv \Sigma W_i H_i$, where i subscripts refer to family member i;

---

[24] See C. Green (1968). Note that, in terms of Figure 6.2, no individual initially below break-even (e.g., at points such as g in Figure 6.2) would ever move to a point on bf after the scheme is introduced, because such an individual considers at least one point below break-even (e.g., the point g) to be superior to all points on bf. Also, although the discussion in the text focuses on the effect on labor supply of introducing a transfer scheme, one might also consider the effect on labor supply of changes in the wage rate or exogenous income in the *presence* of such a transfer scheme. The key to understanding such issues is that, because the scheme makes the budget constraint convex, the graph of labor supply against the wage rate in the presence of the scheme will exhibit discontinuities. For details, see Hanoch and Honig (1978), MacRae and MacRae (1976), and Moffit (1977); the latter two papers are concerned with the Social Security payroll tax, but much of their analysis applies equally well to a negative income tax.

thus, if family income is below Y_B, then (6.24) and (6.25) entail an implicit tax on each family member's earnings and, therefore, reduce each family member's wage rate by the same proportion: $100\tau_Y$ percent. By the composite commodity theorem (see Chapter 1), Figure 6.2, therefore, applies equally well to family as to individual labor supply. The one difference is that, in a family context, the L that appears on the horizontal axis of Figure 6.2 must be interpreted as *composite family* leisure time, L_F. Now, $L_F \equiv \Sigma W_i L_i$, a wage-weighted sum of the leisure times of the individual family members, so L_F may be interpreted as the family's total "expenditure" on leisure. Note that, so long as gross wage rates W_i do not change, an increase (decrease) in L_F must be accompanied by a decrease (increase) in the family's total earnings, $E_F \equiv \Sigma W_i H_i$. Thus, in the conventional static model of family labor supply, arguments identical to those just presented in the context of individual labor supply show that introducing (6.24)–(6.25) will reduce the total earnings E_F and increase the "composite" leisure time L_F of (i) all families initially below break-even and (ii) above-break-even families whose *family* own-wage substitution elasticity of *composite* labor supply is relatively high. (The family own-wage substitution elasticity is a weighted combination of the substitution elasticities of the family's members; see Ashenfelter, 1980b.) On the other hand, above-break-even families with relatively low family own-wage substitution elasticities of composite labor supply will not change their behavior.

These results refer to family behavior (e.g., to family earnings E_F and family composite leisure L_F) and provide little in the way of specific a priori conclusions about the behavior of individual family members. Now, the effect of the transfer program on the labor supply of any given family member i, dH_i^P, may be written as

$$(6.26) \quad dH_i^P = S_{ii}^P + \sum_{j \neq i} S_{ij}^P + I_i^P$$

where S_{ij}^P is the substitution effect on i's labor supply of the program-induced reduction in family member j's wage and I_i^P is the income effect on H_i of the program-induced change in the family's total income. S_{ii}^P (which is proportional to the conventional own-wage substitution effect but opposite-signed) and I_i^P are both negative, but the sign of any S_{ij}^P, $j \neq i$, may be either negative (if the leisure times of i and j are net – income-compensated –

complements) *or* positive (if the leisure times of i and j are net substitutes). If all family member leisure times are complements (so that the sign of the second term in (6.26) is negative) or if family leisure times are "weak" substitutes (i.e., if the second term in (6.26) is positive but smaller in absolute value than the sum of the other two terms), then each individual family member's leisure time will rise and each individual family member's hours of work and earnings will fall in response to the transfer scheme. Otherwise, however, the scheme might raise the earnings and hours of work and reduce the leisure time of some individual family members.[25]

2. *Dynamic models.* Once one considers labor supply in a dynamic context, discussion of the impact of transfer programs becomes somewhat complicated. To simplify exposition, it is useful to distinguish between models in which the wage is exogenous and models in which the wage is endogenous, as in Chapter 5. Also, as before, it is important to distinguish between cases in which income Y initially exceeds break-even and cases in which income initially is less than break-even. (Note that, in a dynamic setting, this entails distinguishing between *periods* when a *given* individual's Y is greater, or less, than Y_B as well as between *individuals* whose Y is greater, or less, than Y_B.) Finally, recall from Chapter 5 that, in dynamic models, property income, the V of Chapter 1, is the endogenously determined amount rZ, where r is the interest rate and Z is the amount of nonhuman wealth.

Exogenous wage models: First, consider a simple dynamic model of an individual who has an *exogenously* given wage $W(t)$ in period t (thus, ignore investment in human capital) and who, in the absence of a transfer program, would have a total income $Y(t) = rZ(t) + W(t)H(t)$ that is always less than Y_B in *each* period t (that is, consider someone who is initially below break-even in all periods). Now, income in any period t is $Y(t) = rZ(t) + W(t)H(t)$. Thus,

---

[25] That is, the scheme reduces all family members' wages; the cross-substitution effect on i's labor supply of the reduction in the wage of some other family member j will be negative if L_i and L_j are complements, but it will be positive if they are substitutes. For example, see Ashenfelter (1978c) and Killingsworth (1976). However, recall that the composite commodity theorem implies that the scheme must reduce *total* family earnings. Hence, the scheme must also reduce the earnings (and thus the labor supply) of at least one family member.

by (6.15), the budget constraint in the presence of the transfer scheme is

$$(6.27) \quad Z(t + 1) - Z(t) = (1 - \tau_Y)[rZ(t) + W(t)H(t)] \\ + G_Y - P(t)C(t)$$

where $Z(0) = Z_0$, a constant, and such that $Z(T + 1) \geq 0$ provided property income $rZ(t)$ *is* included within the "income" that is implicitly "taxed" by the transfer scheme. (Note that in (6.27) I have converted the $\dot{Z}(t)$ of (6.15) into its discrete-time analog, $Z(t + 1) - Z(t)$, for ease of exposition.) If so, then the individual's lifetime budget constraint may also be written as

$$(6.28) \quad Z(0) + \sum_{t=0}^{T} (1 + \hat{r})^{-t}[(1 - \tau_Y)W(t)H(t) \\ + G_Y - P(t)C(t)] \geq 0$$

where $\hat{r} \equiv r(1 - \tau_Y)$. On the other hand, for reasons that will become clear shortly, it is convenient, and perhaps not unrealistic, to assume that property income is not taxed by the transfer scheme.[26] If so, then the individual's lifetime budget constraint is

$$(6.29) \quad Z(t + 1) - Z(t) = rZ(t) + (1 - \tau_Y)W(t)H(t) \\ + G_Y - P(t)C(t)$$

where $Z(0) = Z_0$, a constant, and such that $Z(T + 1) \geq 0$, or, equivalently,

$$(6.30) \quad Z(0) + \sum_{t=0}^{T} (1 + r)^{-t}[(1 - \tau_Y)W(t)H(t) \\ + G_Y - P(t)C(t)] \geq 0$$

provided property income is *not* taxed (in other words, *not* included in the income on the basis of which transfer payments are made). Note that the only difference between (6.28) and (6.30) is that, in the latter, the transfer scheme does not affect the rate of interest the individual can earn on a given amount of property, whereas, in the

---

[26] Particularly at low income levels, much of the income from property, V, that individuals receive takes the form of service flows of income-in-kind, rather than money flows (e.g., services yielded by ownership of consumer durables rather than dividends paid on holdings of shares of stock). For the most part, only the latter kind of income from property is taxed, or would be taxed, under transfer schemes either actual or proposed.

former, the net interest rate $\hat{r} \equiv r(1 - \tau_Y)$ is lower than the gross or pre-tax interest rate r due to the taxation of income from property.

Next, let the individual's lifetime utility function U be given by

$$(6.31) \quad U = U[C(0), \ldots, C(T), L(0), \ldots, L(T)]$$

where $C(t)$ and $L(t)$ are the individual's consumption of goods and leisure, respectively, in any period t, $t = 0, 1, 2, \ldots, T$. Note that, when property income is not taxed by the transfer scheme so that the lifetime budget constraint in the presence of the transfer scheme is as given by (6.30), the "price" of leisure in any period t, $\Pi_{L(t)}$, is $\Pi_{L(t)}$ $\equiv (1 + r)^{-t}(1 - \tau_Y)W(t)$.

This means that, in this particular case, when the transfer program does not tax property income, one may consider the labor supply effects of the transfer program using a straightforward application of the composite commodity theorem. To see this, define *composite* leisure, L_L, as the price-weighted sum of the leisure consumed in all periods from the present through time T, that is, L_L $= \Sigma_{t=0}^{T}(1 + r)^{-t}(1 - \tau_Y)W(t)L(t) = \Sigma_{t=0}^{T}\Pi_{L(t)}L(t)$; and note that the transfer scheme implicit in (6.30) changes the price of leisure in any given period t, $\Pi_{L(t)}$, by the same proportion: $100\tau_Y$ percent. Thus, in this case, the substitution effect of the transfer scheme raises *composite* (that is, *lifetime*) leisure time L_L. Also, by assumption, the individual's earnings in any period t are less than Y_B. Thus, the transfer scheme's *net* income effect on composite leisure L_L (i.e., the sum of the negative income effect attributable to imposition of the marginal tax rate τ_Y and of the positive income effect attributable to introduction of the income guarantee G_Y) will raise composite leisure L_L (and, for that matter, leisure in each period t, $L(t)$) provided leisure in each period t is a normal good.

Next, note that the present value of lifetime earnings, E_L, is simply $E_L = \Sigma_{t=0}^{T}(1 + r)^{-t}W(t)H(t)$. Thus, changes in L_L induced by the transfer scheme embedded in (6.30) will always be accompanied by changes in E_L of opposite sign. So, when the transfer scheme does not tax property income, its introduction will raise the individual's composite (or lifetime) leisure, L_L, and will reduce the present value of the individual's lifetime earnings, E_L. Not surprisingly, then, application of the composite commodity theorem to the present case – a dynamic model of an individual –

yields results that are identical to those derived earlier for the static model of a family, mutatis mutandis. In both cases, the NIT reduces earnings (family earnings, in the static family model; the present value of lifetime earnings, in the dynamic individual model) and increases composite leisure (the price-weighted sum of the leisure times of different family members, in the static family model; the price-weighted sum of the leisure times consumed in different periods, in the dynamic individual model).

Moreover, as in the static family model, it is not possible to say much a priori in the dynamic individual model about the effect of the transfer program on specific components of composite leisure without introducing further assumptions. For example, the effect of the transfer scheme on labor supply in period t, $dH^P(t)$, may be written for this model as

$$(6.32) \quad dH^P(t) = S^P(t, t) + \sum_{q \neq t} S^P(t, q) + I^P(t)$$

which is, of course, very similar to (6.26). The third term on the right-hand side of (6.14) is the income effect on the individual's labor supply in period t resulting from the program-induced increase in lifetime wealth;[27] provided leisure in period t is a normal good, this term will have a negative sign. The first term on the right-hand side of (6.32) is the own-substitution effect on the individual's labor supply in period t resulting from the program-induced reduction in the price of leisure $\Pi_{L(t)}$ during period t; this term will also have a negative sign. However, the sign of the second term − the sum of all compensated cross-substitution effects on labor supply during period t arising from induced reductions in the price of leisure during periods q *other than* period t − is indeterminate a

---

[27] More properly speaking, since this is a dynamic model, this is a "wealth effect" rather than an "income effect." Ignoring the impact of introduction of the tax rate τ_Y, one may write the present value of introducing the guarantee G_Y as

$$G_P = \sum_{t=0}^{T} (1 + r)^{-t} G_Y$$

that is, as the present value of an income stream of G_Y per period paid for a total of T + 1 periods. In the absence of uncertainty, this is equivalent to an increase in initial wealth $Z(0)$ of exactly G_P.

priori. If all leisure times at different dates are substitutes for (complements to) each other, this term will have a positive (negative) sign. Thus, in principle, the transfer scheme embedded in (6.30) could increase labor supply in some periods, if leisure times in different periods are sufficiently substitutable (that is, provided the second or cross-substitution term on the right-hand side of (6.32) is positive and larger in absolute value than the negative own-substitution and income terms).

A moment's reflection suggests that the composite commodity theorem may also be used to derive fairly specific results about the effects of a transfer scheme such as (6.30) in a dynamic model of family, rather than individual, labor supply. Write the family lifetime utility function as $U = U[C(0), \ldots, C(T), \mathbf{L}(0), \ldots, \mathbf{L}(T)]$, where $\mathbf{L}(t) = [L_1(t), \ldots, L_m(t)]$, the vector of labor supplies of the m family members at t. Next, note that if the transfer scheme does not tax family property income, the family's lifetime budget constraint is a straightforward modification of (6.30), in which the term $(1 - \tau_Y)W(t)H(t)$ becomes $(1 - \tau_Y)[\Sigma W_i(t)H_i(t)]$, where i subscripts refer to family member i. The price of i's leisure time during period t is, therefore, $(1 + r)^{-t}(1 - \tau_Y)W_i(t)$. Again, introducing the transfer scheme reduces the prices of all leisure times by the same proportion, so the composite commodity theorem applies once again. Mutatis mutandis, the effects of the transfer program here are, therefore, identical to those in the dynamic model of individual labor supply. Specifically, in the present case, composite leisure is the present value of the price-weighted sum of all family members' leisure times over time; E_L, lifetime family earnings, is the present value of the total lifetime earnings of all family members combined; and the transfer scheme raises L_L and reduces E_L. (However, this assumes that the number of family members at any date is not affected by the transfer scheme. To the extent that the scheme affects fertility or the departure of members from the family unit, analysis becomes more complicated.) To say more than this, it is necessary, as before, to impose some restrictions on the utility function.

Endogenous wage models: In exogenous wage models, the effect of transfer schemes such as (6.30) can readily be analyzed using the composite-commodity theorem because, in such models, the price of leisure is also exogenous. However, if the wage itself is a choice variable then, in general, the composite commodity theorem no longer applies. Hence, analysis of the impact of transfer schemes in endogenous wage models is fairly complicated. Moreover, in order to say anything specific about the impact of transfer programs in such models, it is of course necessary to say something specific about the nature of this endogeneity, that is, about the way in which individuals accumulate human capital.

Perhaps for these reasons, most discussions of the impact of transfer schemes in dynamic endogenous wage models tend to be – because they must inevitably be – somewhat imprecise and discursive. (For example, see J. Smith, 1975, esp. pp. 34–6.) In general, it is possible to derive clear-cut a priori conclusions only by imposing some fairly strong assumptions about functional forms and the like. For example, consider the following Heckmanesque continuous-time model of an individual who maximizes a lifetime utility function that is additively separable in time, goods $C(t)$ and effective leisure $K(t)L(t)$,

$$(6.33) \quad U = \int_0^T e^{-\rho t} \{u[C(t)] + v[K(t)L(t)]\} dt$$

To begin with, assume that the individual's stock of human capital K accumulates according to the relation $\dot{K}(t) = n[I(t)K(t)] - \delta K(t)$ and that the wage $W(t)$ is equal to $kK(t)$, where k is the rental rate on human capital and all symbols are as defined in Chapter 5. (Specifically, ρ is the individual's subjective rate of time preference, I is the fraction of available time per period devoted to investment in human capital, and δ is the rate of decay or obsolescence of human capital.) Let H denote time spent *at* work, consisting of investment time I and time spent actually performing market work M, that is, $H = I + M$, as in Chapter 5. Finally, assume that the individual's total income in each period t, $Y(t) = rZ(t) + W(t)M(t)$, is always below the transfer scheme's break-even income level Y_B and the scheme does not tax property income $rZ(t)$. If so, then the individual's lifetime budget constraint is similar to the one given by (6.30), that is,

$$Z(0) + \int_0^T e^{-rt} [(1 - \tau_Y)W(t)M(t) + G_Y - P(t)C(t)] dt = 0$$

It turns out that, in this particular model, analyzing the effects of the transfer scheme defined by equations (6.24) and (6.25) is surprisingly simple. First, in this particular model, an increase in initial wealth $Z(0)$ has no effect at all on human capital accumulation $\dot{K}(t)$ or, therefore, on effective investment $K(t)I(t)$ at any moment t. (See Heckman, 1976b.) Thus, the income (or, more precisely, wealth) effect on $I(t)K(t)$ and $\dot{K}(t)$ attendant on introducing the scheme's income guarantee G_Y is zero for all t. Second, it also turns out that the amount of effective investment $I(t)K(t)$ and, therefore, of human capital accumulation $\dot{K}(t)$ at any given moment is independent of any marginal tax rate τ_Y embedded in the transfer scheme. Roughly speaking, this is because, in this particular model, the tax rate is neutral, in the sense that it reduces both marginal costs and marginal benefits of investment in human capital in the same proportion.

It follows that, at least in this particular version of the dynamic endogenous wage model of labor supply and human capital accumulation, neither the guarantee G_Y nor the marginal tax rate τ_Y of the transfer scheme embedded in (6.30) will change the individual's investment behavior or wage profile in any way. (Note, however, that this particular version of (6.24) and (6.25) does not tax property income $rZ(t)$.) Thus, in this model, introducing (6.30) will (i) have no effect on the individual's investment behavior or wage profile and, as in other models, (ii) reduce the individual's lifetime earnings.[28]

Of course, these conclusions would not necessarily hold in different models (e.g., ones in which human capital is not neutral, that is, in which a given percentage increase in human capital does not raise the efficiency of time in each of its different uses by the same proportion, as is the case in Heckman's (1976b) model; see Rea (1977). For example, if credit markets are imperfect, individuals may not always be able to devote the optimal amount of time to investment in human capital accumulation. If so, then the increase in lifetime wealth associated with introduction of the

---

[28] Note also that the need to distinguish between hours spent at work H and hours actually worked M (the difference being hours devoted to investment I), mentioned in Chapter 5, is not a problem here because investment hours do not change due to the transfer scheme.

transfer scheme's income guarantee may permit an increase in investment, which will lead to a rise in wages and hence to complicated income and substitution effects on life cycle behavior that could, in principle, entail an increase in labor supply and earnings at some points in time.

Behavior above break-even: Thus far, this discussion has ignored individuals who are above break-even for at least part of their working lives. If, as I have assumed thus far, the transfer program implicitly taxes earnings but does not tax property income, then the only way in which such above-break-even individuals can receive transfer payments under the scheme is to reduce their labor supply. In static models, the question of whether above-break-even individuals will reduce their labor supplies in order to receive such payments is essentially a question about the magnitude of the own-substitution effect – that is, about whether the individual's indifference curve is sufficiently flat. If the life cycle could be regarded as a sequence of single periods in which behavior is as described in the simple static model – in which, in particular, individuals spend all of their income in the period during which it is received – then the decision of above-break-even individuals in dynamic models to reduce their labor supply in order to receive transfer payments could be analyzed in just the same way. However, the life cycle is of course not simply a sequence of single periods as described in the simple static model. In particular, in dynamic models, the individual may choose to save some or all of an exogenous increase in wealth or income occurring in period t in order to permit increased consumption of goods or leisure in later periods. This means that, even when wages are exogenous, events in any given period may have important "spillover" effects, via savings and asset decisions, on subsequent periods. Thus, in dynamic models – unlike static models, or a "pseudo-life cycle" model consisting of a sequence of single-period static models – the rise in income during below-break-even periods attendant upon introduction of a transfer scheme may have negative spillover effects on labor supply during above-break-even periods. Such effects may occur regardless of whether indifference curves are sufficiently flat, in the sense used in the previous discussion of the behavior of above-break-even individuals in a static model. Indeed, they would occur even if indifference curves were rectangular, that is, if the own-substitution effect of a wage change on labor supply were zero – in which case, in a static context, no above-break-even individual would ever reduce labor supply in order to receive transfer benefits.

6.4. Transfer payments and labor supply: empirical analysis

In principle, it is simple to use results of previous studies to determine the labor supply effects of introducing a transfer scheme such as the one given by (6.24) and (6.25). For example, suppose that the labor supply function is $H = a + bW + cV$ if $a + bW + cV$ is positive, and that $H = 0$ otherwise; and suppose further that estimates of the parameters a, b, and c are available. Introduction of (6.2) changes the wage relevant to labor supply decisions from W to $(1 - \tau_Y)W$ and changes exogenous income from V to $V + \tau_Y[(G_Y/\tau_Y) - V] = V + \tau_Y(Y_B - V)$. The change in labor supply associated with these changes is, therefore, given by

$$dH^* = -\tau_Y[bW - c(Y_B - V)]$$

If $c < 0$, that is, if leisure is a normal good, then $dH^* < 0$ also. Persons who were initially below break-even will reduce their labor supply by exactly this much, with two exceptions: persons whose initial hours of work H are smaller than $|dH^*|$ will reduce labor supply by only H to zero, and persons whose initial labor supply is zero will not, of course, change their labor supply. Above-break-even individuals will change their labor supply by dH^* only if the change in labor supply implied by dH^* is sufficiently large to reduce total income exclusive of benefits to a level below the breakeven level: that is, only if $(V + WH) - WdH^* \le Y_B$. Thus, the actual change in labor supply induced by the transfer scheme, (6.2), dH^P, is given by

(6.34) $dH^P = \max(dH^*, -H)$
    if and only if $V + WH - WdH^* \le Y_B$
    and $H > 0$

(6.35) $dH^P = 0$ if and only if $V + WH - WdH^* > Y_B$
    or $H = 0$

where $dH^* = -\tau_Y[bW - c(Y_B - V)]$. Note that $Y_B - V$ must be positive for anyone who receives benefits: if it were negative, an individual could never receive benefits, even if he did not work at all.[29]

However, researchers have long been somewhat skeptical about the use of labor supply parameter estimates to derive estimates of the magnitude of effects of transfer programs. First, as noted in previous chapters, estimates of labor supply function parameters may be systematically biased for one or more of a great variety of reasons. If so, then using such estimates in calculations like those implied by (6.34) and (6.35) may give very misleading implications about the labor supply effects of transfer schemes such as (6.24) and (6.25). Second, even if one can obtain estimates of the labor supply effects of wages and exogenous income (e.g., the parameters b and c of the previous discussion) that are both unbiased and very precise, such estimates do not necessarily constitute unbiased measures of the labor supply effects of transfer payments. This is because transfer programs may involve nonpecuniary effects (feelings of pleasure or displeasure about "living on the dole," etc.) that are either absent, or are both quantitatively and qualitatively different, from the effects of (changes in) wages or exogenous income.

Indeed, some researchers have carried this reasoning one step further, arguing that one may obtain more reliable and less misleading results about *both* conventional income and substitution effects *and* the effect of transfer schemes by conducting a *planned experiment*, consisting of an experimental group (who are eligible to receive transfer payments, provided they wish to do so, under the terms of a scheme such as (6.24) and (6.25)) and also of a parallel, control, sample of persons (who are not eligible to receive such payments). First, these researchers contend, estimates of conventional income and substitution effects derived from experimental data are more likely to be unbiased and consistent than estimates derived from nonexperimental data. The main reason for this, according to these researchers, is that wage rates and property income variables in nonexperimental data are likely to be endogenous: Property income may depend on savings decisions and on unobservable tastes for asset accumulation that are likely to be

[29] For further discussion on using conventional labor supply parameter estimates to simulate the effect on labor supply of a transfer scheme, see Ashenfelter and Ehrenberg (1973) and Cain and Watts (1973a).

correlated with the labor supply error term, wage rates may be chosen as part of an employment package (consisting of wages, hours, and working conditions) whose characteristics may be correlated with the labor supply error term, *net* wage rates are functionally related to labor supply through the marginal rate of tax, and so on. In contrast, planned experiments create substantial and wholly exogenous differences in net wage rates and net property income between experimental and control subjects, differences that are a consequence of exogenously determined eligibility (or ineligibility) for experimental transfer payments rather than of choices made by the subjects themselves. (For statements of this kind, see Danziger, Haveman, and Plotnick, 1981, p. 1015, note 62; Keeley, 1981, p. 106; Weiss, 1981, p. 124.)

Second, proponents of experimental data argue, effects of transfer schemes are likely to be different from effects of changes in wages and in exogenous income as such, due to nonpecuniary aspects (stigma, etc.) of transfer schemes. If so, then simulating the effects of transfer schemes by using parameter estimates generated by nonexperimental data (under the assumption that transfer schemes are no different from anything else that induces the same changes in wages and exogenous income) is likely to produce very misleading estimates of the effects of such schemes. Here, too, experimental data seem preferable to nonexperimental data.

The notion that experimental data are in some sense superior to nonexperimental data for the purpose of estimating structural labor supply parameters (that is, wage and exogenous income effects) seems questionable, however. There are already a variety of different methods for coping with endogeneity of W and V in conventional (i.e., nonexperimental) data; and it is not obvious that mere availability of experimental data is either necessary or sufficient to dispose of the problem of wage endogeneity or of the need to use appropriate statistical methods. The notion that observed wage and property income variables are in some sense "more exogenous" in experimental data than in nonexperimental data ignores the possibility that individuals will make endogenous *adjustments* to the exogenous *impact* of the experimental transfer scheme by changing jobs (thereby changing not only hours of work but also wages and employment conditions), savings behavior (thereby changing property income), and so on. In other words, introduction of an experimental transfer scheme is quite likely to change wages and property income, but there is no reason to suppose that all such changes will be wholly endogenous. To the extent that wages and property income were endogenously chosen prior to the start of the experiment, wages and property income observed during the experiment are likely to be endogenously chosen as well. In sum, as Heckman (1978b) has argued, if one's purpose is to estimate structural labor supply parameters, then the availability of experimental data in no way reduces the need for a carefully specified behavioral model of labor supply or for appropriate estimation techniques.

Advocates of experimental data are on stronger ground in arguing that experimental data may be superior to nonexperimental data for estimating labor supply responses to transfer programs (as opposed to conventional wage and income changes). For example, strictly speaking, Figure 6.2 shows only that if *employers* changed the wage by $-\tau_Y W$ and simultaneously changed exogenous income by $G_Y - \tau_Y V$ at all levels of income below Y_B, then all individuals below break-even will reduce their labor supply and some individuals above break-even will reduce their labor supply. The conclusion that the same effects will occur when the *government* introduces a *transfer program* that generates the same net changes in wage rates and exogenous income of course rests on the implicit assumption that utility depends only on the size of the total consumption–leisure time bundle (C, L) and not on how it is obtained. However, this may not be the case if, for example, individuals "feel bad" (or good) about "taking money from the government." (For discussion of "welfare stigma," see Handler and Hollingsworth, 1971, esp. Chap. 7.) If so, then the utility derived from the (C, L) bundle z shown in Figure 6.2 when one participates in a transfer program will be less than the utility attainable from the same bundle z when one is working (Moffitt, 1981). Moreover, if such "welfare stigma" effects are particularly pronounced, then the utility attainable from consuming z and participating in a transfer program could even be less than the utility attainable from consuming either the bundle x (which involves less C and less L than z but also does not involve "being on the dole") or the bundle a (which might be perceived as inferior to z *if* neither a nor z involved "being on the dole"). Thus, experimental data on actual responses of eligible persons to introduction of a transfer program – accompanied by data on a tandem group of controls not eligible for payments – may be indispensible, or at least particularly valuable, for the purpose of estimating the likely response to such a program, even if it is neither an essential nor a particularly cost-effective way of estimating conventional wage and exogenous income effects.[30]

Experimental data on effects of transfer programs

Perhaps (it is certainly not possible to be sure) with this in mind, in recent years the U.S. government has supported a number of different experimental studies of responses to NIT schemes.[31] These projects – and thus the data collected during them – differ in numerous respects, but they also have a number of important common elements. First, data derived in each experiment refer to persons at specific locations (rather than, say, to a national sample)

---

[30] Unfortunately, however, experimental data may not always lend themselves immediately even to analyses of transfer program responses. First, experimental data may contain behavioral responses attributable to so-called Hawthorne effects (i.e., behavioral changes associated with the mere existence of the experiment) rather than to the provisions of the experimental transfer program as such. Unless such effects alter the behavior of experimental and control subjects equally, it may be difficult to isolate responses attributable to the transfer scheme per se. Second, the stigma of an experimental program may be quite different, both qualitatively and quantitatively, from the stigma of a permanent transfer program. Also, as explained later in this section, several other features of the data generated by the experiments actually undertaken make the task of analyzing such data more complicated than would otherwise be the case.

[31] In the United States, the government has funded four negative income tax or income maintenance experiments: in New Jersey and Pennsylvania; in Gary, Indiana (where virtually all of the participants were black); in rural areas of Iowa and North Carolina; and in Seattle, Washington, and Denver, Colorado. For early discussions of the basic features of these experiments, see Bawden (1969, 1970), Bawden and Harrar (1977a), Browning (1971), Kelly and Singer (1971), Kurz and Spiegelman (1971, 1972), Orcutt and Orcutt (1968), Orr (1969), Spiegelman and West (1976), and Watts (1969, 1971). Aigner (1979), Cain (1975), Conlisk and Watts (1969) and Keeley and Robins (1980) discuss some of the major aspects of the design of the experiments. Aaron and Todd (1979), Boeckmann (1976), Moynihan (1973), and Williams (1975) present interesting discussions of the interplay between this research and the actions – and inactions – of policymakers. Canada conducted a negative income tax experiment in Manitoba during 1975–8 but no research studies of the experiment have yet appeared; see Mason (1982) and Survey Research and Special Projects Directorate (1978) for descriptions of the Manitoba experiment. Whiteford (1981) reviews both the U.S. and Canadian experiments and their relevance to Australia.

who were classified into two distinct categories. Persons in the first category, controls, were simply asked to provide researchers with data on their behavior via periodic interviews and questionnaires in exchange for a small payment for these services; persons in the second category, experimentals, not only provided data but were also eligible to receive payments under one of a variety of distinct versions of the basic NIT scheme embodied in equations (6.24) and (6.25). (Thus, each NIT experiment consisted of several distinct experimental groups – one for each variant of equations (6.24) and (6.25) being considered – and the control group. Note that although only experimentals were *eligible* to receive NIT payments, not all experimentals would choose to do so; some experimentals were recipients, but others were not.)

Second, all such experiments were limited in duration. Most lasted for between three and five years.

Third, neither controls nor experimentals were randomly selected from the population at any given site. Rather, generally speaking, those responsible for the experiments undersampled families judged unlikely to qualify for NIT payments (so as to ensure that a reasonably large number of experimentals would in fact elect to receive such payments). The New Jersey–Pennsylvania experiment used the most stringent undersampling: In order to be included in that experiment, families had to have had an income no greater than 1.5 times as large as the poverty income level in the year immediately before the start of the experiment.

Fourth, persons within the experimental group were not randomly assigned to the various negative income tax schemes whose effects were to be considered by the experiment. Rather, in most cases, those responsible for the experiments systematically assigned experimentals to the different NIT plans being tested on the basis of factors such as preexperiment earnings levels (and, hence, preexperiment labor supply levels).

Finally, in all of the experiments, researchers found that a substantial proportion of both experimentals and controls simply stopped participating in the experiment or disappeared from sight – and thus from the analysis sample – as time went by. (For example, Hausman and Wise, 1979, p. 462, report that attrition rates in their samples of Gary experimentals and controls were about 31 and 41 percent, respectively.)

Each of these features of the experimental NIT data poses problems, of varying degrees of seriousness, for analysis of labor supply responses either to ordinary wage and exogenous income changes or to transfer programs. First, attempts to generalize from the experiments to the country as a whole are somewhat problematic. (Nothing daunted, a number of studies have in fact attempted to make such generalizations. For example, see Keeley et al., 1978a, b, and the studies summarized in Danziger, Haveman, and Plotnick, 1981, pp. 1015–19.)

Second, data derived from the experiments may not provide useful information about *long-run* responses to *permanent* transfer programs, and it is not clear how the experimental response differs from the response to a long-run or permanent program. As several authors have noted, the main reason for this is that, considered as estimates of what would obtain under a permanent NIT scheme, both the effect of the program-induced change in the wage and the effect of the program-induced change in exogenous income are biased – but in different directions. (For example, see Metcalf, 1973, 1974.) On the one hand, availability of benefits under a temporary NIT scheme raises lifetime wealth (and thus exogenous income) relatively little, compared with what would be implied by a permanent program; thus, the wealth (or exogenous–income) effect on labor supply at any time t of a temporary scheme will understate the wealth effect on labor supply at t of a permanent program. On the other hand, whereas a permanent program changes wage rates in all periods in the same proportion (provided individuals are below break-even in all periods), a temporary program of course changes wage rates only in the periods during which the experiment is in operation. Thus, a temporary program creates a pronounced tendency to substitute leisure during post-experiment periods for leisure during within-experiment periods; the substitution effect on labor supply at t of a temporary scheme will, therefore, tend to exaggerate the substitution effect at t of a permanent scheme.

Finally, the three other particular features of the experimental data noted – nonrandom selection of persons for the experimental and control samples, nonrandom allocation of experimentals to the different NIT plans being tested, and nonrandom attrition by experimental and control observations – all raise questions of selectivity bias of the kind discussed in Chapter 4.

In principle, there are solutions – of varying degrees of complexity and precision – for each of these problems. Budgetary and administrative considerations may rule out experiments based on national samples, but conducting experiments at a number of different sites with rather different populations – as has in fact been done – is at least a partial remedy for the fact that it is not always possible to be very confident about drawing general conclusions for the country as a whole on the basis of results for a single site. Heckman (1978b), Metcalf (1973, 1974), and J. Smith (1975) have proposed methods for deriving estimates of responses to a long-run permanent NIT from short-run experimental responses; roughly speaking, Metcalf's results suggest that the *net* bias involved in treating the latter as direct measures of the former is small but both the income and substitution effects comprehended within the short-run response may be fairly substantially biased measures of the income and substitution effects, respectively, underlying the likely response to a permanent NIT.

Finally, Hausman and Wise (1976, 1977, 1979, 1981) and others have developed methods similar to those discussed in Chapter 4 for coping with selectivity bias problems caused by the sample selection rules of the experiments, the procedures used to assign experimentals to alternative experimental NIT plans, and the attrition of both experimentals and controls from the sample. Roughly speaking, these studies suggest that failure to correct for such biases leads to empirical results that may understate, substantially, in some cases, the actual labor supply response to the experimental NIT schemes being considered.

Labor supply in the presence of transfers: econometric specification

At least for purposes of exposition, econometric models of labor supply in the presence of transfer schemes, such as (6.24) and (6.25), may conveniently be grouped under two headings: ad hoc and structural. Such transfer schemes may be either permanent (as with an analysis of labor supply in the presence of the Aid to Families with Dependent Children program) or experimental (as with an analysis of the labor supply effects of the NIT schemes just discussed). In what follows, I will focus on the latter kind of study, since this has been the main concern of most of the work in this area, and I will be concerned with static models, since dynamic empirical models of labor supply – with or without transfers or taxes – are still at an early stage of development. In some respects, models developed to analyze experimental NIT effects carry over without much modification to the case of permanent transfer schemes. In other respects, however, different models are required for analysis of these two different kinds of programs. On the one hand, the experimental NIT programs were temporary, whereas other transfer schemes are more or less by definition permanent; and, as just noted, much has been written about the extent to which one may make inferences about the impact of a permanent program using data on a temporary experimental program. On the other hand, data referring to temporary experimental NIT schemes include control observations, whereas data on permanent transfer schemes do not. Thus, experimental data contain substantial – and seemingly exogenous – variation in net wages and nonwork income, at least in the sense that, in terms of Figure 6.2, such data provide numerous experimental observations along budget line segment bv' and numerous control observations (with identical gross wage rates W and exogenous income V) along budget line segment bv. Other things being equal, this is an important source of information for use in estimating the parameters that determine labor supply.[32]

Ad hoc models. At the simplest level, one might begin empirical analysis of labor supply in the presence of transfers by dividing labor supply in the presence of transfers into two parts: the level that it would have been in the absence of any such transfers and the effect of such transfers on labor supply. Write the former as a linear function $\mathbf{Xb}$ of a vector of variables $\mathbf{X}$ and write the latter as Z; hence, in the most general terms, ad hoc models take the form

$$H = a + \mathbf{Xb} + Z + e$$

where H is labor supply and e is an error term. If $\mathbf{Xb}$ is set at zero, whereas Z is defined as $\mathbf{Td}$, the product of a vector of dummy variables $\mathbf{T}$ (representing eligibility or ineligibility for alternative

[32] However, note that such variation in net wages and nonwork income may only be "seemingly" exogenous and that it is useful "other things being equal." As implied earlier, however, such variation may not be altogether exogenous and other things may not be equal.

(G_Y, τ_Y) combinations provided by the transfer scheme) and a corresponding vector of coefficients **d**, then the investigator is simply comparing mean labor supply differences for persons with different values of **T**. Some investigators estimate **Xb** along with **Td**, resulting in a set of regression-adjusted mean labor supply differences for persons with different **T**: For example, Hausman and Wise (1979) and Robins and West (1980) use a single dichotomous T variable, denoting experimental or control status; Cain et al. (1974, 1977) and Hausman and Wise (1979) use a vector of dichotomous **T** variables, referring to each of the various guarantee–tax rate combinations provided in the New Jersey–Pennsylvania experiment. (Unlike most other studies, the one by Hausman and Wise, 1979, focuses on earnings rather than labor supply as such.) Other researchers define Z to be either $Z = a_1\tau_Y + a_2G_Y$ or $dT + a_1\tau_Y + a_2G_Y$, where τ_Y and G_Y are the tax rate and guarantee, respectively, associated with the particular scheme for which a given individual is eligible; and T is a single dummy variable denoting status as an experimental subject; T, τ_Y, and G_Y are set at zero for controls. For example, see Bawden (1977) and Cain et al. (1974, 1977).

In effect, regression measures of coefficients such as the d or a_i mentioned earlier are summary statistics – "quick and dirty" simple or regression-adjusted measures of the average association between labor supply, on the one hand, and transfer schemes, on the other. Some essentially ad hoc models have, however, attempted to go beyond simple averaging to tackle the "break-even problem" – the fact that the response to a transfer scheme will be zero for persons sufficiently above break-even but will be negative and large in absolute value for others not sufficiently above break-even. For example, Cogan (1978) specifies Z as

$$Z = dT + a_R R$$

where R is a dummy variable indicating actual *receipt* of NIT payments (i.e., an experimental subject who is below break-even *during* the experiment) and, as before, T is a dummy variable indicating experimental status (i.e., *eligibility* for NIT payments). As Moffitt and Kehrer (1981, pp. 126–7) point out, Cogan's least squares estimates of NIT effects using this specification of Z may be severely biased. To see why, note that, *even if the NIT scheme has no effect on labor supply at all*, individuals who actually receive NIT payments (that is, have $R = 1$) will *always* be observed to supply less labor than otherwise comparable individuals who do not receive such payments. Thus, the estimate of a_R is likely to be negative even if there is no response to the NIT scheme. In contrast, Watts and Horner (1977), Watts et al. (1974), and Watts, Poirier, and Mallar (1977) specify the transfer scheme effect Z as

$$Z = (a_{10} + a_{11}\tau_Y + a_{12}G_Y)\theta + (a_{20} + a_{21}\tau_Y + a_{22}G_Y)\theta^2$$

where

$$\theta = (Y_B + 20\widetilde{W} - \widetilde{Y})/10\widetilde{W} \qquad \text{if} \quad Y_B + 20\widetilde{W} > \widetilde{Y}$$
$$\theta = 0 \qquad \text{if} \quad Y_B + 20\widetilde{W} \leq \widetilde{Y}$$

and where $\widetilde{W}$ and $\widetilde{Y}$ are normal wage rate and normal total family income levels, respectively.[33] Thus, θ is a measure of distance from break-even; it increases as the difference between break-even income and actual income increases. For example, $\theta = 0$ for a person whose family's normal income is 20 or more hours' worth of (his) work in excess of the break-even level of income, $\theta = 2$ for a person whose family's total income is normally exactly equal to the break-even level of income, and so on. Under this approach, then, persons who are at least 20 hours' worth of work above break-even are assumed not to respond to the transfer scheme, whereas the response of other persons is assumed to be an increasing function of θ, other things being equal.

Cain et al. (1974, 1977) address the problem somewhat differently. In their work, Z, is given by $Z = dT + a_1\tau'_Y + a_2B'_Y$, where τ'_Y and B'_Y are the tax rate and benefit payment, respectively, that would confront an individual if he were to work exactly the number of hours he worked *before* introduction of the transfer scheme (and so are set at zero for controls and for experimentals who were initially above break-even). Here, the average response of above-break-even experimentals is measured by d, whereas the

---

[33] These normal wage and income variables were derived from regressions for preexperiment values of wages and total family income, in which wages (or total family income) were regressed on a vector of observed characteristics, such as schooling, and which incorporated a variance components scheme designed to estimate person-specific effects.

response of below-break-even experimentals is measured by $d + a_1\tau'_Y + a_2B'_Y$, evaluated at the relevant values of τ'_Y and B'_Y. Kerachsky and Mallar (1976) write Z as

$$Z = dT + a_1\tau_Y + a_2G_Y + a_3p + a_4(TH_p)$$

where p is the probability (computed from a first-stage auxiliary probit analysis) that an observation's initial income was less than the break-even level and where H_p is initial labor supply. Thus, in this case, a_3 and a_4 refer to the effect of the transfer scheme on above-break-even observations, in the sense that someone with a lower p or a higher TH_p value, or both, is more likely to be (well) above break-even and, hence, less likely to respond to the transfer scheme.

Estimates of parameters such as d or the a_i in these ad hoc models may provide some information on the average relation between labor supply and transfer program parameters. However, they obviously do not provide information about the structural parameters (e.g., utility function parameters) that actually generate labor supply decisions or that determine changes in labor supply in response to introduction of a transfer scheme. Ad hoc models, therefore, may suffer from specification error (in the sense that they do not reflect accurately the processes that actually generate labor supply responses to transfer programs) and inefficiency (in the sense that using such models may require estimating more parameters than are really necessary in order to represent the structural determinants of labor supply decisions).

Structural models. In contrast, structural models have somewhat more analytical content and represent an attempt to say something about labor supply and its relation to transfers in terms of structural (e.g., utility function) parameters – albeit, at times, in a nonrigorous fashion. A natural starting point for models of this kind is the linearized budget constraint approach, discussed in Chapter 4. This exploits the fact that, no matter how complicated the actual budget constraint facing an individual may be, an individual's ultimate indifference curve–budget constraint equilibrium can always be written in terms of tangency with a linearized budget constraint line, that is, in terms of a line that is tangent to the equilibrium indifference curve at the point of ultimate equilibrium.

This means that the labor supply function may be written in general terms as

$$H = f[(1 - \tau^*)W, V + \tau^*(Y_B - V)]$$

where τ^* is the marginal tax rate actually observed at the individual's equilibrium *after* introduction of the transfer scheme. Thus, for an experimental subject who receives payments under the scheme, τ^* is the marginal tax rate of that scheme, whereas $\tau^* = 0$ both for experimental subjects who do not receive payments and for all control subjects.

Now, τ^* is determined along with H and so is endogenous. Just as in studies of the effect of the positive income tax, as discussed (see Chapter 4), appropriate implementation of the linearized budget constraint approach here requires an instrumental variable for τ^* (or, alternatively but more or less equivalently, a model that describes the joint determination of H and τ^*). Johnson and Pencavel (1982b) proceed in just this manner, deriving an instrumental variable for τ^* using general "free-form" specifications. Most other researchers have used various proxy or substitute measures for τ^* rather than an instrument per se. For example, Moffitt (1979a) uses an averaged marginal tax rate, $\bar{\tau}$, which, for any given individual, is computed as an hours-weighted average of the various marginal tax rates applicable along the various segments of that individual's budget constraint. On the other hand, as their substitute measure of any given individual's τ^*, Rosen (1976b) and Hausman and Wise (1976) use the tax rate $\tau_{\overline{H}}$ that individuals would face if they were to work exactly 1,500 hours per year.

Since $\bar{\tau}$ and $\tau_{\overline{H}}$ are not really instruments for τ^*, using them as substitutes for τ^* does not really follow the linearized budget constraint approach and, in particular, does not directly address the break-even problem.[34] Keeley et al. (1978a, b) and Robins and West

---

[34] Using the labor supply function $H = f[(1 - \tau_{\overline{H}})W, V + \tau_{\overline{H}}(Y_B - V)]$ ignores the fact that introduction of a transfer scheme (and hence a change in an individual's $\tau_{\overline{H}}$) may produce either no change in H (if the individual is sufficiently above break-even) or a large drop in H (if the individual is "close to" break-even). In principle, the problem is little different from the one that would arise in the absence of any transfers if one had data on W and V for all observations and used the simple function $H = f(W, V)$ to describe labor supply. In this simple case, under certain conditions (when the wage is less than the reservation level), a change in the wage will not affect hours

(1980), who also use a "substitute" variable τ_p (rather than an instrument) for τ^*, attempt to remedy this problem by including above-break-even variables.[35] Robins and West (1980) first use logit analysis to compute a variable p, a measure of each individual's probability of actually receiving benefits under the transfer scheme (that is, of being below break-even *after* introduction of the scheme) and then estimate

$$H = f[p(1 - \tau_p)W, V + p\tau_p(Y_B - V)]$$

– that is, they interact the wage and income variables in the labor supply function with p, the predicted probability of being below break-even in *final* (not initial) equilibrium. On the other hand, Keeley et al. (1978a, b) and Keeley and Robins (1980) include a set of three separate above-break-even variables, denoting (i) whether a given observation was initially above break-even, (ii) the amount of initial income (if any) in excess of break-even, and (iii) the level of break-even income as such. Roughly speaking, both these specifications permit the impact of the transfer scheme to be small for persons initially above break-even (and for the impact to be progressively smaller for persons further and further above break-even). However, note that these procedures "smooth" the labor supply discontinuity of persons initially above break-even; they do not represent it explicitly. Moreover, these procedures are inefficient, in the sense that they involve estimating more parameters (e.g., the vector of above-break-even parameters) than

of work, whereas under other conditions (when the wage is greater than the reservation level), a wage change will lead to a change in labor supply. In both cases, the problem is that simple functions with smooth derivatives ignore the fact that labor supply can have either a positive or a zero derivative with respect to some variable (W or $(1 - \tau_{\overline{H}})W$), depending on whether another variable (the difference between the offered and the reservation wage or the difference between utility with and without benefits from the transfer program) is positive. Similar remarks apply as regards the use of $\bar{\tau}$. In each case, the problem is to develop a model that describes the way in which the individual simultaneously makes both a discrete choice (to work or not to work; to accept or decline transfer benefits) and a continuous choice (the level of hours of work).

[35] In both studies, τ_p is the marginal tax rate that a given individual would face under the transfer scheme if he were to work the number of hours he supplied prior to introduction of the scheme, H_p.

are really necessary in order accurately to describe labor supply behavior.

In contrast, Ashenfelter (1980b) and Burtless and Hausman (1978) devise procedures for analyzing the discontinuous nature of the labor supply response of initially above-break-even individuals (and, in the latter case, for analyzing the choice of hours of work of individuals along either segment of budget lines such as fbv' of Figure 6.2). In the absence of "welfare stigma," Ashenfelter notes, individuals will choose to accept benefits under the transfer scheme if their income exclusive of transfer benefits Y is less than some critical amount Y^* and will decide not to accept such benefits otherwise. Ashenfelter specifies the natural logarithm of Y as a function of a vector of variables $\mathbf{X}$ and a normally distributed error term e and uses a conventional model of utility maximization to show that $\ln Y^*$ is approximately equal to $\ln Y_B + 0.5 s\tau_Y$, where s is the uncompensated own-wage elasticity of labor supply and Y_B and τ_Y are the break-even income level and marginal tax rate of the NIT plan for which the individual is eligible. Thus, if $\ln Y \geq \ln Y^*$, then the individual will choose segment fb of Figure 6.2 (and thus will choose not to accept transfer payments); otherwise, the individual will choose segment bv' (and so will accept payments).

This leads immediately to a simple probit model for the decision of experimentals to receive, or not to receive, payments under the transfer scheme: The probability that an individual will accept payments and locate along budget line segment bv' is given by $\text{Pr} \{\ln Y - \ln Y^* \leq 0\} = \text{Pr} \{e/\sigma_e \leq [\ln Y_B + 0.5 s\tau_Y - \mathbf{Xb}]/\sigma_e\}$, where σ_e is the standard deviation of e; hence,

$$\text{Pr} \{\text{individual is on segment } bv'\}$$
$$= F[(\ln Y_B + 0.5 s\tau_Y - \mathbf{Xb})/\sigma_e]$$

where F is the standard normal cumulative density function. Together with the complementary expression for the probability that an experimental is on segment fb, this forms a simple probit model that can be estimated using data on experimental observations only. On the other hand, the probability density of earnings for any control observation is the conventional expression $f[(\ln Y - \mathbf{Xb})/\sigma_e]/\sigma_e$, where f is the standard normal density function; note that the parameters $\mathbf{b}$ and σ_e are also in the expressions for experimentals. Thus, one can also form a complete likelihood function that can be estimated using the entire sample of experimentals and controls.[36]

This provides a simple method for analyzing an experimental's choice of budget line segment using specifications derived using considerations of utility maximization. It does not, of course, permit one to analyze hours of work given choice of budget line segment. However, Burtless and Hausman (1978) derive a model for analyzing both aspects of behavior. In its essentials, their model is a variant of the complete budget constraint (cbc) procedures used to analyze labor supply in the presence of taxation, as discussed in Chapter 4. (Indeed, Burtless and Hausman show how it may be used to analyze taxation effects on labor supply as well as transfer effects.) The key difference between behavior in the presence of taxation and behavior in the presence of transfers is that budget lines with taxes but not transfers are generally concave (as shown, e.g., in Figure 4.3), whereas budget lines with transfers are not (see, e.g., Figure 6.2) – so that in the latter case, a local utility maximum is not necessarily a global utility maximum. (The break-even problem, discussed earlier, is one manifestation of this fact.) This means that, in analyzing labor supply in the presence of transfers, it is in general necessary to locate all local optima and then check each to see which is the global optimum. (In contrast, in the presence of taxes but not transfers, there is one local optimum, which is also the global

---

[36] Like most other work on this issue, the approach as outlined in the text ignores welfare stigma and, in effect, assumes that the decision to accept payments under the transfer scheme is no different from the decision to accept a wage of $(1 - \tau_Y)W$ and exogenous income $V + \tau_Y(Y_B - V)$ rather than a wage of W and exogenous income of V. However, as Ashenfelter observes, the probit model for the decision of experimentals to accept or not accept transfer benefits can be estimated separately from the earnings function for controls; this allows the parameters of the model to differ as between experimentals and controls and may be one way to see if welfare stigma is present. However, Ashenfelter (1980b) concludes that there is little evidence to suggest that strong stigma effects are present. Moffitt (1979a) takes a somewhat different approach: In analyzing hours of work, he adopts a specification in which the net wage is not $W(1 - \tau_Y - \tau_Z)$, where τ_Y is the NIT marginal tax rate and τ_Z is the marginal tax rate of other programs for which the individual is eligible, but rather $W(1 - s\tau_Y - \tau_Z)$, where s is a stigma parameter. (Exogenous income is treated in a comparable manner.) The net wage is then split into two components, a non-NIT net wage, $W(1 - \tau_Z)$, and an NIT net wage, $-s\tau_YW$; and similarly for exogenous income. As shown in Table 6.2, the coefficients on NIT and non-NIT wage rates and exogenous income are rather different from each other, but there is no particular pattern to these differences.

optimum for the individual.) Thus, for example, in the case of a two-segment budget line like the one shown in Figure 6.2, one would first locate the individual's local optimum along bv', then locate the individual's local optimum along the second segment bf, and, finally, determine which of these two local optima is the optimum optimorum.

Burtless and Hausman (1978), however, work with a specific functional form in which this laborious procedure can be considerably simplified: They make indirect utility u^* on budget line segment s a function of the net wage $W(s)$ and exogenous income $V(s)$ applicable to that segment and of a random taste variable e; and, for their particular functional form, e values larger (smaller) than a critical value e^* always imply that the individual will choose the second (first) segment of the budget line, bf (bv'). By Roy's Identity, hours worked when an individual chooses segment s are given by

$$H(s) = \{\partial u^*[W(s), V(s), e]/\partial W(s)\}$$
$$\div \{\partial u^*[W(s), V(s), e]/\partial V(s)\}$$
$$= H[W(s), V(s), e]$$

This implies that expected hours of work for a given individual eligible for the transfer scheme are

$$H_p = \int_{-\infty}^{e^*} H(1) f(e)\, de + \int_{e^*}^{\infty} H(2) f(e)\, de$$

whereas expected hours of work for any control observation are $\int_{-\infty}^{+\infty} H(2) f(e)\, de$, where 1 refers to the first segment bv' and 2 refers to the second segment bf (or, in the case of controls, to the *only* segment, vbf) of the budget line. In either case, if there are errors of measurement or of optimization ν, then actual hours of work H are simply $H = H_p + \nu$; hence one may estimate the parameters of the indirect utility function u^* and of the distributions of ν and e by minimizing the value of $\sum_{i=1}^{N} (H - H_p)^2$ over the entire sample of N individuals (including both experimentals and controls) with respect to these parameters. (If ν is assumed to be normally distributed, this is equivalent to maximum-likelihood estimation.)

The particular functional form of Burtless and Hausman constrains labor supply to be positive for all individuals (although

Hausman, 1980, 1981a, has modified their cbc procedure to allow for zero hours of work). A more serious limitation is that the relative simplicity of the estimation procedure depends heavily on the specific form of the indirect utility function u^* and, in particular, on the fact that the probability that a given experimental observation will choose segment fb (or bv') is uniquely determined by that observation's value of e (and, in particular, by whether that observation's e exceeds or is less than the critical value e^*). For other specifications of the indirect utility function, estimation will usually be more cumbersome; in particular, in the more general case, the observation's e will determine only one or more local optima, and it will typically be necessary to determine which of the local optima is the global optimum. (For details, see Heckman and MaCurdy, 1981.) Alternatively, one might use two-stage procedures similar to those discussed in Chapter 4 (e.g., by using an approach like Ashenfelter's to determine the probability of occupying either budget line segment and then using selectivity bias-corrected regression to fit hours of work functions for observations on each segment).

6.5.   Negative income tax experimental results

With Section 6.4 as prologue, I now summarize and discuss some of the results – both on conventional labor supply parameters and on the labor supply effects of transfer schemes – that appear in studies of the experimental NIT data. The number of such studies is vast;[37] although this summary, therefore, cannot pretend to be

---

[37] For a survey of studies of the NIT experiments, see Moffitt and Kehrer (1981). The experiments have spawned a vast array of publications, including (i) official summary reports by the U.S. Department of Health, Education and Welfare; (ii) "final reports," consisting of multivolume collections of studies and descriptive material; (ii) special issues or symposia in the *Journal of Human Resources*; (iv) collections of selected studies, taken from the final reports, in book form; (v) conference volumes, consisting of papers presented at conferences sponsored by the Brookings Institution; and (vi) innumerable research memoranda, working papers, and journal articles. References of type (vi) are mentioned in the text, passim. A brief listing of references of type (i) −(v) by experiment is as follows: *New Jersey–Pennsylvania*: Mathematica Policy Research (1976), Pechman and Timpane (1975), Rees (1974), Rees and Watts (1973), U.S. Department of Health, Education and Welfare (1973), and Watts and Rees (1977). *Rural*: Bawden and Harrar, eds. (1977b), Palmer and Pechman (1978), and U.S. Department of Health, Education and Welfare (1976). *Gary*: Kehrer (1979) and Kehrer, McDonald, and Moffitt (1980). *Seattle–Denver*: Robins et al., eds.

exhaustive, it is nevertheless representative of the wide range of results that have appeared to date.

Table 6.1 sets out some of the principal features of many of the main studies of labor supply based on the experimental data.[38] As Table 6.1 implies, virtually all of the studies are concerned, either implicitly or explicitly, with obtaining estimates of the parameters of static labor supply models; to date, empirical analysis of dynamic labor supply models using the NIT experimental data is in its infancy.[39] Accordingly, I focus on estimates derived from static models.

First, consider Table 6.2, which summarizes the results of a representative group of studies of the experimental data regarding uncompensated and compensated own-wage elasticities and exogenous income elasticities of labor supply.[40] On the whole, the results for husbands shown in Table 6.2 agree with those derived in first-generation studies: Each of these three elasticities is usually rather small in absolute value. However, the range of estimates for each of these elasticities is hardly trivial: The uncompensated

(1980), Spiegelman and Yaeger (1980), and U.S. Department of Health, Education and Welfare (1978).

[38] Like everything else in this section, Table 6.1 is a summary; for details, one must consult each specific study. The descriptions in Table 6.1 (and the estimates in Tables 6.2 and 6.3) refer to what appear to be (and, in many cases, to what are explicitly labeled) the central findings of each study; however, it is worth noting that in many cases the authors of each study also present alternative estimates and use alternative methodological approaches in addition to the ones discussed here.

[39] For an exception, see Moffitt (1980).

[40] In most cases, the results shown in Table 6.2 are taken directly from the papers cited. In other cases, I have calculated these elasticities myself, using the approximate means of the sample(s) used in each study; see note 41. In still other cases, the information required for calculation of some elasticities implied by the results of a given study is simply not available, either because the relevant labor supply parameters were not estimated (e.g., Burtless and Hausman, 1978, do not consider the labor supply of wives or of single female household heads) or because authors do not provide information (e.g., sample mean values of the variables) required for calculation of certain elasticities. It should, therefore, be stressed that the figures presented in Table 6.2 are approximate and that Table 6.2 is a summary; for details, one must consult each specific study. (See Tables 4.2 and 4.3 for further results derived from the experimental data by Burtless and Hausman, 1978; Hausman, 1980; Hausman and Wise, 1976, 1977.) As emphasized in Chapters 4 and 5, the elasticities may differ from one study to another – even when they obtain the same point estimates – if the sample means differ.

Table 6.1. *Major characteristics of experimental NIT data studies*

Author(s)	Characteristics of sample; dependent variable	Budget line specification	Estimation technique
New Jersey–Pennsylvania			
Watts et al. (1974)	White, black and Hispanic men remaining as husbands and in panel throughout experiment and not in the two "least-generous" experimental NIT plans; hours of work per week (with hours of nonworking persons set at zero)	"θ, G, τ" specification (see text)	Least squares
Cain et al. (1974)	White, black, and Hispanic women remaining as wives and in panel throughout experiment; hours of work per week (with hours of nonworking persons set at zero)	"T, τ_p, B_p" specification (see text)	Least squares
Rees (1974)	White, black, and Hispanic husband–wife families remaining as husband–wife families and in panel throughout experiment; hours of work per week (with hours of nonworking persons set at zero)	Dummy variable, $= 1$ if eligible for an NIT payment, $= 0$ otherwise	Least squares
Kerachsky & Mallar (1976)	White husbands and wives both of whom are at work; hours of work per week	See text	2SLS
Hausman & Wise (1976)	White husbands; hours of work per week (computed as ratio of earnings to a computed wage rate)	Linearized budget constraint with tax rate set at $\tau_{\bar{H}}$ (see text)	FIML, with correction for truncation bias due to exclusion of persons with prior incomes $\geq 1.5 Y_B$

Study	Population; dependent variable	Role of taxes	Estimation method
Hausman & Wise (1977)	Husbands; hours worked per year (computed as ratio of earnings to a computed wage rate)	Role of taxes ignored	Same as Hausman & Wise (1976)
Cogan (1978)	White husbands; hours of work per week	Dummy variables for eligibility for and receipt of NIT payments	Least squares
Rural Ashenfelter (1978c)	Husbands and wives (pooled observations for each year of experiment); change in earnings from one year to the next	i. G and τ entered linearly ii. τ and B_p entered linearly	Least squares
Gary Burtless & Hausman (1978)	Black husbands (nonworkers excluded); hours worked per week	Linearized budget constraint with tax rate set at its current value (see text)	FIML (see text), with income effect constrained to be negative
Moffitt (1979a)	Husbands, wives, single female heads; hours worked per month	"Averaged" tax rate $\bar{\tau}$ calculated separately for NIT and for other tax/transfer schemes	Tobit (to correct for fact that hours worked can never be negative)
Hausman & Wise (1979)	Black males; monthly earnings	Dummy variable, = 1 if eligible for NIT payment, = 0 otherwise	FIML, with correction for attrition of experimental and control subjects (or GLS, without attrition correction)
Greenberg, Moffitt, & Friedmann (1981)	Husbands, wives, single female heads (pooled quarterly observations for middle two years of experiment); quarterly earnings	Dummy variable, = 1 if eligible for an NIT payment, = 0 otherwise	Tobit (to correct for fact that earnings can never be negative)

Table 6.1. *(cont.)*

Author(s)	Characteristics of sample; dependent variable	Budget line specification	Estimation technique
Seattle–Denver			
Keeley et al. (1978a, b)	Persons classified as husbands/wives/single female household heads as of start of experiment; hours worked per year	Linearized budget constraint with tax rate set at τ_p, and supplementary vector of above-break-even variables	Tobit (to correct for fact that hours worked can never be negative)
Burtless & Greenberg (1982)	Same as Keeley et al. (1978a, b)	Same as Keeley et al. (1978a, b) but with linearized budget constraint variables interacted with dummy variable = 1 if in five-year experiment, = 0 if in three-year experiment	Same as Keeley et al. (1978a, b)
Robins & West (1980)	Same as Keeley et al. (1978a, b)	Linearized budget constraint with tax rate set at τ_p, interacted with a measure of probability of being above break-even during the experiment	Tobit (to correct for fact that hours worked can never be negative)
Keeley & Robins (1980)	Same as Keeley et al. (1978a, b) but with Hispanics included	Same as Keeley et al. (1978a, b)	Same as Keeley et al. (1978a, b)

Johnson & Pencavel (1982a)	Husband--wife families (both spouses working), single female heads who work; change in earnings	Linearized budget constraint (with tax rate set at τ_p), Stone–Geary utility function	Nonlinear least squares with selectivity bias correction for exclusion of nonworkers and instruments for linearized budget constraint variables
Johnson & Pencavel (1982b)	Same as Johnson & Pencavel (1982a) but with level of earnings as dependent variable	Linearized budget constraint (with tax rate set at τ^*), modified Stone – Geary utility function	Same as Johnson & Pencavel (1982a)

Table 6.2. *Summary of wage and exogenous income elasticities reported in experimental NIT data studies*

Author(s), reference	Husbands			Wives			Single female household heads		
	$\eta(W)$	$\eta_{\underline{U}}(W)$	$\eta(V)$	$\eta(W)$	$\eta_{\underline{U}}(W)$	$\eta(V)$	$\eta(W)$	$\eta_{\underline{U}}(W)$	$\eta(V)$
New Jersey–Pennsylvania									
Watts et al. (1974, p. 193)									
Whites	– 0.06	– 0.11 to – 0.07	0.02 to 0.10						
Blacks	– 0.07 to – 0.03	– 0.05 to – 0.01	– 0.05 to – 0.03						
Hispanics	0.01 to 0.28	0.07 to 0.30	– 0.09 to – 0.04						
Kerachsky & Mallar (1976, Tables B1, B2)	nc	– 0.68 to – 0.37	≈ 0	nc	0.93 to 1.48	≈ 0			
Hausman & Wise (1976, p. 436)	0.14	nc	– 0.02						
Hausman & Wise (1977, p. 932)	0.10	nc	– 0.02						
Rural									
Ashenfelter (1978c, p. 127)									
i.	0.21	nc	0 to 0.02	0.84	nc	0 to 0.01			
ii.	0.17	nc	– 0.01 to 0	0.94	nc	0 to 0.01			

398

Gary

Burtless & Hausman (1978, p. 1123)	0.00	nc	-0.05*						
Moffitt (1979a, p. 484)									
NIT effect	-0.01	0.02	-0.05	0.16	0.07	0.07	-0.12	-0.04	-0.23
Non-NIT effect	-0.01	0.76	-0.13	0.46	0.43	0.45	-0.27	-0.18	-0.20

Seattle-Denver

Keeley et al. (1978a, p.882; 1978b, p. 12)	0.02	0.10	-0.13	-0.00	0.22	-0.95	-0.03	0.12	-0.32
Burtless & Greenberg (1982, p. 490)									
3-year experiment	0.08	0.11	-0.06	0.19	0.37	-0.78	0.05	0.17	-0.26
5-year experiment	-0.12	0.06	-0.30	-0.36	-0.05	-1.32	-0.23	0.01	-0.46
Robins & West (1980, p. 521)	0.06	0.12	-0.08	0.13	0.30	-0.61	-0.05	0.09	-0.24
Keeley & Robins (1980, p. 317)	-0.09	0.05	-0.21	-0.00	0.17	-0.64	-0.08	0.07	-0.24
Johnson & Pencavel (1982a, p. 228)	-0.19	0.10	-0.15	0.09	0.18	-0.12	-0.01	0.12	-0.17
Johnson & Pencavel (1982b, p. 20)									
Short run	-0.06	0.13	-0.10	0.08	0.16	-0.11	0.07	0.15	-0.11
Long run	0.02	0.19	-0.08	0.12	0.18	-0.07	0.20	0.29	-0.12

Note: $\eta(W) = (\partial H/\partial W)(W/H)$, where W is the net wage (adjusted for taxes, etc.) and H is hours of work, that is, $\eta(W)$ is the uncompensated own-wage elasticity of labor supply.

$\eta_{\bar{U}}(W) = (\partial H/\partial W)_{\bar{U}}(W/H)$, where W and H are as just defined and subscript $\bar{U}$ means "with income adjusted so as to keep utility constant," that is, $\eta_{\bar{U}}(W)$ is the compensated own-wage elasticity of labor supply.

$\eta(V) = (\partial H/\partial V)(V/H)$, where V is exogenous income (adjusted for taxes, etc.) and H is as previously defined, that is, $\eta(V)$ is the exogenous income elasticity of labor supply.

nc, Not computed due to insufficient information; *, constrained to be negative.

own-wage elasticity ranges from -0.19 (Johnson and Pencavel, 1982a, Seattle–Denver husbands) to $+0.21$ (one of Ashenfelter's estimates for rural husbands); the compensated own-wage elasticity estimates lie between -0.68 (Kerachsky and Mallar, New Jersey–Pennsylvania white husbands) and $+0.76$ (Moffitt, Gary black husbands); the estimated exogenous income elasticity of labor supply goes from -0.21 (Keeley Robins, Seattle–Denver husbands) to $+0.10$ (Watts et al., New Jersey–Pennsylvania white husbands). A number of the results shown in Table 6.2 appear to suggest that the uncompensated own-wage elasticity of husbands is positive. This appears to be in conflict with first-generation results (in which this elasticity is generally negative or zero). However, in principle much of the difference could be attributable to mere sampling variation or to differences in the samples being studied: Many of the results in Table 6.2 are imprecisely estimated, and such results, of course, refer to relatively low-wage, low-income samples, whereas most first-generation studies were concerned with a somewhat broader spectrum of the population. Differences in estimation technique may also be part of the explanation: As noted in Table 6.1, several of the studies use an estimation method such as Tobit or selection bias-corrected regression (Moffitt, Keeley et al., and Johnson and Pencavel), whereas virtually all first-generation studies use ordinary least squares.

Next, consider the elasticities obtained from the experimental studies for married women. With some significant exceptions to be noted presently, the broad implications of the results shown in Table 6.2 agree with those of previous studies. Here, as in earlier studies, the labor supply of married women appears to be fairly elastic with respect to wage rates (on either an uncompensated or an income-compensated basis) and to exogenous income. Again, however, the range of values for each elasticity in Table 6.2 is fairly wide: The uncompensated own-wage elasticity of married women's labor supply ranges between -0.00 (Keeley et al., Seattle–Denver) and $+0.94$ (Ashenfelter, rural wives); the estimated compensated own-wage elasticity is between $+0.07$ (Moffitt, Gary wives) and $+1.48$ (Kerachsky and Mallar, New Jersey–Pennsylvania wives); the exogenous income elasticity estimates are between -0.95 (Keeley et al., Seattle–Denver) and $+0.45$ (Moffitt, Gary wives).

Because the number of unmarried female family heads was not

particularly large in the New Jersey–Pennsylvania and rural experiments, elasticity estimates for this group are relatively few in number and appear to be available only for the Gary and Seattle–Denver experiments. Estimates of the exogenous income elasticity for this group are between – 0.11 (Johnson and Pencavel, 1982b, Seattle–Denver) and – 0.32 (Keeley et al., Seattle–Denver). The range of estimates of the compensated and uncompensated wage elasticities for this group is rather wide: The latter is estimated at between – 0.27 (Moffitt, Gary) and + 0.20 (Johnson and Pencavel, 1982b, Seattle–Denver), whereas the former is between – 0.18 (Moffitt, Gary) and + 0.29 (Johnson and Pencavel, 1982b, Seattle–Denver).

The ranges of these estimated elasticities for any given demographic group are not only considerable; they also include magnitudes that can only be called anomalous. For example, Moffitt, Watts et al., and Kerachsky and Mallar report negative compensated own-wage labor supply elasticities; Kerachsky and Mallar, Watts et al., Ashenfelter, and Moffitt report exogenous income elasticities that are either positive or zero. Finally, both the results of Keeley and Robins and the results of Keeley et al. appear to contradict one stylized fact that has generally been an article of faith among researchers: In these studies, the uncompensated own-wage elasticity of labor supply of married women is virtually zero. (Indeed, in the Keeley et al. studies, this elasticity is actually slightly smaller for married women than it is for married men.)[41]

---

[41] The elasticities shown in Table 6.2 for six different studies based on the Seattle–Denver experimental data provide an example of the extent to which estimates can differ even when different studies consider the same experimental site. Several factors may help account for these differences (see Johnson and Pencavel, 1980, pp. 37–9; 1982a, pp. 230–1, for further discussion). First, both Johnson–Pencavel studies (1982a, b) allow for intrafamily cross-substitution effects, whereas the other Seattle–Denver studies constrain such effects to equal zero (that is, assume that each family member treats the earnings of other family members as equivalent to property income). (Also, recall from Chapter 3 that, in models with zero intrafamily cross-substitution effects, the "property income" variable – actual property income plus earnings of other family members – is endogenous. However, Burtless and Greenberg, 1982; Keeley et al., 1978a, b; Keeley and Robins, 1980; and Robins and West, 1980; ignore this endogeneity.) Second, both Johnson–Pencavel studies use selection bias-corrected regression (Procedure VIII, in terms of Table 4.1), whereas the other Seattle–Denver studies use Tobit (Procedure III, in terms of Table 4.1).

Burtless and Greenberg (1982) provide both a confirmation and a contradiction in their study, which differentiates between persons eligible for a three- and for a five-year NIT in the Seattle–Denver experiment. Their results appear to support Metcalf's (1973, 1974) hypothesis that a longer-run NIT should have both a larger income effect and a smaller substitution effect than a short-run NIT. (However, Burtless and Greenberg derive their estimates in the context of a single-period, not a life cycle, model. Moreover, a finding that the substitution *parameter* is smaller and the income *parameter* is larger for five-year *as opposed* to three-year *experimentals* is not quite a demonstration that a *given* set of individuals would have different substitution and income *responses* to NIT programs of different *durations*.) Unfortunately, their results only deepen the mystery about the uncompensated own-wage elasticity of married women's labor supply. The study most comparable to theirs, Keeley et al. (1978a, b), yields a zero elasticity, whereas Burtless and Greenberg (1982) get estimates of 0.19 and – 0.36 for the three- and five-year groups, respectively. To some extent, this simply reflects the fact that their parameter estimates are

(As Johnson and Pencavel, 1982a, p. 231, observe, in this setting Tobit is a special case of selection bias-corrected regression, in the sense that the latter does not assume that hours worked fall continuously to zero as the wage falls to the reservation level.) Third, both Johnson–Pencavel studies allow for errors in the measurement of, for example, net wage rates and, in particular, for the possibility that these errors may be endogenous to labor supply; the other Seattle–Denver studies do not. Fourth, the Johnson–Pencavel studies use variants of the Stone–Geary utility function, in which husbands' and wives' leisure times are constrained to be net (income-compensated) substitutes and in which income and substitution effects are nonlinear functions of the wage and of hours of work; in contrast, the other Seattle–Denver studies use linear approximations in which income and substitution effects are parameters. Fifth, the six studies consider somewhat different samples. Burtless and Greenberg (1982) and Keeley et al. (1978a, b) do not include Hispanics, whereas the other studies do; Robins and West (1980) exclude control subjects, whereas the remaining studies do not; both Johnson–Pencavel studies refer to persons whose marital status remained unchanged over the period of observation, whereas the other four studies categorize individuals according to marital status as of the *start* of the period of observation and do not require that marital status remain the same over time. Finally, Burtless and Greenberg (1982) distinguish between different experimental durations; the other five studies do not. That these differences in procedures might lead to differences in results is clear. What is much less clear is why these differences in procedure have led to the differences in results that actually occurred and that are shown in Table 6.2.

imprecise (most of the differences in the parameter estimates between the three- and five-year groups would not be judged statistically different from zero at reasonable levels of significance). However, imprecision is one of the main problems besetting analysts who hope to use nonexperimental estimates. Although not exactly unexpected, its appearance in the experimental studies is hardly comforting.

In sum, it appears that, considered as a whole, analyses of the experimental data have produced a range of labor supply elasticities that is at least as wide as that generated by first-generation studies and have produced at least an equal number of puzzles and anomalies. The variation in elasticities implied by estimates based on the experimental data is all the more surprising because the experiments were concerned with relatively homogeneous subsets of the total population (for the most part, with poor people), for which one might have expected to obtain stable estimates falling in a fairly narrow range.[42]

Table 6.3 summarizes some of the main experimental data results on the labor supply effects of the NIT experiments themselves. Except in a few instances (notably for blacks in New Jersey–Pennsylvania), all of the estimated experimental effects shown in Table 6.3 are negative. Most, particularly those for husbands, are rather small in absolute value; the estimated response of wives or unmarried female family heads to a given experiment is generally somewhat larger in absolute value than the estimated response of husbands. Finally, broadly speaking the range of estimates of these experimental effects is also rather small, particularly for husbands, both across experiments and for different studies of a given experiment.

However, Greenberg, Moffitt, and Friedmann (1981) raise the possibility that systematic underreporting of earnings by experimentals may have exaggerated the absolute magnitude of the reductions in earnings and in labor supply induced by the NIT

---

[42] Moffitt and Kehrer (1981, p. 143) write that "the evidence so far seems to indicate fairly conclusively that experimental estimates [of income and substitution effects] are both smaller [in absolute value] and more robust [i.e., less subject to variation] than non-experimental estimates." (For similar statements, see Danziger, Haveman, and Plotnick, 1981, p. 1015, note 62; Keeley, 1981, p. 172.) In view of the results shown in Table 6.2, however, such remarks seem somewhat overstated.

Table 6.3. *Summary of estimates of proportionate changes in labor supply induced by NIT experiments reported in experimental NIT data studies (%)*

Author(s), reference	Husbands	Wives	Single female household heads
New Jersey–Pennsylvania			
Rees (1974, pp. 174–5)			
Whites	− 5.6	− 30.6	
Blacks	+ 2.3	− 2.2	
Hispanics	− 0.7	− 55.4	
Watts et al. (1974, as summarized			
by Kerachsky & Mallar, 1976, p. 8.22 +)			
Whites – with $H > 0$	− 1.3		
Whites – with $H \geq 0$	− 5.8		
Blacks – with $H > 0$	+ 1.6		
Blacks – with $H \geq 0$	+ 3.4		
Cain et al. (1974, as summarized by			
Kerachsky & Mallar; 1976, p. 8.22 +)			
Whites – with $H \geq 0$		− 17.0	
Blacks – with $H \geq 0$		+ 10.4	
Kerachsky & Mallar (1976, p. 8.22 +			
(husbands) and p. 8.26 + (wives))			
Whites – with $H > 0$	− 4.4 to − 6.9	− 10.2	
Whites – with $H \geq 0$	− 8.4 to − 10.7	− 39.7	
Blacks – with $H > 0$	+ 3.5 to + 6.4	− 7.5	
Blacks – with $H \geq 0$	+ 11.1 to + 14.4	+ 0.6	

Hausman & Wise (1976, p. 437)			
With earnings as dependent variable	− 5.8		− 25.9 to − 30.0
With hours as dependent variable (below break-even observations only)	− 16.1		
With hours as dependent variable (single dummy to represent experimental effect)	− 3.8		
Cogan (1978, Tables 3 and 15) (Whites)	− 16.2		
Rural			
Ashenfelter (1978c, p. 123)		− 30.5	
With earnings as dependent variable	− 5.9		
Gary			
Burtless & Hausman (1978, p. 1124)	− 7.7		
Moffitt (1979a, p. 482)	− 2.9 to − 6.5	+ 1.0 to + 5.0	
Hausman & Wise (1979; refers to effect on earnings)			
P. 464 – analysis of variance model	− 6.5		
P. 465 – analysis of variance model with individual error component	− 6.2		
P. 466 – regression, without attrition correction	− 7.9		
P. 468 – regression, with attrition correction	− 8.2		
Greenberg, Moffitt, & Friedmann (1981, p. 586)			
With earnings as dependent variable			
Interview data	− 3.9	− 2.7	− 23.2
Employer data	+ 0.3	+ 14.3	+ 0.3

Table 6.3. *(cont.)*

Author(s), reference	Husbands	Wives	Single female household heads
Seattle–Denver			
Keeley et al. (1978a, p. 14)	− 5.3	− 22.0	− 11.2
Keeley et al. (1978b, p. 884)	− 6.0 to − 7.0	− 16.0 to − 17.0	− 12.0 to − 15.0
Robins & West (1980, p. 521)	− 7.0	− 25.0	− 15.0
Keeley & Robins (1980, pp. 319, 330)	− 8.2 to − 8.7	− 18.2 to − 19.1	− 9.5 to − 10.0

Note: Entries in this table give estimates derived in selected studies of the experimental NIT data of the percentage change in hours of work (relative to comparable individuals in the control group) associated with eligibility for NIT payments, other things (as controlled for by regression) being equal, *except that* in some instances noted in the table (e.g., Ashenfelter, 1978c, and some estimates presented by Hausman and Wise, 1976, 1979) the "experimental effect" refers to the percentage change in *earnings* associated with the experimental "treatment."

experiments. They were able to estimate the effect of the Gary NIT experiment on earnings using two different measures of earnings: first, as reported by experimentals and controls themselves in periodic interviews conducted during the course of the Gary experiment; and, second, as reported by the employers of the experimentals and controls. Greenberg, Moffitt, and Friedmann (1981, p. 585) found that both experimentals and controls did not report all of their earnings (as recorded in the employer data) when they were interviewed and also found greater underreporting among experimentals than among controls. (For example, experimental husbands did not report 29.8 percent of their earnings vs. 27.7 percent for control husbands. The comparable figures for wives are 48.9 and 37.1 percent, whereas the comparable figures for female family heads are 45.4 and 36.4 percent.) As shown in Table 6.3, estimated NIT effects derived from the interview data are negative, but estimated effects on earnings derived from the employer data are either approximately zero or else positive. Although their data do not permit them to check for underreporting of hours worked, Greenberg, Moffitt, and Friedmann conclude that estimates of experimental effects on labor supply derived from interview data may seriously overstate the actual effect.

Subject to this caveat, which raises important questions that deserve much further study, it appears that the experimental studies have been fairly successful in providing measures of the impacts of the experiments they were designed to evaluate, even if they have not done much to clarify various unresolved questions about conventional labor supply elasticities. Estimates of experimental effects derived from the experimental data generally fall within a relatively narrow range, even though estimates of wage and income effects derived from the same data frequently do not. Thus, errors and anomalies in estimates of conventional wage and income effects may have more or less offset each other: It may be easier to estimate the experimental response itself than it is to estimate the wage and income effects (and, perhaps, stigma effects) that underlie this response.

Is it, therefore, correct to conclude that the experimental studies' estimates of experimental effects are useful for purposes of analysis and policy even if these studies' estimates of income and substitution effects – like those derived in first-generation work – span too broad a range to be of much use for analysis or policy? Many researchers would answer this question in the negative. As Ashenfelter (1978c, p. 125) points out, one important reason for the experiments was (or, at least, should have been) to estimate "the effects of variations in the tax rate and guarantee levels of the various experimental plans" and, thus, to estimate not only the net outcomes (in terms of labor supply changes) of the experiments but also the structural determinants – substitution and income elasticities or, more or less equivalently, tax rate and guarantee effects – that generated those net outcomes. Ashenfelter goes on to add:

> The importance of accurate estimates of these [tax rate and guarantee] effects cannot be overstated. First, they are needed for consideration of the impact of other potential programs. Since tax and guarantee levels in any actual negative income tax program are a subject for public decision, it could be argued that obtaining reliable estimates of the labor supply effect of variations in these parameters is the entire rationale for the experiment and that failure to obtain such estimates would constitute a major failure of the experiment. Second, it is important to verify through variation in the tax and guarantee level whether income and substitution effects were what lay behind the observed response to the experiment. Otherwise, there always remains the possibility that the experimental effect was due to some other causal mechanism altogether.

> It is important to have this issue clarified since it has wide implications for the study of labor supply behavior as well as many normative aspects of both taxation and welfare policy. In effect, the experimental data offer an extraordinary opportunity to put some quite basic theoretical structures to a test and this opportunity should not be missed.

> As it turns out, this issue does not seem to have received nearly the attention it deserves by the authors of the reports on either the [New Jersey–Pennsylvania] or the rural negative income tax experiments.

6.6. Social Security and labor supply

Having discussed taxes in Section 6.2 and transfers in Sections 6.3–6.5, I will now consider the Social Security system, which is a combination of taxes *and* transfers: In general terms, the Social Security system levies taxes on earnings and makes transfer payments according to age *and* earnings.

The tax component of the Social Security system is simple to describe: Working individuals, regardless of age, pay a flat proportion τ_P of their earnings up to a maximum earnings amount (called the *wage base*) E_M, and pay $\tau_P E_M$ if their earnings exceed E_M. Thus, regardless of age, *payments to* Social Security are given by

$$(6.36) \quad \Lambda_P(t) = \tau_P W(t) H(t) \quad \text{if} \quad W(t) H(t) \le E_M$$
$$\Lambda_P(t) = \tau_P E_M \quad \text{if} \quad W(t) H(t) > E_M$$

where t refers to age. Note that someone who earns less than the wage base E_M faces a marginal rate of Social Security tax of τ_P, whereas someone who earns more than E_M faces a zero marginal tax rate. In 1983, E_M was \$35,700, whereas τ_P was 0.067.

The transfer component of Social Security is somewhat more complicated to describe, since *receipts from* Social Security depend on one's current earnings, one's past earnings history, and the age at which one elects to start receiving benefits. In most cases, persons age 61 or less receive no payments at all from Social Security. (For exceptions, see note 43.) Benefits paid to persons age 62 or more depend on the maximum benefit amount they can receive and on their current earnings – the so-called earnings test. In turn, the maximum benefit amount Λ_{t^*} depends on prior earnings and the age t^* at which one elects to start receiving benefits: The higher the level of prior earnings or t^*, the higher Λ_{t^*} is. However, benefits actually paid Λ_R depend not only on Λ_{t^*} but also on current age t and on current earnings (if any) in excess of an age-dependent value $E_D(t)$ known as the "earnings disregard": Benefits are reduced below Λ_{t^*} by an amount τ_R (the benefit reduction rate) for each dollar of earnings in excess of $E_D(t)$. In 1983, E_D and τ_R were both zero for persons age 70 or over (who therefore receive Λ_{t^*} regardless of current earnings); were \$6,600 and .50, respectively, for persons age 65–69; and were \$4,920 and .50, respectively, for persons age 62–64. Finally, the value of Λ_{t^*} at each initial benefit age t^* was a complex function of one's previous earnings history and, of course, of t^* itself. Thus, *receipts from* Social Security are typically given by

(6.37) $\Lambda_R(t) = 0$ if $t \leq 61$

(6.38) $\Lambda_R(t) = \Lambda_{t^*}$ if $62 \leq t \leq 69$ and
                                     $W(t)\,H(t) - E_D(t) < 0$

$\Lambda_R(t) = \Lambda_{t^*} - \tau_R[\,W(t)\,H(t) - E_D(t)]$
                    if $62 \leq t \leq 69$ and
                    $\Lambda_{t^*}/\tau_R \geq W(t)\,H(t) - E_D(t) \geq 0$

$\Lambda_R(t) = 0$ if $62 \leq t \leq 69$ and
                                     $W(t)\,H(t) - E_D(t) > \Lambda_{t^*}/\tau_R > 0$

(6.39) $\Lambda_R(t) = \Lambda_{t^*}$ if $t \geq 70$

Thus, most individuals age 61 or less make payments to, but do not receive any benefits from, Social Security. Individuals age 62 or more make payments to Social Security according to their earnings, as given by (6.36); such individuals may or may not also receive benefits, depending on their current earnings and on the age at which they choose to start receiving benefits, as given by (6.37)–(6.39).[43]

---

[43] This sketch of the main features of the Social Security system simplifies in at least two significant respects. First, it ignores *employer* contributions to the system, which are determined by the same formula, (6.36), governing employee contributions. To the extent that employers shift their Social Security tax liability onto employees, the actual tax rate the employee pays is larger than the rate τ_P. Second, contrary to (6.37) –(6.39), some individuals age 61 or less do in fact receive payments *from* the system; usually, these recipients are disabled persons and some survivors (usually, widows and minor children) of workers covered by the system. (For a discussion of some of the effects of the system's disability provisions, see Parsons, 1982.) For useful background on the Social Security system, see Diamond (1977); for surveys of Social Security and of pensions (some of whose effects are similar in nature to those of Social Security that are discussed here), see Fields and Mitchell (1982), Honig and Hanoch (1980a, b) and Mitchell and Fields (1981). Diamond and Mirrlees (1978), Sheshinski (1978), and Sheshinski and Weiss (1980) discuss questions about the financing of Social Security and about risk and uncertainty, both of which are more or less ignored in the discussion in the text. Although the present discussion is concerned with the U.S. Social Security system, it is worth noting that the social security systems of other countries are basically fairly similar to the U.S. system; for example, see the capsule summary of the U.K. system in Zabalza, Pissarides, and Barton (1980).

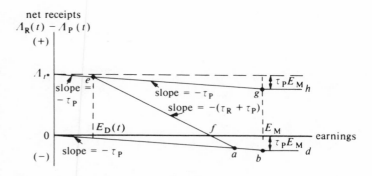

Figure 6.3. Relation between earnings and net receipts from Social Security

To see this in detail, first consider Figure 6.3, which shows the *net* receipts of individuals from Social Security, $\Lambda_R(t) - \Lambda_P(t)$, that is, the difference between receipts from and payments to Social Security. (Note that net receipts are the *negative* of the individual's liability to the Social Security system, and so are the equivalent of $-\Lambda(t)$ in expressions such as (6.9).) As before, let t^* denote the age at which the individual starts to receive Social Security benefits. Then an individual has negative net receipts at each age prior to t^* (that is, is a net contributor to the Social Security system) as given by the line 0*abd*. However, net receipts at each age between t^* and 69 are given by the line $\Lambda_{t^*}efabd$, whereas on or after age 70 receipts at each age are given by the line $\Lambda_{t^*}egh$.

Figure 6.4 expresses the same relationships shown in Figure 6.3 in terms of budget lines. In Figure 6.4, the price of the consumer good C is normalized to unity, property income is V, and the wage rate is W; $(1 - L_D)W$ is equal to E_D, the earnings disregard, whereas $(1 - L_M)W$ is equal to E_M, the wage base. In the absence of any taxes or transfers, the budget line is $1Vfq$. In the presence of Social Security taxes and transfers, however, the budget line depends on age. In particular:

(i) The budget line at each age prior to t^* is $1Vabd$, where the vertical distance between $1Vfq$ and $1Vabd$ gives the amount of Social Security taxes paid.

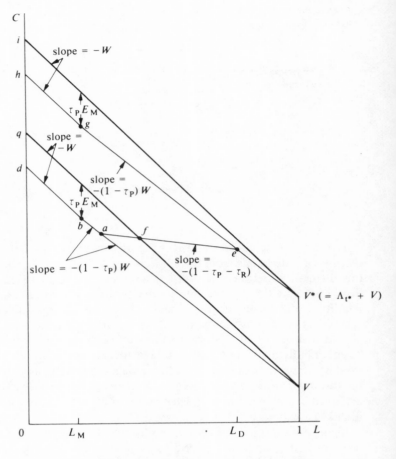

Figure 6.4.   Budget lines in the presence of Social Security taxes and transfers

(ii)   The budget line at each age between t^* and 69 is $1V^*efabd$, where the vertical distance between this line and $1vfq$ gives the net amount of Social Security benefits received. (When $1V^*efabd$ lies above $1Vfq$, the individual is a net recipient from Social Security; when it lies below $1Vfq$, the individual is a net contributor to Social Security. The break-even point, at which net contributions and receipts are zero, is f.)

(iii)   The budget line at each age starting at age 70 is $1V^*egh$, where the vertical distance between $1V^*i$ and $1V^*egh$ gives the amount of Social Security taxes paid.

Now, Figure 6.4 reduces the rather complex set of Social Security tax and transfer rules, (6.36)–(6.39), to something quite familiar: the budget line of a simple one-period labor supply model. At first glance, Figure 6.4, might, therefore, appear to be an eminently suitable point of departure for deriving theoretical predictions (e.g., about whether changing parameters such as E_D or τ_R will affect labor supply). Perhaps not surprisingly, then, Figure 6.4 or something like it has figured in a number of recent discussions of the impact of Social Security on labor supply. (For example, see Boskin, 1977; Boskin and Hurd, 1978; Browning, 1975; Keeley, 1981; Quinn, 1977.) Figure 6.4 also might seem tailor-made as a basis for developing empirical models – and, again, not surprisingly, two recent empirical studies have used empirical procedures similar to the ordered probit analysis discussed in Chapter 4 (in particular, see equation (4.51) and Figure 4.4) to see how individuals facing a "Social Security budget line" such as V^*efabd choose from among the various segments of that line that involve work (V^*e, efa, ab, or bd) or else decide not to work at all (that is, choose the point V^*). (See Pellechio, 1978; Zabalza, Pissarides, and Barton, 1980.)

Unfortunately, however, simpleminded use of the single-period budget constraint of Figure 6.4 to analyze questions about labor supply in the presence of Social Security is inappropriate. The basic reason for this is that labor supply decisions in the presence of Social Security taxes and transfers are inherently multiple-period – that is, dynamic – decisions that cannot be shoe-horned into a single-period framework, such as the one shown in Figure 6.4. This is most easily seen by considering the meaning of Λ_{t^*} and of V.

First, consider Λ_{t^*}. Contrary to what Figure 6.4 seems to imply, Λ_{t^*} is not a constraint (that is, exogenous) but a choice variable (that is, endogenous): The individual is free to decide t^* (the date on which benefits will commence), and changing t^* automatically changes Λ_{t^*}. This occurs as a result of two separate features of the Social Security system: the *actuarial adjustment* (AA) and the *automatic benefit recomputation* (ABR). The purpose of the AA provision is to ensure that postponing t^* does not change the discounted present value of the stream of future Social Security benefits that the individual will receive over the rest of his life. If so – for example, if the present value of the benefits that someone age 62 will receive over the rest of his life if he retires now is the same as the present value of the (higher, but deferred) benefits that he would receive were he to retire next year – then the actuarial adjustment to benefits is said to be "actuarially fair."[44] There is some controversy about whether benefit adjustments under the AA provision are indeed actuarially fair; Burkhauser (1980) and Burkhauser and Turner (1978, 1980a, 1981) say no, whereas Blinder, Gordon, and Wise (1980, 1981) suggest that in many cases AA is either fair or a little more than fair, at least up to $t^* = 65$.

It is, therefore, not clear whether AA does or does not discourage postponement of t^*. There is also controversy about the extent to which the second kind of adjustment of Λ_{t^*}, ABR, encourages postponement (Blinder, Gordon, and Wise, 1980, 1981; Burkhauser and Turner, 1981; Reimers, 1980). Under ABR, Λ_{t^*} is based on one's earnings during one's "best earnings years." Thus, in an era of inflation and secular real wage growth, one can raise one's Λ_{t^*} by working another year at a relatively high wage, thereby substituting a year of high(er) earnings for the worst of the prior years that would otherwise have been included in the best earnings years used under ABR to calculate Λ_{t^*}.

In any event, both the AA and ABR provisions of the Social Security system mean that the individual must compare the costs and benefits of setting t^* at 62, 63, . . . : If he chooses to start receiving benefits at age 62, then he gets a lower Λ_{t^*}, Λ_{62}, immediately; if he waits another year, then he gets a higher Λ_{t^*}, Λ_{63}, next year; and so on. (More precisely, the individual must compare

---

[44] Note that this definition of actuarial fairness, which is used in most discussions of the subject, ignores the fact that someone who postpones receiving benefits for another year also, in effect, elects to go on paying contributions to the system for another year. If receipt of benefits is taken to be synonymous with retirement (that is, with zero hours of work and, thus, zero earnings), however, then someone who starts receiving benefits now not only starts to receive benefits sooner but also stops paying contributions sooner. In other words, actuarial fairness should entail constancy in the present value of the stream of benefits *net of* contributions, rather than of the stream of benefits as such.

the maximized stream of utility he will enjoy over the rest of his life, which depends on his consumption and leisure at all future dates, if he sets t^* at 62, 63, . . . , with the stream he will enjoy if he sets t^* at 63, 64, ...) Clearly, there is no sensible way to treat such intertemporal trade-offs in a single-period model.

Now consider V. Contrary to what Figure 6.4 seems to imply, V, like Λ_{t^*}, is not a constraint but a choice variable: As emphasized in Chapter 5, V (property income) is proportional to asset holdings Z, where the factor of proportionality is r, the rate of interest; and Z is in turn a function of life cycle choices subject to constraints, including, of course, those implicit in the Social Security system. (See J. Smith, 1975.) In general, then, changing the parameters of the Social Security system (e.g., making benefits more generous by raising Λ_{t^*} at all initial benefit ages t^*, reducing τ_R, etc.) will change the location of V as well as the rest of the budget line(s) shown in Figure 6.4. Treating V as exogenous and using Figure 6.4 to discuss the impact of changing Social Security benefits is, therefore, likely to produce misleading results, both in theoretical analyses[45] and in empirical work.

To highlight some of the basic analytical issues, consider a hypothetical social security system that is much less complicated than the "real-world" one whose provisions are summarized by (6.36)–(6.39): a scheme that sets t^* at 65. (Thus, assume that individuals have no choice about when they will start to receive benefits and that there is, therefore, no AA.) As before, earnings below E_M at any age are taxed at the rate τ_P, whereas benefits (whose maximum amount is now a fixed number, Λ_{65}, for everyone) are still reduced by an amount τ_R for every dollar of earnings in excess of E_D. To simplify matters considerably (at the cost of a not inconsiderable

---

[45] For example, suppose the value of Λ_{t^*} at *each* t^* is increased by an amount $d\Lambda_{t^*}$. Simpleminded analysis based on Figure 6.4 would treat the impact of this on labor supply as the approximate equivalent of an increase in V of the same amount. However, such analysis ignores the possibility that people who have *anticipated* the increase in Λ_{t^*} will have reduced asset accumulation in prior periods, making $V + \Lambda_{t^*}$ in the *current* period not much different from what it would otherwise have been. Ehrenberg and Smith (1982, pp. 197–201) discuss changes in Social Security parameters of this kind using a diagram similar to Figure 6.4, but they are careful to emphasize that their analysis refers only to the "immediate effects on older workers," for example, persons who are currently age t^* who did not anticipate the change in Λ_{t^*}.

loss of generality), assume further that Λ_{t^*} ($= \Lambda_{65}$) is independent of one's earnings history *prior* to age 65 (so that there is no ABR), and restrict the discussion to an "intramarginal" individual who, both before *and* after introduction of this scheme, will always and in each period earn slightly more than E_D and substantially less than E_M. Then, at all ages t before 65, this individual's net wage is reduced from $W(t)$ to $W_1\widehat{(t)} \equiv (1 - \tau_P) W(t)$, whereas at age 65 and beyond his net wage is reduced from $W(t)$ to $W_2\widehat{(t)} \equiv (1 - \tau_P - \tau_R) W(t)$. Finally, in keeping with most discussions of this issue,[46] assume that introduction of this hypothetical social security scheme represents a net increase in the individual's *lifetime* wealth, that is, that the present value of the payments he will make to the system will be smaller than the present value of the payments he will receive from it.

Under these assumptions, one can analyze the impact of the Social Security scheme using an old friend – the composite commodity theorem – in much the same way that one can discuss the life cycle effects of a negative income tax (see section 6.3). The scheme reduces the price of leisure (relative to consumption goods) at *each* age t prior to 65 by the *same* relatively small proportion, τ_P, whereas

---

[46] Financing of the Social Security system is intended to be on a "pay as you go" basis, that is, total payments into the system each year and total disbursements from the system each year are intended to be equal. (Thus, Social Security is *not* intended to be, and will not necessarily operate as if it were, financed on an "insurance" basis, under which total payments made into the system by an individual over his lifetime, appropriately discounted, would equal total payments made to the same individual over his lifetime, again appropriately discounted.) Relatively high rates of population growth, which the United States has enjoyed until recently, imply a youthful population, one that makes a sizable (and increasing) net contribution *to* the system each year. This permits high (and rising) payments to benefit recipients each year, and, thus, a sizable intergenerational transfer from young to old: Today's oldsters will receive more *from* the system (that is, from today's young) than they paid *into* the system (that is, to yesterday's oldsters) when *they* were young, implying a net increase in lifetime wealth for today's oldsters. For discussion, see Sheshinski (1978). (The resemblance between Social Security, chain letters, and Ponzi schemes is, therefore, not entirely accidental.) However, Barro (1974, 1978) argues that people will respond to a Social Security-induced increase in their lifetime wealth by making offsetting transfers – bequests, gifts, and the like – to their children. Moreover, as anyone who has read a newspaper in the past several years is aware, the objective of pay-as-you-go financing of the Social Security system has not always been achieved, particularly recently, and the population growth that has helped stimulate increases (if any) in the net wealth of today's oldsters has been slowing down.

it reduces the price of leisure (relative to consumer goods) at *each* age t starting at age 65 by the same larger proportion, $\tau_P + \tau_R$. Also, by assumption, the scheme increases lifetime wealth (in other words, net receipts from the scheme are positive). Now define composite leisure prior to age 65, L_1, to be the discounted wage-weighted sum of leisure times consumed at all ages prior to age 65, that is, $L_1 \equiv \Sigma_{t=0}^{64} (1 + r)^{-t} W(t)L(t)$, and similarly for composite leisure during or after age 65, $L_2 \equiv \Sigma_{t=65}^{T} (1 + r)^{-t} W(t)L(t)$, where T is the age of death. Then, for the reasons noted in Section 6.3, L_1 and L_2 are composite commodities, in the sense of the composite commodity theorem. In particular, introducing the hypothetical Social Security scheme considered here will have the following effects on L_i, $i = 1$ *or* 2:

(i) A substitution effect on L_i, arising from the equiproportionate decrease in the price of each of the components of L_i (= $-100\tau_P$ percent, for $i = 1$; = $-100(\tau_P + \tau_R)$ percent, for $i = 2$). This will raise consumption of the *composite*, L_i.

(ii) A cross-substitution effect on L_i, arising from the equiproportionate decrease in the price of each of the components of the *other* leisure composite, $L_j, j = 2$ or 1 (= $-100(\tau_P + \tau_R)$ percent, for $j = 2$; = $-100\tau_P$ percent, for $j = 1$). This will reduce or increase consumption of the *composite*, L_i, depending on whether L_i and L_j are net substitutes or complements.

(iii) A wealth effect, arising from the Social Security-induced increase in lifetime wealth. This will raise consumption of the *composite*, L_i, provided L_i is a normal good.

If leisure times at all dates are complements to each other, then all three of these effects on both L_1 and L_2 are positive signed. In this case, then, the scheme will increase composite leisure – and, therefore, reduce the present value of earnings – both before and after age 65. On the other hand, if leisure times at all dates are substitutes for each other, then the own-substitution and wealth effects on L_1 (and L_2) are positive signed, whereas the cross-substitution effect on L_1 (and L_2) is negative signed. Here it is not possible to say how the scheme will affect either L_1 or L_2 (or, therefore, the present value of earnings either before or after age 65) without introducing additional assumptions (e.g., about the magnitudes of the cross-substitution terms). Also, in either case, it is not possible to say how the scheme will affect leisure (or, therefore, earnings or labor supply) at any particular age *t* without introducing additional assumptions.

As this exercise illustrates, deriving unambiguous predictions about the impact of Social Security on leisure or labor supply at specific ages – even in the context of the model considered here – is no simple task. (Deriving predictions about composites, such as the L_1 and L_2 of the previous discussion, does not seem a very simple matter either.) As with other questions of a similar nature, empirical analysis is the most obvious way to try to dispose of some of the ambiguity. A number of recent analyses suggest that the Social Security system has substantially reduced labor supply (e.g., by inducing retirement at age 62 or 65 to a greater extent than would otherwise be the case) among older workers; for example, see Boskin (1977) and Boskin and Hurd (1978). Burkhauser and Turner (1978, 1982) present results that appear to suggest that Social Security has also *increased* labor supply among *younger* workers (i.e., "prime-age" workers age 25–64). Hence, the available evidence seems to suggest that the Social Security system has increased L_2, while simultaneously reducing L_1.

Unfortunately, however, much of the available evidence is at best rather unconvincing. Most of the studies of Social Security consider only transfers *to* individuals and ignore Social Security taxes paid *by* individuals; generally ignore most of the intertemporal aspects of Social Security discussed earlier in this section and treat both Λ_{r} and *V* as exogenous;[47] and, finally, model benefits paid by the system in a rather crude fashion. For example, several time-series studies of Social Security (Burkhauser and Turner, 1978, 1982; Feldstein, 1974b, 1982; Leimer and Lesnoy, 1982) collapse the complex of maximum benefit amounts, earnings disregards, tax rates, benefit reduction rates, and so forth into a single variable, "Social Security

---

[47] Studies of the impact of Social Security on labor supply that treat a measure of property income as an exogenous right-hand-side variable include Boskin (1977), Boskin and Hurd (1978), Burkhauser and Turner (1978), Pellechio (1978), Quinn (1977), and Zabalza, Pissarides, and Barton (1980). Studies that treat a measure of wealth or assets as an exogenous right-hand-side variable include Burkhauser (1980) and Hall and Johnson (1980). To the extent that private pensions are a form of savings, they are also a form of (endogenous) wealth; studies that treat a measure of private pension eligibility as an exogenous right-hand-side variable include Burkhauser (1979, 1980) and Hall and Johnson (1980).

wealth." Reimers (1980, p. 147) notes that the construction of this variable is such that it is "essentially proportional to a time trend multiplied by real per capita disposable income, which is the real disposable wage times hours worked,"[48] and adds:

> With the real (gross) wage also in the equation, it should surprise no one that this variable is significantly positively related to the dependent variable, hours worked. It is as if we were to regress hours worked on both earnings and the wage rate – we would "discover" that earnings are positively related to hours!

A more promising – but also considerably more challenging – line of attack is to embed the provisions of the Social Security system in a formal life cycle model (e.g., one of those discussed in Chapter 5). This is essentially the approach that Gordon and Blinder (1980) take: They extend, to the dynamic case, Heckman's static model of an individual who decides whether (and how much) to work via a comparison of his market and his reservation wage. Their results suggest that Social Security benefits have at best a minor effect on labor supply and retirement decisions. However, like several other authors, they use a Social Security wealth variable rather than a fully specified intertemporal budget constraint. Their specification of the dynamic reservation wage function, though derived from a careful treatment of the dynamic optimization problem, also raises some awkward empirical problems: The reservation wage at any date t depends, in part, on whether the individual works at *other* dates $t' \neq t$. (To see why, note by way of analogy that, in a family labor supply model, family member i's reservation wage will in general depend on the labor supply of other family members.) To derive period t's reservation wage by treating work at other dates as exogenous is obviously incorrect (to do so would amount to assuming that labor

---

[48] In a rejoinder to Reimers (1980), Burkhauser and Turner (1980b) note that their Social Security wealth variable (introduced by Feldstein, 1974b) includes property income. (More precisely, it includes nonwage income, which, although they do not say so explicitly, would seem to include not only dividends, rent, and interest but also transfer payments, including current Social Security benefit payments.) This may weaken somewhat the notion that the partial correlation between hours and Social Security wealth with wages constant is really just a simple correlation between hours and hours. However, in view of the discussion in the text about property income (V), it does little to increase confidence in the Social Security wealth variable.

force participation is exogenous, contradicting the model's assumption that participation is a choice made by comparing market and reservation wages). To measure work at other dates using an instrument is obviously correct but, unfortunately, requires that the investigator have available such an instrument for work at other dates *before* the analysis of current work effort begins! As an "empirical compromise," Gordon and Blinder (1980, p. 294, note 30) construct a reservation wage function assuming full-time work at 2,000 hours per year until age 67 and complete retirement thereafter. Whether this compromise (which is similar in nature to H. Rosen's, 1976b, procedure of evaluating tax rates at a "standard" number of hours of work) is satisfactory is an open question. An alternative is to use the COLISPIA approach to specification, in which the reservation wage at any date t may be written in terms of only one endogenous variable, the fixed effect μ. (For an application, see Heckman and MaCurdy, 1980, in press.) However, implementation of the COLISPIA approach requires longitudinal data, rather than a single cross-section data set (which is what Gordon and Blinder, 1980, use).

6.7. Other transfer programs and labor supply

The unrestricted income-related transfer schemes that have been the focus of this chapter are the predominant kind of transfer payment in the U.S. economy. (For example, according to Danziger, Haveman, and Plotnick, 1981, Table 1, such programs accounted for over 70 percent of all Federal expenditures for income transfers during Fiscal Year 1981.) However, other kinds of transfer schemes are either currently in effect or have been proposed. In this section, I will consider current restricted income-related transfers and proposals for wage-related transfers.

Restricted income-related transfers

Although unrestricted income-related transfers may be used by recipients for any expenditures they wish to make, restricted transfers may be used only for certain kinds of expenditures. (Recall note 21.) Thus, any model of restricted income-related transfers must consider at least three different kinds of "commodities": leisure and two market goods, one of which is subsidized (that is, may be purchased using grants under the restricted transfer scheme) and the other of which is not.

Such schemes differ in terms of the way in which the particular subsidy in question is determined. Letting the price and amount purchased of market good i be P_i and C_i, respectively, where $i = s$ or u (for subsidized or unsubsidized), one may write a reasonably[49] general version of the formula for restricted benefits B_R paid under such schemes as

$$B_R = \min (P_s C_s, B_R^\circ)$$

where

$$B_R^\circ = G_R - F(Y) \qquad \text{if} \quad G_R - F(Y) > 0$$

$$B_R^\circ = 0 \qquad \text{if} \quad G_R - F(Y) \leq 0$$

---

[49] For example, under the Food Stamp program, eligible families may make a payment $F(Y)$ whose amount is based on income Y, and, in exchange, receive coupons that may be used to purchase a total of G_R worth of domestically produced food items (but not imported food, tobacco, alcoholic beverages, or nonfood items); the "Food Stamp benefit" is, therefore, $B_R = G_R - F(Y)$. Similarly, under the Medicaid program (a program that subsidizes housing costs), eligible families who purchase G_R worth of medical care (housing) receive $G_R - F(Y)$ from the government; the benefit under such programs is, again, $B_R = G_R - F(Y)$. Thus, as noted in the text, the benefit formulas under such programs are very similar in form to those used in cash or unrestricted subsidy schemes, such as the NIT. However, other kinds of in-kind or restricted subsidy schemes, present or proposed, have somewhat different benefit formulas. For example, Friedman and Hausman (1974) and Murray (1980) consider *price subsidy* schemes, under which eligible individuals pay only $\theta P_s (0 < \theta < 1)$ rather than P_s per unit of the subsidized good; and Murray (1980) considers *fixed quantity voucher* schemes under which eligible individuals receive a fixed amount C_s of the subsidized good in exchange for a payment π_s that is less than the market value of C_s (so that $\pi_s < P_s C_s$). Similarly, Heckman (1974a, p. S137–40) considers various alternative schemes for subsidizing expenditures on child care: One might (i) provide a voucher, entitling the recipient to v_C worth of child-care services, for *each hour* the recipient works; (ii) provide a voucher, entitling the recipient to V_C worth of child-care services, *provided* the recipient works at least H_C hours per year; or (iii) permit either tax *deductions* or tax *credits* for some (or all) child-care expenses, provided, for example, the amount deducted or credited is less than the earnings of the spouse with lower earnings (in the case of a two-spouse family) or is less than the individual's earnings (in the case of a single parent). Finally, see Akerlof (1978) for discussion of categorical or "tagged" subsidies, paid on the basis of demographic or personal characteristics (age, handicap, etc.).

and where $Y_R \equiv F^{-1}(G_R)$ is the scheme's break-even level of income. Thus, by analogy with equations (6.24) and (6.25), if $F(Y)$ is simply $\tau_R Y$ then τ_R is the marginal tax rate of the restricted subsidy scheme, G_R is the guarantee level of the scheme, and $Y_R = G_R/\tau_R$. In this case, the scheme can be written in terms of the formula

$$(6.40) \quad B_R = \min (P_s C_s, B_R^\circ)$$

$$(6.41) \quad \begin{aligned} B_R^\circ &= \tau_R(Y_R - Y) \quad &\text{if} \quad Y < Y_R \\ B_R^\circ &= 0 \quad &\text{if} \quad Y \geq Y_R \end{aligned}$$

For simplicity, I shall use this formulation in what follows.

To fix ideas, consider the individual's choice problem when he faces the scheme given by (6.40) and (6.41) and assume – temporarily, and for purposes of illustration only – that the individual does not work and that his income Y is, therefore, fixed at V. Figure 6.5 shows the essential nature of the choice problem under these conditions. The line $v_s v_u$ shows the set of alternative (C_s, C_u) bundles from which the individual can choose in the absence of the scheme; the line $v_s' n v_u'$ shows the budget line he would face were he to receive an unrestricted cash grant sufficient to permit the purchase of $v_s' - v_s$ worth of C_s (or, equivalently, $v_u' - v_u$ worth of C_u) through a scheme such as (6.24) and (6.25). Finally, the broken line $v_s' n v_u$ shows the budget line the individual would face were he eligible for a restricted scheme such as (6.40) and (6.41), with the same guarantee and tax rate as the unrestricted scheme.

In other words, as (6.40) and (6.41) imply, the terms of the restricted subsidy B_R are such that the individual can never consume more than v_u worth of the unsubsidized good, even after he gets the benefit payment: At point n, his payment can buy nv_u worth of C_s, and any attempt to increase consumption of C_u by cutting C_s below this amount (as would be possible under an unrestricted scheme, which permits the individual to travel down nv_u') will only result in a reduction in the restricted grant amount by a sum equal to the reduction in C_s. This means that, at point n, the individual who receives a restricted transfer can reduce C_s only by moving straight down along nv_u toward v_u with no corresponding increase in C_u.

Thus, unless consumption goods are perfect substitutes, a transfer scheme restricted to purchases of certain kinds of goods will typically have different effects on labor supply and consumption than will an unrestricted scheme, at least for certain individuals.

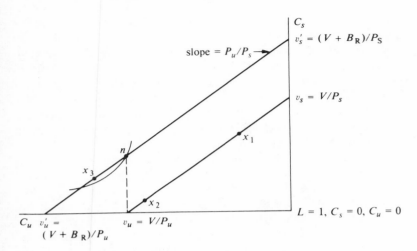

Figure 6.5. Unrestricted versus restricted transfers

This and related notions figured fairly prominently in early discussions of the negative income tax and other proposals for unrestricted transfer schemes[50] but have largely been ignored in subsequent work. (For example, see Danziger, Haveman, and Plotnick, 1981.) One possible reason for this is that it seems reasonable to suppose

[50] The standard microeconomics textbook result that "one can make a man happier by giving him cash and letting him spend it as he thinks best than by forcing him to take all his relief in the form of one commodity" (Scitovsky, 1971, p. 71) is, of course, well known. For example, in terms of Figure 6.5, the individual who is initially at x_2 and who receives a grant of nv_u that is restricted to C_s and locates at point n would be able to locate at a point such as x_3 – and, thus, be better off – if the government were to pay him a lump-sum *cash* grant equal to nv_u (or, equivalently, if the government were to relax its restriction and permit him to convert some of his C_s into C_u). (Scitovsky's discussion of Food Stamps on pp. 70–1 is somewhat misleading: He analyzes the program as if it subsidized the *price* of food but placed no restrictions on individuals' ability to purchase food at the subsidized price. In fact, as implied by (6.40) and Figure 6.5, the program subsidizes food *purchases* rather than food *prices*, and is "just as good" as a cash subsidy for individuals at points such as x_1.) Friedman and Hausman (1974) show that at least some price subsidies can raise hours of work relative to the level that would prevail under a negative income tax involving the same cost to the government. Murray (1980) shows that, provided the utility function is separable in leisure (on the one hand) and consumer goods C_s and C_u (on the other hand), subsidizing the price of C_s will always raise hours of work

that many individuals are at points such as x_1 in Figure 6.5, that is, already consume more C_s than the maximum amount nv_u that the restricted subsidy would provide. For such individuals, restricted transfer schemes are not, in fact, much different from unrestricted schemes: If both C_s and C_u are normal goods, then the restricted subsidy, in shifting the individual's budget line from $v_s v_u$ to $v'_s nv_u$, would not increase consumption of the unsubsidized good C_u beyond v_u, in which case the individual will act "as if" the restricted scheme were an unrestricted scheme.

However, some individuals may be at points such as x_2 in Figure 6.5 (e.g., if C_s is medical care and C_u is all other goods). In this case, the effects of introducing a restricted subsidy will differ from the effects of introducing an unrestricted subsidy. For example, an individual initially at x_2 who receives an unrestricted subsidy equal to nv_u might desire to move to x_3, but this obviously would not be possible if the subsidy were restricted to purchases of C_s, that is, if the subsidy were subject to the terms of (6.40) and (6.41). In the restricted case, the best the individual can do would be to move to point n. Note that the indifference curve that passes through n has a slope that is steeper than the line $v'_s v'_u$, implying that the individual would like to exchange some of his C_s for C_u. (Indeed, accounts of operations under the Food Stamp program suggest that some individuals sell their Food Stamp coupons for cash, that is, organize black market trades that will reduce C_s – food – and increase C_u – other commodities.)

Thus far, the discussion has taken labor supply and income as given, using the two-dimensional diagram in Figure 6.5. To consider labor supply in addition to the two market goods C_s and C_u, it is of course necessary to use a three-dimensional diagram, as in the three panels of Figure 6.6. In each panel, C_s is measured along the vertical axis, L is measured along the easterly axis, and C_u is measured along the southerly axis. In the absence of any subsidy, the individual's budget line (more accurately, budget plane or frontier) is the plane $f_s v_s v_u f_u$, as shown in Figure 6.6(a). In the presence of an unrestricted subsidy such as the one defined by (6.24) and (6.25), the budget

relative to the level that would prevail under a program of lump-sum transfers involving the same cost to the government. Roughly speaking, the intuition underlying both results is that a price subsidy increases the real or purchasing-power reward for work.

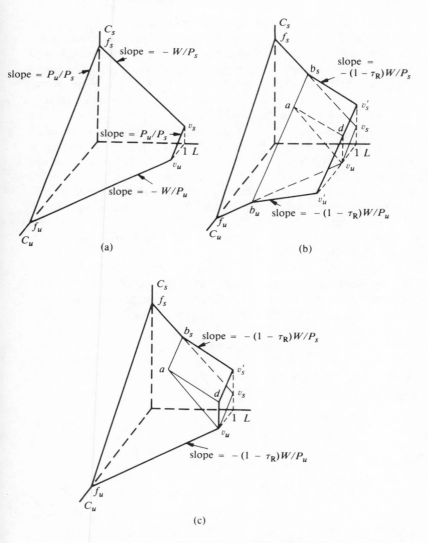

Figure 6.6. Budget frontiers, leisure and two-market goods

frontier is the plane $f_s b_s v'_s dv'_u b_u f_u$ shown in Figure 6.6(b); note that the line $f_s b_s v'_s$ lies on the (C_s, L) plane and is identical in nature to the line fbv' in Figure 6.2 (in which all consumption goods are taken to be homogeneous, i.e., perfect substitutes). Moreover, the plane $1 v_s v_u$, which is parallel to the (C_s, C_u) plane, is the same as the triangle formed by the line $v_s v_u$ and the C_s and C_u axes in Figure 6.5, since they both refer to the combinations of C_s and C_u available to the individual when $L = 1$. Finally, in the presence of a restricted subsidy, the individual's budget frontier is $v_u f_u f_s b_s v'_s da$ shown in Figure 6.6(c), that is, is the surface formed by the intersection of the planes adv_u, $ab_s v'_s d$, and $ab_s f_s f_u v_u a$. Thus, in terms of Figure 6.6(b), after introduction of an unrestricted subsidy, an individual who is initially at a point within the plane $ab_s v_s v_u$ may move to a point within the plane $adv_u v'_u b_u$, whereas in the presence of a subsidy restricted to purchases of C_s, such an individual can only move to points along the line ad.

Hence, individuals who are in fact restricted by a restricted subsidy would, in general, change their labor supply if the subsidy were converted into an unrestricted subsidy with the same tax rate τ_R and guarantee level G_R. As a simple example, consider someone who would work (have $L < 1$) under either kind of subsidy, and assume that utility is separable in L, C_s, and C_u, so that $u_i > 0$, $u_{ii} < 0$, and $u_{ij} = 0$, where i and j refer to L, C_s, and C_u. Figures 6.5 and 6.6(c) indicate that for someone who is restricted by a restricted subsidy (and who is, therefore, located along the line ad in Figure 6.6(c))

$$u_{C_u} / u_{C_s} > P_u / P_s$$

$$u_L / u_{C_s} = \hat{W} / P_s$$

where $\hat{W} = (1 - \tau_R)W$. Consequently,

$$u_L / u_{C_u} < \hat{W} / P_u$$

Dropping the restriction, that is, abandoning the requirement that the subsidy amount B_R must be used to purchase C_s, permits the individual to move from ad to a point within the plane $adv'_u b_u$; note that this must always mean an increase in consumption of the unsubsidized good C_u provided hours of work remain positive, as assumed. However, both before and after the restriction is dropped, the individual faces the *same* budget constraint,

$$P_uC_u + P_sC_s + \hat{W}L = \hat{V} + \hat{W}$$

where $\hat{V} = (1 - \tau_R)V + G_R$: All that is being changed is the requirement that benefits B_R must be spent on C_s. It follows that the individual's increased consumption of C_u must be accompanied by a decrease in expenditure on C_s and L combined – in other words, $P_sC_s + \hat{W}L$ must fall. Moreover, the decrease in combined expenditure on C_s and L will always occur via reductions in *both* C_s and L (rather than via increases in one accompanied by offsetting decreases in the other): If C_s and L were to change in opposite directions, then the marginal rate of substitution between C_s and L, u_L/u_{C_s}, would change and this would violate the first-order condition $u_L/u_{C_s} = \hat{W}/P$ (which must hold both before and after the restriction is dropped). As L falls and C_u rises, the marginal rate of substitution between C_u and L rises, yielding $u_L/u_{C_u} = \hat{W}/P$ at the final optimum; as C_u rises and C_s falls, the marginal rate of substitution between C_s and C_u falls, yielding $u_{C_u}/u_{C_s} = P_u/P_s$ at the final optimum.

In sum, *provided* the utility function is separable in L, C_u, and C_s, converting the restricted subsidy into an unrestricted subsidy (that is, a negative income tax) will increase purchases of the unsubsidized good and will reduce both leisure time and purchases of the subsidized good for persons initially restricted by the restricted subsidy (that is, persons initially located along the line *ad* in Figure 6.6(c)). Persons who are not restricted by the terms of the restricted subsidy (that is, persons initially located within the plane $adv_s'b_s$ in Figure 6.6(c)) will not change their behavior. However, note that these results depend on the assumption of separability; more complex cases are less clear-cut.

Although these conclusions pertain only to the static case, it is clear that the same basic issues arise in the context of dynamic models. However, it is interesting to note that such issues are important in a dynamic setting even if the benefits under an in-kind transfer scheme are "restricted" to consumption spending of *all* kinds. That is, the analysis implicit in Figure 6.6(c) carries over to this case even if C_s is defined to be consumption of *all* consumer goods whereas C_u, the "unsubsidized" good, is defined to be savings.

To date, empirical analyses of transfers have largely ignored the distinction between in-kind and unrestricted cash transfers and have treated benefits under the former as if they were the equivalent of cash benefits paid out under the latter. In most cases (e.g., persons initially at points such as x_1 in Figure 6.5), this is appropriate, but in other cases, noted above, it may not be. However, in principle, empirical models such as the ones discussed earlier can be modified so as to allow for in-kind transfer schemes. In essence, the idea is to calculate the optimal (C_u, C_s, L) bundle both on the no benefits segment $f_u v_u v_s b_s f_s$ of the budget frontier in Figure 6.6(c) and on the benefits portion $a d v_s' b_s$ of that frontier and then determine which bundle yields greater utility. The main complication introduced by restricted transfers is that equilibrium can occur at a corner of the budget frontier that involves *positive* hours of work (e.g., along the line ad in Figure 6.6(c)); under an unrestricted transfer, the only kind of corner equilibrium that can occur is one involving zero hours of work (e.g., along the line $v_u' v_s'$ in Figure 6.6(b)).

Wage subsidies

Schemes such as (6.24) and (6.25) and (6.40) and (6.41) define payments whose amount is related to income (or, more accurately, to the amount, if any, by which income falls short of a poverty-line or break-even level). Recent years have seen considerable interest in and discussion of wage subsidies – payments whose amount is related to wage rates (or, more accurately, to the amount, if any, by which one's wage rate falls short of a poverty-line or break-even level). A simple prototype wage subsidy scheme is given by

$$(6.42) \quad B_W = G_W - \tau_W W = \tau_W (W_B - W)$$
$$\text{if} \quad G_W - \tau_W W = \tau_W (W_B - W) > 0$$

$$(6.43) \quad B_W = 0$$
$$\text{if} \quad G_W - \tau_W W = \tau_W (W_B - W) \le 0$$

where B_W is the amount of benefit paid per hour of work, G_W is the scheme's wage guarantee, τ_W is the scheme's implicit marginal tax rate (or rate of hourly wage subsidy reduction), W_B is the break-even wage level, and W is the wage paid to the individual by his employer.

Individuals whose wage exceeds the break-even level W_B would never give up their high-wage job and "drop down" to a job paying a lower wage rate in order to receive wage subsidy payments: Higher wages are always better than lower wages.[51] Hence, the subsidy would not change the behavior of persons with wage rates above the break-even level. On the other hand, for individuals with wage rates below the break-even level, the effect of the scheme will be identical to the effect of an increase in the wage rate of B_W, since the scheme pays such individuals B_W per hour of work. As such, the wage subsidy scheme will have not only a negative income effect on labor supply (if leisure is a normal good) but also a positive substitution effect.

Because both the income effect *and* the substitution effect on labor supply of a NIT or similar income-related transfer scheme are negative, it would, therefore, seem that wage subsidies will at least reduce labor supply by less than income-related transfers and that wage subsidies could even increase labor supply. (See Browning, 1973; Zeckhauser, 1971.) However, wage subsidies could also be more expensive, that is, involve a greater total amount of benefit payments, than an NIT or other income-related transfer scheme: A wage subsidy scheme would make payments to all persons whose wage is below break-even, even if their hours of work are high and even if their incomes are well above the break-even income level of an NIT. Indeed, wage subsidies could actually reduce labor supply by *more* than an NIT, if there are large numbers of persons who (i) have wage rates that are below the break-even level W_B, (ii) work sufficiently many hours to earn incomes that are well above the NIT break-even level Y_B, and (iii) have backward-bending labor supply curves. Such persons would not change their labor supply in response to introduction of an NIT (in effect, they are initially on segment *fb* in Figure 6.2 and have indifference curves that are sufficiently curved so as to mean that points on *bv'* are less attractive than the point on *fb* that they chose prior to the NIT) but will reduce their labor supply in response to the wage increase generated by introduction of the wage subsidy scheme. Comparing the relative

---

[51] Provided jobs differ only in terms of wages. If jobs differ in terms of non-pecuniary characteristics, a wage subsidy might encourage persons to take low-wage jobs.

labor supply effects of wage subsidy programs such as (6.42) and (6.43) with income-subsidy programs such as (6.24) and (6.25) is, therefore, somewhat difficult, even in the context of static models (Garfinkel, 1973b).[52]

[52] Hurd and Pencavel (1981) consider alternative ways of setting the wage subsidy scheme parameters G_W and τ_W using criteria that are related to the notion of a poverty line: One such scheme would set G_W and τ_W so as to raise families to a level of *income* equal to the poverty-line level of income, another would set these parameters so as to raise families to the level of *utility* enjoyed by a "reference" family that receives the poverty-line level of income, and so on. In effect, this amounts to modifying the wage subsidy scheme discussed in the text so as to cut off all wage subsidies when some threshold – either the poverty-line level of income or the poverty-line level of utility – is crossed. Cutting off such subsidies to persons who enjoy more than the poverty-line level of utility is likely to prove somewhat difficult from an administrative standpoint. Limiting such subsidies to persons who receive less than the poverty-line level of income may also create incentives for reductions in labor supply that would not be present in a "straight" wage subsidy scheme of the kind discussed in the text.

7

Conclusion

Much has been accomplished in the theoretical and empirical analysis of labor supply, particularly in the past half-dozen years or so. As noted in Chapters 1, 2, and 5, researchers may now choose from a wide variety of quite elaborate theoretical models in starting any analysis of labor supply. The developments surveyed in Chapters 3, 4, and 6 have led to a set of econometric techniques that are remarkably well suited to estimation of − because they were developed along with − behavioral models of labor supply and provide a solid intellectual framework for empirical inquiry. Finally, as implied in Chapters 3, 4, and 6, the amount of data now available for empirical investigation is much greater than was available even a few years ago.

However, most theoretical or empirical papers in economics conclude with the comment, "More research is needed," and this survey of work on labor supply does so also. Indeed, it would be difficult *not* to do so. Compared with disciplines such as mathematics, economics is a very young field indeed (after all, Euclid flourished in 300 B.C., and Newton in 1700, whereas Adam Smith published *The Wealth of Nations* in 1776); and the subspecialty of labor supply had its earliest beginnings only in the 1930s, with the appearance of studies of Robbins (1930) and Schoenberg and Douglas (1937). Although the past decade has seen many important developments, it is, therefore, hardly surprising that much remains to be done. Accordingly, in this concluding chapter, I will consider two questions: What do (and don't) we know now about labor supply? Where should future research take us?

7.1.   **What we do (and don't) know about labor supply**

A glance at first- and second-generation results for static labor supply models (see particularly Tables 3.2 and 4.3), results for dynamic labor supply models (see particularly Table 5.1), and results derived from the NIT experiments (see particularly Table 6.2) shows that there is now a great deal of empirical evidence about labor supply behavior. First, and of crucial importance, pecuniary variables – wage rates and property income – do generally seem to have something to do with labor supply. That this should be so is hardly earth-shattering; that it should need to be said may seem somewhat surprising – until one recalls the many eloquent criticisms, some now quite venerable and some of much more recent vintage,[1] that have cast doubt on this notion and, more generally, on the concept of *Homo economicus*. Second, and of almost equal importance, most of the available evidence suggests that female labor supply, measured either as labor force participation or as hours of work, is considerably more wage and property income elastic than male labor supply. Finally, as second-generation research has begun to recognize explicitly, unobservable factors – taste differences, nonpecuniary components of pay, hard-to-measure pecuniary influences – play a substantial role in labor supply.

Thus, some extremely important brute facts about labor supply seem quite firmly established. A closer look at the evidence, however, argues for caution in treating these results as "facts" and underscores the most obvious reason why more research is needed: On the whole, the evidence on labor supply is rather imprecise, and available quantitative estimates of any given labor supply elasticity typically cover a wide range. Moreover, second-generation research methodology seems to have raised the midpoint of some estimates (e.g., of the wage elasticity of female labor supply) and lowered others (e.g., exogenous income elasticity of labor supply is estimated at approximately zero in several such studies) without appreciably narrowing their range. At least temporarily, then, uncertainty about, and variation in, actual magnitudes of labor supply parameter estimates seems larger than it used to be.

---

[1] For example, see Lampman (1956), Parnes (1960, p. 30; 1970, pp. 65–6), and Piore (1979, p. 53).

As another way of understanding both what we do and what we don't know about labor supply, consider what light econometric studies of labor supply shed on important secular trends in labor supply in the U.S. economy. One important stylized fact about labor supply trends is particularly arresting: Since about 1890, labor force participation has gradually, but perceptibly, declined for men as a whole, whereas female labor force participation has risen substantially, particularly since about 1940. (For example, see U.S. Department of Labor, 1976, p. 381.) Does the research discussed in previous chapters provide at least a partial explanation for this?

Even the simplest labor supply model, coupled with the fact that real wages have risen steadily since the turn of the century, provides a fairly plausible account of the trend in female labor force participation: Given the wealth of empirical evidence that suggests that not only participation, but also hours of work, among women are an increasing function of real wages (and numerous estimates implying a negative but rather small response to rises in property income), anyone familiar with the results of previous chapters would hardly be surprised to find that female labor force participation has in fact increased over time. Second-generation notions can carry this story a bit further: If one assumes that – given observable characteristics such as schooling, age, and so on – female reservation wages follow something like a normal distribution, then second-generation models of participation, such as the ones discussed in Chapter 5, imply that, over time, *given* successive increases in wage rates will be accompanied by successively *larger* increases in female labor force participation, provided the female participation rate is low "at first" (as was indeed the case around the turn of the century). This is shown in Figure 7.1. (See Ben-Porath, 1973, for elaboration on the links between wages, reservation wages, and participation, particularly as regards the nonlinearity of the wage–participation relationship.)

However, any explanation of increases in female participation that relies on rising wage rates for women must also explain why male participation has not also increased, at least among men as a whole, in the face of rises in male wages.[2] Here, it is worth noting

---

[2] In other words, ceteris paribus, an increase in the wage rate necessarily increases (i) the probability that any given individual will be employed and, thus, (ii) the proportion of individuals that is employed. (The ceteris that are paribus include such factors as property income, tastes, etc., that affect reservation wages.)

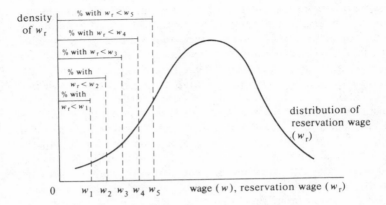

Figure 7.1.   Changes in participation associated with wage changes.

that much of the decline in male participation that has occurred seems to have occurred mainly among men under 25 or over 64: The limited available evidence seems to suggest that participation rates for men age 25–64 have actually increased somewhat since 1890 (Mincer, 1968, p. 474). The drop in male participation at the lower end of the age range is manifested largely in the form of increased school enrollment, which raises dynamic or life cycle considerations that are discussed in more detail in Chapter 5. The fall in participation among older men[3] and the slight increase in participation by men age 25–64 may both be explained, at least in part, by factors that have raised male reservation wages relative to market wages for older men, such as increases in transfer benefits such as Social Security (see, in particular, Burkhauser and Turner, 1978, 1980a; Parsons, 1980a, b): In effect, men may be replacing leisure between the age of 25 and 64 with leisure after age 65. To be sure, such transfer programs also seem to reduce female participation (Butler and Heckman, 1977). However, Social Security and other transfer

[3] It is interesting to note, however, that the decline in labor force participation among older men does not seem to be the result of a decrease in the age of retirement, defined to mean "permanent withdrawal from the labor force." See Reimers (1976), who shows that the conditional mean retirement age for cohorts born between 1866 and 1909 was stable around age 65 (the *variance* of the retirement age has, however, fallen secularly).

benefit increases may have had a greater impact on male reservation wages (relative to market wages) than on female reservation wages (relative to market wages). This is because, at least to some extent, eligibility for increased benefits (and even the size of benefit increases) is a function of previous participation, which is lower, on average, for women than for men.

Thus, simple notions about labor supply may well provide an explanation of these trends in male and female participation. However, to date, there appears to be no comprehensive study that attempts to provide an accounting for both trends. Moreover, the declines in participation by older and younger men and increases in participation by women (and, to a lesser extent, "intermediate-age" men) that have occurred since 1890 were underway *before* the 1930s, when most transfer programs were introduced on a large scale and had been in motion well before the 1960s and 1970s, when such programs were substantially expanded.

On the other hand, to the extent that these trends simply mean that women are now working more, and men less, in *paid* employment than was the case in the 1890s, the results of recent cross-section studies of male and female labor supply easily account for these secular trends: As previously noted, such studies typically imply that male labor supply schedules are gently backward bending, whereas female labor supply schedules are strongly forward sloping. However, this serves to highlight another basic question to which I will return presently: If the long-run leisure demand schedule for men seems to be positively sloped with respect to the wage (see, in particular, Lewis, 1957), then why does this not seem to be the case for women?

A second stylized fact about labor supply trends is that the average workweek appears not only to have (i) fallen fairly steadily between about 1890 and 1940, but also (ii) remained roughly constant since about that time, particularly among intermediate-age men. A number of authors have presented a variety of different (but not mutually exclusive) explanations of this pattern. Kniesner (1976b, 1980a) emphasizes the changing role of women in the labor market (and, thus, the potential importance of intrafamily substitution effects) and changes in overall educational attainment. Owen (1969, 1971, 1976) points to increases in the cost of raising children and other uses of nonwork time (and, thus, to the potential importance of time allocation models of the kind discussed in Chapter 2). Burkhauser and Turner (1978, 1980a) stress changes in fertility and the role of Social Security benefit increases. They put special emphasis on the possibility that the Social Security system has twisted life cycle patterns of labor supply, simultaneously reducing it after age 65 but also – via an intertemporal cross-substitution effect – inducing men to work *more* during their prime-age years, leading to a flattening of previously pronounced downward trends in the average workweek of prime-age males. (Recall the discussion of Social Security in Chapter 6, however.) Barzel and McDonald (1973) consider implications for secular trends of specific forms of the utility function, some of which entail progressively smaller reductions in hours of work in response to wage increases, that is, a pattern similar to the apparent long-run behavior of the average workweek. Although Hanoch (1980a) does not discuss secular trends in the average workweek, it is clear that his distinction between the length of the workweek and the number of annual weeks of work, and his suggestion that they are not likely to be perfect substitutes, may also be pertinent to analyses of such trends.

However, it may be that the stylized fact of an L-shaped secular pattern for the average workweek is only a "quasi-fact" or a "demi-fact." For example, data on average hours worked per week generally refer to hours *paid for* rather than to hours *actually worked*; thus, such data are not adjusted so as to exclude paid sick and paid vacation time (Rees, 1979, p. 25). There seems to be a general consensus that correction for such factors – to the extent that it is possible – does not alter the basic conclusion that the average workweek within manufacturing fell between 1890 and 1930 and has fallen much less or has even been roughly constant since about the end of Word War II. Also, partially corrected data on the average workweek of men age 25–44 in the total economy show little, if any, trend since about 1956 (Jones, 1980; Kniesner, 1976b, 1980a; Owen, 1969). Reimers (1980, p. 147), however, warns that "we may be wasting a lot of effort trying to explain a spurious 'fact' about the trend of men's annual hours in the United States, produced by the way we collect our data and not by workers' actual behavior." She points out that the correction for vacation, holiday, and sick time that is used in most attempts to measure the *actual* average workweek in effect ignores *all* growth in holiday and vacation time since the 1950s. Stafford and Duncan (1978) produce time budget data that suggest that, because they ignore growth in leisure on the job and in paid vacation, holiday, and sick time, Current Population Survey and other conventional statistical series understate the decline in weekly hours of work. Using Census data, Cain (1977) finds that average weekly hours "worked" (that is, paid-for hours, including paid vacation time and the like) for women have *risen* since 1949 (although the 1939 figure was higher than the 1949 figure). Since *overall* average weekly hours have fallen more or less continuously since 1949, this suggests that average weekly hours worked by men may have fallen.

Growth of "paid leisure," for example, both paid vacations and holidays *from* work, and "goofing-off" and coffee-break time *at* work, is not the only factor that is sometimes neglected or imperfectly taken into account in attempts to understand the apparent (but not necessarily actual) flattening of the downtrend in the average workweek of men. The growth of the tax system and of tax rates means that a given increase in the *gross* wage now entails a smaller increase in the *net* wage, particularly at high marginal tax rates, than it used to. Any apparent "failure" of hours of work to decline in response to increases in gross wages the way they once did may, therefore, simply reflect the fact that such wage increases involve smaller net wage growth than they once did. (On the other hand, growth in various fringe benefits, pension plans, medical care, and the like, may have made up much of the tax-induced increase in the difference between gross and net wages, and to some extent is almost certainly a by-product of this divergence between gross and net wages. Particularly since most fringe benefits are not taxable, it may even be the case that an increase in the net wage entails *greater* growth in *total* marginal compensation, inclusive of fringes, than it used to.)

Another difficulty confronting attempts to understand observed trends in the average workweek is the identification problem. Observed data on the average workweek and the wage rate over time do not necessarily trace out a labor supply schedule; rather, they are points of intersection of the supply and the demand schedule. To identify the observed scatter of average workweek–wage rate points as a supply schedule – as most discussions of the secular behavior of the average workweek tend to do – is to ignore potentially important secular trends in demand.

Finally, as the previous references to fertility, child-bearing, and male–female differences imply, changes in overall aggregates such as the average workweek (or the average workyear or the working lifetime) are presumably the result of, among other things, changes in household behavior. Such microlevel changes involve both income and substitution effects, but they also involve cross-substitution effects, not only on labor supply (of husbands and wives) but also between labor supply (of both husbands and wives) and various nonmarket uses of time (Kniesner, 1976b; Gronau, 1977). In principle, then, a full accounting of past trends in labor supply requires consideration of all these factors and their inter-relationships and, as Finegan (1978) and Jones (1980) point out, ought to measure the relative importance of each of these factors. Not surprisingly, most studies of past trends have not been quite so comprehensive.

Thus, it still seems possible that models of labor supply can provide a satisfactory account of long-run trends in labor supply and leisure demand. Indeed, Barnett (1979a, 1981) argues that there is no evidence of any "pure" time trend in labor supply during the period 1890–1955 over and beyond that implied by the changes in wages and nonlabor income that occurred during the same period: In other words, the whole "trend" in labor supply can be explained solely by income and substitution effects. However, Barnett focuses on aggregate labor supply (thus, he does not consider males and females separately) and does not investigate trends within the period 1890–1955 (e.g., 1890–1945 vs. 1945–55, etc.). Thus, even if it is indeed true that the aggregate amount of labor supply (measured as weekly hours, yearly hours, or lifetime hours) forthcoming at *given* wage rates and property income levels has not changed secularly, it is still necessary to explain why *males'* leisure demand schedules seem to be positive sloped with respect to the wage while females' schedules seem to be negative sloped.[4]

---

[4] Nakamura, Nakamura, and Cullen (1979) appear to disagree with the notion that female hours of work have in fact increased over time. For example, they note that, in Canada, "while both real wages for women and the female labor force participation rate have clearly risen over time, the percent of all female workers working forty weeks per year or more has fallen from 74.4 percent in 1961 to 67.0 percent in 1971 and the percent of all female workers working thirty-five hours per week or more has fallen from 90.0 percent in 1951 to 81.7 percent in 1961 to 71.3 percent in 1971."

In this connection, it is often argued that, due to societal norms and other taste factors, much of the leisure time of females (but little of the leisure time of males) is really nonmarket work. Thus, the secular increase in market work by women may still mean an increase in "true" leisure time among women (as seems to be the case for men), *if* there has been an even greater decrease in nonmarket work among women, spurred by, for example, changes in wage rates and improvements in household technology (home appliances, other labor-saving devices, etc.).

This hypothesis is difficult to test: Long-run data on nonmarket work are even harder to come by than long-run data on market work (e.g., on the average workweek).[5] Moreover, one widely cited study appears to contradict this hypothesis directly: Vanek's (1974) analysis of family "time budgets" appears to suggest both that (i) currently, employed women spend only half as much time doing housework than do women who are not in paid employment and (ii) between the 1920s and the present, time spent doing housework by women who do no market work has stayed more or less the same.

Such evidence, of course, refers to simple average differences in nonmarket work (or in the total of market and nonmarket work) either in cross section (in the case of comparisons between present-day working and nonworking women) or over time (in the case of comparisons between different dates for nonworking women). As such, these differences are the result of not only (i) structural responses to measured (or measurable) changes in wages and household technology (that is, conventional income and substitution

---

(Nakamura and Nakamura, 1981, pp. 480–2, cite the same Canadian evidence and similar figures for the U.S.) However, any inference from these figures that hours of work for women have fallen is a non sequitur: For example, a rise in the number of part-time women workers (and, thus, in the female labor force participation rate) could easily reduce both the *proportion* of women working at least 40 weeks per year and the *proportion* of women working at least 35 hours per week, even if *every* woman *already* at work were to increase both weeks worked per year and hours worked per week.

[5] For example, see Barnett (1981), Kniesner (1976b, 1980a), and Owen (1969), who had to derive time series on the average workweek by painstakingly stitching together or extrapolating a variety of different (and not always readily or directly comparable) time series; and Vanek (1974), whose data on nonmarket work over time come from a variety of different (and, again, not always readily or directly comparable) sources.

effects) but also (ii) unmeasured taste factors. As such, they do not necessarily say much about whether increases in wage rates or improvements in household technology would induce a *given* woman, with *given* tastes for market and nonmarket work, to increase or reduce the total amount of market and nonmarket work she does.

For example, suppose that having a high reservation wage (and thus a low taste for market work) is strongly associated with devoting a large amount of time to nonmarket work, other things (including wage rates and household technology) being equal. Suppose further that, other things (including tastes) being equal, increases in wage rates or household technology increase market work H while reducing nonmarket work N to a greater extent – that is, holding tastes constant, the demand for leisure schedule does indeed slope upward with respect to the wage rate within the relevant range of wage rate values. Now, consider the effect of improvements in household technology or increases in market wage rates. Other things being equal, such changes will reduce N both among women who do not now work and among women who do now work. However, such changes will also induce some nonworking women to work.

These "new workers" have higher reservation wages than the average of all women currently at work and have lower reservation wages than the average of all other women not now working. By assumption, this means that, at any given wage rate and level of household technology, these new workers have lower N than the average of all other women not now working and have higher N than the average of all women now working. Their departure from the group of nonworking women tends to raise average N among that group; their entry into the group of working women tends to raise average N among that group as well. Thus, findings to the effect that increases in wages and improvements in household technology do not seem to change N among nonworking women and do not seem to reduce total labor supply, $H + N$, among working women may simply be evidence of a form of selection bias rather than evidence that the female demand schedule for leisure does not slope upward with respect to the wage. This is because samples of working and nonworking women are selected on the basis of market employment status, which can hardly be considered exogenous to the determination of nonmarket work.

Thus, various important questions about past secular trends in labor supply are still very much open. Getting definite answers to such questions from parameter estimates of simple labor supply models is likely to prove difficult. It is still more difficult to use simple labor supply models to make accurate forecasts of future trends in labor supply. For example, as R.S. Smith (1979) notes, forecasts of female labor supply have usually turned out to be lower than actual labor supply. In part, forecasts may err because the models on which they are based are overly simple. In particular, most forecasts involve simply inserting expected future values (e.g., of wage rates) into a labor supply equation, which implies that given changes in such variables will always produce the same change in labor supply. However, as Figure 7.1 implies, if tastes within the *nonworking* subpopulation do *not* resemble a randomly distributed mean-zero error term – something that most simple labor supply models ignore – then given changes in wage rates or property incomes may not always have the same effect on labor supply. On the other hand, forecasting is bound to be difficult even if one uses a highly sophisticated and detailed labor supply model: Future values of independent variables, such as the wage rate, cannot be known in advance, and factors that may shift little in the short run, such as tastes, may change substantially in the long run.[6]

7.2. Where do we go from here?

Just what the end products of future research will be – for example, whether it will prove possible to narrow the range of parameter estimates of labor supply responses, and what the consensus estimates will be – is, of course, impossible to say. However, it does seem possible to say something about the likely concerns of future work, for here past experience provides a few clues.

First, in very general terms, one might say that the second-generation research discussed in Chapter 4 is based on the simple,

---

[6] For extensive discussion of trends in female labor force participation in developed countries and on use of cross-section participation patterns to forecast time-series behavior of participation, see the papers presented at a June 1983 conference on women's work, education, and family building forthcoming in a special issue of the *Journal of Labor Economics*.

but extremely important, insight that many problems that are essentially empirical in nature (e.g., sample selection, missing wage data, and the like) are intimately connected. Although all predictions are hazardous, it seems at least possible that the next decade or so will see the advent of third-generation research premised on an equally simple, but equally important, unifying concept: Many analytical problems are also intimately tied together. Just as second-generation research was concerned with developing a coherent statistical model in which a wide variety of empirical problems could be analyzed within the same basic framework, third-generation research may be concerned with unifying and regularizing a variety of seemingly unrelated, but fundamentally interconnected, aspects of labor supply.

For example, consider the following set of topics, all of which raise questions of an essentially static nature, and all of which have played a prominent role in recent empirical analyses of labor supply: household behavior, taxation and transfer payments, and fixed costs of labor market entry. On the one hand, as noted in Chapter 2, much recent work has been concerned with the interdependent nature of family labor supply decisions, with intrafamily cross-substitutions of leisure and work time and the like. This work has primarily been theoretical in nature; the relatively small number of empirical studies in this area have focused on testing restrictions (e.g., symmetry) implied by the theoretical models; and questions about taxes, transfers, and fixed costs and their impact on household decisions have generally been ignored or treated in a somewhat cursory manner. On the other hand, as Hausman (1981a) comments, "Fixed costs . . . are particularly important for women because they earn lower wages, work fewer hours and leave the labor force more than men do." Indeed, it may be that fixed costs (and the discontinuities they generate) may help explain the apparently high sensitivity of female labor supply (measured either in terms of participation or in terms of hours of work) to changes in wage rates and the like and may also help explain why empirical estimates based on simple family labor supply models (which typically ignore fixed costs) generally fail to support certain a priori theoretical implications of those models (e.g., symmetry). Taxes and transfers may also play an important role here and magnify the impact of fixed costs of market entry. For example, if many married women are indeed "secondary workers" – perhaps in part because of high fixed costs – then, as Boskin (1974, p. 254) observes, "the progressive rate structure [of present tax laws] combines with the income splitting provision to drive the marginal tax rate on the *first* dollar earned by the second earner in the family – usually the wife – up to the rate on the *last* dollar earned by the first earner" (emphasis original). Indeed, Hausman (1980, 1981a) reports results that imply that taxes, transfers, and fixed costs have quite powerful effects on the labor supply of married women. However, the model of family decision making on which these results are based is rather simple: Marital status and the secondary-worker status of wives are taken as givens on which the rest of the analysis is premised, rather than as outcomes to be explained by that analysis. As Hausman (1981a) points out, the idea that wives are secondary workers (more precisely, the idea that husbands' earnings and labor supplies are independent of the behavior of their wives) may be inaccurate for some households; moreover, it does not emerge naturally from conventional formal models of family labor supply, except perhaps in the male chauvinist model of Chapter 2 (where, strictly speaking, it is again an assumption rather than a conclusion).

Thus, to date, analysis has focused either on joint family decision making to the exclusion (at least in most empirical applications) of taxes, transfers, and fixed costs or on the effects of taxes, transfers, and fixed costs in models in which joint family decision making is largely ignored or treated on an ad hoc basis. The need for a synthesis is apparent. Formulating a coherent picture of the interrelationships between these two sets of factors may be difficult, but recognizing that they are, in fact, interrelated is not. Although these two sets of issues are by no means the only ones where static labor supply analysis would benefit from work aimed at synthesis, they are important examples of topics where such synthesis may figure prominently in future research. The range of empirical issues raised by these questions is extensive and important. For example, to the extent that wives are indeed secondary workers, is this due to role differentiation or a comparative advantage of wives in nonmarket production (e.g., differences in household utility or nonmarket production function coefficients for the nonmarket times of husbands and wives); to differential fixed costs; to unobservable differences in tastes for work that, at least for women, are associated with marital status; or to something else? (See Siegers and Zandanel, 1981, for discussion of similar issues surrounding the relation between labor supply and child-rearing.)

Although the vast array of static labor supply models has developed to the point where synthesis seems likely to be particularly useful, analysis of dynamic labor supply models is still at a stage where extension and elaboration seem at least as important as integration and synthesis. First, so far there has been relatively little empirical work on dynamic labor supply decisions that is comparable, in terms of depth or sophistication, to the recent proliferation of second-generation empirical studies of static labor supply models. Moreover, analytical models of dynamic behavior, for all their occasionally fearsome control-theoretic mathematics, are also still fairly rudimentary – at least when viewed in relation to observed facts about the life cycle that they might be called upon to explain. For example, life cycle relationships between fertility, labor force participation (including, in particular, discontinuities and gaps in labor force participation, a "cycling" between the market and the home), and wage rates for married women, even if fairly easy to understand at a simple intuitive level, do not seem to emerge readily from available formal models of dynamic optimization. Likewise, most investigations of the labor supply effects of taxes and transfers (see Chapters 4 and 6) have been concerned with induced changes in short-term (e.g., annual) hours of work and have largely ignored life cycle effects on human capital investment, lifetime hours of work, retirement decisions, and so on. As Rosen (1980, p. 175) has warned, short-term labor supply effects of taxes and transfers may be "the tip of an iceberg that is potentially very deep"; but, at the moment, it is not possible to discuss long-run effects with even the somewhat hesitant semicertainty that characterizes most discussions of short-run effects. Heckman (1976b), Heckman and MaCurdy (1980, in press), and MaCurdy (1981 a, b) have made an important beginning in developing formal theoretical life cycle models to address these and similar issues and in designing empirical strategies for estimating the parameters of such models. However, as they themselves are quick to point out, such work has only just begun. Such questions about life cycle behavior have profound implications for analysis and policy concerning, for example, population growth, income distribution, male–female wage differentials, and taxation. One, therefore, runs little risk in predicting that much future work on labor supply will be concerned with just such questions.

Dynamic models of labor supply under conditions of risk and uncertainty are likewise in a very early stage of development and are another likely concern of much future work. Models of labor supply rationing and of an individual's choice of a wage–employment package (see Chapter 2) are explicitly concerned with decisions about hours of work but implicitly raise questions about uncertainty and risk. Models of job search are explicitly concerned with uncertainty and risk and take labor supply as fixed, but they implicitly raise questions about labor supply choices, particularly lifetime labor supply choices. Again, refinement and synthesis seem important and potentially fruitful, since future work on these questions promises to advance understanding not only of micro- and cross-sectional phenomena but also of important macro- and time-series relationships concerning, for example, unemployment and business cycles.

BIBLIOGRAPHY

Aaron, H., and J. Todd (1979). "The Use of Income Maintenance Experiment Findings in Public Policy, 1977–78," in Industrial Relations Research Association, *Proceedings of the Thirty-First Annual Meeting*, pp. 46–56. Madison, Wisc.: Industrial Relations Research Association.

Abbott, M., and O. Ashenfelter (1976). "Labour Supply, Commodity Demand and the Allocation of Time." *Review of Economic Studies* 43:389–411.

(1979). "Labour Supply, Commodity Demand and the Allocation of Time: Correction." *Review of Economic Studies* 46:567–9.

Abowd, J. M., and O. Ashenfelter (1979). "Unemployment and Compensating Wage Differentials," Working Paper No. 120. Industrial Relations Section, Princeton University.

(1981). "Anticipated Unemployment, Temporary Layoffs and Compensating Wage Differentials," in S. Rosen, ed., *Studies in Labor Markets*, pp. 141–70. Chicago: University of Chicago Press.

Aigner, D. J. (1974). "An Appropriate Econometric Framework for Estimating a Labor Supply Function from the SEO File." *International Economic Review* 15:59–68.

(1979). "A Brief Introduction to the Methodology of Optimal Experimental Design," *Journal of Econometrics* 11:7–26.

Akerlof, G. (1978). "The Economics of 'Tagging' as Applied to the Optimal Income Tax, Welfare Programs, and Manpower Planning." *American Economic Review* 68:8–19.

Akerlof, G., and H. Miyazaki (1980). "The Implicit Contract Theory of Unemployment Meets the Wage Bill Argument." *Review of Economic Studies* 47:321–38.

Allen, R. G. D. (1938). *Mathematical Analysis for Economists*. London: Macmillan Press.

Allen, S. G. (1981). "An Empirical Model of Work Attendance." *Review of Economics and Statistics* 63:77–87.

Allingham, M. G. (1972). "Progression and Leisure." *American Economic Review* 62:447–50.

Altman, S. H., and R. Barro (1971). "Derivation of a Nursing Supply Function," in S. H. Altman, ed., *Present and Future Supply of Registered Nurses*, pp. 117–40. Bethesda: U. S. Department of Health, Education and Welfare.

Altonji, J. G. (1982). "The Intertemporal Substitution Model of Labour Market Fluctuations: An Empirical Analysis." *Review of Economic Studies* 49 (Supplement): 783–824.

  (1983). "Intertemporal Substitution in Labor Supply: Evidence from Micro Data." Paper prepared for Hoover Institution Conference on Labor Economics.

Amemiya, T. (1973). "Regression Analysis When the Dependent Variable Is Truncated Normal." *Econometrica* 41:997–1017.

  (1975). "Qualitative Response Models." *Annals of Economic and Social Measurement* 4:363–72.

  (1981). "Qualitative Response Models: A Survey." *Journal of Economic Literature* 19:1483–536.

Andersen, P. (1977). "Tax Evasion and Labor Supply." *Scandinavian Journal of Economics* 79:375–83.

Anderson, F. J. (1974). "Pecuniary Externalities and Referent Groups in the Operation of the Price System." *Southern Economic Journal* 40:442–6.

Annable, J. E., Jr. (1977). "A Theory of Downward Rigid Wages and Cyclical Unemployment." *Economic Inquiry* 15:326–44.

  (1980). "Money Wage Determination in Post Keynesian Economics." *Journal of Post Keynesian Economics* 2:405–19.

Arrow, K. J. (1962). "The Economic Implications of Learning by Doing." *Review of Economic Studies* 29:155–73.

  (1963). "Comment." *Review of Economics and Statistics* 45 (Supplement):24–7.

Arrow, K. J., and F. H. Hahn (1971). *General Competitive Analysis*. San Francisco: Holden-Day.

Arrow, K. J., and M. Kurz (1970). *Public Investment, the Rate of Return, and Optimal Fiscal Policy*. Baltimore: Johns Hopkins University Press.

Ashenfelter, O. (1978a). "Unemployment as a Constraint on Labour Market Behaviour," in M. J. Artis and A. R. Nobay, eds., *Contemporary Economic Analysis*, pp. 149–81. London: Croome Helm.

  (1978b). "What Is Involuntary Unemployment?" *Proceedings of the American Philosophical Society* 122:135–8.

  (1978c). "The Labor Supply Response of Wage Earners," in Palmer and Pechman, eds. (1978), pp. 104–38.

  (1980a). "Unemployment as Disequilibrium in a Model of Aggregate Labor Supply." *Econometrica* 48:547–64.

  (1980b). "Discrete Choice in Labor Supply: The Determinants of Participation in the Seattle-Denver Income Maintenance Experiments." Working Paper No. 136. Industrial Relations Section, Princeton University. (Forthcoming in *Journal of the American Statistical Association*.)

Ashenfelter, O., and R. Ehrenberg (1973). "Using Estimates of Income and Substitution Parameters to Predict the Work Incentive Effects of Various Income Maintenance Programs: A Brief Exposition and Partial Survey of the Literature." Technical Analysis Paper No. 2. Office of Evaluation, Office of the

Assistant Secretary for Policy, Evaluation and Research, U. S. Department of Labor.

Ashenfelter, O., and J. Ham (1979). "Education, Unemployment and Earnings." *Journal of Political Economy* 89:S99–116.

Ashenfelter, O., and J. J. Heckman (1973). "Estimating Labor Supply Functions," in Cain and Watts, eds. (1973b), pp. 265–78.

(1974). "The Estimation of Income and Substitution Effects in a Model of Family Labor Supply." *Econometrica* 42:73–85.

Ashworth, J., A. McGlone, and D. Ulph (1977). "Uncertainty, Overtime and the Demand for Labor." *Zeitschrift fur Nationalokonomie* 37:323–36.

Ashworth, J. S., and D. T. Ulph (1981a). "Endogeneity I: Estimating Labour Supply with Piecewise Linear Budget Constraints," in Brown, ed. (1981), pp. 53–68.

(1981b). "Household Models," in Brown, ed. (1981), pp. 117–33.

Atkinson, A. B., and N. H. Stern (1980). "On the Switch from Direct to Indirect Taxation." *Journal of Public Economics* 14:195–224.

(1981). "On Labour Supply and Commodity Demands," in A. Deaton, ed., *Essays in the Theory and Measurement of Consumer Behaviour in Honour of Sir Richard Stone*, pp. 265–96. Cambridge: Cambridge University Press.

Atrostic, B. K. (1982). "The Demand for Leisure and Nonpecuniary Job Characteristics." *American Economic Review* 72:428–40.

Axelsson, R., R. Jacobsson, and K.-G. Löfgren (1981). "A Note on the General Equilibrium Effects of Taxes on Labor Supply in Sweden." *Scandinavian Journal of Economics* 83:449–56.

Azariadis, C. (1975). "Implicit Contracts and Underemployment Equilibria." *Journal of Political Economy* 83:1183–202.

(1976). "On the Incidence of Unemployment." *Review of Economic Studies* 43: 115–25.

(1977). "R. J. Gordon [1977] on Unemployment Theory." *Journal of Monetary Economics* 3:253–5.

(1981). "Implicit Contracts and Related Topics: A Survey," in Hornstein, Grice, and Webb, eds. (1981), pp. 219–48.

Bailey, M. J. (1954). "The Marshallian Demand Curve." *Journal of Political Economy* 62:255–61.

(1962). *National Income and the Price Level*, 1st ed. New York: McGraw-Hill.

Baily, M. N. (1974). "Wages and Employment under Uncertain Demand." *Review of Economic Studies* 41: 37–50.

(1977). "On the Theory of Layoffs and Unemployment." *Econometrica* 45: 1043–63.

(1981). "Comment [on Azariadis, 1981]," in Hornstein, Grice, and Webb, eds. (1981), pp. 254–7.

Baldry, J. C. (1979). "Tax Evasion and Labor Supply." *Economics Letters* 3: 53–6.

Barnett, W. A. (1977). "Pollak and Wachter on the Household Production Function Approach." *Journal of Political Economy* 85:1073–82.

(1979a). "The Joint Allocation of Leisure and Goods Expenditure." *Econometrica* 47:539–604.

(1979b). "Theoretical Foundations for the Rotterdam Model." *Review of*

Economic Studies 46:109–30.

(1981). *Consumer Demand and Labor Supply*. Amsterdam: North Holland.

Barro, R. J. (1974). "Are Government Bonds Net Wealth?" *Journal of Political Economy* 82:1095–117.

(1977). "Long-Term Contracting, Sticky Prices and Monetary Policy." *Journal of Monetary Economics* 3:305–16.

(1978). *The Impact of Social Security on Private Saving*. Washington, D. C.: American Enterprise Institute.

Barro, R. J., and H. I. Grossman (1971). "A General Disequilibrium Model of Income and Employment." *American Economic Review* 61:82–93.

(1974). "Suppressed Inflation and the Supply Multiplier." *Review of Economic Studies* 41:87–104.

(1976). *Money, Employment and Inflation*. Cambridge: Cambridge University Press.

Barten, A. P. (1977). "The System of Consumer Demand Functions Approach: A Review." *Econometrica* 45:23–51.

Barth, P. S. (1967). "A Cross-Sectional Analysis of Labor Force Participation Rates in Michigan." *Industrial and Labor Relations Review* 20:234–49.

Barzel, Y. (1973). "The Determination of Daily Hours and Wages." *Quarterly Journal of Economics* 87:220–38.

Barzel, Y., and R. J. McDonald (1973). "Assets, Subsistence and the Supply Curve of Labor." *American Economic Review* 63:621–33.

Battalio, R. C., L. Green, and J. H. Kagel (1981). "Income-Leisure Tradeoffs of Animal Workers." *American Economic Review* 71:621–32.

Bawden, D. L. (1969). "A Negative Tax Experiment for Rural Areas," in *Proceedings of the Social Statistics Section, American Statistical Association, 1969*, pp. 157–62.

(1970). "Income Maintenance and the Rural Poor: An Experimental Approach." *American Journal of Agricultural Economics* 52:438–41.

(1977). "Income and Work Response of Husbands," in Bawden and Harrar, eds. (1977b), Chap. 3.

Bawden, D. L., and W. Harrar (1977a). "Purpose and Design of the Rural Income Maintenance Experiment." *American Journal of Agricultural Economics* 59: 855–8.

eds. (1977b). *Rural Income Maintenance Experiment: Final Report*. Madison: Institute for Research on Poverty, University of Wisconsin.

Becker, G. S. (1965). "A Theory of the Allocation of Time." *Economic Journal* 75: 493–517.

(1974). "A Theory of Marriage," in T. W. Schultz, ed., *Economics of the Family*, pp. 293–344. Chicago: University of Chicago Press.

(1975a). "A Theory of Social Interactions." *Journal of Political Economy* 82: 1063–93.

(1975b). *Human Capital*, 2nd ed. New York: Columbia University Press.

(1975c). "The Allocation of Time over the Life Cycle," in G. Ghez and G. S. Becker, *The Allocation of Time and Goods over the Life Cycle*, pp. 83–132. New York: Columbia University Press.

(1977). "A Theory of the Production and Allocation of Effort." Unpublished manuscript, Department of Economics, University of Chicago.

(1981). *A Treatise on the Family*. Cambridge, Mass.: Harvard University Press.

Benham, L. (1971). "The Labor Market for Registered Nurses: A Three-Equation Model," *Review of Economics and Statistics* 53:246–52.

Ben-Porath, Y. (1967). "The Production of Human Capital and the Life Cycle of Earnings." *Journal of Political Economy* 75 (Supplement):352–65.

(1970). "The Production of Human Capital over Time." in Hansen, ed. (1970), pp. 129–47.

(1973). "Labor-Force Participation Rates and the Supply of Labor." *Journal of Political Economy* 81:697–704.

Berch, B. (1977). "Wages and Labour," in F. Green and P. Nore, eds., *Economics: An Anti-Text*, pp. 89–104. London: Macmillan Press.

Bienefield, M. A. (1969). "The Normal Week under Collective Bargaining." *Economica* 36:172–92.

Bishop, C. E. (1973). "Manpower Policy and the Supply of Nurses." *Industrial Relations* 12:86–94.

Blaug, M. (1976). "The Empirical Status of Human Capital Theory: A Slightly Jaundiced Survey." *Journal of Economic Literature* 14:827–55.

Blinder, A. S., R. H. Gordon, and D. E. Wise (1980). "Reconsidering the Work Disincentive Effects of Social Security." *National Tax Journal* 33:431–42.

(1981). "Rhetoric and Reality in Social Security Analysis — A Rejoinder [to Burkhauser and Turner, 1981]." *National Tax Journal* 34:473–8.

Blinder, A. S., and Y. Weiss (1976). "Human Capital and Labor Supply: A Synthesis." *Journal of Political Economy* 84:449–72.

Bloch, F. (1973). "The Allocation of Time to Market and Nonmarket Work within a Family Unit." Technical Report No. 114. Institute for Mathematical Studies in the Social Sciences, Stanford University.

Block, M. K., and J. M. Heineke (1972). "A Comment on Uncertainty and Household Decisions." *Review of Economic Studies* 39:523–5.

(1973). "The Allocation of Effort under Uncertainty: The Case of Risk-Averse Behavior." *Journal of Political Economy* 81:376–85.

Bloom, D. E., and M. R. Killingsworth (1982). "Pay Discrimination Research and Litigation: The Use of Regression." *Industrial Relations* 21:318–39.

Blundell, R. W. (1980). "Estimating Continuous Consumer Equivalence Scales in an Expenditure Model with Labor Supply." *European Economic Review* 14:145–57.

Blundell, R. W., and I. Walker (1982). "Modelling the Joint Determination of Household Labour Supplies and Commodity Demands." *Economic Journal* 92:351–64.

Boeckmann, M. E. (1976). "Policy Impacts of the New Jersey Income Maintenance Experiment." *Policy Sciences* 7:53–76.

Bognanno, M. F., J. S. Hixson, and I. R. Jeffers (1974). "The Short-Run Supply of Nurse's Time." *Journal of Human Resources* 9:80–94.

Borjas, G. J. (1980). "The Relationship between Wages and Weekly Hours of Work: The Role of Division Bias." *Journal of Human Resources* 15:409–23.

Borjas, G., and J. J. Heckman (1979). "Labor Supply Estimates for Public Policy Evaluation," in Industrial Relations Research Association, *Proceedings of the*

Thirty-First Annual Meeting, pp. 320–31. Madison, Wisc.: Industrial Relations Research Association.

Boskin, M. J. (1967). "The Negative Income Tax and the Supply of Work Effort." *National Tax Journal* 20:353–67.

(1969). "The Negative Income Tax and the Supply of Work Effort: Reply [to Kesselman, 1969]." *National Tax Journal* 22:417.

(1973). "The Economics of Labor Supply," in Cain and Watts, eds. (1973b), pp. 163–81.

(1974). "The Effects of Government Taxes and Expenditures on Female Labor." *American Economic Review* 64:251–6.

(1977). "Social Security and Retirement Decisions." *Economic Inquiry* 15:1–25.

Boskin, M. J., and M. D. Hurd (1978). "The Effect of Social Security on Early Retirement." *Journal of Public Economics* 10:361–77.

Boskin, M. J., and E. Sheshinski (1979). "Optimal Tax Treatment of the Family: Married Couples." Working Paper No. 368. National Bureau of Economic Research.

Bosworth, D. L., and P. J. Dawkins (1980). "Compensation for Workers Disutility: Time of Day, Length of Shift and Other Features of Work Patterns." *Scottish Journal of Political Economy* 27:80–96.

Bowen, W. G., and T. A. Finegan (1965). "Labor Force Participation and Unemployment," in A. M. Ross, ed., *Employment Policy and the Labor Market*, pp. 115–61. Berkeley: University of California Press.

(1966). "Comment [on Mincer, 1966]," in R. A. Gordon and M. S. Gordon, eds., *Prosperity and Unemployment*, pp. 113–31. New York: Wiley.

(1969). *The Economics of Labor Force Participation*. Princeton, N. J.: Princeton University Press.

Bowers, J. K. (1975). "British Activity Rates: a Survey of Research," *Scottish Journal of Political Economy* 22:57–90.

Brown, A., and A. Deaton (1972). "Models of Consumer Behaviour: A Survey." *Economic Journal* 82:1145–236.

Brown, C. (1976). "A Model of Optimal Human-Capital Accumulation and the Wages of Young High School Graduates." *Journal of Political Economy* 84:299–316.

Brown, C. V., ed. (1981). *Taxation and Labour Supply*. London: Allen & Unwin.

Brown, C. V., E. Levin, and D. T. Ulph (1976). "Estimates of Labour Hours Supplied by Married Male Workers in Great Britain." *Scottish Journal of Political Economy* 23:261–77.

(1981), "The Basic Model," in Brown, ed. (1981), pp. 35–52.

Browning, E. K. (1971). "Incentive and Disincentive Experimentation for Income Maintenance Policy Purposes: Note." *American Economic Review* 61:709–12.

(1973). "Alternative Programs for Income Redistribution: The NIT and the NWT." *American Economic Review* 63:38–49.

(1975). "Labor Supply Distortions of Social Security." *Southern Economic Journal* 42:243–52.

Bryant, J. (1978). "An Annotation of 'Implicit Contracts and Underemployment Equilibria.' " *Journal of Political Economy* 86:1159–60.

Buchanan, J. M. (1971). "The Backbending Supply Curve of Labor: an Example of

Doctrinal Retrogression." *History of Political Economy* 3:383–90.

Burdett, K., and D. T. Mortensen (1978). "Labor Supply under Uncertainty," in R. G. Ehrenberg, ed., *Research in Labor Economics,* Vol. 2, pp. 109–58. Greenwich, Conn.: JAI Press.

Burkhauser, R. V. (1979). "The Pension Acceptance Decision of Older Workers." *Journal of Human Resources* 14:63–75.

(1980). "The Early Acceptance of Social Security: An Asset Maximization Approach." *Industrial and Labor Relations Review* 33:484–92.

Burkhauser, R. V., and J. A. Turner (1978). "A Time-Series Analysis of Social Security and Its Effect on the Market Work of Men at Younger Ages." *Journal of Political Economy* 86:701–15.

(1980a). "The Effects of Pension Policy through Life," in Clark, ed. (1980), pp. 128–42.

(1980b). "Rejoinder [to Reimers, 1980]," in Clark, ed. (1980), pp. 150–4.

(1981). "Can Twenty-Five Million Americans Be Wrong? A Response to Blinder, Gordon and Wise [1980]." *National Tax Journal* 34:467–72.

(1982). "Social Security, Preretirement Labor Supply, and Saving: A Confirmation and a Critique." *Journal of Political Economy* 90:643–646.

Burtless, G., and D. Greenberg (1982). "Inferences Concerning Labor Supply Behavior Based on Limited-Duration Experiments." *American Economic Review* 72:488–97.

Burtless, G., and J. A. Hausman (1978). "The Effect of Taxation on Labor Supply: Evaluating the Gary Income Negative Income Tax Experiment." *Journal of Political Economy* 86:1103–30.

Burton, J. (1977). "A Critique of the Relative Deprivation Hypothesis of Wage Inflation." *Scottish Journal of Political Economy* 24:67–76.

Butler, R., and J. J. Heckman (1977). "The Government's Impact on the Labor Market Status of Black Americans: A Critical Review," in L. J. Hausman, O. Ashenfelter, B. Rustin, R. F. Schubert, and D. Slaiman, eds., *Equal Rights and Industrial Relations*, pp. 235–81. Madison, Wisc.: Industrial Relations Research Association.

Cain, G. G. (1966). *Married Women in the Labor Force.* Chicago: University of Chicago Press.

(1975). "Regression and Selection Models to Improve Nonexperimental Comparison," in C. A. Bennett and A. A. Lumsdaine, eds., *Evaluation and Experiment: Some Critical Issues in Assessing Social Programs*, pp. 297–317. New York: Academic Press.

(1976). "The Challenge of Segmented Labor Market Theories to Orthodox Theories: A Survey." *Journal of Economic Literature* 14:1215–57.

(1977). "New Data and Old Issues in the Study of Labor Force Behavior." Unpublished manuscript, Department of Economics, University of Wisconsin.

Cain, G. G., W. Nicholson, C. Mallar, and J. Wooldridge (1974). "The Labor-Supply Response of Married Women, Husband Present." *Journal of Human Resources* 9:201–22.

Cain, G. G., W. Nicholson, C. Mallar, and J. Wooldridge (1977). "Labor-Supply Response of Wives," in Watts and Rees, eds. (1977), pp. 115–62.

Cain, G. G., and H. W. Watts (1973a). "Toward a Summary and Synthesis of the

Evidence," in Cain and Watts, eds. (1973b), pp. 328–67.

eds. (1973b). *Income Maintenance and Labor Supply*. New York: Academic Press.

Calvo, G., and E. S. Phelps (1977). "Appendix: Employment-Contingent Wage Contracts," in K. Brunner and A. H. Meltzer, eds., *Stabilization of the Domestic and International Economy*, pp. 160–8. New York: North Holland.

Cassidy, H. J. (1970). "Work Effort under Proportional and Progressive Taxation." *Journal of Political Economy* 78:1163–7.

Cazenave, P., and C. Morrison (1973). "Fonctions d'Utilite Interdependantes et Theorie de la Redistribution en Economie de Production." *Revue Economique* 24:725–60.

Chase, E. S. (1967). "Leisure and Consumption," in K. Shell, ed., *Essays on the Theory of Optimal Economic Growth*, pp. 175–80. Cambridge, Mass.: MIT Press.

Chiang, A. (1974). *Fundamental Methods of Mathematical Economics*, 2nd ed. New York: McGraw-Hill.

Cichetti, C. J., and V. K. Smith (1973). "Interdependent Consumer Decisions: A Production Function Approach." *Australian Economic Papers* 12:239–52.

Clark, K. B., and L. H. Summers (1982). "Labour Force Participation: Timing and Persistence," *Review of Economic Studies* 49 (Supplement): 825–44.

Clark, R. L., ed. (1980). *Retirement Policy in an Aging Society*. Durham, N. C.: Duke University Press.

Clower, R. (1965). "The Keynesian Counter-Revolution: A Theoretical Appraisal," in F. H. Hahn and F. P. R. Brechling, eds., *The Theory of Interest Rates*, pp. 103–25. London: Macmillan Press.

Cogan, J. F. (1978). "Negative Income Taxation and Labor Supply: New Evidence from the New Jersey-Pennsylvania Experiment." Report R-2155-HEW. The Rand Corporation.

(1980a). "Married Women's Labor Supply: A Comparison of Alternative Estimation Procedures," in Smith, ed. (1980c), pp. 90–118.

(1980b). "Labor Supply with Costs of Labor Market Entry," in Smith, ed. (1980c), pp. 327–64.

(1981). "Fixed Costs and Labor Supply." *Econometrica* 49:945–64.

Cohen, M. S., S. A. Rea, and R. I. Lerman (1970). *A Micro Model of Labor Supply*. BLS Staff Paper No. 4, U. S. Department of Labor. Washington, D.C.: Government Printing Office.

Cohen, M. S., and F. P. Stafford (1974). "A Life Cycle Model of the Household's Time Allocation." *Annals of Economic and Social Measurement* 3:447–62.

Conant, E. H. (1963). "Worker Efficiency and Wage Differentials in a Clerical Labor Market." *Industrial and Labor Relations Review* 16:428–33.

Conlisk, J., and H. W. Watts (1969). "A Model for Optimizing Experimental Designs for Estimating Response Surfaces," in *Proceedings of the Social Statistics Section, American Statistical Association, 1969*, pp. 150–6.

Cotterman, R. F. (1981). "The Role of Assets in Labor Supply Functions." *Economic Inquiry* 19:495–505.

Cowell, F. A. (1981a). "Income Maintenance Schemes under Wage Rate

Uncertainty." *American Economic Review* 71:692–703.

(1981b). "Taxation and Labour Supply with Risky Activities," *Economica* 48: 365–79.

Dankert, C. E. (1962). "Shorter Hours — In Theory and Practice." *Industrial and Labor Relations Review* 15:323–49.

Danziger, S., R. Haveman, and R. Plotnick (1981). "How Income Transfers Affect Work, Savings and Income Distribution." *Journal of Economic Literature* 19: 975–1028.

Darrough, M. N. (1977). "A Model of Consumption and Leisure in an Intertemporal Framework: A Systematic Treatment Using Japanese Data." *International Economic Review* 18:677–96.

DaVanzo, J., D. DeTray, and D. Greenberg (1973). "Estimating Labor Supply Response: A Sensitivity Analysis." Report R-1372-OEO. The Rand Corporation.

(1976). "The Sensitivity of Male Labor Supply Estimates to Choice of Assumptions." *Review of Economics and Statistics* 58:313–25.

Deardorff, A. V., and F. P. Stafford (1976). "Compensation of Cooperating Factors." *Econometrica* 44:671–84.

Deaton, A. (1974). "A Reconsideration of the Empirical Implications of Additive Preferences." *Economic Journal* 84:338–48.

(1981). "Optimal Taxes and the Structure of Preferences." *Econometrica* 49: 1245–60.

Deaton, A., and J. Muellbauer (1981). "Functional Forms for Labour Supply and Commodity Demands with and without Quantity Restrictions." *Econometrica* 49:1521–32.

DeSerpa, A. C. (1971). "A Theory of the Economics of Time." *Economic Journal* 81:828–46.

Diamond, P. A. (1968). "Negative Taxes and the Poverty Problem — A Review Article." *National Tax Journal* 21:288–303.

(1977). "A Framework for Social Security Analysis." *Journal of Public Economics* 8:275–98.

Diamond, P. A., and J. Mirrlees (1978). "A Model of Social Insurance with Variable Retirement." *Journal of Public Economics* 10:295–336.

Diamond, P. A., and J. E. Stiglitz (1974). "Increases in Risk and in Risk Aversion." *Journal of Economic Theory* 8:337–60.

Dickinson, J. G. (1975). "Theoretical Labor Supply Models and Real-World Complications." Working Paper No. 312–75, Institute for Research on Poverty, University of Wisconsin.

(1979). "Revealed Preferences, Functional Form and Labor Supply." Discussion Paper No. 546–79. Institute for Research on Poverty, University of Wisconsin.

(1980). "Parallel Preference Structures in Labor Supply and Commodity Demand: An Application of the Gorman Polar Form." *Econometrica* 48:1711–26.

Diewert, W. E. (1974). "Intertemporal Consumer Theory and the Demand for Durables." *Econometrica* 42:497–516.

Dixit, A. K. (1976). *Optimization in Economic Theory*. Oxford: Oxford University Press.

Doeringer, P., and M. Piore (1971). *Internal Labor Markets and Manpower Analysis.* Lexington, Mass.: Heath.

Dooley, M. D. (1982). "Labor Supply and Fertility of Married Women: An Analysis with Grouped and Individual Data from the 1970 U. S. Census." *Journal of Human Resources* 17:499–532.

Driffill, E. J. (1980). "Life-Cycles with Terminal Retirement." *International Economic Review* 21:45–62.

Duesenberry, J. (1949). *Income, Spending and the Theory of Consumer Behavior.* Cambridge, Mass.: Harvard University Press.

Duncan, G. J., and F. P. Stafford (1980). "Do Union Members Receive Compensating Wage Differentials?" *American Economic Review* 70:355–71.

Dunn, L. F. (1978). "An Empirical Indifference Function for Income and Leisure." *Review of Economics and Statistics* 60:533–40.

(1979). "Measurement of Internal Income-Leisure Tradeoffs." *Quarterly Journal of Economics* 93:373–93.

Easterlin, R. A. (1968). *Population, Labor Force and Long Swings in Economic Growth: The American Experience.* New York: Columbia University Press.

Eaton, J., and R. E. Quandt (1980). "A Quasi-Walrasian Model of Rationing and Labor Supply: Theory and Estimation." Research Memorandum No. 251. Econometric Research Program, Princeton University.

Eaton, J., and H. S. Rosen (1980a). "Optimal Redistributive Taxation and Uncertainty." *Quarterly Journal of Economics* 94:357–64.

(1980b). "Labor Supply, Uncertainty and Efficient Taxation." *Journal of Public Economics* 14:365–74.

(1980c). "Taxation, Human Capital and Uncertainty." *American Economic Review* 70:705–15.

Eckaus, R. S. (1963). "Investment in Human Capital: A Comment." *Journal of Political Economy* 71:501–4.

Eckstein, O., and T. Wilson (1962). "The Determination of Money Wages in American Industry." *Quarterly Journal of Economics* 72:110–18.

Eden, B. (1980). "Stochastic Dominance in Human Capital." *Journal of Political Economy* 88:135–45.

Eden, B. and A. Pakes (1979). "Using Consumption Data for Measuring the Time Resolution of Uncertainty." Discussion Paper No. 792. Falk Institute, Hebrew University of Jerusalem.

Edlefsen, L. E. (1982). "The Effects of Taxation and Other Government Activity on Price and Quantity in General Equilibrium." Unpublished manuscript, Department of Economics, University of Washington.

Ehrenberg, R. G. (1970). "Absenteeism and the Overtime Decision." *American Economic Review* 60:352–7.

Ehrenberg, R. G. and R. S. Smith (1982). *Modern Labor Economics.* Glenview, Ill.: Scott, Foresman.

Fan, L.-S. (1972). "Leisure and Time Elements in the Consumer Behavior." *Southern Economic Journal* 38:478–84.

Faurot, D. J., and G. H. Sellon, Jr. (1981). "Analyzing Labor Supply without Considering Income from Assets." *Review of Economics and Statistics* 63:458–62.

Feldstein, M. S. (1968). "Estimating the Supply Curve of Working Hours." *Oxford Economic Papers* 20:74–80.

(1974a). "Unemployment Compensation, Adverse Incentives and Distributional Anomalies." *National Tax Journal* 37:231–44.

(1974b). "Social Security, Induced Retirement and Aggregate Capital Accumulation." *Journal of Political Economy* 82:905–26.

(1976). "Temporary Layoffs in the Theory of Unemployment." *Journal of Political Economy* 84:937–57.

(1982). "Social Security and Private Saving: Reply [to Leimer and Lesnoy, 1982]." *Journal of Political Economy* 90:630–42.

Feldstein, M. S., ed. (1983). *Behavioral Simulation Methods in Tax Policy Analysis.* Chicago: University of Chicago Press. Forthcoming, 1983.

Fields, G. S., and O. S. Mitchell (1982). "Economic Determinants of the Optimal Retirement Age: An Empirical Investigation." Working Paper No. 876. National Bureau of Economic Research.

Finegan, T. A. (1962a). "Comment [on Vatter, 1961]: The Backward Sloping Supply Curve." *Industrial and Labor Relations Review* 15:230–4.

(1962b). "Hours of Work in the United States — A Cross-Sectional Analysis." *Journal of Political Economy* 70:452–70.

(1978). "Hours of Work in the Long Run," in U. S. National Commission for Manpower Policy, *Work Time and Employment.* Washington, D. C.: Government Printing Office.

(1981). "Discouraged Workers and Economic Fluctuations." *Industrial and Labor Relations Review* 35:88–102.

Fisher, M. R. (1968). "Selection of Skill, Training and Occupational Mobility." *Manchester School* 36:111–30.

(1971). *The Economic Analysis of Labour.* London: Weidenfeld & Nicolson.

Fleisher, B., and T. J. Kniesner (1980). *Labor Economics.* Englewood Cliffs, N.J.: Prentice-Hall.

Fleisher, B., D. Parsons, and R. D. Porter (1973). "Asset Adjustment and Labor Supply of Older Workers," in Cain and Watts, eds. (1973b), pp. 279–327.

Flueckiger, G. E. (1976). "Specialization, Learning by Doing and the Optimal Amount of Learning." *Economic Inquiry* 14:389–409.

Forbes Magazine (1972). "Plucking the Goose." Vol. 109 (February 15), p. 22.

Franz, W. (1981). "Schatzung Regionaler Arbeitsangebotsfunktionen mit Hilfe der Tobit-Methode und des Probit-verfahrens unter Berucksichtigung des sog. 'Sample Selection Bias'." Discussion Paper No. 171–81. Institut für Volkswirtschaftslehre und Statistik, University of Mannheim.

Franz, W., and S. Kawasaki (1981). "Labor Supply of Married Women in the Federal Republic of Germany: Theory and Empirical Results from a New Estimation Procedure." *Empirical Economics* 6:129–43.

Friedman, B. L., and L. J. Hausman (1974). "Income Conditioning in a System of Transfer Programs." *American Economic Review* 64 (May):175–80.

Friedman, M. (1949). "The Marshallian Demand Curve." *Journal of Political Economy* 57:463–94.

(1957). *A Theory of the Consumption Function.* Princeton, N. J.: Princeton University Press.

(1962). *Capitalism and Freedom*. Chicago: University of Chicago Press.

Fullerton, D. (1982). "On the Possibility of an Inverse Relationship between Tax Rates and Government Revenues." *Journal of Public Economics* 19:3–22.

Futia, C. (1977). "Excess Supply Equilibria." *Journal of Economic Theory* 14:200–20.

Garfinkel, I. (1973a). "On Estimating the Labor Supply Effects of a Negative Income Tax," in Cain and Watts, eds. (1973b), pp. 205–64.

(1973b). "A Skeptical Note on 'The Optimality' of Wage Subsidy Programs." *American Economic Review* 63:447–53.

Gayer, D. (1977). "The Effects of Wages, Unearned Income and Taxes on the Supply of Labor." *International Economic Review* 18:101–16.

Ghez, G. (1975). "The Allocation of Goods over the Life Cycle," in G. Ghez and G. S. Becker, *The Allocation of Time and Goods over the Life Cycle*, pp. 46–82. New York: Columbia University Press.

Ghez, G., and G. S. Becker (1975). "A Theory of the Allocation of Time and Goods over the Life Cycle," in G. Ghez and G. S. Becker, *The Allocation of Time and Goods over the Life Cycle*, pp. 1–45. New York: Columbia University Press.

Gilbert, F. L., and R. L. Pfouts (1958). "A Theory of the Responsiveness of Hours of Work to Changes in the Wage Rate." *Review of Economics and Statistics* 40:116–21.

Glaister, K., A. McGlone, and R. J. Ruffell (1981). "Preferences," in Brown, ed. (1980), pp. 69–100.

Goldberger, A. (1967). "Functional Form and Utility: A Review of Consumer Demand Theory." Workshop Paper No. 6703. Social Systems Research Institute, University of Wisconsin.

Gordon, D. F. (1974). "A Neo-Classical Theory of Keynesian Unemployment." *Economic Inquiry* 12:431–59.

Gordon, R. H., and A. S. Blinder (1980). "Market Wages, Reservation Wages and Retirement Decisions." *Journal of Public Economics* 14:277–308.

Gordon, R. J. (1976). "Aspects of the Theory of Involuntary Unemployment: A Comment," in K. Brunner and A. H. Meltzer, eds., *The Phillips Curve and Labor Markets*, pp. 98–119. Amsterdam: North Holland.

(1977). "Aspects of Unemployment Theory: Reply to Azariadis [1977]." *Journal of Monetary Economics* 3:257–60.

Gramm, W. L. (1974). "The Demand for the Wife's Nonmarket Time." *Southern Economic Journal* 41:124–33.

(1975). "Household Utility Maximization and the Working Wife." *American Economic Review* 65:90–100.

Green, C. (1967). *Negative Taxes and the Poverty Problem*. Washington, D. C.: Brookings Institution.

(1968). "Negative Taxes and Monetary Incentives to Work: The Static Theory." *Journal of Human Resources* 3:280–8.

Green, H. A. J. (1971). *Consumer Theory*. London: Penguin Books.

Greenberg, D. H. (1971). "Income Guarantees and the Working Poor in New York City: The Effect of Income Maintenance Programs on the Hours of Work of Male Family Heads." Report R-658-NYC. The Rand Corporation.

(1972). "Problems of Model Specification and Measurement: The Labor Supply

Function." Report R-1085-EDA. The Rand Corporation.

Greenberg, D. H., and M. Kosters (1973). "Income Guarantees and the Working Poor: The Effect of Income-Maintenance Programs on the Hours of Work of Male Family Heads," in Cain and Watts, eds. (1973b), pp. 14–101.

Greenberg, D., R. Moffitt, and J. Friedmann (1981). "Underreporting and Experimental Effects on Work Effort: Evidence from the Gary Income Maintenance Experiment." *Review of Economics and Statistics* 63:581–9.

Greenhalgh, C. A. (1977). "A Labour Supply Function for Married Women in Great Britain." *Economica* 44:249–65.

   (1979). "Male Labour Force Participation in Great Britain." *Scottish Journal of Political Economy* 26:275–86.

   (1980). "Participation and Hours of Work for Married Women in Great Britain." *Oxford Economic Papers* 32:296–318.

Gronau, R. (1973a). "The Effect of Children on the Housewife's Value of Time." *Journal of Political Economy* 81:S168–99.

   (1973b). "The Intrafamily Allocation of Time: The Value of the Housewives' Time." *American Economic Review* 63:634–51.

   (1973c). "The Measurement of Output in the Non-Market Sector — The Evaluation of Housewives' Time," in M. Moss, ed., *The Measurement of Economic and Social Performance*, pp. 163–90. New York: Columbia University Press.

   (1974). "Wage Comparisons — A Selectivity Bias." *Journal of Political Economy* 82:1119–43.

   (1977). "Leisure, Home Production and Work — The Theory of the Allocation of Time Revisited." *Journal of Political Economy* 85:1099–124.

Grossman, H. I. (1977). "Risk Shifting and Reliability in Labor Markets." *Scandinavian Journal of Economics* 79:187–209.

   (1978). "Risk Shifting, Layoffs and Seniority." *Journal of Monetary Economics* 4:661–86.

   (1981). "Risk Shifting, Unemployment Insurance and Layoffs," in Hornstein, Grice, and Webb, eds. (1981), pp. 259–77.

Hadley, G., and M. C. Kemp (1971). *Variational Methods in Economics.* Amsterdam: North Holland.

Haley, W. (1973). "Human Capital: The Choice between Investment and Income." *American Economic Review* 63:929–44.

   (1976). "Estimation of the Earnings Profile from Optimal Human Capital Accumulation." *Econometrica* 44:1223–38.

Hall, A., and T. R. Johnson (1980). "The Determinants of Planned Retirement Age." *Industrial and Labor Relations Review* 33:241–54.

Hall, R. E. (1973). "Wages, Income and Hours of Work in the U.S. Labor Force," in Cain and Watts, eds. (1973b), pp. 102–162.

   (1980a). "Employment Fluctuations and Wage Rigidity." *Brookings Papers on Economic Activity* 1980(1):91–123.

   (1980b). "Labor Supply and Aggregate Fluctuations." *Journal of Monetary Economics* 12:7–33.

Hall, R. E., and D. M. Lillien (1979). "Efficient Wage Bargains under Uncertain Supply and Demand." *American Economic Review* 69:868–79.

Ham, J. C. (1982). "Estimation of a Labour Supply Model with Censoring Due to Unemployment and Underemployment." *Review of Economic Studies* 49:333–54.

Hamermesh, D. S. (1974). "Enjoyable Work and Labor Supply: A Pedagogical Note." Unpublished manuscript, Department of Economics, Michigan State University.

(1975). "Interdependence in the Labour Market." *Economica* 42:420–9.

Handler, J. F., and E. J. Hollingsworth (1971). *The "Deserving Poor."* Chicago: Markham.

Hanoch, G. (1965). "The 'Backward-Bending' Supply of Labor." *Journal of Political Economy* 73:636–42.

(1980a). "Hours and Weeks in the Theory of Labor Supply," in Smith, ed. (1980c), pp. 119–65.

(1980b). "A Multivariate Model of Labor Supply: Methodology and Estimation," in Smith, ed. (1980c), pp. 249–326.

Hanoch, G., and M. Honig (1978). "The Labor Supply Curve under Income Maintenance Programs." *Journal of Public Economics* 9:1–16.

Hansen, W. L., ed. (1970). *Education, Income and Human Capital.* New York: National Bureau of Economic Research.

Hartley, M. J., and N. S. Revankar (1974). "Labor Supply under Uncertainty and the Rate of Unemployment." *American Economic Review* 64:170–5.

Hashimoto, M., and B. T. Yu (1980). "Specific Capital, Employment Contracts and Wage Rigidity." *Bell Journal of Economics* 11:536–49.

Hausman, J. A. (1979). "The Econometrics of Labor Supply on Convex Budget Sets." *Economics Letters* 3:171–4.

(1980). "The Effect of Wages, Taxes and Fixed Costs on Women's Labor Force Participation." *Journal of Public Economics* 14:161–94.

(1981a). "Labor Supply," in H. Aaron and J. Pechman, eds., *How Taxes Affect Economic Behavior*, pp. 27–72. Washington, D.C.: Brookings Institution.

(1981b). "Income and Payroll Tax Policy and Labor Supply," in L. H. Meyer, ed., *The Supply-Side Effects of Economic Policy*, pp. 173–202. St. Louis, Mo.: Center for the Study of American Business, Washington University.

(1981c). "Stochastic Problems in the Simulation of Labor Supply." Paper presented at National Bureau of Economic Research Conference on Behavioral Simulation Methods in Tax Policy Analysis, Palm Beach, Fla. (forthcoming in M. S. Feldstein, ed., 1983).

Hausman, J. A., and D. A. Wise (1976). "The Evaluation of Results from Truncated Samples: The New Jersey Negative Income Tax Experiment." *Annals of Economic and Social Measurement* 5:421–46.

(1977). "Social Experimentation, Truncated Distributions and Efficient Estimation." *Econometrica* 45:919–38.

(1979). "Attrition Bias in Experimental and Panel Data: The Gary Income Maintenance Experiment." *Econometrica* 47:455–75.

(1981). "Stratification on Endogenous Variables and Estimation: The Gary Income Maintenance Experiment," in D. McFadden and C. Manski, eds., *Statistical Analysis of Discrete Data with Econometric Applications*, pp. 365–91. Cambridge, Mass.: MIT Press.

Heavy, R. (1971). "Effects of Improved Housing on Worker Performance." *Journal of Human Resources* 6:297–308.

Heckman, J. J. (1971). *Three Essays on the Supply of Labor and the Demand for Goods.* Unpublished Ph.D. dissertation, Department of Economics, Princeton University.

(1974a). "Effects of Child Care Programs on Women's Work Effort." *Journal of Political Economy* 82:136–63.

(1974b). "Life Cycle Consumption and Labor Supply: An Explanation of the Relationship between Income and Consumption over the Life Cycle." *American Economic Review* 64:188–94.

(1974c). "Shadow Prices, Market Wages and Labor Supply." *Econometrica* 42:679–94.

(1976a). "Estimates of a Human Capital Production Function Embedded in a Life Cycle Model of Labor Supply," in Terleckyj, ed. (1976), pp. 227–58.

(1976b). "A Life Cycle Model of Earnings, Learning and Consumption." *Journal of Political Economy* 84:S11–44.

(1976c). "The Common Structure of Statistical Models of Truncation, Sample Selection, and Limited Dependent Variables and a Simple Estimator for Such Models." *Annals of Economic and Social Measurement* 5:475–92.

(1978a). "A Partial Survey of Recent Research on the Labor Supply of Women." *American Economic Review* 68:200–7.

(1978b). "Comment [on Ashenfelter, 1978c]," in Palmer and Pechman, eds. (1978), pp. 138–47.

(1979). "Sample Selection Bias as a Specification Error." *Econometrica* 47:153–62.

(1980). "Sample Selection Bias as a Specification Error," in Smith, ed. (1980c), pp. 206–48.

(1981). "Comments on the Hausman [1981c] Paper." Paper presented at National Bureau of Economic Research Conference on Behavioral Simulation Methods in Tax Policy Analysis, Palm Beach, Fla. (forthcoming in M.S. Feldstein, ed., 1983).

Heckman, J. J., M. R. Killingsworth, and T. E. MaCurdy (1981). "Empirical Evidence on Static Labour Supply Models: A Survey of Recent Developments," in Hornstein, Grice, and Webb, eds. (1981), pp. 75–122.

Heckman, J. J., and T. E. MaCurdy (1980). "A Life Cycle Model of Female Labour Supply." *Review of Economic Studies* 47:47–74.

(1981). "New Methods for Estimating Labor Supply Functions: A Survey," in R. G. Ehrenberg, ed., *Research in Labor Economics*, Vol. 4, pp. 65–102. Greenwich, Conn.: JAI Press.

(in press). "A Life Cycle Model of Female Labour Supply: Corrigendum." *Review of Economic Studies* 49.

Heckman, J. J., and R. J. Willis (1977). "A Beta-Logistic Model for the Analysis of Sequential Labor Force Participation by Married Women." *Journal of Political Economy* 85:27–58.

(1979). "Reply to Mincer and Ofek [1979]." *Journal of Political Economy* 87:203–11.

Heffernan, W. J., Jr. (1973). "Variations in Negative Tax Rates in Current Public

Assistance Programs: An Example of Administrative Discretion." *Journal of Human Resources* 8(Supplement):56–68.

Hemming, R. (1980). "Income Tax Progressivity and Labour Supply." *Journal of Public Economics* 14:95–100.

Henderson, J. M., and R. E. Quandt (1971). *Microeconomic Theory: A Mathematical Approach.* New York: McGraw-Hill.

Hicks, J. R. (1932). *The Theory of Wages.* London: Macmillan Press.

(1946). *Value and Capital,* 2nd ed. Oxford: Oxford University Press.

(1965). *Capital and Growth.* Oxford: Oxford University Press.

Hill, C. R. (1971a). "Education, Health and Family Size as Determinants of Labor Market Activity for the Poor and Nonpoor." *Demography* 8:379–88.

(1971b). "Wage, Income Interactions in a Micro Model of Labor Supply," in *Proceedings of the Business and Economics Statistics Section, American Statistical Association, 1971,* pp. 378–82.

(1973). "The Determinants of Labor Supply for the Working Urban Poor," in Cain and Watts, eds. (1973b), pp. 182–204.

Himmelweit, S., and Mohun, S. (1977). "Domestic Labour and Capital." *Cambridge Journal of Economics* 1:15–31.

Hoel, P. G. (1971). *Introduction to Mathematical Statistics,* 4th ed. New York: Wiley.

Holmes, J. M. (1972). "The Keynesian Aggregate Supply Function for Labor." *Journal of the American Statistical Association* 67:797–802.

Honig, M., and G. Hanoch (1980a). "Estimation of Labor Supply and Retirement Behavior." Paper prepared for Brookings Institution Conference on Research in Retirement and Aging.

(1980b). "A General Model of Labor-Market Behavior of Older Persons." *Social Security Bulletin* 43(4):29–39.

Horney, M. J., and M. B. McElroy (1978). "A Nash-Bargained Linear Expenditure System." Unpublished manuscript, Department of Economics, Duke University.

Hornstein, Z., J. Grice, and A. Webb, eds. (1981). *The Economics of the Labour Market.* London: Her Majesty's Stationery Office.

Houthakker, H. S. (1961). "The Present State of Consumption Theory: A Survey Article." *Econometrica* 29:704–40.

Howard, D. H. (1977). "Rationing, Quantity Constraints and Consumption Theory." *Econometrica* 45:399–412.

Huang, Y. (1976). "Backward-Bending Supply Curves and Behaviour of Subsistence Farmers." *Journal of Development Studies* 12:191–211.

Hughes, B. (1971). "Direct Income and Substitution Effects in Participation Decisions." *Journal of Political Economy* 80:793–5.

Hunt, J. C., C. D. DeLorme, Jr., and R. C. Hill (1981). "Taxation and the Wife's Use of Time." *Industrial and Labor Relations Review* 34:426–32.

Hunter, L. C. (1970). "Some Problems in the Theory of Labour Supply." *Scottish Journal of Political Economy* 17:39–59.

Hurd, M. D. (1978). "Estimating the Family Labor Supply Function Derived from the Stone-Geary Utility Function." Working Paper No. 228. National Bureau of Economic Research.

Hurd, M. D., and J. H. Pencavel (1981). "A Utility-Based Analysis of the Wage Subsidy Program." *Journal of Public Economics* 15:185–201.

Industrial Relations (1967). "A Symposium on Negative Income Tax Proposals." Vol. 6(2), pp. 121–65.

Isachsen, A. J., and S. Strøm (1980). "The Hidden Economy: The Labor Market and Tax Evasion." *Scandinavian Journal of Economics* 82:304–11.

Johnson, G. E. (1976). "Evaluating the Macroeconomic Effects of Public Employment Programs," in O. Ashenfelter and J. Blum, eds., *Evaluating the Labor-Market Effects of Social Programs*, pp. 90–123. Princeton, N.J.: Industrial Relations Section, Princeton University.

Johnson, M. B. (1966). "Travel Time and the Price of Leisure." *Western Economic Journal* 4:135–45.

Johnson, N. L., and S. Kotz (1972). *Distributions in Statistics: Continuous Multivariate Distributions*. New York: Wiley.

Johnson, T. R., and J. H. Pencavel (1980). "Utility-Based Hours of Work Functions for Husbands, Wives and Single Females Estimated from Seattle-Denver Experimental Data." Research Memorandum 71. Stanford Research Institute.

(1982a). "Forecasting the Effects of a Negative Income Tax Program." *Industrial and Labor Relations Review* 35:221–34.

(1982b). "Dynamic Hours of Work Functions for Husbands, Wives and Single Females." Unpublished manuscript, Stanford Research Institute.

Johnson, W. R. (1980). "The Effect of a Negative Income Tax on Risk-Taking in the Labor Market." *Economic Inquiry* 18:395–407.

Johnson, W. T. (1970). "Returns from Investment in Human Capital." *American Economic Review* 60:546–60.

Jones, E. B. (1980). "The Fulltime Workweek in the United States, 1900–1970: Comment [on Kniesner, 1976b]." *Industrial and Labor Relations Review* 33: 379–84.

Jones, E. B., and W. F. Barnes (1973). "Robbins, Hicks, Buchanan and the Backward-Bending Labor Supply Curve." *Mississippi Valley Journal of Business and Economics* 9:76–82.

Joshi, H., R. Layard, and S. Owen (1981). "Female Labour Supply in Post-War Britain: A Cohort Approach." Discussion Paper No. 79, Centre for Labour Economics, London School of Economics.

Kalachek, E. D., W. Mellow, and F. Q. Raines (1978). "The Male Labor Supply Function Reconsidered." *Industrial and Labor Relations Review* 31: 356–67.

Kalachek, E. D., and F. Q. Raines (1970). "Labor Supply of Lower-Income Workers," in President's Commission on Income Maintenance Programs, *Technical Studies*, pp. 159–86. Washington, D.C.: Government Printing Office.

Kalachek, E. D., F. Q. Raines, and D. Larson (1979). "The Determination of Labor Supply: A Dynamic Model." *Industrial and Labor Relations Review* 32: 367–77.

Kalman, P. J. (1968). "Theory of Consumer Behavior When Prices Enter the Utility Function." *Econometrica* 36:497–510.

Kasper, H. (1966). "Assets and the Supply of Labor: A Note." *Southern Economic Journal* 33:245–51.

Katzner, D. (1970). *Static Demand Theory*. New York: Macmillan.

Keeley, M. C., (1981). *Labor Supply and Public Policy*. New York: Academic Press.

Keeley, M. C., and P. K. Robins (1980). "The Design of Social Experiments: A Critique of the Conlisk-Watts Assignment Model and Its Application to the Seattle and Denver Income Maintenance Experiments," in R. G. Ehrenberg, ed., *Research in Labor Economics, Vol. 3*, pp. 293–333. Greenwich, Conn.: JAI Press.

Keeley, M., P. Robins, R. Spiegelman, and R. West (1978a). "The Labor Supply Effects and Costs of Alternative Negative Income Tax Programs." *Journal of Human Resources* 13:3–36.

 (1978b). "The Estimation of Labor Supply Models Using Experimental Data." *American Economic Review* 68: 873–87.

Kehrer, B. H. (1976). "Factors Affecting the Incomes of Men and Women Physicians: An Exploratory Analysis." *Journal of Human Resources* 11: 526–45.

Kehrer, K. C. (1979). "Introduction." *Journal of Human Resources* 14:431–3.

Kehrer, K. C., J. McDonald, and R. Moffitt (1980). *Final Report of the Gary Income Maintenance Experiment: Labor Supply*. Princeton, N.J.: Mathematica Policy Research.

Keller, W. J. (1977). "Savings, Leisure, Consumption and Taxes: The Household Expenditure System." *European Economic Review* 9:151–67.

Kelly, T. F., and L. Singer (1971). "The Gary Income Maintenance Experiment: Plans and Progress." *American Economic Review* 61:30–8.

Kerachsky, S., and C. Mallar (1976). "Alternative Parameterizations of Labor-Supply Reponses in the Presence of Welfare," in Mathematica Policy Research (1976), Chap. 8.

Kesselman, J. (1969a). "The Negative Income Tax and the Supply of Work Effort: Comment [on Boskin, 1967]." *National Tax Journal* 22:411–16.

 (1969b). "Labor-Supply Effects of Income, Income-Work and Wage Subsidies." *Journal of Human Resources* 4:275–92.

 (1973). "Incentive Effects of Transfer Systems Once Again." *Journal of Human Resources* 8:119–29.

 (1976). "Tax Effects on Job Search, Training and Work Effort." *Journal of Public Economics* 6:255–72.

Kesselman, J., and I. Garfinkel (1978). "Professor Friedman, Meet Lady Rhys-Williams: NIT vs. CIT." *Journal of Public Economics* 10:179–216.

Keynes, J. M. (1936). *The General Theory of Employment, Interest and Money*. New York: Harcourt, Brace & World.

Kiefer, N. M. (1976). "Quadratic Utility, Labor Supply and Commodity Demand," in S. M. Goldfeld and R. E. Quandt, eds., *Studies in Nonlinear Estimation*, pp. 167–79. Cambridge, Mass.: Ballinger.

 (1977). "A Bayesian Analysis of Commodity Demand and Labor Supply." *International Economic Review* 18:209–18.

Kihlstrom, R., and L. Mirman (1974). "Risk Aversion with Many Commodities." *Journal of Economic Theory* 8:361–88.

Kiker, B. F. (1966). "The Historical Roots of the Concept of Human Capital." *Journal of Political Economy* 74:481–99.

Killingsworth, M. R. (1976). "Must a Negative Income Tax Reduce Labor Supply?

A Study of the Household's Allocation of Time." *Journal of Human Resources* 11:345–65.

(1981). "A Survey of Labor Supply Models: Theoretical Analysis and First-Generation Empirical Results," in R. G. Ehrenberg, ed., *Research in Labor Economics,* Vol. 4, pp. 1–64. Greenwich, Conn: JAI Press.

(1982a). " 'Learning by Doing' and 'Investment in Training': A Synthesis of Two 'Rival' Models of the Life Cycle." *Review of Economic Studies* 49:263–71.

(1982b). "Labor Supply, Risk and Risk Aversion." Unpublished manuscript, Department of Economics, Rutgers–The State University.

Kisker, K. P. (1967). "A Note on the Negative Income Tax." *National Tax Journal* 20:102–5.

Klemesrud, J. (1981). "Where Are All the Women Who Fell for 007?" *The New York Times,* June 21, Section 2, pp. 1; 17.

Kmenta, J. (1971). *Elements of Econometrics.* New York: Macmillan.

Kniesner, T. J. (1976a). "An Indirect Test of Complementarity in a Family Labor Supply Model." *Econometrica* 44:651–9.

(1976b). "The Full-Time Workweek in the United States, 1900–1970." *Industrial and Labor Relations Review* 30:3–15.

(1980a). "The Full-Time Workweek in the U. S., 1900–1970: Reply [to Jones, 1980]." *Industrial and Labor Relations Review* 33:385–9.

(1980b). Review of *Working Hours* by J. Owen (1979). *Industrial and Labor Relations Review* 33:576–8.

Knight, F. H. (1921). *Risk, Uncertainty and Profit.* Boston: Houghton Mifflin.

Kosters, M. (1966). "Income and Substitution Effects in a Family Labor Supply Model." Report No. P-3339. The Rand Corporation.

(1969). "Effects of an Income Tax on Labor Supply," in A. C. Harberger and M. J. Bailey, eds., *The Taxation of Income from Capital,* pp. 301–24. Washington, D.C.: Brookings Institution.

Kraft, A. (1973). "Preference Orderings as Determinants of the Labor Force Behavior of Married Women." *Western Economic Journal* 11:270–84.

Kraus, M. (1979). "On Pareto-Optimal Time Allocation." *Economic Inquiry* 17: 142–5.

Krueger, A. O. (1962). "The Implications of a Backward Bending Labor Supply Curve." *Review of Economic Studies* 29:327–8.

Kurz, M., and R. G. Spiegelman (1971). "The Seattle Experiment: The Combined Effect of Income Maintenance and Manpower Investments." *American Economic Review* 61: 22–9.

(1972). "The Design of the Seattle and Denver Income Maintenance Experiments." Research Memorandum 18. Stanford Research Institute.

Lampman, R. J. (1956). "On Choice in Labor Markets: Comment." *Industrial and Labor Relations Review* 9:629–36.

Lancaster, K. J. (1966). "A New Approach to Consumer Theory." *Journal of Political Economy* 74:132–57.

Landsberger M. (1971). "An Integrated Model of Consumption and Market Activity: The Children Effect," in *Proceedings of the Social Statistics Section, American Statistical Association, 1971,* pp. 137–42.

(1973). "Children's Age as a Factor Affecting the Simultaneous Determination of

Consumption and Labor Supply." *Southern Economic Journal* 40:279–88.

Landsberger, M., and U. Passy (1973). "Human Capital, Its Shadow Price and Labor Supply." Operations Research, Statistics and Economics Mimeograph Series No. 138. Faculty of Industrial and Management Engineering, Technion-Israel Institute of Technology.

Larson, D. A. (1979). "Taxes in a Labor Supply Model with Joint Wage-Hours Determination: A Comment." *Econometrica* 47:1311–13.

(1981). "Labor Supply Adjustment over the Business Cycle." *Industrial and Labor Relations Review* 34:591–5.

Lau, L. J., W-L. Lin, and P. A. Yotopoulos (1978). "The Linear Logarithmic Expenditure System: An Application to Consumption-Leisure Choice." *Econometrica* 46:843–68.

Layard, R. (1978). "Hours Supplied by British Married Men, with Endogenous Overtime." Discussion Paper No. 30. Centre for Labour Economics, London School of Economics.

Layard, R., M. Barton, and A. Zabalza (1980). "Married Women's Participation and Hours." *Economica* 47:51–72.

Leibenstein, H. (1950). "Bandwagon, Snob and Veblen Effects in the Theory of Consumers' Demand." *Quarterly Journal of Economics* 64:183–207.

(1974). "Towards a Significantly (but Not Radically) New Theory of Consumption." Discussion Paper No. 343. Harvard Institute of Economic Research, Harvard University.

Leibowitz, A. (1974). "Production within the Household." *American Economic Review* 64(2):243–50.

Leijonhufvud, A., and J. M. Buchanan (1973). "The Backbending Supply Curve of Labor: Comment on Buchanan [1971], with his Reply." *History of Political Economy* 5:261–7.

Leimer, D. R., and S. D. Lesnoy (1982). "Social Security and Saving: New Time-Series Evidence." *Journal of Political Economy* 90:606–29.

Leuthold, J. H. (1968). "An Empirical Study of Formula Income Transfers and the Work Decision of the Poor." *Journal of Human Resources* 3:312–23.

(1978a). "The Effect of Taxation on the Probability of Labor Force Participation by Married Women." *Public Finance* 33:280–94.

(1978b). "The Effect of Taxation on the Hours Worked by Married Women." *Industrial and Labor Relations Review* 31:520–6.

Leveson, I. F. (1967). "Reductions in Hours of Work as a Source of Productivity Growth." *Journal of Political Economy* 72:199–204.

Lewis, H. G. (1957). "Hours of Work and Hours of Leisure," in Industrial Relations Research Association, *Proceedings of the Ninth Annual Meeting*, pp. 195–206. Madison, Wisc.: Industrial Relations Research Association.

(1972). "Income and Substitution Effects in Labor Force Participation and Hours of Work." Unpublished manuscript, Department of Economics, University of Chicago.

(1974). "Comments on Selectivity Biases in Wage Comparisons." *Journal of Political Economy* 82:1145–55.

Lillard, L. A. (1978). "Estimation of Permanent and Transitory Response Functions in Panel Data: A Dynamic Labor Supply Model." *Annales de l'INSEE* 30–1:367–94.

Linder, S. B. (1971). *The Harried Leisure Class*. New York: Columbia University Press.

Lippman, S. A., and John J. McCall (1976a). "The Economics of Job Search: A Survey, I." *Economic Inquiry* 14:155–89.

(1976b). "The Economics of Job Search: A Survey, II." *Economic Inquiry* 14: 347–68.

Lloyd, C. B., E. S. Andrews, and C. L. Gilroy, eds. (1979). *Women in the Labor Market*. New York: Columbia University Press.

Lluch, C. (1973). "The Extended Linear Expenditure System." *European Economic Review* 4:21–32.

Long, C. D. (1958). *The Labor Force under Changing Income and Employment*. Princeton, N.J.: Princeton University Press.

Lucas, R. E., and L. Rapping (1970). "Real Wages, Employment and Inflation," in E. S. Phelps, A. A. Alchian, C. C. Holt, D. T. Mortensen, G. C. Archibald, R. E. Lucas, Jr., L. A. Rapping, S. G. Winter, Jr., J. P. Gould, D. F. Gordon, A. Hynes, D. S. Nichols, P. J. Taubman, and M. Wilkinson, *Microeconomic Foundations of Employment and Inflation Theory*, pp. 257–305. New York: Norton.

Lundberg, S. (1981). "The Added Worker Effect: A Reappraisal." Working Paper No. 706. National Bureau of Economic Research.

Lurie, I. (1974). "Estimates of Tax Rates in the AFDC Program." *National Tax Journal* 27:93–111.

Mabry, B. D. (1969). "Income-Leisure Analysis and the Salaried Professional." *Industrial Relations* 8:162–73.

(1970). "An Analysis of Work and Other Constraints on Choice of Activities." *Western Economic Journal* 8:213–25.

(1971). "An Analysis of Work and Other Constraints on Choice of Activities: Reply [to Ng, 1971]." *Western Economic Journal* 9:318.

MacCrimmon, K. R., and M. Toda (1969). "The Experimental Determination of Indifference Curves." *Review of Economic Studies* 36:433–51.

McElroy, M. B. (1981). "Appendix [to Killingsworth, 1981]: Empirical Results from Estimates of Joint Labor Supply Functions of Husbands and Wives," in R. G. Ehrenberg, ed., *Research in Labor Economics*, Vol. 4, pp. 53–64. Greenwich, Conn.: JAI Press.

McElroy, M. B., and M. J. Horney (1981). "Nash-Bargained Household Decisions: Toward a Generalization of the Theory of Demand." *International Economic Review* 22: 333–49.

McGuire, T. W., and L. A. Rapping (1968). "The Role of Market Variables and Key Bargains in the Manufacturing Wage Determination Process." *Journal of Political Economy* 76:1015–36.

(1970). "The Supply of Labor and Manufacturing Wage Determination in the United States: An Empirical Examination." *International Economic Review* 11:258–68.

MacKay, R. J., and G. A. Whitney (1980). "The Comparative Statics of Quantity Constraints and Conditional Demands: Theory and Applications." *Econometrica* 48:1727–44.

MacRae, C. D., and E. C. MacRae (1976). "Labor Supply and the Payroll Tax." *American Economic Review* 66:408–9.

MacRae, C. D., and A. M. J. Yezer (1976). "The Personal Income Tax and Family Labor Supply." *Southern Economic Journal* 43:783–92.

MaCurdy, T. E. (1981a). "An Empirical Model of Labor Supply in a Life-Cycle Setting." *Journal of Political Economy* 89:1059–85.

(1981b). "An Intertemporal Analysis of Taxation and Work Disincentives: An Analysis of the Denver Income Maintenance Experiment." Working Paper No. 624. National Bureau of Economic Research. (Forthcoming in *International Economic Review*.)

(in press). "An Empirical Model of Labor Supply in an Environment of Uncertainty," in B. Singer and J. J. Heckman, eds., *Longitudinal Studies of the Labor Market*. New York: Academic Press.

Manser, M., and M. Brown (1979). "Bargaining Analyses of Household Decisions," in Lloyd, Andrews and Gilroy, eds. (1979), pp. 3–26.

(1980). "Marriage and Household Decision-Making: A Bargaining Analysis." *International Economic Review* 21:31–44.

Markusen, J. R. (1979). "Personal and Job Characteristics as Determinants of Employee-Firm Contract Structure." *Quarterly Journal of Economics* 93:255–79.

Martin, D. L., (1977). "The Economics of Employment Termination Rights." *Journal of Law and Economics* 20:187–204.

Mason, G. (1982). "The Manitoba Basic Annual Income Experiment (MINCOME)." Unpublished manuscript, Institute for Social and Economic Research, University of Manitoba.

Masters, S., and I. Garfinkel (1977). *Estimating the Labor Supply Effects of Income Maintenance Alternatives*. New York: Academic Press.

Mathematica Policy Research (1976). *Follow-Up Studies Using Data Generated by the New Jersey Negative Income Tax Experiment*. Princeton, N.J.: Mathematica Policy Research.

Maurizi, A. (1966). "Empirical Evidence on Labor Supply: The Case of Dentists," in Industrial Relations Research Association, *Proceedings of the Nineteenth Annual Winter Meeting*, pp. 354–64. Madison, Wisc.: Industrial Relations Research Association.

Meissner, M. (1971). "The Long Arm of the Job: A Study of Work and Leisure." *Industrial Relations* 10:239–60.

Metcalf, C. (1973). "Making Inferences from Controlled Income Maintenance Experiments." *American Economic Review* 63:478–83.

(1974). "Predicting the Effects of Permanent Programs from a Limited Duration Experiment." *Journal of Human Resources* 9:530–55.

Metcalf, D., S. Nickell, and R. Richardson (1977). "The Structure of Hours and Earnings in British Industry." *Oxford Economic Papers* 28:284–303.

Meyers, F. (1965). "The Economics of Overtime," in C. E. Dankert, F. C. Mann, and H. L. Northrup, eds., *Hours of Work*, pp. 95–110. New York: Harper & Row.

Michael, R. T., and G. S. Becker "On the New Theory of Consumer Behavior." *Swedish Journal of Economics* 75:378–96.

Mincer, J. (1962). "Labor Force Participation of Married Women: A Study of Labor Supply," in National Bureau of Economic Research, *Aspects of Labor Economics*, pp. 63–97. Princeton, N.J.: Princeton University Press.

(1963). "Market Prices, Opportunity Costs and Income Effects," in C. F. Christ, M. Friedman, L. A. Goodman, Z. Griliches, A. C. Harberger, N. Liviatan, J. Mincer, Y. Mundlak, M. Nerlove, D. Patinkin, L. G. Telser, and H. Theil, eds., *Measurement in Economics*, pp. 67–82. Stanford, Calif.: Stanford University Press.

(1966). "Labor Force Participation and Unemployment: A Review of Recent Evidence," in R. A. Gordon and M. S. Gordon, eds., *Prosperity and Unemployment*, pp. 73–112. New York: Wiley.

(1968). "Labor Force: Participation," in D. L. Sills, ed., *International Encyclopedia of the Social Sciences*, pp. 474–81. New York: Macmillan Free Press.

(1970). "Comment [on Ben-Porath, 1970]," in Hansen, ed. (1970), pp. 147–51.

(1974). *Schooling, Experience and Earnings*. New York: National Bureau of Economic Research.

Mincer, J., and H. Ofek (1979). "The Distribution of Lifetime Labor Force Participation of Married Women: Comment." *Journal of Political Economy* 87:197–201.

Mincer, J., and S. Polachek (1974). "Family Investments in Human Capital: Earnings of Women," in T. W. Schultz, ed., *Economics of the Family: Marriage, Children and Human Capital*, pp. 397–429. New York: Columbia University Press.

(1978). "The Theory of Human Capital and the Earnings of Women: Women's Earnings Reexamined." *Journal of Human Resources* 13:118–34.

Mirrlees, J. A. (1971). "An Exploration in the Theory of Optimum Income Taxation." *Review of Economic Studies* 38:175–208.

Mitchell, O. S., and G. S. Fields (1981). "The Effects of Pensions and Earnings on Retirement: A Review Essay." Working Paper No. 772. National Bureau of Economic Research.

Moffitt, R. (1977). "Labor Supply and the Payroll Tax: Note." *American Economic Review* 67:1004–5.

(1979a). "The Labor Supply Response in the Gary Experiment." *Journal of Human Resources* 14:477–87.

(1979b). "A Note on the Effect of Taxes and Transfers on Labor Supply." *Southern Economic Journal* 45:1266–73.

(1980). "Limited-Duration NIT Experiments and Life-Cycle Labor Supply." Unpublished working paper, Department of Economics, Rutgers–The State University.

(1981). "Participation in the AFDC Program and the Stigma of Welfare Receipt: Estimation of a Choice-Theoretic Model." *Southern Economic Journal* 47:753–62.

(1982). "The Tobit Model, Hours of Work and Institutional Constraints." *Review of Economics and Statistics* 54:510–15.

Moffitt, R., and K. C. Kehrer (1981). "The Effect of Tax and Transfer Programs on Labor Supply: The Evidence from the Income Maintenance Experiments," in

R. G. Ehrenberg, ed., *Research in Labor Economics*, Vol. 4, pp. 103–50. Greenwich, Conn.: JAI Press.

Mood, A. M., F. A. Graybill, and D. C. Boes (1974). *Introduction to the Theory of Statistics*, 3rd ed. New York: McGraw-Hill.

Morgan, J. N. (1968). "The Supply of Effort, the Measurement of Well-Being, and the Dynamics of Improvement." *American Economic Review* 58(2):31–39.

Mortensen, D. (1978). "On the Theory of Layoffs." Discussion Paper No. 322. Center for Mathematical Studies in Economics and Management Science, Northwestern University.

Mosbaek, E. (1959). "Fitting a Static Supply and Demand Function for Labor." *Weltwirtschaftliches Archiv* 82:132–40.

Moses, L. (1962). "Income, Leisure and Wage Pressure." *Economic Journal* 72:320–34.

Mossin, J., and M. Bronfenbrenner (1967). "The Shorter Work Week and Labor Supply." *Southern Economic Journal* 33:322–31.

Mosteller, F., and P. Nogee (1951). "An Experimental Measurement of Utility." *Journal of Political Economy* 59:371–404.

Moynihan, D. P. (1973). *The Politics of a Guaranteed Income: The Nixon Administration and the Family Assistance Plan*. New York: Random House.

Muellbauer, J. (1981). "Linear Aggregation in Neoclassical Labor Supply." *Review of Economic Studies* 48:21–36.

Murray, M. P. (1980). "A Reinterpretation of the Traditional Income-Leisure Model, with Application to In-Kind Subsidy Programs." *Journal of Public Economics* 14:69–81.

Musgrave, R. A. (1959). *The Theory of Public Finance*. New York: McGraw-Hill.

Muth, R. F. (1966). "Household Production and Consumer Demand Functions." *Econometrica* 34:699–708.

Nakamura, A., and M. Nakamura (1981). "A Comparison of the Labor Force Behavior of Married Women in the United States and Canada, with Special Attention to the Impact of Income Taxes." *Econometrica* 49:451–90.

Nakamura, M., A. Nakamura, and D. Cullen (1979). "Job Opportunities, the Offered Wage, and the Labor Supply of Married Women." *American Economic Review* 69:787–805.

Neary, J. P., and K. W. S. Roberts (1980). "The Theory of Consumer Behavior under Rationing." *European Economic Review* 13:25–42.

New York Times (1979). "I. R. S. and Couple Waging 'Tax Divorce' Test Case." September 11, Section A, p. 11.

Ng, Y-K. (1971). "An Analysis of Work and Other Constraints on Choices of Activities: Comment [on Mabry, 1970]." *Western Economic Journal* 9:226–9.

Nickell, S. J. (1976). "Wage Structure and Quit Rates." *International Economic Review* 17:191–203.

Nordhaus, W. D., and J. Tobin (1972). "Is Growth Obsolete?" in National Bureau of Economic Research, *Economic Growth: 50th Anniversary Colloquium V*, pp. 1–80. New York: Columbia University Press.

Olsen, E. O. (1976). "The Effort Level, Work Time, and Profit Maximization." *Southern Economic Journal* 42:644–52.

Olsen, R. J. (1977). *An Econometric Model of Family Labor Supply*. Unpublished

Ph.D. dissertation, Department of Economics, University of Chicago.

Orcutt, G. K., and A. G. Orcutt (1968). "Incentive and Disincentive Experimentation for Income Maintenance Policy Purposes." *American Economic Review* 58:754–72.

Orr, L. L. (1969). "Strategy for a Broad Program of Experimentation in Income Maintenance," in *Proceedings of the Social Statistics Section, American Statistical Association, 1969*, pp. 163–73.

Owen, J. D. (1969). *The Price of Leisure*. Rotterdam: Rotterdam University Press.

(1971). "The Demand for Leisure." *Journal of Political Economy* 79:56–76.

(1976). "Workweeks and Leisure: An Analysis of Trends, 1948–1975." *Monthly Labor Review* 99(8):3–8.

(1979). *Working Hours*. Lexington, Mass.: Heath.

Palmer, J., and J. A. Pechman, eds. (1978), *Welfare in Rural Areas: The North Carolina-Iowa Income Maintenance Experiment*. Washington, D.C.: Brookings Institution.

Parker, J. E., and L. B. Shaw (1968). "Labor Force Participation in Metropolitan Areas." *Southern Economic Journal* 34:538–47.

Parnes, H. S. (1960). "The Labor Force and Labor Markets," in H. G. Heneman, Jr., L. C. Brown, M. K. Chandler, R. Kahn, H. S. Parnes, and G. P. Shultz, eds., *Employment Relations Research*, pp. 1–42. New York: Harper & Brothers.

(1970). "Labor Force Participation and Labor Mobility," in W. L. Ginsburg, E. R. Livernash, H. S. Parnes, and G. Strauss, eds., *A Review of Industrial Relations Research*, Vol. 1, pp. 1–79. Madison, Wisc.: Industrial Relations Research Association.

Parsons, D. O. (1977). "Health, Family Structure and Labor Supply." *American Economic Review* 67:703–12.

(1980a). "The Decline in Male Labor Force Participation." *Journal of Political Economy* 88:117–34.

(1980b). "Racial Trends in Male Labor Force Participation." *American Economic Review* 70:911–20.

(1982). "The Male Labour Force Participation Decision: Health, Reported Health and Economic Incentives." *Economica* 49:81–91.

Pechman, J. A., and P. M. Timpane, eds. (1975). *Work Incentives and Income Guarantees: The New Jersey Negative Income Tax Experiments*. Washington, D.C.: Brookings Institution.

Peisa, P. (1977). "Wages and the Demand for Labor in Unemployment Equilibria." *Scandinavian Journal of Economics* 79:227–38.

Pellechio, A. (1978). "The Social Security Earnings Test, Labor Supply Distortions and Foregone Payroll Tax Revenue." Working Paper No. 272. National Bureau of Economic Research.

(1979). "The Estimation of Labor Supply over Kinked Budget Constraints: Some New Econometric Methodology." Working Paper No. 387. National Bureau of Economic Research.

Pencavel, J. (1977). "Work Effort, on-the-Job Screening, and Alternative Methods of Remuneration," in R. G. Ehrenberg, ed., *Research in Labor Economics*, Vol. 1, pp. 225–58. Greenwich, Conn.: JAI Press.

(1979). "A Note on Income Tax Evasion, Labor Supply and Nonlinear Tax Schedules." *Journal of Public Economics* 12:115–24.

Perlman, R. (1966). "Observations on Overtime and Moonlighting." *Southern Economic Journal* 33:237–44.

(1968a). "A Negative Income Tax Plan for Maintaining Work Incentives." *Journal of Human Resources* 3:289–99.

(1968b). "Moonlighting and Labor Supply — Reply." *Southern Economic Journal* 35:82–4.

(1969). *Labor Theory*. New York: Wiley.

Pfouts, R. W. (1955). "Some Difficulties in a Certain Concept of Community Indifference." *Metroeconomica* 7:16–26.

(1960). "Hours of Work, Savings and the Utility Function," in R. W. Pfouts, ed., *Essays in Economics and Econometrics in Honor of Harold Hotelling*, pp. 113–32. Chapel Hill: University of North Carolina Press.

Phlips, L. (1974). *Applied Consumption Analysis*. Amsterdam: North Holland.

(1978). "The Demand for Leisure and Money." *Econometrica* 46:1025–43.

Piore, M. (1979). *Birds of Passage*. Cambridge: Cambridge University Press.

Pissarides, C. A. (1976). *Labour Market Adjustment*. Cambridge: Cambridge University Press.

(1979). "Contract Theory, Temporary Layoffs and Unemployment: A Critical Assessment." Discussion Paper No. 48. Centre for Labour Economics, London School of Economics.

Polemarchakis, H. (1979). "Implicit Contracts and Employment Theory." *Review of Economic Studies* 46:97–108.

Polemarchakis, H., and L. Weiss (1978). "Fixed Wages, Layoffs, Unemployment Compensation and Welfare." *American Economic Review* 68:909–17.

Pollak, R. A. (1976). "Interdependent Preferences." *American Economic Review* 66:309–20.

Pollak, R. A., and M. R. Wachter (1974). "The Relevance of the Household Production Function and Its Implications for the Allocation of Time." *Journal of Political Economy* 83:255–77.

Pollak, R. A., and T. J. Wales (1980). "Comparison of the Quadratic Expenditure System and Translog Demand Systems with Alternative Specifications of Demographic Effects." *Econometrica* 48:595–612.

(1981). "Demographic Variables in Demand Analysis." *Econometrica* 49:1553–8.

Portes, R. D., and J. Muellbauer (1978). "Macroeconomic Models with Quantity Rationing." *Economic Journal* 88:788–821.

Powell, A. A. (1979). "The Theory of Labour Supply and Commodity Demand with an Endogenous Marginal Wage Rate." Preliminary Working Paper No. BP-19. Impact Research Centre, Industries Assistance Commission, Melbourne.

Pratt, J. (1964). "Risk Aversion in the Small and in the Large." *Econometrica* 32:122–36.

Psacharopoulos, G., and R. Layard (1979). "Human Capital and Earnings: British Evidence and a Critique." *Review of Economic Studies* 46:485–503.

Quinn, J. F. (1977). "Microeconomic Determinants of Early Retirement: A Cross-Sectional View of White Married Men." *Journal of Human Resources* 12:329–46.

Radford, R. A. (1945). "The Economics of a Prisoner-of-War Camp." *Economica* 12:189–201.

Ransom, M. R. (1982). "Estimating Family Labor Supply Models under Quantity Constraints." Working Paper No. 150. Industrial Relations Section, Princeton University.

Rayner, A. C. (1969). "On the Identification of the Supply Curve of Working Hours." *Oxford Economic Papers* 21:293–8.

Rea, S. A. (1977). "Investment in Human Capital under a Negative Income Tax." *Canadian Journal of Economics* 10:607–20.

Rees, A. (1974). "An Overview of the Labor-Supply Results." *Journal of Human Resources* 9:158–80.

(1979). *The Economics of Work and Pay*, 2nd ed., New York: Harper.

Rees, A., and H. W. Watts, eds. (1973). *Final Report of the Graduated Work Incentive Experiment*. Madison: Institute for Research on Poverty, University of Wisconsin.

Reimers, C. W. (1976). "Is the Average Age at Retirement Changing?" *Journal of the American Statistical Association* 71:552–8.

(1980). "Labor Supply: Discussion." in Clark, ed. (1980), pp. 143–50.

Rein, M. (1973), "Recent British Experience with Negative Income Tax." *Journal of Human Resources* 8(Supplement):69–89.

Robbins, L. (1930). "Note on the Elasticity of Demand for Income in Terms of Effort." *Economica* 10:123–9.

Robins, P. K., and R. W. West (1980). "Program Participation and Labor-Supply Response." *Journal of Human Resources* 15:499–523.

Robins, P. K., R. G. Spiegelman, S. Weiner, and J. G. Bell, eds. (1980). *A Guaranteed Annual Income: Evidence from a Social Experiment*. New York: Academic Press.

Rosen, H. S. (1976a). "Tax Illusion and the Labor Supply of Married Women." *Review of Economics and Statistics* 58:167–72.

(1976b). "Taxes in a Labor Supply Model with Joint Wage-Hours Determination." *Econometrica* 44:485–507.

(1978). "The Measurement of Excess Burden with Explicit Utility Functions." *Journal of Political Economy* 86:S121–35.

(1980). "What Is Labor Supply and Do Taxes Affect It?" *American Economic Review* 70(2):171–6.

Rosen, H. S., and R. E. Quandt (1978). "Estimation of a Disequilibrium Aggregate Labor Market." *Review of Economics and Statistics* 60:371–9.

Rosen, S. (1969). "On the Interindustry Wage and Hours Structure." *Journal of Political Economy* 77:249–73.

(1972a). "Learning and Experience in the Labor Market." *Journal of Human Resources* 7:336–42.

(1972b). "Learning by Experience as Joint Production." *Quarterly Journal of Economics* 86:366–82.

(1975). "Measuring the Obsolescence of Knowledge," in T. F. Juster, ed., *Education, Income and Human Behavior*, pp. 199–234. New York: McGraw-Hill.

(1976). "A Theory of Life Earnings." *Journal of Political Economy* 84:S45–68.

Rosen, S., and F. Welch (1971). "Labor Supply and Income Redistribution." *Review of Economics and Statistics* 53:278–82.

Rothschild, M., and J. E. Stiglitz (1970). "Increasing Risk. I. A Definition." *Journal of Economic Theory* 2: 225–43.

(1971). "Increasing Risk. II. Its Economic Consequences." *Journal of Economic Theory* 3:66–84.

Rousseas, S. W., and A. G. Hart (1951). "Experimental Verification of a Composite Indifference Map." *Journal of Political Economy* 59:371–404.

Rowlatt, J. D. (1972). "An Estimate of the Tax Rate in a Public Assistance System." *Canadian Journal of Economics* 5:84–95.

Roy, R. (1947). "La Distribution du Revenue Entre les Divers Biens." *Econometrica* 15:202–25.

Ruffell, R. J. (1981). "Endogeneity II: Direct Estimation of Labour Supply Functions with Piecewise Linear Budget Constraints," in Brown, ed. (1981), pp. 101–16.

Ryder, H. E., F. P. Stafford, and P. Stephan (1976). "Labor, Leisure and Training over the Life Cycle." *International Economic Review* 17:651–74.

Sadka, E. (1976a). "On Income Distribution, Incentive Effects and Optimal Income Taxation." *Review of Economic Studies* 43:261–7.

(1976b). "On Progressive Taxation." *American Economic Review* 66:931–5.

Samuelson, P. A. (1956). "Social Indifference Curves." *Quarterly Journal of Economics* 70:1–22.

(1969). "Lifetime Portfolio Selection by Dynamic Stochastic Programming." *Review of Economics and Statistics* 51:239–46.

Sandmo, A. (1976). "Optimal Taxation — An Introduction to the Literature." *Journal of Public Economics* 6:37–54.

(1981). "Income Tax Evasion, Labour Supply and the Equity-Efficiency Tradeoff." *Journal of Public Economics* 16:265–88.

Sattinger, M. (1977). "Compensating Wage Differences." *Journal of Economic Theory* 16:496–503.

Schelling, T. C., ed. (1973). "Symposium: Time in Economic Life." *Quarterly Journal of Economics* 87:627–75.

Schoemaker, P. J. H. (1982). "The Expected Utility Model: Its Variants, Purposes, Evidence and Limitations." *Journal of Economic Literature* 20:529–63.

Schoenberg, E., and P. Douglas (1937). "Studies in the Supply Curve of Labor: The Relation between Average Earnings in American Cities and the Proportion Seeking Employment." *Journal of Political Economy* 45:45–62.

Schultz, T. P. (1976). "Comments on 'Estimates of a Human Capital Production Function Embedded in a Life-Cycle Model of Labor Supply' [by Heckman, 1976b]," in Terleckyj, ed. (1976), pp. 259–64.

(1980). "Estimating Labor Supply Functions for Married Women," in Smith, ed. (1980c), pp. 25–89.

Schultz, T. W. (1961). "Investment in Human Capital." *American Economic Review* 51:1–17.

ed. (1962). "Investment in Human Beings." *Journal of Political Economy* 70 (Supplement):1–157.

(1971). *Investment in Human Capital: The Role of Education and Research.* New

York: Free Press.

(1972). "Human Capital: Policy Issues and Research Opportunities," in National Bureau of Economic Research, *Human Resources: 50th Anniversary Colloquium VI*, pp. 1–84. New York: Columbia University Press.

Scitovsky, T. (1971). *Welfare and Competition*, Revised ed. Homewood, Ill.: Irwin.

Sharir, S. (1975). "The Income-Leisure Model: A Diagrammatic Extension." *Economic Record* 51:93–8.

Sherman, R., and T. D. Willett (1972). "The Standardized Work Week and the Allocation of Time." *Kyklos* 25:65–82.

Sheshinski, E. (1968). "On the Individual's Lifetime Allocation between Education and Work." *Metroeconomica* 20:42–9.

(1978). "A Model of Social Security and Retirement Decisions." *Journal of Public Economics* 10:337–60.

Sheshinski, E., and Y. Weiss (1980). "Uncertainty and Optimal Social Security Systems." *Quarterly Journal of Economics* 96:189–206.

Shishko, R., and B. Rostker (1976). "The Economics of Multiple Job Holding." *American Economic Review* 66:298–308.

Shulenberger, D. E. (1978). "A Contour-Theoretic Approach to the Determination of Negotiated Wage Change in the Building Construction Industry." *Economic Inquiry* 16:395–410.

Siegers, J. J., and R. Zandanel (1981). "A Simultaneous Analysis of the Labor Force Participation of Married Women and the Presence of Young Children in the Family." *De Economist* 129:382–93.

Sjoquist, D. L. (1976). "Labor Supply under Uncertainty: Note." *American Economic Review* 66:929–30.

Slutzky, E. E. (1915). "Sulla Teoria del Bilancio del Consumatore," *Giornale degli Economisti* 51:1–26. (Reprinted as "On the Theory of the Budget of the Consumer," Olga Ragusa, tr., in G. J. Stigler and K. Boulding, eds., *Readings in Price Theory*, pp. 27–56. Homewood, Ill.: Irwin.)

Smith, A. (1776). *The Wealth of Nations*. Reprint ed., E. Cannan, ed. New York: Modern Library, 1937.

Smith, J. P. (1973). "A Life Cycle Family Model." Working Paper No. 5. National Bureau of Economic Research.

(1975). "On the Labor Supply Effects of Age-Related Income Maintenance Programs." *Journal of Human Resources* 10:25–43.

(1977a). "Assets, Savings and Labor Supply." *Economic Inquiry* 15:551–73.

(1977b). "Family Labor Supply over the Life Cycle." *Explorations in Economic Research* 4:205–76.

(1980a). "Introduction," in Smith, ed. (1980c), pp. 3–23.

(1980b). "Assets and Labor Supply," in Smith, ed. (1980c), pp. 166–205.

ed. (1980c). *Female Labor Supply: Theory and Estimation*. Princeton, N. J.: Princeton University Press.

Smith, R. S. (1979). "Projecting the Size of the Female Labor Force: What Makes a Difference," in Lloyd, Andrews, and Gilroy, eds. (1979), pp. 45–65.

Spiegelman, R. G., and R. W. West (1976). "Feasibility of a Social Experiment and Issues in Its Design: Experiences from the Seattle and Denver Income Maintenance Experiment," in *Proceedings of the Business and Economic*

Statistics Section, American Statistical Association, 1976, pp. 168–76.

Spiegelman, R. G., and K. E. Yaeger (1980). "Overview." *Journal of Human Resources* 15:463–71.

Stafford, F. P., and G. Duncan (1978). "The Use of Time and Technology by Households in the United States," in R. G. Ehrenberg, ed., *Research in Labor Economics*, Vol. 3, pp. 335–75. Greenwich, Conn.: JAI Press.

Strotz, R. (1956). "Myopia and Inconsistency in Dynamic Utility Maximization." *Review of Economic Studies* 23:165–80.

Strotz, R. H. (1957). "The Empirical Implications of a Utility Tree." *Econometrica* 25:269–80.

(1959). "The Utility Tree — A Correction and Further Appraisal." *Econometrica* 27:482–8.

Stuart, C. E. (1981). "Swedish Tax Rates, Labor Supply and Tax Revenues." *Journal of Political Economy* 89:1020–38.

Subcommittee on Fiscal Policy, Joint Economic Committee, U. S. Congress (1972). *Studies in Public Welfare*, Paper No. 2, *Handbook of Public Income Transfer Programs*. Washington, D.C.: Government Printing Office.

Survey Research and Special Projects Directorate (1978). *Manitoba Basic Annual Income Experiment*. Ottawa: Department of National Health and Welfare.

Takayama, A. (1974). *Mathematical Economics*. Hinsdale, Ill.: Dryden Press.

Tella, A., D. Tella, and C. Green (1971). *The Hours of Work and Family Income Response to Negative Income Tax Plans*. Kalamazoo, Mich.: Upjohn Institute.

Terleckyj, N., ed. (1976). *Household Production and Consumption*. New York: Columbia University Press.

Theeuwes, J. (1981). "Family Labour Force Participation: Multinomial Logit Estimates." *Applied Economics* 13:481–98.

Theil, H. (1975). *The Theory and Measurement of Consumer Demand*, Vol. 1. Amsterdam: North Holland.

(1976). *The Theory and Measurement of Consumer Demand*, Vol. 2. Amsterdam: North Holland.

(1978). *Introduction to Econometrics*. Englewood Cliffs, N.J.: Prentice-Hall.

Thurow, L. C. (1970). *Investment in Human Capital*. Belmont, Calif.: Wadsworth.

Thurstone, L. L. (1931). "The Indifference Function." *Journal of Social Psychology* 2:139–67.

Tinbergen, J. (1956). "On the Theory of Income Distribution." *Weltwirtschaftliches Archiv* 77:155–73.

Tintner, G. (1938). "The Maximization of Utility over Time." *Econometrica* 6:154–8.

Tobin, J. (1952). "A Survey of the Theory of Rationing." *Econometrica* 20:521–53.

(1958). "Estimation of Relationships for Limited Dependent Variables." *Econometrica* 26:24–36.

(1964). "Improving the Economic Status of the Negro." *Daedalus* 94:889–95.

Tobin, J., and H. S. Houthakker (1951). "The Effects of Rationing on Demand Elasticities." *Review of Economic Studies* 18:140–53.

Trevithick, J. A. (1976), "Money Wage Inflexibility and the Keynesian Labour Supply Function." *Economic Journal* 86:327–32.

Trussell, T. J., and J. M. Abowd (1980). "Teenage Mothers, Labour Force

Participation and Wage Rates." *Canadian Studies in Population* 7:33–48.

Ulph, D. (1978). "On Labour Supply and the Measurement of Inequality." *Journal of Economic Theory* 19:492–512.

U. S. Department of Health, Education and Welfare (1973). *Summary Report: New Jersey Graduated Work Incentive Experiments*. Washington, D.C.: Government Printing Office.

——— (1976). *Summary Report: Rural Income Maintenance Experiment*. Washington, D.C.: Government Printing Office.

——— (1978). *The Seattle-Denver Income Maintenance Experiment: Mid-Experimental Labor Supply Results and a Generalization to the National Population*. Washington, D.C.: Government Printing Office.

U. S. Department of Labor (1976). *Employment and Training Report of the President 1976*. Washington, D.C.: Government Printing Office.

Vahovich, S. G. (1977). "Physicians' Supply Decisions by Specialty: 2SLS Model." *Industrial Relations* 16:51–60.

Vanek, J. (1974). "Time Spent in Housework." *Scientific American* 231 (November):116–20.

Varian, H. (1977). "Non-Walrasian Equilibria." *Econometrica* 45:573–90.

Vatter, H. G. (1961). "On the Folklore of the Backward Sloping Supply Curve." *Industrial and Labor Relations Review* 14:578–86.

——— (1962). "Rejoinder [to Finegan, 1962a]." *Industrial and Labor Relations Review* 15:234–6.

Veblen, T. (1934). *The Theory of the Leisure Class*. New York: Modern Library.

von Weiszäcker, C. C. (1967). "Training Policies under Conditions of Technical Progress: A Theoretical Treatment," in Organization for Economic Co-operation and Development, *Mathematical Models in Educational Planning*, pp. 245–57. Paris: Organization for Economic Cooperation and Development.

Wales, T. J. (1973). "Estimation of a Labor Supply Curve for Self-Employed Business Proprietors." *International Economic Review* 14:69–80.

——— (1978). "Labor Supply and Commuting Time." *Journal of Econometrics* 8:215–26.

Wales, T. J., and A. D. Woodland (1976). "Estimation of Household Utility Functions and Labor Supply Response." *International Economic Review* 17:397–410.

——— (1977). "Estimation of the Allocation of Time for Work, Leisure and Housework." *Econometrica* 45:115–32.

——— (1979). "Labour Supply and Progressive Taxes." *Review of Economic Studies* 46:83–95.

——— (1980). "Sample Selectivity and the Estimation of Labor Supply Functions." *International Economic Review* 21:437–68.

Wallace, M.S. (1981). "A Backward Bending Supply of Labor Schedule and the Short Run Phillips Curve." *Southern Economic Journal* 48:502–5.

Wallace, T. D., and L. A. Ihnen (1975). "Full-Time Schooling in Life-Cycle Models of Human Capital Accumulation." *Journal of Political Economy* 83:137–55.

Wallis, W. A., and M. Friedman (1942). "The Empirical Derivation of Indifference Functions," in O. Lange, F. McIntyre, and T. Yntema, eds., *Studies in Mathematical Economics and Econometrics in Memory of Henry Schultz*, pp. 175–89. Chicago: University of Chicago Press.

Watts, H. W. (1969). "Graduated Work Incentives: An Experiment in Negative Taxation." *American Economic Review* 59(2):463–72.

(1971). "The Graduated Work Incentive Experiments: Current Progress." *American Economic Review* 61:15–21.

Watts, H. W., R. Avery, D. Elesh, D. Horner, M. J. Lefcowitz, J. Mamer, D. Poirier, S. Spilerman, and S. Wright (1974). "The Labor-Supply Response of Husbands." *Journal of Human Resources* 9:181–200.

Watts, H. W., and D. Horner (1977). "Labor-Supply Response of Husbands," in Watts and Rees, eds. (1977), pp. 57–114.

Watts, H. W., D. Poirier, and C. Mallar (1977). "Sample, Variables and Concepts Used in the Analysis," in Watts and Rees, eds. (1977), pp. 33–56.

Watts, H. W., and A. Rees, eds. (1977). *The New Jersey Income-Maintenance Experiment*, Vol. II, *Labor-Supply Response*. New York: Academic Press.

Weiss, Y. (1971). "Learning by Doing and Occupational Specialization." *Journal of Economic Theory* 3:189–98.

(1972). "On the Optimal Pattern of Labour Supply." *Economic Journal* 82:1293–1315.

(1981). "Comment [on Heckman, Killingsworth and MaCurdy, 1981]." in Hornstein, Grice, and Webb, eds. (1981), pp. 123–24.

Whiteford, P. (1981). "Work Incentive Experiments in the United States and Canada." Research Paper No. 12. Research and Statistics Branch, Development Division, Department of Social Security, Woden, Australia.

Whybrew, E. (1968). "Overtime Working in Britain." Research Paper No. 9. Royal Commission on Trade Unions and Employers' Associations. London: Her Majesty's Stationery Office.

Wilensky, H. L. (1963). "The Moonlighter: A Product of Relative Deprivation." *Industrial Relations* 3:105–24.

Williams, W. (1975). "The Continuing Struggle for a Negative Income Tax: A Review Article." *Journal of Human Resources* 10:427–44.

Winston, G. C. (1965a). "Income and the Aggregate Allocation of Effort." *American Economic Review* 55(2):375–85.

(1965b). "Taxes, Leisure and Public Goods." *Economica* 32:65–9.

(1966). "An International Comparison of Income and Hours of Work." *Review of Economics and Statistics* 48:28–39.

Wonnacott, T. H., and R. J. Wonnacott (1977). *Introductory Statistics for Business and Economics*, 2nd ed. New York: Wiley.

Yaniv, G. (1979). "Labor Supply under Uncertainty: Note." *American Economic Review* 69:203–5.

Yotopoulos, P. A. (1965). "The Wage-Productivity Theory of Underemployment — A Refinement." *Review of Economic Studies* 32:59–65.

Zabalza, A. (1982). "Compensating and Equivalent Variation, and the Deadweight Loss of Taxation." *Economica* 49: 355–59.

(1983). "The CES Utility Function, Nonlinear Budget Constraints and Labour Supply: Results on Female Participation and Hours." *Economic Journal* 93: forthcoming.

Zabalza, A., C. A. Pissarides, and M. Barton (1980). "Social Security and the

Choice between Full-Time Work, Part-Time Work and Retirement." *Journal of Public Economics* 14:245–76.

Zeckhauser, R. (1971). "Optimal Mechanisms for Income Transfer." *American Economic Review* 61:324–34.

(1977). "Taxes in Fantasy, or Most Any Tax on Labor Can Turn Out to Help the Laborers." *Journal of Public Economics* 8:133–50.

NAME INDEX

479

SUBJECT INDEX

absenteeism, 18, 48, 51–2
age, 75, 79, 84, 86, 100, 148, 154–5,
   200, 208, 274, 282, 319, 323–4,
   328, 335–6, 409, 421, 433
Aid to Families with Dependent
   Children (AFDC), 361, 382
assets, *see* property income

bequests, 221, 223–4, 233, 277–8
bias, 82–7, 99, 108, 148, 279, 376,
   384; sample selection (selectivity),
   79, 85, 93, 96, 101, 105, 109, 139,
   145, 150, 152, 155, 160, 205–6,
   222, 266–7, 284–5, 317, 329–30
borrowing and saving, 2, 210–11,
   214, 241–2, 247–8, 251, 254, 260–2,
   273, 281–2, 302, 354, 362, 374,
   376–7
brute force specification of dynamic
   labor supply function, 267–70,
   283, 284
budget constraint, 4–11, 14, 16, 18,
   22, 40–1, 45–6, 68–9, 89, 132, 168,
   172, 178, 205, 209–12, 223–5, 231,
   293, 332–9, 344–7, 368, 372, 394–7,
   411–13, 415, 422, 426–7;
   discontinuous, 18, 45–66, 127;
   dynamic, 335–8, 419; family, 30;
   government, 349–50; kink point
   on, 170, 174, 177–8; kinky, 46, 95;
   linearized, 90–91, 178–9, 204–5,
   280, 332–9, 344, 357, 364, 386;
   linearized dynamic, 335–8;

linearized lifetime, 281–2;
   linearized static, 332–5, 338;
   segment of, 168–77, 389–92, 413;
   static, 332–5
budget frontier, 424, 426, 428
budget line, *see* budget constraint,
   budget frontier
business cycle, 17, 61, 105, 216, 445;
   see also macroeconomics

cbc (complete budget constraint)
   estimation procedure, 177–9, 204–
   5; *see also* budget constraint
change, anticipated vs.
   unanticipated, 218–20; *see also*
   entries for specific variables, e.g.,
   wage
change, evolutionary, *see* movement
   along time profile
change, parametric, *see* shift in time
   profile
child care, 28
COLISPIA specification of dynamic
   labor supply function, 267, 274–8,
   283, 296, 420
comparative dynamics, 212–13, 215–
   16, 218–22, 225, 227, 230–6, 238–9,
   270, 274, 276, 292, 297–301
comparative statics, 212–14
complements, 32, 72, 219–21, 367,
   371, 417
complete budget constraint, *see*
   cbc

DATE DUE